AN OUTLINE

OF

SHIP BUILDING,

THEORETICAL AND PRACTICAL.

In Five Divisions.

BY

THEODORE D. WILSON,

ASSISTANT NAVAL CONSTRUCTOR, U. S. NAVY; INSTRUCTOR OF NAVAL CONSTRUCTION, U. S. NAVAL ACADEMY; MEMBER OF THE INSTITUTION OF NAVAL ARCHITECTS, ENGLAND.

NEW YORK:
JOHN WILEY & SON,
15 ASTOR PLACE.
1873.

POOLE & MACLAUCHLAN,
PRINTERS AND BOOKBINDERS,
205–213 *East 12th St.*,
NEW YORK.

To

My Tried and Sincere Friend,

COMMANDER JOSEPH S. SKERRETT, U. S. NAVY,

This Book is Dedicated.

T. D. W.

JANUARY, 1873.

CONTENTS.

Division First.

NAVAL ARCHITECTURE.

CHAPTER I.

PAGE

Qualities sought in a Ship—Buoyancy—Stability—Speed—The Quality of Working Well........ 1

CHAPTER II.

Buoyancy—Displacement........ 3

CHAPTER III.

Centres of Gravity and of Buoyancy........ 8

CHAPTER IV.

Stability in Smooth Water........ 10

CHAPTER V.

Steadiness in Rough Water—Easy Rolling—Speed and Resistance........ 13

CHAPTER VI.

Fairness—Models—Propulsion by Machinery, 17—Propulsion by Sails........ 19

CHAPTER VII.

Working or Manœuvring Qualities of a Ship-Design........ 21

CHAPTER VIII.

Areas of Arbitrary Plane Figures, 22—Trapezoidal Rule—Simpson's First and Second Rules........ 23

CHAPTER IX.

Volumes of Solid Figures—Direct Measurements of Volumes, 27—Measurement of Volumes in Layers, or in Rectangular Divisions........ 28

CHAPTER X.

Rules for Moments and Centres of Plane Areas—Rules for Moments and Centres of Volumes........ 30

CHAPTER XI.

PAGE

Centres of Gravity and Moments of Bodies.............................. 33

CHAPTER XII.

Displacement and Centre of Buoyancy, 38—Methods of Computing Displacement, 39—Curve and Scale of Displacement, 40—Computation of Cross-Sections, 40—Computation of Water-Sections, 41—Computation of Displacement in Layers, 41—Appendages, 41—Computation of Midship-Section in Layers, 41—Determination of Centre of Buoyancy............... 42

CHAPTER XIII.

Co-efficient of Fineness, 44—Tonnage, 45—Burden.........................45

CHAPTER XIV.

Combined Calculations of Buoyancy and Stability, 47—Object of this Chapter, 47—Arrangement of the Data, 47—Arrangements of the Results of Calculations, 47.. 50

CHAPTER XV.

Practical Method of Ascertaining the Height of the Centre of Gravity of a Vessel Equipped and Ready for Sea................................. 53

CHAPTER XVI.

Rule for Computing the Register Tonnage of all United States Vessels, 61—Calculations of Register Tonnage of the U. S. Steamers *Omaha* and *Brooklyn*..66–69

CHAPTER XVII.

On the Longitudinal Metacentre of a Ship.............................. 70

CHAPTER XVIII.

Geometrical Construction of Sails, 81—Method of Determining the Position of the Centre of Effort of the Sails of a Ship, 82—Manœuvring by Sail, 85—Calculations for the Position of the Centre of Effort of the Sails of the U. S. Steamer *Brooklyn* 87

CHAPTER XIX.

On the Limits of Safety of Ships as regards Capsizing, 88—Distribution of Weight and Buoyancy in Ships, 92—Measure of Fighting Efficiency of Sea-going Iron-clads.. 96

CHAPTER XX.

On the Designing of Ships, 98—General Design, 98—Principal Dimensions, 99—Keel, Stem, Stern-Post, and Rudder, 100—Moulded Dimensions and Displacement, 100—Midship Section, 101—Leading Water-Line, 102—Balance-Sections, 102—Additional Water-Lines, 103—Buttock-Lines, 103—Additional Cross-Sections, 104—Main-Breadth-Line, 104—Sheer-Lines, 104—Gunwale—Rail—Head and Stern, 104—Use of Models in Designing Ships, 105—Summary of Calculations....................... 107

CHAPTER XXI.

PAGE
The Wave-Line System of Construction and its Advantages................ 109

CHAPTER XXII.

Propelling Power and Speed, 123—Resistance due to Frictional Eddies, 123 —Computation of Augmented Surface, 124—Computation of Probable Resistance, 125—Computation of Engine Power required at a Given Speed, 125—Computation of probable Speed, 126—Example of Calculation of Probable Speed of H.B.M. Ship *Warrior*..........................126–127

Division Second.

"LAYING DOWN AND TAKING OFF" SHIPS.

Introductory Observations.. 131
1. Process of "laying down" so as to forward the conversion of the different timbers.. 131
2. Laying down upon the Mould-Loft Floor.. 132
3. Definitions of the Sheer Plan.. 132
4. " " Body Plan.. 133
5. " " Half-Breadth Plan.. 133
6. Profile and other plans.. 134
7. Mould-Lofts.. 135
8. Base Line.. 135
9. To place the Foremost and Aftermost Perpendiculars, and get the Stations of the Timbers on the Floor.. 135
10. To run in the Horizontal and Sheer-Lines.. 136
11. To get the shape of the Forward Edge of the Rabbet of the Stem...... 137
12. To get the Shape of the After Edge of the Rabbet of the Stern-Post and Centre-Counter-Timber.. 137
13. To run in the Half-Breadth Plan.. 137
14. Ending of Water-Lines and Sheer-Lines Forward.. 138
15. Ending of Water-Lines and Sheer-Lines Aft.. 138
16. To Construct the Square-Body-Plan.. 138
17. To obtain the Shape of the Transverse Section or Moulding-Edges of the Frames in the Square-Body-Plan.. 139
18. To obtain the Bearding or Stepping-Line.. 140
19. Vertical Longitudinal Sections or Buttock and Bow-Lines.............. 141
20. Method of taking off the Vertical Longitudinal Sections or Buttock and Bow-lines.. 142
21. Ending of Vertical Longitudinal Sections or Buttock and Bow-Lines.. 142
22. Diagonal-Lines.. 142
23. Method of Taking Off Diagonal-Lines.. 143
24. To End the Diagonal-Lines.. 143

PAGE
25. Joints of Alternate Square Frames 144
26. Cutting-Down or Deadwood-Line 145
27. To make the Moulds for the Square-Body 145
28. To take the Bevellings of the Square-Body 147
29. Bevelling Boards 149
30. Nature and use of Cant-Timbers 149
31. To Lay Down the Cant-Timbers in the Half-Breadth-Plan, Forward.... 150
32. Horizontal Ribbands 151
33. To Lay Down Cant-Timbers by Horizontal Ribbands 152
34. To End the Heels of Cant-Timbers 152
35. To Lay Down the Cant-Timbers by Water-Lines 153
36. To Correct the Sheer-Lines for a Flaring-Bow 154
37. To Correct the Cant-Timbers by Vertical Sections or Buttock-Lines 154
38. To Make the Moulds for the Cant-Timbers 155
39. Scantling-Lines 155
40. To Lay Down the Bevelling-Edges of the Cant-Timbers 156
41. To End the Bevelling-Edges of the Cant-Timbers 157
42. To take the Bevellings of the Cant Timbers 157
43. Harpins 158
44. Laying Down a Harpin to a Sheer-Line 159
45. Laying Down a Harpin to a Water-Line 159
46. Knight-Heads 159
47. Laying Down Fore-and-Aft Knight-Heads 160
48. Laying Down Canted-Knight-Heads 161
49. To Lay Down Fore-and-Aft Hawse-Pieces 162
50. Laying Down the Centre and Side-Counter-Timbers 163
51. To Lay Down the Side-Counter-Timbers when they form the sides of the Propeller-Well 163
52. To Lay Down the Head 165
53. Taking off from the Mould-Loft Floor 168
54. Correct Method of Ending Level-Lines 168
55. Ending of Level-Lines 169
56. Bearding-Line 170
57. To Find the Foci of the Ellipse 170
58. Dimensions for Laying-Down a Steam Screw Sloop-of-War *Antietam* and Class 171

Division Third.

SHIP-BUILDING.

CHAPTER I.

Building Slip, 183—Building Blocks, 184—Keel, 185—Rabbet of Keel, 187—False Keel or Shoe, 187—Bilge Keels, 187—Stem, 188—Apron, 189—Forward Deadwood, 189—Stemson, 190—Stern-Post, 190—Counter-Timbers, 191—Stern-Post Knee, 191—Inner-Post, 191—After Deadwood.. 191

CHAPTER II.

PAGE

After Stern-Post or Rudder-Post, 193—Stern-Framing required for a Lifting-Screw, 193—Stern-Frames of Square-Sterned Ships, 194—Transoms, 195—The Fashion Pieces, 195—Frame, 196—Floors, 196—Method of Framing 198

CHAPTER III.

Regulating the Frame, 200—Knight-Heads, 201—Cants, 202—Hawse-Pieces, 203—Chocks, 203—Fillings, 204—Keelsons, 205—Main Keelson, 205—Sister Keelsons, 206—Boiler or Bilge Keelsons 206

CHAPTER IV.

Capping on Main Keelson, 207—Water Courses, 207—Diagonal Braces, 207—Diagonal Bracing on Outside of Vessels, 209—Breast-Hooks, Stern-Hooks, and Deck-Hooks, 210—Port-Sills, 211—Deck Clamps, 212—Bilge-Strakes, 213—Thick Strakes, 213—Ceiling 213

CHAPTER V.

Outside Planking, 215—Main Wales, 216—Channel Wales, 217—Middle Wales, 217—Sheer-Strakes, 217—Outside Battery Plank, 217—Garboard Strakes, 217—Bottom Plank, 218—Preparations for and Method of Planking, 218—Upon the Fastening of the Outside Planking, 219—Deck Plans, 221—Deck Beams, 221—Two-Piece Beam, 223—Iron Beams, 223—Knees used to Secure the Beams to the Side of the Ship, 224—The Fastenings of the Knees, 225—Regulating the Beams, 226—Framing of Decks, 226—Carlings, 227—Framing of Mast-Partners, 227—Ledges, 227—Waterways, 228—Deck Thick Strakes, 228—Framing of Hatches, 229—Spirketting, 230—Inside Battery Plank, 230—Deck Stringers, 230—Deck Plank, 230—Stanchions 231

CHAPTER VI.

Rule to obtain the Scantling or Siding Sizes of the Timber used in the Construction of Wooden Vessels-of-War, 232—Fastenings near the Binnacles, 232—Bitts, 232—Bowsprit Bitts, 232—Mooring or Cable Bitts 233—Topsail Sheet-Bitts, 234—Towing Bitts, 234—Orlop-Decks, 234—Bulkheads, 235—Poop and Top-Gallant Forecastle-Decks, 235—Number and Names of Decks, 236—Bulwarks, 237—Hammock-Nettings, 237—Hawse Holes, 238—Manger-Board and Manger, 239—Scuppers, 239—Air-Ports, 239—Controllers, 240—Compressor, 240—Channels, 240—Cutwater or Head, 242—Gripe, 244—Caulking, 244—Sheathing Vessels with Copper and Yellow-Metal 245

CHAPTER VII.

Mast Steps, 247—Capstans, 247—Wooden Rudders, 250—Iron Rudders, 252—Equipoise or Balance Rudders, 254—Steering Wheels, 255—Cat-heads, 255—Boats, 256—Ventilators 259

CHAPTER VIII.

Internal Arrangements of the *Antietam*, 260—Berth-Deck of the *Antietam*, 263—Main, or Gun-Deck of the *Antietam*, 263—Spar-Deck of the *Antietam*, 264—Magazines, 264—Lighting the Magazine, 266—Shell Rooms, 267—Areas Occupied by one Tier of Shell Boxes, 268—Dimensions, &c.,

PAGE

of Powder Tanks, 268—Dimensions of Boxes for Boat Ammunition, 268 —Gun-Tackle Bolts, 268—Spaces required for Working Guns on Truck Carriages, 269—Spaces required for Working different Classes of Guns on Pivot Carriages, 269—Sizes of Sockets and Pivot Bolts, 270—Position of Gun-Tackle Bolts for Broadside Guns, 270—Fife Rails, 270—Fore and Main Sheet-Chocks, 271—Top-sail Sheets, 272—Bolts for Jib-and Top-mast Stay-sail Sheets, 272—Bolts for Fore and Main Try-sail and Spanker Sheets, 272—Bolts for Leaders for Top-sail Halliards, 273—Main-brace Bumpkins, 273—Fore-Stay Bolts, 273—Main-Stay Bolts, 274—Bolts for Top-Tackles and Leaders for Top-Tackles, 274—Bolts for Leaders for Yard and Stay Tackle-Fall, 274—Bolts for a Leader for Fore-Stay Tackle-Fall, 274—Bolts for Main-Yard and Main-Stay Tackle-Fall, 274—Chock for Fore-Topmast Studding-sail Tack and Boom Brace, 274—Bolts in Channels for Pendant Tackles, 274—Bolts for Leaders for Fore and Main Topmast and Fore and Main Top-Gallant Studding-sail Halliards, 275—Bolts for Leaders for the Mast-Ropes, 275—Bolts for Leaders for Main Topmast and Main Top-Gallant Stay-sail Sheets, 275—Bolts for Hooking the Cat-Backs, 275—Bolts for Sheet-Chain Stops, 275—Bolts for Rudder-Pendant Stops, 275—Bolts for Securing the Ends of Rudder-Chains, 275 —Bolts in Lower Brackets for Securing Whisker-Jumpers, 275—Bolts for Jib and Flying-Jib Guys, Fore Topmast-Stays, Back-ropes and Bowsprit Shrouds, and Links for Bobstays, 276—Method of Setting up the Jib and Flying-Jib Stays, Fore Top-Gallant and Royal Stays, 276—Bolt for the Fore-Yard Tackle, 276—Bolts for Fore and Main Lifts, 276—Bolts for Securing Main Topmast-Stays, 276—Bolts for Leaders for Boats' Falls, —Miscellaneous Fittings.......... 276

CHAPTER IX.

IRON SHIP BUILDING, 278—Preparation of Model and Arrangement of Outside Plating, 278—Mode of Ordering Plates and Angle-Irons, 279—Laying off of the Ship, 279—Preparation of Frame Angle-Irons, 280—Preparation of Keel-Work, Stem and Stern-Posts, 281—Stems, 282—Forging and Planing of Stems, 283—Stern-Posts, 283—Iron Beams, 283 —Preparation of Beams, 284—Process of Framing, 285—Preparations of Floor-Plates and Reversed Angle-Irons, 285—Description of Ordinary Mode of Plating a Ship, 286—Mode of Working Deck-Stringers, 288—Method of Taking the Shape for and Working Plates with a large Amount of Curvature and Twist, 289—Ordinary Arrangements of Riveting in Outside Plating, 290—Deck-Planking for Iron Vessels, 290—Preparation of Bulkheads, 290—Putting in and Testing Rivet Work, 291—Caulking Laps and Butts of Plating.......... 291

Bracket Plate System of Framing Iron Ships, 292—Laying off of Ships, 292 —Preparation of Model, 292—Disposition of Butts of Keel Work, Bottom-Plating, &c., 292—Arrangements of Butts and Edges of Skin-plating and Outside-plating, 293—Preparation of Moulds for Stem and Stern-Post, 294—Preparation of the Keel Work, 294—Preparation of Short Transverse Plate and Bracket Frames, 295—Preparation of Longitudinal Frames, 296 —Process of Framing, 297—Working of Bottom Plating, 299—Fitting of Skin-Plating and Girders behind Armor, 300—Preparation of Beams, 300 —Preparation of Bulkheads, 301—Arrangement of Deck-Stringers and Plating, 301—Armor Plating.......... 302

PAGE

CHAPTER X.

Composite Ships, 303—Jordan's System of Constructing Composite Ships, 303—McLain's System of Constructing Composite Ships, 304—Descriptive Particulars of McLain's System, 304—Scott's System of Constructing Composite Ships, 305—Daft's Method of Sheathing Iron Ships, 306—Grantham's Method of Sheathing Iron Ships, 306—English Admiralty Method of Sheathing Iron Ships.... 307

Docks, 307—Wet Docks, 307—Dry Docks, 308—Method of Docking a Vessel in a Dry Dock, 308—Floating Sectional Dry Docks, 309—Method of Docking a Vessel on a Sectional Dock, 310—Marine Railway, 310—Balance Floating Dock, 311—Method of Docking a Vessel on a Balance Dock..... 311

Launching, 312—The Ways, 313—Breadth of Surface of Ways, 314—Distance of Ways Apart, 315—Launching Ribbands, 315—Ribband Shores, 315—Back Shores, 316—The Cradle, 316—Bilge Ways, 316—Packing or Fillings, 317—Poppets, 317—Poppet Ribbands, 318—Lashing for Packing, 318—Poppet Lashing, 318—Preparations for Launching, 319—Launching of Iron-Clad Ships, built on the Longitudinal System, 322—On Completing the Launching of Ships which have Stopped on their Launching Ways, 323—Launching of the *Great Eastern*.... 324

Division Fourth.

MAST AND SPAR-MAKING.

---

1. Remarks on the Benefit of having Masts Elastic, 329. — 2. Main Mast, 329. — 3. Fore Mast, 330. — 4. Mizzen Mast, 330. — 5. Bowsprit, 330. — 6. Main-Topmast, 330. — 7. Fore-Topmast, 330. — 8. Mizzen-Topmast, 331. — 9. Jib-Boom, 331. — 10. Flying-Jibboom, 331. — 11. Jib-Boom (again), 331. — 12. Main Top-gallant-Mast, 331. — 13. Fore Top-gallant-Mast, 331. — 14. Mizzen Top-gallant-Mast, 332. — 15. Main Royal-Mast, 332. — 16. Fore Royal-Mast, 332. — 17. Mizzen Royal-Mast, 332. — 18. Main-Yard, 332. — 19. Fore-Yard 332. — 20. Cross-Jack Yard, 332. — 21. Main-Topsail Yard, 333. — 22. Fore-Topsail Yard, 333. — 23. Mizzen-Topsail Yard, 333. — 24. Main Top-gallant Yard, 333. — 25. Fore Top-gallant Yard, 333. — 26. Mizzen Top-gallant Yard, 333. — 27. Main Royal-Yard, 333. — 28. Fore Royal-Yard, 333—29. Mizzen Royal-Yard, 334. — 30. Spanker-Boom, 334. — 31. Spanker-Gaff, 334. — 32. Main and Fore-Gaffs, 334. — 33. Dolphin-Striker, 334. — 34. Whisker-Booms, 335. — 35. Notes on Yards, 335. — 36. Top-sail Yards, 335. — 37. Ensign-Staff, 335. — 38. Jack-Staff, 335. — 39. Cap-Shores, 335. — 40. Swinging-Booms, 335. — 41. Topmast Studding-Sail Booms, 335. — 42. Top-gallant Studding-Sail Booms, 336. — 42½. Topmast Studding-Sail Yards, 336. — 43. Main-Top, 336. — 44. Fore-Top, 337. — 45. Mizzen Top, 337. — 46. Lower Trestle-trees, 337. — 47. Topmast Trestle-trees, 337. — 48. Lower Cross-trees, 337. — 49. Top-mast Cross-trees, 337. —

PAGE

50. Caps, 338. — 51. Bibbs, 338. — 52. Long Bees on Bowsprit, 338. — 53. Notes on Masts and Bowsprits, 338. — 54. Notes on Bibbs, 339. — 55. Notes on Scarphs and Hoops, 339. — 56. Nibs of Scarphs of Masts, 339. — 57. Chafing Battens, 339. — 58. Square Hole in Lower Masts, 339. — 59. Preparing to Build a Mast, 340. — 60. Fastenings for Masts, 340. — 61. Futtock-Band, 340. — 62. Truss-Band, 340. — 63. Notes on Yards, 340. — 64. Iron Work for Yards, 341. — 65. Top-sail Yards, 341. — 66. Quarter-Irons, 342. — 67. Boom-Irons, 342. — 68. Burton-Bands, Lower Yards, 342. — 69. Burton-Bands Top-sail Yards, 342. — 70. Distance between Masts and Yards, 342. — 71. Iron Jacks, 342. — 72. Iron Fids, 342. — 73. Notes on Tops, 343. — 74. Top Tables, 342. — 75. Top Stanchions and Rails, 343. — 76. Converting and lining Timber for Masts and other Spars, 344. — 77. Notes and explanations on the following Tables of Dimensions.... 344

78. Tables of Dimensions Nos. 1 and 2. Lower Masts—Lower Yards.... 345
79. " " " " 3 " 4. Topmasts—Top-sail Yards..... 346
80. " " " " 5 " 6. Top-gallant Masts—Top-gallant Yards.... 347
81. " " " " 7 " 8. Royal-Masts—Royal-Yards...... 348
82. " " " " 9 " 10. Bowsprit—Dolphin-Striker and Whisker-Booms.... 349
83. " " " " 11 " 12. Jib-Boom—Flying Jib-Boom... 350
84. " " " " 13 " 14. Spanker-Boom—Spanker-Gaff.. 351
85. " " " " 15 " 16. Swinging-Booms—Lower Studding-Sail Yard.... 352
86. " " " " 17 " 18. Top-mast Studding-Sail Boom— " " " Yard.. 353
87. " " " " 19 " 20. Top-gallant Studding-Sail Boom —Top-gallant " " Yard 354
88. Notes on the following Tables of Lower Masts.... 355
89. Notes on Topmasts.... 355
90. Notes on Top-gallant Masts.... 355

Tables of Dimensions of the several parts of Lower Masts.... 356
" " " " Topmasts.... 357
" " " " Top-gallant Masts.... 358
" " " " Lower Top-sail, Top-gallant, and Royal-Yards, with Cleats 359
" " " " Yards with Shoulders, Lower Top-gallant and Royal...... 360
" " " " Yards with Shoulders. Top-sail Yards.... 361
" " " " Jib-Booms.... 362
" " " " Flying Jib-Boom and Bowsprit. 363
" " " " Spanker-Booms.... 363
" " " " Spanker-Gaff and Dolphin-Striker.... 364
" " " " Whisker-Booms, Main and Fore-Gaff.... 364
" " " " Swinging-Booms — Fore and Main Topmast — Studding-Sail Boom.... 365

PAGE

Tables of Dimensions of the several parts of Fore and Main Top-gallant Studding-Sail Boom—Lower and Topmast Studding-Sail Yards 365

103. A Plan for Iron Screw-Fids for Topmasts, and Wooden Wedge-Fids for Top-gallant Masts, by Rear Admiral T. O. Selfridge, U.S.N. 366

Masts and Spars for Revenue Cutters and other Schooners. — 104. Wood-wedge Fids for Top-gallant Masts, 366. — 105. Main-Mast, 366. — 106. Fore-Mast, 366. — 107. Bowsprit, 366. — 108. Main Topmast, 367. — 109. Top-gallant Masts, 367. — 110. Fore Topmast, 367. — 111. Jib-Boom, 367. — 112. Flying-Jib-Boom, 367. — 113. Main-Boom, 368. — 114. Main-Gaff, 368. — 115. Fore-Gaff, 368. — 116. Fore-Yard, 368. — 117. Fore Top-sail Yard, 368. — 118. Fore Top-gallant Yard, 369. — 119. Square-Sail Yard 369

Masting of Boats.. 369

Table giving the Lengths of the Masts, Yards, etc., of different Rigged Boats.. 371

Boats as Schooners.—Length of Booms, Gaffs, and Bowsprits 372

Boats with Sprit-sails.—Boats with Lug-sails.........................373–375

Vocabulary of Terms Used.. 377

PREFACE.

In offering this work on Ship-Building to officers of the naval service and to others of my profession, the author has no apology to make for its production. Information on this subject has been sought from every available source, with a view of rendering this work useful for the purposes of elementary instruction as well as to the practical builder. The result of the undertaking is humbly submitted, trusting that it will meet with indulgence for such faults as it may contain.

The First Division has been compiled chiefly from Rankine's Ship-Building, Theoretical and Practical. Credit for articles taken from other authors is given in foot-notes.

The Second Division is based upon the actual practice of the public and private Ship-Yards of this country; but the treatises on this subject, of Rankine, Scott Russell, Knowles, and Fincham have been freely used and portions incorporated whenever it seemed desirable to do so.

The Third Division describes the processes of shaping and of putting together the materials of which a United States Vessel of War is composed, and explains the structure, building, and fitting up of a ship in detail, as well as the process of launching and docking her. The articles on Iron Ship-Building are from the standard work on Ship-Building in Iron and Steel, by E. J. Reed, Esq., late Chief Naval Constructor of the English Navy. The articles on Composite Ship-Building are from the Transactions of the Institute of Naval Architects.

The Fourth Division is a Treatise on the Masting and Sparring of United States Vessels of War, by Titus Evans Dodge, Esq., Foreman of Sparmakers, Navy Yard, Brooklyn, N. Y., who invented and constructed the first "round made masts" used in the Naval service of this country, in 1839. These masts are now used in all our Ships of War. To Mr. Dodge the author is indebted for permission to include his treatise in this work. The article on the Masting of Boats is included at the suggestion of Mr. John Southwick, Carpenter, U. S. Navy. It is hoped that it will prove useful to Carpenters in the Navy and to Boat-Builders.

The Fifth Division is a vocabulary of the terms used.

DIVISION FIRST.

NAVAL ARCHITECTURE.

NAVAL ARCHITECTURE.

CHAPTER I.

Qualities sought in a ship.

The qualities sought in a ship depend mainly on the fact, that the ship, with her burden, has to be safely and steadily carried by, and propelled through, the water, her movements being at all times under control. Setting aside, then, for the present, the qualities of strength and durability, the qualities of a ship which conduce to her efficient support by and propulsion through the water may be thus summed up:—

Buoyancy, to enable her to carry her burden without either sinking too deep in the water, or floating too lightly on it.

Stability, that she may tend to "right herself" when disturbed from an upright position, and may never, under the action of winds, waves, or other disturbing causes, deviate further from that position than is consistent with convenience and safety; and also, that her movements may neither be so extensive nor so abrupt as to strain or damage her structure or contents.

Speed sufficient for her purpose, with due regard to economy in the means whereby such speed is obtained.

The quality of working well, which it would be difficult to find any single word to express. In a vessel propelled by steam alone, it consists chiefly in ready and quick answering to the helm; in a sailing vessel, it embraces also "weatherliness," and the performing of various manœuvres with promptness and certainty.

All those qualities depend mainly on forces exerted between the ship and the fluids by which it is surrounded—viz., the water and the air; and therefore the means of obtaining them depend to a great extent on principles belonging to the sciences of hydrostatics, or the balance of fluids, and hydrodynamics, or the motion of fluids. The practical application of those branches of science is commonly known by the term "hydraulics."

Besides knowing how to obtain separately each of the qualities that are sought in a ship, it is necessary that the naval architect should know how to combine those qualities in the manner best suited for the use to which the ship is to be applied, and how to insure that the means adopted for obtaining one of them shall not be injurious to the others. This is the kind of knowledge whose application constitutes *Design* in naval architecture.

The following seven chapters will be devoted to a general account of the principles to be observed in designing a ship, leaving the details of their application to be explained further on.

CHAPTER II.

Buoyancy—Displacement.

THE buoyancy of a ship depends on the following principles :—

I. That in order that a body may remain steady in a given position, the forces acting upon it must be balanced; which, in the case of there being two forces, means that they must be equal, and directly opposed, to each other.

II. That a body plunged into a still fluid is urged downwards by its own weight, and pressed upwards by the fluid with a force equal and opposite to the weight of the volume of fluid which the body displaces.

III. That consequently, in order that a given body, such as a ship, may float steadily in a given position in smooth water, the weight of the volume of water displaced must be equal to the weight of the body; and the total upward pressure of the water,

FIG. 1.

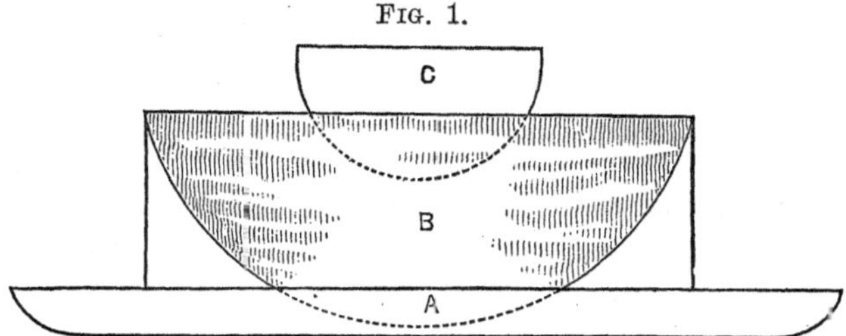

which is equal and opposite to the weight of the water displaced, must be directly opposed to the weight of the body.

The quantity of water displaced by a ship is called her *displacement*, and may be expressed either by its volume (for example, as so many cubic feet), or by its weight (for example, as so many tons, a ton being the weight of 35 cubic feet of ordinary sea-water, or 35.9 cubic feet of fresh water).

The principle No. II. above stated is easily demonstrated by the following reasoning. The total pressure exerted on the solid body by the neighboring particles of fluid is the same with that which was previously exerted on the mass of fluid whose place the solid body occupies; and that mass of fluid was *in equilibrio;* therefore the total pressure exerted on it was equal and directly opposed to its weight.

That the weight of the water displaced by a floating body is equal to that of the body and all its contents, may be experimentally proved by apparatus within the reach of every one.

Take two vessels, A and B, as represented in Fig. 1; place one within the other, and fill the upper one with water to the brim; then take another empty vessel, C, and lower it gradually into the water in B, until it is supported by the pressure of the water. When C is at rest, a volume of water equal to that displaced by it has run over into A; and if this water be placed in one side of a pair of scales, and the vessel C in the other, they will be found to balance each other. Replace C in the water, and gently drop some heavy material, such as sand or shot, into it, and more water will overflow; remove C with the material it contains carefully to one end of the balance, and add to the water before put in that which was caused to overflow by the introduction of the material into C, and, as before, the water will balance the vessel and its contents. This may be often repeated, until C sinks nearly to its upper part, and it will be found in every experiment that the weight of the water which has overflowed from B is always equal to that of C, and of the material it contains, provided great care be taken that none of the water is lost, and that none adheres to the outside of the vessels. From these practical proofs of the equality which always exists between the weight of the floating body with its contents and that of the water displaced, we also learn that for every weight put on board of a ship there is an equal weight of water displaced by it.

In consequence of the necessity for this equality of the weight of the ship and of the water displaced, we perceive that, if the water in which a ship floats at different times differs in density, there will be a corresponding difference in the immersion of the ship. Now, the weight of a cubic foot of sea water is a little more than 64 lbs., and the weight of a cubic foot of river water about one-fortieth less. A line-of-battle ship, when ready for sea, weighing about 5,000 tons, requires 26 tons to increase her immersion one inch; consequently, were such a ship to come direct from sea into the river, keeping precisely the same weights on board, she would sink $\frac{5000}{40 \times 26}$ inches, or 5 inches (very nearly) deeper in the river than when at sea. Ships which have flat floors, and are full forward and aft—approximating, in fact, to the form of a rectangular box—as are some colliers, barges, &c.—will sink just one-fortieth deeper when in river water than when at sea.

We have already proved that a floating body presses downwards, and is pressed upwards, by forces equal to its weight. If, now, a light air-tight vessel, such as an empty cask, be placed in the water, it will float until it is loaded with a weight equal to the difference between its weight and that of an equal volume of water. Let one end of a rope be secured to the weight, and the other end to the air-tight vessel; throw the weight into the water, and as soon as the equilibrium has been restored, it will be found that the vessel is nearly at the surface of the water, and the weight hanging vertically under it, supported by the tension of the rope. It would be entirely immersed, were it not for the effect which the immersion of the weight and the rope has on the vessel, that effect being to raise it a little out of the water—the part emersed being equal to the volume of the weight and of the rope, diminished by a quantity of fluid the weight of which is the same as that of the rope.

On this principle, sunken vessels are often recovered in the following manner:—At low water a number of empty casks, air-tight caissons, or one or two ships or barges, are attached by strong ropes or hawsers to parts of the sunken ship, and the ropes are hove in tight. As the tide rises, the vessels become more and more emersed in the water until the weight of the additional volume of water displaced by the whole of them equals the force necessary to raise the ship. When the tide is nearly at its height, the vessels, with the sunken ship under them, are removed towards the shore until she touches the ground again. If the ship be then in such a position that the falling tide will leave her above water when at its lowest, the vessels are cast off; but if not, they are hove down as before, and the process described is repeated.

The number of air-tight vessels necessary to raise a sunken ship may be thus approximated to. On the sunken ship the pressure downwards is the weight of the ship and of the cargo; and the pressure upwards is the weight of a volume of water equal to that occupied by the materials of the ship and by the cargo. If the ship be built of wood, the specific gravity of the mass does not much exceed unity—that is, the weight of the whole mass would be about the same as that of an equal volume of water. There would then remain to be overcome by the water-tight vessels a pressure equal to the weight of the cargo when placed in water. This pressure can often be found very readily. When known, we must have a number of water-tight vessels, such that their weight, together with the weight of cargo when in water, shall equal the weight of the volume of water displaced by these vessels. If the ship be built of iron, with the usual amount of wood-work, the weight of the whole is about five times the weight of a volume of water equal to the bulk of the materials. In addition, therefore, to the difference between the weight of the cargo and that of a volume of water equal to it—that is, to the weight of the cargo in water—four-fifths of the entire weight of the ship has to be overcome by the pressure of the immersed water-tight vessels. To find the weight of a vessel by computing the weight of the several parts composing it would be a problem almost impracticable, because of its complexity. But, after the ship is completed and floating in the water, since we know that her weight is equal to that of the water she displaces, we have only to find the cubic contents of the part immersed, multiply it by the weight of a unit of volume of water, and the product is the weight of the ship and everything in it.

When the ship is of any regular form, the volume of displacement may be found by certain mathematical rules. Ships are, however, usually of no regular figure, their sections conforming to no other law than the will of the constructor; consequently, whatsoever methods may be employed to find the displacement, they cannot be more than approximations. Those approximations, however, as we shall hereafter show, may be made to approach the exact displacement as nearly as we please.

In determining how much the displacement of a proposed ship ought to be, the naval architect will consider, in the first place, what burden the vessel is to carry, whether in the shape of cargo, stores, armament, or otherwise; and then, knowing from experience what proportion the weight of a ship of the kind intended, with her equipments, bears to her lading, he will calculate that weight, and thence the whole displacement required. In steam-vessels provision must be made in the total lading for the weight of engines and fuel, which will depend on the dimensions and form of the vessel, the intended speed, the length of voyage, and the construction and economy of the engine.

Particulars of the proportionate weights of ships and their lading will be given further on in the treatise; in the meanwhile it may be stated, that the weight of a ship, with her equipments (engines not included), usually ranges from about *one-third* to *one-half* of the whole displacement; iron vessels in general approaching the lighter of those limits, and wooden vessels the heavier.

CHAPTER III.

Centres of Gravity and of Buoyancy.

In the previous chapter have been considered the consequences of the principle, that the weight of the ship and the pressure of the water must be *equal*. We have now to consider the consequences of the principle, that they must be *directly opposed;* which, as both forces act vertically, the weight downwards and the pressure upwards, means that they must act *in the same vertical line.*

A force acting in a single line, or, what is the same thing, at a single point, is purely imaginary, being an idea introduced in order to make mechanical calculations possible. The action of every force is diffused throughout some space: for example, the action of a body's weight is diffused throughout the whole bulk of the body; and the action of a pressure, over the surface of contact of two bodies or parts of a body which press each other. Nevertheless it is always possible to find a single point in a body acted upon by gravity or by pressure, such that the effect of the weight or pressure on the body as a whole is the same as if its action were really concentrated at that point. That point, in the case of a body's weight, is called the *centre of gravity* of the body; in the case of a pressure, it is called a *centre of pressure;* and when the pressure is that of a fluid in which a solid body floats, *the centre of buoyancy.* The single or concentrated force which is thus conceived to be equivalent to a given diffused force, is called the *resultant* of the diffused force.

It is a necessary consequence of the principle No. II., stated at the beginning of the preceding chapter, that the centre of buoyancy of a floating body must occupy the place of the centre of gravity of the mass of fluid displaced; and hence that point is sometimes called the *centre of displacement.* Let Fig. 2 represent a ship, floating in smooth water, of which YY is the surface. The weight of the whole ship acts as if it were concentrated at the centre of gravity of the ship, G, and may be represented by the arrow, W, pointing vertically downwards. The immersed part of the ship, DDDD, displaces a volume of water whose weight is equal to that of the ship. Let C be the centre of gravity of that volume of water, that is, the centre of buoyancy; then the pressure of the water against the ship acts as if it were a single force,

FIG. 2.

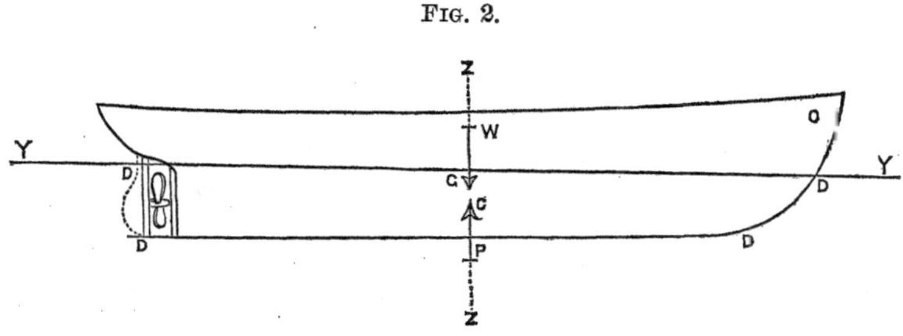

P, equal to the ship's weight, acting vertically upwards through the centre of buoyancy, C; and as the weight and pressure must be directly opposed, the centres of gravity, G, and of buoyancy, C, must be in the same vertical line, ZZ.

It may here be explained, that the particles of water press against the ship's bottom horizontally and obliquely, as well as vertically; the direction of the pressure exerted by each particle being at right angles to that part of the ship's bottom which it touches; but the horizontal parts of the whole pressure exactly balance each other; so that the resultant acts vertically upwards, as already stated.

The precise position of the centre of gravity of a ship is always to a certain extent capable of adjustment; that is, the ship's "*trim*" may be altered after she is afloat, by suitable stowage of her lading; but a skilful naval architect will always be able to fix on the "*trim*" beforehand, in designing a ship, to such a degree of approximation that the subsequent adjustment shall not cause any inconvenience.

CHAPTER IV.

Stability in Smooth Water.

A BODY which is free to move, is said to be *stable*, if, when disturbed from its position of balance or steadiness, it tends to *right itself*, or return to that position. If, on the other hand, it tends to deviate further from that position, or upset, it is said to be *unstable*.

A ship is always stable as regards vertical disturbances, that is, rising above or dipping below her position of steady floating; for when she rises out of the water, her displacement is diminished, and there is an excess of the weight over the supporting pressure, tending to bring her down again; and when she dips deeper into the water, her displacement is increased, and there is an excess of the supporting pressure over the weight, tending to make her rise again.

The kind of disturbance of a ship's position which it is of primary importance to consider, is that which consists in *heeling*, or leaning over to one side. Similar disturbances in a longitudinal plane, known as *pitching* and *scending*, have also to be considered, although they are of less importance than heeling. All these are disturbances of angular position, and stability against them all depends on similar principles; so that it will be sufficient for the purposes of the present chapter to explain on what stability against heeling, or transverse stability, depends.

It has already been stated, that in order that a pair of forces applied to one body may balance each other, they must not only be equal in amount and opposite in direction, but *directly* opposed to each other—that is, they must act in opposite directions along the *same* straight line. When a pair of equal forces act in opposite directions along *parallel*, but not identical lines, they no longer balance each other, but constitute what is called a *couple*, tending to turn the body into a new angular position. When the angular position of such a body as a ship is disturbed, the weight and the supporting pressure, which originally were a pair of directly opposed equal forces, producing balance, become a couple;

and the body is stable or unstable, according as that couple is a *righting couple*, or an *upsetting couple*.

It may facilitate the understanding of this subject to give an illustration taken from the mechanics of solid bodies. Figs. 3 and 4 represent two blocks, each with a rounded base, resting on a level platform. Either of those blocks may be balanced on its rounded end, by so placing it that the upward pressure of the platform, exerted against the point of support, may act in a line passing through the centre of gravity of the block. If the block with the sharper curvature at the base, Fig. 3, is disturbed, the weight, W, acting through the centre of gravity, G, and the pressure exerted by the platform at the point of support, C, form an *upsetting couple*, which makes the block fall over on its side. If the block with the flatter base, Fig 4, is disturbed, the weight acting through G, and the pressure of the platform acting through C, form a *righting couple*, which makes the block return to its position of balance. The condition of a ship as regards stability is analogous to that of the latter block.

Fig. 5 represents an end view of a ship floating upright in

FIG. 3. FIG. 4.

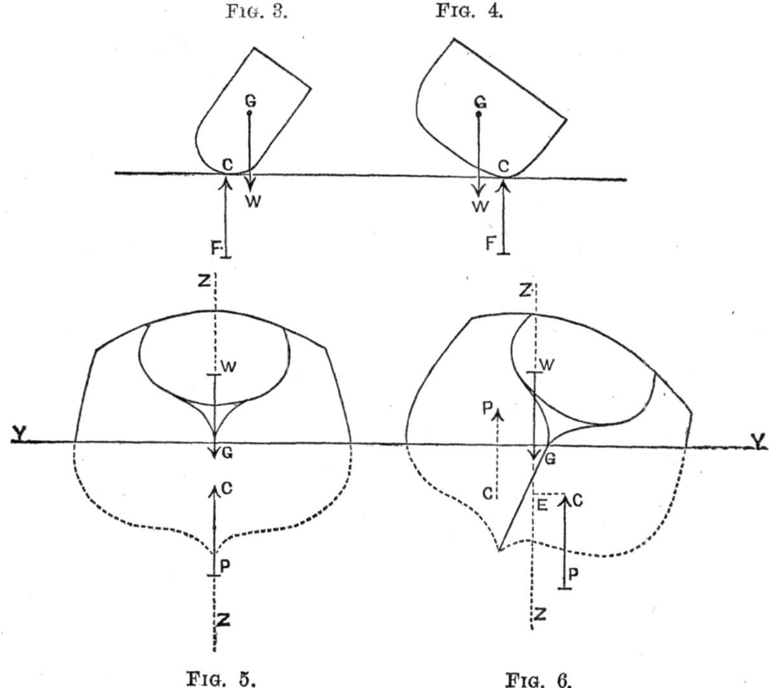

FIG. 5. FIG. 6.

smooth water, of which YY is the surface. G is the ship's centre of gravity; C the centre of buoyancy, in the same vertical line ZZ; W represents the weight of the ship, exactly balanced by the equal and opposite resultant pressure P. Fig. 6 represents the same ship, having heeled over through a certain angle towards the right. The weight of the ship, W, continues to act through the same centre of gravity, G, in the same vertical line, ZZ; but in consequence of the new form assumed by the immersed part of the ship, or displacement, the centre of buoyancy shifts into a new position, C′; and in a properly designed ship, that new position lies to the same side of the vertical line, ZZ, as that towards which the ship has heeled; so that the weight, W, and the resultant pressure, P, form a *righting couple*, tending to bring the ship back to the upright position. Had the new centre of buoyancy, through a faulty design, lain to the other side of ZZ, as at *c*, the weight and pressure would have formed an upsetting couple.

The *moment* of a couple is the name given to the magnitude of its tendency to turn the body on which it acts, and is computed by multiplying either of the two equal forces of which the couple consists, by the perpendicular distance between the parallel lines of action of the forces, which distance is called the *arm* or *leverage* of the couple. The moment of the righting couple which acts on a ship at some fixed angle of heel, is called her *moment of stability* at that inclination. For example, in Fig. 6, the moment of stability is the weight of the ship, W, multiplied by the horizontal distance of the new centre of buoyancy, C′, from the vertical line, ZZ, traversing the ship's centre of gravity; that is—$W \times EC'$. The moment of stability required for different sorts of vessels has been ascertained by practical experience. An account of the experiments for ascertaining the stability of a ship will be found in Chapter XV. For the present, it may be stated, by way of illustration, that a common value for the moment of stability in large vessels at an angle of heel of fifteen degrees, is the weight of the ship acting with a leverage of one foot. The power of a vessel to carry sail obviously depends mainly on her stability.

CHAPTER V.

Steadiness in Rough Water.

Although a certain amount of stability in a ship is absolutely necessary, an excess of that quality becomes an evil, for the following reasons:—

I. A ship of great stability is quick in her rolling motion; and if the stability be excessive, the rolling may be so quick as to strain and damage her structure and contents.

II. The same form and proportions which make a ship very stable in smooth water, tend also to make her accompany the waves in their motions. This, to a certain extent, is necessary, but if it goes too far, causes inconvenience and danger.

III. It is dangerous for a ship in rolling to *keep time* with the waves, because in that case each successive wave increases the extent of the ship's rolling; and the best way to avoid that danger is to take care that the ship shall roll more slowly than the waves. The time of a ship's rolling is affected by the distribution of the weight of the ship and lading, as well as by the stability. To distinguish the tendency of a ship to keep *upright to the surface of the water*, whether level or sloping, from the tendency to keep *truly upright* in rough water, the former may be called *stiffness*, and the latter *steadiness*.

Easy Rolling is insured by avoiding excessive quickness of rolling, as already mentioned; and also by so designing the form of the ship's hull, that when she heels over, the pressure of the water shall tend to make her simply roll back again, and shall not tend at the same time to make her pitch, scend, or rise and fall bodily.

Speed and Resistance.—The resistance opposed by the water to the progress of a ship depends on the speed with which the ship moves through the water, and on the figure and dimensions of the vessel, and the smoothness of her immersed surface. So far as the resistance depends upon speed, it is well ascertained by experience that for a given vessel, and within the limits of speed to which that vessel is suited, the resistance is sensibly proportional to the square of the speed, being fourfold for a double speed, ninefold for a triple speed, and so on; in other words, it is proportional to the height from which a body must fall to acquire the velocity of the vessel. When the speed of the vessel, however, is urged beyond certain limits depending on her dimensions and figure, the resistance begins to increase sensibly faster than the square of the speed; the reason being, that the wave or swell raised in front of the vessel begins to have a sensible effect in adding to the extent of surface acted upon by the resistance. Our knowledge of the manner in which the resistance is affected by the dimensions and figure of the vessel is still imperfect, although it has of late made much progress. During the last century attempts were made to deduce a theory of the resistance of ships from that of the impulse of jets of water against flat surfaces; but the results arrived at were so utterly inconsistent with those of practical experience that the theory has long ago been abandoned as useless; and indeed this was to have been expected, from the want of resemblance between the circumstances of the two cases compared together. Better success has attended the theory which considers the resistance as being analogous to that met with by a stream in flowing along a channel; that is to say, as depending on a certain degree of viscosity, or stiffness, in the water; and by means of that theory, marine engineers have of late years been enabled in various instances to compute beforehand the engine-power required to drive an intended vessel at a given speed with accuracy sufficient for practical purposes. The viscosity of the water acts in two ways; by producing a direct backward drag, exerted by the particles of water on the skin of the vessel, and by causing a heaping-up of water against the bow of the vessel as compared with the stern. Independently of any knowledge of the particular mode of action of the water in resisting the progress of a vessel, it is obvious, and must always have been obvious to common observation, that the vessel which makes the least commotion in the water is the least resisted. Thus it has been known from remote antiquity that the length of a ship should be greater than her breadth; and that fine ends, both at the bow and stern, causing the particles of water to be displaced and replaced gradually, are favorable to speed. It has been left for correct theoretical views to show conclusively, what had already been only partially and imperfectly known through practical experience, that there are limits beyond which great length as compared with breadth ceases to be an advantage, and becomes a cause of increased resistance.

In the proportion of the length of a ship to her breadth, the ratio of 4 : 1 was seldom exceeded until after the introduction of steam navigation. Then gradually increasing proportions were introduced, with continually improving results, until the ratio of 7 : 1 was reached; and it was naturally taken generally for granted that an unlimited increase of length and slenderness would cause an unlimited diminution of resistance. This, however, was not found to be the case in practice, which concurs with theory to show that the proportion of 7 : 1, or thereabouts, is very nearly the utmost that is attended with advantage in vessels whose draught of water is not specially limited; and that greater proportions, such as 8 : 1, 9 : 1, or 10 : 1, are advantageous under special conditions only, such as limited draught of water, or limited breadth of channel.

Another principle which is known independently of the precise mode of action of the particles of water is this—that the resistances of vessels of *similar figures*, but different dimensions, at the same speed, are nearly proportional to their *surfaces*—that is, to the squares of their linear dimensions, or to the squares of the cube roots of their displacements; so that, for example, if there be two ships of precisely similar figures, one of 1,000 tons displacement, and the other of 1,331 tons, which are to each other as the cube of 10 to the cube of 11; then the resistances of those vessels at the same speed will be to each other nearly as the square of 10 to the square of 11; that is, as 100 to 121. This principle, however, ceases to be exact in extreme cases; so that it is not applicable, for instance, to the comparison of real ships with small models. To make experiments on the resistance of models available for arriving at correct conclusions respecting vessels on the large scale, the velocities of the models must be kept within certain limits, to be afterwards specified.

It is evident that the smoothness or roughness of a vessel's bottom must materially affect her resistance. The bottom of every ship, how smooth soever it may have been originally, tends to become crusted in time with shells and weeds, which increase the adhesion of the water. It is very common to find the resistance increased by about a fourth from this cause; and occasionally it is increased more. The means of preventing or removing such incrustation consists mainly in coating the vessel with some substance which shall from time to time scale off in thin flakes, carrying the incrustation with it, and leaving the bottom clean.

Such is the action of the copper-sheathing of wooden ships, and of various paints and other compositions used for protecting iron ships.

CHAPTER VI.

Fairness—Models—Propulsion by Machinery—Propulsion by Sails.

ALTHOUGH some knowledge has been gained of the effect of using certain definite curves, such as the curve of versed-sines or harmonic curve, the trochoid or rolling-wave curve, and some others, for the water-lines or horizontal sections of ships; and although the effect of those and various other forms on the motion of the water has been theoretically investigated, it cannot yet be said that any particular form has been conclusively demonstrated to be the form of least resistance for a given displacement. Still, it has always been admitted by all naval architects, that the figure of a ship should be what mathematicians call "*continuous*" and shipbuilders "*fair*." A *fair line* is a line in which there is not only no sudden change of direction, but no sudden change of curvature; and a *fair surface* is one whose sections are all fair lines. The fairness of the water-lines, or horizontal sections, is of the highest importance in the form of a ship; next in importance is the fairness of the vertical longitudinal sections, called *bow* and *buttock lines;* and sometimes, to test the fairness of the intended form of a ship still further, oblique sections, called *diagonal* or *riband lines*, are drawn. The naval architect judges of the fairness of lines by the eye; and sometimes, if a model of the vessel is before him, by the sense of touch. To show the form of lines distinctly, models are made of layers of differently colored wood.

Propulsion by machinery, although of more modern invention (if we except rowing and paddling by hand) than propulsion by sails, is much simpler in its principles, and will therefore be considered first. The fundamental principle of the action of every propeller is the same, whether it is an oar, a paddle, a screw, a jet, or any other contrivance. The propeller drives backwards a certain quantity of water at a certain speed; in so doing, it presses backwards against the water with a force depending on the quantity of water driven back, and the speed impressed upon it. The water presses forward against the propeller with an equal force; and that force (which is called the "reaction" of the water), being transmitted to the framework of the machinery and thence to the vessel, is what drives her forward. When the ship is starting from a state of rest, or increasing her speed, the driving force must be greater than the resistance; but so long as the speed is uniform, the driving force and the resistance are equal.

Some propellers act directly backwards on the water, or nearly so, like the feathering paddle; some, like the common paddle, act more or less obliquely in a vertical plane; some, like the screw, act obliquely in various directions. Due regard must be given to those circumstances, and also to that of the working of the propeller in water which has already been disturbed by the vessel.

The *engine-power* required to drive a given vessel at a given speed depends on a mechanical principle which governs the actions of all machines whatsoever—*the equality of the energy exerted to the work performed.* The *useful* part of the work performed in driving a vessel during a given time (such as a second), is found by multiplying the resistance by the distance through which the vessel is driven. To this has to be added the *wasteful work*, one part of which is performed in the following manner:—The propeller exerts backwards a force equal to that with which the vessel is driven forwards; but it exerts that force through a greater distance, viz.:—the *sum* of the distance through which the vessel is driven forward, and the water backward (the latter distance is called the *slip*); so that the total work performed by the propeller is greater than the useful work, in the proportion in which the total backward speed of the propeller exceeds the forward speed of the ship—a proportion which ranges from $1\frac{1}{10}$: 1 to 2 : 1. Some additional work is wasted in giving lateral and vertical motions to the water, and in overcoming the friction of the machinery. The sum of all those quantities of work, useful and wasteful, which are performed in a given time, is equal to the energy which must be exerted in the same time by the engine. The ratio which the useful work bears to the energy exerted, is called the *efficiency* of the propeller and its machinery; in some of the best examples of economy of power in steam-vessels it is about 3 : 5; in less economical examples it is sometimes as low as 2 : 5, and perhaps even less.

When resistances are expressed in pounds, and are multiplied by the distances through which they are overcome, in feet, the products, or quantities of work, are said to be expressed in "*foot-pounds*." If the total number of foot-pounds of energy exerted per second in driving a vessel be divided by 550, the quotient is the *real* or *indicated horse-power* of her engine.

Upon the power of the engine, and its system of construction and working, depends its weight (including that of its boilers), for which, as well as for the store of fuel, provision must be made in the displacement of the vessel, and to which regard must be had in considering questions of stability.

Propulsion by Sails depends upon more complex principles than propulsion by machinery; because the direction of the wind, which supplies the propelling force, is seldom the same with that of the vessel's course, and often makes a great angle with it. The pressure of the air on the sails, moreover, does not depend on the *real* direction and velocity of the wind relatively to the ocean, but on its *apparent* direction and velocity relatively to the moving ship, and also on the position of the sails themselves.

The pressure of the wind, diffused over the surface of the sails, is capable, like the pressure of water and the force of gravity (see Chap. III.), of having its action on the ship as a whole represented by one resultant, traversing a point called the *Centre of Effort*, which is at a height above the deck depending on the figure, dimensions, and positions of the sails. When that resultant is oblique to the ship's course, it is resolved, according to well-known principles, into two *component forces*—the longitudinal component, acting forwards parallel to the keel, which is the effective effort that drives the ship forward against the resistance of the water; and the transverse component, acting at right angles to the keel, which drives the ship to leeward; so that her real course or direction of motion, instead of being parallel to the keel, makes a small angle to leeward of that line, called the *angle of leeway*.

The angle of leeway depends on the proportion borne by the velocity with which the ship drifts to leeward, to her forward velocity; and the velocity with which she drifts to leeward is such that the resistance to her *transverse* motion through the water is exactly equal to the transverse component of the pressure of the wind on the sails. Those two forces, though equal and opposite, are not directly opposed; for the resistance acts below water, and the transverse pressure of the wind high above water; they therefore form a *couple* (Chap. IV.), tending to make the vessel heel over; and the vessel does heel over to leeward until the moment of the righting couple, or moment of stability, is sufficient to balance the heeling moment. Thus the power of a vessel to carry sail depends on her stability, and must be kept in view in designing her.

It is evident that, for the purpose of propulsion by sails, it is not sufficient that the hull of the vessel should be of such a shape as to meet with little resistance to forward motion through the water; its shape should also be such as to meet with great resistance to transverse motion or leeway.

CHAPTER VII.

Working or Manœuvring Qualities of a Ship-Design.

THE working or manœuvring qualities of a ship depend on the combined action of the rudder, the propelling apparatus, the sails, and the figure of the ship's hull. In vessels under steam alone, the working qualities chiefly required are those of going readily astern as well as ahead, and of turning quickly and accurately, and in as small a circle as possible, under the action of the rudder. Sometimes, as in vessels driven by two screws with independent engines, the propelling apparatus may be used so as to turn the ship when required.

In vessels under sail, a much more complex combination of qualities is required. One of the most important is that of working well to windward, for which purpose it is essential that the ship should make little leeway, and should carry a *weather helm;* that is to say, that the action of the sails, unaided by that of the helm, should tend of itself to bring the ship's head towards the point from which the wind blows; this property, when in excess, is called *ardency.* It depends in a great measure on the position of the centre of effort of the sails, relatively to the resultant of the resistance to leeway. The manœuvring of a ship under sail, too, depends not merely on the action of the rudder and of the ship's hull on the water, but on the positions of the masts, and the figure and dimensions of the sails.

The working qualities of a ship are materially affected by her *trim*, or the position in which she floats. This depends on the position of her centre of gravity relatively to her centre of buoyancy; and the position of the centre of gravity depends partly on the stowage of the lading, as has been already stated in Chap. III.

Design.—From the brief summary which has been given of the qualities sought in a ship, and the means of obtaining them, it is evident that every one of those qualities is more or less affected by every circumstance in the figure and dimensions of the ship, the distribution of her weight, and the nature and arrangement of her means of propulsion; and, consequently, that the naval architect must keep the whole of those qualities, and the whole of those circumstances, before his mind at once, in designing a ship.

CHAPTER VIII.

Areas of Arbitrary Plane Figures—Trapezoidal Rule—Simpson's First and Second Rules.

THE area of a plane figure bounded by a curved line of arbitrary form, such as a frame or a water-line of a ship, is found by measuring a sufficient number of parallel and equidistant ordinates, conceiving the figure to be divided by certain of those ordinates into figures of the parabolic kind, computing the areas of those figures, and adding them together; or else computing the sum of those areas at one operation.

In Fig. 7, let ABCD be the plane figure whose area is to be measured, bounded by the straight base-line or axis of abscissæ,

FIG. 7.

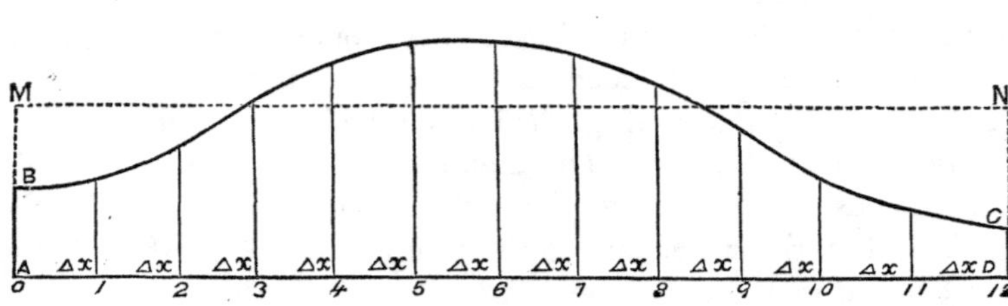

AD, by two ordinates, AB and DC, at right angles to the base, and by the curved line, BC.

Divide the base into a sufficient number of equal intervals, and draw and measure ordinates at the points of division. The total number of ordinates, including the two endmost ordinates, will of course be one more than the number of intervals.

If the area is to be measured by conceiving it to be divided into trapezoids (that is, by conceiving BC to be made up of straight lines), the number of intervals into which the base is divided may be either odd or even.

If the area is to be measured by conceiving it to be divided into parabolic areas of the second order, the number of intervals must be even; if into parabolic areas of the third order, the number of intervals must be a multiple of three.

In the example represented in the figure, the base is divided into twelve equal intervals, which will suit any one of those three methods.

For the sake of uniformity in stating the rules for calculation, the ordinates which separate the parabolic areas into which the figure is conceived to be divided from each other will be called *dividing ordinates*, and all the other ordinates, except the endmost ordinates, *intermediate ordinates*.

I. *Trapezoidal Rule.*—Here every ordinate, except the endmost ordinates, is a dividing ordinate.

Add together all the dividing ordinates, and one-half of the endmost ordinates; multiply the sum by the common interval: the product will be the required area, nearly. This is the simplest rule; but for figures whose boundaries present long sweeps of convexity or concavity, it is only a rough approximation.

II. *Parabolic Rule of the Second Order, or Simpson's First Rule.*—Here the number of intervals must be even; and the dividing ordinates are at the distance of a double interval from each other, being those at the points 2, 4, 6, &c., in Fig. 7. The intermediate ordinates are those at 1, 3, 5, &c.

Add together the endmost ordinates, double the dividing ordinates, and four times the intermediate ordinates; multiply the sum by one-third of the common interval: the product will be the required area, nearly. This is the most generally useful of all rules for measuring areas. It is capable of any required degree of accuracy, if the ordinates are made numerous and close enough.

III. *Parabolic Rule of the Third Order, or Simpson's Second Rule.*—Here the number of intervals must be a multiple of three; and the dividing ordinates are at the distance of a treble interval from each other, being at the points marked 3, 6, 9, in Fig. 7. The intermediate ordinates are at 1, 2, 4, 5, &c.

Add together the endmost ordinates, double the dividing ordinates, and three times the intermediate ordinates; multiply the sum by three-eighths of the common interval: the product will be the required area, nearly.

This rule is more complex than Simpson's first rule, and not more accurate.

[In algebraical symbols, those three rules for mensuration are expressed as follows:—Let L denote the whole length of the base, and n the number of intervals into which it is to be divided; then the *common interval* is given by the formula—

$$\triangle x = \frac{L}{n};$$

n being a multiple of 2 or 3, according to the order of the parabolic curves of which the boundary of the figure is held tc consist.

Let the ordinates corresponding to the following abscissæ,

$$0, \triangle x, 2\triangle x, 3\triangle x, \&c. \quad . \quad . \quad . \quad . \quad n\triangle x = L,$$

be denoted as follows—

$$y_1, y_2, y_3, y_4, \&c. \quad . \quad . \quad . \quad . \quad y_{n+1}.$$

This mode of numbering the ordinates is that practised by naval architects. Amongst pure mathematicians it is more common to number them as follows—

$$y_0, y_1, y_2, y_3, \&c. \quad . \quad . \quad . \quad . \quad y_n;$$

because of the convenience of having each ordinate marked by a number proportional to the corresponding abscissa; but the former method of numbering is adopted in the following equations:—

I. *Trapezoidal Rule*—

$$\int y dx = \triangle x \left(\frac{y_1 + y_{n+1}}{2} + y_2 + y_3 + \&c.\right).$$

II. *Simpson's First Rule*—

$$\int y dx = \frac{\triangle x}{3}(y_1 + 4y_2 + 2y_3 + 4y_4 + 2y_5 + \&c. \quad . \quad . \quad .$$
$$+ 2y_{n-1} + 4y_n + y_{n+1}).$$

III. *Simpson's Second Rule*—

$$\int y dx = \frac{3\triangle x}{8}(y_1 + 3y_2 + 3y_3 + 2y_4 + 3y_5 + 3y_6 + 2y_7 + \&c.$$
$$. \quad . \quad . \quad . \quad . \quad . + 2y_{n-2} + 3y_{n-1} + 3y_n + y_{n+1}).]$$

Mathematical principles might here be explained, for determining how close together the ordinates ought to be, in order to give an approximate area of any required degree of accuracy; but it is unnecessary to do so; because the constructor, after a little experience in the use of the rules, learns to judge by the eye whether the ordinates are close enough.

Where the curved boundary of the figure is nearly at right angles to the ordinates, and where it is nearly straight, the ordinates may be far apart. Where the curved boundary is very oblique to the ordinates, and where its curvature is sharp, the ordinates must be closer together.

Much time is saved in calculation by the use of *subdivided intervals*, as follows:—

In those parts of the figure where close ordinates are required, the ordinary intervals may be subdivided into half-intervals, quarter-intervals, or smaller subdivisions if necessary; each ordinate belonging to a set of subdivided intervals having its multiplier diminished in the same proportion in which the intervals are subdivided. Thus, the series of multipliers for ordinates at whole intervals being—

1, 4, 2, 4, 2, &c.,

the series of multipliers for ordinates at half-intervals will be—

$\frac{1}{2}$, 2, 1, 2, 1, &c.,

and at quarter-intervals,

$\frac{1}{4}$, 1, $\frac{1}{2}$, 1, $\frac{1}{2}$, &c.

When an ordinate stands between a larger and a smaller interval its multiplier will be the sum of the two multipliers which it would have had as an end-ordinate for each interval. Thus, for an ordinate between a whole-interval and a half-interval, the multiplier is $1+\frac{1}{2}=1\frac{1}{2}$; for an ordinate between a whole-interval and a quarter-interval, $1+\frac{1}{4}=1\frac{1}{4}$; for an ordinate between a half-interval and a quarter-interval, $\frac{1}{2}+\frac{1}{4}=\frac{3}{4}$, &c. The ordinates having been multiplied by their proper multipliers, and the products added together, the sum is to be multiplied by *one-third* of a *whole-interval*, to find the area.

In the following Table, those rules are applied to the calculation of the approximate area of a quadrant of a circle of 12 feet radius (Fig. 9).

This figure is chosen, because its true area to the 100th of a square foot is otherwise known to be $12 \times 12 \times .7854 = 113.10$ square feet, and this affords the means of testing the degree of approximation attained by the rules.

The ordinates are computed, to the accuracy of the 100th of a foot, by the formula, Ordinate$=\sqrt{(\text{radius}^2 - \text{abscissa}^2)}$.

In the first division of the Table, the base of the figure is divided into six intervals of two feet each. This gives an error of nearly $\frac{1}{100}$ of the whole area. In the second division of the Table, the last two intervals, where the curve becomes very oblique to the ordinates, are subdivided into four half-intervals, and the error is reduced to about $\frac{1}{250}$ of the whole area. In the third division of the Table, the last two half-intervals are further subdivided into four quarter-intervals; and the error in the area becomes only $\frac{1}{600}$ of the whole.

FIG. 9.

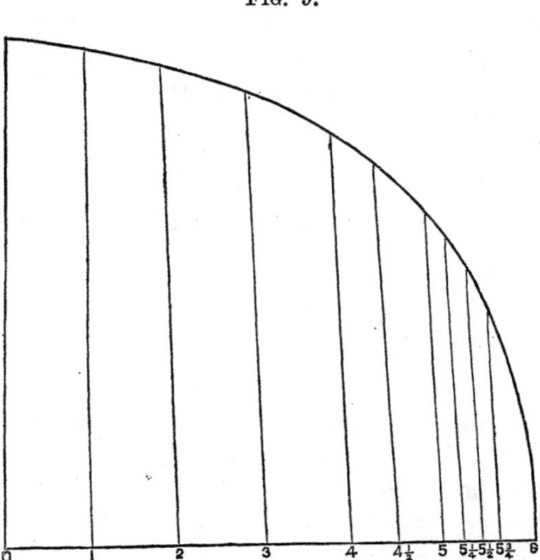

Approximate Area of the Quadrant of a Circle of 12 *feet Radius.*

I. Six Intervals.				II. Four Whole-Intervals, and Four Half-Intervals.				III. Four Whole-Intervals, Two Half-Intervals, and Four Quarter-Intervals.			
Number of Intervals from Origin.	Ordinates.	Multipliers.	Products.	Number of Intervals from Origin.	Ordinates.	Multipliers.	Products.	Number of Intervals from Origin.	Ordinates.	Multipliers.	Products.
0	12·00	1	12·00	0	12·00	1	12·00	0	12·00	1	12·00
1	11·83	4	47·32	1	11·83	4	47·32	1	11·83	4	47·32
2	11·31	2	22·62	2	11·31	2	22·62	2	11·31	2	22·62
3	10·39	4	41·56	3	10·39	4	41·56	3	10·39	4	41·56
4	8·94	2	17·88	4	8·94	1½	13·41	4	8·94	1½	13·41
				4½	7·94	2	15·88	4½	7·94	2	15·88
5	6·63	4	26·52	5	6·63	1	6·63	5	6·63	¾	4·97
								5¼	5·81	1	5·81
				5½	4·80	2	9·60	5½	4·80	½	2·40
								5¾	3·43	1	3·43
6	0	1	0	6	0	½	0	6	0	¼	0
			167·90				169·02				169·40
		× $\frac{\text{Interval}}{3}$,	⅔			× $\frac{\text{Interval}}{3}$,	⅔			× $\frac{\text{Interval}}{3}$,	⅔
Approximate Area			111·93	Approximate Area			112·68	Approximate Area			112·93
True Area			113·10	True Area			113·10	True Area			113·10
Error			—1·17	Error			—0·42	Error			—0·17
Or nearly $\frac{1}{100}$				Or nearly $\frac{1}{250}$				Or nearly $\frac{1}{600}$			

CHAPTER IX.

Volumes of Solid Figures—Direct Measurement of Volumes—Measurement of Volumes in Layers or in Rectangular Divisions.

THE *Volumes of Solid Figures* are computed as follows:—

Conceive the figure to be traversed in a convenient direction by a straight line, as base-line or axis of abscissæ, on which line divide the length of the solid into a sufficient number of equal intervals, and let the solid be conceived to be traversed by a series of plane cross-sections at the points of division of the base-line. If the solid figure has flat ends perpendicular to the base-line, those ends themselves will be the endmost sections. If it is pointed, wedge-shaped, or rounded at the ends, each of the endmost sections will be 0. Measure and compute the areas of the cross-sections by the rules applicable to plane figures.

Then conceive the areas of the sections to represent the ordinates of a plane curve of the same length with the solid figure; compute the area of that ideal curve by the rules applicable to plane curves: the area so computed will be equal to the volume of the solid figure.

The curve whose ordinates represent areas of sections is sometimes drawn on paper, and is then called the "*curve of areas.*" If drawn with sufficient accuracy, it obviously enables the volume of a figure to be found by means of the platometer.

In determining the closeness of the cross-sections, and subdividing, if necessary, the intervals between them, the same rules are to be followed as those which are applicable to the ordinates of plane figures.

Direct Measurement of Volumes.—A solid, standing on a rectangular plane base, may have its volume computed directly, without the intermediate process of finding sectional areas, by the following rule, which is founded on Simpson's first rule:—

Divide each side of the rectangular base into an even number of equal intervals, and through the points of division draw a network of lines, so as to divide the base into a number of equal rectangular subdivisions. At the angles of those subdivisions measure ordinates, which multiply by the factors shown in the following table, and add the products together. Multiply the sum by one-ninth of the product of the longitudinal and transverse intervals; the product will be the volume required.

Table of Multipliers for Ordinates.

For 2 × 2 Subdivisions.

1	4	1
4	16	4
1	4	1

For 4 × 6 Subdivisions.

1	4	2	4	2	4	1
4	16	8	16	8	16	4
2	8	4	8	4	8	2
4	16	8	16	8	16	4
1	4	2	4	2	4	1

For any number of Subdivisions.

1	4	2	4	2	&c.	2	4	1
4	16	8	16	8	&c.	8	16	4
2	8	4	8	4	&c.	4	8	2
4	16	8	16	8	&c.	8	16	4
2	8	4	8	4	&c.	4	8	2
&c.	&c.	&c.	&c.	&c.	&c.	&c.	&c.	&c.
"	"	"	"	"	"	"	"	"
"	"	"	"	"	"	"	"	"
"	"	"	"	"	"	"	"	"
2	8	4	8	4	&c.	4	8	2
4	16	8	16	8	&c.	8	16	4
1	4	2	4	2	&c.	2	4	1

Measurement of Volumes in Layers, or in Rectangular Divisions.

The volume of a solid may be computed in separate layers; the thickness of each layer being, if the trapezoidal rule is employed, one interval of the length; if Simpson's first rule, two intervals; if Simpson's second rule, three intervals. The trapezoidal rule is not always sufficiently exact; Simpson's first rule is the most generally useful. Supposing, then, that this rule is to be adopted, each layer will be bounded by two of the plane sections of the body to be measured, and will have a third plane section at the middle of its thickness. Then,

I. *Add together the two outer sections and four times the middle section: one-third of the sum multiplied by the interval of the sections (or half-thickness of the layer) will be the volume of the layer:*—Or otherwise, *one-sixth of the sum will be the mean sectional area of the layer, which multiplied by its thickness, will give its volume.*

The volume of a layer whose thickness is one interval, may be computed by the following rule, viz.:

To eight times the middle ordinate add five times the near end ordinate, and subtract the far end ordinate: multiply the remainder by one-twelfth of the common interval; the product will be the area required.

The volume of a solid standing on a rectangular base may also be computed in separate rectangular prisms, each standing on one or more rectangular subdivisions of the base. If Simpson's first rule be taken as the foundation of the method, each prism will stand on four subdivisions of the base, measuring two longitudinal intervals lengthwise by two transverse intervals breadthwise, and will have its curved boundary defined by nine ordinates; one in the centre, one in the middle of each of the four sides, and four at the corners. Then,

II. *Add together, the corner ordinates, four times the side ordinates, and sixteen times the middle ordinate; one-ninth of the sum, multiplied by the longitudinal and transverse intervals, will be the volume*:—Or otherwise, *one thirty-sixth part of the sum will be the mean ordinate, which multiplied by the area of the base of the prism, will give its volume.*

The rectangular divisions at the edges of the base may sometimes become wedge-shaped instead of prismatic, by their outer ordinates becoming $= 0$.

When the volume of a solid has thus been computed in rectangular divisions, these may be added together so as to give either longitudinal or transverse layers.

CHAPTER X.

Rules for Moments and Centres of Plane Areas—Rules for Moments and Centres of Volumes.

RULES FOR MOMENTS AND CENTRES OF PLANE AREAS.

LET the plane figure in question be such as that represented in Fig. 8, Chapter VIII., its curved boundary being defined by means of a series of equidistant ordinates; and let it be required to find the moment of that figure relatively to a transverse axis, AB, traversing the origin; its moment relatively to the base-line, AD; and the abscissa and ordinate of its centre. The rules for those purposes are as follows:—

I. To find the Moment relatively to the transverse Axis: *Multiply each ordinate by the corresponding abscissa; treat the products as if they were the ordinates of a curve, of the same length with the given figure; the area of that curve, found by the proper rule, will be the moment required.*

II. To find the Abscissa of the Centre: *Divide that moment by the area of the figure.*

In applying Rule I. it is often convenient to multiply each ordinate first by its proper multiplier, according to Simpson's rule, and then, not by the abscissa itself, but by the *number of intervals* contained in the abscissa, whether integral or fractional. The sum of the products is finally to be multiplied by *one-third of the square of a whole interval*, to obtain the moment required.

III. To find the Moment relatively to the Base-line or Axis of Abscissa: *Take the half-square of each ordinate; treat those half-squares as if they were the ordinates of a curve, of the same length with the given figure; the area of that curve, found by the proper rule, will be the moment required.*

IV. To find the Ordinate of the Centre: *Divide the last-mentioned moment by the area of the figure.*

RULES FOR MOMENTS AND CENTRES OF VOLUMES.

I. To find the Moment relatively to the Transverse Plane traversing the Origin: *Multiply each sectional area by the corresponding abscissa; treat the products as if they were the ordinates of a curve of the same length with the given figure; the area of that curve, found by the proper rule, will be the moment required.*

II. To find the Abscissa of the Centre: *Divide that moment by the volume of the figure.*

In applying Rule I. it is often convenient to multiply each sectional area, first by its proper multiplier according to Simpson's rule, and then by the number of intervals in the abscissa. The sum of the products is finally to be multiplied by *one-third of the square of a whole interval.*

The usual method of finding the moment of a solid figure relatively to a plane different from that first chosen, and the distance of the centre from that plane, is to conceive the solid to be divided into layers by transverse sections parallel to the new plane of moments, and proceed as in Rules I. and II. above stated.

Example.—Quarter-Spheroid as in Fig. 10.

FIG. 10.

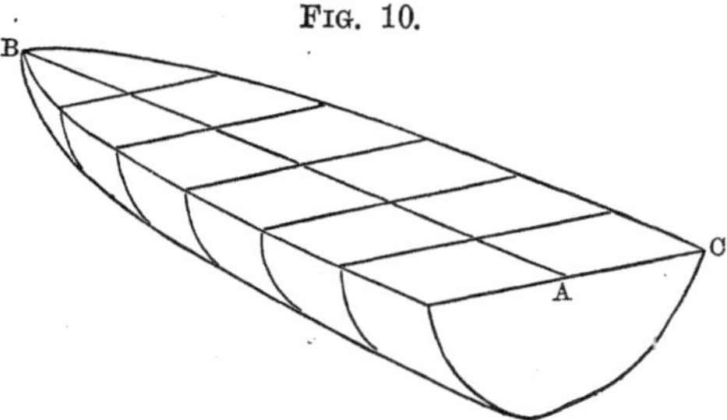

Calculation of the moment relatively to the transverse plane traversing A, and of the distance of the centre of mean distances from the plane. Length 120 feet, in six intervals of 20 feet; radius of greatest section 12 feet.

Number of Intervals from End Plane.	Sectional Areas.	Multipliers.	Products.	Products × Intervals from End Plane.
0	226·20	1	226·20	0
1	219·91	4	879·64	879·64
2	201·06	2	402·12	804·24
3	169·65	4	678·60	2035·80
4	125·66	2	251·32	1005·28
5	69·12	4	276·48	1382·40
6	0	1	0	0
				6107·36

$\times \frac{\text{Interval}^2}{3} = \frac{400}{3} =$ .... $133\frac{1}{3}$

Moment relatively to end plane at A 814315

$\frac{\text{Moment, } 814315}{\text{Volume, } 18096} = 45$, abscissa of centre of mean distances, being its distance from the end plane.

To find the moment relatively to the longitudinal plane through A and B, and the ordinate, or distance of the centre, from that plane, conceive the solid to be divided into six horizontal layers by horizontal plane sections at intervals of 2 feet, and proceed as above. It is unnecessary to give the details of the calculation.

The results are—

Moment, 81431.5 ;
Ordinate of centre, 4.5.

CHAPTER XI.

Centre of Gravity—Centres of Gravity and Moments of Bodies.

THE *Centre of Gravity* of a heavy body, or of a system of heavy bodies, is a point which is always traversed by the resultant of the weight of the body or system. Supposing a set of weights to act at detached points, their common centre of gravity is found by the following:—

RULE I.—*Having chosen a fixed plane to which to refer the positions of the weights, take their moments relatively to that plane by multiplying each weight by its perpendicular distance from the plane; find the resultant of those moments, and divide it by the sum of the weights; the quotient will be the distance of their common centre of gravity from the fixed plane. By a similar process, find the distances of the same point from two other fixed planes at right angles to the first plane and to each other; the position of the centre of gravity will then be completely known.*

The three planes are called, as in other cases, *co-ordinate planes*, and the distances of the weights and of their centre of gravity from those planes, *co-ordinates.*

The weights and their resultant (or sum) are to be regarded as all positive; but if some of the weights lie at one side, and some at the opposite side of a co-ordinate plane, their co-ordinates and moments relatively to that plane must be distinguished into positive and negative.

The sign of the resultant moment will show at which side of the plane the centre of gravity lies. When the resultant moment relatively to a plane is nothing, the centre of gravity is in that plane; and when each of the resultant moments is nothing, the centre of gravity is at the point of intersection of the three planes, or *origin of co-ordinates.* In other words, *the moment of a set of weights relatively to their common centre of gravity is nothing.*

The two following particular cases are useful:—

II.—*The common centre of gravity of two weights divides the straight line joining them into parts inversely proportional to the weights respectively furthest from them.* For example, in Fig. 11, let A and B be the two weights; join AB; the centre of gravity, G, divides that line in the following proportion:—

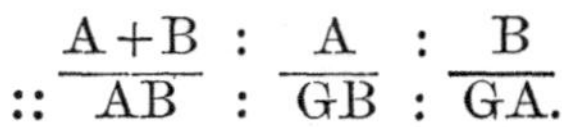

$$\mathrm{A+B} : \mathrm{A} : \mathrm{B} :: \overline{\mathrm{AB}} : \overline{\mathrm{GB}} : \overline{\mathrm{GA}}.$$

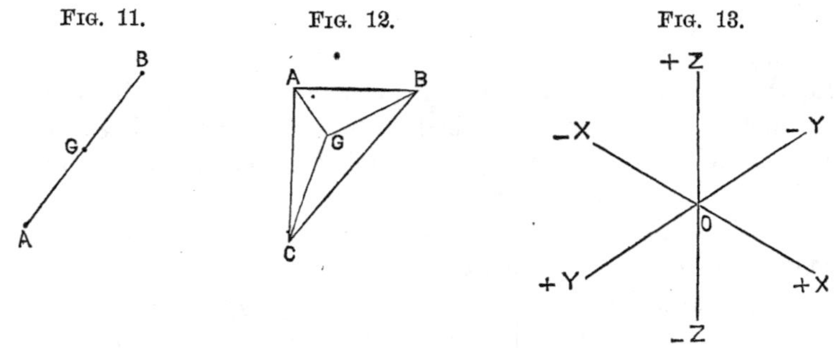

FIG. 11. FIG. 12. FIG. 13.

III.—*The common centre of gravity of three weights is in the same plane with them; and if from the centre of gravity three straight lines be drawn to the three weights, those lines will divide the triangle formed by the weights into three triangles, each of an area proportional to the weight furthest from it.*

In Fig. 12, let A, B, C, be the weights, G their common centre of gravity; then,

$$\mathrm{A+B+C} : \mathrm{A} : \mathrm{B} : \mathrm{C} :: \text{Triangle ABC} : \mathrm{GBC} : \mathrm{GCA} : \mathrm{GAB}.$$

[In algebraical symbols, the general problem of finding the common centre of gravity of a set of weights is expressed as follows:—In Fig. 13, let $-\mathrm{XO}+\mathrm{X}$, $-\mathrm{YO}+\mathrm{Y}$, $-\mathrm{ZO}+\mathrm{Z}$, be the axes of co-ordinates, being the three straight lines in which the three co-ordinate planes cut each other. The distance or ordinate of any point from the plane $\left\{\begin{matrix}\mathrm{YOZ}\\ \mathrm{ZOX}\\ \mathrm{XOY}\end{matrix}\right\}$ is denoted by $\left\{\begin{matrix}x\\ y\\ z\end{matrix}\right\}$, and regarded as positive or negative, according as the point lies to one side of the plane or to the opposite side.

Let the weights be denoted by W_1, W_2, W_3, &c.; their co-ordinates by x_1, y_1, z_1; x_2, y_2, z_2; x_3, y_3, z_3; &c.; and the co-ordinates of their common centre of gravity by x_G, y_G, z_G; then

$$x_G = \frac{W_1 x_1 + W_2 x_2 + W_3 x_3 + \&c.}{W_1 + W_2 + W_3 + \&c.};$$

$$y_G = \frac{W_1 y_1 + W_2 y_2 + W_3 z_3 + \&c.}{W_1 + W_2 + W_3 + \&c.};$$

$$z_G = \frac{W_1 z_1 + W_2 z_2 + W_3 z_3 + \&c.}{W_1 + W_2 + W_3 + \&c.}.]$$

Example.—Suppose that as the co-ordinate planes are taken, a horizontal plane in a ship's engine-room; a vertical longitudinal plane traversing that room amidships; and a transverse plane in a convenient assumed position; and that the weights under consideration are four portions of the engine, of the weights and in the positions stated in the following Table:—

Weights.		Co-ordinates.					
		Longitudinal.		Transverse.		Vertical.	
No.	Lbs.	Forward.	Backward.	Right.	Left.	Up.	Down.
1	1000	2	..	3	..	5	..
2	500	..	1	..	3	5	..
3	250	2	..	3	..	..	2
4	500	..	3	..	6	0	0
Total Weight.	2250						

Then the following Table shows the calculation of the moments and resultant moments, and of the co-ordinates of the centre of gravity:—

	Moments Relatively to					
	Transverse Plane.		Longitudinal Plane.		Horizontal Plane.	
No. of Weight.	Positive.	Negative.	Positive.	Negative.	Positive.	Negative.
1	2000	....	3000	....	5000	....
2	....	500	....	1500	2500	....
3	500	....	750	....	....	500
4	....	1500	....	3000	0	0
Sums..................	2500	2000	3750	4500	7500	500
Subtract...............	2000	....	....	3750	500	....
Resultant Moments.....	500	....	....	750	7000	....

Divide by total weight, 2250, giving for the co-ordinates of the centre of gravity... } Forward, $0.2\dot{2}$ | Left, $0.3\dot{3}$ | Up, $3.1\dot{1}$

IV. To find the effect upon the position of the centre of gravity of a set of weights, of shifting one of those weights into a new position, *multiply the weight shifted by the distance through which it is shifted, and divide by the sum of all the weights:* the quotient will be the distance through which the centre of gravity will be shifted, in a direction parallel to that in which the weight is shifted.

V. To find how far a given single weight must be shifted, in order to shift the common centre of gravity through a given distance in the same direction, *multiply the sum of the weights by the distance through which their common centre of gravity is to be shifted, and divide by the single weight.*

For example, if weight No. 3 of the preceding table, 250 lbs., be shifted in any direction through $4\frac{1}{2}$ feet, the centre of gravity will be shifted in the same direction through

$$\frac{250 \times 4\frac{1}{2}}{2250} = \frac{1}{2} \text{ foot.}$$

Centres of Gravity and Moments of Bodies.—The supposition of the weight of a body being concentrated at a point is a mathematical fiction, as has been already stated in Chap. III.; but the centre of gravity of a body, at which its weight may be conceived to be concentrated, without error as regards its mechanical action as a whole, can always be found.

When the body is *homogeneous,* or composed of material of uniform heaviness throughout, the following principles serve to determine the centre of gravity and the moment of its weight relatively to a given plane.

I. *The centre of gravity of a homogeneous body is its centre of figure, or of mean distances.*

II. *The moment of the weight, or statical moment, of a homogeneous body, relatively to a given plane, is equal to the product of its geometrical moment relatively to that plane into the heaviness of the material.*

The rules which have reference to *plane areas* are applicable to plates or prismatic bodies of uniform thickness, having those areas for bases. In computing statical moments by means of them, the following rule is to be used:—

III. *Multiply the geometrical moment of the plane base by the thickness, and by the heaviness of the material.* The product of the thickness into the heaviness is the weight per unit of area. In all such calculations, if the dimensions are expressed in feet, and the heaviness in lbs. to the cubic foot, the moment is expressed in *foot-pounds.* If the heaviness is *that of sea-water,* the geometrical moment itself is the statical moment *in cubic feet of sea-water at a leverage of a foot;* which may be multiplied by 64 for *foot-pounds*, or divided by 35 for *foot-tons.*

When a body is *heterogeneous*, or consists of parts of different heaviness, the following rule is to be applied:—

IV. *Divide the body into parts, each of which is of uniform or sensibly uniform heaviness; find the centre of gravity of each such part separately; conceive the weight of each part to be concentrated at its own centre of gravity, and treat those weights as detached weights* (according to rules before given in this chapter).

The *Resultant of a Pressure* distributed over a *plane surface* is found by the following rules:—

I. If the intensity is uniform, *muliply the area of the surface by the intensity.*

II. If the intensity is not uniform, *conceive that the surface lies horizontal, and that a solid stands upon it, whose height at each point represents the intensity of the pressure at that point. Then the volume of that solid will represent the amount of the pressure.* As to finding the volume of such a solid, see Chapter IX.

The *Centre of Pressure* means, a point traversed by the resultant of a pressure that is distributed over a surface. When the surface pressed upon is plane, the centre of pressure is a point in that surface itself, and is found according to the following rules:—

III. When the intensity of the pressure is uniform, *the centre of figure is the centre of pressure.*

IV. When the intensity of the pressure is not uniform, *find the centre of the solid of Rule* II., *from which let fall a perpendicular on the pressed surface; the foot of that perpendicular will be the centre of pressure;* or otherwise, *find the co-ordinates of the centre of that solid relatively to two axes in the plane of the pressed surface: these will be the co-ordinates of the centre of pressure.*

V. If the pressure is that of a fluid upon a solid immersed on it, then, as already stated (Chaps. I., II., and III.), *the Resultant Pressure is equal and opposite to the weight of the volume of fluid displaced; and the centre of pressure is the centre of that volume, or* CENTRE OF DISPLACEMENT.

CHAPTER XII.

Displacement and Centre of Buoyancy—Curve and Scale of Displacement—Methods of Computing Displacement—Computation of Cross Sections—Computation of Water Sections—Computation of Displacement in Layers—Appendages—Computation of Midship Section in Layers—Determination of Centre of Buoyancy.

DISPLACEMENT, AND CENTRE OF BUOYANCY.

THE drawings of a proposed ship, from which measurements for finding the displacement and stability of the ship are made, consists of three plans, viz.:—Sheer, Half-Breadth, and Body Plans. A great variety of lines are shown on these plans. Some of those lines are specially connected with the practical execution of the ship, and will be fully treated of in the following division of this work. In connection with displacement, two sorts of lines only have to be considered; and those are *Water-lines* and *Vertical Cross Sections.*

The water-lines of the immersed part of the ship are first drawn to the outside of plank, as represented in the accompanying plan of the U. S. steamer *Antietam* *, Plate 6, drawn on a scale of one-quarter of an inch to a foot, or $\frac{1}{48}$th of the real dimensions, which scale is commonly employed. The 16th water-line is the load-water line. To obviate the necessity of having to take off the half-breadths of the ordinates in order to compute the displacement, centre of buoyancy and metacentre, a Table of the ordinates as taken off is appended.

A WATER-LINE is the outline of a horizontal section of the ship; being the line in which the surface of the water either actually meets the skin of the ship when she floats upright at a certain depth of immersion, or would meet the skin of the ship if she were to float to a certain supposed depth.

The vertical depth between the highest and lowest water-lines is divided into a number of equal intervals by the intermediate water-lines, which are numbered in succession 2 W. L., 4 W. L., 6 W. L., &c. If considered necessary in calculating the displacement, those intervals may be subdivided, according to the principles explained in Chapter VIII. This is often required at those parts

* The plan in the book is reduced from this scale.

of the vessel's bottom which are rapidly curved, such as the *bilge*, being the part which connects the nearly upright side with the comparatively flat *floor*. The plane horizontal area enclosed within a water-line is called a *Water-section* or a *Plane of Flotation.*

As a *base-line*, or *longitudinal axis*, for all the measurements of the ship, there is taken the *Centre-Line of the Load-water-section*, marked AB in the sheer and half-breadth plans. It is held to extend from the forward edge of the rabbet of the stem at A, to the after-edge of the rabbet of the stern-post at B, being the points where the surface of the vessel meets the stem and stern-post respectively; and that distance is divided into a sufficient number of equal intervals, which may be subdivided where the figure of the vessel requires it.

When the vessel has two stern-posts, a main stern-post and a rudder-post, as in the case of most screw steamers, it is at the foremost of the two, or main stern-post, that the length of the load-water-section is held to terminate. In the plan, the base-line is divided into twenty intervals from the centre of the length each way. In vessels having a full bow and stern, several of the foremost and aftermost intervals should be subdivided into half-intervals, because of the rapid curvature of the water-lines. In vessels with fine entrances and runs to the water-lines, like the plan given, such subdivision is unnecessary. By calculating the displacement of the fore and after bodies separately, their relative capacities may be ascertained.

The *ordinates of a ship* are all *half-breadths;* that is to say, horizontal lines, measured from the central vertical longitudinal plane traversing the axis AB (*Antietam's* Plan) to the outside surface of the plank on the vessel. Each ordinate belongs at once to the water-section and to the vertical section of which it is the intersection; and by Simpson's rules, it has two multipliers, according as it is to be used in computing the area of the water-section, or that of the vertical section.

METHODS OF COMPUTING DISPLACEMENT.

There are two processes for computing the displacement of a ship, both of which should always be gone through; because the intermediate steps of both processes are necessary in the subsequent operation of finding the centre of buoyancy; and also because the agreements of their final results form a check on the accuracy of the calculations.

One process consists in first computing, by Simpson's rules, the areas of the several vertical sections; and then treating those areas as the ordinates of a new curve upon the base, AB, in order to compute the volume of the displacement, by the method of Chapter IX. Sometimes, though not always, that curve is drawn to a scale, and is called "Peak's Curve," or the Curve of Sectional Areas. The other process consists in computing the areas of the several water-sections, and then treating those areas as the ordinates of a new curve upon a base equal to the distance between the load-water-line and the lowest water-line, in order to compute the displacement, not only up to the load-water-section, but up to each water-section of the series.

The area of a given water-section represents also the *displacement in cubic feet per vertical foot of immersion* at that water-section; which, being divided by 35, gives the *displacement in tons per foot of immersion.* This again, being divided by 12, gives the *displacement in tons per inch of immersion.*

$$= \frac{\text{Water-section in square feet}}{420}.$$

It is customary, in drawing the curve of water-sections on the plans of a ship, to lay down its horizontal ordinates to such a scale that they shall represent, not the areas of the water-sections themselves, in square feet, but the 420th parts of those areas, or the *tons per inch immersion.* The use of that quantity has already been illustrated in Chapter II. It enables us to calculate how much deeper a given ship will be immersed by a given addition to her lading.

Curve and Scale of Displacement.—(Fig. 15.) The displacements themselves, in tons of 35 cubic feet, corresponding to different draughts of water, are laid down on the drawing as the horizontal ordinates of a curve, O*d*D. For example, the ordinate, HD, represents the load displacement, and the ordinate, *hd*, the displacement at the draught, O*h*. A scale of tons is marked along the longest ordinate, HD.

Computation of Cross-Sections.—As each vertical cross-section consists of two similar halves, it is customary to begin by computing the half area of each vertical section, and afterwards to multiply it by 2. The appearance of the vertical sections upon the body-plan enables the naval architect to judge where and to what extent subdivisions of the vertical intervals is required; and that subdivision should be made by means of intermediate water-sections running the whole length of the ship, for the sake of uniformity in the calculations, the neglect of which is apt to lead to confusion and mistakes.

Computation of Water-Sections.—The water-sections, like the cross-sections, consist of two similar halves; and therefore, in general, the half areas are computed first, and afterward multiplied by 2. The process of measurement and calculation requires no special remark, being almost always performed by means of Simpson's First Rule, with subdivided intervals where they are required (Chapter VIII.), of which the naval architect judges from the appearance of the half-breadth plan.

Computation of Displacement in Layers.—The computation of the load displacement presents no peculiarity; it is performed by treating the areas of the water-sections just as the ordinates are treated in computing areas of cross-sections, the series of multipliers being exactly the same.

In computing the series of displacements up to the other water-sections, the particular rule employed must be varied according to the circumstances of the particular calculation.

If the displacement up to the 7th W.L. was required, the water-line next below the load-water-line, it could be computed by the following rule, and subtracted from the load displacement, viz.: To *five* times the area of the L.W.L. add *eight* times the area of the 6th W.L. and substract the area of the 5th W.L.; multiply the remainder by one-twelfth of the vertical interval or depth of the layer: the product will be the volume of the layer.

The volume of any even number of equally deep layers is to be computed by Simpson's First Rule, and that of three equally deep layers by Simpson's Second Rule.

The name of *Appendages* is given to small portions of the ship which project beyond the net-work of water-sections and cross-sections, and whose volume must therefore be found by special calculations, and added to the main part of the displacement. They usually consist of the keel below its rabbet, the false keel (if any), part of the stem, part of the stern-post, the rudder and the rudder-post in screw steamers.

Computation of Midship-Section in Layers.—It is a common practice to compute the area of immersed midship-section for a series of different draughts of water, like the displacement; and the process is perfectly analogous. The areas can then be represented by the horizontal ordinates of a curve, which usually in general appearance is somewhat like the curve of displacement. It was formerly supposed that the resistance of a given ship at the same speed, and at different immersions, varied proportionally to the area of the immersed midship-section; but that supposition was founded on an imperfect theory of the resistance of fluids, and has not been corroborated by experience.

Determination of Centre of Buoyancy.—The nature of the centre of buoyancy, and the use of finding its position, has been explained in Chapter III.

As the immersed part of a ship floating upright consists of two symmetrical halves, one on each side of the central vertical plane which traverses AB, Figs. 1 and 2, Plate 6, it is obvious that the centre of buoyancy of a ship floating upright must be in that plane; so that in order to find the position of that centre completely, it is only necessary to find its horizontal distance from the plane of the cross-section through A, and its vertical depth below the load-water-section.

To find the horizontal distance of the centre of buoyancy from a transverse vertical plane through A, the first step is to compute the *moment* of the volume of displacement relatively to that plane by the rule for moments and centres of volumes, page 30, Chapter X.; that is to say, the area of each cross-section is to be multiplied by its distance from A, and the products treated as the ordinates of a new curve. The moment thus found, being divided by the volume of the displacement, gives the distance required.

To find the depth of the centre of buoyancy below the load-water-section, the first step is to compute the moment of the volume of the displacement relatively to the plane of that section, by the rule just referred to; that is to say, the area of each water-section is to be multiplied by its depth below the load-water-section, and the products treated as the ordinates of a new curve. The moment thus found, being divided by the volume of the displacement, gives the depth required.

In performing these calculations, time is saved by the method already explained in Chapter X., of multiplying the sectional areas in the first instance not by the leverages themselves, but by the number of intervals to which those leverages are proportional, and performing a multiplication by the common interval after the addition has been made.

Half Breadths of Ordinates for Computing the Displacement of the U. S. Steamer "Antietam."

Fore Body.	2 ft. W. L.	4 ft. W. L.	6 ft. W. L.	8 ft. W. L.	10 ft. W. L.	12 ft. W. L.	14 ft. W. L.	16 ft. W. L.
Section No. 1	.....	.....	.....	.....	.....	.....	.....	0.66
" " 2	.....	0.79	1.17	1.50	1.79	2.08	2.37	2.66
" " 3	1.08	1.66	2.33	2.92	3.42	3.92	4.37	4.83
" " 4	1.75	2.75	3.66	4.50	5.25	5.92	6.50	7.08
" " 5	2.50	4.00	5.21	6.21	7.17	8.00	8.66	9.29
" " 6	3.42	5.39	6.83	8.00	9.12	10.04	10.83	11.50
" " 7	4.42	6.75	8.58	9.87	11.08	12.08	12.87	13.50
" " 8	5.50	8.25	10.25	11.66	12.92	13.92	14.75	15.37
" " 9	6.62	9.70	11.83	13.42	14.70	15.62	16.37	16.96
" " 10	7.83	11.21	13.42	15.00	16.33	17.17	17.83	18.25
" " 11	9.08	12.66	14.92	16.58	17.66	18.50	19.12	19.50
" " 12	10.33	14.04	16.21	17.75	18.87	19.62	20.12	20.42
" " 13	11.58	15.33	17.42	18.83	19.83	20.50	20.96	21.21
" " 14	12.75	16.46	18.50	19.75	20.70	21.25	21.58	21.83
" " 15	13.83	17.42	19.33	20.54	21.33	21.83	22.08	22.25
" " 16	14.75	18.25	20.08	21.17	21.87	22.21	22.47	22.58
" " 17	15.42	18.83	20.62	21.58	22.21	22.50	22.70	22.83
" " 18	15.92	19.29	21.00	21.92	22.46	22.70	22.87	22.96
" " 19	16.25	19.62	21.25	22.12	22.58	22.83	22.96	23.00
" " 20	16.42	19.75	21.37	22.21	22.75	22.87	22.96	23.00
Centre No. 21	16.50	19.87	21.42	22.29	22.75	22.87	22.96	23.00

After Body.	2 ft. W. L.	4 ft. W. L.	6 ft. W. L.	8 ft. W. L.	10 ft. W. L.	12 ft. W. L.	14 ft. W. L.	16 ft. W. L.
Section No. 1	0.66	0.79	1.08	1.47	0.87	0.66	0.66	0.66
" " 2	0.79	1.00	1.47	1.92	2.12	2.46	3.37	4.87
" " 3	0.97	1.46	2.17	2.87	3.67	4.87	6.58	8.67
" " 4	1.25	2.00	3.04	4.25	5.75	7.58	9.66	11.92
" " 5	1.66	2.83	4.33	6.00	8.00	10.17	12.33	14.33
" " 6	2.25	3.92	5.92	8.00	10.29	12.58	14.58	16.25
" " 7	3.08	5.29	7.79	10.17	12.50	14.66	16.42	17.75
" " 8	3.96	6.83	9.66	12.25	14.50	16.42	17.92	18.87
" " 9	5.00	8.42	11.50	14.12	16.25	17.83	18.00	19.70
" " 10	6.21	10.17	13.33	15.79	17.66	19.00	19.92	20.42
" " 11	7.58	11.87	15.00	17.25	18.83	20.00	20.62	21.00
" " 12	9.08	13.50	16.50	18.46	19.83	20.75	21.25	21.50
" " 13	10.58	15.00	17.75	19.46	20.62	21.33	21.66	21.87
" " 14	12.04	16.29	18.79	20.25	21.21	21.83	22.08	22.25
" " 15	13.37	17.42	19.62	20.92	21.70	22.17	22.37	22.54
" " 16	14.50	18.25	20.29	21.42	22.04	22.42	22.58	22.70
" " 17	15.33	18.92	20.79	21.79	22.29	22.66	22.79	22.87
" " 18	15.92	19.37	21.12	22.00	22.50	22.79	22.87	22.92
" " 19	16.25	19.66	21.33	22.17	22.62	22.87	22.92	22.96
" " 20	16.42	19.75	21.37	22.21	22.75	22.87	22.96	23.00
Centre No. 21	16.50	19.87	21.42	22.29	22.75	22.87	22.96	23.00

Piece of the stem forward of Section No. 1, to be added to the total displacement.

To be added to the area of 2 ft. W. L. Fore Body.......

To be added to the area of 4 ft. W. L. Fore Body.......

To be added to the area of 6 ft. W. L. Fore Body......

To be added to the area of 8 ft. W. L. Fore Body........

To be added to the area of 10 ft. W. L. Fore Body..

To be added to the area of 12 ft. W. L. Fore Body..

To be added to the area of 14 ft. W. L. Fore Body..

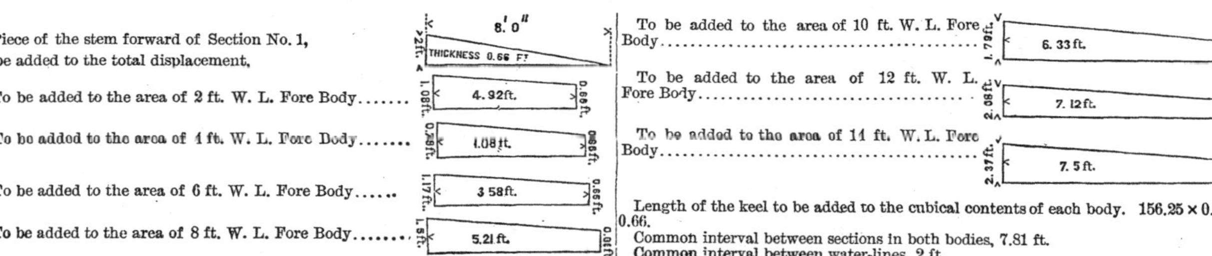

Length of the keel to be added to the cubical contents of each body. 156.25 × 0.83 × 0.66.

Common interval between sections in both bodies, 7.81 ft.

Common interval between water-lines, 2 ft.

CHAPTER XIII.

Coefficients of Fineness—Tonnage—Burden.

If two ships have figures so far similar, that every ordinate or half-breadth in one of them bears an uniform proportion to the corresponding or similarly situated ordinate in the other ship, it is evident that the displacements of those two ships will be to each other simply in the proportion of the products of their lengths, extreme breadths, and immersed depths or draughts of water; that is, of the rectangular solids circumscribed about their respective immersed bodies.

Hence, if it has been ascertained that the displacement of a given ship is a certain fraction of the circumscribed rectangular solid, the displacement of any other ship of similar figure (as above defined) may be found by multiplying the product of her length, extreme breadth, and immersed depth, by the same fraction. That fraction is called a *coefficient of fineness;* because, by being greater in ships with bluff ends and flat floors, and smaller in ships with fine ends and rising floors, it furnishes a sort of indication of the general character of a ship's figure.

Examples of the coefficient of fineness will be given in the sequel. Amongst its commonest values are those which range from 0.5 to 0.66; but it is occasionally as low as 0.3, and as high as 0.8.

Besides the just-mentioned coefficient of fineness of the displacement, coefficients of fineness may also be computed for cross-sections and for water-sections. Thus the midship section, being divided by the rectangle of its extreme breadth and immersed depth, gives a coefficient which ranges from 0.5 to very near 1. The coefficients of fineness of water-lines, obtained by dividing the area of a water-section by the rectangle of its length and extreme breadth, range in extreme cases from 0.5 to 0.9, the more common proportions being from 0.6 to 0.75.

The mean coefficient of fineness of all the water-lines of a ship is obtained as follows: multiply the greatest immersed area of midship-section by the length of the load-water-line, and divide the load displacement by the product.

The coefficient of fineness of the displacement is equal to the product of the coefficient of fineness of the midship-section, multiplied by the mean coefficient of fineness of the water-lines.

The *Tonnage* of a ship, according as the word is qualified, may mean either the Displacement in Tons, the Burden, the Registered Tonnage, or the Tonnage by "Builders'" old measurement.

The *Burden* means the number of tons of lading which the ship is able to carry, in addition to the weight of her hull and equipments. It is obviously equal to the difference between the displacement when light, and the displacement when loaded; and, on the scale of displacement, supposing OH, Fig. 15, to represent the load draught of water, and *oh* the light draught, the burden is represented by the difference between the ordinates, HD and *hd*. Hence the burden of a ship, whose dimensions and figure, and light and load draughts are given, can always be calculated with precision. According to what has already been stated in Chapter II., the burden of a ship ranges from about one-half to two-thirds of her load-displacement, according to the heaviness or lightness of her construction. Wooden ships are heavier than iron ships of the same load displacement, and ships of war heavier than merchant ships. The following may be taken as ordinary proportions:—

	Per Cent. of Load Displacement.	
	Ship.	Lading.
Iron Merchant Ships	35	65
Wooden Merchant Ships	40	60
Ships of War, from	40	60
" " to	50	50

Large ships, to be equally strong with small ships, must be made proportionally heavier; so that the weight of a large ship will form a greater percentage of the displacement, and that of a small ship a smaller, than the average stated above. This applies especially to the skin, the keel, and all longitudinal parts of the framing, whose weight should vary nearly *as the displacement multiplied by the length*, or, in similarly shaped vessels, *as the displacement multiplied by its own cube root.*

The total burden of a steam-vessel includes her engines and store of fuel; hence, to find her net burden, available for cargo, those weights must be subtracted from the total burden. The proportion which they bear to the displacement varies very much in different cases, according to the speed, the figure of the ship, and the construction and efficiency of the engine; and it is likely to undergo very great diminution when improvements in design and in economy shall have been generally adopted in practice. The results of present practice, with moderately good design and economy, may be roughly approximated to by the following rules:—

A steamer of 1000 tons' displacement, to go at a full speed of ten knots under steam, requires engines of the weight (including boilers) of about 125 tons, and a store of coal of one ton per hour of the voyage, or one-tenth of a ton per nautical mile.

The weight of engines, and of fuel consumed *per hour*, varies nearly as the square of the cube root of the displacement, and as the cube of the speed; but the weight of fuel *for a given trip* varies as the square of the speed.

[In algebraical symbols, let V denote the speed in knots per hour, and D the displacement in tons; then—

$$\text{Tons' weight of engines and boilers} = \frac{V^3 D^{\frac{2}{3}}}{800} \text{ nearly;}$$

$$\text{Tons coal per hour} \quad . \quad . \quad . \quad . = \frac{V^3 D^{\frac{2}{3}}}{100{,}000} \text{ nearly;}$$

$$\text{Tons coal per nautical mile} \quad . \quad . = \frac{V^2 D^{\frac{2}{3}}}{100{,}000} \text{ nearly.]}$$

Such calculations as these, however, give but a loose approximation; for the actual weight of engines and boilers, even according to ordinary examples, may range from four-fifths to once and a quarter of that given by the above rule, and the consumption of fuel within even wider limits (say from two-thirds to once and a half in ordinary cases, and from half to double in extreme cases), owing to the great differences in the economy of engines.

The burden of a ship may be computed approximately, by multiplying the area in square feet of the water-section midway between the load and light water-lines, by the difference between the load and light draught in feet, and dividing by 35 for tons. The area of that water-section may also be approximated to with considerable accuracy by a practised measurer, by measuring simply its extreme length and breadth, and multiplying their product by a coefficient of fineness, estimated by the eye at the commencement of this chapter; and this was the method of measuring the burden of ships introduced by Chapman into Sweden.

CHAPTER XIV.

Combined Calculations of Buoyancy and Stability—Object of this Chapter—Arrangement of the Data—Arrangement of the Results of Calculations.

COMBINED CALCULATIONS OF BUOYANCY AND STABILITY.

The *object of the present section* is to illustrate by an example, the manner in which the calculations of displacement, and of the positions of the centre of buoyancy and metacentre, can be conveniently combined in one tabular arrangement for practical purposes.

The methods of doing this are, of course, all identical in principle; but during the progress of naval architecture they have varied considerably in detail, and have been from time to time rendered more simple and concise. The arrangement adopted in this section is the most simple and concise yet known.*

The cross-sections are numbered from 1 to 17, commencing at the stern.

The ordinates or half-breadths at the intersections of the cross-sections and water-sections, having been measured, are set down in the Table given at the end of this chapter.

The column on the extreme left of that Table contains the numbers of the cross-sections 1, 2, 3, 4, &c.

The next column contains Simpson's Multipliers, in their order, agreeably to the rules given in Chap. VIII.

Then follow the columns containing the ordinates.

Of these columns there are as many as there are water-sections; that is, in the present case, nine, including the base-line.

The columns containing ordinates are headed at the top with the numbers of the water-sections, and immediately below these with Simpson's Multipliers. The ordinates are ranged in as many lines as there are cross-sections; that is, in the present case, seventeen: being at whole-intervals apart.

Arrangement of Results of Calculation.—Immediately *to the right* of each ordinate is written, in differently-sized or differently-colored figures, its product by the Simpson's multiplier proper to the *line* to which the ordinate belongs.

Immediately *below* each ordinate is written, in differently-sized

* This method was devised by the late Mr. John Wilson, chief draughtsman in the Surveyors' department of the English Admiralty.

or differently-colored figures, its product by the Simpson's multiplier proper, to the *column* to which the ordinate belongs. For example, at the intersection of the line belonging to the cross section 3 (for which the Simpson's multiplier is 2), and the column belonging to the water-section 3 W.L. (for which the Simpson's multiplier is 4), is the ordinate 9.87. Immediately to the right of that ordinate is written its product by the multiplier 2, viz., 19.74, and immediately below it is written its product by the multiplier 4, viz., 39.48.

The products written *below* the ordinates are added in *lines;* and the sum of each line of products is written in the column headed "Half Areas $\div \frac{\text{V.I.}}{3}$," under the general heading "Vertical Sections." The numbers in this column are proportional to the areas of the several vertical cross-sections; but to give the absolute values of those areas, they still require to be multiplied by 2, and by one-third of the vertical interval of the ordinates, (abbreviated into $\frac{\text{V.I.}}{3}$).

Each of those numbers proportional to the areas of the cross-sections is then multiplied by the proper Simpson's multiplier, found in the second column from the extreme left of the Table; and the products are written in the column headed "Multiples of Areas." These multiples being added up, their sum (viz., 16563.20) is written at the foot of the column. It is then multiplied successively by one-third of the vertical interval $\left(\frac{\text{V.I.}}{3}=\frac{2.12}{3}\right)$ and by one-third of the horizontal interval $\left(\frac{\text{H.I.}}{3}=\frac{14.5}{3}\right)$ The product (56572.52961) is one-half of the load displacement, in cubic feet, which being multiplied by 2 gives 113145.05922 cubic feet, the whole *load displacement;* and this being divided successively by 7 and by 5 gives 3232.71597, the *Load Displacement in Tons.*

Each of the numbers in the column headed "Multiples of Areas" is next multiplied by the proper "Multiplier for Leverage," contained in the column on its right. The multiplier for leverage for a given cross-section is the number of intervals by which that cross-section is distant from the first cross-section or commencement of the base-line.

The products are set down in the column headed "*Moments;*" and having been added up, their sum (131032·80), at foot of column) is multiplied by the horizontal interval (H.I. = 14.5). The product (1899975·60) is not the absolute value of the moment of the displacement relatively to the first cross-section; but it bears the same proportion to that moment which the sum of the column headed "Multiples of Areas" (16563.20) bears to the displacement.

Dividing, therefore, that product by that sum, the quotient (1899975.60 ÷ 16563.20 = 114.7) is *the horizontal distance in feet of the centre of buoyancy forward of the first cross-section.*

Returning to the columns containing the ordinates, the products written immediately to the *right* of the ordinates are added in *columns*, and the sum of each column of products is written at the foot of the column, in the line marked "Half-Water-Sections $\div \frac{\text{H. I.}}{3}$." The numbers in this line are proportional to the areas of the several water-sections; but to give the absolute values of those areas, they still require to be multiplied by 2, and by one-third of the horizontal interval between the ordinates (here abbreviated into $\frac{\text{H. I.}}{3}$). Each of those numbers proportional to the areas of the water-sections is then multiplied by the proper Simpson's multiplier, as written in the line below it. The products are written in the next line again, marked "Multiples of Water-Sections," and being added together, their sum (16563·20) is written to their left. If the calculations have been correctly made, that sum ought to agree *exactly* with the sum of the column headed "Multiples of Areas."

Each of the numbers in the line of "Multiples of Water-Sections" is next multiplied by the proper "Multiplier for Leverage," contained in the line immediately below. The multiplier for leverage for a given water-section is the number of intervals by which that water-section is below the load-water-section. The products are set down in the line marked "Moments;" and having been added together, their sum (57775·68) at the left end of the line, is mutiplied by the (V. I. = 2·12). The product (122484·4416) is not the absolute value of the moment of the displacement relatively to the load-water-section; but it bears the same proportion to that moment which the sum of the line marked "Multiples of Water-Sections (16563·20) bears to the displacement. Dividing, therefore, that product by that sum, the quotient (122484·4416 ÷ 16563·2 = 7·39) is *the depth, in feet, of the centre of buoyancy below the load-water-section.*

Below the calculations of moments just described, are written the calculations of the *displacement up to the several water-sections* between the load-water-section and the keel. The calculator here employs various rules according to his judgment, so as to save labor as much as possible. In the present case the displacement up to the 2d, 4th, and 6th water-sections is computed by Simpson's First Rule.

The area of each water-section in square feet being divided by 35, gives the *tons displacement per foot of immersion*, which is divided by 12 for the *tons displacement per inch of immersion.*

The *areas of the midship-section* (No. 9) up to the several water-lines, are computed from its ordinates, just as the displacements are computed from the water-sections; and those areas are written at the foot of the Table.

The two columns at the right-hand side of the Table, headed "Metacentre," contain the *calculations of stability*, estimated from the expression $\frac{2}{3}\int\frac{y^3dx}{D}$, in which

y=The ordinates of the half-breadth, load-water-section.

dx=The increment of the length of the load-water-section.

D=Displacement of the immersed portion of the body in cubic feet.

The first of those columns, headed "Cubes," contains the cubes of the ordinates, or half-breadths, of the load-water-section.

Each of those cubes is multiplied by the proper Simpson's multiplier (found in the second column from the left of the Table), and the products are written in the column headed "Multiples of Cubes." Those products having been added up, their sum (326006·757804) is multiplied by one-third of the horizontal interval $\left(\frac{\text{H.I}}{3}=\frac{14.5}{3}\right)$ giving the area of the curve whose ordinates are the cubes of the half-breadths (1575699·329386). Two-thirds of that area is the *coefficient of surface stability* (1050466·219590); which, being divided by the displacement in cubic feet, (113145·05922) gives the *height of the metacentre above the centre of buoyancy* (9.28) feet.

From that height, at the lower left-hand corner of the Table, is subtracted the depth of the centre of buoyancy below L. W. L. (7·39 feet); leaving the *height of the metacentre above* L. W. L. (1·89 feet).

FIG. 15.

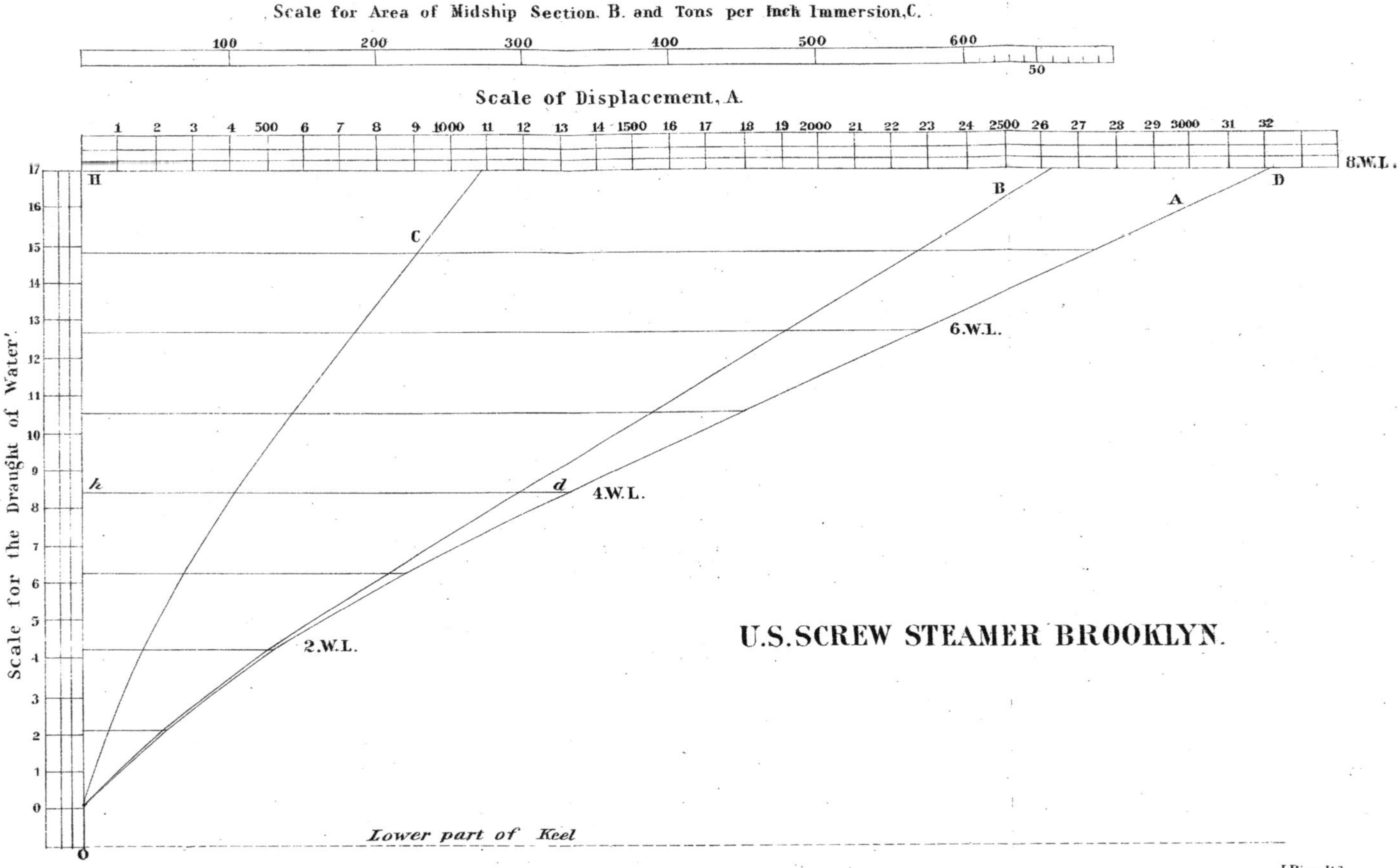

U.S. SCREW STEAMER BROOKLYN.

J. Bien, lith.

CHAPTER XV.

Practical Method of ascertaining the Height of the Centre of Gravity of a Vessel Equipped and Ready for Sea.

THE position of the centre of gravity of a vessel may be found by direct calculation. Still the results cannot be regarded with much confidence. When the difficulties which beset this method of ascertaining the centre of gravity of a ship were understood, it was seen that, as in any small body which is symmetrical with respect to a plane passing through it, its centre of gravity may be found by suspending it from two points in that plane by means of a string, and obtaining the point in which two vertical lines drawn through the points of suspension intersect, so, by altering the *line of support* of a ship, *i.e.*, the vertical lines through the centres of gravity and buoyancy, and obtaining the point in which two such verticals intersect, the position of the centre of gravity of the ship may be found. Any person possessed of a small amount of mathematical knowledge, and having the drawings of the ship, could ascertain for himself the position of the centre of gravity of the ship in a very short time.

The rationale of the method may be briefly given as follows:

Let ACD, Fig. 14, represent the transverse section of a ship through G, the common centre of gravity of the hull and every article on board; WL the load-water-line when the ship is floating in the upright position; CBGM the middle line, which is therefore perpendicular to WL, and also contains G, the centre of gravity of the ship, and B, the centre of buoyancy (or centre of gravity of the displacement); let, also, P represent a weight or weights on any or all of the decks, such as the guns, shot, ballast, &c., capable of being readily transported to the opposite side of the deck or decks.

If the weight or weights P be moved across the deck to P′ the ship will incline through an angle WSW′, the amplitude of which will depend, *cœteris paribus*, upon the weight or weights moved, and the distance through which they have been moved.

When the ship has taken up the new position of equilibrium, the centre of buoyancy will have moved from B to B′, and the centre of gravity of the ship from G to G′; so that the line joining B′ and G′ will be vertical, and therefore perpendicular to W′L,′ the new water-line, and will make the same angle BMB′ with the middle line BGM as the water-lines do with each other; and B′G′ produced will meet the middle line in a point M. This point, in ships of the usual form, may, without any appreciable error, be assumed to coincide with the *metacentre* when the inclination does not exceed 4° or 5°.

From a general and well-known property of the centre of gravity of a system of bodies, such as a ship, we know that since the weight or weights P have been moved in a horizontal direction to P′, the centre of gravity has also moved in the same direction; therefore GG′, the line joining the original and the new centres of gravity, will be horizontal; and from another property of the centre of gravity we have, that the weight of the ship × GG′ = P × distance through which it has been moved; or, if W represent the total weight of the ship, and c the distance through which the centre of gravity of the weight or weights P has been moved,

$$W \times GG' = P.c$$

$$\text{and } GG' = \frac{P.c}{W}$$

Now by trigonometry GG′= GM × tangent of the angle between the middle line and the new vertical line B′G′M, *i.e.*, the angle of the ship's inclination from the upright; or representing the angle of inclination by θ,

$$GG' = GM \tan\theta$$

Equating the two values of GG′ thus obtained,

$$\frac{P.c}{W} = GM, \tan\theta$$

$$\text{or, } GM = \frac{P.c}{W \tan\theta} \qquad (1)$$

The right-hand member of this equation (1) will contain all known quantities after the ship has been inclined; and since the *metacentre* corresponding to any draught of water is easily obtained by calculation from the drawings of the ship, and its position fixed, the distance GM set off below it will give the position of the centre of gravity of the ship.

Should the inclination obtained by the movements of the

weights on board be greater than the limit before mentioned, the vertical through the new centre of buoyancy may not pass through the *metacentre*, but through another point of the middle-line, found in the following manner:—

Through B draw BP parallel to W′L′, and therefore perpendicular to B′G′. Let A represent the weight of the water displaced by either of the equal wedges WSW′, LSL′, of which the centres of gravity are g and g' respectively. From g and g' let fall the perpendiculars gh and $g'h'$ upon W′L′ and let b represent the distance hh'. The product bA may be found by the ordinary methods of calculation, and is, in fact, the first part of the expression representing the moment of stability of the ship.

Now, by the general property of the centre of gravity before made use of, since the wedge WSW′ concentrated in g, its centre of gravity, has been moved in the direction W′ L′, through a distance b, to LSL′ concentrated in g', the distance BP through which the centre of buoyancy has moved in the same direction is

equal to $\frac{b.\text{A}}{\text{W}} = \text{BP}$

But by trigonometry $\text{BP} = \text{BM} \sin\theta$

$$\text{BP} = \text{GM} \sin\theta + \text{BG}. \sin\theta$$

$$\text{Again, GM} \sin\theta = \frac{\text{GG}'}{\tan\theta}.\sin\theta = \text{GG}' \cos\theta = \frac{\text{P}.c}{\text{W}} \cdot \cos\theta$$

$$\therefore \quad \frac{b\text{A}}{\text{W}} = \frac{\text{P}c}{\text{W}}. \cos\theta + \text{BG} \sin\theta$$

$$\text{and BG} = \frac{b\text{A} - \text{P}.c. \cos\theta}{\text{W}. \sin\theta} \qquad (2)$$

G

The right-hand side of this equation (2) contains all known quantities after the experiments have been made, and the distance BG thus found, set off above the centre of buoyancy B, will determine the position of the centre of gravity of the ship.

In equations (1) and (2), since W represents the displacement of the ship, calculated to the draught of water taken at the time of the experiment, the greatest possible care should be taken to obtain the correct draught of water, and also to obtain a close approximation to the cubic contents of the part of the ship immersed; any errors made in either will affect the assigned position of the centre of gravity. The same care should also be taken to obtain the correct positions of the centre of buoyancy and metacentre, since these points are taken as origins from which the distances to the centre of gravity, as found above, are set off.

Again, P being the sum of all the weights moved, and which alone is assumed to have caused the inclination, all weights moved should be accurately known, and also the distance c, measured transversely, through which the centre of gravity of the same has moved in a horizontal direction; and every precaution should be taken to prevent the motion of any article which cannot be thus estimated. The ship should therefore be pumped out dry, coals and such other articles prevented from shifting, and at the several times of making the observations every man on board should be in a given position.

Finally, the angle of inclination (θ) is found with the greatest exactness in the following manner:—

A thick board, about twenty feet long, is nailed to the combings in the main hatchway in a vertical position when the ship is upright, and on its lower end a straight batten is nailed at right angles to the board, or horizontally; from the upper part of the batten a distance of twenty feet is carefully set off upwards, and at the height thus obtained a nail is driven into the board, and to it is attached a plumb-line, the plummet hanging freely at some distance below the batten. When the vessel is upright, and the experiment about to be commenced, the point where the plumb-line intersects the upper edge of the batten is carefully marked; and when the ship has attained her new position of equilibrium, by the movement of the weights, the new point of intersection of the plumb-line and the upper edge of the batten is marked in like manner; the distance in feet between the two points marked on the batten, divided by twenty, will clearly give the tangent of the angle of the ship's inclination.

In the experiments hereinafter described two plumb-boards were nailed to the hatchways—one amidships, and the other about midway between it and one of the extremities of the ship. The two boards, being independent of each other, were intended to serve as mutual checks, and also to point out any racking of the ship which might be occasioned by the movement of the weights on board. It may be well to mention here, that as the plummet is nearly always in a state of vibration, the extreme positions of the plumb-line on the upper edge of the batten can be best observed, and the mean position obtained, from them.

The following is a detailed account of the experiment as performed upon the English screw line-of-battle-ship *Conqueror.* The vessel was lying in Plymouth Sound, not far distant from the Breakwater; and on the day of the experiment there was but little wind, thus affording an excellent opportunity of taking the draught of water very correctly. The ship was completely fitted and rigged; the topsail yards were on the caps; all the sails were furled; the two bower anchors were down; and the guns were run out. She had on board a crew of 508 men, with provisions for the full complement for about three months; 60 tons of water in the tanks; 517 tons of coal in the bunkers; and two of the boilers were full.

After the usual preparations had been made, such as fixing the two plumb-boards, marking the position of the trucks of the guns on the decks, and pumping out the ship, the men were ordered to take up positions, at their ease, one-half on either side of the deck, and each man to note for himself such position, with a view of his taking up the same when again ordered to do so. The draught of water was also taken at the time.

When all were quiet, and the ship steady, the points in which the plumb-lines crossed the upper edges of the cross-battens were carefully marked, as already described; an operation which occupies scarcely half a minute, and it is only during the short intervals when the marks are being made that the men need be under any constraint. The men were then immediately ordered to move the guns of all the decks on one side of the ship as far as practicable to the other side of the decks, and nearly opposite their respective ports, with the axes of the guns in the same directions as they were before, so as to simplify the calculations as much as possible. As the guns were moved to the other sides of the decks, the same part of the trucks was again marked on the deck; and after all the guns had been moved the men were ordered to resume their stations as before directed.

When all was again quiet, the points in which the plumb-lines crossed the upper edges of the cross-battens were marked at the same time; and the deflection of the plumb-lines read off from both plumb-boards was found to be $12\frac{1}{4}$ inches.

The men were next ordered to replace the guns, and to move those on the other side of the ship in the same manner as the first had been moved. As these were moved the positions of their trucks were marked on the decks, and when all the movements were completed, the men once more took up their proper positions, and the deflection of the plumb-lines from the upright in 20 feet, taken with the usual precautions, was found to be $15\frac{3}{8}$ inches, corresponding to an inclination of about 3° 40′.

The work of the crew here terminated; and by the movements of the guns above described two registered inclinations were obtained, and data furnished from two independent experiments, by which the centre of gravity might be found.

An account of the weights moved, and the distance through which each was moved, had next to be taken, which was a more troublesome business than when pig-ballast was used for obtaining the inclinations. The guns, however, have their respective weights marked on them, and the average weight of the different kinds of carriages of any particular ship can also be obtained; hence the weight of each article moved is known.

The weight of each gun is taken down, and the distance through which it has been moved in a transverse direction is very carefully measured and recorded.

This concludes the requisite operations for our purpose at the ship. It will be readily seen, from the foregoing description of the movements required, that the active co-operation of the commander of the ship is absolutely necessary for the successful completion of the experiments; and unless such could be insured, it would be useless to attempt to carry them out.

The recorded draught of water at the time of the above experiment was: forward, 23′ 10″; abaft, 26′ 5″.

Displacement to the above line in tons, 5610 tons.

Metacentre above the water-line, 4.229 feet.

Metacentre above the lower edge of the keel, 29.354 feet.

The sum of the products of each weight, and the distance through which it was moved in the first experiment was (in tons and feet) 1288.0595; and the deflection of the plumb-line from the upright in 20 feet was $12\frac{1}{4}$ inches.

$$\text{Therefore GM} = \frac{GG'}{\tan\theta} = \frac{1288.0595}{5610} \div \frac{49}{4\times12\times20}$$
$$= 4.4983 \text{ feet.}$$

From the second experiment, GM was found to be equal to 4.4083 feet.

Taking the mean of the two experiments, the centre of gravity of the ship at the time of the experiment was 4.45 feet below the metacentre, or 29.904 feet above the lower edge of the keel, and $2\frac{5}{8}$ inches below the corresponding water-line.

The *Conqueror*, when completely equipped for sea, had on board 167 tons more than she had at the time of the experiment, giving a draught of water, forward, 24′ 5″; abaft, 26′ 10″, with all the boilers full.

Making the necessary calculations consequent on the introduction of the above known weights, the centre of gravity was found to have fallen (with reference to any point in the ship) through a distance of .1770 feet.

The centre of gravity of the ship, when fully equipped for sea, above the lower edge of the keel, is therefore 24.727 feet.

The corresponding metacentre above the lower edge of the keel is also 29.3167.

Consequently, the metacentre of the ship, when fully equipped for sea, is 4.5897 feet above the centre of gravity; and the centre of gravity is $25.625' - 24.727' = 0.898$, or $10\frac{3}{4}$ inches below the water-line.*

Many of the vessels in our navy have had a light spar deck put on, in the course of repairs, during the past five years, viz.: the *Hartford*, *Brooklyn*, *Tennessee*, and several others; had it been considered necessary to ascertain whether their stability would admit of it, an experiment could have been made upon one of the same class, fully equipped for sea: we have no accounts of any such experiment ever having been made on any vessel in the U. S. Navy.

† The best distance between the centres of gravity and the metacentre in rigged sea-going ships ranges between 2 feet and 3 feet 6 inches. The result to be aimed at is, that the metacentric height should not fall below the lower amount when the ship is light, and should not exceed the higher amount when she is deep; but the variation in weight of materials used from those estimated from the specifications, and the changes made in the design in the course of building must always interfere with accuracy in this respect.

---

* The above experiment was made by Assistant Naval Constructor F. K. Barnes, H. B. M. Navy, and is recorded in the Transactions of the Institution of Naval Architects for 1860.

† Opinion expressed by the Council of Construction: Messrs. Barnaby, Barnes and Crossland, Assistant Naval Constructors, H.B.M. Navy.

The sail power should also be kept down in armored ships, so that the number indicating the power of the ship to resist inclination under her canvas, at deep draught, may not be less than 20.

FIG. 14.

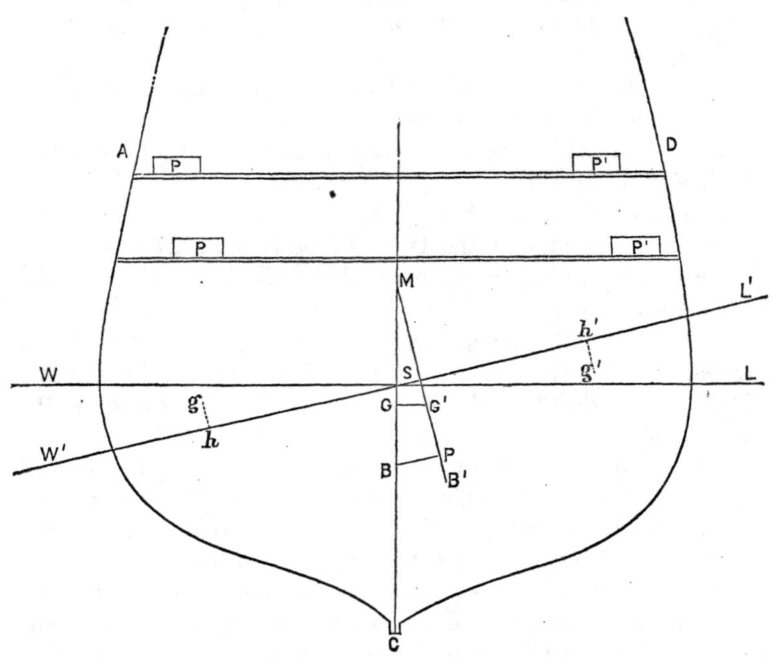

CHAPTER XVI.

Rule for Computing the Register Tonnage of all United States Vessels—Calculation of Register Tonnage of the U. S. Steamers *Omaha* and *Brooklyn*.

Be it enacted by the Senate and House of Representatives of the United States in Congress assembled, That every ship or vessel built within the United States, or that may be owned by a citizen or citizens thereof, on or after the 1st day of January, 1865, shall be registered and measured in the manner hereinafter provided; also, every ship that shall be owned by a citizen or citizens of the United States shall be remeasured and registered upon her arrival, after said day, at a port of entry in the United States, and prior to her departure therefrom, in the same manner as hereinafter described: Provided, That any ship or vessel built within the United States, after the passage of this act, may be measured and registered in the manner herein provided.

Section 2. And be it further enacted, That the register of every vessel shall express her length and breadth, together with her depth, and the height under the third or spar deck, which shall be ascertained in the following manner: The tonnage-deck, in vessels having three or more decks, shall be the second deck from below; in all other cases the upper deck is to be the tonnage-deck. The length from the fore-part of the outer planking, on the side of the stem, to the after-part of the main stern-post of screw steamers, and to the after-part of the rudder-post of all other vessels measured on the top of the tonnage-deck, shall be accounted the length of the vessel. The breadth of the broadest part on the outside of the vessel shall be accounted the vessel's breadth of beam. A measure from the under side of the tonnage-deck plank amidships to the ceiling of the hold (average thickness) shall be accounted the vessel's depth. If the vessel has a third deck, then the height from the top of the tonnage-deck plank to the under side of the upper-deck plank shall be accounted as the height under the spar-deck. All measurements to be taken in feet and fractions of feet; all fractions of feet to be expressed in decimals.

SEC. 3. And be it further enacted, That the register tonnage of a vessel shall be her entire internal cubic capacity in tons of one hundred cubic feet each, to be ascertained as follows: Measure the vessel in a straight line, along the upper side of the tonnage-deck, from the inside of the inner plank (average thickness), at the inside of the stem to the inside of the plank on the stern-timbers (average thickness), deducting from this length what is due to the rake of the bow in the thickness of the deck, and what is due to the rake of the stern-timbers in the thickness of the deck, and also what is due to the rake of the stern-timber in one-third the round of the beam; divide the length so taken into the number of the equal parts required by the following table, according to the class in such table to which the vessel belongs:

TABLE OF CLASSES.

Class 1. Vessels of which the tonnage length, according to the above measurement, is fifty feet or under, into six equal parts.

Class 2. Vessels above fifty feet, and not exceeding one hundred feet, into eight equal parts.

Class 3. Vessels above one hundred feet, and not exceeding one hundred and fifty feet, into ten equal parts.

Class 4. Vessels above one hundred and fifty, and not exceeding two hundred feet, into twelve equal parts.

Class 5. Vessels above two hundred feet, and not exceeding two hundred and fifty feet, into fourteen equal parts.

Class 6. Vessels above two hundred and fifty feet, into sixteen equal parts. Then the hold being sufficiently cleared to admit of the required depths and breadths being taken, find the transverse area of such vessel at point of division of the length as follows:

Measure the depth at each point of division from a point at a distance of one-third the round of the beam below such deck, or, in case of a break, below a line stretched in continuation thereof, to the upper side of the floor-timbers, at the inside of the limber-strake, after deducting the average thickness of the ceiling, which is between the bilge planks and the limber-strakes; then, if the depth at the midship division of the length does not exceed sixteen feet, divide each depth into four equal parts; then measure the inside horizontal breadth, at each of the three points of division, and also at the upper and lower points of the depths, extending each measurement to the average thickness of that part of the ceiling which is between the points of measurement; number these breadths from above (numbering the upper breadth one, and so on down to the lowest breadth); multiply the second and fourth by four, and the third by two: add these products together, and to sum add the first breadth and the last, or fifth; multiply the quantity thus obtained by one-third the common interval between the breadths, and the product shall be deemed the transverse area; but if the midship depth exceed sixteen feet, divide each depth into six equal parts, instead of four, and measure as before directed, the horizontal breadths at the five points of division and also at the upper and lower points of the depths; number them from above as before; multiply the second, fourth and sixth, by four, and the third and fifth, by two; add these products together and to the sum add the first breadth and the last, or seventh; multiply the quantities thus obtained by one-third the common interval between the breadths, and the product shall be deemed the transverse area.

Having thus ascertained the transverse area at each point of division of the vessel, as required above, proceed to ascertain the register-tonnage of the vessel in the following manner:

Number the areas successively one, two, three, &c., number one being at the extreme limit of the length at the bow, and the last number at the extreme limit of the length at the stern; then, whether the length be divided according to table, into six or sixteen parts, as in classes one and six, or any intermediate number, as in classes two, three, four and five, multiply the second and every even-numbered area, by four, and the third, and every odd-numbered area (except the first and last) by two; add these products together, and to the sum add the first and last if they yield anything; multiply the quantities thus obtained by one-third of the common interval between the areas, and the product will be the cubical contents of the space under the tonnage-deck; divide this product by one hundred, and the quotient being the tonnage under the tonnage-deck, shall be deemed to be the register tonnage of the vessel, subject to the additions hereinafter mentioned.

If there be a break, a poop, or any permanent closed-in space, on the upper decks, available for cargo, or stores, or for the berthing or accommodation of passengers or crew, the tonnage of such place shall be ascertained as follows:

Measure the internal mean length of such space in feet, and divide it into an even number of equal parts, of which the distance asunder shall be most nearly equal to those into which the tonnage-deck has been divided; measure at the middle of its height the inside breadths, namely, one at each end and at each of the points of division, numbering them in succession, one, two, three, &c.; then to the sum of the end breadths add four times the sum of the even-numbered breadths, and twice the sum of the odd-numbered breadths, except the first and last, and multiply the sum by one-third the common interval between the breadths; the product will give the mean horizontal area of such space; then measure the mean height between decks, and multiply by it the mean horizontal area; divide the product by one hundred, and the quotient shall be deemed the tonnage of such space, and shall be added to the tonnage under the tonnage-decks, ascertained as aforesaid.

If a vessel has a third or spar deck, the tonnage of the space between it and the tonnage-deck shall be ascertained as follows: Measure in feet the inside length of the space at the middle of its height from the plank at the side of the stem to the plank on the stern, and divide the length into the same number of equal parts that the tonnage-deck is divided; measure (also at the middle of its height) the inside breadths of the space at each point of division; also the breadth at the stem and breadth at the stern; number them one, two, three, and so forth, commencing at the stern: multiply the second and all other even-numbered breadths by four, and the third and all other odd-numbered breadths (except the first and last) by two; to the sum of these products add the first and last breadth, multiply the whole sum by one-third the common interval between the breadths, and the result will give in superficial feet the mean horizontal area of such space; measure the mean height between the planks of the two decks, and multiply by it the mean horizontal area, and the product will be the cubical contents of the space; divide the product by one hundred, and the quotient shall be deemed the tonnage of such space, and shall be added to the other tonnage of the vessel, ascertained as aforesaid. And if the vessel has more than three decks, the tonnage of each space above the tonnage-deck shall be severally ascertained in the manner above described, and shall be added to the tonnage of the vessel ascertained as aforesaid.

In ascertaining the tonnage of open vessels, the upper edge of the upper strake is to form the boundary line of measurement, and the depth shall be taken from an athwartship line, extending from edge of said strake at each division of its length.

The register of the vessel shall express the number of decks, the tonnage under the tonnage-deck, that of the between-decks above the tonnage-deck; also that of the poop or other enclosed space above the deck, each separately.

In every registered United States ship or vessel the number denoting the total registered tonnage shall be deeply carved, or otherwise permanently marked, on her main beam, and shall be so continued; and if at any time cease to be so continued, such vessel shall no longer be recognized as a registered United States vessel.

Approved May 6th, 1864.

U. S. Screw Steamer "Omaha."

Built at the Navy Yard, Philadelphia, launched May, 1869.
Has two (2) decks and a knuckle stern.

	Feet.
Length on the tonnage-deck from outside of plank at the bow to the back of the stern-post..................	251.83
Extreme breadth from outside of plank	38.
Hull from under side of the tonnage-deck to the limber-strake (5½ inches allowed)........................	18.70

Dimensions for Calculations for the Tonnage:—

Length from the inside of inner planking at the bow to the inner inside of the inner planking of the stern, at the lower side of the tonnage-deck plank...............	257.5
This length divided into 16 equal parts.	
Class (VI.) The common interval between the areas...	16.09

Calculations of the Areas of Cross-Sections under the Tonnage-Deck. U. S. S. S. "Omaha."

No. of Ordinate			No. 17 or Stern.		16		15		14		13		12		11		10	
Depth			0		9.75		15.58		18.		18.50		18.52		18.45		18.50	
Common Interval between Breadth			0		1.62		2.59		3.		3.08		3.08		3.07		3.08	
	Number.	Multiplier.	Ord.	Prod.	Ord.	Prod.	Ord.	Prod.	Ord.	Prod.	Ord.	Prod.	Ord.	Prod.	Ord.	Prod.	Ord.	Prod.
	1	1	0	0	10.92	10.92	13.25	13.25	14.50	14.50	15.25	15.25	15.92	15.92	16.33	16.33	16.50	16.50
	2	4	0	0	9.68	38.72	12.75	51.	14.54	58.16	15.75	63.	16.29	65.16	16.83	67.32	17.	68.
	3	2	0	0	7.16	14.32	11.08	22.16	13.83	27.66	15.50	31.	16.33	32.66	16.92	33.84	17.16	34.32
	4	4	0	0	4.50	18.	8.16	32.64	11.58	46.32	14.23	57.32	15.75	63.	16.50	66.	16.92	67.68
	5	2	0	0	2.33	4.66	5.08	10.16	7.87	15.74	11.75	23.50	14.33	28.66	15.29	30.58	15.92	31.84
	6	4	0	0	.92	3.68	2.58	10.32	4.	16.	7.08	28.32	10.92	43.68	13.16	52.64	14.08	56.32
	7	1	0	0	.16	.16	.50	.50	.58	.58	.68	.68	1.	1.	2.25	2.25	3.	3.
Sum of Products						90.46		140.03		178.96		219.07		250.08		268.96		277.66
Multiply by ⅓ Com. Interval						.54		.86		1.		1.02		1.02		1.02		1.02
						36184		84018		178.96		43814		50016		53792		55532
						45230		112024				21907		25008		26896		27766
						48.8484		120.4258		178.96		223.4514		255.0816		2743392		283.2132
						2		2		2		2		2		2		2
Total Areas						97.6968		240.8516		357.92		446.9028		510.1632		548.6784		566.4264

No. of Ordinate			9		8		7		6		5		4		3		2		1 or Bow.	
Depth			18.60		18.68		18.75		19.		19.16		19.60		19.68		18.33		0	
Common Interval between Breadth			3.10		3.11		3.12		3.16		3.19		3.26		3.28		3.05		0	
	Number.	Multiplier.	Ord.	Prod.	Ord.	Prod.	Ord.	Prod.	Ord.	Prod.	Ord.	Prod.	Ord.	Prod.	Ord.	Prod.	Ord.	Prod.	Ord.	Prod.
	1	1	16.70	16.70	16.62	16.62	16.58	16.58	16.33	16.33	15.50	15.50	14.16	14.16	11.41	11.41	6.92	6.92	0	0
	2	4	17.20	68.80	17.16	68.64	16.87	67.48	16.58	66.32	15.58	62.32	13.83	55.32	10.71	42.84	6.	24.	0	0
	3	2	17.37	34.74	17.33	34.66	16.92	33.84	16.50	33.	15.33	30.66	13.20	26.40	9.80	19.60	5.16	10.32	0	0
	4	4	17.08	68.32	17.	68.	16.68	66.72	16.08	64.32	14.70	58.80	12.16	48.64	8.50	34.	4.16	16.64	0	0
	5	2	16.12	32.24	16.	32.	15.83	31.66	15.08	30.16	13.41	26.82	10.41	20.82	6.85	13.70	3.08	6.16	0	0
	6	4	14.64	58.56	14.41	57.64	14.16	56.64	11.92	47.68	10.68	42.72	7.68	30.72	4.54	18.16	1.83	7.32	0	0
	7	1	3.	3.	2.75	2.75	2.	2.	1.75	1.75	1.16	1.16	.58	.58	.54	.54	.41	.41	0	0
Sum of Products				282.36		280.31		274.92		259.56		237.98		196.64		140.25		71.77		
Multiply by ⅓ Com. Interval				1.03		1.03		1.04		1.05		1.06		1.08		1.09		1.01		
				84708		84093		109968		129780		142788		157312		126225		7177		
				28236		28031		27492		25956		23798		19664		14025		7177		
				290.8308		288.7193		285.9168		272.5380		252.2588		212.3712		152.8725		72.4877		
				2		2		2		2		2		2		2		2		
Total Areas				581.6616		577.4386		571.8336		545.0760		504.5176		424.7424		305.7450		144.9754		

Cubic Contents and Register-Tonnage. U. S. S. S. "Omaha."

Under Tonnage-Deck.

Number of Ordinate.	Multiplier.	Areas brought forward.	Products.
1 or Bow	1	0	0
2	4	144.9754	579.9016
3	2	305.7450	611.4900
4	4	424.7424	1698.9696
5	2	504.5176	1009.0352
6	4	545.0760	2180.3040
7	2	571.8336	1143.6672
8	4	577.4386	2309.7544
9	2	581.6616	1163.3232
10	4	566.4264	2265.7056
11	2	548.6784	1097.3568
12	4	510.1632	2040.6528
13	2	446.9028	893.8056
14	4	357.9200	1431.6800
15	2	240.8516	481.7032
16	4	97.6968	390.7872
17	1	0	0

Sum of Products.............	19298.1364
Multiply by ⅓ Com. Interval.	5.363
	578944092
	1157888184
	578944092
	964906820
Cubic Contents. Divide by 100)	103495.9055132
Tonnage under Tonnage-deck..	1034.96
Add Tonnage under Poop-deck.	47.60
Total Tonnage...............	1082.56

Poop-Cabin.

Mean Length.			33.
Common Interval below the breadth.			16.50
Height bet. decks.			6.67
No. of Ordinate.	Multiplier.	Breadth.	Product.
1	1	25.67	25.67
2	4	22.33	89.32
3	1	00	00
Sum of Products............			114.99
Multiply by ⅓ Com. Interval.			5.50
			574950
			57495
			632.4450
Multiply by height between decks			6.67
			44271150
			37946700
			37946700
			4218.408150
Add two projecting Rooms....			541.93750
Divide by 100)			47603.45650
			47.603

U. S. Screw Steamer "Brooklyn."

Built by Jacob Westervelt, New York, 1859.
Launched,
Has two decks and a round stern.

	Feet.
Length on the tonnage-deck from outside of plank at the bow, to the back of the forward-stern-post..........	237.5
Extreme breadth from outside of plank..............	43.
Hold from under side of the tonnage-deck to the limber-strake (7 inches allowed)......................	21.71

Dimensions for Calculations for Tonnage:—

Length from the inside of inner planking at the bow, to the inside of the inner planking at the lower side of the tonnage-deck plank........................ .... 248.33

This length divided into 14 equal parts Class (V.)

The common interval between the areas will be....... 17.736

The middle depth exceeding 16 feet will be divided into (6) equal parts.

Calculations of the Areas of Cross-Sections under the Tonnage-Deck. U. S. S. S. "Brooklyn."

No. of Ordinate			No. 15 or Stern.		14		13		12		11		10		9	
Depth			0		13.75		21.85		21.60		21.54		21.50		21.50	
Common Interval bet. breadths			0		2.29		3.64		3.60		3.59		3.58		3.58	
	Number.	Multiplier.	Ord.	Prod.	Ord.	Prod.	Ord.	Prod.	Ord.	Prod.	Ord.	Prod.	Ord.	Prod.	Ord.	Prod.
	1	1	0	0	13.25	13.25	15.75	15.75	16.92	16.92	17.75	17.75	18.	18.	18.50	18.50
	2	4	0	0	11.83	47.32	15.25	61.	16.92	67.68	17.96	71.84	18.50	74.	18.92	75.68
	3	2	0	0	9.33	18.66	13.83	27.66	16.50	33.	18.	36.	18.83	37.66	19.25	38.50
	4	4	0	0	6.	24.	11.	44.	15.41	61.64	17.64	70.56	18.83	75.32	19.33	77.32
	5	2	0	0	3.12	6.24	7.75	15.50	13.41	26.82	16.58	33.16	18.41	36.82	19.	38.
	6	4	0	0	1.20	4.80	4.41	17.64	9.67	38.68	13.83	55.32	16.58	66.32	17.68	70.72
	7	1	0	0	.16	.16	.75	.75	1.	1.	1.50	1.50	2.50	2.50	3.75	3.75
Sum of Products						114.43		182.30		245.74		286.13		310.62		322.47
Multiply by ⅓ of Com. Interval						.76		1.21		1.20		1.19		1.19		1.19
						68658 80101 86.9668 2		18230 36460 18230 220.5830 2		491480 24574 294.8880 2		257517 28613 28613 340.4947 2		279558 31062 31062 369.6378 2		290223 32247 32247 383.7393 2
Total Areas						173.9336		441.1660		589.7760		680.9894		739.2756		767.4786

No. of Ordinate			8		7		6		5		4		3		2		1 or Bow.	
Depth			21.58		21.70		21.92		22.25		22.68		23.16		22.83		0	
Common Interval bet. breadths			3.59		3.61		3.65		3.70		3.78		3.86		3.80		0	
	Number.	Multiplier.	Ord.	Prod.	Ord.	Prod.	Ord.	Prod.	Ord.	Prod.	Ord.	Prod.	Ord.	Prod.	Ord.	Prod.	Ord.	Prod.
	1	1	18.58	18.58	18.50	18.50	18.50	18.50	18.08	18.08	17.70	17.70	16.75	16.75	13.58	13.58	0	0
	2	4	19.08	76.32	19.	76.	18.92	75.68	18.58	74.32	17.70	70.80	16.	64.	11.41	45.64	0	0
	3	2	19.45	38.90	19.41	38.82	19.25	38.50	18.68	37.36	17.37	34.74	14.83	29.66	9.25	18.50	0	0
	4	4	19.54	78.16	19.41	77.64	19.25	77.	18.41	73.64	16.60	66.40	13.23	52.92	7.	28.	0	0
	5	2	19.33	38.66	19.16	38.32	18.92	37.84	17.68	35.36	15.16	30.32	10.92	21.84	5.	10.	0	0
	6	4	18.08	72.32	17.83	71.32	17.50	70.	15.75	63.	12.41	49.64	7.75	31.	2.92	11.68	0	0
	7	1	4.75	4.75	4.	4.	3.	3.	2.	2.	1.50	1.50	.92	.92	.68	.68	0	0
Sum of Products				327.69		324.60		320.52		303.76		271.10		217.09		128.08		
Multiply by ⅓ of Com. Interval				1.19		1.20		1.21		1.23		1.26		1.28		1.26		
				294921 32769 32769 389.9511 2		649200 32460 389.5200 2		32052 64104 32052 387.8292 2		91128 60752 30376 373.6248 2		162660 54220 27110 341.5860 2		173672 43418 21709 277.8752 2		76848 25616 12808 161.3808 2		
Total Areas				779.9022		779.0400		775.6584		747.2496		683.1720		555.7504		322.7616		

Cubic Contents and Register Tonnage. U. S. S. S. Brooklyn.

Under Tonnage-Deck.

Number of Ordinate.	Multiplier.	Areas brought forward.	Products.
1 or Bow.	1	0	0
2	4	322.7616	1291.0464
3	2	555.7504	1111.5008
4	4	683.1720	2732.6880
5	2	747.2496	1494.4992
6	4	775.6584	3102.6336
7	2	779.0400	1558.0800
8	4	779.9022	3119.6088
9	2	767.4786	1534.9572
10	4	739.2756	2957.1024
11	2	680.9894	1361.9788
12	4	589.7760	2359.1040
13	2	441.1660	882.3320
14	4	173.9336	695.7344
15 or Stern.	1	0	0

Sum of Products............. 24201.2656
Multiply by ⅓ Com. Interval.. 5.912

484025312
242012656
2178113904
1210063280

143077.8822272

Cubic Contents. Divide by 100.. 1430.77
Add Tonnage under Poop-Cabin, 67.12

Total Tonnage. .... 1497.89 Tons.

Poop-Cabin.

Mean Length........................	39.75
Common Interval bet. the breadths..	19.87
Height between decks...............	6.79

Number of Ordinate.	Multiplier.	Breadth.	Product.
1	1	32.33	32.33
2	4	29.25	117.
3	1	0	0

Sum of Products............... 149.33
Multiply by ⅓ Com. Interval... 6.62

29866
89598
89598

988.5646
Multiply by height bet. decks.. 6.79

88970814
69199522
59313876

Cubic Contents under Poop.. 6712.353631

Divide by 100.... .... 67.12 Tons.

CHAPTER XVII.

On the Longitudinal Metacentre of a Ship.

THE effect of shifting a large weight in a fore-and-aft direction, of putting a large weight on board, or of taking a large weight out of a ship, must be dealt with by the naval architect, and he must take into account the form of the transverse sections of the ship between the original and new water-lines, and the calculations must be made by a tentative process. With this I shall not now occupy myself; my object will be to show that the effect of a moderate weight on the trim of a ship may be readily calculated, when it is either shifted in a fore-and-aft direction, or put on board, or taken out of that ship.

To proceed first with the case where a weight in the ship is shifted in a fore-and-aft horizontal direction. Let ABWL, Fig. 16, represent a ship floating at the water-line, WL; B her centre of buoyancy; G her centre of gravity; BGM the vertical line through these points; and M (a point in BGM) the longitudinal metacentre—all corresponding to the above draught of water. Let now some of her weights be shifted in a horizontal direction —say further aft. The effect of this removal is that the centre of gravity of the ship (G) moves horizontally aft to G_1, and the centre of buoyancy from B to some point B_1; and when the ship has reached the new position of equilibrium (W_1L_1 being the new water-line) and a vertical line B_1G_1 be drawn through the new centres of buoyancy and gravity, this line will cut the original vertical BGM in some point M, and will make with it the angle B_1MB equal to the angle LSL_1—between the two water-lines. Now, when the weight moved is very small, and also the distance through which it has been moved is very small, the angle between the water-lines WL and W_1L_1, and therefore between the verticals BM and B_1M, is very small also, and the point M in which the two verticals intersect is called the *longitudinal* "*metacentre*," corresponding to the water-line, WL. Through B draw BQ perpendicular to BM, cutting B_1M in the point Q. Then $BQ = BM \tan I$, if I represent the inclination of the two verticals.

Since the displacement of the ship to the water-line WL, is the same as that to the water-line W_1L_1, take away the common part $AWSL_1B$; and the wedge WSW_1, remaining in one case, is equal to the wedge LSL_1, remaining in the other case. Also by a well-known property of the centre of gravity of bodies, since the wedge LSL_1 may be conceived to have been shifted to the position WSW_1, therefore BQ (the distance through which the centre of buoyancy moves in the direction WL) is equal to either of the wedges WSW_1 or LSL_1 multiplied by the horizontal distance between their centres of gravity, divided by the whole volume of the displacement, or BQ, which is equal to BM tan I =

$$\frac{\text{Moment of wedge } LSL_1 \text{ about } S + \text{Moment of } WSW_1 \text{ about } S}{\text{Volume of the displacement}}$$

To find the moments of the wedges WSW_1 and LSL_1, about S. Let PQMN, Fig. 17, represent the section of the wedge $LSOL_1$ by a plane perpendicular to the load-water-section WL, and also to the longitudinal plane which divides the ship into two equal and symmetrical parts. Let MN be the section of the ship's side by this plane. Let the distance SP of this plane from the intersection of the load-water-sections be represented by x, and PM by y. Let also another plane, parallel to this one, be drawn at a very small distance PP_1, from it, and let PP_1 be represented by dx ; let M_1N_1 be the section of the ship's side by this plane. Then since PQ and PP_1 are both very small, the volume of the small prism PM_1 is nearly equal to $PQ.PP_1\, y$. Now $PQ = x \tan I$ where I is the very small inclination of the load-water-sections. Therefore the volume of the prism PM_1 is equal to $\tan I\; y\, x\, dx$. But $y\, x\, dx$ is the moment of the small area PP_1MM_1 about the axis SO ; therefore the volume of the small prism PM_1 is equal to the moment of the small area forming its base on the load-water-section about the axis SO multiplied by the tangent of the small inclination of the water-lines. Again, if the whole wedge LSL_1 be imagined to be cut up into a very large number of small prisms similar to PM_1, their sum, or the volume of the whole wedge, would be equal to the sum of the moments of all the very small areas into which the load-water-section would be divided about the axis SO multiplied by tan I ; that is, the volume of the wedge LSL_1, is equal to the moment of the fore-part SOL of the load-water-section about SO.

In the same manner it can be shown that the volume of the wedge WSW_1 is equal to the moment of the after-part WOS of the load-water-section about SO. But the wedge $LOSL_1$ has been shewn to be equal to the wedge $WOSW_1$, therefore the moment of the part SOL of the load-water-section before SO is equal to the moment of the part WOS abaft SO; that is, the two water-sections intersect in a line passing through the centre of gravity of either. Again, the moment of the small prism PM_1 about SO is equal to its volume multiplied by its distance from SO $= \tan I\ y\ x\ dx\ x = \tan I\ y\ x^2\ dx =$ moment of inertia of the small portion PN_1 of the load-water-section forming its base about the axis SO multiplied by tan I; and the moment of the whole wedge $LSOL_1$ is equal to the sum of the moments of inertia of all such small portions into which the water section is divided; that is, it is equal to the whole moment of inertia of the part LOS of the load-water-section before SO about the transverse axis passing through its centre of gravity. This may be represented by the symbol $\tan I \Sigma_S^L y^2\ x\ d\ x$.

In the same manner it can be shown that the moment of the wedge WOS about OS is equal to the moment of inertia of the after-part WOS of the load-water-section about SO multiplied by tan I. This may be represented by $\tan I \Sigma_S^W y\ x^2\ dx$. Therefore the moment of the two wedges $LOSL_1$ and $WOSW_1$ about OS is equal to the moment of inertia of the whole load-water-section about SO multiplied by tan I; observing that the axis OS passes through the centre of gravity of the load-water-section.

Therefore the value of BQ above given =

$$\frac{\text{Moment of inertia of the load-water-section about SO} \times \tan I}{\text{Volume of the displacement}}$$

But BQ = BM tan I, therefore dividing each side of the equation by tan I,

$$BM = \frac{\text{Moment of inertia of the load-water-section about SO}}{\text{Volume of the displacement}} =$$

$$\frac{\Sigma_S^L y\ x^2\ d\ x + \Sigma_S^W y\ x^2\ d\ x}{D}$$

where D represents the displacement of the ship.

It would be very inconvenient in practice, if it were necessary, first, to find the centre of gravity of the load-water-section, and then to arrange the ordinates, for making the calculations, with reference to this point; but if the moment of inertia be obtained with reference to any axis, the moment of inertia about an axis parallel to it through the centre of gravity can be readily found. Let $\Sigma_S^L\, y\, x^2\, dx + \Sigma_S^W\, y\, x^2\, dx$ represent the moment of inertia of the load-water-section about a transverse axis, distant a feet from the centre of gravity; and let X represent the distance of the ordinate y from the centre of gravity, then for one part of the water-section $x = \text{x} - a$, and for the other part of the water-section $x = \text{x} + a$.

$$\therefore \left. \begin{array}{l} \Sigma_S^L\, y\, x^2\, dx + \Sigma_S^W\, y\, x^2\, dx \\ = \Sigma\, y\, (\text{x} - a)^2\, dx + \Sigma y\, (\text{X} + a)\, dx \end{array} \right\} \text{taken between the same limits,}$$

$$= \Sigma\, y\, \text{x}^2\, dx - 2a\, \Sigma\, y\, \text{x}\, dx + a^2\, \Sigma\, y\, dx + \Sigma\, y\, \text{x}^2\, dx + 2\, a\, \Sigma\, y\, \text{x}\, dx + a^2\, \Sigma\, y\, d$$

$$= \Sigma\, y^2\, dx + \Sigma\, y\, \text{x}^2\, dx + 2a\, \{\Sigma\, y\, \text{x}^2\, dx - \Sigma\, y\, \text{x}\, dx\} + a^2\, \{\Sigma\, y\, dx + \Sigma\, y\, d\, x\},$$

all taken between the same limits respectively.

Now the two first terms of the last line of the above equation represent the moment of inertia of the load-water-section about a transverse axis through the centre of gravity: the next two terms the difference of the moments of the fore and after portions of the load-water-section about an axis passing through the centre of gravity, which is zero: and the last two terms the whole area of the load-water-section multiplied by the square of the distance between the axes. The moment of inertia of the water-section, therefore, about a transverse axis through its centre of gravity is equal to its moment of inertia about any other transverse axis, diminished by the product of its area and the square of the distance between the axes. To find the moment of inertia of the load-water-section about any transverse axis: Like all other calculations in naval architecture, this is found by obtaining a curvilinear area, the ordinate to which at any point represents the product of the ordinate of the load-water-section at the same point, and the square of its distance from the axis of moments. Let WL, Fig. 18, be taken as the axis of co-ordinates, where WL is equal to the length of the ship, and let any ordinate SO be taken as the axis of moments, the parts before and abaft SO being divided into equal intervals, and their number such as Simpson's rules can be applied to them. Let SNL represent the curvilinear area required, then any ordinate PN represents the ordinate to the load-water-section at the point P multiplied by SN^2. Let m represent the common interval between the ordinates, then the several ordinates of the load-water-section must be multiplied by 0, m^2, $(2m)^2$, $(3m)^2$, $(4m)^2$, etc., to obtain the ordinates of the area SNL. But, since m^2 is common to all, this may be suppressed until the final result is obtained; and the ordinates of SNL would, therefore, represent the ordinates of the load-water section multiplied by the square of the number of intervals between the the ordinate and the axis of moments SO. It will, however, be more convenient to proceed in the manner hereafter described, since in order to obtain the curvilinear area required, we can also obtain at the same time the area of the load-water-section, and the distance of its centre of gravity from the axis of moments. This will be best described by means of the following table, in which the necessary calculations are made for the armor-plated ship *Warrior*, at her load-draught of water. The ordinate No. 12, of the load-water-section is taken as the axis of moments; and the ordinates of the water-section before and abaft it are so arranged that one of Simpson's Rules can be applied to find the area. Taking the part before ordinate No. 12; in the first column are written down the numbers of the several ordinates. In the second column, the lengths of the corresponding ordinates of the water-section. The third column contains the multipliers according to Simpson's rule for finding the area. The fourth column contains the products of the ordinates and these multipliers: and it is evident that the sum of the quantities in this column, if multiplied by $\frac{m}{3}$, will give one-half the area of the fore-part of the load-water-section. The fifth column contains the number of the intervals between the several ordinates and the ordinate No. 12. The sixth column contains the continued product of the several quantities in No. 4 column, and the respective numbers in No. 5 column. It is clear, also, that the sum of the quantities in this column, if multiplied by m, and again by $\frac{m}{3}$, the result will be the moment of one-half of the load-water-section about No. 12 ordinate. The seventh column also contains the number of intervals between the several ordinates and the ordinate No. 12. The eighth column contains the continued products of the quantities in the sixth column, and the numbers opposite to them in the seventh column; and the several quantities are clearly the same as would have been obtained if the quantities in the fourth column had been multiplied by the square of the respective number opposite to them, as found in either of the columns 5 or 7. Further, it is evident, that if the sum of the quantities in the eighth column be multiplied by m^2, and again by $\frac{m}{3}$, the result will be the moment of inertia of one-half of the fore part of the load-water-section about ordinate No. 12.

Proceeding in the same manner with the after body, the area of one-half of the after-part of the load-water-section will be obtained; also its moment about ordinate No. 12, and also its moment of inertia about the same ordinate. Let the sums for the fore and after bodies in column 8 be added together and multiplied by m^2, $\frac{m}{3}$, and by 2, the result will give the moment of inertia of the load-water-section about ordinate No. 12. Now, if the sum of the moments in the sixth column for the fore body be equal to those in the same column for the after body, then the ordinate about which the moments were taken passes through the centre of gravity of the load-water-section; and the sum of the quantities in the eighth column for the fore and after bodies added together and multiplied by m^2, by $\frac{m}{3}$, and by 2, will give the moment of inertia required. But if the sum of the moments in the sixth column for the fore body be not equal to the same for the after body, let their difference be taken, and multiply it by the common interval.

This product, divided by the sum of the quantities in the fourth column for the fore and after bodies, will give the distance of the centre of gravity of the water-section from the ordinate taken as the axis of moments. In the table, the distance of the centre of gravity of the load-water-section before ordinate No. 12 is found to be equal to 7.42 feet. Also the area of the load-water-section, found by adding together the quantities in the fourth column for the fore and after bodies, and multiplying by $\frac{m}{3}$ and by 2, is equal to 17366.09. Multiplying this area by $(7.42)^2$ or 55, the product 955134.95 is the quantity to be taken away from the moment of inertia of the load-water-section about ordinate No. 12. Let this deduction be made, and the difference is the moment of inertia of the water-section about a transverse axis through its centre of gravity. This moment divided by the volume of the displacement gives the value of BM (the height of the longitudinal metacentre above the centre of buoyancy), which in the table is equal to 483.2 feet. Now the centre of gravity of the *Warrior* is about 8.2 feet above the centre of buoyancy, therefore the distance GM of the longitudinal metacentre above the centre of gravity of the ship is 475 feet. Referring to Fig. 16, in ships of the usual form when the trim has been altered to a moderate extent, the vertical through the new centre of buoyancy B_1 always passes through the longitudinal metacentre M. Consequently, if the moment of the weights to be moved in a horizontal direction on board the ship to produce an alteration of trim of say one foot be found, the effect of the removal of any weight through any distance may also be readily known. Let w be the weight or weights moved on board through the mean distance, a; then by a property of the centre of gravity, $GG_1 = \frac{wa}{D}$, where D is the displacement of the ship in the same unit as w is taken. But since the angle between GM and G_1M is the same as that between the two water-lines, $GG_1 : WW_1 + LL_1 :: GM :$ length of the ship $\therefore GG_1 = (WW_1 + LL_1)\frac{GM}{WL}$; also $WW_1 + LL_1 = GG_1 \times \frac{WL}{GM}$. If the trim be altered 1 foot, $WW_1 + LL_1 = 1$, and $GG_1 = \frac{GM}{WL}$; also $D \times GG_1 = D \times \frac{GM}{WL}$. In the case of the *Warrior* taking D in tons, $D = 8625$. Consequently the moment in foot tons to alter the trim of the *Warrior* at her load-draught of water 1 foot $= 8625 \times \frac{475}{380} = 10781$. If this result be obtained in all ships, the effect of moving any moderate weights on board of them may be readily found. Let M represent this moment. The alteration of trim for any other moment (wa, suppose,) $= \frac{wa}{M}$.

Example.—Six of the *Warrior's* guns, each weighing, say 6 tons, has to be moved further aft through a distance of 248 feet, required the new draught of water, supposing the original draught of water to be $\begin{cases} \text{Forward, } 25'\ 0'' \\ \text{Aft, } 26'\ 0'' \end{cases}$

Here $\frac{wa}{M} = \frac{6 \times 6 \times 248}{10781} = .83$ feet $\therefore$ alteration of trim $= 9.86$ inches $= 10$ inches nearly; and since the centre of gravity of the water-section, or the line in which the two water-sections intersect is near the middle of the length, thus giving the elevation of the bow equal to the depression of the stern = 5 inches each nearly, the new draught of water will therefore be $\begin{cases} \text{Forward, } 24'\ 7'', \\ \text{Aft, } 26'\ 5''. \end{cases}$

When the centre of gravity of the load-water-section is not near the middle of the length of the ship, then the elevation of the bow $= (WW_1 + LL_1)\frac{SL}{WL}$, and the depression of the stern $= (WW_1 + LL_1)\frac{SW}{WL}$.

To find the effect of putting additional weights on board of a ship. Let P be the weight in tons, and b the horizontal distance of its centre of gravity, in a fore-and-aft direction from the centre of gravity of the load-water-section. If the weight P (supposed to be moderate) were placed directly over the centre of gravity of the load-water-section, it is clear that the ship will sink down in the water until the additional water displaced is equal to the weight put on board, and the new water-line will be parallel to the original water-line. Then if the weight P be shifted horizontally to the position intended, distant b feet from the centre of gravity of the water-section, the problem resolves itself into the question of the alteration of a ship's trim, when a given weight on board is moved through a given distance in a fore-and-aft direction, account being taken of the increased immersion by first putting the weight, P, on board over the centre of gravity of the load-water-section.

It may be mentioned here, and could also be readily proved, that in a ship whose water-section is invariable in the parts subject to immersion or emersion, if a weight be placed on board of her or a weight be taken out of her, thereby increasing or diminishing the displacement to any extent, and the centre of gravity of the weights added or taken out be situated at the same height as the centre of gravity of the displacement added or lost, then the moment to alter the trim of the ship to any given extent will always remain the same.

Also, if the weight added be above the centre of gravity of the displacement added, the moment required to alter the trim to any given extent will be slightly less than before the weight was put on board. If the centre of gravity of the weight added be below the centre of gravity of the displacement added, the moment required to alter the trim to any extent will be slightly increased by putting the weights on board. In the case of weights taken out of a ship, if the centre of gravity of the weights taken out be above the centre of gravity of the lost displacement, the moment to alter the trim to any given extent will be slightly increased; and if the centre of gravity of the weights be below the centre of gravity of the lost displacement, this moment will be slightly diminished. In ordinary cases, however, where neither the alteration of the trim nor the alteration of the form of the load-water-section is considerable, the effect produced in elevating or depressing the centre of gravity of the ship is very slight; and since its position is not often known to any degree of accuracy, if the moment required to alter the trim (say 1 foot) be calculated for the load-water-line, this will be sufficiently near for calculating the alteration of the trim when at any other water-line not far removed from that for which the calculations have been made.

Example.—A weight 82.7 tons has to be put on board of the *Warrior*, at a distance of 70 feet before the centre of gravity of her load-water-section, when she is floating at her constructed draught of water. Required the new draught of water.

The displacement per inch immersion is found from the table to be 41.35 tons nearly. Therefore, when the weight is placed on board, immediately over the centre of gravity of the load-water-section, the draught of water would be increased forward and aft 2 inches, and it would be

Forward, ... 25′ 2″,
Aft, ... 26′ 2″.

If the weight be now moved forward through the distance 70 feet, the moment in foot tons will be $70 \times 82.7 = 5789$. Now, the moment to alter the trim 1 foot in foot tons is 10781. Therefore the alteration of the trim by the removal of the weights will be $\frac{5789}{10781} = .537$ feet $= 6\frac{1}{2}''$ nearly; and since the centre of gravity of the load-water-section is situated near the middle of the ship, making the depression of the bow and the elevation of the stern nearly equal, the elevation of stern is equal to the depression of the bow $= 3\frac{1}{4}$ inches nearly. Therefore the new draught of water will be

$$\left.\begin{array}{l}\text{Forward, } 25'\ 2'' + 3\frac{1}{4}\text{ inches,}\\ \text{Aft, ... } 26'\ 2'' - 3\frac{1}{4}\quad\text{"}\end{array}\right\}\text{ or }\left\{\begin{array}{l}\text{Forward, } 25'\ 5\frac{1}{4}'',\\ \text{Aft, ... } 25'\ 10\frac{3}{4}''.\end{array}\right.$$

To find the effect of taking out a given weight from on board of a ship—Let Q represent the given weight, and c the distance in a fore-and-aft direction of its centre of gravity from the centre of gravity of the load-water-section. Imagine the weight Q to be moved on board of the ship horizontally until its centre of gravity is nearly in the same vertical with the centre of gravity of the load-water-section. The effect of such removal is found by the method already described, and the draught of water corresponding is also known. When this has been found, if the weight be taken out of the ship, she will rise evenly in the water until the loss of displacement is equal to the weight taken out. The new draught of water corresponding will therefore be completely known.

When therefore the moment required to alter the trim of any ship (say 1 foot) has been calculated, and the displacement per inch immersion, and also the position of the centre of gravity of the load-water-section have been ascertained, the alteration of the ship's trim, made either by shifting a moderate weight on board of her in a horizontal direction, by putting an additional weight on board of her in any position, or by taking a weight out of her, can be found sufficiently exact for all practical purposes in a few minutes. Also by referring to the Table containing all the calculations for the height of the longitudinal metacentre, it will be seen that the calculations for a large ship like the *Warrior*, can be made in a very short time.

Longitudinal Metacentre of H. M. S. "Warrior," at { 25′0 / 26′0 } *draught of water.*

Displacement of the Ship, 301870 *cubic feet*=8625 *tons.* *Distance between Ordinates*, 18.3 *feet.*

No. of Ordinates.	Ordinates.	Simpson's Multipliers.	Products.	No. of Intervals from 12 Ordinates.	Products for Moments.	No. of Intervals from 12 Ordinates.	Products for the Moments of Inertia.
FORE BODY.							
1	1.2	½	.6	11	6.6	11	72.6
1½	4.1	2	8.2	10½	86.1	10½	904.1
2	7.2	1½	10.8	10	108.0	10	1080.0
3	13.8	4	55.2	9	496.8	9	4471.2
4	19.4	2	38.8	8	310.4	8	2483.2
5	23.5	4	94.0	7	658.0	7	4606.0
6	26.1	2	52.2	6	313.2	6	1879.2
7	27.7	4	110.8	5	554.0	5	2770.0
8	28.6	2	57.2	4	228.8	4	915.2
9	28.9	4	115.6	3	346.8	3	1040.4
10	29.0	2	58.0	2	116.0	2	232.0
11	29.0	4	116.0	1	116.0	1	116.0
12	29.0	1	29.0	0	0	0	0
Totals for Fore Body...			746.4		3340.7		20569.9
AFTER BODY.							
12	29.0	1	29.0	0	0	0	0
13	28.9	4	115.6	1	115.6	1	115.6
14	28.7	2	57.4	2	114.8	2	229.6
15	28.3	4	113.2	3	339.6	3	1018.8
16	27.6	2	55.2	4	220.8	4	883.2
17	26.5	4	106.0	5	530.8	5	2650.0
18	25.0	1½	37.5	6	225.0	6	1350.0
18½	23.9	2	47.8	6½	310.7	6½	2019.55
19	22.7	1	22.7	7	158.9	7	1112.3
19½	20.9	2	41.8	7½	313.5	7½	2351.25
20	18.4	1	18.4	8	147.2	8	1177.6
20½	14.5	2	29.0	8½	256.5	8½	2180.25
21	6.9	½	3.45	9	31.05	9	279.45
Totals for After body....			677.05		2763.65		15367.6
Fore body.....			746.4	Fore body	3340.7		20569.9
			1423.45		577.05	Diff'nce.	35937.5
			6.1	m=	18.3		18.3=m
			8683.045	1423.45)10560.015(			657656.25
			2				18.3 =m
			7)17366.090	Area of L. W. Section.	7.42 feet Centre of Gravity of L. W. Section before No. 12 Ordinate.		12035109.375
			5)2480.87				6.1= $\frac{m}{3}$
Tons per inch immersion =			12)496.174				73414167.1875
			41.3478				2 For both sides of ship.
							146828334.375
							955134.95 Deduct $17366.09 \times (7.42)^2$
						301870)	145873199.425(
							483.2 Long. Metacent. above Centre of Buoyancy.
							8.2 Centre of Gravity above ditto.
							475.0 Long. Metacent. above Centre of Gravity.

Moment in foot tons to alter the trim one foot $=8625 \times \frac{475}{380}=10781.$

NOTE.—[From Transactions of the Institute of Naval Architects. Vol. 5. 1864. By F. K. Barnes, Esq., Asst. Naval Constructor H.B.M.N.]

FIG. 16.

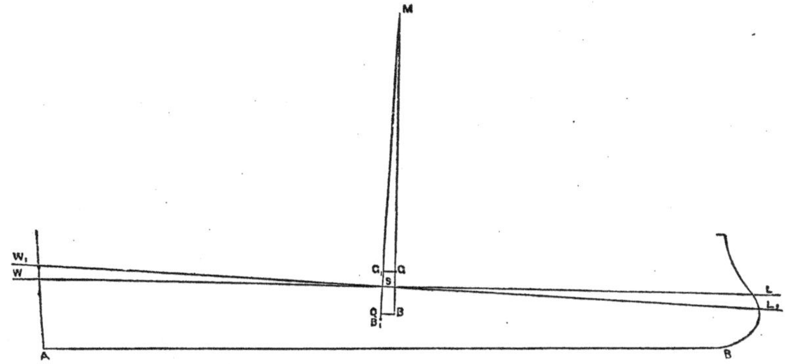

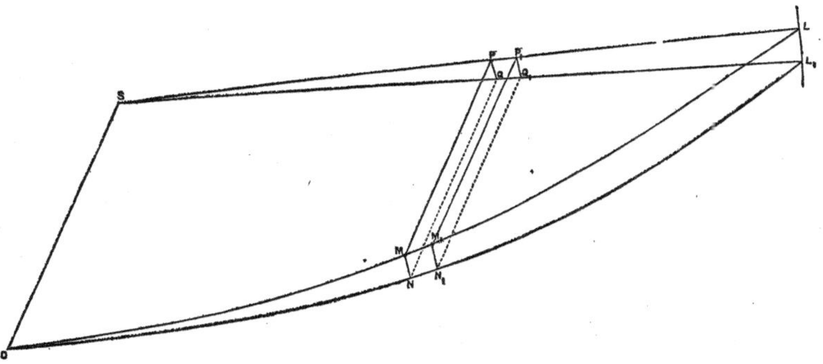

FIG. 17.

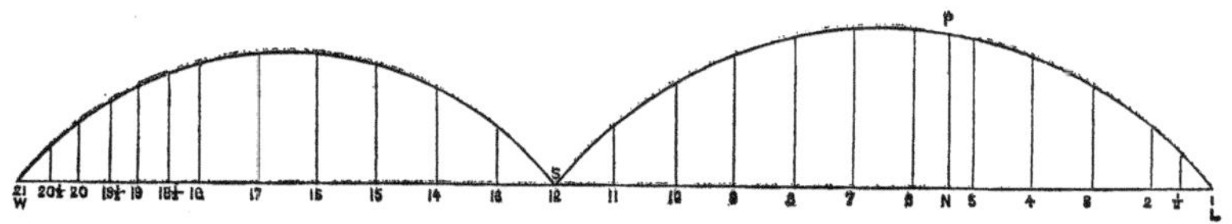

FIG. 18.

CHAPTER XVIII.

Geometrical Construction of Sails—Method of Determining the Position of the Centre of Effort of the Sails of a Ship—Calculations for the Position of the Centre of Effort of the Sails of the U. S. Steamer *Brooklyn*—Manœuvring by Sail.

GEOMETRICAL CONSTRUCTION OF SAILS.

The following rules may sometimes be useful:—

I. Square Sail (Fig. 19).—*Given, the foot,* BB, *the depth,* AC, *and the area of a square sail: to construct its figure.* Divide

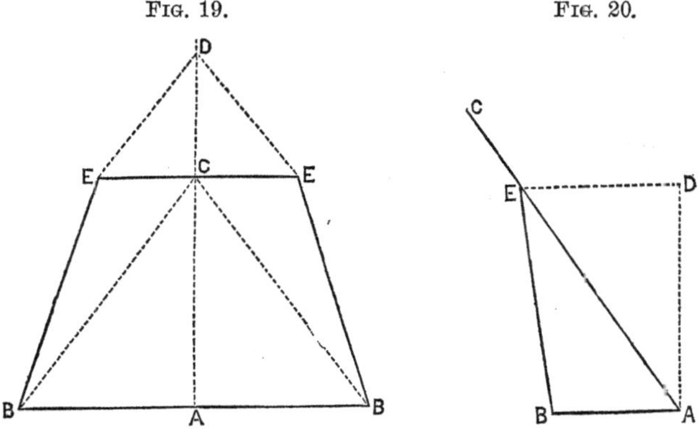

the area by half the breadth at foot; lay off the quotient, AD, upwards from the foot on the upright centre-line. Join CB, CB; and parallel to those lines, draw DE, DE. Through C draw a straight line parallel to BB, cutting the two oblique lines from D in E, E; join EB, EB; then EE will be the head of the sail, and EB, EB, its leeches.

II. Triangular Sail (Fig. 20).—*Given the foot,* AB, *the direction of one leech,* AC, *and the area of a triangular sail: to construct its figure.* Divide the area by half the foot, and set up the quotient as a perpendicular, AD, to AB. Through D draw DE parallel to AB, cutting AC in E; join EB: ABE will be the required figure.

III. Quadrangular Fore-and-Aft Sail (Fig 21).—*Given the foot,* AB, *the weather-leech,* AC, *the direction,* CH, *of the head, and the area of a quadrangular sail: to construct its figure.* Divide the area by half the foot, and set up the quotient as a perpendicular, AD, to AB. Through D draw DE, cutting AC produced in E. Join CB; and parallel to it, through E, draw EK, cutting CH in K. Join KB. Then ABKC will be the required figure.

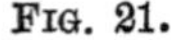
FIG. 21.

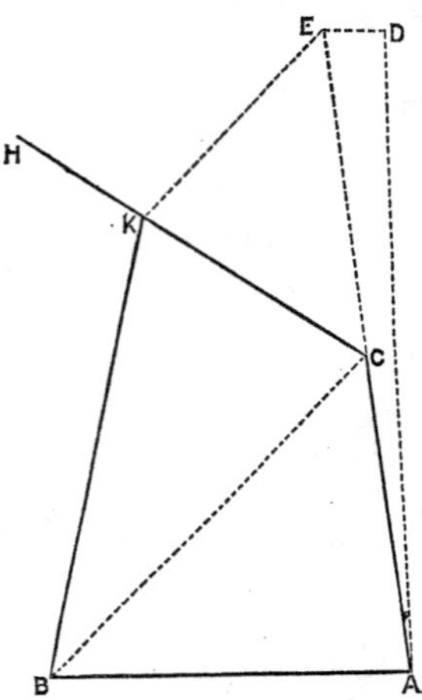

Having made the principal calculations on the immersed portion of a ship or her displacement, the quantity of sail and its distribution, or the moving force required with relation to the form of the vessel, is the next subject that demands the attention of the naval architect.

A plan of the sails having been delineated by the draughtsman, the areas, centres of gravity, and centre of effort, or the centre of pressure of them, are found in the following manner:—

AREAS.

I. *Square Sails.*—Multiply the depth by the half-sum of the breadths at the head and foot.

II. *Triangular Fore-and-Aft Sails.*—Multiply any side by half its perpendicular distance from the opposite corner.

III. *Four-sided Fore-and-Aft Sails.*—Multiply either diagonal by the half-sum of its perpendicular distance from the opposite corners.

The *centre* of each sail is then to be found by one or other of the following rules:—

IV. *Triangular Sails* (Fig. 22).—From any two of the corners draw straight lines to the centres of the opposite sides; the intersection, G, of those lines will be the centre of the sail or otherwise, from any corner draw a straight line to the middle of the opposite side, and cut off one-third from that line, beginning at the side.

FIG. 22.

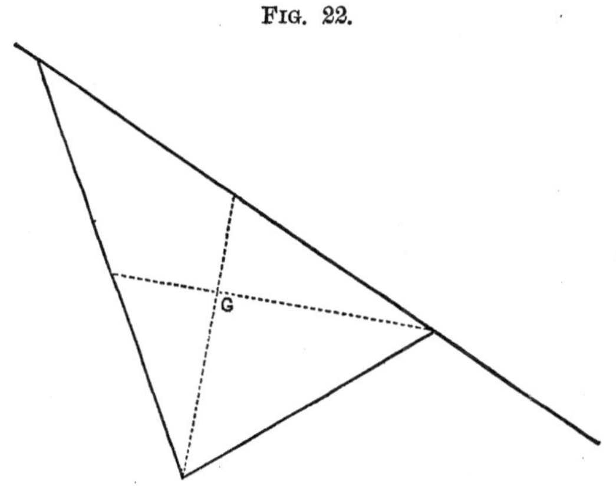

V. *Four-sided Sails—Case First* (Fig. 23).—Draw the diagonals, AB and CD, cutting each other in E; make BF=AE, and DH=CE; then, by Rule IV., find the centre, G, of the triangle, EFH, which will be the centre required.

FIG. 23.

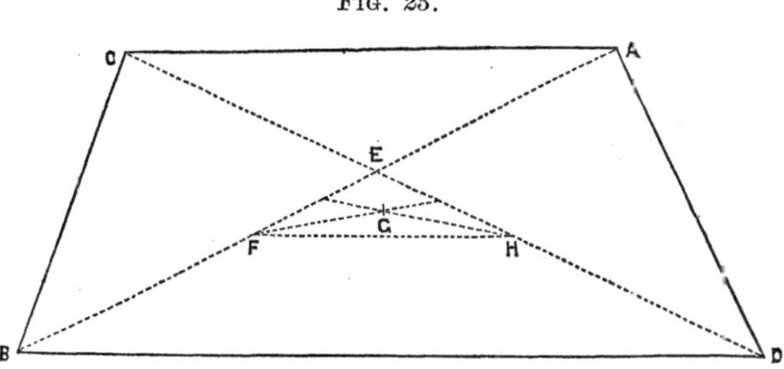

VI. *Four-sided Sails—Case Second* (Fig. 24).—First divide it into two triangles, *azd* and *azg*, by drawing the diagonal *az*; the centres of each triangle are found by Rule IV. and a line *hl*, is drawn to pass through them; this figure is then again formed into the two triangles *dga*, *dgz*, by drawing the diagonal *dg*, from the two other angles *d* and *g*, the centre of these is found as before, and a line, *of*, drawn to pass through them; the intersection *m* of the two lines *of* and *hl*, is the centre required.

FIG. 24.

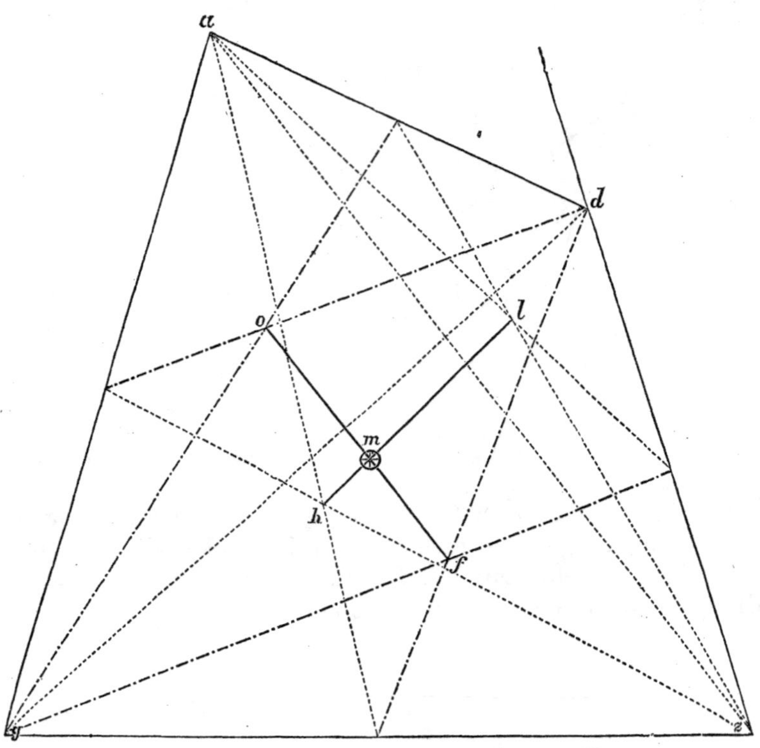

When a sail is bounded by slightly curved lines, an approximation near enough for the present purpose may be made by drawing straight boundaries, so as to inclose, as nearly as can be judged by the eye, an equal area having the same centre.

The areas of the sails and their centres having been individually determined by one of the foregoing rules, the *centre of effort* of them is usually found by assuming, but not necessarily so, an initial plane at the fore extreme of the load-water-line; from this plane (which will be represented by a line on the drawing) the distances, by a scale of parts, are taken to the respective centres of the several sails shown on the drawing, which distances, when multiplied into the respective areas of those sails, give the moment of each sail from the assumed plane; and the sum of these moments being divided by the sum of the areas of the respective sails, or the total area of sail, will give the distance of the common centre of gravity of the sails from it. This is supposing that the centres of the respective sails are all situated on the one side of the assumed plane; should the contrary be the case, and that some of them are on the reverse side of the plane, then the difference between the moments of those which fall on either side, divided as before by the whole area of sails, will give the distance the common centre of gravity of them is from the initial plane. This gives the position of the centre of effort of sail with respect to the length of the load-water-section. To find its height from that plane, the load-water-section, take from the drawing of the sails, by a scale of parts, the height of the centre of each sail from the load-water-line: this distance for each sail multiplied by the area of the same, will give its moment of height from that plane; and the sum of such moments for all the sails, being divided by the whole area of sails, will give the height of the centre of gravity of them from the load-water-line. The position of the centre of effort of the sails will thus be fixed; for the centre of gravity of the same systems of areas having been ascertained for length and height, it follows that the point in which these co-ordinates meet is the common centre of gravity of that system, and thence the centre of effort of the sails which it represents.

Accompanying this work is a sail-plan of the U. S. Steamer *Antietam*, on which is marked the dimensions of the several sails, and the distance of their several centres forward or aft, as the case may be, of an initial plane supposed to pass through the centre of the length of the load-water-line, and their distance above the load-water-line.

Manœuvring by Sail is effected by trimming the different sails, or sets of sails, so that the wind shall act upon them with different forces and in different directions. For purposes of manœuvring, the sails are distinguished into *head-sail* and *after-sail*—head-sail comprehending all sails whose centres lie before the general centre of effort of all the sails; and after-sail, all sails whose centres lie abaft that point. By "shivering" either of those two sets of sails (that is, placing them edgewise towards the wind), the other set is left to act alone; by "backing" one set, and "filling" the other, the wind can be made to act upon them in contrary directions; and by these, and other changes, a good seaman can make a ship perform a great variety of manœuvres with very little assistance from the rudder.

The capacity which a ship possesses for being thus manœuvred depends on the proportionate areas and moments of the head and after sail, and on the position of the two separate centres of effort of those two sets of sails.

Fincham, in his treatise on the "Masting of Ships," compares together the respective moments of the head and after sail relatively to a vertical axis standing in the middle of the length of the load-water-line; and shows, that in good examples of *square-rigged ships*, the *moment of after-sail varies from $\frac{72}{100}$ths to $\frac{77}{100}$ths of the moment of head-sail*, relatively to that axis; and that in *fore-and-aft rigged vessels*, the moment of after-sail varies *from once to* 1.3 *times the moment of head-sail.*

But what the power of manœuvring by sail must principally depend upon, is the *horizontal distance between the separate centres of effort of the head-sail and after-sail:* for that distance is the lever at the two ends of which those two sets of sails act in turning the vessel. Its ordinary value, as computed from some practical examples, appears to be from *$\frac{6}{10}$ths to $\frac{7}{10}$ths of the length on the load-water-line.*

The *areas* of head-sail and after-sail are of course to each other inversely as the distances of their respective centres from the centre of effort. Their relative proportions varies very much in the smaller classes of vessels; in ships, however, it is more nearly uniform; the area of after-sail being greater than the area of head-sail in a ratio which ranges from 3 : 2 to 5 : 3. The greater area of after-sail is advantageous as counteracting the tendency to check the ship's headway, which is produced when the head-sail, or part of it, is taken aback during the operation of *tacking*, or going about with her head to windward.

Calculations for determining the Position of the Centre of Effort of the Sails of the U. S. Steam Sloop-of-War "Brooklyn."

AREAS AND POSITIONS OF THE CENTRE OF GRAVITY AND MOMENTS OF SAIL.

Species of Sails.	In relation to the load-water-line.			In relation to a section passing through the centre of the load-water-line.		
	Areas.	Height of centre of gravity.	Moments.	Distance of centre of gravity from the centre.	Moments before.	Moments abaft.
Flying Jib..........	940.13 ×	58.58=	55072.8154	159. 5b	149950.735	
Jib..........	1184.48 ×	51.25=	60704.6000	135. 0b	159904.80	
Fore Staysail........	956.42 ×	46.25=	44234.4250	118. 0b	112857.56	
" Course.........	2360.63 ×	36.25=	85572.8375	75.42b	178038.7146	
" Topsail........	2575.72 ×	76.42=	196836.5224	74.42b	191685.0824	
" Top-gallant sail	1274.71 ×	116.58=	148605.6918	71. 5b	91141.765	
" Royal..........	627.75 ×	144.92=	90973.5300	69.58b	43678.8450	
Main Course........	3314.82 ×	37.17=	123211.8594	7.25a		24032.4450
" Topsail........	2562. ×	82.42=	211160.04	11. 0a		28182.
" Top-gallant sail	1283.35 ×	122.83=	157633.8805	14.25a		18287.7375
" Royal.........	633.02 ×	150.83=	95478.4066	16.82a		10646.3964
Spanker............	1625.88 ×	39.33=	63945.8604	95.75a		155678.0100
Mizzen Topsail......	1473.95 ×	72.33=	106610.8035	73. 0a		107598 35
" Top-gallant sail	689.20 ×	101.83=	70181.236	76.42a		52668.664
" Royal.........	352.35 ×	120.66=	42514.5510	78.33a		27599.5755
	21854.41		1552737.0595		927257.5020	424693.1784

Height of Centre of Effort, above the load-water line $= \dfrac{1552737.0595}{21854.41} = 71.04$ ft.

Centre of Effort before the centre of the load-water line $= \dfrac{927257.5020 - 424693.1784}{21854.41} = 22.99$ ft.

CHAPTER XIX.

On the Limits of Safety of Ships as Regards Capsizing—Distribution of Weight and Buoyancy in Ships—Measure of Fighting Efficiency of Sea-Going Iron-Clads.

ON THE LIMITS OF SAFETY OF SHIPS AS REGARDS CAPSIZING.*

If we consider a ship heeling over in still water, and have regard simply to the statical effects of the pressure of the water and the action of gravity, we observe that these effects are the same as would be produced by a pair of parallel and equal forces. The force of gravity may be replaced by a single force acting downwards at the centre of weight of the ship, and the pressure of the water by a single force acting upwards at the centre of figure of the displaced water, or centre of buoyancy. These forces therefore constitute a *couple*, the axis of which is in the direction of the vessel's length; the arm is the horizontal distance between the centres of weight and buoyancy, and the moment is the product of this arm into the weight of the vessel, or, what is the same, into the weight of the water which it displaces, called the displacement. The question whether this couple is an upsetting or righting one depends upon the centre of buoyancy moving out from the middle-line plane slower or faster than the centre of weight. With a ship which has both sides alike, these are in the same vertical line when she is upright.

The determination of their motion, as the ship heels, is one of pure geometry. For the present we are only concerned with its effects. Whatever may be the details, the instant after the centre of weight has overtaken the centre of buoyancy in moving out towards the direction of heeling, there is a tendency to upset, even without any extraneous force, such as that of the wind. The action of a steady wind, after all oscillations have disappeared, and steady motion has been obtained, consists partly of linear motion of the ship and partly of another couple, formed by the resistance of the water to the lateral motion of the ship, as one

* From the Annual of the Royal School of Naval Architecture. 1871. By C. W. Merrifield, F.R.S., Principal of the School.

force, and by the resolved pressure of the wind on the sails as the other. This wind-couple, if the vessel maintains a steady inclination, must be exactly equal to the righting-couple due to the stiffness of the ship; for if we have regard only to the tendency to capsize, or the reverse, we need only consider the resolved wind-couple acting in a plane parallel to that of the stiffness-couple. The statical measure of either of these couples is its moment, expressed in foot-tons, or some equivalent unit.

The knowledge of a ship's statical stability at any particular angle is not sufficient to determine the practical question of her capsizing. Dynamically, the difference between the moments of the wind-couple and the stiffness-couple is simply an accelerating or retarding force. Even in smooth water the effects of a varying wind, or of the sudden application of a steady wind, as may happen when a vessel passes a high head-land, depend upon the equation of work, not on the vanishing of the applied couple. Let us suppose that we have calculated the moment of the righting-couple for all possible angles of inclination, and that, setting out equal angles at equal distances along a base-line, we set off the corresponding moments as ordinates. We then obtain the curve of stability or stiffness. I will suppose it to be as in Fig. 25. The ordinate, always beginning from zero, is here supposed to reach its maximum at 23°, when the stiffness is 1,850 foot-tons; and the stiffness vanishes at 60°. At this point there is unstable equilibrium, and if the vessel be *slowly* pushed beyond it, she must continue to heel until she reaches another position of stable equilibrium. If there be such a position, short of her being bottom up, she is said to be "on her beam ends."

Now consider the vessel to be suddenly exposed to the action of a steady breeze, producing an upsetting couple of 1,000 foot-tons. This wind-couple will be in excess of the righting-couple until 11° 30′ of heel. It will then be balanced by the righting-couple; but the vessel will not stop at that point, because it will have accumulated a quantity of mechanical work, represented by the area of the triangle *Owp;* it will continue to heel, with diminishing velocity, until this work has been expended by the action of the righting-couple in excess of the wind-couple. This will take place at about 21° of heel, when the area *ptr*, is equal to the area *Owp*, or, what is the same thing, when the total work done by the wind, represented by the rectangle *Owth*, is equal to the total work done against it by the righting-couple, represented by the area *Orh*. The vessel will then begin a return oscillation against the wind, the applied force with which it tends to return being then measured by the line *tr*. Suppose now that the steady pressure of the wind-couple is 1.300 foot tons, and that the wind is again suddenly applied, the applied couple will vanish when the angle of heel is 15°, but the vessel will continue to go over beyond this until the area of the rectangle OWTH is equal to the curvilinear area OPDRH. The righting force against the wind will then be represented by the line RT, and since the points R and T are here coincident, their force vanishes, and there is nothing whatever to right the vessel. Therefore, although her statical stability does not vanish until 60° of heel, a wind which would give her a steady heel beyond 15° would capsize her if it came as a sudden gust.*

Through what follows, I neglect the diminution of the effect of the wind on the sails, by the vessel's heeling. This is not sensible until very large angles are reached, especially when bellying of the sails is taken into consideration. Besides this, the reasoning involves several assumptions which are not in accordance with observation, and it omits others which ought not to be neglected.

We assume that the displacement remains invariable, and we neglect all keel-resistance and friction. Evidently, if part of the work done by the wind be taken up by these obstructions, the result will be more favorable for the vessel. Again, we assume the gust to be suddenly applied,—that is, bursting suddenly from a calm into its full force, and lasting long enough to upset the ship. Now this is quite contrary to what we know of the propagation of atmospheric waves, especially away from the coast. Therefore, the work done by the wind should be represented, not by a rectangle, but by a curve beginning from 0. Thus, the curve of stability being given by the plain line in Fig. 26, the wind curve would be given by the chain line, and safety would depend upon the area OMP being less than PNR. On the other hand, we have entirely neglected the effect of waves. These will sometimes tend to right the ship, and sometimes to upset her. In considering the limit of safety we must take the worst case.

In a stormy sea, with waves, the *statical* stability of a ship may be supposed to oscillate about the calm-water stability or stiffness.

---

* According to the data stated at the court martial, this would have happened at 13° with H.B.M. ship *Captain*.

Thus for a particular amplitude of wave-motion we may have something of this kind:—NP (Fig. 27) being the righting moment for still water, this moment will oscillate from Np_1 to Np_2 in wave water. We have no means of calculating what this oscillation may be, because it depends upon the mechanical composition of the wave as well as on the geometrical form.

Of course, if a ship lurches beyond her proper statical heel, the curve of righting moments in wave water will oscillate about the still-water curve, like Fig. 28, which, however, represents only one particular combination of phase between the wave and the lurch. But if we could draw all the curves corresponding to every variety of phase, we should obtain a belt, the inner edge of which (envelope of the different oscillatory curves) would give a limit within which none of them would pass. If we then apply

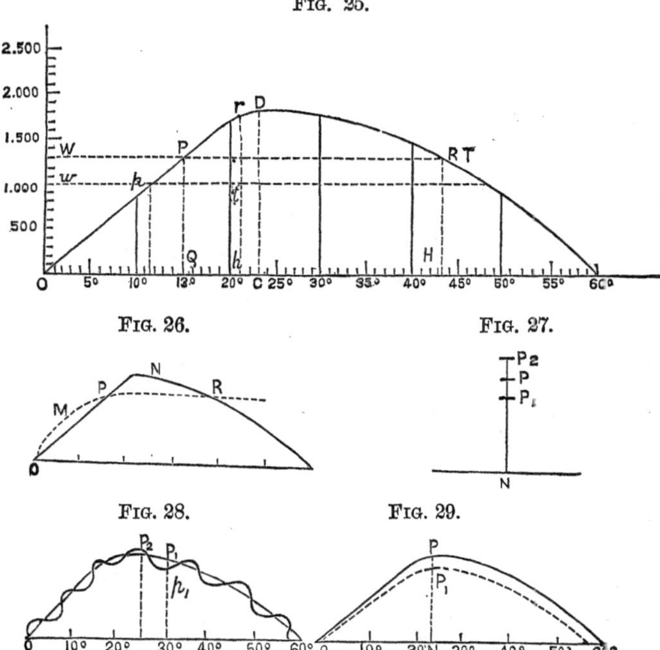

to this curve the construction first used, we shall obtain an inferior limit to the capsizing angle—that is to say, a limit of heel short of which the righting-moment will still exceed the upsetting-moment of the wind-couple. But we have no means at present known of setting off the curve Op, and the object here is simply to call attention to the fact that it must lie within the curve OP and *considerably within it* in very rough water.

This includes the rolling of the ship, so far as relates to the angle which she will bear without risk of capsizing. But it has no reference at all to the dynamical stability, or stored work, inasmuch as the phase of the wave does not remain unaltered during the period of heeling. Evidently the accumulation of work depends on the individual curve, and its limiting conditions are not to be inferred from the envelope of the family of curves.

Reverting to Fig. 26, we conclude, that for the curve OPNR, we must take, not the curve of stability given in Fig. 25, but the inner curve of Fig. 29.

It follows that the angle at which the statical stability altogether disappears may very easily be three or four times the angle of safety due to the wind measured statically. That is to say, in a stormy sea, it is conceivable that a vessel might capsize with a gust equal in force to a steady wind which would heel the vessel 15°, while yet the statical stability would not vanish until an angle of 60° was attained. For small angles a sudden gust pushes a vessel to double the statical angle; but for critical angles the statical angle has to be considered at both ends of the curve of stability. Moreover, although there is no such thing practically as an absolutely sudden gust, yet the gradual increase of the wind may be much more than compensated for by the possible diminution of stability due to the waves.

DISTRIBUTION OF WEIGHT AND BUOYANCY IN SHIPS.*

The testimony of early writers on this subject puts it almost beyond doubt that in the older types of wood sailing-ships there was generally a great excess of buoyancy in the middle, and deficiencies of buoyancy at the ends only. In later sailing-ships there were portions of the amidship length (in wake of water, ballast, and other concentrated weights) of which the weight exceeded the buoyancy; and this excess, as well as that due to the heavy extremities, was counterbalanced by the surplus buoyancy of the portions of the ship intermediate between the middle and the extremities. With the introduction of steam as a propelling agent, and of very largely increased lengths and proportions for ships, a vastly different state of things has been brought

* From Naval Science for July, 1872.

about in the distribution of weight and buoyancy. At the ends of ships there still remains an excess of weight, exaggerated in many cases by the adoption of very fine under-water lines in combination with heavy bows and sterns above water; but the distribution of weights in the fuller parts of the ship becomes much changed. How great the change has been we may infer from the fact that at present merchant steamships are in actual employment of which the length is 400 feet, and the proportion of length to breadth exceeds 10 to 1, both length and proportion having been more than doubled since the introduction of iron into ship construction and steam into ship propulsion.

We usually find the weights of engines, boilers and coals concentrated at some part of a ship. In a paddle-steamer they are found near the middle of the length, in full-powered screw-steamers rather abaft the middle, and in auxiliary screw-steamers very far aft. Wherever they come, their weight obviously increases the downward pressure at that part very considerably; in some cases they cause, while in others they exaggerate, an excess of weight over buoyancy, and in others they bring up the weight very nearly to an equality with the buoyancy. No general law can now be laid down for the strains of all ships and no general statement can be made to include all the conditions in which any particular ship may be placed by means of variations in her stowage or in the weights she has on board. Having given the details of the weights and buoyancies of various parts, however, the calculation of the resulting still-water strains is practicable, but involves considerable labor. We have taken the cases of one or two typical ships, and have had the distribution of the weight and buoyancy very carefully calculated and graphically recorded. Each example is a ship of modern type, and the results are wholly unlike any which have before been published. In fact, owing to the great labor involved, or to some other cause, only the most meagre and unsatisfactory attempts to discover and exhibit the actual strains of ships have previously been made and recorded.

The first case represents the conditions of long, fine paddle-steamers, of high speed, employed as yachts, or blockade-runners, or on other services where great cargo-carrying power is of comparatively minor moment. The case we have selected is that of the royal yacht *Victoria and Albert*, and Fig. 30 has been prepared in order to indicate the distribution of weight and buoyancy. In making the calculations required for this purpose, the total length (300 feet) has been divided into 20-feet spaces, and transverse planes of division have been supposed to be drawn, in order to form the foremost and aftermost boundaries of the spaces. For each division of the ship, the buoyancy, the weight of the hull, and the weight of the equipment have been determined; and the sum of the two latter qualities, of course, gives the total weight of ship and lading for any particular 20-feet space.

A base-line, AB (Fig. 30), has been taken to represent the ship's length, and a series of equidistant ordinates has been erected, each ordinate representing, in position, the centre plane of a 20-feet space.

The positions of the imaginary planes of division in the ship are indicated in the figure at the middle points of the parts of AB, lying between the feet of the ordinates; and the distance between consecutive ordinates is, we need hardly say, 20 feet on the scale by which AB is set off. Upon these ordinates, there have been set off, on a certain scale of tons per inch*—(1), a length representing the buoyancy of the division of the ship, with which the ordinate corresponds, divided by the length of the division; the ordinate will therefore represent the average buoyancy of the division per unit of length; (2), a length representing in a similar way, and on a similar scale, the average weight of hull per unit of length for that division: (3), a length similarly representing the weight of hull and equipment for that division. Through the three sets thus obtained, three curves have been drawn. The curve DD represents the displacement or buoyancy, the curve HH represents the weight of hull, and the curve WW represents the total weight of hull and equipment. From this explanation it will be obvious that, by choosing a proper scale, the areas lying above the line AB, and inclosed by the various curves as well as by any two ordinates, may be taken as representatives of the buoyancy, total weight, and weight of hull, respectively, for the corresponding part of the ship. Hereafter it will appear preferable to adopt the latter mode of representation, and in the various diagrams of a character similar to Fig. 30, this plan is followed.

These curves are not minutely accurate representations of the distribution of weight and buoyancy; but for our present pur-

* For areas of curves, 3 square inches = 8,000 tons. For lengths along line AB, 3 inches = 200 feet.

pose they are sufficiently close approximations to such representations. Our chief interest centres in the comparison of the curve of buoyancy with the curve of total weight of hull and equipment; but the curve HH of weight of hull has an interest attaching to it also, as it enables us to determine the straining-effect of the equipment, and to illustrate the importance of careful stowage of the weights carried. For the present we shall only make an examination of the distribution of the weight and buoyancy, and for this purpose shall compare the curves WW and DD. These curves, it will be noticed, cross each other at four points marked R^1, R^2, R^3, R^4, in Fig. 30; at these stations the weight equals the buoyancy, and the ship is there "water-borne." Before the foremost water-borne section R^1R^1, which is 50 feet from the bow, the weight exceeds the buoyancy by 85 tons; between this section and the water-borne section R^2R^2 next abaft it, a length of about 68 feet, the buoyancy exceeds the weight by 225 tons; between the two water-borne sections, R^2R^2 and R^3R^3, a length of 82 feet of the midship length (in which come the engines, boilers, and coals), the weight exceeds the buoyancy by 210 tons; and from R^3R^3 to R^4R^4, a length of 70 feet, the buoyancy exceeds the weight by 130 tons; while abaft R^4R^4, which is 30 feet from the stern, the weight exceeds the buoyancy by 60 tons. These excesses and defects of buoyancy are graphically represented by the areas of the spaces inclosed by the two curves DDD and WWW between their various points of intersection. The hydrostatical conditions of equilibrium are, of course, satisfied by the distribution of the weight and buoyancy.

These figures will show the vastly different condition of many modern steamships as compared with the older types of sailing-ships, which had an excess of weight only at the extremities.

Some modern ships, however, have a distribution of weight and buoyancy similar in kind, although extremely different in degree, to that of their predecessors; and, as an example of these, we have taken the iron-clad frigate *Minotaur*. This ship is armored throughout the length; or, to use a more common phrase, is "completely protected," and may be considered a fair representative of extremely long, fine ships so protected, with V-shaped vertical transverse sections at the bow. Her length is 400 feet; the heavy weights of engines, boilers, water, powder, and provisions are distributed over a considerable portion of the length; the guns are also distributed along the broadside; and the weight of hull is nearly uniform, except at the extremities. We should naturally expect, therefore, that the weight would considerably exceed the buoyancy at the bow and stern, and that the buoyancy would exceed the weight throughout the amidship section. The curves in Fig. 31 show that this is actually the case. They are constructed and marked similarly to those of the *Victoria and Albert.* In this case there are only two water-borne sections, $R^1 R^1$, $R^2 R^2$. The first is about 80 feet from the stem, and before it the weight exceeds the buoyancy by about 420 tons; the second is 70 feet from the stern, and on this length there is an excess of weight of about 450 tons; between $R^1 R^1$ and $R^2 R^2$, a length of 250 feet, the buoyancy exceeds the weight by the sum of these excesses—870 tons. It will be observed that at the stern the curve of buoyancy DD is ended at some distance before the curve of total weight WW, in Fig. 30. The overhang of the stern above water is the cause of this method of ending the curves; and in the *Minotaur* the distance between the points where they terminate is greater than in the *Victoria and Albert*, because she is a larger ship, and has a screw propeller.

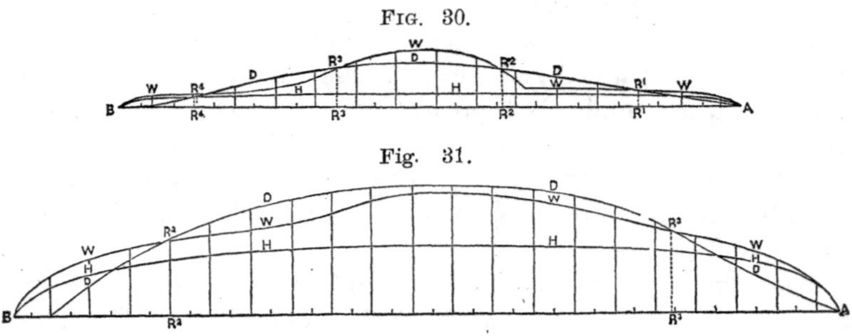

FIG. 30.

Fig. 31.

MEASURE OF FIGHTING EFFICIENCY OF SEA-GOING IRON-CLADS.

It is very difficult to express by a coefficient the several elements which constitute efficiency in a ship of war; but the principal elements of fighting efficiency in a sea-going iron-clad may, we think, be said to be—

1. The weight of armor per ton of ships' measurement.
2. The weight of the protected guns and ammunition carried.
3. The height of the battery port-sills above the load-line.
4. The speed in knots at the measured mile.
5. Handiness and quickness in manœuvring.

A coefficient of fighting efficiency may be constructed from these elements if the following assumptions are made:—

First. That the efficiency will vary directly as the first three of these elements. If an objection is made against the third on the ground that in a turret-ship the guns have the advantage of being withdrawn further from the water in rolling by being placed centrally, and that this advantage is not shown, it may be answered that neither is the advantage possessed by the broadside ship of having a greater number of guns, and that these advantages may be set off one against the other.

Secondly. That the efficiency will vary as the cube of the speed. This power of the speed is taken because the difference in speed among the ships compared are very small; but even small differences may have great results in an engagement.

Thirdly. That, other things being the same, handiness and quickness in manœuvring will vary inversely as the length of the ship.

On these assumptions we get the following measures of fighting efficiency:—

Proposed approximate measure of fighting efficiency in fully-rigged iron-clads, as given by the expression—

$$\frac{A \times G \times H \times S^3}{L}$$

Where A is the weight of armor per ton of ship's measurement.
G is the weight of protected guns and ammunition.
H is the height of battery port-sills above load-water-line.
S is the speed in knots at the measured mile.
L is the length of the ship.

Ship's Name.	Tonnage.	Complete Cost of Ships and Engines.	Measure of Fighting Efficiency.
Monarch	5,102	£345,540	149.8
Hercules	5,234	360,147	113.4
Captain	4,272	330,000	83.3
Vanguard	5,774	255,000	83.0
Minotaur	6,621	430,000	61.1
Bellerophon	4,270	343,076	58.6
Achilles	6,121	458,000	42.9

NOTE.—Extract from report of the English Naval Construction Bureau, as given before the Committee appointed to examine designs upon which ships of war have recently been constructed.

CHAPTER XX.

On the Designing of Ships—General Design—Principal Dimensions—Keel, Stem, Stern-Post and Rudder—Moulded Dimensions and Displacement—Midship Section—Leading Water-Lines—Balance Sections—Additional Water-Lines—Buttock-Lines—Additional Cross-Sections—Main Breadth Line—Sheer-Lines—Gunwale—Rail—Head and Stern—Use of Models in Designing Ships—Summary of Calculations.

ON THE DESIGNING OF SHIPS.

General Design—Outside Dimensions.—It would not be desirable, even if it were possible, to lay down an invariable system of rules as to the method and order to be followed in designing a ship. All that can be done in the present Chapter is to indicate, in a general way, the nature of the processes; the best way of arranging them, and the omission of some of them, are matters to be decided by the judgment of the naval architect in each particular case.

One of the principal conditions to be fulfilled by a proposed ship almost always is, that she shall be capable of carrying a certain burden, or load, in tons of 2240 lbs., and shall be of a certain internal capacity in tons of 100 cubic feet. Hence, by the aid of principles explained in Chap. IX., the naval architect can estimate what her *displacement* ought to be.

The *Outside Dimensions* of a ship's displacement are: the *length* on the plane of flotation, the extreme *breadth*, and the *mean load draught* of water or *immersed depth* amidships, down to the lower edge of the rabbet, where the skin of the vessel joins the keel. The product of those three dimensions gives the volume of a certain rectangular solid; and that volume, multiplied by a certain *co-efficient of fineness* (as explained in Chap. IX.), is equal to the displacement. As a step, therefore, towards determining the three outside dimensions, it is necessary that the naval architect should decide what co-efficient of fineness the ship is to have. That will depend on the figures which he intends to adopt for the midship-section, and for the water-lines; for (as stated in Chap. IX.) the co-efficient of fineness of the displacement is the product of the co-efficient of fineness of the midship-section, and of the mean co-efficient of fineness of the water-sections. It appears that a close approximation to the mean co-efficient of fineness of all the water-sections is obtained in ordinary cases by taking the co-efficient of fineness of a water-section situated at *one-third of the immersed depth* below the load-water-section.

The water-lines of the fore-body and after-body may, and very often do, differ in fineness; and they may or may not have the straight water-lines of a middle body between them. To find the co-efficient of fineness of an entire water-section from those of its parts, the naval architect must decide what proportions of the whole length are to belong to the fore-body, the middle-body, and the after-body respectively; then, multiplying each division of the length by its proper co-efficient of fineness, and dividing the sum of the products by the whole length, the quotient is the co-efficient of fineness of the whole water-section. The co-efficient of fineness of the straight middle division is always *unity*. The displacement in cubic feet being divided by the co-efficient of fineness of the whole immersed body, gives *the product of the three outside dimensions.* In order to find those three dimensions separately, when no conditions are laid down to limit their absolute values, the naval architect must decide what proportions they are to bear to each other. Then multiplying together the proportions which the length and the immersed depth are respectively to bear to the breadth, a divisor is obtained, by which the volume of the rectangular solid is to be divided; and the *cube root of the quotient will be the extreme breadth.* The ordinary proportions of length to breadth may be taken as ranging from 3 to 7 in sailing vessels, and from 5 to 12 in steamers; those of immersed depth to breadth, from $\frac{1}{2}$ downwards. In certain cases, limits may be put to the absolute values of the outside dimensions. For example:—

I. The *least length of fore-body* and *after-body* consistent with economy of power, at the greatest intended speed of the vessel, may be determined by the principles as explained in Scott Russell's wave-line theory.

II. The depth of immersion may be limited by the shallowness of the water which the vessel is to navigate.

When the quality aimed at in the vessel to be designed is speed under sail, irrespective of other qualities (as in the case of sailing yachts), the primary condition to be fulfilled may be, that the plane of flotation shall have a given area (for to that area the area of sail is nearly proportional). In this case, the naval architect, so soon as he has fixed the co-efficient of fineness of the load-water-section, can at once calculate the area of its circumscribed rectangle, which is the product of the length and breadth. He has next to decide what proportion the length is to bear to the breadth; and then the absolute length and breadth are to be computed. The midship-draught of water will then be fixed, according to the form and proportion chosen for the midship-section, with a view to weatherliness, handiness, and steadiness.

The ordinary proportion of midship depth of immersion to breadth in sailing yachts ranges from $\frac{1}{2}$ to $\frac{1}{3}$. When it is $\frac{1}{4}$, or smaller, lee-boards or a centre-board are in general required.

Keel, Stem, and Stern-post.—The determination of the length and midship-draught of water gives the dimensions of the immersed part of the midship longitudinal section of the vessel, bounded by the forward-edge of the rabbet of the stem, the lower edge of the rabbet of the keel, and the after-edge of the rabbet of the stern-post; and the naval architect is then enabled to decide upon the figure of that section with a view to the position of the centre of lateral resistance, and the action of the rudder. He will fix, for example, whether the ship is to float on an even keel, by the stern, or by the head; whether the keel is to be straight or curved, of uniform or of varying depth; whether the stern-post is to be upright or raking; whether the stem is to be straight or curved, upright or raking, etc.

Moulded Dimensions and Displacement.—It is more convenient for practical purposes, though less scientifically exact, to design the figure, not of the outer surface of the ship, but of the *inner surface of her skin;* because upon the figure of that inner surface the shapes of all the pieces of the frame directly depend.

The principal dimensions of the inner surface of the skin of a vessel are called her *moulded dimensions,* to distinguish them from her outside dimensions. The *breadth moulded* is the extreme breadth from inside to inside of the skin; the *moulded length* is measured from the after-edge of the rabbet of the stem to the forward-edge of the rabbet of the stern-post; and the *moulded depth of immersion* amidships is measured from the plane of flotation down to the upper edge of the rabbet of the keel. By the *moulded displacement* is meant, the internal capacity of the skin of the vessel, below the plane of flotation.

When the naval architect makes his design represent the

moulded figure and dimensions of the ship, it is necessary that he should consider in what proportions the real displacement, stability, and other quantities for the real external figure, will be greater than the corresponding quantities as computed for the moulded figure.

The *bends* or *wales*, being the part of the skin of the vessel at and near the load-water-line, depend for their thickness upon the material of the skin, and the strength which it is required to have.

In wooden vessels, that thickness may be estimated as ranging from $\frac{1}{30}$th to $\frac{1}{50}$th of the *extreme half-breadth, moulded;* and in iron ships, at from $\frac{1}{6}$th to $\frac{1}{8}$th of the thickness proper for wooden ships of the same size. The thickness of the bends having been determined, let the proportion which it bears to the *mean half-breadth of the plane of flotation* (or extreme half-breadth × coefficient of fineness of the load-water-section) be denoted by m; also let the thickness of the skin of the floor be determined, and let the proportion which it bears to the midship draught of water be denoted by n; and let the fraction by which the real length on the load-water-line is to exceed the moulded length be denoted by p. Then the following proportions will be correct enough for a first approximation :—

	Moulded : Real.
Area of Plane of Flotation........	$:: 1 : 1 + m + p$
Displacement....................	$:: 1 : 1 + m + n + p$
Surface Stability................	$:: 1 : 1 + 3m + p$
Augmented Surface..............	$:: 1 : 1 + \frac{m+n}{2} + p$

Midship-section.—The upper diagram in Fig. 32 represents the sheer-plan of a ship, in which the figure and dimensions of the longitudinal section have been laid down, and the length, AB, has been divided into fore-body and after-body (there being no middle-body in the example chosen). The lower diagram represents the half-breadth plan, which at first contains only the length, AB, divided at ⊕ into fore-body and after-body; a straight line drawn parallel to AB, at a distance representing the half-breadth (or "half siding" as it is called) of the keel; and a third straight line, ⊕ C, representing the extreme half-breadth of the ship.

The next step is usually to design the midship section, CC ⊕ CC. The general character of this section below water is supposed to have been already so far determined, that its co-efficient of fineness is known, at least approximately. In designing its figure in detail, the naval architect has to keep in view at once stiffness, steadiness, easy rolling, economy of power, and, in sailing vessels, weatherliness. As regards the figure of the midship-section between wind and water, two main classes of vessels may be distinguished; those which are to float at a nearly constant draught of water (as ships-of-war and yachts), and in which the best forms are unquestionably those which roll isochronously, and those which are to float at a variety of different draughts (as merchant ships), and in which, in order that the stability may vary as little as possible, it is preferable to make the section between wind and water straight and vertical, or nearly so.

As regards the *floor*, or lowest part of the section, a sharp or rising floor is favorable to steadiness and to sailing; a flat floor is convenient for stowage, for the arrangement of engines, and for taking the ground, and is sometimes necessary when the draught of water is limited.

The *bilges*, which unite the floor with the sides, are said to be "hard" or "easy" according as their curvature is more or less sharp. A hard bilge is considered to promote steadiness and weatherliness, so as to make up somewhat for flatness of the floor: but it is unfavorable to the fairness of the lines of the fore and after-body: an easy bilge is, on the whole, the most favorable to good forms of water-line.

The *leading water-line* is that whose figure is first designed. It may be the load-water-line; but inasmuch as the water-line (DD in the figure) at one-third of the immersed depth, is approximately a mean of the other water-lines as to fineness, it is advisable to begin with it. The influence of the forms of water-lines upon resistance and speed has been explained.

The fairness of this leading water-line is of primary importance to speed and economy of power. The variety of curves possessing the requisite quality of fairness is infinite; and the naval architect may prefer to be guided wholly by his eye in designing this and other lines of the ship; but should he choose to avail himself of certain definite curves, he may be aided by some mechanical and geometrical processes as the Wave-line theory of Scott Russell, or Chapman's Parabolic theory.

Balance Sections.—The term "balance-sections" is applied to a pair of vertical cross-sections, one near each end of the vessel, which are designed after the midship-section and leading water-line. Their position is optional; but in most cases it is convenient to place them (as directed by Fincham in his Outlines of Naval Architecture) at *one-third of the length of the fore-body and after-body respectively, from the ends of the line of flotation*, AB. They are so placed in the figure, where the forward balance-section is marked E, and the after balance-section, F. In vessels with very fine and sharp ends, it may sometimes be convenient to place the balance-sections at the middle of the length of the fore-body and after-body respectively. One half-breadth in each of those sections is already determined—viz., where they intersect the leading water-line, DD. The sections are completed according to the judgment of the naval architect; and their form is generally such as to give sharpness to the floor for resisting rolling and leeway, to make the water-lines gradually become finer from above downwards, and to flare out above water, for the sake of liveliness in pitching and scending, and of giving sufficient breadth to the decks, especially towards the stern of the vessel.

Additional Water-lines (such as ACB, and GG) can now be designed in any required number above as well as below water, by drawing (either by the eye, or by process described in Wave-Line theory,) a series of fair curves through the points where a series of horizontal planes cut the midship and balance-sections.

Vertical Longitudinal Sections.—Additional longitudinal sections, or bow and buttock-lines, can now be laid down, by first drawing straight lines (such as those marked H) on the half-breadth plan and body-plan to represent the planes of those sections, and then marking on the sheer-plan the points where those planes intersect the midship and balance-sections, and the water-lines, and drawing fair curves through those points. An example of a longitudinal section is represented by the dotted line, marked HH in the sheer-plan, Fig. 32.

The fairness of the buttock lines, or after-parts of the longitudinal sections is so important, that the naval architect may sometimes find it advisable to design a *leading buttock-line* before any of the water-lines, and then adapt the water-lines of the after-body to it.

Riband or *Diagonal Lines* are oblique longitudinal sections, sometimes used in testing the fairness of the body; but it is unnecessary to refer to them further here, as their construction will be described in a subsequent division of this work.

Additional Cross-sections, in any number that may be considered necessary, can now be constructed, so as to complete the body plan, by taking their half-breadths at the several water-lines from the half-breadth plan. None of these are shown in Fig. 32, but numerous examples of them are contained in the other plates.

By *the Main-breadth-line* is meant, a line on the surface of the vessel, cutting each of the cross-sections at the point where its breadth is greatest. Its figure can be constructed on the three plans after the cross-sections have been completed. It is represented in Fig. 32 by the dotted curves marked L. It forms, of course, the outline of the half-breadth plan, in which it very often coincides with the load-water-line in the middle part of its length, and with the gunwale or the plank-sheer, near the head and stern. In former times, one of the first steps taken in designing a ship was to assume a figure for the main-breadth-line; but, as its shape has little direct influence on the qualities of the ship, that method is seldom followed now.

When a ship has a "straight of breadth" vertically; that is, when her cross-sections are partly vertical at the sides, there are two main-breadth-lines at the upper and lower boundary of the straight of breath respectively.

Sheer-lines.—Head and Stern.—The under side of the *gunwale*, marked K in the figure, is designed so as to form a fair curve on the half breadth plan. Its form near the bow is like that of a water-line; but in most cases somewhat fuller. Near the stern, its figure is fuller still, with a view to giving a convenient breadth to the after-part of the decks. It may sometimes be advisable to design the gunwale before completing the cross-sections.

In almost every vessel the gunwale has an upward curvature longitudinally, called the *sheer*. The true practical object of this is, to protect the vessel against waves breaking over her, by giving her greater height out of water at the bow and stern, where her vertical motion relatively to the water is greatest.

The bow, as having more vertical motion relatively to the water than the stern, and also as being more exposed to the waves, requires the greater height of sheer. This may be effected by making the curvature of the sheer vanish, or nearly so, at the stern, and increase gradually in sharpness towards the bow.

The less lively a vessel is in pitching and scending, the more sheer does she require; and it is specially needed at the bow of a vessel with fine lines, and little or no flaring out above the water-line. Large vessels have proportionately less sheer than small vessels, and ships-of-war than merchant-ships. The reason in the latter case is, that the decks follow the form of the sheer, and that decks with much sheer are inconvenient for working guns.

The design of the *figure-head or cut-water*, and that of the stern, are matters to be regulated chiefly by the taste of the naval architect. In many vessels the figure-head is dispensed with, as was the case in many of our naval vessels.

Use of Models in Designing Ships.—A model, to be used by a naval architect in designing a ship, is usually composed of two sorts of soft wood of different colors, such as pine and cedar, in alternate layers, screwed, pinned or glued together. The seams between the layers represent water-lines. The model usually represents the starboard half of the vessel, and has a plane side, representing the longitudinal midship-plane, on which the sheer-plan is drawn. Its curved side is then gradually carved, shaved, and filed to such a form as to satisfy the eye and the judgment of the designer; the touch also is used, by passing the hand over the model, as a test of the fairness of its figure.

The co-efficient of fineness of a model may be determined by filling a trough with water exactly to the level of a suitable outlet, carefully lowering the model into the water until it is immersed exactly to the load-water-line, and finding, by measurement or by weighing, the volume of water which is made to run over. That volume will be equal to the displacement of the model; and being divided by the product of the principal dimensions of the model, the quotient will be the co-efficient of fineness.

Another mode of roughly determining the displacement of a model is to separate the part below the load-water-line from the rest, weigh that part, and compare its weight with that of a rectangular block made up of the same materials in the same way; when the proportion of the volumes may be taken as approximately the same with that of the weights.

To find approximately the centre of buoyancy of a model, hang up the part below the load-water-line by a fine thread to a single pin in an exactly vertical board, so that the plane side of the model shall be in contact with the board. Mark the two points where a plumb-line hanging from the same pin passes the edges of the model, and draw a straight line on the plane side of the model through those two points. Repeat the experiment with the model hanging in a position as nearly as may be at right angles to its former position; the intersection of the two lines on its plane side will correspond to the centre of buoyancy of the vessel represented by the model. In models whose layers are screwed together, the accuracy of the result of this process may be interfered with by unequal distribution of the screws; hence, for the purpose of finding the centre of buoyancy, the best fastening is made with wooden pins or glue.

Models are sometimes built up of small prismatic bars of wood, so as to show the figures of vertical and oblique as well as horizontal sections.

A model may be used either to construct drawings from, or directly in laying off the figures of the pieces of the ship on the mould-loft, without the intervention of drawings.

After a ship has been designed, and the sheer, body, and half-breadth plans all faired, it may sometimes be requisite to alter the form of the ship slightly, so as to obtain an increased or diminished displacement.

This may often be effected by retaining the water-lines in the half-breadth plan, and increasing or diminishing the common intervals between the water-lines; or the transverse sections of the body-plan may remain unaltered, but the interval between them be increased or diminished.

Case I.—Let D represent the displacement according to the prepared plan, $\triangle$ the increase or decrease of the displacement, d the common interval between the horizontal sections, and z the quantity by which this common interval is increased or diminished. Then $z=d.\frac{\triangle}{D}$; also, since the number of intervals will remain unaltered, the increase or decrease in the whole distance between the extreme horizontal sections will be

$$= \text{Original distance between extreme horizontal sections} \times \frac{\triangle}{D}.$$

Again, the distance of the centre of gravity of the displacement, bounded by the extreme longitudinal section, will be to the original distance as $D+\triangle : D$, or as $d+z : d$.

Also, the moment of inertia of the load-water-section remaining the same, the height of the metacentre above the centre of buoyancy will be to the original height as D to $D+\triangle$.

Case II.—When the forms of the vertical sections are retained, but the interval between them is altered, let l represent the interval between the vertical sections, and y its increase or decrease, when the displacement is increased or decreased by the quantity, $\triangle$. Then

$$y = l \times \frac{\triangle}{D}.$$

The depth of the centre of buoyancy below the load-water-line remains unaltered, as also the height of the metacentre above the centre of buoyancy.

Statement of Dimensions, Weights, &c., for an Iron Corvette of 3,978 *tons.*

Length between the perpendiculars		333 ft. 0 in.
Breadth, extreme		50 " 1 "
Depth in hold		17 " 5½ "
Burden in tons		3,978$\frac{42}{94}$
Draught of water	Forward	22 ft. 0 in.
	Aft	24 " 0 "
Displacement in tons		5,495
Area of midship-section in feet		926
Height of midship-port		10 ft. 3 in.
Nominal horse-power		1,000
Estimated speed in knots per hour		15
Coals, No. of tons		600
Water	No. of tons	68
	No. of weeks' consumption	4
Provisions	No. of tons	88
	No. of weeks' consumption	16
Complement of men		550
Armament	10 guns on main deck.	
	4 guns on upper deck.	
	14	

	Tons.
Water for one month	68
Tare of tanks	14
Provisions for four months	88
Tare of casks	17
Officers' stores and slops	12
Wood, sand, and holystones	4
Officers, men, and effects—550 in number	69
Masts and yards	87
Rigging and blocks	59

	Tons.
Sails	$8\frac{1}{2}$
Chain cables / Hempen "	$67\frac{1}{2}$
Anchors	18
Boats	10
Warrant-officers' stores	65
Guns and Carriages { 10 on main deck / 4 on upper deck — 14; Shot, shell, and powder	381
Small arms, &c	8
Grape and canister	6
Galley	6
Condensers	6
Engineers' stores	16
Engine, boilers, &c., for 1,000 horse-power	1,000
Extra weights for engines	20
Coals	600
Total of equipment	2,629
Hull	2,810
Displacement required	5,439
Displacement as per drawing	5,495
Surplus	56

Fig. 32.

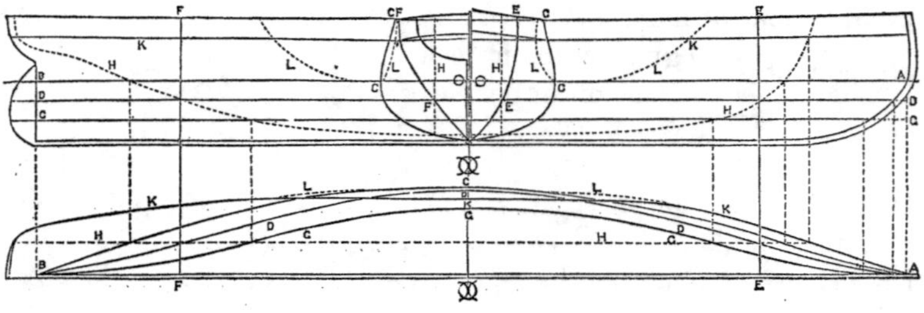

CHAPTER XXI.

The Wave-Line System of Construction and Its Advantages.

IT requires a man of fully as much wisdom and knowledge of his profession to turn the wave principle to account, and build a ship, promising every good quality it can give, as to build a vessel of traditional form. All it does is to enable an accomplished naval architect to combine with certainty the properties of high speed, small resistance, economical transport, and sea-going qualities, under circumstances where formerly it was guesswork merely.

Practical constructors should alter their system with great caution. It is quite possible to understand the wave principle and yet to design a bad ship. Knowledge of the wave principle does not supersede the knowledge of other principles of naval construction; it merely adds to their number.

There is hardly a vessel in the naval or mercantile marine in the world at the present day, possessing *high speed* with a *moderate* consumption of fuel, which does not possess a number of the characteristics of the "wave" principle.

The following are the main points of practical construction determined by the "wave" principle.

1. *The entrance of a Ship designed on the Wave Principle may have a hollow water-line.*

With a hollow water-line, one can obtain many qualities irreconcilable with a convex bow-line. In the materials of wood, the structure is much more easy and stronger with a hollow than a convex bow water-line; and in any structure the hollow line has the virtue of diminishing the room for carrying weights in those parts of a ship where it is injurious to sea-going qualities to carry much weight. In releasing us from the dominion of the convex bluff bow, the wave-principle has left us free from much that tended to bad ships and slow ones. To carry weights near the middle, and relieve the ends, is to give a ship some of the best qualities we are able to bestow.

2. *The run of a ship may have a convex water-line.*

The same maxims which used to prescribe a full bluff bow,

prescribed with equal force the long, fine run of the water-lines of the stern. "Cod's Head and Mackerel Tail," was the motto of the "old school," which happily now retains few disciples. The importance of this maxim was, however, not founded on fancy merely, but on a practical wish to improve the steering of the bluff-bowed ships. It is now most certain, that bluff, full bows have a great tendency to make vessels, forced through the water with great power, steer very wild, and obey their rudder inefficiently. It was to counteract this fault of the bluff bow that the extremely fine run was contrived.

The fault of the extremely fine run was not merely that it sacrificed a great deal of the excellent stowage of the ship in a place where it was much wanted, by making the whole of the after-body meagre and thin, but that it failed to cure the fault of steering wildly under heavy press of sail or steam. The wave principle provides for a fine run, and admits of it; but it does so in the right manner and at the right place. It approves of fineness of water-line aft, and gives as much deadwood before the rudder as the old school could desire. But it shows that the place where the fineness should lie is below the surface, deep down, and not higher up. It shows that fineness below should be well aft, and not where capacity is wanted.

Fulness for capacity, it gives in the after-body, well up towards the surface of the water, and gives a large, capacious, upper after-body, exactly in the place where room in a ship is valuable—valuable in money, valuable in convenient stowage, and valuable in reference to those movements of a vessel which test the excellence of her performance in a heavy sea.

3. *The entrance of a ship designed on the wave principle may be as long as the run, and even longer.*—This is also the contrary of the maxims of naval architecture of the old school. That the run must be long and fine, and the bow comparatively short and full, was nearly the universal system adopted. The question left open to opinion and discussion, was merely whether the length of the after-body should be longer than that of the fore-body in some one proportion rather than another. I have seen ships designed with nearly every variety of practice in this respect, some in a proportion of 2 to 1, others 3 to 2, others 4 to 3, and others 5 to 4. Nearly every builder had his own special proportion for this purpose.

The wave principle releases us from this maxim also: The

bow may be made as long as the stern of a ship. This proportion has the advantage of enabling the designer to obtain balance of weights in the varying circumstances of lading and draft of water more easily than with an excess of length at one end.

There is a class of vessels which require this exact balance; and especially where it is reckoned important that a vessel should navigate either end foremost, such an arrangement is very useful. The wave principle leaves us free to adopt this arrangement. I have found it useful to design a number of vessels in this manner, with the hollow wave-lines at both ends of equal length and width. And further, the entrance of a ship may be made longer than the run. This is especially valuable where the length is very limited, so that it is difficult to obtain by any means a fine hollow bow. By giving greater length to the bow than to the run, a long fine water-line of entrance may be obtained, with its widest part nearer the stern, and its length therefore exceeding half the length of the ship. To gain capacity, the lines of the after-body may be made extremely full above, and may be fine only below. In circumstances of very limited length, this treatment may be turned to great account; especially in building the smaller class of sailing vessels, yachts and steamers, where good speed is wanted under restricted dimensions.

4. *The main breadth of a ship may, therefore, be placed nearer the stern than the bow of a ship.*—This is almost an evident consequence of what precedes. The chief water-line of entrance being made longer than the run, naturally throws the main midship-section further back than the middle. This, however, may be only partially true; because it by no means follows that the greatest breadth shall be necessarily found in the same position in all the water-lines; it may be further forward in the upper water-lines, and further aft in the lower, or the contrary. I have often seen it expedient to place the greatest breadth well abaft the middle in the upper water-lines of a ship, and well forward of the middle in the lower water-lines of the same ship. This expedient will be found especially useful in forming designs for speed upon dimensions that are much restricted. This distribution of main breadths, fore and aft the middle, is indicated clearly by the wave principle; and I am not aware that it is to be found in any other system of scientific construction.

5. *The foregoing maxims release us from the trammels of previous systems;* and so enable us to give to a vessel forms

which may suit the specific objects we may wish to attain. This alone is a great boon to the shipbuilder, who wishes power to adapt the shape of his vessel to the various uses of nautical and mechanical art.

The maxims which follow do much more than release us from impediments. They enable us to accomplish definite objects of practical value in an exact method. One of the most important practical qualities of a ship is that which enables her to carry her profitable load at least cost. Cost in a ship, propelled by steam or other power, has, as one of its main elements, the resistance which the water opposes to the passage of the ship. This resistance is little for slow velocities, and very great for high velocities; increasing generally as fast as the square of the velocity, and in many shapes of vessel much faster.

It has always been of great value to know how to give a vessel, of given length and breadth, such lines as should enable her to divide the water in the easiest way, so as to experience least resistance from the water moved by the ship out of her path. But now, and especially of late years, the demand for high velocities in vessels propelled by steam, has given this problem of the form of least resistance paramount importance in naval architecture, especially with reference to ships of war.

The problem is frequently presented in this shape: A vessel is to be built of a given breadth, of a given length of bow, and a given length of run; and the question is, what kind of lines will give this vessel the power to divide the water so as to suffer least resistance, and waste least power; or, it may be, to attain the highest possible velocity with a given propelling power. The following maxims of the wave system show how this is to be done:

6. When it is required *to construct the water-lines of the bow of a ship, of which the breadth and length of bow are given*, so as to give the vessel the form of least resistance to passage through the water, or to obtain the highest velocity with a given power:

Take the greatest breadth of the vessel on the main section of construction, or midship breadth, and halve this breadth. At right angles to this, draw the centre line of length of the bow. On each half-breadth, describe a half-circle, dividing its circumference into (say) eight equal parts. Divide also the length into an equal number of equal parts. The divisions of the circle, reckoned successively from the extreme breadth, indicate the breadths of the water-line at the successive corresponding points of the line of length. Thus in Fig. 33, MM is the midship breadth of the proposed water-line; OX is the length of bow intended. Semicircles M, 1, 2, 3, 4, 5, 6, 7, 0, and M′, 1′, 2′, 3′, 4′ 5′, 6′, 7′, 0′, are described on the half-main-breadths, MO, and M′ O′. OX, is divided into the same number of equal parts. Through the divisions of the circles lines are to be drawn parallel to AX; and through the divisions of AX, lines parallel to MM′. These intersecting one another, show the successive points in the required water-line. This process may be carried to any degree of subdivision and precision. The line traced through all these points is the water-line of least resistance for a given length of bow, and breadth of body. The form thus described is the wave water-line. The half-breadths of the water-line are the versed sines of arcs of the circle described on the half-breadth, corresponding in order to the places where these half-breadths lie on the length. *The wave water-line of least resistance is*, therefore, geometrically considered, a curve of versed sines,—or simply *a curve of sines.* This water-line is of a similar form to *a wave of the first order*, propagated through water of considerable depth.

7. *Comparative qualities of the Wave Water-line, Convex Water-line, and Straight Water-line of Entrance.*—The full bow, the straight bow, and the hollow bow, have each had, for some years, their respective advocates and parties among professional shipbuilders. The wave form has some advantages and some disadvantages; and the various forms of various lines give various qualities, which different constructors prize more or less, and which suit them to various uses. The practical problem is to select those forms most fit for special uses.

In regard to the wave-line, it must be conceded that in one point it is inferior to the convex, or bluff bow. It is inferior in capacity, or displacement, to a vessel with a full convex water-line on the same midship breadth and length of entrance. The convex water-line made of the parabolic form (Fig. 34) has a larger area than the water-line, in the proportion of 6.66 to 5.00.

For a slow vessel the parabolic entrance may have an advantage in point of capacity. But that will be a mercantile point of comparison between the value of speed and capacity in the conditions of a given case.

The straight line entrance (Fig. 35) has no greater capacity than the wave-line entrance. There is no advantage with which I am acquainted possessed by a straight-line bow over the wave-line. On the other hand, the advantages, in a sea-going point of view, of the wave-line bow over the straight-line bow are great. The wave water-line has, it is true, no greater area than the straight water-line, but it has that area in a much better place. It carries its cargo and weights in the right place, near the middle of the ship, while the straight bow, as well as the convex bow, carry their weights nearer the ends of the ship. To remove weights out of the ends of his ship, and to carry them near the middle, is exactly what the wise constructor aims at in a good design, and what the wise captain tries to arrange in his practical stowage. The extent to which this is carried out in practice is a main point in the sea-worthiness of a ship, especially in heavy weather. This excellent disposition of weights, the wave form accomplishes better than any other form. It takes weight out of the bow, to carry it near the middle.

In the Parabolic line the centre of weight is 0.37 from the middle.
In the Straight line the centre of weight is 0.33 from the middle.
In the Wave line the centre of weight is 0.29 from the middle.

Next, I may notice, that in point of stability the wave-bow is superior to the straight bow. In the drawings it is shown that the centres of gravity of the wave-line are further from the middle than in the straight-line bow. (Fig. 36.) Thus, although the areas of water-line are equal, the stability of the wave-line is greater than that of the straight-line bow.

But in regard to the motion of pitching in a heavy sea, the wave-line is, beyond all question, much easier in its motions than the straight-line, or than the convex. This arises from its capacity for weight lying nearer to the centre of the ship, and also from the weight of the hull itself lying much nearer the centre. This prevents the ends from being loaded. Moreover, the very fact of there being little displacement near the ends deprives the sea of power either to move the ship vertically in the longitudinal direction, or to act upon it with injurious force to the same degree as either the straight-line or the convex bow. Hence, the wave-bow makes the ship not only easier, but stronger and safer, than a ship of the same length with either the convex or the straight-water-line.

The advantages and disadvantages of the three classes of bow are nearly as follows:—

CONVEX PARABOLIC.	STRAIGHT LINE.	WAVE LINE.
Greatest capacity, 0.66.	Less capacity, 0.5.	Less capacity, 0.5.
Greatest resistance.	Less resistance.	Least resistance.
Greatest stability.	Least stability.	Mean stability.
Greatest pitching.	Less pitching.	Least pitching.
Worst place for weights.	Mean place for weights.	Best place for weights.
Worst for strength.	Mean for strength.	Best for strength.
Worst for injury at sea.	Mean for injury at sea.	Safest at sea.
Least speed.	Mean speed.	Greatest speed.
Most waste of power.	Mean waste of power.	Least waste of power.

8. *The Wave-Lines of the After-Body.*—The wave-line of the fore-body of a ship is a simple geometrical line of unvarying form and appearance, unmistakable in its characters, and perfectly definite and precise in all its elements. On a given length and breadth it has a given invariable measure of convexity and concavity, and characters which do not change.

The wave-line of the after-body is less definite in some of its characters, and admits of variations which allow greater freedom of choice.

The reason of this difference arises mainly out of the different conditions of the water as it is acted on by the bow, and as it acts on the stern. The bow strikes water in a condition which (in smooth water at least) is uniform, definite, and exactly foreknown. The particles of water are at rest in front of the bow, and the only choice we have in designing a bow is whether we shall give them one motion or another.

But the after-body is in quite different conditions from the fore-body. It moves in troubled water. Instead of finding particles of water at rest, it finds them with motion already given to them, and the first question to be asked is, what state does the fore-body leave the water in when the after-body has to follow it up? The problem is, therefore, more complicated.

And further, the after-body really finds itself in a cavity, or hole, ready made for it by the fore-body, and the question is rather this, What shape will the water itself take? than this, What shape shall we give the water? In the case of the fore-body, the water must suit itself to the shape of that body which is forced into it. But in the case of the after-body the water is free to follow the shape of the after-body or not, according as it may, or may not, find the shape of the after-body suited to it. The run of the water may, or may not, choose to follow the shape of the after-body of the ship. We must, therefore, fit the after-body to the run of the water in the wake.

The after-body must, therefore, fit the water, and fill the run which the water may take. And the question next has to be asked,—How does the water which has been parted and moved out of the way of the bow of a ship behave itself in the process of refilling the hole which has been made? We have seen, in a previous part of this inquiry, that the water in filling a wake abaft the midship section of a ship takes the form of a wave of the second order. In order to fit it the line of the ship ought to fit the line of the wave of the second order.

In order to apply this in practice to the after-body of a ship of a given length and breadth, and of which we have already formed the water-line of entrance, we take the main breadth and length of run chosen. (Fig. 37.) We divide the length of run into 1, 2, 3, 4, 5, 6, 7, 8, equal parts; we place a semi-circle on half the main breadth, abaft it, as shown in the drawing; we divide the circumference into the same number of equal parts as the length of run; and in the same order we draw a fore-and-aft line from each point in the circle equal the parts 0, 1, 2, 3, 4, 5, 6, 7, on the length. The ends of these parallels are points in the water-line required.

The curve of the after-body is, therefore, of the kind commonly called cycloidal, or *trochoidal*, and though not identical with the curve of the bow, belongs to the same family. Such curve may, however, be called *wave-lines* better than by any other Greek, or Latin name, as the forms are best known to every body from the shape of the waves on the surface of the sea. The curve just described is the same as *the curve of the front of a common sea wave* approaching a shore, and it is the curve which water filling up an opening artificially made in it, naturally assumes in the process of filling up.

It should be carefully noted that, in the case of the fore-body, the water-line has an invariable *concavity*. In the after-body, on the contrary, it may be even quite *convex* (see Fig. 38), in extreme cases. This depends on the relative length and breadth in the after-body, while in the fore-body it is constant. It is also to be noted, that in every case the after water-line thus constructed is fuller than the corresponding water-line of entrance. Another point of distinction between the wave-line fore-body and after-body is this, that the whole of the wave water-lines of the fore-body may be constructed so as to follow closely all the characters of that line which is taken as the principal water-line. On the contrary, the character of the wave water-lines of the after-body, which are lower down than the principal water-line, may, and in many cases must and should, vary entirely from that of the principal water-line, which is to be taken at, or near, the surface of the water. The reason of this difference is cogent. The particles of water at the bow, acted on by a wave fore-body, do in general take motions which closely resemble each other from the bottom to the top of the water. On the contrary, the particles entering the run take motions in entirely different planes. Their motions vary as follows:—Those on the surface move more nearly in a horizontal plane; those near the bottom of the ship move nearly in a vertical plane. For the same reason, also, the depth of the ship materially affects the direction of motion of the particles in the wake. In a shallow ship much of the motion of the particles is in a vertical plane, and little of it horizontal. In a deep ship much of it is horizontal, and less of it vertical. The shape of the midship section also affects powerfully the direction of the particles starting on their run into the wake.

To determine the best form of after-body it is, therefore, expedient to construct a vertical wave-line on the run, as well as a horizontal one (see Fig. 39), and in designing two vessels, to give more weight to the vertical wave-line and less to the horizontal one. Great use may be made of this in shallow vessels, to give them good qualities, by filling the horizontal water-lines and fining only the vertical ones.

We have, therefore, *in the after-body, a wave buttock-line,* as well as a wave water-line to assist us. It is fortunate, indeed, for us, that we have two lines to help us instead of one; and that we are able to use our judgment in the degree by which we lean more on the one of these, or more on the other. For the run of a ship is more complex than the bow, in consequence of the place of the rudder being aft; and the best action of the rudder is a point to which minor considerations must give way. The two lines we possess enable us to give more or less fineness one way than another, according as we find it to affect steering power.

The case of screw vessels, also, which have the propeller in the stern, requires a judicious choice to be made between vertical fineness and horizontal. The result of my experience is, that fineness below is much more valuable, both for the good action of rudder and screw, than fineness above. I, therefore, am guided mainly by the vertical wave-line in giving fineness to the after-body.

The practical advantages to be given to a ship, by means of the wave-line after-body, are as follows :—

Great capacity of after-body ;

A very fine run below-water ;

Great area of water-line near the surface, where it is most valuable for use ;

Great stability, given in a good place, and of a good sort, for sea-going qualities ;

Least resistance, and greatest economy of power.

9. *A definite proportion of the length of fore-body of a ship is given by the wave principle.*—Different naval constructors have adopted different methods of proportioning the fore and after-bodies ; but no one of these has borne the test of practical trial at considerable velocity. I was educated in the dogma that the greatest beam, or main breadth of construction, should be exactly one-third of the length from the stem, and exactly two-thirds of the length from the stern ; making the after-body double the length of the fore-body. Later, the advancement of steam navigation compelled the abandonment of this idea ; and with a straight bow and a straight run, there came into use a fore and after-body more nearly equal.

The wave principle has reversed the old inequality between the fore and after-body of a ship, by allowing the after-body to be even shorter than the fore-body. The degree to which the after-body may be shortened, without injury to speed and power, is also defined ; being, in round numbers, one-third shorter than the fore-body.

Hence the after-body of a wave-line ship may be shorter than the fore-body, in the proportion of two to three. This gives the following proportions :—

Fore-body = three-fifths.
After-body = two-fifths.
Whole length = five-fifths.

10. There is no principle given by the wave method of construction more important than the following : That there is *a fixed proportion between the speed for which a ship is to be*

designed, and the length of entrance and run which must be given to her in order to fit her for that speed. The importance of obtaining such definite proportions had long been felt by practical men. It was known that it was very difficult, by any amount of power, to push vessels of certain length and shape through the water at a high velocity. Power and money were wasted in vain attempts to make ships of unsuitable dimensions attain high speed. Vessels were filled with boilers and machinery, designed to compel the performance of high velocities. Instances are well known where a double amount of steam boiler had been provided to compel high speed in an unsuitable vessel, and afterwards these boilers had to be removed, the higher speed being found impossible in that kind of ship, and the highest speed of which the ship was capable was afterwards brought out with half the power. It is, in general, most unwise to attempt, by excess of steam-power, to compel vessels to perform speeds to which their dimensions and form are unsuited; only in rare cases is such a sacrifice of power excusable, when circumstances render it impossible to have the proper length and form. The wave principle at once gives us the following information:—

For a speed of 10 statute miles an hour, the entrance of a ship should have a length of not less than 35 feet, and the run should have a length of 20 feet.

For a speed of 15 statute miles an hour, the entrance of a ship should have a length of not less than 95 feet, and the run should have a length of 68 feet.

For a speed of 20 statute miles an hour, the entrance of a ship should have a length of 170 feet, and a length of run of 120 feet.

The cause which fixes this proportion is obvious. The length of the fore-body of a ship designed on the wave principle must be the same as the length of a wave of the first order which moves with that speed. The length of the after-body must be the same as the length of front face of the wave of the second order moving with that velocity.

Hence the following table:—

Lengths of Entrance and Run for Given Speeds.

Statute Miles per Hour.	Length of Entrance.	Length of Run.
1	.42	.3
2	1.68	1.2
3	3.78	2.7
4	6.72	4.8
5	10.50	7.5
6	15.12	10.8
7	20.58	14.7
8	26.88	19.2
9	34.02	20.5
10	42.00	30.0
11	50.82	36.3
12	60.48	43.2
13	70.98	50.7
14	82.32	58.8
15	94.50	67.5
16	107.52	76.8
17	121.38	86.7
18	136.08	97.2
19	151.62	108.3
20	168.00	120.0

11. The wave system of construction releases us from the trammels of another very old and time-revered prejudice. It used to be imagined that there was a *fixed proportion of breadth and length* in a ship which was essential to her attaining high speed. For example, a proportion of three breadths to her length was reckoned a good proportion for a sailing-vessel of moderate speed, four to one was used for a higher speed, and six breadths to her length was considered a high proportion. Next came the demands of steam navigation, and it was considered necessary for high speeds, that a proportion of 8 to 1, 9 to 1, 10 to 1, and even 15, 18 and 20 to 1 would be required for the highest speeds.

The wave system destroys all idea of any proportion of breadth to length being required for speed. An absolute length is required for the entrance and run; but these being formed in accordance with the wave principle for any given speed, the breadth may have any proportion to that which the uses of the ship and the intentions of the constructor require. A vessel meant to go ten knots can be efficiently propelled at that speed if her length and form be right, whether she is 3 feet beam or 30 feet.

12. The wave system of construction fortunately leaves us *free to adopt any form of midship-section* we require for the other qualities of the ship, and it is nearly equally easy to design a

ship according to the wave principle on any one midship-section which gives us the good qualities we want as on any other.

13. In conclusion. The wave system allows us to give the vessel as much length as we please to the middle-body. It is by this means that we can give to a vessel of the wave form the capacity we may require, but which the ends may not admit. Thus the *Great Eastern*, which is a pure example of the wave form, has an entrance, or fore-body, of 330 feet; a run, or after-body, of 220 feet; and a middle-body of 120 feet, which was made of this length merely to obtain the capacity required.

In designing wave vessels, it is necessary to distinguish carefully the *three great elements of construction*, viz.: the *fore-body*, the *after-body*, and the *middle-body*. The lengths of the fore and after-body are indicated by the required speed, and if the beam is fixed, it is only by means of a due length of middle-body that the required capacity, stability, and such other qualities are to be given, which will make the ship, as a whole, suit its use. Middle-body is therefore an element demanding the careful study of the designer on the wave system, and it will well reward his pains.

It only remains now to notice the errors which a young naval constructor, trained in the old school, is likely to commit in his first use of the wave principle. One of the most common of these errors is to exaggerate the wave principle, and to caricature it. Finding that a hollow water-line is admissible, he rushes to the extreme, and makes it too hollow, and gets increased resistance. Finding that a long entrance is good, he makes it too long, and gets increased surface. Finding that a full after-body is admissible, he makes it too full, and injures steering. On the other hand, instead of going too far, he may stop short too soon. When the water-line near the bow is made fine, and the deck allowed to remain full, the end of the ship is overloaded, and so the value of carrying weights in the centre is sacrificed to a custom. It is most unwise not to reduce the weight and bulk carried out of the water, in like proportion to the weight and bulk by which they are carried in the water. No error is more common than to give a wave-line vessel greater fineness than is required for the special case, to the sacrifice of the carrying qualities of the ship. The best way of avoiding these errors, is for the constructor not to adopt the system too hurriedly, nor to introduce it too largely in his first constructions. Let him take the lines of a ship he has already built, and only alter them in a small degree the first time in the direction which the wave principle indicates. He will find out thus how far he has made improvement, and how far he has altered the ship's practical points. Next time he may make a further change in the same direction. Thus he will avoid the error of rushing to an extreme—than which there is nothing more fatal to the success of a new method. A ship all ends, with no middle—all top, with no bottom—all deadwood, with no capacity, is precisely one of those caricatures of the wave principle of which we have seen a great many misnamed clippers, in which the true purposes and uses of a ship have been lost sight of; and the attempt to achieve a sudden and fruitless victory in speed has been made at the expense of every quality which makes speed desirable and remunerative.

To guard against such errors let it never be forgotten, that the end of all shipbuilding is to work out the purposes of the shipowner. A ship of war has to fight guns, and a merchantman to carry freight. To build the former so as not to fight her guns, is a much greater fault than to make her slow. To build the latter so as to have great speed at great cost, without the capacity necessary to repay the owner his outlay, is a folly. Freight is the owner's object, and to earn the greatest freight is the problem submitted to the designer of his ship. To this object the wave principle, well understood, gives a safe and certain guide. When you know the speed wanted for the trade, the wave principle will give you the length of entrance and run to gain that speed. When you know the cargo to be carried, you are able to say what buoyancy you want, and what length of middle-body will carry the bulk and weight. When you know what draught of water the intended navigation admits, you are ready to decide what form of midship-section will give the stiffness and weatherliness wanted. When you know the weights to be carried, and the bulks to be stowed, you must take care that you carry them where they are supported by the water, and not where, being unsupported, they weaken the ship and increase its strains. If you thus keep the uses of the ship steadily in view, you will find the principles of the wave system a safe guide to enable you to give your design those qualities, without a sacrifice of those other qualities which can alone enable the shipowner to continue to avail himself of your science and skill.

NOTE.—[From Transactions of the Institute of Naval Architects, Vol. II., 1861.]

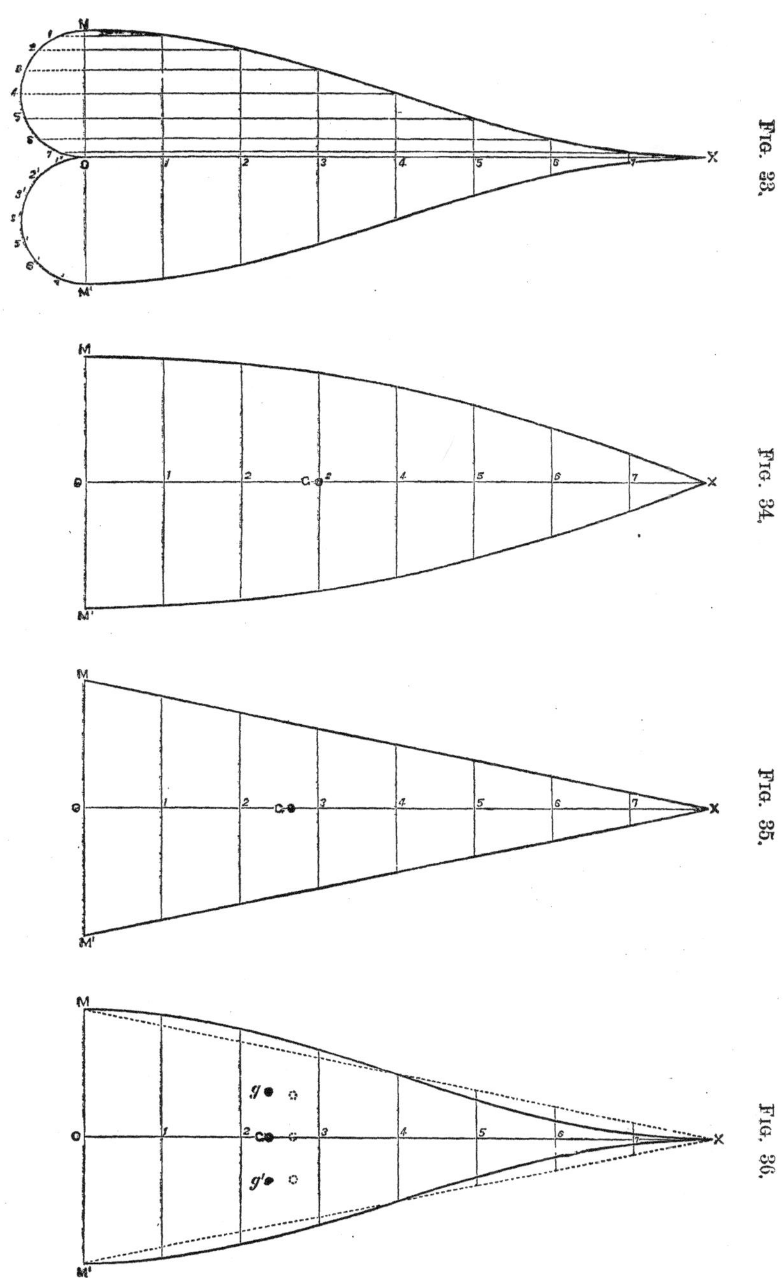

FIG. 33.

FIG. 34.

FIG. 35.

FIG. 36.

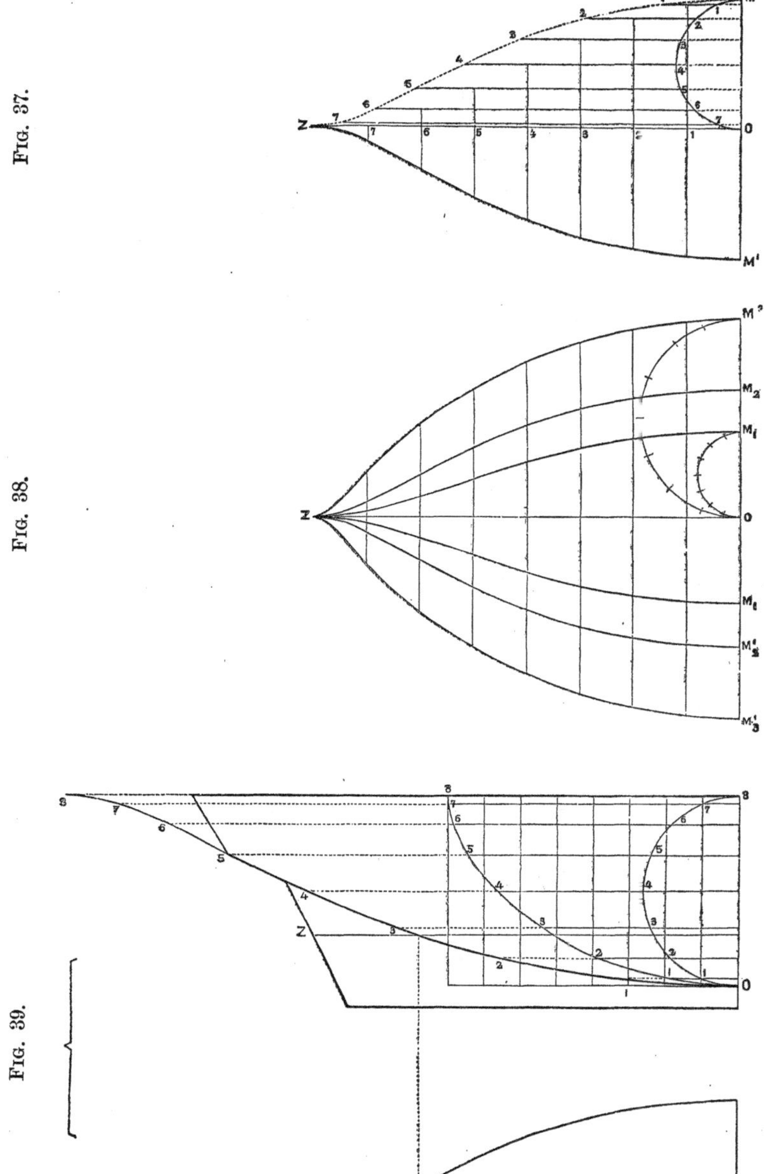

FIG. 37.

FIG. 38.

FIG. 39.

CHAPTER XXII.

Propelling Power and Speed—Resistance due to Frictional Eddies—Computation of Augmented Surface—Computation of Probable Resistance—Computation of Engine Power required at a Given Speed—Computation of Probable Speed—Example of Calculation of Probable Speed of H. M. S. *Warrior*.

THE *resistance to the motion of a ship due to the production of frictional eddies by a given portion of her skin* is the product of the following factors :—

I. The area of the portion of the ship's skin in question;

II. The *cube* of the ratio which the velocity of gliding of the particles of water over that area bears to the speed of the ship, being a quantity depending on the figure of the ship and the position of the part of her skin under consideration;

III. The height due to the ship's speed; that is (in feet)

$$\frac{(\text{speed in feet per second})^2}{64.4}, \text{ or } \frac{(\text{speed in knots})^2}{22.6}:$$

IV. The heaviness (or weight of an unit of volume) of the water (64 lbs. per cubic foot of sea-water); and

V. A factor called the *coefficient of friction*, depending on the material with which the ship's skin is coated, and its condition as to roughness or smoothness.

The sum of the products of the factors I. and II. for the whole skin of the ship, has of late been called her *Augmented Surface;* and the *Eddy-Resistance* of the whole ship may therefore be expressed as the product of her Augmented Surface; by the factors III., IV., and V., above mentioned.

[In algebraical symbols, let $d\ s$ denote the area of a small portion of the ship's skin, q the ratio which the velocity of gliding of the water over that portion bears to the speed of the ship, c the speed of the ship, g gravity, w the heaviness of the water, f the coefficient of friction: then,

Eddy-Resistance $= f\ w \frac{c^2}{2g} \int q^3\ d\ s$; $\int q^3\ d\ s$ being the *Augmented Surface.*]

The resistance thus determined, being deduced from the work performed in producing eddies, includes in one quantity both the direct adhesive action of the water on the ship's skin and the indirect action, through increase of the pressure at the bow and diminution of the pressure at the stern.

The constant part of the expression deduced by Professor Weisbach, from experiments on the flow of water in pipes, viz., $f = .0036$, has given a coefficient of friction, corroborated by practice, for surfaces of clean painted iron.

For clean copper sheathing, it appears probable that the coefficient of friction is somewhat smaller, but there are not yet sufficient experimental data to decide that question exactly. Experimental data are also wanting to determine the précise increase of the coefficient of friction produced by various kinds and degrees of roughness and foulness of the ship's bottom, but it is certain that that increase is sometimes very great.

The preceding value of the coefficient of friction leads to the following very simple rule:—*At ten knots, the eddy-resistance of a clean iron ship is one pound avoirdupois per square foot of augmented surface; and it varies, for other speeds, as the square of the speed.*

Computation of Augmented Surface.—To compute the *exact* augmented surface of a vessel of any ordinary shape, would be a problem of impracticable labor and complexity. The method employed, therefore, as an approximation for practical purposes, is to choose in the first instance a figure approximating to the actual figure, but of a kind such that its augmented surface can be calculated by a simple and easy process, and to use that augmented surface instead of the exact augmented surface of the ship; care being taken to ascertain, by comparison with experiments on ships of various sizes and forms, whether the approximation so obtained is sufficiently accurate.

The figure chosen for that purpose is the trochoïd, or rolling-wave curve, extending between a pair of crests; for by an easy integration, it is found, that the augmented surface of a trochoïdal riband of a given length in a straight line, and of a given breadth, is equal to the product of that length and breadth, multiplied by the following *coefficient of augmentation:* $1 + 4$ (sine of greatest obliquity)^2 + (sine of greatest obliquity)^4; the *greatest obliquity* meaning the greatest angle made by the riband with its straight chord.

In approximating to the augmented surface of a given ship by the aid of that of a trochoïdal riband, the following values are employed:—I. For the length of the riband, the length of the ship on the plane of flotation; II. For the total breadth of the riband, the *mean immersed girth*, found by measuring, on the body plan, the immersed girths of a series of cross-sections, and taking their mean by Simpson's Rule; III. For the *coefficient of augmentation*, the mean of the values of that coefficient as deduced from the greatest angles of obliquity of the series of water-lines of the fore-body, as shown on the half-breadth plan. The augmented surface is then computed by multiplying together these three factors.

The Computation of the Probable Resistance (in lbs.), at a given speed, is performed according to the rule already stated, by *multiplying the augmented surface by the square of the speed in knots, and dividing by* 100 (for clean painted iron ships).

In Computing the Probable Engine-Power required at a given Speed, allowance must be made for the power wasted through slip, through wasteful resistance of the propeller, and through the friction of the engine. The proportion borne by that wasted power to the effective or net power, employed in driving the vessel, of course varies considerably for different ships, propellers, and engines; but in several good examples it has been found to differ little from 0.63; so that as a probable value of the *indicated power* required, in a well-designed vessel, we may take net power $\times 1.63$.

Now an indicated horse-power is 550 foot-pounds per second, and a knot is 1.688 feet per second; therefore an indicated horse-power is $\frac{550}{1.688} = 326$ knot-pounds, nearly; or 326 lbs. gross resistance overcome through one nautical mile in an hour. If we estimate, then, the *net* or *useful* work done in propelling the vessel as being equal to the total work of the steam divided by 1.63, we shall have $\frac{326}{1.63} = 200$ knot-pounds of net work done in propulsion for each indicated horse-power. Hence the following rule:—*Multiply the augmented surface in square feet by the cube of the speed in knots, and divide by* 20,000; *the quotient will be the probable indicated horse-power.*

The divisor in this rule (20,000) expresses the *number of square feet of augmented surface, which can be driven at one knot by one indicated horse-power:* it may be called the "coefficient of propulsion."

It is, of course, to be understood that the exact divisor ("or coefficient of propulsion") differs in different vessels, according to the smoothness of the skin, the nature of its material, and the efficiency of the engines and propellers; it being greatest in the most favorable examples.

The value 20,000 may be taken as a probable and safe estimate of the divisor in any proposed vessel designed on good principles. For copper sheathing and smooth pitch, the coefficient of propulsion is certainly greater than 20,000, but in what precise proportion it is at present difficult to decide.

Computation of Probable Speed.—When the augmented surface of a ship has been determined, her probable speed, with a given power, is computed as follows:—*Multiply the indicated horse-power by* 20,000; *divide by the augmented surface, and extract the cube root of the quotient for the probable speed in knots.*

Example.—Calculation of Probable Speed of H. M. S. Warrior.—Displacement on trial, 8,997 tons; draught of water forward, 25.83 feet; aft, 26.75 feet:—

Water Lines.	Sine of Obliquity.	Square of Sine.	Fourth Power of Sine.
L.W.L.	.370	.1369	.01874
2 W.L.	.315	.0992	.00984
3 W.L.	.290	.0841	.00707
4 W.L.	.265	.0702	.00492
5 W.L.	.235	.0552	.00304
6 W.L.	.165	.0272	.00074
Keel	.000	.0000	.00000
Means		.0674	.00583

1 + (4 × .0674) + .0058 = 1.275, Co-efficient of Augmentation.

Half-Girths from Body Plan.	Simpson's Multipliers.	Products.
Feet.		
21.0	1	21.0
27.2	4	108.8
30.8	2	61.6
34.6	4	138.4
38.8	2	77.6
41.5	4	166.0
42.6	2	85.2
44.0	4	176.0
44.0	2	88.0
44.0	4	176.0
43.3	2	86.6
42.1	4	168.4
40.3	2	80.6
38.1	4	152.4
36.0	2	72.0
35.0	4	140.0
32.0	1	32.0

Divide by 3)1830.6 sum.

Divide by half number of Intervals 8)610.2

Mean Immersed Girth 76.3
× Length 380

Product 28994
× Coefficient of Augmentation 1.275

Augmented Surface 36979 square feet.

Indicated Horse-Power, on trial, 5,471
× Coefficient of Propulsion, 20,000

Divide by Augmented Surface, 36,979)109,420,000 product.

Cube of Probable Speed, 2,959

Probable Speed, Computed, 14.356 knots.
Actual Speed, on trial, 14.354

Difference, .002

NOTE.—From Transactions of the Institute of Naval Architects. Vol. v., 1864.

DIVISION SECOND.

DIRECTIONS FOR

"LAYING DOWN" AND "TAKING OFF" SHIPS

ON

THE MOULD-LOFT FLOOR.

INTRODUCTORY OBSERVATIONS.

1. *Laying down* consists in drawing the lines of the ship on the *mould-loft floor*, to the *full size*. The body-plan forms the most prominent part, and the sections which are shown in it are moulding-lines or outside the timber, and are measured with a scale from the drawing or model, and with these measures the lines are laid down. When a model is used in laying down, a series of vertical lines representing generally every fourth frame, or at least a sufficient number for ascertaining correctly the figure of the vessel, are to be drawn upon the vertical side of it. The measurements for constructing the sheer-plan can now be obtained by taking the height of the several sheer and water-lines from the base-line or lower edge of the model, and the distances forward or aft of some given vertical line on each water and sheer-line, of the fore-edge of rabbet of stem, and after-edge of rabbet of stern-post and centre-counter timbers. The next operation is to take the model apart, and draw upon each lift, ordinates at the stations of the frames already marked. These ordinates, being measured by the proper scale, give the half-breadths at the points where the several frames intersect the several water-lines and sheer-lines; and all the dimensions as taken off are to be written in a Table prepared for that purpose and intended to be used in transferring the lines to the full size on the mould-loft floor. These Tables are known as "Tables of Ordinates." In many cases, the desired form of the vessel is first drawn on paper, the lines proved and all the necessary calculations made before making a model, the necessary dimensions are then taken off and written in the Tables as before described. The reader is referred to the "Tables of Ordinates" for laying down a steam screw-corvette of the *Antietam* class, which were taken from a drawing and show exactly what data is required before commencing the work in the mould-loft. A great deal of trouble may be saved in the fairing-in of the lines, by reading with the scale on the drawing as accurately as possible, so that when these measures

are laid down on the floor, and a batten passed through, the curve drawn along its edge will form a fair curve.

Unless due attention be paid to laying-down, considerable injury may be done to a good design, by deviating from the drawings. Accuracy in making the moulds is also necessary, in order to insure the economical appropriation of timber; and it also facilitates the execution of the workmanship.

In proceeding with the explanations required for laying down the body of a ship, it is taken for granted that the student is conversant with the names of the various timbers of the frame, and the manner in which they are combined; if not, it is necessary to study these points first, which may be done by referring to the Third Division of this work on Shipbuilding.

2. The laying-down upon the mould-loft floor should be proceeded with in such a manner as to be least subject to error, and, as far as practicable, that the conversion of the timbers may go on at the same time, to prevent any delay in proceeding with the structure. The moulds, therefore, should be made for the different timbers as they are laid down, beginning with the stem, stern-post, forward and after deadwoods and fore-foot; which, with a plan of the shift of deadwood, should be sent at once into the shipyard for providing the pieces. In order to economize time, the keel-scarphs are laid down and a mould made for them; the after-piece of the scarph always overlaps the foremost piece; the scarphs are what are termed "plain horizontal scarphs" and should be long enough to admit of the fastening of four frames through each, the nibs of the scarphs should come under a futtock or filling timber. Two long battens, having the distance between the joints of the square frames painted upon them, called "room and space battens," are accurately marked; one is sent to the foreman of shipwrights to be used in laying off the stations of the frames on the keel, the duplicate is retained and used in the mould-loft in laying down the vessel.

In laying down a vessel there are three principal plans made use of which are distinguished by the names of sheer, body and half-breadth plans. These combined constitute what is termed the draught of a ship. We will describe each separately.

SHEER PLAN.

3. The sheer-plan (Plates I. and II., Fig. 1) is the representation of an imaginary longitudinal section, dividing the ship into two

equal parts, by a vertical plane passing through the middle of the keel, stem, and stern-posts. This section is bounded by the fore-part of the head, under-side of the keel, aft side of the rudder, rake of the stern, and sheer of the upper part of the top-side.

Besides this plan being a section of the ship amidships, showing the sheer of the decks, rails, port-sill, cutting-down or throating-line, bearding-line, &c., on it are also projected, in lines perpendicular to the aforesaid longitudinal section, the stations of the frames, the ports, cathead, head-rails, side counter-timber, &c.

From this we see that upon this plan all lines are projected as to height and length; it gives the vertical longitudinal form, and from it lines are transferred to the half-breadth as to length, and to the body as to height.

The lines of the sheer-plan are transferred to the body-plan by means of their heights taken at various parts on the sheer-plan, and those same heights measured off as heights on the body-plan from the base-line. All horizontal lines on the sheer-plan will be horizontal on the body-plan, as the water-lines when parallel to the base-line.

BODY-PLAN.

4. The body-plan (Plates I. and II., Fig. 2) is simply a representation of the form of the ship by transverse sections perpendicular to the keel, before, at, and abaft the greatest transverse section, which is termed "dead-flat," and usually denoted by the symbol ⊖. These transverse sections are transferable to the half-breadth plan as to breadth, and to the sheer-plan as to height.

HALF-BREADTH PLAN.

5. The half-breadth plan (Plate VII., Figs. 1 and 2) is that on which is shown the form of the body by horizontal and diagonal longitudinal sections, from which are obtained other sections in the body-plan,—such as the intermediate transverse sections, and the oblique sections as the cant timbers. Besides the above the form of the decks, port-sill and rail-lines, may be also delineated on the half-breadth plan.*

* The lines of the half-breadth plan are transferred to the body-plan by means of their distances taken at various parts on the half-breadth plan, and those same distances measured off from the centre line of the body-plan, either in a horizontal or diagonal direction. All lines parallel with the centre

The transverse sections in the body-plan and their corresponding stations in the half-breadth and sheer-plans are generally distinguished by letters, A, B, C, &c., those in the after-body by figures, 1, 2, 3, &c., although in very many cases figures are used for both fore and after-bodies, commencing to number from forward, omitting the greatest transverse section, which is invariably denoted by the symbol ⊕, and should there be more than one of that form they are denoted as ⊕1, ⊕2, ⊕3, &c.

It must be understood that the sections in the body-plan on the right of the centre-line represent the starboard fore-body, whilst those on the left of the centre-line represent the port after-body of the ship.

It will be perceived from the preceding remarks that

The sheer-plan	is a projection	on a vertical longitudinal plane;
The body-plan		on a vertical athwartship plane;
The half-breadth plan		on a horizontal plane.

The three plans above described constitute the draught of a ship. We shall see presently their mutual dependence on each other, so that any two being given, the third may be obtained.

PROFILE AND OTHER PLANS.

6. Besides the sheer-plan, it is customary to furnish the builder with a profile of the inboard works, on which is shown the stations of the masts, catheads, channels, chain-plates, head, head-rails, cheeks and brackets, engine keelsons, shaft bearings, water-tight bulkheads, &c. A plan of the midship section should be furnished, showing the moulding or athwartship size of the timbers, the thickness of the exterior and interior planking, the connections of the beams to the sides, the dimensions of the waterways, thick-strakes, description and fastening of the knees, the position and fastening of the keelsons, &c. A plan should be furnished for the several decks, showing the positions of the beams, carlings, ledges, hatches, skylights, cabin, wardroom, steerages, warrant-officers' quarters, sick-bay, dispensary, yeoman's and other store rooms; also one for the hold, showing the position of the engines, boilers, magazines, shell-rooms, shot-lockers, chain-lockers, stores, etc. These, together with the "building direc-

---

line in the half-breadth plan are equally parallel with and equidistant from the centre line of the body-plan as the vertical longitudinal section or buttock and bow lines.

tions," which is a document containing the dimensions and general directions for combining and fastening together the principal pieces that enter into the construction of the vessel, constitute all the preparatory information required by the builder.

MOULD-LOFTS.

7. Mould-lofts in private ship-building establishments are seldom long enough to admit of laying down any large vessel in one length; in small lofts they are laid down in three or four lengths. In the government yards, the length of the mould-loft generally admits of laying the vessel down in one length.

BASE-LINE.

8. The mould-loft floor being cleared, begin the process of laying down, by striking a straight line from one end to the other, or as long as the length of the vessel requires, called the base-line (Plates I. and II., Fig. 2), leaving space below, next the side of the loft, to strike in the depth of the keel.

The base-line will represent the lower edge of the garboard strake on the side of the keel, in the sheer and body-plans, above which all heights are to be set up;* and it will represent, also, the centre-line of the half-breadth plan, unless the half-breadth plan is laid down separately from the sheer-plan, in which case, the half-breadth is placed below the sheer-plan, and a line is struck in for the centre-line, parallel to the base-line, and, at a parallel distance below it, equal to one-half the greatest transverse section of the vessel.

To each of these lines, a broad batten with a straight edge is fixed for the convenience of butting the measuring batten against when setting off the distances.

TO PLACE THE FOREMOST AND AFTERMOST PERPENDICULARS, AND GET THE STATIONS OF THE TIMBERS ON THE FLOOR.

9. Set off on the base line the position of the foremost and aftermost perpendiculars, also the station of every fourth frame;

---

* See Plates III. and IV.

NOTE.—In the Plates, Nos. I. and II., accompanying this work, the reader will observe that the half-breadth (VII.) plan is laid down below the sheer-plan. My object in doing this is to make the lines used appear as distinct from each other as possible, and still be able to show as clearly as possible their intimate relation to each other.

these stations answer both for the sheer and half-breadth plans. The foremost perpendicular must be drawn in at such a distance from the end of the floor as to allow room for laying down the head, provided the length of the floor will admit; if not, leave room for the stern only. The length between the perpendiculars is generally measured on the load-water-line, from the fore-side of the rabbet of the stem to the after-side of the stern-post in sailing vessels, and after-side of main or forward stern-post in screw vessels having a forward and after-post. From the aftermost perpendicular, set forward the distance of dead-flat, and, as a proof of its correctness, try how the distance to some station abaft it corresponds; and if the whole distance—that is, if from the foremost perpendicular to dead-flat, added to the distance of the aftermost perpendicular from some station, together with the distance from this station to dead-flat, make the whole space between the perpendiculars as given in the "tables of ordinates"—these stations are correct. The stations of the perpendiculars are marked respectively FP and AP. The greatest transverse section, or, as it is termed, dead-flat, is invariably denoted by the symbol ⊕; as has been stated before, the stations of the frames or joints of the timbers are generally denoted by letters in the fore-body—that is, all frames forward of dead-flat, and by figures in the after-body of all frames abaft dead-flat, or by figures in both bodies, commencing to number them from forward, omitting dead-flat.

TO RUN IN THE HORIZONTAL AND SHEER LINES.

10. From the Tables, take the parallel distance of the water-lines from the base-line, set them up on the perpendiculars, and strike in the lines. Next take the heights of the several sheer-lines, set them up on their respective stations from the base-line, and mark the height. Nail a batten on the floor, corresponding to the spots already obtained, see that the curve is perfectly fair, and mark it in—the round edge of the batten is the best to look at in fairing the sheer or other lines on the floor, and they should lay on their flat, the edge to the spots. The battens to one or all of the sheers may be placed on the floor at the same time. If, however, the sheers taper, one at a time is sufficient; when they are parallel, they may all be regulated to advantage at the same time.

TO GET THE SHAPE OF THE FORWARD EDGE OF THE RABBET OF THE STEM.

11. To get the shape of the forward edge of the rabbet of the stem in the fore-body; take from the Tables the distance on each sheer and water-line that the edge of the rabbet is forward or aft, as the case may be, of the forward perpendicular; place a batten to the points thus obtained, fair the curve, and mark it in on the floor. This is the boundary line of the forward part of the sheer-plan. The distance that the fore-side of the stem and gripe are forward of this line can be struck in now, or when ready to make the moulds for the stem-pieces.

TO GET THE SHAPE OF THE AFTER-EDGE OF THE RABBET OF THE STERN-POST AND CENTRE-COUNTER-TIMBER.

12. To get the shape of the after-edge of the rabbet of the stern-post and centre counter-timber; take from the Tables the distances on each sheer and water-line that the after-edge of the rabbet of the stern-post and centre counter-timber are forward or aft, as the case may be, of the after perpendicular; place a batten to the points thus obtained, fair the curve and mark it in on the floor. This is the boundary line of the after-part of the sheer-plan. The distance that the stern-post is aft of the rabbet can be struck in now or when ready to make the mould for it.

TO RUN IN THE HALF-BREADTH PLAN.

(Plate VII., Figs. 1 and 2.)

13. Having struck in a line for the centre-line of the half-breadth plan as before described, and marked the stations of the frames in the sheer-plan down to it, proceed as follows:—

Set up from the centre-line and parallel to it at either extremity of the vessel, one-half the siding size of the stem and stern-posts, as given in the building instructions, and draw in a line for several feet from the extremities: this will be called the side-line. The general practice is to strike the side-line in at a distance from the centre-line equal to one-half the siding size of the keel, and has been drawn in in this way on the accompanying plan. From the Tables set off from the centre-line the half-breadths of the water-lines and sheer-lines at their proper stations, and proceed to find their ending forward and aft.

ENDING OF WATER-LINES AND SHEER-LINES FORWARD.

(Plate IV., Fig. 1.)

14. To end the water-lines and sheer-lines forward; square down the intersection of the several lines with the fore-edge of the rabbet of the stem in the sheer-plan, on to the side-line in the half-breadth plan; with this point as a centre and the thickness of the plank at that point as a radius, describe an arc towards the centre-line, and let the lines end tangent to, or touch this arc.

ENDING OF WATER-LINES AND SHEER-LINES AFT.

(Plate III., Fig. 1.)

15. To end the water-lines and sheer-lines when they cross above the rabbet of the post; square down the intersection of these lines with the after-edge of the centre counter-timber in the sheer-plan on to the side-line in the half-breadth and end the lines at those points. The water-lines that intersect the after-edge of the rabbet of the stern-post in the sheer-plan will be ended by squaring down their several points of intersection on to the side-line, and, with these points as centres and the thickness of plank as the radius, describe an arc towards the centre-line, and let the lines end tangent to, or touch this arc. Proceed now to place battens to the spots on the stations of the frames, obtained as before described. It is desirable to regulate all the water-lines at the same time, or to have all the battens on the floor at the same time, as one line determines, to some extent, the correctness of the other. If proper care is taken in taking off the Tables from the model or plan, the variations will be inconsiderable; the battens will have to be reduced at the ends and made wedge-shaped, in order that they may be secured at their proper ending, or they can lay one above the other until regulated.

Proceed now to construct and lay down the body-plan in order that it may be regulated at the same time and made to correspond with the half-breadth.

TO CONSTRUCT THE SQUARE BODY-PLAN.

(Plates I. and II., Fig. 2.)

16. If the length of the floor will admit of it, extend the base-line of the sheer-plan out forward for the base-line of the body-

plan; on this erect a perpendicular as centre-line for both forward and after-bodies, the half-siding size of the keel must be struck in on either side of the centre-line; these are called side-lines, and in a propeller the swell of the post in the vicinity of the shaft must be drawn in, in the after-body plan. Draw from the base-line two lines parallel to the centre-line, one on either side of it, at a distance equal to one-half the breadth of the greatest transverse section; these are termed boundary-lines of the body-plan. Next set up the height of the water-lines from the base-line on the boundary-lines and draw or strike in the lines across both bodies.

TO OBTAIN THE SHAPE OF THE TRANSVERSE SECTIONS OR MOULDING EDGES OF THE FRAMES IN THE SQUARE BODY-PLAN.

17. Having provided a number of small pine battens about one-half of an inch square, and long enough to take off the greatest half-breadth and depth of the vessel, proceed as follows:—Hold one end of the batten against the strip placed to the centre-line in the half-breadth plan, at the perpendicular or station of the joint of the frame, and mark the intersection of each water-line and sheer-line; transfer these half-breadths to the body-plan and set them off from the centre-line on their corresponding water-lines, being careful to set off the half-breadths accurately and in their proper body,—that is, all those forward of dead-flat in the fore-body, and those abaft it in the after-body.

Before the half-breadths of the sheer-lines can be set out in either body, the proper height for setting them out must be obtained, viz.: Place one end of the batten against the base-strip in the sheer-plan and mark the intersection at the height of each sheer-line; transfer these heights to the body-plan and set them up on the side and boundary-lines in their respective bodies, and draw or strike in level lines at these heights; then, upon these lines set off the corresponding half-breadths as already obtained from the half-breadth plan; by this means a spot is obtained in the body-plan at the height of the breadth for every frame.

To end the heels of the square frames; set down below the base-line at its intersection with the side-line in each body the thickness of the rabbet of the bottom plank, as taken from the building instructions; take a pair of dividers and open them to correspond with this distance: one leg is placed at the intersection of the base and side-lines; the second leg is placed on the side-line below, and an arc is swept from the base-line inward, the compasses turning on the lower leg below the base-line. It must be observed that in the case above the base-line was the upper edge of the rabbet on the side of the keel; in the plan it is the lower edge of the rabbet on the side of the keel, consequently the thickness of the rabbet must be swept in above the base-line. It is assumed that the keel is of a parallel thickness, consequently but one sweep is necessary for ending all the square frames in either body. The frame-lines all end tangent to, or touch, this arc. By cutting out a thick piece of plank with the proper sweep, and screwing it down on the floor in the body-plan at its proper place, it will be found very handy to place the lower end of the frames' battens against, as they can then lay over each other and also be ended properly.

The battens, which should be about one-half to three-fourths of an inch square, may now be placed on the floor and secured by nails driven in at short intervals on either edge of the battens; the rounding side of the battens being set to correspond with the half-breadths as before obtained,—the lower end secured at the ending marked for them. The battens should now be made perfectly fair in both the half-breadth and body-plans, any alteration in one body being made at the corresponding place in the other. The water-lines cut the frames in the body-plan so obliquely, as to point out readily any unfairness; at the same time, act with the greatest caution, in order to preserve the shape of the body as nearly as possible. Before marking in the shape of the frames proceed to prove the heels of the timbers by getting in the bearding-line.

TO OBTAIN THE BEARDING OR STEPPING-LINE.

(Plates I., II., and VII., Figs. 1 and 2.)

18. The bearding or stepping-line is obtained from the body and half-breadth plans, by taking from the body-plan, on a batten, the heights above the base-line to the intersection of each joint of frames with the side-line, and setting them up on their corresponding stations from the base-line in the sheer-plan; squaring up also from the half-breadth plan, the points where the several water and sheer-lines intersect the side-line, on to their corresponding lines in the sheer-plan; a curve passed through the points thus obtained, breaking in fair with the after-edge of the

rabbet of the stem forward, and fore-edge of the rabbet of the stern-post aft, will give the bearding or stepping-line in the sheer-plan, which is run in as a broken, not a full line.

The heels of the timbers being found to agree with this line by the fairness of the curve, the frames may now be marked in with pencil or chalk on the body-plan, and the water-lines and sheer-lines in the half-breadth, and the battens taken up.

The rising or height of the bearding-line above the base-line will be found in the Tables, these measurements having been taken from a draught; but, in working from a set of Tables taken from a model, and laid down direct on the floor, no measurements for this line would appear.

VERTICAL LONGITUDINAL SECTIONS, OR BUTTOCK AND BOW-LINES.

(Plates I., II., and VII., Figs. 1, 2.)

19. The water-lines being horizontal sections, proceed to prove the frames in the body-plan again by vertical longitudinal sections. They are the boundaries of planes which are supposed to pass fore-and-aft through the whole length of the ship, and parallel to the middle plane of her; these lines, by projection, are indicated by straight lines in the body, and half-breadth plans laid off at equal distances from the centre-line, generally the same distance as the water-lines, so that where the half-breadth is laid down that the base of the sheer-plan answers for the centre-line of the half-breadth, less lines would be required as the water-lines in the sheer-plan would answer for the projection of the sections in the half-breadth plan. In the sheer-plan they are curves bounding the sectional areas, and denoting by their form and regularity the symmetry of the vessel as well as the fairness of her. Though it may not be desirable to run in on the floor no more lines than necessary, both on account of despatch and to prevent confusion, yet, as a fair body is the main object, we must spare no pains nor number of lines to effect it.

These section-lines are distinguished as being dotted or broken lines in all three plans, and are marked according to their distance from the centre-line, viz., 2 ft., 4 ft., 6 ft., &c., Vertical Section-Lines.

METHOD OF TAKING OFF THE VERTICAL LONGITUDINAL SECTIONS OR BUTTOCK AND BOW-LINES.

20. The method of setting off these lines upon the sheer-plan is, by taking off the heights from the base-line in the body-plan, on a batten where the lines drawn for the sections intersect the transverse sections or frame-lines, and transferring these heights to the corresponding stations in the sheer-plan, setting them up from the base-line. Other points may be obtained for running this curve from the half-breadth plan, by squaring up the intersection of the water and sheer-lines with the section-lines on to their corresponding lines in the sheer-plan; and, if correct, the same water and section-lines will be found to intersect on the sheer-plan in that perpendicular.

ENDING OF VERTICAL LONGITUDINAL SECTIONS OR BUTTOCK AND BOW-LINES.

21. The ending of these lines is obtained by squaring up from the half-breadth plan the intersection of these lines with the half-breadth of rail on to the corresponding line in the sheer-plan, and ending the battens at that point. Now pin battens to the spots before set up, and to the last squared up as the ending, which should produce fair curves representing the body cut in that direction in the sheer-plan. Then, if these lines prove fair, the frame-lines in the body will be fair, and, likewise, the water-lines in the half-breadth plan; but if these lines to be made fair curves require alteration from the spots before set off, then the frame-lines in the body-plan must be altered accordingly, and, consequently, the water-lines.

The rising or height of these section-lines appear in the Tables having been obtained from the draught, no such measurements can be got direct from the model.

We will now proceed to prove the correctness of the body for the second and last time, by diagonal lines.

DIAGONAL LINES.

(Plates I. and II., Fig. 2.)

22. A diagonal-line is a curved line bounding a section or area of the body in an oblique direction, passing through the vessel longitudinally, and meeting the centre-line its entire length, parallel to the base-line. They are usually drawn in red on the body-plan of the draught where they are made to denote the lengths of

the timbers forming the frame of the vessel, and by projection they are in that plan represented as straight lines running in an oblique direction from the centre-line, each line crossing the forward and after body at a corresponding angle with the centre-line marking the heads and heels of the frame timbers. These lines are considered the most effectual towards fairing the body of the ship, or making the one portion of her assimilate with the other. It may here be observed that the diagonal-lines standing square to the frame-lines, or nearly so, upon the body-plan, are the least to be depended upon for pointing out any unfairness in the formations of the frame-lines, because they may really appear as fair lines on the half-breadth-plan, while the body itself is unfair. Therefore the diagonals can be first struck in at the discretion of the draughtsman, and after taking them off and proving the fairness of the body, these lines may be erased, and the diagonals drawn in red ink on the draught, or red chalk or pencil on the floor, strictly adhering to what has been said on this subject. Between the diagonals drawn at the heads and heels of the frame timbers, draw other diagonals for the sirmarks or stations of the ribbands which are placed between the heads of the respective frame timbers, in order to give support to the ship whilst in frame. A diagonal should also be marked between the floor-sirmark and keel for the floor guide. The diagonals are distinguished as 1st, 2d, etc., diagonals. The sirmarks are distinguished as floor-sirmark, 1st, 2d, 3d, etc., sirmarks. Having explained the nature and use of the diagonals, I will now proceed to explain the method of taking them off from the body-plan, and developing their curves in the half-breadth-plan.

METHOD OF TAKING OFF DIAGONAL-LINES.

23. The diagonals are taken off from the body-plan, for the form of the diagonal section to be shown on the half-breadth-plan, where it will be developed as a curve; by taking on a batten in the direction of the diagonal, the distances or intersections of each frame line with the diagonal from the centre-line, and setting them off from the centre-line of the half-breadth plan on their corresponding stations, and pinning a batten to these spots.

TO END THE DIAGONAL-LINES.

24. Diagonal-lines may be ended on the bearding-line, as the harpins, the form of which the diagonals are intended to de-

termine, do not go beyond it, but turn off at it, and follow the side of the stern or stern-post. The ending of any of the diagonals may be obtained if the bearding-line has been run in, by measuring in the body-plan the height of the intersection of the diagonal with the side-line, setting it up from the base-line until it intersects the bearding-line in the sheer-plan, squaring this point down to the side-line in the half-breadth plan, at which point the batten ends. A curve passed through the points before obtained and properly ended, will be the boundary of a plane cutting the frames of the ship obliquely, or of a plane that, if it were hung with hinges at the centre-line of the vessel, would, when allowed to fall to the given angle from the horizon, be found to coincide with the proposed form of the body of the vessel.

We may safely assume that the ship is fairly proved on the floor if the diagonals agree with the water-lines; we fairly conclude that there has been nothing left undone to insure the fairness and accuracy of the work. The diagonal-lines are found to be useful, not only as a proof line, and for the better distribution of the sirmarks, but they aid in the planking of the ship. By following the sirmarks we are enabled to make a proper distribution of surface, and reduce the opening in due proportion, before we may have proceeded far enough to make a division of the same. The diagonal-lines are of no further use in the half-breadth plan after the frames are faired.

JOINTS OF ALTERNATE SQUARE-FRAMES.

25. When the body is perfectly fair on the floor it becomes necessary to get in all the alternate timbers, or rather joints of frames which were omitted in the commencement of the work on the floor. In the half-breadth and sheer-plans bisect the spaces between every joint already laid down, and strike in the new joints; the half-breadths of which will be taken off the same as the others and transferred to and set off on their corresponding lines in the body-plan. Curves passed through the series of points thus obtained and ended the same as the other square frames, will represent the new joints, when the moulding edges of all the square frames in the body-plan will be complete.

Should the timbers taken from the draught not be sufficient to prove the body at the extremities, other timbers, called proof-timbers, must be got in forward and aft nearer to the extremities, and the horizontal, vertical, and diagonal sections corrected by them. The frame lines and all sections that are necessary to be preserved are now razed in on the floor.

Before commencing to make moulds for the square frames, we will first mention that the whole length of the ship is divided into three parts, viz., the "square body," "fore-cant body," and "after-cant body." With our modern hollow and fine lines the fore-cant body could almost be done away with. The cant bodies generally begin where the lines of the ship begin to deviate *greatly* from parallelism with the centre-line. Having settled where the square-body terminates and the cant-bodies commence (which is shown on the building draught of the lines in the half-breadth plan), we next proceed to find the "cutting-down line." It is nearly identical with the bearding or stepping-line. The first is the lowest point of the inside of the frame, and the last is the lowest point of the outside, or moulding side of the frame.

DEADWOOD LINE.*

(Plates I. and II., Fig. 1.)

26. This line is obtained by drawing the scantling of each frame at its lowest point, or its inner side, and where this intersects the side-line in the body-plan it will give a point at each frame; these distances taken off, on a batten, from the base-line, and set up on their corresponding stations in the sheer-plan, will give a series of points to place the batten to, forming a curve, called the "cutting-down line." The midship part of the cutting-down line in most ships runs along the lower surface of the keelson, which is parallel to and directly above the keel; the forward and after parts mark the height that it is required to build up the deadwood, for the purpose of securing the heels of the cant-timbers.

TO MAKE THE MOULDS FOR THE SQUARE-BODY.

27. The form of a vertical transverse section in the body-plan gives the shape of two assemblages of timbers; and that strength may be given by the connections of the timbers that compose one frame, the heads and heels of those in one assemblage are brought near the middle of those in the other; the moulds, therefore, which are made from the body-plan, and which are thin pine boards formed to the curve of each transverse section, must have

* Usually called the throating-line.

one set to overrun the other, agreeable to the shift determined. In the modern system of framing, when the frame is of white oak, the floor timbers are made with a short and a long arm, and the first futtock is dispensed with; the continuous line of butts made by the abutment of the first-futtocks at the centre-line of the keel, as is the case when a floor-timber is used extending equally on either side of the centre-line, as in vessels having live-oak frames, is thus obviated; the second-futtock butts the short-arm of the floor-timber; the third-futtock butts the long-arm of the floor-timber; the fourth-futtock butts the head of the second-futtock; the fifth-futtock butts the head of the third-futtock, and so on to the top and half-top. In the government yards a mould is made for the floor-timber, futtocks, top and half-top timbers, each edge of each mould giving a timber and its opposite. These moulds are made of pine boards, well seasoned, having painted upon them the name, floor, futtock, top and half-top, and the frame to which it belongs; upon these moulds are marked the diagonals, which are the stations of the ribbands, heads, and heels, and at which places the bevellings of the timbers are given. The heads and heels are distinguished upon the moulds by a single line in the direction of the diagonals, while the sirmarks or stations of the ribbands are marked by a line crossed thus (✱).

Upon the floor-mould is marked the centre and side lines. These moulds must all be marked on both sides, as the timbers of both sides of the ship are moulded by them. The heads of the frame timbers are cut off square from the curve in-and-out, at the intersection of the diagonal with the moulding edge, which marks the head and heel of the timber, and fore-and-aft, square from the side of the joint. In giving out the moulds it is also customary to send the foreman a board on which is drawn a longitudinal distribution of the frames, with ports, showing where the timbers are cut off for them, and what timbers form sides of ports, whether moulding edge or bevelling edge.

In trimming the timbers of the frame, it is necessary that they should be sided straight and out of winding, or else there can be no certainty in the application of the moulds and bevellings. In moulding the timbers, the mould is laid on the stick, and the moulding and scantling edges razed in; the diagonals and sirmarks are also razed in from the moulds, and marked to correspond with them, the timbers having marked on them the name of the frame to which they belong, the timber of the frame, and whether a forward or after timber, as every mould gives a timber and its opposite. The bevellings for each timber are taken from the bevelling-boards; the bevel is laid with the angle made by the tongue and stock, so as to intersect the moulding edge of the timber at the station of the diagonal or sirmark where it belongs; and the angle or bevel made by the outside edge of the stock and tongue of the bevel is razed in. In getting out the timbers, the shipwright trims the edge of the stick according to the moulding lines; and having set his pocket bevel to correspond with the bevelling as razed in, he applies it at that point square to the curve, and trims it through at each bevelling spot; the timber is then canted over and counter-moulded, and trimmed through fair to the lines. By means of large and heavy rotary planing machines and bevel futtock-saws, used in most of our navy-yards, the timbers are first planed to the proper siding size, and, after being moulded, are sawed out to the correct bevel, which is undoubtedly a saving in time and money.

The moulds for the timbers of the square-body being made, I shall, in the next place, show in what manner their bevellings may be taken; for, until then, the timbers which have bevellings cannot be cut out.

The term "bevelling" denotes the angle which two surfaces make with each other at the line where they intersect. In speaking of the pieces of the frame of a ship, it is applied to the angle made by the surface at which the piece touches the skin, with the moulding plane of the piece.

TO TAKE THE BEVELLINGS OF THE SQUARE-BODY.

28. The square-body being a projection of all the timbers or transverse sections upon a vertical plane, it will give the distance that each section is within or without the other in the distance they are apart; these distances, therefore, set within or without a square, at the distance the sections are apart, or the room-and-space, will give the angles formed by the plane of the sides of the timbers with the body longitudinally.

The method frequently pursued to obtain these angles, or bevellings, is by marking in the half-breadth plan the siding size of the timbers on each side of the joint, taking the distances from the centre-line to the intersection with the diagonal, water, and sheer lines, and setting them off on their corresponding lines in the body-plan; with a pair of compasses take the shortest distance of these spots so obtained, from the joint or timber, and set them off within or without a square at the siding of the timber, which gives the different bevellings. But as this process is tedious, the following is given as sufficiently accurate for practice, and that which is now in general use :—

Make a bevelling-frame (Plate IV. Fig. 2) by securing, either on top of a table or some other convenient place, two straight-edges, about four feet in length, parallel to each other, at a distance from outside to outside equal to the room-and-space; square a line across the upper part; take a straight-edge long enough to take the greatest bevel, and pin the end of it at the out-edge of the left-hand batten, being careful to get the pin in line with the upper edge. The straight edges or sides of the bevelling-frame are made the same thickness as the bevel-boards, so as to admit of the arm moving freely over them.

Take from the body-plan, at the diagonals and sirmarks, the shortest distance of the frame-lines from each other (using a pair of compasses for the purpose), the standing bevellings being obtained by beginning with the foremost frame in the fore-body, and the aftermost frame in the after-body, taking the graduations of every frame as far as the midship one; the under bevellings are obtained by beginning with the midship one and proceeding forward and aft to one frame beyond the foremost and aftermost sections, setting off those graduations for the under bevellings below the square line on the bevelling-frame, and those for the standing bevellings above it. Bring the arm so that its upper edge is to the spot set above or below the square line (as the case may be), and draw the lines across the bevelling board, (shoving the board up a little as each bevel is marked); the angle formed by these lines with the edge of the board will give the angles made by the planes of the sides of the timbers with sections square to the curve.

If the body should have a considerable curvature, these lines for obtaining the bevellings must be considered only as chords; in such a case, to obtain the bevelling, a straight-edged batten must be applied to the extremities of the curve between the two joints in the half-breadth, taking the round at the distance of the siding of the timber from the joint, setting it off at the same distance from the edge of the board from the corresponding chord, which will give the bevelling at that place.

This method of taking the round is not perfectly correct, because the lines drawn on the board are chords to sections square to the body, whereas the lines in the half-breadth-plan seldom are; it is, however, near enough for all practical purposes, as the difference would be inconsiderable. This curvature may be noticed at the extremities; in other parts it is not worthy of attention. The method very often pursued to allow for this round is, to take the under bevellings and reverse them for the standing bevellings; this will certainly leave wood on the obtuse side, but there will be a deficiency of wood on the acute.

The second method, that of taking both the standing and under bevellings, is the most correct method that has yet been adopted, and of course requires two sets of bevelling-boards for each body.

The difference, however, between this and the method of taking the under bevellings and then reversing them, is inconsiderable, and would not compensate for the extra work; it can only be perceived at the extremities, and is so small that it is not worthy of notice.

BEVELLING-BOARDS.

(Plate IV., Fig. 3).

29. Bevelling-boards are made usually ten inches in width,—a separate set for each body. They should be marked in the following manner: first, name the board that it may be known; then mark a square line across just below the name, marking this set of bevels First Diagonal. The bevels will now be marked in regular succession; the first will be ⊕, and whether in the fore or after body, we continue on until we reach the highest number or letter, as the case may be, in the alphabet, or in the numbered square-body. Thus we have all the bevels of the square-body at the first diagonal together. The same may be said of all the remaining diagonals, sirmarks, and sheer-lines or breadths. Two sets of bevelling boards are always prepared—one set for the mould-loft, the duplicate for the use of the foreman in the ship-yard.

NATURE AND USE OF CANT-TIMBERS.

30. Hitherto we have considered the timbers as having their planes perpendicular both to the sheer and half-breadth plans, and have, consequently, termed them square-timbers, but cant-timbers have their planes inclined to the sheer (or *canted*, as shipwrights term it), but perpendicular to the half-breadth plan. To illustrate this further, so that the student will fully understand

the nature of cant-timbers, I will describe them in the following manner:—Observe in the half-breadth plan where the joint of the cant-timber intersects the centre-line; at which place suppose it hung on a hinge, moving fore-and-aft, and also imagine the lines drawn for the cant-timbers in the half-breadth plan to represent the upper edge of a large surface, the breadth of which is equal to the distance of the line of the same cant-timber on the body-plan from the centre-line; and, supposing the horizontal view of that surface to be represented by that one line, it immediately follows that the surface must stand perpendicular to the upper edge of the keel, similar to a door swinging on its hinges; and, if we draw the proper shape of the cant-timber, according to the shape of the body upon this surface, from the keel to the top of the side (not moving its position), and then cut it out, we shall have the true position of the cant-timber in its position on the ship, which will stand in a perpendicular direction; we may also (supposing it to be hung), swing it either forward or aft, and it will maintain its perpendicularity with respect to the keel.

The canting of the timbers are of great utility, as they contribute greatly to the strength of the vessel in the forward and after parts, and likewise greatly assist the conversion of the timbers. For, in the first place, by canting the plane of the sides of the timbers gradually from an athwartship line, we thereby bring each timber nearer to a square with the outside planking, which is not only best for the security of the planking, but the timbers are also better able to bear that security. And, secondly, were all the timbers of the bow and stern to be placed square, as those of the square body, though the scantling of the square timbers on a square should be equal to the scantling of the timbers, if canted, yet the bevelling of the bow and stern timbers would be so great that the consumption, in some places, in order to get the timber clear of sap, would be greater by one-half than that in the timber when canted.

TO LAY DOWN THE CANT-TIMBERS IN THE HALF-BREADTH-PLAN FORWARD.

(Plate IV., Fig. 1.)

31. The number of cant-frames will be governed partially by the rake of the stem and fullness of the bow; if the bow is full and the stem rakes, the cant-timbers require to be carried further aft, or else there will be too much opening at the main-breadth, or the timbers will be too much reduced at the heel.

Having determined how far to run the knight-head down for the strength of the stem; square that point down on to the side-line in the half-breadth plan; this fixes the forward edge of the forward cant on the side of the deadwood or side-line; draw a line from this point to the rail-line in the half-breadth plan, the direction of the line being as square as possible to the ribband-lines; this line represents the forward-edge of the forward-cant. In all our sharp vessels of war, having very little, if any, flare to their bows, the cant-timbers have gradually been canted or swung forward to meet the stem, the plane of whose side is fore-and-aft.

Set forward from the joint of the forward square frame, the siding size of the floor-timber, the opening or space three or four inches, and the siding size of the cants at the heels; this gives a point for the joint of the after-cant on the side-line; having decided how much it is necessary to swing it, draw a line from this point to the half-breadth of rail, which will represent the joint of the after-cant, or the last cant in the fore-body. The remaining cants are then struck in, taking into consideration the location of the ports and the proper distribution of the timbers; each cant-line should cut across the ribband lines as square as possible.

In laying down the cant timbers, the whole of the lines before run off in the half-breadth plan for fairing the square-body, may now be brought into use; but to get their form by the diagonals, a projection of these lines, which are called horizontal ribband-lines, must first be obtained in the half-breadth plan.

HORIZONTAL RIBBANDS.

32. The lines formed by the projection of the diagonals are called horizontal ribbands; they are laid off by taking the distance square from the centre-line in the body-plan, to where each square frame cuts the several diagonals, and setting them off from the centre-line, on their corresponding stations in the half-breadth plan, passing curves through the points thus obtained, and ending them as follows:—Take the height from the base-line in the body-plan to where the diagonal intersects the side-line, and set this up from the base-line in the sheer-plan until it intersects the fore-edge of the rabbet; square this point down on to the side-line in the half-breadth plan; with this point as a centre and the

thickness of the plank at that point as the radius, describe an arc towards the centre-line ; the line ends tangent to, or touches it.

TO LAY-DOWN CANT-TIMBERS BY HORIZONTAL RIBBANDS.

33. The horizontal ribbands being laid off as before described, and the cant-timbers struck in, proceed to lay them off, viz. :—

Commencing with the first cant, take the distance square from the centre-line in the half-breadth plan to the intersection of each ribband-line with the joint of the cant, and set these distances out square from the centre-line in the cant-body until they intersect their corresponding diagonals, at which place run in a short level line ; then take the distance in the half-breadth plan in the direction of the cant, from the centre-line to their intersection with the ribband-lines, and set them off from the centre-line in the cant-body on their corresponding level-lines before obtained, which will give the points for running the curve at each diagonal ; but as the diagonals do not extend sufficiently high to give the form of the timbers at the sheer-heights, other points must be obtained for them ; to obtain which, square up from the half-breadth plan, where the cant-line intersects the half-breadths of the several sheer-lines on to their corresponding lines in the sheer-plan, and transfer these heights to the cant-body-plan, drawing level lines through the points so determined ; then, in the half-breadth-plan, take the half-breadths of these lines respectively from the centre-line on a line with the cant, and set them off from the centre-line of the cant-body-plan on the heights or level lines just obtained, which will give the points for continuing the curve to the extreme height of those frames. It only remains now to find the ending for the heel in order that we may run in the joint or moulding edge.

TO END THE HEELS OF CANT-TIMBERS.

(Plate IV., Fig. 1.)

34. Where the joint of the cant-timber intersects the side-line in the half-breadth-plan, square up the intersection on to the bearding-line in the sheer-plan ; which height take off from the base-line and set up on the centre-line of the cant-body-plan, squaring a line out from it for a short distance. Next, take the distance from the centre-line in the half-breadth to where the cant-line intersects the side-line, in the direction of the cant-line, and set it off from the centre-line of the cant-body-plan, on the

line last squared out, which will give the point at which the heel of the cant-timber ends. A batten can now be pinned to the points obtained and the line razed in on the floor.

It will be unnecessary to describe the method for taking off any other cant-frame, as the remaining cants can be laid down either in the fore or after bodies by proceeding in a similar manner.

TO LAY DOWN THE CANT-TIMBERS BY WATER-LINES.

(Plate IV., Figs. 1 and 4.)

35. The reader will observe that two processes were necessary in laying down cant-timbers by the horizontal ribbands: for, first, we had to take the square distances of the intersection of the timbers with each horizontal ribband from the centre-line in the half-breadth-plan, and transfer these distances to the corresponding diagonals in the cant-body-plan; and, secondly, we had to take the oblique or cant-distances of the timbers, with the same horizontal ribbands in the half-breadth-plan, and transfer them to the cant-body-plan. But the method of laying off these timbers by water-lines, is far more simple, only one process being required. Thus, to lay off the joint of any cant, take the distances on a line with the cant from the centre-line in the half-breadth-plan to the intersection of the joint with each water-line, and transfer these distances to, and set them off on their corresponding lines from the centre-line in the cant-body-plan. A curve passed through the points thus obtained gives the true form of the timber.

In considering these two methods of laying-off cant-timbers, the reader will remark, that the difference between them consists in this particular, viz., in the first method, or by horizontal ribbands, the heights in the body-plan along which the cant-distances are set off, are procured from the half-breadth-plan; whereas, in the second method, or by water-lines, these heights are already given in the cant-body-plan.

But, it may be naturally asked, which is the preferable method? To this we reply, if the student can rely on the fidelity of his labors, let him by all means lay-off the cant-timbers by water-lines; if, however, he mistrusts the accuracy of his work, let him adopt the plan by horizontal ribands. The reason of this opinion is, that as the water-lines cut the body obliquely, any inaccuracy is more magnified by them than by the diagonals, which cut the body nearly at right angles. With this explanation we leave the choice of these plans to the discretion of the student.

TO CORRECT THE SHEER-LINES FOR A FLARING BOW.

36. In laying down vessels having considerable flare to the bow, it will be found necessary to run in new sheer-lines, in order to make an allowance for this, or, in other words, to raise the sheer to make the necessary allowance for this curve or flare.

To obtain the true sheer-heights, lay a batten with the edge against the forward square frame in the half-breadth plan, and pin it around to the shape of the sheer-lines to the rabbet; mark on this batten the intersection of all the square (fictitious) frames. Take this batten to the sheer-plan and set it to the sheer-lines as run from the model or draught, keeping the after-end to the forward square frame, letting the other end extend as far forward as it will. Mark these stations as taken from the half-breadth-plan and take up the battens; take off the heights of the stations from the base-line, and set them up on the old stations; take the height at the extreme fore end of the batten and set it up on the fore-edge of the rabbet; by drawing new sheer lines through all these points we obtain the exact sheer required for the cants.

Now take off the new heights of the sheer-lines and set them up in the square-body-plan above the heights of the corresponding frames, and on the side-line, and draw a fair line through these points. New sheer-lines may now be taken off as before and run in the half-breadth plan. Having obtained this new line, take off the distances square from the centre-line at each cant station at the sheer-lines, and set them off in the body-plan until they intersect the line just found there for the sheer; at the point of intersection level out a line; now take off the half-breadths for the sheers in the direction of the cant-lines, and take them to the body-plan, setting the spots off on the lines just leveled out, which are the true heights of the cants.

TO CORRECT THE CANT-TIMBERS BY VERTICAL SECTIONS OR BUTTOCK-LINES.

(Cant No. 12. Plate III., Figs. 1 and 2.)

37. To correct the cant-timbers by these lines will only be necessary when there is a considerable distance between any of the points that have been obtained by the water or ribband lines in the after-body, as these vertical sections or buttock-lines are seldom run off forward; these corrections are got by squaring the intersection of the cants with the buttock-lines in the half-

breadth-plan, to the corresponding buttock-lines in the sheer-plan, which will give the disposition of the timbers, and transfer the heights where the squarings-up cut the buttock-lines to the cant-body plan, and draw horizontal lines. Then, in the direction of the cant, take the distance from the centre-line to where the cant of the timbers cuts the buttock-lines in the half-breadth-plan, and set them off from the centre-line in the cant-body-plan, on the level-lines before obtained; these distances should correspond to the curves of the frames as got in by water and ribband lines.

TO MAKE THE MOULDS FOR THE CANT-TIMBERS.

38. The moulds for the cant-timbers are made the same as those for the square-body, each edge of each mould giving a timber and its opposite. The heads and sirmarks, rail, port-sills, and decks, and as many level-lines as may be necessary for levelling spots, are marked upon the moulds; the stations of the diagonals are determined by drawing horizontal lines from where the projection of the cant-timbers cross the diagonals to the extended cant-timbers, and the direction will be obtained by drawing lines from these points to where the diagonal cuts the centre line.

To get the direction of the heel on the stepping or bearding, square up from the half-breadth-plan where the joints of the cant-timbers cuts the side-line to the bearding in the sheer-plan, and transfer these heights to the centre-line in the cant-body-plan, and draw lines from these heights to the ending of the cant-timbers, which will give the direction on the bearding sufficient for all practical purposes, and will also give the line for cutting off the lower part of the moulds. The direction of the bearding is also marked for cutting off their heels in-and-out, also a line parallel to the centre-line at a distance from it equal to the bearding-line, taken in the direction of the cant of the timber from the centre-line of the half-breadth; this line gives the cutting-off of the heels up-and-down—the depth of the boxing-wood is left inside this line; the height of the throating-line is also marked.

SCANTLING-LINES.

39. In order to obtain the points for running in the inside of the cant-timbers, a new set of lines, called scantling-lines, must be got in, viz.:—

Set off the scantling size of each square (fictitious) frame (making an allowance for increased bevel) on the diagonal-lines in the body-plan, and run in curves to these points; next, take off the half-breadth of each line in the body-plan, transfer them to and set them off on their corresponding frames in the half-breadth plan; put down battens to these points, fairing them and those in the body to correspond, and when perfectly fair mark the lines in the body and half-breadth plans; the scantling-lines taken off on a line with the cant, and transferred to and set-off on their corresponding lines in the cant-body (the points being set off while the cant-mould is in position on the floor, having been got out to the moulding or outside edge), and curves passed through the points thus obtained, will give the inside or scantling edge of the cant-timbers.

TO LAY DOWN THE BEVELLING-EDGES OF THE CANT-TIMBERS.

(Plate IV., Figs. 1 and 4.)

40. In the half-breadth-plan draw lines to represent the bevelling edges of the timbers, parallel to the joints, and at a distance from them on each side equal to the siding size of the timbers, and square the heels at the centre-line. From and perpendicular to the centre-line in the half-breadth-plan, take the distances to where the horizontal ribbands and bevelling-edges intersect, and set them off from, and perpendicular to, the centre-line in the body-plan, to cut the corresponding diagonals and draw level-lines through them; then, in the direction of the bevelling-edges, and from the lines drawn perpendicular to the joints at the heel, take the distance in the direction of the bevelling-edges to the intersection with each of the horizontal ribbands, and set them off from the centre-line of the body-plan on the short level-lines just drawn for them: this will give spots for the bevelling-edges by the horizontal ribbands. Other spots can be obtained from the water and sheer lines, the same as for the joints, excepting that the distances in the direction of the cant in the half-breadth-plan must be taken from the line drawn perpendicular to the joint, instead of from the centre-line, to give in the body-plan the relative position of the bevelling-edges with their joints, that the angle formed by the plane of their sides and the outer surface of the body may be got. The bevelling-edges of the cants are distinguished from the joints or moulding-edges, by being run in in broken or ticked lines.

TO END THE BEVELLING-EDGES OF THE CANT-TIMBERS.

(Plate IV., Figs. 1 and 4.)

41. Where the bevelling-edges in the half-breadth-plan intersect the side-line, square them up to the bearding-line in the sheer-plan; take off these heights from the base-line, transfer them to and set them up from the base-line on the centre-line in the cant-body; then from the line drawn perpendicular to the joint at the centre-line, in the half-breadth plan, take the distance in the direction of the bevelling-edge to where they intersect the side-line, and set them off square from the centre-line at their corresponding heights in the body-plan: these points will give the endings. Battens may now be put down to the several points before obtained, and the bevelling-edges be marked in.

TO TAKE THE BEVELLINGS OF THE CANT-TIMBERS.

(Plate IV., Figs. 1 and 4.)

42. The bevellings of the cant-timbers are obtained by taking the shortest distances between the curves got in for the joints and bevelling-edges in the body-plan, at the heads, sirmarks, level-lines, sheer-heights, and as many other places as may be necessary; and by setting them off above or below a square line, according as the bevels are standing or under—that is, as they are within or without the joint in the body-plan, on a board equal in width to the siding-size of the cant as shown in the half-breadth plan.

For trimming and cutting off the heels two bevellings are necessary. The bevelling against the deadwood is simply the angle formed in the half-breadth-plan by the direction of the timbers and a fore-and-aft line, and is therefore taken by placing the stock of the bevel to the cant of the timber and the tongue to the side-line. The bevellings on the stepping or bearding is obtained by squaring up from the half-breadth-plan where the joints intersect the side-line, and drawing a line upwards as far as the cutting-down line, perpendicular to the base-line; then the stock of the bevel is applied against this line, and the tongue to the bearding, forward for the foremost timber, and aft for the aftermost. The bevelling at the throating or cutting-down line is obtained by placing the stock of the bevel against this line, and the tongue to the cutting-down line, forward for the foremost timber, and aft for the aftermost timber

HARPINS.

43. The ribbands in the fore and after cant-bodies are called "harpins," and on account of their sudden curvature, have to be shaped to their actual shape. The harpins, as they are shown in the plate, present themselves in horizontal projection: to get, therefore, the true shape, we have to imagine a plane in the direction of the harpin, and to go through the centre-line; when, therefore, this plane is turned upwards, so as to come in full view, it will be in a horizontal position, and the true shape of the harpin will be shown. We might construct the true shape of the second sirmark. We might take for that purpose, in the body-plan, the distances of the second sirmark from the centre-line in the direction of the diagonal by that name at each cant-frame, and set these distances off in the half-breadth plan on the corresponding cant-timbers; a curve passed through these points would give the actual shape of the second sirmark harpin. These harpins generally constitute different lengths; they are made of two or more thicknesses of oak plank, the lengths overlapping each other, and being secured together with screw-bolts and nuts. Where they come against the stem, there the bevel of the stem is taken; and to get the other bevels, they are obtained through means of a bevelling-edge. This bevelling-edge is laid off in the body-plan parallel to the topside of the harpin, and at a distance equal to the sidings; it is further laid down in the half-breadth-plan, the process of taking it off being precisely like that of the harpin. The bevelling will be the distance between the two edges as laid down set off in the square or siding of the harpin.

It is optional at which of the sheer-lines the harpins shall be placed; but one is generally placed at the height of the rail and port-sill, forward and aft. The harpins should be placed at the sheer-heights, so that the sheer-strakes may be worked without interfering with them, when they can be taken off, as they were only required to regulate the cants, and give them a landing when raised. The harpins placed at the sheer-heights aft are continued around the stern of the ship; they are not, however, worked out to the shape of the ship any further than is actually required, or until a ribband may be bent the remaining distance amidships.

LAYING DOWN A HARPIN TO A SHEER-LINE.

44. Having decided on the height to run it, first lay it off in the half-breadth-plan, as any other sheer-line. In order to make the mould correctly, take a batten, and lay its edge well with the sheer-line in the sheer-plan; proceed to mark its intersections with the cants and square-frames as the batten lays to the sheer-line. Keep the forward end fast, and raise the after end level: from this level-line square down the new positions of cants and square-frames to the half-breadth-plan, crossing the line laid out for the harpin; level aft-lines from the intersection of the cants and square-frames with the harpin-line in the half-breadth-plan, as first laid out, until it intersects the lines just squared down from the sheer-plan; pin a batten to the new points, and draw in a line for the harpin-mould, and mark the last spots for the position of cants and square-frames when the harpin is in place.

The bevels of the harpin can be taken in the following manner: Apply the stock of the bevel to a level line at the height at which the mould is made in the body-plan. The tongue should then extend downwards with the frame—this operation is performed on every cant-frame, and on every square-frame, as far as they extend. The fore-edge of rabbet of stem is squared down from the sheer-plan, and marked on the mould as a sirmark; the fore-and-aft part of the harpin against the stem is cut off well with the half-siding, parallel to the centre line.

LAYING DOWN A HARPIN TO A WATER-LINE.

45. The mould is made to the half-breadth of the water-line in the half-breadth-plan. To obtain the bevelling, strike a line across the body-plan, below the water-line, corresponding to the depth or thickness of the harpin; take off the half-breadth of this new line, and set them off from the centre-line on their corresponding frames in the half-breadth-plan; the distance between these lines on a square will give the bevel in the thickness of the harpin. The joints of the cants and square-frames should be marked on the mould, and transferred to the harpin.

KNIGHT-HEADS.

46. The knight-heads are the first timbers on either side of the stem; they are either placed fore-and-aft or canted, according as

the vessel is full or very sharp at the bow: they form the sides of the seat or bed for the reception of the bowsprit, the top of the stem itself forming the actual resting-place or bed. The boundaries of the knight-head are the extreme height, the vertical line of the keel, inner side to the cutting-down line, and the outside edge to the bearding-line; when the mould is made (which is to the lines above-mentioned in the sheer-plan), a projection for the boxing is left on the mould inside and out to the thickness of the plank, extending downwards some distance below the stem-head, so that there may be as few joints as possible in the bed of the bowsprit.

When the knight-heads are sided, the mould is laid on, and the level-lines and sirmarks marked upon the piece; and the stock of the bevel, when the bevellings are pricked off, is kept in the direction of the level-lines and the tongue horizontal.

LAYING DOWN FORE-AND-AFT KNIGHT-HEADS.

(Plate IV., Fig. 1.)

47. To lay down a fore-and-aft knight-head, it will first be necessary to obtain in the sheer-plan the disposition of the fore-edge of the foremost cant-frame for the knight-head to form an abutment against. To get the disposition, square up where the foremost bevelling-edge of the foremost cant-frame in the half-breadth-plan cuts the horizontal or projection of the ribbands, level-lines, and sheer-lines, to their corresponding sheer of the ribbands, level-lines, and sheer-lines, in the sheer-plan, and where it cuts the side-line, in the half-breadth plan, to the stepping or bearding-line in the sheer-plan; and a curve passed through all these squarings-up will give the disposition of the fore-edge of the cant-frame.

Next, set off the siding size of the knight-heads from the side-line in the half-breadth plan, and parallel to it. The moulding-edge is shown by the bearding-line; the bevelling-edge is obtained by squaring up the intersection of the several lines in the half-breadth-plan with the bevelling-edge on to the corresponding lines in the sheer-plan, the intersection of the bevelling-edge with the fore-edge of the foremost cant in the half-breadth plan squared up to the disposition of the cant in the sheer-plan will give the ending; a curve passed through the points thus obtained will give the bevelling-edge of the knight-head. A line drawn perpendicular to the base-line, at the point for the ending of the moulding-edge, shows not only the length of the knight-head, but that its heel cuts square from the base. The bevel of the heel is obtained by applying the stock of the bevel against the side-line in the half-breadth-plan, the heel of which must be forward; we then close the bevel until the tongue ranges outboard and with the side of the cant; this is the bevel of the heel of the knight-head, to be applied from the moulding-side or face of the timber, the bevel or angle the other way having been shown to be at right angles with the base-line. The bevels of the outside, or what is usually termed the back of this timber, are obtained from the half-breadth-plan by placing the stock of the bevel parallel to the centre-line and the tongue in the direction of the water-lines; this method saves the trouble of laying down a bevelling-edge, and is equally well applied by the workmen. Where both edges of the timber have been laid down, we may take the bevel anywhere, and may take it off by measuring the distance the bevelling-edge falls aft of the moulding-edge in the siding size laid down—the knight-head bevels under just that distance.

On very sharp vessels it may be found advantageous to cant the knight-heads, for the reason that a smaller piece of timber will make them.

LAYING DOWN CANTED KNIGHT-HEADS.

48. The knight-heads are laid down with any cant we please; square up the points at which they intersect the sheer, horizontal ribbands and water-lines in the half-breadth-plan on to their corresponding lines in the sheer-plan; pass a curve through these points; and we have their athwartship view in the sheer-plan as though they were cants, which they virtually are; the shape on the face of canted knight-heads is obtained in the same manner as a cant is, by taking the distance in the half-breadth-plan from the centre-line on the line showing their face to the crossing of the several sheer and water lines; setting them off in the body-plan on their corresponding lines the same as though they were cants; they are cants in all respects, and should be so laid down and bevelled, as also all the hawse-timbers that are canted. The bevelling of the heels of the canted knight-heads and hawse-pieces is also obtained like those of the cants; their heels end on the bearding-line, the same as the cants; all of which may be obtained from the sheer-plan, by placing the stock of the bevel to

the vertical line squared up from the half-breadth plan for the ending of the heel, and the tongue in the direction of the bearding. To obviate the trouble of laying down a bevelling-edge, the bevellings can be taken from the half-breadth-plan, where the knight-head is shown in projection, by placing the stock of the bevel parallel to the centre-line, while the tongue is put against the level-lines.

TO LAY DOWN FORE-AND-AFT HAWSE-PIECES.

(Plate IV., Fig. 1.)

49. When the hawse-pieces are not carried down to take the common stepping of the cant-timbers, they have the planes of their sides fore-and-aft, when they are called fore-and-aft hawse-pieces. The disposition of the fore-edge of the foremost cant-frame having been obtained for the fore-and-aft knight-head, the work of laying the hawse-pieces down can be proceeded with, otherwise that should first be obtained.

To lay down the fore-and-aft hawse-pieces, will only require to obtain a projection of them in the sheer-plan, as the plane of their side is fore-and-aft; draw, therefore, in the half-breadth-plan their stations by lines parallel to the centre-line; where these lines intersect the level-lines, horizontal ribbands, and sheer-lines, square them up to their corresponding lines in the sheer-plan, and draw curves through them; it will be to these curves that the moulds are to be made. The moulds are in general made to the fore-side of each hawse-piece, and are cut off at the lower end, by squaring up from the half-breadth-plan, where the fore-side cuts the fore-edge of the cant-timber, to the disposition of the fore-edge of the cant-timber in the sheer-plan, and there drawing a line perpendicular to the keel. Upon the moulds are marked the height of the sheer and bevelling-spots. The bevelling can be got in the sheer-plan by taking the shortest distance between the fore and after edges, which is from the fore-edge of one hawse-piece to the fore-edge of the other, at each bevelling-spot, and setting them below a square in the siding of the hawse-piece; and when applied, the stock is kept square to the curve. For the heel, the bevelling is taken by placing the stock of the bevel to the station of the hawse-piece, or fore-and-aft, in the half-breadth-plan; and the tongue to the cant-timber, and applying it horizontal, or perpendicular to the heel up and down. The bevellings can all be obtained from the half-breadth-plan as well as from the sheer-plan, by following the same directions as in taking the bevellings for fore-and-aft knight-heads.

LAYING DOWN THE CENTRE AND SIDE-COUNTER-TIMBERS.

(Plate III., Figs. 1 and 2.)

50. The operation of laying down the centre and side-counter timbers of a round-sterned ship, is precisely the same as that of laying down the fore-and-aft knight-heads and hawse pieces; the bevellings are also taken in a similar manner.

In laying down the stern-frame of a vessel designed to have a propeller triced up, instead of disconnecting it when under sail, it is necessary that an aperture should be allowed for this purpose. The side-counter timbers, which in the stern before laid down were placed on either side of and close to the centre-counter timber, are now spread apart a parallel distance from the centre-line, which in this case is two feet and nine inches, and are designed to form the sides of the aperture or propeller well, extending from the aftermost cant or square frame that heels on the deadwood; against which their heels form an abutment, to the rail height: against the sides of these side-counter-timbers the heels of the cant-timbers coming aft of the forward stern-post are bolted. This side-counter-timber is laid down in all three plans, body-plan, sheer, and half-breadth plans.

TO LAY DOWN THE SIDE-COUNTER-TIMBERS WHEN THEY FORM THE SIDES OF THE PROPELLER WELL.

(Plate III., Figs. 1 and 2.)

51. In the half-breadth-plan strike in a line parallel to the centre-line, and at a distance from it equal to the half-opening required; and parallel to this, another line equal to the siding-size of the counter-timber, these lines extend from the rail half-breadth to the timber against which the heel abuts. Next, lay down the form of the timber against which the heel of the side-counter timber abuts, in the body-plan, as any other timber, and set off, parallel to the centre-line, the half opening of the aperture and siding-size of the counter-timber, and draw the straight lines corresponding to these settings off from the rail until they intersect the frame last laid down: the inside line in both plans is the moulding, the outside the bevelling-edge; it is against this bevelling-edge that the further cant-timbers end in both plans.

Strike in the cants in the half-breadth-plan, taking into consideration the location of the ports; laying them off as single timbers, ending against the bevelling-edge; strike in also the siding-size of the after-transom, which is placed against the after-stern-post, and is tenoned into the side-counter-timbers, keeping them the proper distance apart, and forming the after-part of the aperture or well, against which the heels of the centre-counter-timbers abut; this transom appears in this plan perpendicular to the centre-line; the centre-counter-timbers are parallel to the centre-line, and are shown heeling or abutting against it.

In the previous explanation of the method of taking off and ending cants, we took them off from the centre-line, and ended them by ascertaining their proper height on the bearding and new side-line; in this case the side-line and centre-line are one, which is the bevelling-edge of the counter-timber, and the half-breadths are taken off from this line in the half-breadth, in the direction of the cant, and set off from the same edge on their corresponding lines in the body-plan; the heights for setting out the half-breadths of the sheer-lines are obtained as for any other cant; the ending cannot be obtained until we obtain the disposition of the bevelling-edge of the side-counter-timber in the sheer-plan, which is obtained by squaring up the intersection of the bevelling-edge in the half-breadth on to the corresponding lines in the sheer-plan, and through these points passing a curve; the intersection of the heel of the cant in the half-breadth with the bevelling-edge of the side-counter timber, squared up to the corresponding line in the sheer-plan, will give the point for the ending; take off this height from some level-line and set it up from the corresponding level-line in the body-plan, on the bevelling-edge of the side-counter-timber, and it will be the point for the ending of the heel of the cant. The bevelling-edge is taken off by squaring the heel, striking in the siding-size of the timber, and proceeding as before described for the moulding-edge. The distance between the two lines taken off, and set above or below a square equal to the siding-size of the cant, will give the bevelling.

The moulding-edge of the side-counter-timber is squared up, from the half-breadth to the sheer-plan, the same as the bevelling-edge, and the mould is made to this line; a boxing is added to it equal to the thickness of the plank, the boxing only extending up as high as the transom, above which the plank runs round the stern. The mould is made above the boxing, equal to the moulding of the timber, and the bevels are taken the same as any other counter-timber when laid in parallel to the centre-line.

The moulding and bevelling-edges of the transom are squared up on the centre-line of the stern and bevelling-edge of the side-counter-timber in the sheer-plan. To obtain the moulding-edge, take the height where it intersects the centre-line and bevelling-edge of the side-counter-timber, from some level-line, and set them up on the centre and side-lines and bevelling-edge of side-counter-timber in the body-plan; connect the bevelling-edge and side-line by a straight-line at these heights, and then square to the centre-line, and we will obtain the moulding-edge of this transom. The bevelling-edge is obtained in a similar manner. The bevelling can be taken off square from the moulding-edge and applied in the siding-size of the transom.

A disposition of the moulding-edges of the centre-counter-timbers can be obtained the same as for the side-counter-timbers in the sheer-plan, to which lines the moulds are made; they all heel against the after-transom.

TO LAY DOWN THE HEAD.

(Plate V., Fig. 1.)

52. If there is room upon the floor forward of the vessel as already laid down, strike in the moulding-size of the stem forward of the rabbet, and transfer from the draught to the floor, in a proper position, with the stem, as just drawn, the outline of the head, the flight of the cheek-knees and brackets, and head-rails; and, in the half-breadth-plan, lay down half-breadth lines, taken at the upper side of the upper and lower cheeks, and upper part of head-rails; and without these half-breadth lines, draw, in parallel, the thickness of the outside planking at those heights.

Square down from the sheer to the half-breadth-plan, the fore-side of the head, and fore-end of main-rail where it lands against the head, and draw in, above the centre-line of the half-breadth-plan, the half-siding of the head, by setting it off at the fore-part, and as squared down at the stem, and drawing a straight line; draw in, likewise, the half-siding of the lacing-piece from the centre-line.

The most important pieces of the head are the cheek-knees: they are placed in the angle made by the bows of the ship and sides of the cutwater or head, connecting them both by means of bolts. The after-part or body, comes against the bows of the ship, while the fore-part, or arm, is bolted to the head. The moulding is generally taken two-and-a-half times the depth at the throat. To get the shape of the cheeks and brackets, we square down from the sheer-plan their extremities on the bow of the ship, on to their half-breadth lines as laid down in the half-breadth-plan. We then put down the moulding-size at the throat, and keep nearly the same width of cheek against the bow, the extension of the cheeks or brackets taper gradually forward on the side of the head: the end of the cheek against the bow is rounded off. The bevels necessary to shape their inner sides can be taken from the cant-timbers against which they are bolted, or on a board. At the width equal to the distance between the two main-breadth lines can be laid down a horizontal line; the shortest distance between these two lines, as taken from the half-breadth-plan, put down below the extremity of this horizontal line: this point, joined with the other extremity of the same line, will give the bevel for the insides of the cheeks, viz.: apply the tongue of the bevel to the line on the board, and the stock against the edge of the board.

Square down from the sheer-plan the extremity of the main-rail on to its half-breadth line in the half-breadth-plan; square down also the intersection of the fore-end of the rail with the head in the sheer-plan on to the half-siding of the lacing-piece in the half-breadth-plan; these two points being determined, the half-breadth shape of the rail can be run in to correspond with the views of the constructor.

To obtain the lower edge, that the rail may have the regular tapering and proper moulding, pin a batten round the curve for the upper part, as drawn in the half-breadth-plan, and mark the position of several ordinates correspondingly upon the curve and batten, and the fore and after-ends; then, upon a straight line, in some convenient part of the floor, place the batten and mark upon it the fore and after-ends, and the intermediate spots or positions of the ordinates as taken on the batten. At the fore and after-ends set off the sizes of the rail, and draw another line to give the tapering of the rail; and between these two lines take the distances at the intermediate spots, and set them off in the half-breadth-plan square to the curve drawn in for the upper side of the rail, at their corresponding stations, and draw in a curve to them, for the lower side, ending it at the square line for the after-end, at a distance from the upper side equal to the moulding of the rail. The other rails are run in a similar manner. The moulds for the rails are made to the curves in the half-breadth-plan; and the moulds for the cheeks and brackets are made the moulding way to the lines, as got in the half-breadth plan, and for the flight as got in the sheer-plan.

The mould for the head is a batten mould; one batten is placed with its after-edge to the fore-side of the stem and extends from within a short distance of the under-side of the bowsprit, down to the scarph of the stem, and one to the fore-side of the head, which extends from the seat of the billet to scarph of the gripe; but as the head at the scarph of the gripe is narrow the mould is made to form the scarph at that point, and the two battens forming the fore and after parts scarph into it. The upper part is made to the top of the head or lacing, and shows the seat of the figure or billet. The mould is supported by cross battens, which are in breadth the half-siding of the head. To get the breadths of the battens, mark first upon the mould their positions, and determine, at the lower end of the head, or, if the gripe mould is to be made at the same time, at the lower part of the gripe, the taperings from the rabbet of the stem; then, pin a batten round the fore-side of the head, and gripe if the mould is to be made, and mark upon it the upper and lower parts and stations of the battens. Then, just before the head, or, on some convenient part of the floor, let the batten fly straight, or place it against some straight line, and mark the upper and lower parts and stations of the battens; and at the upper and lower parts set off the half-size of the head; the upper part is taken from the half-siding at the fore-part of the head, as shown in the half-breadth-plan, and the lower part from the tapering obtained at the lower part of the head or gripe, as just got in the sheer-plan, and strike the lines, the distances between will give the half-siding of the fore-part of the head, at any of the intermediate parts or stations of the battens and the half-breadth of these battens at the fore-part.

To obtain the half-breadth at the after-part, take the heights in the sheer-plan where the stations of the battens cut the fore-edge of the rabbet, and at these heights take the half-siding of the stem for the breadth of the battens at the rabbet; then, from this breadth to the one obtained at the fore-part of the head, draw a straight line, which will give the breadth of the cross battens and the half-siding of the head; but that the head under the cheeks may have the greater substance, or the surface under them be in the same plane, square down where the stations of the battens cut the lower side of the lower cheek, and cutting down to the half-breadth-plan, and the half-siding of the head, before got in, at the squarings-down, will give the breadth of the battens, or the half-siding of the head in the wake of the cheeks. The upward flight of the cheeks and brackets, and the direction in which the several pieces forming the cutwater or head are placed and their breadth, are marked on the mould for the head.

"TAKING OFF" FROM THE MOULD-LOFT FLOOR.

53. The only thing remaining to be done, is to take off all the dimensions from the mould-loft floor, so that, if desired, there would be no difficulty in building another vessel of the same model. The U. S. steamer *Oneida*, built at the commencement of the rebellion, was a duplicate of the U. S. steamer *Iroquois* built in 1858. The U. S. steamers *Florida* and *Tennessee* were also built from one set of moulds. The latter vessel has lately been altered, by having another deck put on her.

I have thus described the principal operations of laying down and taking off a vessel in detail; and although there may be some things omitted, it will be found to embrace all those points which are likely to occur in the building of a ship at the present day, or at least render them comparatively easy.

CORRECT METHOD OF ENDING LEVEL-LINES.

(See Fig. 40.)

The usual mode of ending a level-line, is to find where it cuts the outer-edge of the rabbet in the sheer-plan, square it down to the side-line in the half-breadth-plan, describe an arc with the thickness of plank at that point as radius, and let the level-line be tangent to, or touch, this arc.

Although this is the general practice, it is not strictly correct, although it has the advantage of leaving an excess of wood in the rabbet. If the fore-edge of the rabbet were vertical, and the stem did not taper, there would be no error, for the surface of the planking would be perpendicular to the horizontal plane; and any inclination in this surface arising either from the obliquity of the fore-edge of the rabbet, or the taper of the stem, increases the thickness of the horizontal section of the planking. When this mode is not considered sufficiently accurate, greater precision may be obtained in the following manner.

It will be seen that if the fore-edge of rabbet of stem represented the axis of a curved cylinder—if the term may be allowed—the radius of which was equal to the thickness of the plank, the side of such a cylinder, or rather series of cylinders, would be in contact with the surface of the timber all down the stem, whatever might be the obliquity of the fore-edge of the rabbet or taper of the stem.

Now, any level plane would cut this cylinder obliquely, and the section in which it would cut it would be an ellipse; from which we see, that the line in which the level plane cuts the surface of the timbers should be ended in the half-breadth plane on the back of an ellipse, such as we have described.

Diagonal lines and water-lines would be ended in a similar manner.

ENDING OF LEVEL-LINES.

55. Thus, to end level-lines, and obtain points in the bearding-line, observe that if AB is a portion of the fore-edge of rabbet of stem, and, therefore, of the axis of the cylinder of which we have spoken, then CD, drawn parallel to AB, and at a distance from it equal to the thickness of the planking, is the side of the cylinder. The longer semi-diameter, or the semi-major axis of the section, made by the level plane AE, is AC; while the shorter is, as before, the radius of the cylinder, or thickness of the plank. To end the level-line AE, or BF, we have then to construct a segment, *a c o*, or *b d o*, of the ellipse, and end the lines as shown.

Then G and H, obtained by squaring up the points *g* and *h*, where the lines cut the siding of the stem, are points in the bearding-line, and so on for any number of points which may be required.

It is not necessary to construct the required ellipse on the floor at each of the endings in the half-breadth plan; the matter is managed very simply, by drawing on a brass-plate, or piece of thin board, PP, a number of elliptic quadrants for the same thickness of plank; increasing the longer or semi-major axes, gradually, by perhaps half-an-inch at a time, from the thickness of plank.

Take the plate which is made for the particular thickness of plank of bottom to be dealt with, and at each level-line—BF, for example—mark on the board or plate PP from *s*, the distance *s d* equal to BD; the point D being found by setting off the thickness of the plank from the fore-edge of rabbet in the sheer, square to the curve. Then nail the plate PP upon the floor, with its edge fore-and-aft, and the point *s* at the point in the fore-edge of the rabbet in the half-breadth plan, and let the penning batten pass over the plate and touch the curve next within the point *d*.

BEARDING-LINE.

56. In the manner above stated, the endings of all the level lines may be easily obtained, and the bearding-line got in. It would require a very complicated construction to determine the exact points in which the lines touch the ellipse, in order to discover the middle of the rabbet; but if we can get in the bearding-line correctly, nothing more is required.

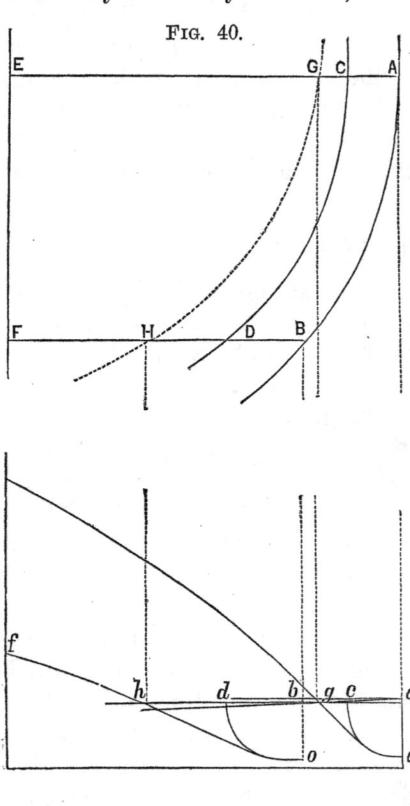

Fig. 40.

TO FIND THE FOCI OF THE ELLIPSE.

57. The foci of the ellipse may be found in each case from the axes, by sweeping from the extremity of the shorter axis, with a radius equal to half the larger, an arc of a circle, cutting the longer axis in two points.

These two points are the foci or centres of the ellipse, from which it may be swept in the usual way. When the bearding-line has been obtained for the stem, it may be found for the stern-post and after-deadwood in the same manner.

58. DIMENSIONS FOR LAYING DOWN A STEAM SCREW SLOOP-OF-WAR.

*(For Plans, See Plates I., II., and VII.)†

Length between perpendiculars........................ 300′ 0
Beam moulded 45 feet, extreme .... 46′ 0
Hold from throat-line to gun-deck...................... 21′ 2″

The base-line is the lower edge of the rabbet of the keel.

The fore-side of the rabbet of stem crosses the forward-perpendicular 16 feet above the base-line.

The after-perpendicular is the aft side of the main stern-post.

The water-lines are parallel 2 feet asunder above the base-line.

The perpendicular sections are 4 feet asunder—set off from the centre-line.

The frame spaces are 30 inches from frame 28 to frame 92 (or 80 feet each way from the centre of the length), and from thence towards the ends they are 32 inches.

Distance from the forward-perpendicular to frame 4.......... 6′
" " 4 to frame 60............................ 144′
" " 60 to " 116 .... 144′
" " 116 to the after-perpendicular................ 6′
Between perpendiculars * .... 300′

Keel, fore-deadwood, apron, and head and heel of post side, 16½ inches. Stem sides, 16 inches; rabbet on keel, 4½ inches; on stem and post, 4 inches.

HEIGHTS ABOVE BASE-LINE ON FRAME 72 OR LOWEST PLACE.

Garboard strake (top of keel).............................. 8½″
Throat of floors.. 1′ 5″
Hold to the berth-deck-beams.......................... 13′
" " " moulded.................... 11½″
" " plank............................ 4″
Height under the gun-deck-beams...................... 5′ 10″
" " " moulded................. 1′ ½″
" " plank......................... 4½″

---

* 12 feet 6 inches additional length was put in amidships in laying down this class of vessels, thus making them 312 feet 6 inches between perpendiculars.

† These plans are on a scale of one inch = 5 feet.

Height to top of gun-deck amidships .... 23′ 8″
" under spar " beam.......................... 6′ 2″
" " " moulded .... 8½″
" " plank.......................... 3½″

Height to top of the spar-deck amidships............... 30′ 10″

Lower side of plank-sheer above the top of deck. 4½″
Plank-sheer in thickness.................... 5½″

Top of plank-sheer above the top of deck...... 10″

Height of top of the gun-deck-plank amidships.......... 23′ 8″
Deduct spring of beam (in length 44 feet)................ 5½″

Top of gun-deck in the side .... 23′ 2½″
Port-sill above the deck................................ 1′ 8″
Port in depth.. 3′ 2″
Port-head to top of the plank-sheer.................... 3′ 3½″
Height of top of the plank-sheer above the base-line....... 31′ 4″

Keel, sided 16½ inches; in depth at the fore-end 20½ inches, at the after-end under the stern-post 21 inches; the lower side of the main keel will be at the forward-perpendicular 4 inches below the rabbet of the keel, and at the after-perpendicular 12 inches, exclusive of the depth of the false keel, that is, below the rabbet at the forward square-frame 5 inches; at frame 60 8 inches, and at the after square-frame 11½ inches. Scarphs in length 10 feet.

Apron, sided 16½ inches, of live or white oak.

Stem, sided 16 inches.

Stern-post, sided at head 16½ inches.

Rabbet on stem and post, 4 inches.

Deadwood, sided 16½ inches.

FRAME.

Floors sided..........	12 to 15 inches.	Top Timbers..............	10 inches.
1st Futtocks sided	11 "	Moulding size in throat.....	17 "
2d " "	10½ "	2d Futtock head...........	12¼ "
3d " "	10½ "	At Gun-deck port-sill........	7 "
4th " "	10 "	At Spar " sill............	5½ "
5th " "	10 "		

ENDING OF LINES MEASURED FROM FORWARD-PERPENDICULAR.

	Front of Stem Gripe.	Fore Side of Rabbet of Stem.	Bearding 8 inches from Centre Line.	Throat Line Aft side of Apron.	4 feet out from Centre Line.	8 feet out from Centre Line.	12 feet out from Centre Line.
	Before.		Abaft.				
Lower Side of Hammock Rail..........	2′ 8″	7″	1¾″	11″	6′ 7½″	15′ 9¾″	28′ 1″
Top of Plank Sheer...	2′ 7½″	6⅝″	3″	1′ 4¾″	7′ 3⅝″	17′ 1⅝″	29′ 7⅝″
Port Head...........	2′ 6¾″	5⅝″	4½″	1′ 10⅝″	8′ 1⅝″	18′ 7⅛″	31′ 5⅛″
Port Sill.............	2′ 6″	5⅛″	6″	2′ 5¼″	9′	20′ 1¼″	33′ 4⅝″
24 ft. Water Line.....	2′ 5″	4¼″	8½″	3′ 2½″	10′ ⅞″	21′ 3½″	35′ 1″
22 " "	2′ 4⅝″	3⅝″	10⅜″	3′ 8⅝″	10′ 10⅜″	23′	
20 " "	2′ 4¼″	3″	1′ ¼″	4′ 3⅝″	11′ 9⅜″	24′ 4¾″	
18 " "	2′ 3″	1¾″	1′ 2¾″	5′ ½″	12′ 10½″	26′ 1″	
16 " "	2′ 1″		1′ 6″	5′ 10¾″	14′ 1⅝″	28′ ¼″	
14 " "	1′ 10¼″	3¼″	1′ 11¼″	6′ 11″	15′ 10¼″	30′ 3¼″	
12 " "	1′ 6″	8⅝″	2′ 7½″	8′ 3½″	17′ 7″	33′ 1¼″	
10 " "	11⅛″	1′ 5¼″	3′ 7″	10′ ¾″	19′ 11⅜″	36′ 3″	
8 " "	1⅜″	2′ 7″	4′ 11¾″	12′ 4¼″	23′		
6 " "	1′ 1½″	4′ 3″	6′ 11½″	15′ 9″	27′ 2½″		
4 " "	2′ 11½″	6′ 8½″	9′ 10″	21′ 7½″	33′ 9½″		
2 " "	5′ 10½″	10′ 8½″	15′ 3″				
Base Line............	13′	27′ 4″					

ENDING OF LINES MEASURED FROM AFTER-PERPENDICULAR.

	After Side of Rabbet of Post.	Centre of Counter Moulding Edge.	Bearding Line at Siding of Deadwood.	Throat Line inside of Counter Timber.	4 feet out from Centre Line.	8 feet out from Centre Line.	12 feet out from Centre Line.
		Abaft.					
Lower Side of Hammock Rail..........		18′ 3¾″		17′ 10½″	17′ 1¾″	12′ 7″	11″
Top of Plank Sheer...		17′ 2¾″		16′ 8″	16′ 1½″	12′ 2⅞″	1′ 4½″
Port Head...........		15′ 7″		14′ 10⅓″	14′ 5⅜″	10′ 10¾″	1′ 8″
Port Sill............	13′ 8″	13′ 1½″		12′ 0¾″	11′ 9″	7′ 11¾″	8⅛″
24 feet Water Line....	11′ 2″	10′ 6½″	10′ 6½″	9′ 1″	8′ 7½″	4′ 4½″	3′ 10¼″
						Before.	
22 " "	8′	7′ 2½″	7′ 2½″	5′ 5″	4′ 5″	2¾″	8′ 7⅝″
20 " "	4′ 4″	3′ 5″	3′ 5″	1′ 5½″	4¾″	5′ 1½″	14′ 0¼″
18 " "	1′ 1¼″		3″	2′	3′ 8½″	10′ 3½″	19′ 11″
		Before.					
16 " "	7⅞″		1′ 5⅜″	4′ 2½″	7′ 3½″	15′ 5½″	26′ 0½″
14 " "	1′ 1¼″		2′ 2″	6′ 1″	10′ 10½″	21′ 1½″	32′ 9″
12 " "	1′ 2″		2′ 7¾″	8′ 10″	14′ 7″	26′ 11½″	
10 " "	1′ 2¾″		4′ 5½″	13′ 5″	19′ 1″	33′ 7″	
8 " "	1′ 3½″		7′	18′ 4½″	24′ 8″		
6 " "	1′ 4¼″		8′ 1¼″	23′ 3″	32′ 1″		
4 " "	1′ 5″		9′ 7″	31′ 3″			
2 " "	1′ 5¾″		17′ 8″				
Base Line............	1′ 6½″						

STATIONS OF DIAGONALS IN BODY-PLAN FOR HEADS AND HEELS OF TIMBERS.

	Up Centre Line.	On Base Line.	Up Side Line.
1st Diagonal short Floor Head........	10′ 4″	12′ 10″	
2d " long " "	16′ 6″	20′ 8½″	
3d " 2d Futtock.	22′ 3″		5′ 3″
4th " 3d "	26′ 9″		12′ 3″
5th " 4th "	29′		19′

Frames that cut off for Ports—9, 18, 27, 37, 47, 57, 67, 77, 87, 97, 106, 114, and 122.

FRAMES IN THE FORE-BODY.

	Fore-Side of Rabbet.	F. P.	4	8	12	16	20	24	28	32	36	40	44	48	52	56	60
Rising of lower side of Hammock Rail…………	37′ 5″	37′ 4¾″	37′ 1¼″	36′ 8¼″	36′ 4″	36′ ¼″	35′ 9″	35′ 6¼″									
" of Top of Plank Sheer….	34′ 2″	34′ 1¾″	33′ 10¼″	33′ 5¼″	33′ 1″	32′ 9¼″	32′ 6″	32′ 3¼″	32′ 1⅛″	31′ 11¼″	31′ 9⅝″	31′ 8¼″	31′ 7⅓″	31′ 6⅛″	31′ 5⅝″	31′ 4¾″	31′ 4⅜″
" of Port Head………	30′ 10½″	30′ 10¼″	30′ 6¾″	30′ 1¾″	29′ 9½″	29′ 5¾″	29′ 2½″	28′ 11¾″	28′ 9⅝″	28′ 7¾″	28′ 6⅛″	28′ 4¾″	28′ 3⅝″	28′ 2⅝″	28′ 1⅞″	28′ 1¼″	28′ ⅞″
" of " Sill…………	27′ 8½″	27′ 8¼″	27′ 4¾″	26′ 11¾″	26′ 7½″	26′ 3¾″	26′ ½″	25′ 9¾″	25′ 7⅝″	25′ 5¾″	25′ 4⅛″	25′ 2¾″	25′ 1⅝″	25′ ⅝″	24′ 11⅞″	24′ 11¼″	24′ 10⅞″
Half Breadth of Hammock Rail			3′ 8½″	8′ 4″	11′ 9¾″	14′ 3⅜″	15′ 11″	16′ 11⅛″									
" of Plank Sheer….			3′ 5″	7′ 10⅝″	11′ 4½″	14′ ¼″	15′ 10⅝″	17′ 2½″	18′ 1⅛″	18′ 8″	19′ ¾″	13′ 4″	19′ 6″	19′ 7¼″	19′ 8″	19′ 8⅜″	19′ 8⅝″
" of Port Head…..			3′ 1½″	7′ 4⅛″	10′ 10¾″	37′ 7⅜″	15′ 8¾″	17′ 3¾″	18′ 5¾″	19′ 3⅜″	19′ 9¾″	20′ 2⅓″	20′ 5⅜″	20′ 7⅓″	20′ 8½″	20′ 9¼″	20′ 9⅝″
" of " Sill……			2′ 10¼″	6′ 10″	10′ 3¾″	13′ 2″	15′ 5½″	17′ 3½″	18′ 8″	19′ 8″	20′ 4¼″	20′ 10½″	21′ 2½″	20′ 4⅞″	21′ 6⅜″	21′ 7½″	21′ 8″
" 24 ft. Water-Line..			2′ 6½″	6′ 3¾″	9′ 9½″	12′ 9″	15′ 2⅞″	17′ 2½″	18′ 8¼″	19′ 9″	20′ 6″	21′ ¾″	21′ 5″	21′ 7½″	21′ 9″	21′ 10⅓″	21′ 10⅝″
" 22 " " ..			2′ 4⅜″	5′ 11⅓″	9′ 4″	12′ 4″	14′ 11″	17′ ¼″	18′ 7½″	19′ 9″	20′ 7½″	21′ 2¾″	21′ 7⅞″	21′ 11″	22′ ⅞″	22′ 2¼″	22′ 2⅞″
" 20 " " ..			2′ 2″	5′ 6¾″	8′ 10⅜″	11′ 10¼″	14′ 6⅝″	16′ 9″	18′ 5⅜″	19′ 8″	20′ 7⅓″	21′ 3¼″	21′ 9″	22′ ½″	22′ 2¾″	22′ 4¼″	22′ 5″
" 18 " " ..			1′ 11½″	5′ 1⅓″	8′ 4⅛″	11′ 4″	14′ 1″	16′ 4⅛″	18′ 2⅓″	19′ 6⅓″	20′ 6⅓″	21′ 3″	21′ 9″	22′ 1″	22′ 3⅜″	22′ 5⅓″	22′ 5⅞″
" 16 " " ..			1′ 9″	4′ 8⅛″	7′ 9½″	10′ 8¾″	13′ 5⅝″	15′ 10″	17′ 9½″	19′ 2¾″	20′ 4″	21′ 1¾″	21′ 8″	22′ ⅜″	22′ 3⅓″	22′ 5⅓″	22′ 6″
" 14 " " .			1′ 6¾″	4′ 2¾″	7′ 2″	10′ ⅝″	12′ 9¼″	15′ 2½″	17′ 3⅝″	18′ 10¼″	20′ ⅝″	20′ 11⅝″	21′ 6⅞″	21′ 11¾″	22′ 2⅞″	22′ 5″	22′ 6″
" 12 " " ..			1′ 4″	3′ 8⅞″	6′ 5¾″	9′ 3⅓″	11′ 11⅜″	14′ 5″	16′ 7⅓″	18′ 3⅓″	19′ 7″	20′ 7½″	21′ 4″	21′ 10″	22′ 1⅝″	22′ 3⅞″	22′ 5″
" 10 " " ..			1′ 1¼″	3′ 2⅞″	5′ 8⅞″	8′ 4½″	10′ 11¼″	13′ 5″	15′ 8″	17′ 5⅜″	18′ 11″	20′ 7⅓″	20′ 11″	21′ 6¼″	22′ 10¾″	22′ 1½″	22′ 2¾″
" 8 " " ..			10⅜″	2′ 8¼″	4′ 11″	7′ 4⅜″	9′ 9½″	12′ 2⅝″	14′ 5⅝″	16′ 4″	17′ 11″	19′ 2⅜″	20′ 2⅓″	20′ 10½″	21′ 4¼″	21′ 7½″	21′ 9″
" 6 " " ..			6⅞″	2′ 1¼″	3′ 11⅞″	6′ 1½″	8′ 4½″	10′ 7⅝″	12′ 10″	14′ 8¾″	16′ 5″	17′ 10″	18′ 11¾″	19′ 9⅜″	20′ 4⅝″	20′ 8⅞″	20′ 10½″
" 4 " " ..				1′ 6¼″	2′ 11½″	4′ 7⅞″	6′ 7⅞″	8′ 6¾″	10′ 7″	12′ 5″	14′ 1¾″	15′ 8″	16′ 11⅜″	17′ 11″	18′ 7⅝″	19′ ¼″	19′ 1⅞″
" 2 " " ..				9⅞″	1′ 8¾″	2′ 9½″	4′ ¾″	5′ 6⅜″	7′ 1″	8′ 7⅓″	10′ 1¼″	11′ 6⅜″	12′ 9¾″	13′ 11⅜″	14′ 8⅜″	15′ 1⅜″	15′ 3″
Rising of Fore-Side of Rabbet of Stem………		16′	4′ 6″	7¼″	0												
" of Bearding-Line………			6′ 11″	1′ 8″	7″	5″	4½″										4½″
" of Section 4 feet out from Centre Line………				13′	5′ 11¾″	3′ 2¾″	1′ 11¾″	1′ 3⅞″	11½″	9⅝″	8½″	7⅞″	7⅝″	7½″	7½″	7½″	7½″
" of Section 8 feet out from Centre Line………				34′ 7¼″	16′ 7½″	9′ 3″	5′ 6⅜″	3′ 6⅝″	2′ 5″	1′ 9¼″	1′ 5″	1′ 2⅛″	1′ ½″	11⅝″	11¼″	11″	11″
" of Section 12 feet out from Centre Line………						20′ 5⅛″	12′ 1⅓″	7′ 8″	5′ 2″	3′ 8¾″	2′ 9½″	2′ 2⅛″	1′ 9⅜″	1′ 6½″	1′ 5″	1′ 4⅜″	1′ 4⅓″
" of Section 16 feet out from Centre Line………								16′ 6⅝″	10′ 7⅝″	7′ 6⅛″	5′ 7″	4′ 3¾″	3′ 4⅞″	2′ 9¾″	2′ 5½″	2′ 3½″	2′ 3″
" of Top of Deadwood, (Keel)						10″	8½″										8½″
" of Throat-Line…… …			15′ 9½″	5′ 7½″	3′ ½″	2′ 3″	2′ 1½″										2′ 1½″
" of Top of Keelson………				5′ 5″	4′ 7⅝″	4′ 3″	4′ 1½″										4′ 1½″

FRAMES IN THE AFTER-BODY.

	60	64	68	72	76	80	84	88	92	96	100	104	108	112	116	A. P.	8 Feet Abaft.	Centre of Stern.	Siding of Post.
Rising of lower side of Hammock Rail…………											34′ 10⅝″	34′ 11⅞″	35′ 1⅜″	35′ 3¼″	35′ 5¼″	35′ 6¼″	35′ 8¼″	35′ 11¼″	
" of Top of Plank Sheer…	31′ 4¾″	31′ 4⅛″	31′ 4⅛″	31′ 4″	31′ 4⅛″	31′ 4¼″	31′ 4⅝″	31′ 5⅛″	31′ 5¾″	31′ 6½″	31′ 7⅝″	31′ 8⅞″	31′ 10⅜″	32′ ¼″	32′ 2¼″	32′ 3¼″	32′ 5¼″	32′ 7¾″	
" of Port Head…………	28′ ⅞″	28′ ⅝″	28′ ½″	28′ ½″	28′ ⅝″	28′ ¾″	28′ 1⅛″	28′ 1⅝″	28′ 2¼″	28′ 3″	28′ 4⅛″	28′ 5⅝″	28′ 6⅞″	28′ 8¾″	28′ 10¾″	28′ 11¾″	29′ 1½″	29′ 4¼″	
" of " Sill…………	24′ 10⅞″	24′ 10⅝″	24′ 10½″	24′ 10½″	24′ 10⅝″	24′ 10¾″	24′ 11⅛″	24′ 11⅝″	25′ ¼″	25′ 1″	25′ 2⅛″	25′ 3⅜″	25′ 4⅞″	25′ 6¾″	25′ 8¾″	25′ 9¾″	26′	26′ 2¼″	
Half Breadth of Hammock Rail.											16′ 4¾″	15′ 9⅝″	15′ ½″	14′ 1″	12′ 9¾″	11′ 10″	9′ 10¾″		
" of Plank Sheer….	19′ 8⅝″	19′ 8⅛″	19′ 7¼″	19′ 5⅞″	19′ 4⅛″	19′ 1⅜″	18′ 11″	18′ 7⅝″	18′ 3⅝″	17′ 10½″	17′ 4⅛″	16′ 8⅛″	15′ 10⅝″	14′ 10⅛″	13′ 5⅛″	12′ 3⅞″	10′ 1″		
" of Port Head….	20′ 9⅝″	20′ 9⅛″	20′ 8¼″	20′ 6⅝″	20′ 4⅜″	20′ 1⅞″	19′ 10¾″	19′ 7″	19′ 2¼″	18′ 8¾″	18′ 1⅝″	17′ 5⅛″	10′ 0¼″	15′ 4⅛″	13′ 9″	12′ 5⅞″	9′ 9⅛″		
" of " Sill……	21′ 8″	21′ 7⅛″	21′ 6½″	21′ 4¾″	21′ 2⅝″	20′ 11¾″	20′ 8⅛″	20′ 3⅞″	19′ 10⅝″	19′ 4⅜″	18′ 8″	17′ 10¼″	16′ 9¾″	15′ 4⅞″	13′ 5″	11′ 9¼″	7′ 11⅞″		
" 24 ft. Water-Line..	21′ 10⅝″	21′ 10⅛″	21′ 9″	21′ 7¼″	21′ 4⅞″	21′ 2″	20′ 10⅜″	20′ 6⅛″	20′ ⅞″	19′ 6⅛″	18′ 9⅝″	17′ 11″	16′ 9″	15′ 1⅝″	12′ 8″	10′ 5¾″	4′ 8½″		8¼″
" 22 " " ..	22′ 2⅞″	22′ 2¼″	22′ 1″	21′ 11¼″	21′ 8¾″	21′ 5¾″	21′ 1⅞″	20′ 9⅜″	20′ 3⅝″	19′ 7¾″	18′ 10¼″	17′ 10″	16′ 4¾″	14′ 4″	10′ 11¾″	7′ 10″			8¼″
" 20 " " ..	22′	22′ 4⅜″	22′ 3⅛″	22′ 1¼″	21′ 10¾″	21′ 7½″	21′ 1⅜″	20′ 10½″	20′ 4⅛″	19′ 7⅜″	18′ 8″	17′ 5⅛″	15′ 7″	12′ 10⅜″	8′ 5½″	4′ 4½″			8¼″
" 18 " " ..	22′ 5⅞″	22′ 5¼″	22′ 4″	22′ 2⅛″	21′ 11⅜″	21′ 7¾″	21′ 3⅜″	20′ 9¾″	20′ 2½″	19′ 4⅜″	18′ 2″	16′ 6¾″	14′ 3″	10′ 9½″	5′ 6½″	1′			8¼″
" 16 " " ..	22′ 6″	22′ 5⅜″	22′ 4″	22′ 2⅛″	21′ 11⅛″	21′ 7″	21′ 2⅛″	20′ 7½″	19′ 10¾″	18′ 10″	17′ 4¼″	15′ 3″	12′ 4⅛″	8′ 6″	3′ 3″				8¼″
" 14 " " ..	22′ 6⅝″	22′ 5¼″	22′ 2¾″	22′ 1⅝″	21′ 10¼″	21′ 5⅜″	20′ 11¼″	20′ 3⅛″	19′ 4″	17′ 11¼″	16′ ⅞″	13′ 6″	10′ 2¾″	6′ 4½″	2′ 1″				8¼″
" 12 " " ..	22′ 5″	22′ 4¼″	22′ 2½″	22′	21′ 7⅞″	21′ 2″	20′ 6″	19′ 7″	18′ 4½″	16′ 7½″	14′ 4¼″	11′ 5½″	8′ 1⅜″	4′ 8″	1′ 7⅝″				10″
" 10 " " ..	22′ 2¼″	22′ 1⅞″	21′ 11¾″	21′ 8⅛″	21′ 2⅞″	20′ 7⅛″	19′ 8⅛″	18′ 6½″	16′ 11⅜″	14′ 10″	12′ 3″	9′ 3½″	6′ 2¼″	3′ 5″	1′ 5½″				1′ 2½″
" 8 " " ..	21′ 9″	21′ 8⅛″	21′ 5⅜″	21′ ¾″	20′ 5⅜″	19′ 7″	18′ 5″	16′ 11¼″	15′	12′ 7⅝″	9′ 10¾″	7′ 1⅜″	4′ 6⅛″	2′ 6⅛″	1′ 3¼″				1′ 4¼″
" 6 " " ..	20′ 10½″	20′ 9¼″	20′ 5¼″	19′ 10⅞″	19′ ⅝″	17′ 10¾″	16′ 5″	14′ 7⅝″	12′ 6″	10′	7′ 5⅛″	5⅞″	3′ 1″	1′ 9¼″	1′ ⅝″				1′ ¼″
" 4 " " ..	19′ 1⅞″	19′ ⅜″	18′ 6¾″	17′ 9½″	16′ 7½″	15′ 1⅞″	13′ 4¾″	11′ 4½″	9′ 3⅛″	7′ ⅜″	4′ 11⅜″	3′ 2½″	1′ 11⅛″	1′ 2″	6⅞				9″
" 2 " " ..	15′ 3″	15′ ½″	14′ 4″	13′ 3¼″	11′ 10″	10′ 2″	8′ 4½″	6′ 8¼″	5′ ¾″	3′ 7½″	2′ 5½″	1′ 7⅛″	1′ ⅛″	8⅛″	5″				8¼″
Rising of aft side of Rabbet…..																17′	22′		
" of Bearding Line………	4½″								4½″	5″	6¼″	8⅝″	1′ 1⅞″	2′ 1⅝″	9′ ¼″	17′ 9½″	22′ 5⅛″		
" of Section 4 feet out from Centre Line………	7½″	7½″	7½″	7⅝″	8″	9″	11″	1′ 2″	1′ 6⅞″	2′ 3″	3′ 3″	4′ 10¼″	7′ 3⅞″	11′ ⅜″	16′ 9″	19′ 9½″	33′ 7¾″		
" of Section 8 feet out from Centre Line………	11″	11¼″	11¾″	1′ ¾″	1′ 2⅝″	1′ 5¾″	1′ 10⅜″	2′ 5⅛″	3′ 4″	4′ 7⅜″	6′ 5⅜″	8′ 9⅜″	11′ 10⅝″	15′ 6¾″	19′ 7¾″	22′ 1″	26′ ⅝″		
" of Section 12 feet out from Centre Line………	1′ 4⅛″	1′ 4⅝	1′ 6″	1′ 8½″	2′ ⅝″	2′ 7″	3′ 4″	4′ 3⅜″	5′ 8″	7′ 6″	9′ 9″	12′ 5¾″	15′ 7⅝″	19′ 1⅜″	23′ 1″	26′ 4⅞″			
" of Section 16 feet out from Centre Line ………	2′ 3″	2′ 3¾″	2′ 6⅛″	2′ 11″	3′ 7⅛″	4′ 5⅝″	5′ 7½″	7′ 1½″	8′ 11″	11′ 2½″	13′ 10⅝″	17′ 3⅜″	20′ 10″						
" of Top of Deadwood (Keel)	8½″								8½″	9¼″	1′	1′ 7½″							
" of Throat Line………	2′ 1½″								2′ 1½″	2′ 2¼″	2′ 5″	3′ 1″	4′ 10″	8′ 9″	14′ 1″	19′ 3″			
" of Top of Keelson…….	4′ 1½″								4′ 1½″	4′ 2¼″	4′ 4¾″	4′ 10½″	5′ 11″						

DIVISION THIRD.

SHIP BUILDING.

CHAPTER I.

Building Slip—Building Blocks—Keel—Rabbet of Keel—False Keel or Shoe—Bilge Keels—Stem—Apron—Forward Deadwood—Stemson—Stern-Post—Counter-Timbers—Stern-Post Knee—Inner Post—After Deadwood.

BUILDING SLIP.

SHIPS are generally built upon inclined surfaces, called slips, which slope gently towards the water. The foundation of the slip must not be neglected. Too much care cannot be given to this, as without a firm foundation we cannot answer for the ship being properly built, or successfully launched; but, of course, the class of ship intended to be built, must, in a great measure, determine this. In the case of an iron-clad ship, piling should be resorted to; but in whatever way it is formed, care should be taken to insure its being of one uniform solidity; for, unless this precaution be taken, it is not at all certain that the launch will be successful. Ships have been known to stop half-way down the ways, and, in some cases, have broken their backs, owing, probably, to the weight of the ship when transferred from the keel-blocks to the launching ways, having produced unevenness, through certain parts of the foundation, being less consolidated than others, causing the grease between the two surfaces of the ways in launching to exude more freely at some places than at others, whereby the ways fire in consequence of the friction thus produced.

The building slips in all of the English dockyards, and most all in our own navy-yards have granite foundations. Building slips are usually covered with what are called ship-houses. This is essentially necessary where a wooden ship is to be left "in frame" to season for any considerable length of time.

Exposure to the alternate action of sun and rain is very injurious, and will cause the vessel to decay in a very short time. Where vessels have been built outside of the ship houses in our navy-yards, and left to season for a time, temporary houses have been placed over them for their protection. Most of the

English iron-clads are built in granite dry-docks. The advantages derived over that of building on slips are as follows:—

1st. No weights are required to be raised to elevated positions—an important item in building heavy vessels.

2d. The workmen within and without the vessel are under the eye of the foreman; for, from the edge of the dock he can, up to the time that the decks are laid, view all of them.

3d. In building the vessel, she lies on an even keel; all the work, therefore, can be fitted to correspond with plumb-lines.

4th. The most important point of all gained is, that the severe strains a vessel is subjected to in launching are avoided, the vessel being floated out of dock when completed.

BUILDING BLOCKS.

(See Frontispiece.)

The blocks on which the keel of the ship is laid are piles of short and thick pieces of timber, placed one above the other, to a height determined by the declivity of the slip upon which they are placed. The lowest piece of each tier is the largest, and is called the bed-block; it extends out far enough on either side, in a temporary building-slip, to admit of the bilge and bottom shores being stepped upon it. In a temporary building-slip it is buried nearly its depth in the earth, and oftentimes piles are driven down in the slip and sawed off even with the surface—the bed-blocks being placed on the heads of them—thus affording a permanent and safe foundation to build upon. The upper block of all is called the cap-block. When the blocking is first set up, the cap-block is put in of a parallel thickness; but previous to launching it has to be removed, for the purpose of clinching the keelson bolts over it; and when completed, it is replaced by two wedge-blocks, the latter being much easier to remove in launching.

The blocks are set up from four to six feet apart.

When the height of the blocks exceed six feet, recourse is had to "cribbing," which is piling long pieces of timbers in a fore-and-aft direction and athwartships, until the requisite height is obtained—cap-blocks being placed on top of all. Three rates of inclination have to be attended to in building a ship; that of her keel, that of the sliding-way on which she is to be launched, and that of the slip. The inclination of the keel varies according to

1. Capstans.
2. Galley.
3. Cable Bitts.
4. Water Closets.
5. Sick Bay.
6. Magazine.
7. Magazine Light-Box.
8. Fore-Peek.
9. Shell-Room.
10. Provisions.
11. Water Tanks.
12. Chain Lockers.
13. Sail-Room.
14. Bread-Room.
15. Sail-Room.
16. General Store-Room.
17. Paint-Room.
18. Upper Pieces of the Keel.
19. Lower Pieces of the Keel.
20. False Keel or Shoe.
21. Floor-Timbers.
22. Main Keelson.
23. Forward Deadwood.
24. Stemson.
25. Apron.
26. Upper Piece of the Stem.
27. Lower Piece of the Stem.
29. Upper Piece of the Gripe.
28. Lower Piece of the Gripe.
30. Breast-Hooks.
31. Deck-Hooks.
32. Seating-Rail of the Head.
33. Main-Rail of the Head.
34. Planking of the Head.
35 & 37. Upper and Lower Brackets.
36. Trail-Board.
38. Spirketing.
39. Waterways.
40. Dagger-Knees.
41. Lodging-Knees.

the dimensions of the vessel. The inclination of the sliding-ways is greater for light vessels than for heavy ones, ranging from half-an-inch to one-inch-and-a-half to the foot, being made less for larger vessels to prevent them from acquiring an excessive speed when they are launched.

The height of the after-block (see Fig. 2, Plate V.) is determined by constructing a sheer-plan of the ship, as shown, in which H H represents a horizontal line, K F the lower side of the keel at the intended inclination, and W W the intended inclination of the sliding-ways, the distance that the fore-foot of the vessel is below the line showing the inclination of the sliding-ways at that point, plus nine inches, will be the height required for the after-block, in order that the fore-foot of the vessel will not touch at this point in launching. The remainder of the blocks will be regulated from the after one of all. Several monitors have been built with their after-block the highest; but the forward-block must be high enough to prevent the fore-foot of the vessel from touching in launching, and one of the *Colossus* class is now on the stocks at Charlestown navy-yard, which sits nearly level on her blocking. The object of building in this way was, that in launching, the vessel would be water-borne at all points at the same time, and the danger of straining, by having the after part water-borne before she was entirely clear of the ways, would be prevented. A number of heavy armor-plated ships have been launched in the usual way, and with perfect success.

KEEL.

(Fig. 41, Nos. 18 and 19. Plates I. and II., Fig. 1.)

The keel is the first timber placed on the blocks, and forms the lower boundary of the longitudinal section.

Keels for all vessels in the naval service are made of white oak. The pieces are obtained in as long lengths as possible, varying in size according to the size of the ship. The siding-size of a keel may be obtained by multiplying the breadth of beam of the vessel by .42 (giving the size in inches and parts of an inch).* The several pieces forming the keel are joined together by plain horizontal scarphs. The scarphs should be long enough to admit of the fastening of four frames through each. (Fig: 42.) The nibs of the scarphs should come under a filling timber. Two rows of square coaks are let into the lips of the scarphs. The

* Rule given by Naval Constructor, Samuel M. Pook, U. S. N.

keel, when dressed up by the carpenters, and the scarphs cut, is placed on the blocks, the lips of the scarph painted, a piece of felt cut over the coaks, and the pieces forced together by means of clamp-screws. They are fastened by driving two copper bolts through each nib, clinching them on composition plates, and not less than four copper bolts through each scarph under the filling, and clinched on rings on the under-side of the keel. The size of the fastening varies according to the size of the vessel. The keel is now regulated, *i. e.*, centered properly on the blocks, and secured by cleats fastened to the cap-blocks on either side of it. A centre line is now marked on top of the keel, and from a batten, called a "room-and-space batten," the position of the joint of each frame is transferred to the centre line of keel, squared across the top and down each side of it, the number corresponding to the frame being painted on either side of the keel, according to the marks on the batten. The stations of the frames on the batten were obtained from the mould-loft-floor, where the vessel is laid down to her full size. About three inches above the lower side of the keel, and about five feet apart, or under every other joint of a frame, a bolt is driven and clinched on rings on alternate sides of the keel, to prevent splitting from the large number of heavy bolts that will pass through it, and as a security from splitting when taking the ground. When the depth of the keel is such as to require it to be in more than one depth, the pieces should be coaked together, the scarphs properly shifted and fastened with copper bolts, taking care to keep them clear of the keelson bolts. (See Figs. 41 and 43.)

In some instances the keel is joined together by vertical scarphs, the nibs of the scarph being fastened by driving two copper bolts through each and clinching them on rings. The lips of the scarph are coaked, and fastened by driving three or four bolts through, and clinching them on rings. Before raising the frames, the upper joint of the scarph is caulked, and a strip of sheet-lead is let in over it, and nailed down. The lower joint of the scarph is caulked as the plank of the bottom.

It is thought by many persons that horizontal scarphs tend to weaken the keel in the direction in which it is most subject to strain, more than the vertical scarphs; for the keel bends vertically, which brings a tension on the upper or lower fibres, according as hogging or sagging takes place; but at the present time but few keels are scarphed in this manner.

Fig. 42.

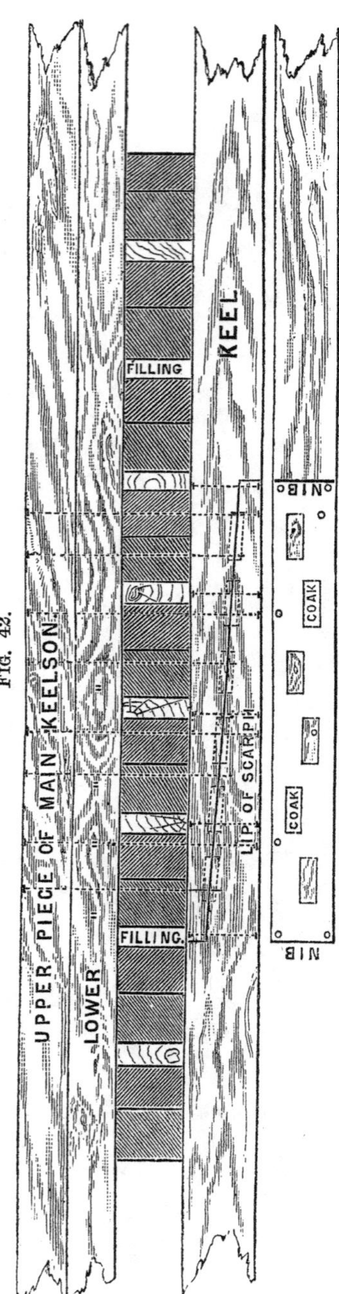

Keel Scarph.

RABBET OF KEEL.

(Fig. 48.)

A wooden keel has in each side a triangular groove or rabbet to receive the edge of the first strake of planking or garboard strake.

In the construction of many of our vessels, the garboard strakes, two in number, on each side were secured to the keel previous to raising the frame; they could be worked much better at that time, and they made a good support for the frame in raising it.* The garboard strakes are secured by driving bolts edgewise through the first strake of plank and keel at intervals of five feet, or under the joint of every other frame, and clinching them on rings on alternate sides; the second strake fastens through the first and keel, under the joint of the intermediate frames, the bolts being driven and clinched on alternate sides. The thickness of the garboard strakes is greatest amidships, and next to the keel, but diminishes gradually, so as to correspond with the thickness of the plank fore-and-aft, and on the bottom.

FALSE KEEL OR SHOE.

(Figs. 41 and 43.)

The false keel or shoe is a piece of oak plank, from two to four inches in thickness, placed underneath the keel; it is put on in lengths of 12 to 16 feet, having square butts (no scarphs), and the butts placed so as to clear the lower nibs of the keel scarphs. The false keel is not put on until all the keelson bolts are driven and clinched, and before it is put on it is covered with two thicknesses of sheathing copper, and secured to the main keel with composition spikes, so that it could be forced off without much damage to the main keel. The main keel has two thicknesses of sheathing copper put on it before the false keel is secured.

BILGE KEELS.

These keels have become very common since the introduction of iron-clad ships. Such keels only extend over a portion of the length of the ship, at the midship part, stopping where the rise of the body, forward and aft, renders them no longer necessary. They, no doubt, check the tendency of a ship to make lee-way

* Since the building of the *Severn* and *Antietam* class of vessels, this method has been partially abandoned on account of the difficulty experienced in regulating the frame.

when under canvas; they tend to check rolling; and, if suitably fitted, add greatly to the chances of safety for a ship in the event of her going ashore. In fixing the position and direction of these keels, it is desirable, of course, to so place them that they shall move truly endwise through the water when the ship is steaming or sailing ahead without encountering pressure upon either side, as that would check the progress of the ship. With this view it is usual to place them in planes parallel to the direction of motion or at right angles to the midship-section. It is also customary to reduce the width and depth of these keels at the fore and after ends, in order to avoid the direct resistance of the fluid. The most of the armor-clad ships of the English navy have angle irons tap-bolted to the outside plating, and between the falling flanges of these angle irons are bolted timber keels, to which again false keels are lightly attached, after the manner of false keels of wooden ships, these keels and false keels being sheathed with thin iron plating. The monitors of the *Miantonomah* and *Colossus* class have bilge keels, moulded and sided about 12 inches at the deepest part, running off to nothing forward and aft.

STEM.

(Plate I., Fig. 1, and Fig. 41, Nos. 26 and 27.)

The stem is the foremost boundary of the ship, being a continuation of the keel to the height of the vessel at the fore extreme of her; in vessels built for naval purposes it is composed of white or live oak timber, and receives in a groove taken out of it, technically called a rabbet, the whole of the fore-ends of the outside planking, called fore-hoods. In large vessels the stem is, from the difficulty of finding timber of sufficient dimensions, composed of two pieces, distinguished as being the upper and lower pieces of stem; these are united to each other and to the fore-end of the keel by hooked-scarphs. These scarphs have round, instead of flat-coaks; the nibs are fastened with two copper bolts in each, riveted on composition plates. The scarphs are fastened with four copper bolts in each, clinched on rings, care being taken to keep them well clear of those of the apron and the deadwood. The stem is sided the same size as the keel, and should be of a parallel size from the fore-foot to the stem-head. The stem is reduced in thickness forward of the rabbet, technically called bearding it. The hooked-scarphs joining the upper and lower stem-pieces and the stem to the keel, are further secured by having large composition-rings let in flush on each side of the stem over the scarphs, and secured with copper bolts driven and clinched on alternate sides. The root end of the tree should be the lower end of the stem, where it will join to the keel.

APRON.

(Plate I., Fig 1, and Fig. 41, No. 25.)

The apron is placed next aft of the stem to strengthen it, and afford wood for the reception of the outside-planking and the heels of the foremost timbers; it is either of white or live oak. The apron may be justly considered as a portion of the fore deadwood, being a continuation of it in a similar way that the stem is a prolongation of the keel; the size of it, in the siding or athwartship direction, is the same as that of the stem, and in large ships, where from necessity it is composed of two or more pieces, the pieces are made to shift scarphs with those of the stem; by shift is meant that it is placed intermediate between the scarphs of the keel and stem to ensure the greatest strength under the required combination of materials. The apron is secured to the stem with round coaks and bolts about 20 inches asunder, clinched on rings on the front of the stem, care being taken to keep the fastening clear of the breast-hook bolts. The stem and apron are got out to the required shape and size from moulds furnished from the mould-loft, and in accordance with the building instructions; when completed and secured together, they are raised to position by means of a derrick, regulated and then secured to the keel. Shores or supports are placed forward, and on either side of it, to keep it securely in place when regulated.

FORWARD DEADWOOD.

(Plate I., Fig. 1, and Fig. 41, No. 23.)

The extremes of the ship, or the fore and after ends of her, have a form given to them that causes the floor-timbers gradually to become more rising or V-like in appearance, which renders them first difficult to be obtained, and finally, not within the natural growth of timber, it then becomes necessary to have recourse to other methods to continue the assemblage of timber which compose the frame of a ship. The position in the length of the frame of the ship, where it would be advisable that the floor-timbers should be discontinued, must be determined by the practical builder with reference to the capabilities of his stock of timber; having fixed that point, called the position of the last square frame, the deadwood becomes the foundation, against which the heels of the remaining timbers or cants are abutted. The deadwood is composed either of white or live oak timber and is coaked to the keel, stem and to each other with round coaks.

STEMSON.

(Plate I., Fig. 1, and Fig. 41, No. 24.)

The stemson is a curved piece of white or live oak timber placed in the angle formed by the apron and upper piece of deadwood or keelson* as a further support to the stem; it is coaked to the deadwood or keelson and apron. The stem, apron, deadwood and stemson are secured together with through-bolts about 20 inches asunder, clinched on rings on the front of the stem and bottom of the keel, all the bolts below the copper line being of copper and above that of iron. The position of all these through-bolts are marked after the several pieces are got in place and bored through each piece separately, so as to avoid bad holes. The necessity for this precaution is greater aft where the fastenings must be got in, so as to be clear of the shaft hole.

STERN-POST.

(Plate II., Fig. 1, and Fig. 43, No. 15.)

The stern-post forms the after boundary of the frame of the ship, being the after-continuation of the keel to the height of the deck, and forming, similarly to the case of the stem and planking forward, the receptacle for the after-ends of the outside planking, a groove being taken out of it called a rabbet to receive these ends, which are technically termed after-hoods. The stern-post is made either of white or live oak, sided at the heel the same as the keel, but in a screw-steamer it is increased in size at the position of and above the shaft, as may be required. The stern-post is in one piece, having two tenons cut on the heel of it, and let into the keel and additionally secured by a composition dovetailed plate let in flush on each side and through bolted.

---

* In the plan shown the stemson is placed on top of the upper piece of main keelson; in many cases the keelson would not run so far forward, when it would come directly on the deadwood.

3. Ward-Room.
4. Steerage.
5. Bread-Room.
6. Magazine.
7. Magazine Light-Box.
8. Store-Rooms.
9. Purser's Clerk's-Room.
10. Sail-Room.
11. Engineer's Store-Room.
13. Shell-Room.
14. Side-Counter-Timber.
15. Forward Stern-Post.
16. After Stern-Post or Rudder-Post.
17. Stern-Post Knees.
18. Inner-Post.
19. After Deadwood.
20. Deadwood-Knee.
21. Stern-Hooks.
22. Rudder-Stock.
23. Backing-Piece.
24. Filling-Pieces.
25. Shoe.
26. Pintle and Strap.
27. Brace or Gudgeon.
29. Saucers.
30. Preventer Tiller.
31. Rudder Yoke.
32. Quadrant on the Head of the Rudder.
33. Inside Spar-Deck Batteries.
34. Inside Gun-Deck Batteries.

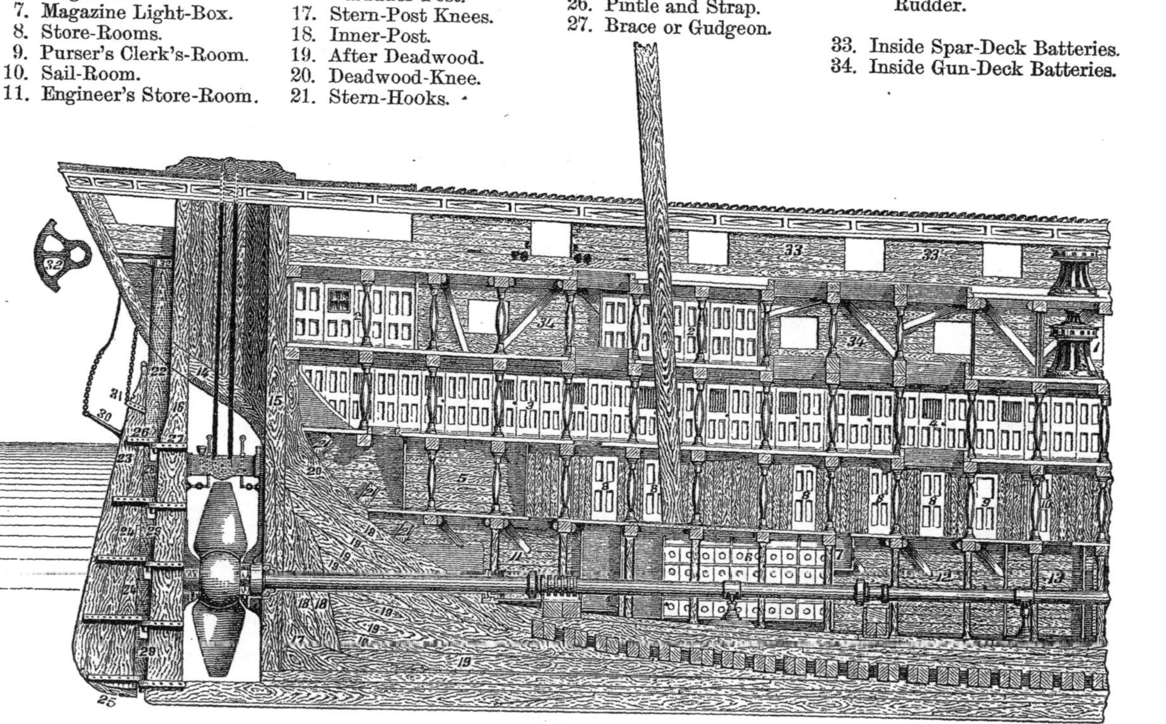

FIG. 43.—Vertical Longitudinal Section U. S. Steamer *Wabash* and Class.

COUNTER-TIMBERS.

(Plate II., Fig. 1.)

In all round and elliptical sterns, timbers called side-counter-timbers are worked on each side of the stern-post, to form the rake and contour of the stern; these timbers abut against the last cant frame, which heels on the deadwood. Between these side-counter-timbers there is a centre-counter-timber large enough to fill up the space between them; upon this centre-counter-timber, there is sufficient wood left in which a rabbet is cut for the bottom plank. These counter-timbers are securely bolted to the stern-post and to each other. The upper end of the counter-timbers extend up to the height of the gun-deck port-sills, and the rudder-port is cut through the centre one. The counter-timbers are worked out and secured to the stern-post and to each other before it is raised to position on the keel.

STERN-POST KNEE.

(Plate II., Fig. 1, and Fig. 43, No. 17.)

The stern-post knee is placed in the angle formed by the keel and stern-post; it is bolted through the stern-post and keel with two copper bolts in each end before the deadwood is put on; it is also coaked to the keel and stern-post. In some cases the inner post runs down to the top of the keel; when this is the case, as in the *Iroquois* and *Oneida* class of vessels, the stern-post knee is placed in the angle formed by the inner stern-post and top of the keel.

INNER-POST.

(Plate II., Fig. 1, and Fig. 43, No. 18.)

The inner stern-post is worked on the inside of the main post running down to the throat of the stern-post knee, and is coaked and temporarily fastened to them. It is made either of white or live oak, and is of the same siding size as the main post.

AFTER-DEADWOOD.

(Plate II., Fig. 1.)

The position of the last-square-frame having been determined the after-deadwood may be got out and put in place, being run up to the height of the floor-timbers, and when the frames are raised the after-piece of keelson will run aft on top of the deadwood, the several pieces being coaked together and fastened as shown in the plan. On top of the deadwood comes the shaft-box, which is generally built and secured together as shown on the plan. In the angle formed by the inner-post and shaft-box, a large knee or piece of curved timber is placed, called the after-deadwood knee, it is coaked to the post and shaft-box. The fastenings are marked off and bored through each piece separately as before described.

In many vessels the deadwood aft is built up as shown in Fig. 3, No. 19, the pieces in wake of the shaft-hole being got out of a sufficient size to admit of cutting the shaft-hole through them, the shaft-box as shown in (Plate II., Fig. 1,) is thus dispensed with.

CHAPTER II.

After Stern-Post or Rudder-Post—Stern-Framing required for a Lifting Screw—Stern-Frames of Square-Sterned Ships--Transoms--The Fashion Pieces—Frame—Floors—Method of Framing.

AFTER STERN-POST OR RUDDER-POST.

(Fig. 43, No. 16.)

In all screw steamers having propeller wells, a second or after stern-post is required; in vessels of the *Wabash*, *Juniata* and *Iroquois* class, it is made of white or live oak, tenoned and secured to the keel with composition dove-tailed plates, let in flush, and through-bolted with copper bolts, countersunk and riveted flush. The heels of these two stern-posts are further secured to the keel and to each other, by composition castings extending along the keel and running up to the castings for the propeller-shaft on each post, they are in two halves and secured with copper bolts driven from alternate sides and flush riveted. The rudder is hung to this after post. In vessels of the *Plymouth* and *Omaha* class (see Fig. 44) the after-stern-post is made of copper, and is connected with the forward post by a composition casting extending to the propeller bearing on the main-stern-post, and on each side of the after-end of the keel; under the middle of the propeller opening it is about four inches in thickness. The width fore-and-aft of this metal-post is two feet; the two plates of copper of which it is made, on the forward and after sides measures seven inches. The head of the metal stern-post is secured to a composition plate fastened to the counter, and the keel secured to the composition casting or shoe, and so fitted that the post can be removed when it becomes necessary to remove the propeller. The rudder is made of composition, and hung in the usual way.

STERN-FRAMING REQUIRED FOR A LIFTING-SCREW

(See Fig. 43.)

The disconnected lifting-screw used in the *Franklin*, *Wabash*, *Hartford*, *Juniata*, *Wyoming*, *Iroquois*, and vessels of their class, is detached altogether from the propeller-shaft and works on a short axis of its own, in a frame of its own, and a couple of beadings of its own; all of which are let down and taken up by means of two grooves cut in the forward and after stern-posts, and they are merely dropped into a seat, which forms a continuous line with the propeller shaft. The revolution of the screw is simply accomplished by a feather on the end of the propeller dropping into a slot in the end of the propeller-shaft; so that, like a screw-driver and screw, they must revolve together. In framing a stern where a lifting-screw is required, the side-counter-timbers (Plate III, Fig. 1) are spread apart far enough to form the sides of the propeller-well, heeling against the after-cant, the after part of the well being formed by a short timber called a transom secured to the after-stern-post; between the side-counter-timbers are several short timbers, heeling on the transom, these are called centre-counter-timbers, and are numbered 1, 2, 3, etc. The *Tennessee*, *Albany*, *Florida*, *Delaware*, *Antietam*, and vessels of their class, have no after-stern-post or rudder-post, an equipoise-rudder being used, the construction and fittings of which will be taken up and described in its appropiate place. The wooden twin-screw monitor *Terror*, *Amphitrite*, *Colossus*, *Thunderer* and vessels of their class have only one stern-post, the rudder being hung to it in the usual way.

STERN-FRAMES OF SQUARE-STERNED SHIPS.

The stern-frame of squared-sterned ships is an assemblage of oak timbers united together, forming the after-part of the ship. It is composed of the stern-post, inner-post, transoms and fashion pieces. They are all secured together before the frame is raised and secured to the keel. The stern-post is united to the keel as before described. At the fore-side of the stern-post an oak timber equal in siding size to the stern-post is placed, called the inner-post, for letting the transoms into. The upper end of this timber formerly abutted under the deck or wing transom, but it is now continued up to the head of the stern-post, and its lower end tenons into the keel with one tenon of the same dimensions as those of the stern-posts.

TRANSOMS.

The transoms in square-sterned ships are transverse timbers connected and placed square with the stern-post. The upper one is called the wing-transom which forms the basis of the upper stern. The after-sides of all the transoms below the wing-transom, and the wing-transom to a short distance below the upper edge, partake of the form of the body, and receive the fastenings of the exterior planking. A short parallel distance below the upper edge of the after-side is called the margin, at the lower part of which the planking ends. A rail called the tuck-rail is fixed on the margin, forming an abutment and finish to the ends of the plank. The next principal transom below is called the deck-transom; it corresponds in height, and supports the after extremity of the lower deck, and has its upper surface of the same round up; this transom is always left as wide as possible for fastening the ends of the deck. Between these two transoms, which are governed as to their situation, one or more transoms are placed according to the distance between them, called filling-transoms; the remaining transoms are distinguished by number, according to their order below the deck-transom. The whole of the transoms are of oak; and are scored, and faced upon the stern and inner-post, to which they are bolted, with one bolt passing through each, driven from the fore-side of the transom and clinched on rings upon the after-part of the post.

THE FASHION-PIECES.

The fashion pieces are timbers having their outward surfaces corresponding to the form of the body, which face over the ends of the transoms, and are secured to them by one bolt in the end of each. The sides of the fashion-pieces are in a vertical plane but oblique to the plane of elevation. The fashion-pieces are from one to three in number on each side. The foremost one extending above the wing transom a sufficient height to form a scarph for the top timber, and to bolt the heels of the side-counter-timber; the second one forms an abutment under the deck-transom; and if three, the after one abuts under the third transom below the deck. The whole of them have their lower ends resting upon a stepping formed in the deadwood, to which they are bolted with one bolt that passes through each fashion-piece and its opposite. Owing to the difficulty of providing timber suited for transoms, the whole of them, except the wing transom, were substituted by timber similar to the fashion-pieces, which formed an abutment under the wing-transom, and were continued to the stern-post. Ships built on the present plan, with elliptical sterns, have the common cant-frames continued round to the stern-post, and up to the top-sides, thus avoiding, entirely, the necessity of transoms.

FRAME.

The frame of a ship is comprised of timbers placed vertically, which give the form of the ship. These timbers are secured together in independent assemblages called frames. It is divided into the square-frame, which is placed transversely, and the cant frame, which is placed obliquely to the longitudinal vertical plane. The timbers of the frame are distinguished by the names, floor, first, second, third, fourth, fifth, etc., futtocks, and long and short top-timbers. These are all the timbers that constitute one frame.

FLOORS.

The floors lay directly across the keel, and have a long and a short arm on either side, and, together with the keel, are those timbers which will have to sustain the body when it takes the ground, and becomes inclined; they should, therefore, extend in the fullest part of the body, beyond the point which would come in contact with the supporting surface. These timbers extend, in general, as far as the square body extends, or as the acuteness of the body will admit of timbers being obtained of the proper shape to form them. The floors of ships commonly extend out from the keel to one-fourth the breadth on each side, and at this place the rise of the floor is usually determined. When they are nearly horizontal from the rabbet of the keel, the ship is said to have a flat-floor; and when the flatness extends for a considerable distance longitudinally, she is said to have a long-floor; and as the floors rise above a horizontal line from the rabbet, the ship is said to have a rising or sharp-floor. The distance from the upper edge of the rabbet of the keel to the upper part of the floors, at the centre line, is called the cutting down or throating; and the line bounding the upper part of the floors, and upper part of the deadwood before and abaft the floor, is called the cutting down or throating-line.

The practice of placing two sets of floors across the keel having a long and a short arm on alternate sides is of recent origin, and is consequent upon the great difficulty in obtaining first futtocks of sufficient length, size and crook for ships of the largest classes. It is regarded as a great improvement, inasmuch as it rids the keel of the range of butts with which it was covered under the old system, which was to have the floor timber extend an equal distance out from the keel on each side of the centre-line and the heels of the first futtock to butt over the centre-line of the keel. This is only the case in vessels having a white-oak frame, as it is next to an impossibility to find live-oak timber that will answer for floors having a long and a short arm.

The futtocks are a continuation of the floor-timbers in the frame, and the upper timbers are the tops and half-tops.

The frames of vessels are composed of live-oak, white-oak, locust, hackmatack and red-cedar; chestnut is also used in merchant vessels.

White and live oak is used for the floors and futtocks; locust and red-cedar for the tops and half-tops. Hackmatack is sometimes used for the upper futtock towards the ends of the vessel.

The timbers of the frame are so disposed, that they give shift to each other; the upper and lower ends of the timbers, which are called the heads and heels, coming near the middle of the adjoining timbers of the frame. The second futtock abuts against the short-floor head; the heel of the third abuts against the head of the long-floor; the heel of the fourth abuts against the head of the second; the heel of the fifth abuts against the head of the third; the heel of the top against the head of the fourth: the heel of the half-top-timber abuts against the head of the fifth. The timbers of the frame are close together, and each lap or scarph is bolted with three iron bolts. These bolts are three inches less in length than the siding size of the frame, and are punched in one and a half inches, taking care to keep them clear of the lodge knee and water-way bolts. The heads and heels of all the timbers are coaked together with round coaks, and there is a three-inch coak between the timbers at each frame bolt; the bolt passing through the timbers and coak. The coaks are made of seasoned oak, locust or lignumvitæ.

The frames are distinguished in two ways, viz., by letters and figures or figures alone. When both are used, those before the greatest transverse section are denoted by letters, and those abaft by figures, beginning from this section, which is called dead-flat, and distinguished thus ⊕ ; but should there be several sections of the same area, which is frequently the case, those before are called A and B, etc., and those abaft 1 and 2, etc., flats, and are marked thus: (1) (2) (A) (B).

METHOD OF FRAMING.

While the work of preparing the keel, stem, and stern-frame has been going on, workmen have also been busy getting the frame-timber out, according to the moulds and directions furnished from the mould-loft. Presuming that this is well underway, preparations are made for putting the frames together and raising them.

For this purpose a platform is built the entire length of the keel at the height of the keel blocks, and wide enough to put the dead-flat frame together on. The floor-timbers are placed across the keel opposite their several stations; and the remaining timbers of the frame on either side of the platform. Blocks are now laid on the platform level with the top of the keel; the lower course of timbers placed on them according to the moulds, and the heads and heels coaked together; the upper course is then put in place, the position of the coaks in the heads and heels and scarph or lap of the timbers are marked; the upper course is then taken off, the holes for the coaks are bored, placed in the lower course and the upper one is driven down upon it. The frame bolts, three in each scarph, are then driven and punched in 1½ inches. Pieces of white or yellow pine plank called cross-spalls are now put on the frames at the proper height for putting on the clamps of the upper and lower deck, and of sufficient strength to build a stage to work on.

These cross-spalls are cut to the proper breadths of the frames at the heights they are put on, as taken from the floor of the mould-loft; the frame is then ready for raising, which is done with two pairs of shears, one pair on each side, standing fore-and-aft and properly guyed. The frame when up is placed in its true position, that is, the joint of the frame to the station marked on the keel, making the plane of its sides athwartships and perpendicular to the keel, and the centre of the cross-spall (which is always marked upon it), vertical to the centre line of the keel;

a plumb-bob is hung to the centre of the cross-spall before raising the frame to centre it by; the frame is then secured by placing shores under it, and at the wale height, and by shores placed at an angle from the head forward-and-aft to hold it firmly in its true position when regulated as those forward-and aft are regulated from it.

The operation of framing is commenced at dead-flat, and carried on both forwards and aft at the same time.

CHAPTER III.

Regulating the Frame—Knight-Heads—Cants—Hawse-Pieces—Chocks—Fillings —Keelsons—Main Keelson—Sister Keelsons—Boiler or Bilge Keelsons.

REGULATING THE FRAME.

WHEN the frames are first raised, they are secured in a temporary manner by placing shores under them, and small pieces of plank, called stay-lathes, are nailed from the head of one frame to another; an iron blunt bolt is then driven through the heel of the first futtock or floor into the keel one-half of its depth. The frames are secured in their position until the outside planking is brought on, by pieces of oak or yellow pine plank, from five to seven inches square, extending the length of the square-body called ribbands, and at the extremities, or where they cross the cant bodies, by pieces formed to the curve of the body called harpins; and at the sirmarks, where the ribbands, and harpins cross the frames, they are attached to them with screw bolts called ribband-screws, the upper end of the ribband-screw having an eye worked in it to admit of turning it in with a lever. The sirmarks spoken of above are transferred from the frame moulds to the timbers of the frame; they mark the point at which the bevellings are to be applied, also the head and heel of each timber of the frame; the lines laid down on the mould-loft floor, called diagonal lines, mark the head and heels of the timbers, and intermediate bevelling spots, and it is to these latter stations called sirmarks* that the ribbands and harpins are put on. On these ribbands and harpins the joint of each frame must be marked, the position of each joint being first transferred from the mould-loft floor to a batten, called a room-and-space batten, from which it is transferred to the ribbands. Moulds are made in the mould-loft, and bevels taken for the purpose of getting out the harpins to the proper shape, and the position of the joint of each cant-frame is marked on it and transferred to the harpins, also the position of the hawse pieces. The floor ribband is the first one put in place. As soon as several frames have been raised, it is put on and shored up to regulate the floor surface, and is of

* The sirmarks are distinguished by being marked thus ✱.

sufficient strength to bear the weight of the entire frame when raised. Harpins are generally placed at the height of the load-water line, port-sill, port-head, and rail-lines.

Staging is erected around the vessel, and the ribbands are put on as soon as a sufficient number of frames have been raised. As soon as the entire square-body is raised, the harpins are secured at their proper stations, the forward ends of those in the fore-body being secured to the stem, and the after ends of those in the after-body to the stern-frame, the other ends generally lapping over three or four frames in the square-body.

A ship may be said to be regulated when the stem and stern-post are found to be plumb, and a line extending from the centre of one to the centre of the other, and at the same time cutting a plumb-line over the centre line of the floors, from the centre of each cross-spawl. When thus bound in ribbands, and securely shored with three tiers of shores set up properly, and their heels secured to prevent them from shifting, the ship may be said to be fairly regulated.

The knight-heads, cants, and hawse-pieces, having been worked out, are now to be raised and regulated, butts chocked and fillings put in.

KNIGHT-HEADS.

(Plate IV, Fig. 1.)

The knight-heads are timbers placed on either side of the apron when the rabbet is on the after edge of the stem and partly on the apron. These timbers give support to the bowsprit, and render more secure the foremost extremities of the exterior planking, called the hooding-ends ; they extend a sufficient height above the bowsprit to receive a chock over it, and sometimes above the chock to form a timber-head, and at other times to receive the planking for the forecastle. When the diameter of the bowsprit exceeds the siding of the stem at the head too much, so that the knight-heads would be cut considerably to allow the bow-sprit to pass between them, which is sometimes the case in sloops-of-war and frigates having a full bow, a piece is then introduced between the apron and stem and knight-heads, called a stem-piece, to give them more spread.

The knight-heads and stem-pieces are of oak or locust, and are made conformably to the scantling of the frame, in and out, except the upper ends where there is an additional substance called the boxing, equal to the thickness of the outside and inside planking, in the make of the bowsprit, extending from about one foot above to one foot below; this wood is left to prevent joints in the hole for the bowsprit.

The knight-heads and stem-pieces are bolted to the stem; when the body is not too acute, the bolts pass through both; the bolts are driven from each side through one knight-head and stem or apron only.

In addition to the bolts, the knight-heads are coaked to the stem or apron according to their position.

CANTS.

(Plates III and IV, Fig. 1.)

A ship is generally spoken of as being divided into fore and after-bodies, and these combined constitute the whole of a ship. They are supposed to be separated by an imaginary athwartship section at the widest part of the ship, called the midship-section or dead flat.

The midship-body is a term applied to an indefinite length of the middle part of the ship longitudinally, including a portion of the fore-body and of the after-body. It is not necessarily parallel or of the same form in its whole length.

Those portions of the ship which are termed square and cant-bodies, may be considered as sub-divisions of the fore and after bodies. There is a square fore-body and a square after-body towards the middle of the ship, and a cant-fore-body and a cant-after-body at the two ends. In the square-body the frames stand at right angles to the centre-line of the keel, and are athwartship vertical planes. In the cant-bodies the joints of the cants are still vertical, but have gradually to be canted or swung around to an angle of 90°, or a quarter of a circle, to meet the stem, the plane of whose sides is fore-and-aft; the heels of them also have a less space for their reception, which causes the practical builder to reduce the cant-timbers in their siding or thickness at the heels, to make them close joints, or, indeed, angle against each other, from a given point, taking the wood away partly from each.

The cants are canted forward in the fore-body, and aft in the after-body. The reasons for the frames in a wooden ship being canted is, that in these parts of the ship, the timbers would be too much cut away, on account of the fineness of the angle formed between an athwartship plane and the outline or water-lines of

FIG. 45.

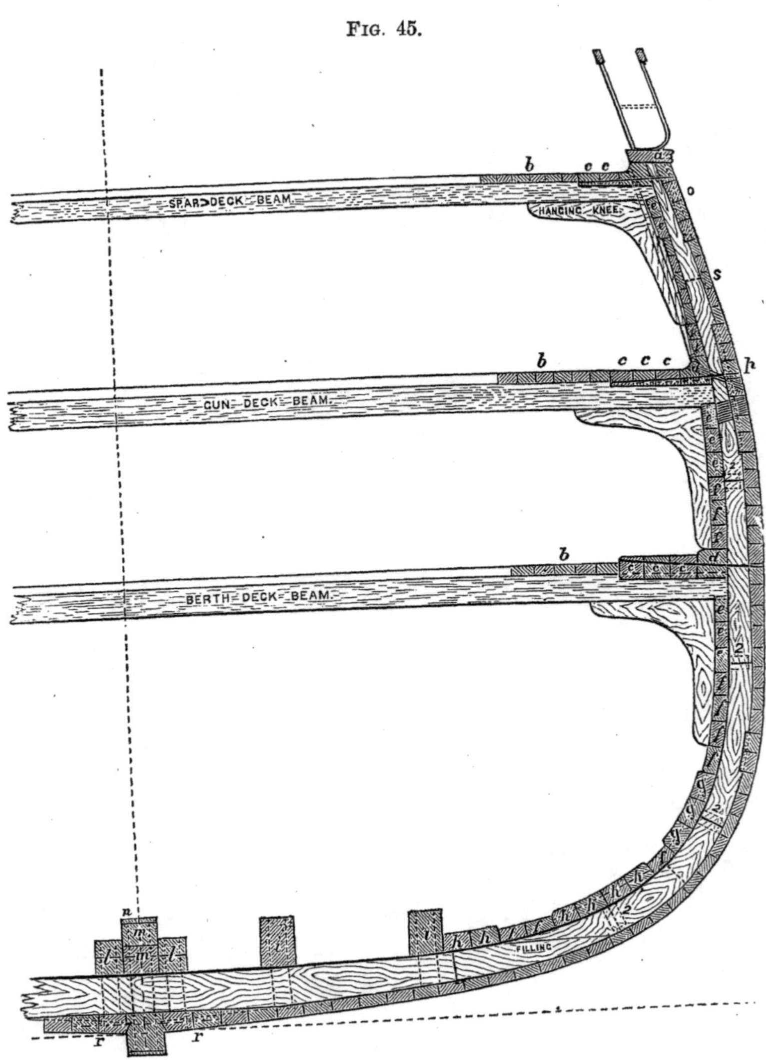

Vertical Transverse Section of the U. S. Steamer *Antietam*, at ⊕.

the ship. The timber is therefore turned partially around till the outside face coincides nearly with the desired outline, and it is by this movement that the side of a frame in the cant-fore-body is made to point forward, and in the cant-after-body to point aft.

The timbers of the cant-frames are close together, coaked and bolted the same as the square-frames. The heels of the cant-frames are boxed into the deadwood about $1\frac{1}{2}$ inches for a length of from 18 to 24 inches but are not cut into the after deadwood in the range of the shaft-hole; the heel of each timber of the cant-frames is bolted through the deadwood with two copper bolts, and riveted on rings on alternate sides.

When the cants are framed, tenons cut on the heel and mortise in the deadwood they are raised, regulated by the stations on the harpins, and heels secured to the deadwood. The cant-frames are designated as Cants Nos. 1, 2, 3, etc., fore-body; Cants Nos. 1, 2, 3, etc., after-body.

HAWSE-PIECES.

(Plate IV. Fig. 1, and Plate VII. Fig. 2.)

The hawse-pieces are the cant-frames to the number of six or seven next aft of the knight-heads; they either heel against the fore-side of the foremost cant-timber, or run down and take the common stepping with the cants.

The hawse-pieces are bolted to the apron and to each other with iron bolts. The bolts should be kept clear of the breast-hooks and hawse-holes.

CHOCKS.

(No. 2, Fig. 45.)

In addition to the coaks, which are placed in the butts of the frame timbers, a seasoned locust or white oak chock is placed between the frames, opposite to each butt; they are six inches in thickness, dove-tailed one-half an inch into the timbers they abut, the grain of the wood is fore-and-aft, and they are driven in tightly over all the butts above the fillings, taking care to keep them about one inch clear of the outside of the frame, to prevent the water from lodging on them, trimming them off fair with the inside of the frame.

FILLINGS.

(Fig. 42.)

In all wooden vessels built for naval purposes, the spaces between the frames are filled up with filling timbers, level athwartships to the height of one foot above the level of the floor timbers, the heads of the fillings rising gradually forward and aft to make a fair line.

These fillings are composed of either white-oak, live-oak, or hackmatack; white-oak in a white-oak frame, live-oak in a live-oak frame amidships, hackmatack or pine forward and aft, and in some vessels pine has been used all through. In getting out the floor-timbers of a frame, they are obtained large enough in siding size to fill up the entire room and space, if possible, amidships, thus obviating the necessity of putting fillings in, but where this cannot be done fillings are put in.

Where the fillings cross the keel they are bolted to it, and they are secured to the frame by driving tree-nails cornerwise into it. The joints of the frames and fillings are caulked inside and outside, so that that part of the vessel would be water-tight, even supposing the bottom plank to be torn off by some accident.

Fillings are placed between the cants and hawse-pieces; in the wake of the fore, main, and mizzen rigging; wherever an airport is located; where the breeching starts or gun-tackle bolts comes between the frames, and wherever a valve connected with the magazines, pumps, boilers, or engines comes through the bottom or side of the vessel, or where a hanging knee comes off a frame.

The advantages obtained by filling in the spaces between the floor-timbers are these:—

To add to the strength and durability of the fabric; to preserve the health of the crew from the effects of the impure air arising from the filth which soon collects in these openings; to render the ship less liable to leakage, as well as to facilitate the stoppage of any leak; and lastly to increase the thickness of the bottom, thereby lessening very considerably the danger to be apprehended from getting on shore or foundering at sea. That it tends also to the durability of the ship will be inferred from the following positions:—

1st. That the openings in the old principle are, after the ship has had any considerable length of service, choked up in many places with an accumulation of filth.

2d. That no free circulation can be obtained in these openings by any means.

3d. That timber, being either freely exposed to, or excluded from, the air, is equally preserved.

4th. That it has been found, on examining the frame and plank of old ships, that those parts (now filled in) generally decay sooner than the rest, viz.: from the floor-heads in the midships, and from the deadwood forward and abaft to the height of the orlop clamps.

The butts of the frames having been chocked, and the fillings all in, the several operations of putting in the keelsons, breast-hooks, riders and diagonal braces may be proceeded with.

KEELSONS.

Keelsons are distinguished as main keelsons, sister keelsons, bilge or boiler, and engine keelsons.

MAIN KEELSON.

(*m m*, Fig. 45.)

The main keelson is a timber in the interior of the ship, placed immediately over the keel, lying upon the upper part of the floors as far as they extend, and before and abaft them upon the deadwood.

It is for uniting in one mass the keel, deadwood, and floors, that a compact union may be formed throughout the system. The keelsons are of white or live oak timber; the main keelson is generally put in in two depths, the scarphs connecting the keelson pieces are cut, coaked, and fastened, the same as those of the keel, care being taken to have the scarphs properly shifted, and clear of each other, and of the keel scarphs.

The lower piece of the main keelson is coaked to the floors and fillings with round coaks, three inches in diameter; the upper and lower pieces are coaked to each other with square coaks in two rows; they are secured by driving through the keelsons and floor timber two copper bolts; where the first futtock do not abut on the keel, but where a long and a short arm floor is used, then there will be two through bolts in each floor timber; these bolts should be driven on the alternate edges, and riveted on composition rings on the lower side of the main keel. One blunt bolt is also driven in each frame. Where cant-frames are, and the keelson forms part of the deadwood, the deadwood bolts take the place of the bolts above named.

When live-oak is used for the main keelson, as shown in Figs. 41 and 43, it is made of pieces six inches in thickness, five in number, the height being thirty inches. The plank is butted together and coaked to each other with square coaks, about fifteen inches apart, in two rows. The lower plank is a little thicker and jogs over the floors and into the futtocks and fillings. These several courses of plank are bolted together with short copper bolts. The sister-keelsons, which in this case are about fifteen inches in depth, are scarphed together.

SISTER KEELSONS.

(*l l*, Fig. 45.)

The sister keelsons are on each side, and close adjacent to the main keelson, extending forward and aft, until the outer edge becomes six inches in depth, the top being parallel with the top of the main keelson, and from six to nine inches below it. These keelsons are coaked to the fillings and floors, as the main keelsons; the scarphs are properly shifted a little less in length than those of the main keelson; coaked and fastened as other scarphs. Through these keelsons, in every timber, there is one copper bolt riveted on rings on the outside of the garboard strake. Where it can be done, these keelsons are bolted athwartships through the lower piece of main keelsons, about five feet asunder, driven and riveted on rings on alternate sides.

BOILER OR BILGE KEELSONS.

(*i i*, Fig. 45.)

In all steamers there are two or more boiler or bilge keelsons on each side, parallel to the sister keelsons, and extending forward and aft until they become on the outer edge six inches in thickness, when they terminate. They are in height and distance asunder to correspond with the plans furnished by the Bureau of Steam Engineering. Short pieces of white oak are placed athwartship between the fore-and-aft line of keelsons, on top of which the engine keelsons are placed, forming a solid foundation for the bed-plates for the engine. (See Fig. 46).

CHAPTER IV.

Capping on Main Keelson—Water-Courses—Diagonal Braces—Diagonal Bracing on Outside of Vessels—Breast-Hooks, Stern-Hooks and Deck-Hooks—Port-Sills—Deck-Clamps—Bilge-Strakes—Thick-Strakes—Ceiling.

CAPPING ON MAIN KEELSON.

(*n*, Fig. 45).

A capping of oak plank, from two to four inches in thickness, is put on top of the main keelson, after all the keelson-bolts have been driven; it is secured with spikes or bolts. The heels of the berth-deck stanchions tenon into this capping.

WATER-COURSES.

The water-courses, under the keelsons, are cut in the fillings between the floor-timbers.

DIAGONAL BRACES.

Sir Robert Steppings, by whom the system known as filling in was introduced into the practice of ship-building, also introduced, as a substitute for a portion of the internal planking, a combination of wood-trussing to strengthen the ship, illustrating the intended effect by a reference to the stability given to a five-barred gate by the bar which is placed across the horizontal portion of it. The illustration would have held good had the strain been similar to that which his trussed frame in the hold of the ship was subjected. In the gate, the stiffness being required in the vertical position, the cross-bar is effective; but the same gate would be found weak if its strength was tested by a force applied to bend it horizontally. This trussing-frame, called, by its projector, a diagonal frame, was composed of timbers nearly equal in dimensions to the lower timbers of the ship, disposed diagonally or athwart the frame of the ship; but in the lower part, or near the keelson, this trussing in flat-floored vessels, was wholly out of comparison with the vertical position of the bar of the gate; and in those ships having a rising floor it only approximated to it. The diagonal framing thus becomes nearly useless as a truss, and its only beneficial effects were to unite the several timbers of the frame together in a horizontal direction. This framing was also found to be subject to early decay, the more especially so where old ship-timber was used for this purpose, as originally suggested by the projector; and, moreover, to yield little strength to the ship.

Modern times have introduced a system of iron diagonal trussing, possessing considerable advantages over all others yet introduced.

The iron diagonal braces vary in thickness from $\frac{5}{8}$ to $\frac{3}{4}$ of an inch, and from 3 to $4\frac{1}{2}$ inches in width, according to the dimensions of the vessel. They are placed on the inside of the frame timbers, so that the timbers of the frame can be more readily removed when repairs are required to be made. There are two sets of braces placed at right angles to each other, one of which lets into the timber, and is laid at an angle of 45° with the joint of the frames; the upper ends being under the head-strap which is at the lower side of the plank sheer* or just below the port-sill on the spar-deck, and the lower ends being below the turn of the bilge, having a bolt in the first futtock and long floor-timbers; the other tier lays on the timbers, the clamps, ceiling, etc., jogging over them. The upper end of the braces are placed between every other frame, or five feet asunder, and they are riveted to the head-strap which runs entirely around the ship on the inside. The head-strap has a bolt in every timber. The braces are bolted to every timber that they cross, and hot riveted to each other at every crossing between the frames; above the copper-fastening the bolts in the timbers go through the outside and inside planking, and iron braces, being riveted on rings on the inside planking thus one bolt secures all three; below the copper fastening one iron bolt is driven in each timber that the brace crosses, being driven from the inside and rivetted on rings on the outside of the timbers before the planking is put on; the tier of braces that let into the timbers act as *struts*, and reach downwards from the ends of the vessel towards amidship below, running past each other alternating amidships.

The tier that lies on the timbers act as *ties*, and reach downwards from amidships towards the ends of the vessel. Great care is requisite in letting these braces closely into the timbers, and in jogging the plank over them. This method has now been abandoned, and in diagonally bracing our naval vessels (Fig. 46,)

* As in the *Antietam* and class.

Fig. 46.

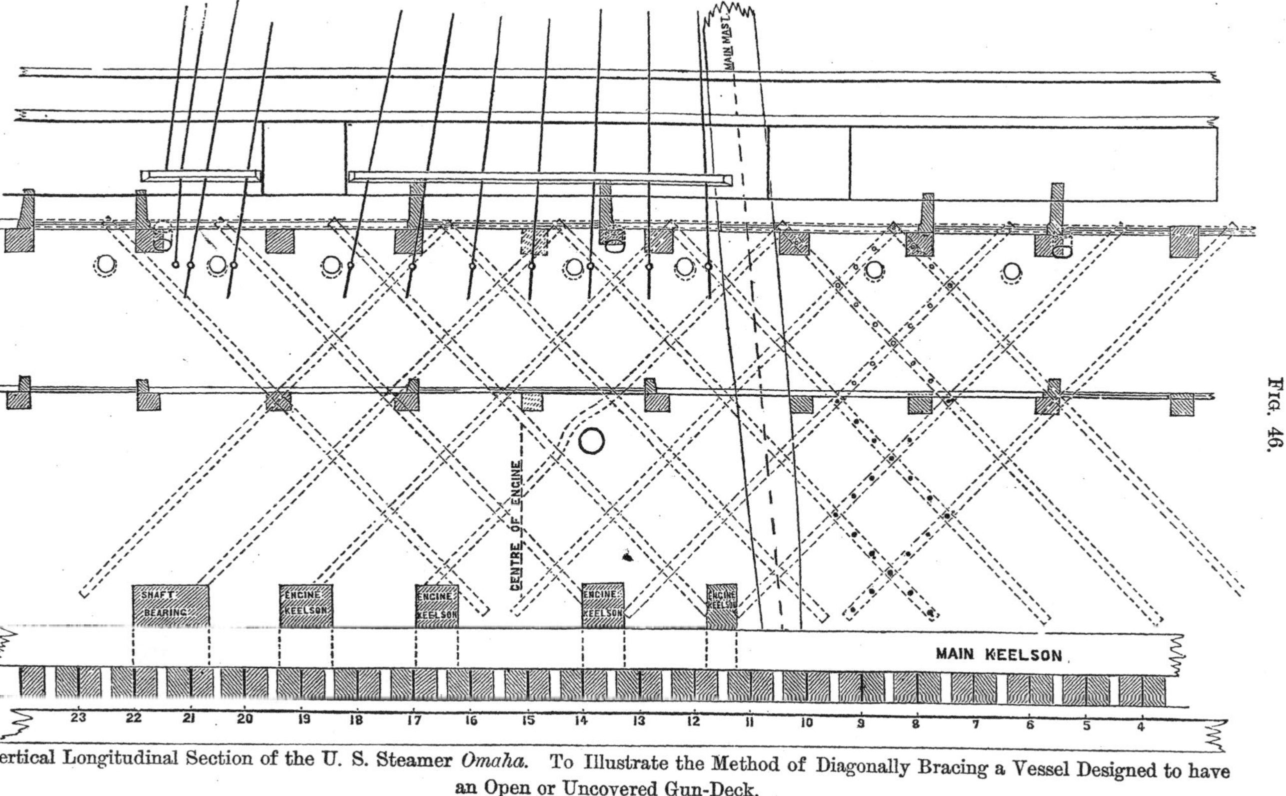

Vertical Longitudinal Section of the U. S. Steamer *Omaha*. To Illustrate the Method of Diagonally Bracing a Vessel Designed to have an Open or Uncovered Gun-Deck.

the old-established system of letting the struts and ties alternate amidships has not been followed out; the general practice now is to let one tier of braces into the frame at an angle of 45° with the joint of the frame, and the other tier to lie on the timbers; the head-strap is let in flush, the head of the *struts* being under and the *ties* over it, one set of braces running from aft the other from forward, but in all other respects as before described. The overhang of the stern is supported by iron straps; one of these is generally placed at or near the poop-deck, one at or near the rail, one at or near the port-sill, and the other near the rudder-port. The upper-straps usually run about twenty-four feet forward of the aft-side of main stern-post; the lower straps reach upwards towards amidships until they reach the upper straps, to which they are hot riveted; the lower one should reach as far forward as the quarter-port will admit; each of these straps is welded in one piece, and fastened to every timber crossed by it, with one iron bolt riveted on the inside of the timbers, or on the inside of the planking where it can be done.

In order to connect the deadwood below the shaft with the frame timbers that are above it, three straps or diagonal braces of composition are placed on each side of the vessel, laying on the deadwood and timbers, and the plank jogging over them, secured with copper bolts driven and riveted on the straps on alternate sides, where it can be done.

DIAGONAL BRACING ON OUTSIDE OF VESSELS.

In addition to the diagonal bracing on the inside of the frames, vessels of the *Congress* and *Severn* class have diagonal braces on the outside, running from the plank-sheer to the turn of the the bilge for a length of 150 feet amidships; one tier of these straps lets into the timbers, the other tier lies on the timbers, the wales jogging over them; they are rivetted together at the crossing between the frames, and all the bolts from the diagonal bracing on the inside rivet on them. The braces are so placed that the bolts securing them to the timbers shall pass through the iron braces on the inside.

In diagonally bracing many of our naval vessels at the present time, and in all merchantmen where iron diagonal braces are used, they are blunt bolted to each timber of the frame that they cross, and hot riveted in the crossings between the frames. This method certainly adds to the amount and weight of material used without adding to the strength of the structure. The plan of making the through fastening above the copper-line answer for the fastening of the braces to the frames is much preferable; it saves expense in fastening, and the frame has less perforations in it.

The *Florida* and *Tennessee*, sister ships, built at the Brooklyn yard by Naval Constructor B. F. Delano, U. S. N., and without any doubt the best constructed vessels in the navy, were diagonally braced on the outside of the frame. The *New York*, now on the stocks, is intended to be braced in a similar manner. There is no advantage in this method; on the contrary, it has many disadvantages. In the event of having to rebuild either of these vessels, should it be necessary to remove any of the frame timbers, it would be necessary to put them in from the inside, and the cost of labor and material would in that case be very much in excess of that where a vessel was braced on the inside, as in the latter case the outside planking would only have to be removed as far down as was required to take the timbers out and replace them. In the case of the *Severn* and *Congress* class, which are braced both *inside* and *out*, and built with white-oak frames, it would cost more to rebuild them than the first cost of such a vessel should be.

BREAST-HOOKS, STERN-HOOKS, AND DECK-HOOKS.

(Plates I and II. Fig. 1, and Figs. 41, 43, and 47.)

To unite the two sides of a ship together at the fore and after ends, or at the head and stern of a ship, in the cant-bodies, where the floors do not cross the keel, inside timbers are worked.

Forward, these are called breast-hooks; aft, they are called stern-hooks. These hooks have equal arms extending across the centre-line of the ship, at which place, or at their throating, they are the widest, or of the most moulding. The lengths given to the arms of these hooks are determined by the store of timber, and the number of them is at the discretion of the practical builder; they are equally spaced between the deck-hooks, which latter may very well be included under the same head with them, with this distinction, that while breast-hooks are generally placed square to the stem and form of the bows, by which position they cross several timbers of the frame and tie them together, the deck-hooks must have their upper surfaces to lie with the round up of

Fig. 47.

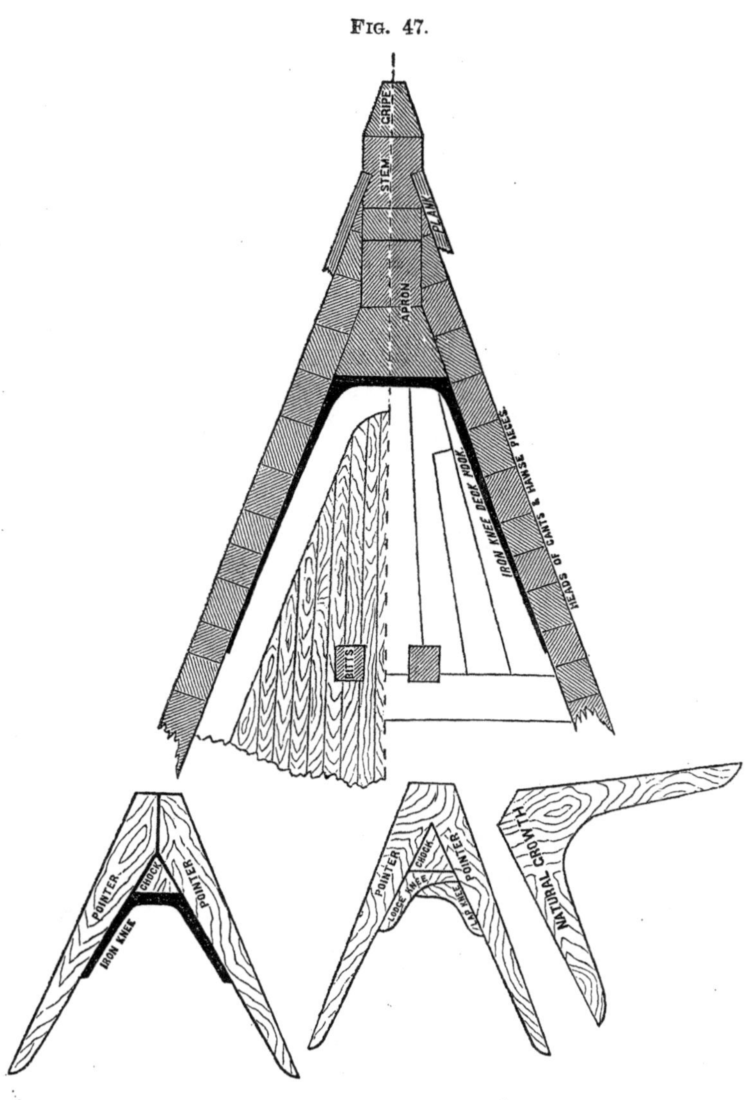

Section at Gun-Deck Height, U. S. Steamer *Antietam*.

the beams, and to the sheer of the decks, and that their positions are fixed, from being at the height of the several decks.

In vessels of the *Wabash* class (Fig. 43) there is a hook over the bowsprit, one to each deck, one to each between decks, and three or four in the hold below the berth-deck forward.

In vessels of the *Antietam* class (Plates I. and II.) forward, there is one hook to each deck, one to each between-decks, and two in the hold below the berth-deck. Aft, there is one at each deck, two between the gun and berth-decks, and two in the hold below the berth-deck.

In the *Wabash* class, the hooks are composed of large pieces of live-oak timber, cut for that purpose, and which can generally be obtained, for full-bowed vessels of the proper shape, in one piece; in sharp-bowed vessels, these hooks are made to the desired shape by placing a piece of timber, called a pointer, on either side, abutting against the apron, with a triangular piece, called a chock, in the angle made by the two pointers, and an iron hook on the inside of the pointers and chock, let in flush, a lodge and a lap-knee is sometimes used instead of the iron hook.

These hooks are fayed against the timbers, and secured with one bolt in the throat and two in every timber that they cross. The throat-bolt is driven from the inside, and rivetted on a ring on the front of the stem; the others are driven from the outside, after the plank is put on, and rivetted on the face of the hook. If iron hooks are used in the hold, then they must be fastened with iron bolts driven from the face of the hook, and rivetted on rings on the outside of the frame before the outside plank is put on.

It may be fairly assumed that the various operations of working out and putting in the port-sills, deck-clamps, bilge-strakes, thick-strakes, ceiling, planking outside, getting out deck-frames, etc., is now fairly under way, and I will describe each part in its turn.

PORT-SILLS.

The port-sills are pieces of white or live oak, forming the upper and lower parts of the ports; they vary in siding size from six to nine inches. They are set with the round of the beam, and dove-tailed to the frame timbers that they cross and abut.

The size of the ports is determined by the calibre of the gun that is to be used in them, and the height of the lower part of the port, or upper side of the lower port-sill from the deck, is determined by the Bureau of Ordnance.

DECK-CLAMPS.

(*e*, Fig. 45.)

The clamps are ranges of thick oak or yellow pine plank, extending the whole length on the inside of the frame, and intended to support the ends of the beams of the different decks; they are in two or more strakes, according to the deck they are connected with.

In vessels of the *Wabash* and *Antietam* class, the berth-deck clamps fill the space amidships, between the thick-strakes and lower side of berth-deck beams; * the gun-deck clamps fill the space amidships between the berth-deck water-way and the under side of the gun-deck beams; the spar-deck clamps fill up the space between the lower side of the upper port-sills and the lower side of the spar-deck beams.

In vessels of the *Omaha* (Fig. 48) class, where iron hanging knees have been substituted for the wooden ones under the forecastle and poop-decks, a shelf-piece has been worked instead of the upper strake of clamps; and in the length of the ship occupied by the engines and boilers, the upper strake of berth-deck clamps has been made considerably thicker than the others, iron hanging knees being used in that space; but in no other cases are shelf-pieces used at the present time. The strakes of clamps are scarphed or plain butted (there being a difference of opinion between constructors as to which is preferable), and carefully cut over the diagonal braces so that they lay close to the frame; enough short fastening is put in to hold the clamps to their place until the outside planking is put on. After three or four strakes have been worked, they are bolted edgewise in every room, and rivetted on rings on the lower edge of the lower strake; the

[NOTE.—The heights of the several decks are transferred from the mould-loft floor to the frame-moulds, and the corresponding sirmarks are cut in on the frame timbers; it is to these sirmarks that the sheer-battens for the several decks are placed, and after being properly regulated, the sheer of the deck is marked across the inside of each frame.]

---

* Properly speaking, only the first three strakes below the beams should be termed clamps, the rest should be termed ceiling.

FIG. 48.

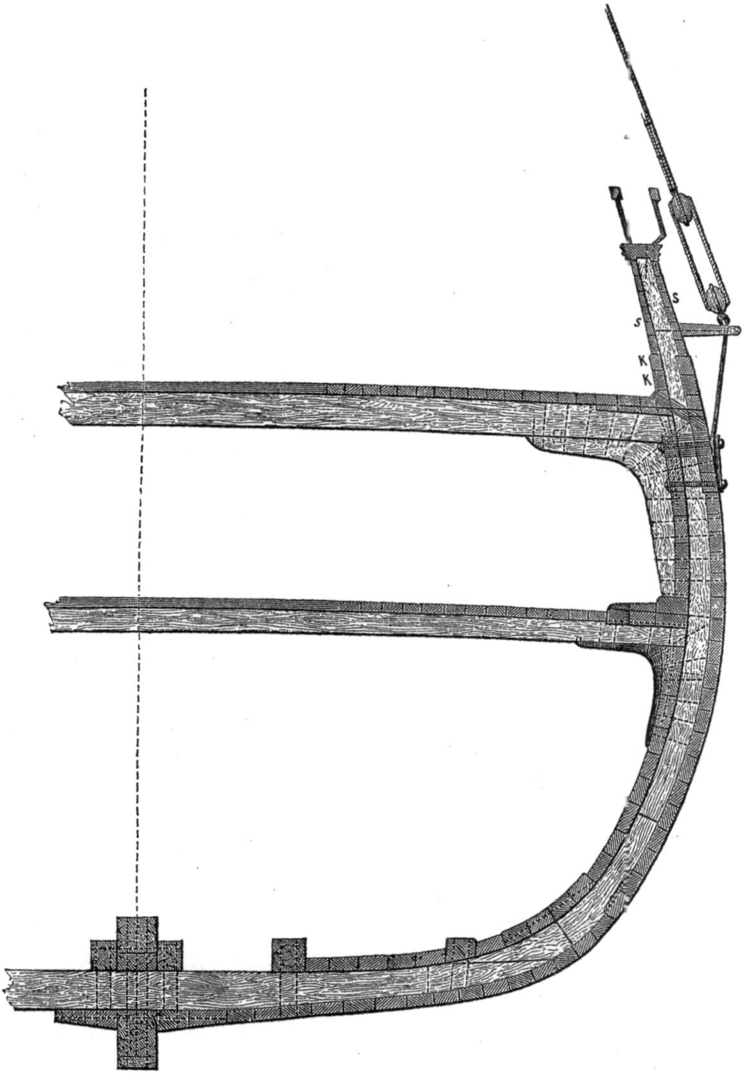

Vertical Transverse Section of the U. S. Steamer *Omaha*, at ⊕

remaining strakes are put in after the decks have been framed, and water-ways put in.

Great care has to be taken *to see that no butt of any inside plank comes on the same frame, and opposite to a butt of the outside planking.*

All short fastening for any inside work is driven near the edge of the plank, but in the middle of the timber, so as not to interfere with the fastening from the outside, as all through bolts from the outside rivet on these planks.

The length of the short fastening is about 2⅛ times the thickness of the plank through which it is driven; but in no case should they go through the frame by one inch after being punched in one-half inch from the face of the plank.

BILGE-STRAKES.

(*h*, Fig. 45.)

Bilge-strakes are strakes of heavy white oak or yellow pine plank worked over the floor-heads and first futtock-heads, running the entire length of the vessel.

In the vessel shown, there are two strakes over the floor-heads, filling the space to the outer keelson, and four strakes at the first futtock-head. Each strake is temporarily fastened with one iron bolt driven near the edge of the strake, but in the middle of each timber, the butts having two bolts in each. These strakes are also bolted edgewise in every room, and rivetted on rings on the lower edge of the bottom strake.

THICK-STRAKES.

(*g*, Fig. 45.)

The thick-strakes are the same thickness as the bilge-strakes, but are worked over the abutments of the second and fourth futtocks; in the plan shown they are three in number, and are secured to the frame, and bolted edgewise, the same as the bilge-strakes. All the thick-strakes rise with the heads and heels of the timber, and abut under the berth-deck clamps.

CEILING.

(*f*, Fig. 45.)

Strakes of white oak plank, called ceiling, are worked between the bilge-strakes and thick-strakes, and thick-strakes and berth-deck clamps, about one inch less in thickness amidships, and short fastening enough is put in to hold it to its place until the outside or bottom plank is worked. The projecting edges of the bilge and thick-strakes are chamfered. Strakes of white oak or yellow pine plank, called ceiling, are also worked between the gun-deck clamps and berth-deck waterways.

CHAPTER V.

Outside Planking—Main Wales—Channel Wales—Middle Wales—Sheer Strakes —Outside Battery Plank—Garboard Strakes—Bottom Plank—Preparations for and Method of Planking—Upon the Fastening of the Outside Planking—Deck Plans—Deck Beams—Two-Piece Beam—Iron Beams—Knees used to secure the Beams to the side of the Ship—The Fastenings of the Knees—Regulating the Beams—Framing the Decks—Carlings—Framing of Mast Partners—Ledges—Waterways—Deck Thick Strakes—Framing of Hatches —Spirketing—Inside Battery Plank—Deck Stringers—Deck Plank—Stanchions.

OUTSIDE PLANKING.

The outside planking in square-sterned ships terminates abaft below the wing transom or gun-deck hook, in the rabbet of the stern-post, on the wing transom at the margin, or at the knuckle of the stern-timbers, and above the wing transom, or knuckle, at the after-edge of the side counter-timber, and forward in the rabbet of the stem.

In vessels with round or elliptical sterns the outside planking terminates abaft, in the rabbet of the stern-post below, and above, in the rabbet formed by a projection of the centre counter-timber, or when the vessel has a propeller well, by allowing the counter-timbers that form the side of the well to project below far enough to form a rabbet; above the projection of the centre counter-timber, the plank runs entirely around the stern. The length of the ship is too great for the strakes to be obtained in one length; each strake is, therefore, composed of several, and the place at which they meet lengthwise is called the butt; the foremost and aftermost plank in each strake are called the fore and after hood, and the extreme ends where they abut against the forepart of the rabbet of the stem and after-part of the rabbet of the stern-post, are called the hooding-ends.

When the edges of the strakes curve up or down, they are said to *hang*, or *sny;* if down, to hang, and if up, to sny.

The strakes are not parallel, but of such a breadth as the form of the place where they are situated, and the circumference of the body at any given distances upon them, may require; narrowing at some places and widening, technically called *fanning*, at others, according as the body requires the form of the edges to hang or sny.

The principal strakes or assemblages of strakes that compose the exterior planking on three-decked ships-of-war, are the channel wales, middle wales, and main wales; in two-decked ships-of-war, such as the *Wabash* and *Franklin*, the channel wales and main wales; in sloops-of-war and all single gun-deck ships, such as the *Omaha* and *Juniata*, the main wales only. Channel wales are often called strings. The other principal strakes which all ships have, are sheer-strakes, bottom-plank, and garboard-strakes.

MAIN WALES.

(*p*, Fig. 45.)

The main wales are an assemblage of planks placed upon the widest part of the body, extending the whole length of the vessel, from the lower port-sill of the gun-deck to the bottom plank; they are the thickest planking and form one of the principal longitudinal ties, as much from their situation as their substance.

The fastening of the principal deck pass through them. The first seven strakes below the gun-deck port-sills in all our steam sloops-of-war and frigates, from abreast the fore-mast to abreast the mizzen-mast, are worked 1¼ inches thicker, and jog that much between the frames, for which the edges of the timbers are carefully trimmed, and sometimes a rabbet is cut for it on the bevelling edge of the timbers. The upper edge of these strakes which project into the room are chamfered, that dirt may not lay on it. The thickness of the wales diminishes gradually from abreast the fore-mast and mizzen-mast to the stem and stern. In like manner, two strakes between the 2d and 3d futtock heads are increased in thickness 1¼ inches amidships and jog that much between the frames. From the port-sill to the light water-line the wale-strakes should not exceed eight inches in width for vessels of the *Omaha*, *Wabash* and *Antietam* class, increasing gradually in width not exceeding twelve inches under the flat of the bottom.

The plank under the bottom and all those subject to compression are in length from 35 to 40 feet, but the wales, clamps and spirketting, which are subject to extension, should be the longest plank, and are from 40 to 50 feet in length. In squaring off the timbers in planking the bottom, the round of the moulding edge is retained, and whatever it is necessary to take away, that the plank may lay solid against the timber, is taken out of the plank.

CHANNEL WALES.

(*o*, Fig. 45.)

The channel wales, sometimes called strings, consist of thick strakes placed between the spar and main-deck ports in ships of three decks, and gun and spar-deck ports in those of two decks; they receive the chain and preventer-plate bolts, and are intended to give strength to the top side or upper works. These strakes are increased 1½ inches in thickness, and jog that much between the frames as far forward and aft as good work can be made. In working the wales they are kept clear of the port-sills about ¾ of an inch to form a stop for the port-shutters.

MIDDLE WALES.

The middle wales consist of thick strakes, in three-decked ships placed between the main and lower gun-deck ports, giving additional strength to this class of ships.

SHEER STRAKES.

The sheer strakes are the first strakes worked, being the upper strake of main wales and upper and lower strake of channel wales or strings. The lower strake of channel wales or strings, and sheer strakes of main wales, can be seen on the frontispiece showing the *Antietam* in frame.

OUTSIDE BATTERY PLANK.

(S, Fig. 45.)

The different strakes that come between the ports are named according as they are situated; if in range of the gun-deck ports, they are called outside gun-deck batteries; if in range of the spar-deck ports, outside spar-deck batteries.

GARBOARD STRAKES.

(*r*, Fig. 45.)

The garboard strakes are the two strakes next the keel on each side, and are made thicker than the rest of the bottom plank.

These strakes diminish gradually in thickness, falling in fair upwards with the bottom plank, and forward and aft these strakes likewise wear into the thickness of the running plank of the bottom.

BOTTOM PLANK.

The bottom plank may be considered as the planking from the main wales to the garboard strakes, and should not exceed twelve inches in width. The thickness of the plank diminishes gradually from the thickness required for the wales to that for the bottom plank.

PREPARATIONS FOR AND METHOD OF PLANKING.

Before commencing to plank a ship, a representation of the plank, or, as it is termed, a shift of the butts of the plank, should be made on a board by the draughtsman, who, in making it, must have reference to the stock of plank in store before he determines the lengths of the plank or shifts to be made in planking the vessel: this board is furnished to the foreman of carpenters as a guide for him to work by. The best shift of butts of plank that can be made, is to have twelve strakes between butts on the same frame; and in no case should there be less than four strakes. (Fig. 49.)

The best plan yet adopted is to have a half-model of the vessel made to a scale and painted white; and on this the position of all the gun-ports, air-ports, scuppers, valves connected with the engines and boilers that will come through the bottom or side, diagonal bracing, lengths, widths, and shifts of butts of planking, can be marked; also the height of the line of copper fastening and copper sheathing line. Models of this description are used in many of our navy-yards.

Before commencing to put on the plank, thin broad battens called sheer battens are nailed around the ship at the sheer heights, and when properly regulated, the line is razed or cut in across each timber; and it is to this line that the edge of the sheer strakes and wales are first set.

A strake of plank can now be worked near each of the ribbands; and when on and fastened, the ribbands can be removed, and several gangs of workmen can be employed advantageously in getting out and working the remainder of the plank required to fill up the openings.

In working the bottom plank and wales, the endeavor of the workmen should be to bring the plank to the timbers without forcing it upwards to the edge of that already worked; or, in other words, edge sets should be used as little as possible, as the

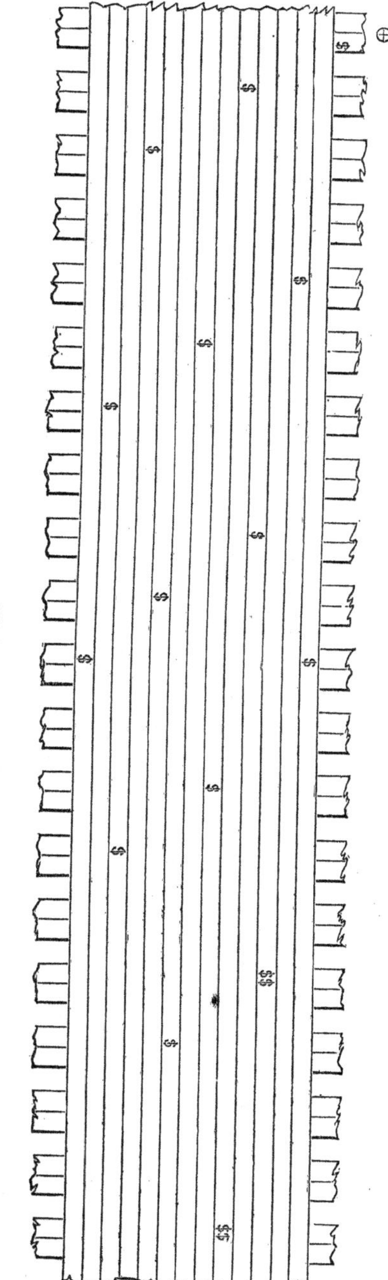

FIG. 49.

planking that would bear bending one way may be easily broken by an attempt to force it in an opposite direction. Moreover, in working the plank, should the edges be bruised, and the bruised portions not removed, early decay will be likely to ensue from the injury that the grain of the wood has received. One reason why the butts of plank are often found to be decayed before the other portion, is, that in working the plank, it is required to be forced towards the plank ahead of it, and by striking with a maul or sledge, in order to diminish the opening of the butt, the grain of the wood is bruised, and early decay ensues, a piece should always be held on the end of the strake to strike against. In working the first strakes of planking, the sirmarks are the best guides to run the strakes on by, as they all give a normal or natural line; and the intermediate strakes, if properly lined and worked, will require little, if any, edge set.

Where the plank requires considerable bending to make it fit to its place, it is got out to the proper shape and bevel, and then placed in a steam-box, and steamed until it can be bent readily to its place, when it is taken out and worked. Enough short fastening is put in the plank as it is worked, to hold it to its place, as it cannot be fastened for good, until the inside planking, water-ways, thick strakes of deck and knees are all worked, as all the through fastening from the outside will rivet on these planks and knees.

UPON THE FASTENING OF THE OUTSIDE PLANKING.

As naval vessels have all the outside planking, strings, wales and bottom plank, double or square fastened, I will describe the manner in which the *Antietam* is fastened, which will answer for all.

All the outside planking, strings, wales and bottom plank, will be double or square fastened, that is, there will be two through and two short fastenings in each frame.

The length of the short fastenings will be about $2\frac{1}{8}$ times the thickness of the plank through which it is driven, but in no case are they to go through the frame timbers by one inch; after being punched in one-half inch from the face of the plank, all through bolts of whatever kind are riveted on rings. Whenever a knee bolt, a water-way, or hook bolt, or any through bolt, will take its place, the fastening from the outside is omitted.

In the frame next on each side that on which the plank butts, in lieu of one of the short fastenings, in the timber next the butt, there is a through bolt placed called a butt-bolt.

In the hood-ends forward and aft, when they can be got through, through-bolts are driven and riveted on alternate sides. When the plank is reduced in width to six inches, one half of the short-fastenings are omitted, and the remainder is placed in the alternate edges.

The copper fastening in the *Antietam* extends up to within six and one-half feet of the lower port-sill, above which it is all of iron, except the counter immediately over the propeller, which is copper fastened.

The battery-plank between the ports have one through bolt and two short fastenings in each frame, called cross-fastenings; but the frame next the ports are square-fastened, care being taken to keep the fastenings in these strakes clear of the gun-tackle bolts.

Below the copper-fastening line, treenails made of seasoned locust are sometimes used; two treenails, one through bolt, and one short fastening, are put in each frame; above the copper line two through bolts and two short fastenings of iron are always used. If treenails are used, five strakes of plank on the turn of the bilge for the length occupied by the engine and boilers, should have two treenails and two through bolts in every other frame. All treenails are caulked outside and wedged on the face of the inside plank.

The heads of all bolts driven from the outside are carefully trimmed and driven home with a swedge or punch, so as not to bruise the plank; no plugs are put over the heads of bolts outside below the lower port-sill.

Where the fillings are of sufficient size, or the floor-timbers fill the space, the plank is fastened to them with additional treenails or bolts.

White oak is used for the strings, wales, bottom plank, and garboard strakes; yellow pine generally for the outside battery plank.

The methods of working plank, denominated "top and butt" and "anchor stock," is never carried out in this country. Many years ago this method was practiced in England, where a great scarcity of timber of the proper length for plank existed; but few, if any, vessels are planked in that way in European countries at the present time.

After the vessel is planked, the projecting edges of the strakes are all trimmed off, called squaring-off; the seams are caulked by

FIG. 50.

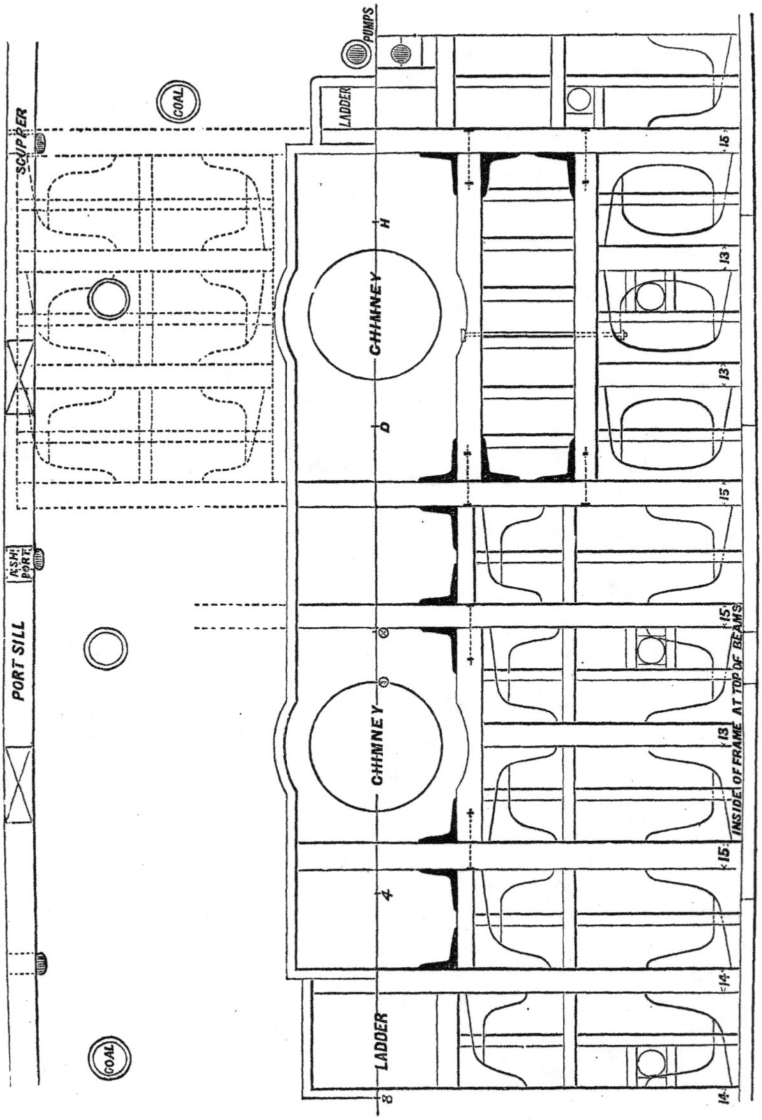
PUMPS
COAL
SCUPPER
LADDER
CHIMNEY
H
D
ASH PORT
PORT SILL
CHIMNEY
4
INSIDE OF FRAME AT TOP OF BEAMS
LADDER
COAL
15
13
13
15
15
13
15
14
14

the caulkers, and afterwards planed smooth and fair, and a coat of paint or oil put on, to keep the air from it, and prevent its rending or splitting.

DECK PLANS.

(Figs. 50, 51, and 52.)

Before the beams can be worked out and the decks framed, a plan must be made for each deck, showing the location of the beams, half-beams, framing for bowsprit-bitts, mooring-bitts, mast partners, nippers, capstan, chain-pipes, pumps, coal-scuttles and towing-bitts, fore-and-aft pieces for hatches, carlings, ledges, deck-hooks, lodging and bosom knees at end of beams, and to fore-and-aft pieces of hatches and mast-partners. On the starboard side of this deck plan, the framing of the parts mentioned above should be shown, and the location of the deck-beams with regard to the joints of the different frames, can be readily ascertained, and their position marked to correspond on top of the deck-clamps; on the port side the deck plan should be represented as laid, showing also the water-ways and deck thick-strakes, with proper shift of butts, position of hawse-pipes, manger-board, nippers, water-closets for officers and men, gun-ports, coal-scuttles, pumps, mast-coamings, bitts and sill-pieces for the bulkheads to cabin and rooms inside, coamings and head ledges of hatches.

That portion of the deck framing on the port-side and inside of the fore-and-aft piece of the boiler and engine hatch, should be framed in such a manner that it can be removed readily to put in the boilers. (Fig. 50.)

DECK BEAMS.

Deck beams are made of yellow pine, white oak, hackmatack and white pine. Yellow pine is used in preference to the others for all the beams of the berth, gun, and spar decks, but hackmatack is sometimes used for the short beams of these decks forward and aft, also for the forecastle deck. White pine or hackmatack is used for the poop-deck beams.

They vary in siding and moulding sizes according to the dimensions of the vessel, and the weight of the battery to be carried on the deck. In the *Wabash* and class, the dimensions for beams are as follows:—Berth-deck, 16×13 inches; gun-deck,

$17 \times 14\frac{1}{2}$ inches; spar-deck, 16×13 inches. In the *Antietam* and class—berth-deck, $13\frac{1}{2} \times 11\frac{1}{2}$ inches; gun-deck, $14 \times 12\frac{1}{2}$ inches; spar-deck, $12\frac{1}{2} \times 8\frac{1}{2}$ inches. *Congress* and class—berth-deck, 13×11 inches; spar-deck, $14 \times 12\frac{1}{2}$ inches. The beams are moulded one inch less at the ends than at the centre. [In the dimensions given above the siding size is given first.] The beams to the engine and boiler hatches, and those next forward and aft of the fore and main masts are made an inch or two larger than the others in siding and moulding sizes.

The deck-beams have to hold the sides of the ship in their places, and prevent them from parting. To make the most effectual combination of the beams with the sides of the ship is of the first consequence, both as regards the safety of the ship and the comfort of the officers and crew, since upon this strength the transverse strength chiefly depends; for it has to sustain the whole force and working of the side, when acted upon by the weight of the guns, stress of the masts when under a press of sail, and pressure of the water when the ship is inclined by the force of the wind or rolling.

The stresses that act upon the side of the ship have a tendency principally to separate the sides from the beams, and to cause successive variation of the angle formed, transversely, by the side of the ship and the beams, which produces the working.

To give the best disposition to the fastenings that form the combination of the side with the beams, so as to oppose the greatest resistance to separation, they must be placed as much in a line with the beams as practicable, for they will be acted upon by a greater force, in degrees proportionate to the distance they are above or below them.

To prevent working, such modes of security should be applied, that while they oppose the change of form, they may resist when motion takes place, the alteration bringing a transverse action on the fastenings, which soon destroys the compactness of the connection.

The stations of the beams having been marked on the top strake of clamps, the length of each one is obtained by first stretching a line across the ship at their several stations, and then sliding out the arms of a rule made for this purpose, called a sliding-rule, until the ends touch the inside of the timbers of the frame, care being taken to keep the rule up to the line.

The lengths of all the beams can be marked on this batten before any of them are marked from it. The ends of each beam are cut to the bevel or angle made by the line and inside of the timber in a vertical direction called the up-and-down bevel and the angle made by the line and inside of timber in a fore-and-aft direction, called the fore-and-aft bevel. The bevels as they are taken are marked on a board called a bevel-board.

The beams are now cut to correspond to the lengths and bevels just obtained, and when completed they are carried to the vessel and placed at their stations on the clamps.

The berth-deck beams are generally got in place first.

The ends of the beams are dove-tailed down into the clamp from one to one-and-a-half inches, the dove-tailed tenon being cut on the lower side of the beam and the corresponding mortise out of the clamp. When the dove-tails are cut the beams are driven down into them and two bolts driven down through it into the clamps.

TWO-PIECE BEAM.

It sometimes happens that the longest beams for vessels of the *Wabash* and *Franklin* class, have to be made in two pieces; in such a case the scarph is vertical and in length one-third the whole length of the beam, the nibs of the scarphs are cut in only one-third of their thickness, or about two inches. The lips of the scarph has two rows of seasoned coaks, $12 \times 8\frac{1}{2} \times 2\frac{3}{4}$ inches, about 12 inches asunder, let in on the alternate edges; fastened with iron bolts about $1\frac{1}{4}$ inches in diameter, about 15 inches asunder and set up with nuts and washers. The nibs are secured with small bolts or spikes.

IRON BEAMS.

Iron beams were first employed in steamships above the engine and boilers, and their superior qualities in respect of strength and durability, together with the facilities presented for firmly connecting them with the sides of the ship, soon led to their general adoption in England and France. According to calculations made by M. Dupuy de Lôme, and given in his report, the weights of iron and wood beams of equal strength (for the section of iron beams then in use) are in the proportion of .65 : 1, or 1.2 : 1. This latter proportion, which makes the iron beam heavier than the wood beam, is deducted from a very defective form of section, and in all other cases given by the author the iron beam is the lighter. On account of the superior fastenings in the hull of an iron ship the number of beams can be considerably decreased, and thus a great reduction of weight be effected, while at the same time the strength of the ship as a whole is considerably greater than could possibly be attained in a wooden ship. During the past year many of our monitors having iron hulls have had the old wooden deck beams removed and replaced by iron ones, and this will require to be done on all of them before they can be again brought into active service.

KNEES USED TO SECURE THE BEAMS TO THE SIDE OF THE SHIP.

(Figs. 50 and 51.)

The mode of securing the beams to the side, in general use, is by lodging, lap and hanging knees, where one of each is placed to every beam end. The hanging knees are secured to the under-side of the beam and to the side of the ship, with the plane of its side vertical or in the same plane with the side of the beam. (See Fig. 45.) That part of the knee which lies under and against the beam is called the arm, and the part which lies against the clamps or side, the body. The lengths of the arms in sloops-of-war and frigates should not be less than 4½ feet, and the bodies 6 feet for those under the berth-deck beams; the bodies of those under the gun-deck beams should reach the berth-deck water-ways, and the bodies of those of the spar-deck beams should reach the spirketting of the gun-deck.

The lodging knees (see Fig. 50) are secured to the forward side of the beams, lying with the body on top of the clamp and fayed out against the inside of the frame. The lap or bosom knees are seen secured to the opposite side of the beams fayed to the inside of the body of the lodging knees.

When a beam comes over a port, so that the plane of the side of the knee could not be in the same plane with the side of the beam without lying before it, the knee is brought with the plane of its side diagonally from the beam, when it is called a dagger knee. (Fig. 41 and 43.)

In the *Wabash*, *Merrimac*, and class, the knees to the beam ends are disposed as follows:—The berth-deck beams have one lodging and one dagger knee to each end of every beam, in addition to which the partner beams of the main-mast and the one next on each side of it has a hanging knee at each end. The dagger knees incline from the aft side of the beams which are forward of the centre of the ship and from the fore side of the beams abaft. The throats of these knees are trimmed so as to look fore-and-aft, that is, in a parallel direction with the bottom of the beam, and with the clamps so that the lower corner on the arm will not hang below the beam.

The gun-deck beams have two lodge and one hanging knee to each end of one beam, and two dagger knees at each end of the next beam; the bodies of the hanging knees run down to the water-ways, the dagger knees mitre against the hanging knees. The spar-deck beams are kneed off precisely the same as those of the gun-deck, with this exception, the hanging knees of this deck are over those beams of the gun-deck which have two dagger knees; and in many cases the dagger knees run down to the water-ways. By this method every other beam has three knees at each end.

The knees are of white oak and hackmatack, and vary in siding size according to the dimensions of the vessel and location of them.

THE FASTENINGS OF THE KNEES.

The arms of the knees, when practicable, have two round coaks in the beams three inches in diameter. The bolts that fasten the bodies of the knees, distinguished as in-and-out bolts, in the hanging knees are generally seven in number, including the throat-bolt. The bodies of the lodge and lap knees have one bolt in each timber of the frame that they cross, also one bolt through the lodging knee into the clamp opposite each opening of the frame. The arms of the hanging knees have not less than five bolts driven from the top of the beams and riveted on rings on the knees. The arms of the lodge and lap knees have not less than five fore-and-aft bolts driven and riveted on rings on alternate sides of the arms of the knees.

All in-and-out bolts are driven from the outside of the wales and riveted on rings on the face of the bodies of the knees, excepting the throat bolts which are blunt bolts, and are driven from the face of the knees.

The knees of the orlop-deck beams, and sometimes those of the berth-deck when below the copper line, are fastened before the vessel is planked outside, as it saves considerable expense, iron fastening being used instead of copper, driven from the outside of frame; when iron hanging knees are used for the berth-deck beams in the space occupied by engine and boilers, the in-

and-out bolts are of iron driven from the outside of frame and riveted on the knees. (See Fig. 48.)

Within the past three years, iron hanging knees have been used for vessels with light spar-decks.

In a side-wheel steamer, the deck beams which project beyond the side of the vessel forward and aft of the paddle-wheels, and forming the foundation on which the guards and paddle-boxes rest, are called the guard-beams; the outside of the paddle-boxes are supported by the spring-beams, the ends resting on and secured to the guard-beam next forward and aft of the wheels. The guards are supported on the outside by hanging knees and heavy iron rods called guard-braces.

REGULATING THE BEAMS.

The beams being in and secured, are temporarily shored up, that is, temporary stanchions are placed under the centre of each beam, commencing with the berth-deck, which are shored from the top of the keelson, and the tops regulated: the beams of the decks above are shored and regulated from those next below. The spring or round-up of beams varies from 3 to 6 inches in the *Wabash* and *Antietam's* decks.

FRAMING OF DECKS.

The deck framing which, in addition to the beams and half-beams, consists chiefly of fore-and-aft pieces for hatchways, carlings and ledges, should now be put in according to the plans furnished for the several decks.

The fore-and-aft pieces of the engine and boiler hatches (Fig. 50), are first put in place in order that the half-beams which have their midships ends let into and supported by them, may be put in place. By reference to the plan (Fig. 50), it will be seen that the half-beams are secured to the fore-and-aft pieces, with a lodging and a lap knee on the outside, at the end of each beam; and an iron knee is placed on the inside of the fore-and-aft piece in either corner of the hatch, and securely fastened through the beams, fore-and-aft pieces and knees, the bolts being driven and riveted on alternate sides.

The fore-and-aft pieces for the remaining hatchways, carlings, framing for bitts, mast partners, nippers, capstan, chain pipes, pumps, &c., are now let down between the beams with a double

MAIN FIFE RAIL
TOPSAIL SHEET
BITT
COAMINGS
HEAD LEDGE
MAST COAMING
MAST
CROSS PARTNER
CORNER CHOCK
FORE AND AFT.
PARTNERS
CARLING
LEDGE
DECK BEAM
CARLING
LEDGE
DECK BEAM
LAPOR BOSOM KNEE
LODGING KNEE
DECK
CLAMPS
72
71
70
69
FRAME

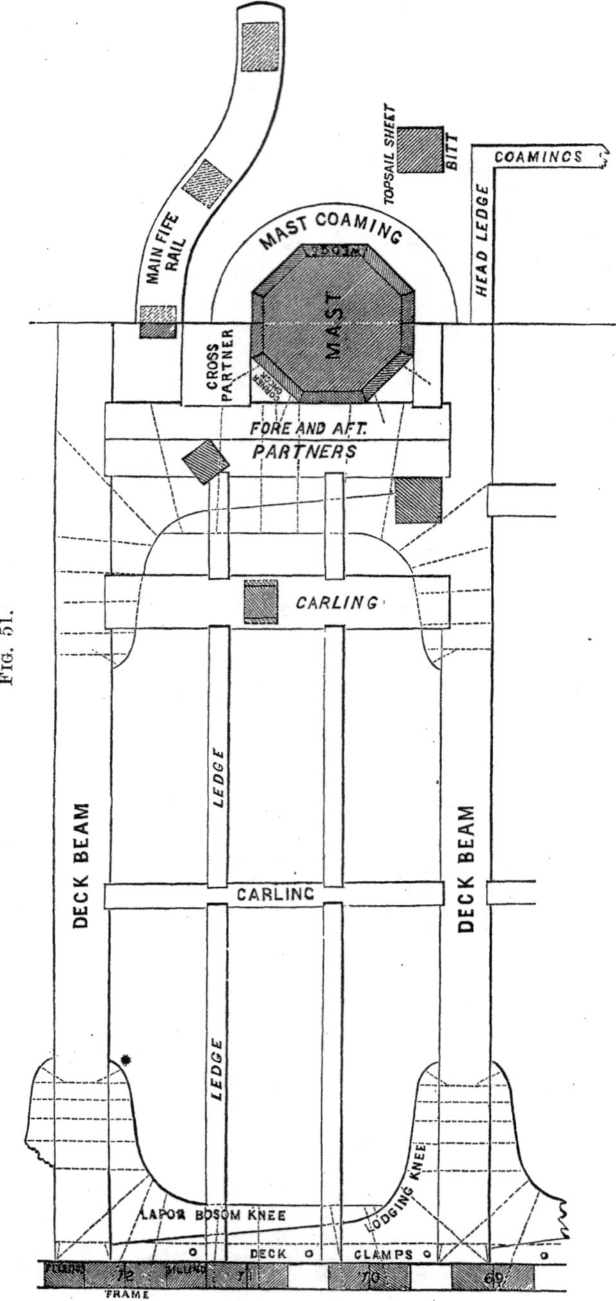

Fig. 51.

jog or shoulder, being cut in on top, from one and one-eighth to one and one-half inches from the face or side of the beam.

CARLINGS.

The carlings are in tiers ranging fore-and-aft between the beams, and vary in number and size according to the deck and dimensions of the vessel. In all sloops-of-war and frigates there are four tiers; the inside ones are kept nearly in line with the fore-and-aft pieces for the hatchways. The outside tiers are arranged in a curved line, keeping nearly parallel to the inside of the frame; this adds to the appearance of the deck-frame, and makes the most economical distribution of timber, inasmuch as the equality of lengths, which there will be in the ledges, is a saving of timber. The carlings are of yellow pine and hackmatack.

FRAMING OF MAST PARTNERS.

(Fig. 51.)

The framing of a mast-hole, where wedges are used, is composed of fore-and-aft partners, cross-partners, and corner-chocks; they are of white or live oak. The ends of the fore-and-aft partners are let down into the beams, and have a lodge and a lap-knee on the outside securely fastened to them. The cross-partners are placed athwartship, between the fore-and-aft partners; they are let down into them at the ends with a double jog. The corner chocks come in the angles made by the insides of the fore-and-aft and cross partners, to which they are secured with blunt bolts. Coamings several inches in height above the deck-plank are placed around each mast-hole and fastened to the partners.

The framing or fore-and-aft stuff forming the beds for bitts, nippers, capstan, and chain pipes are generally of white or live oak. The fore-and-aft pieces of hatches are of white oak or yellow pine, and in some cases mahogany has been used.

In many of our vessels the fore-and-aft pieces to the hatches are secured with a lodge and a lap-knee.

LEDGES.

(Fig. 51.)

The ledges are of yellow pine or hackmatack, and placed between the beams. In some cases there is but one, but many vessels have two between each beam, especially in a deck where a heavy battery is to be carried; they extend from carling to carling, and from carling to the throat of the knees, lying parallel to the beams, and with a common distance between them; they are cut in on to the carlings with a double jog, a little less than the carlings are on to the beams.

The various operations of putting in the water-ways, deck thick strakes, and framing of hatches, may now be proceeded with.

WATER-WAYS.

(*d*, Fig. 45.)

The water-ways are pieces lying in the angle made by the top of the deck beams and the inside of the frame timbers, extending the whole length of the ship; they are bevelled off on their face, on the gun-decks, from the thickness of the spirketing to that of the thick strakes, in order that the forward gun-trucks may lay closer to it, and thus allow of more lateral train to the guns.

On the berth-deck the inside edge is square, and projects above the thick strakes. The pieces forward and aft, where there is considerable shape, are of white or live oak, the remainder are of yellow pine. In some cases the pieces are joined together with a vertical scarph, but generally abut each other. They are dove-tailed down over the ends of the beams two inches, and secured with one up-and-down bolt through each beam; one between the beams through the knees into the clamps, and one in each beam, driven at an angle into the frame.

DECK THICK STRAKES.

(*c*, Fig. 45.)

The deck thick strakes are the first two or three strakes next inside the water-ways, and are generally about two inches thicker than the deck plank; they extend from about twenty feet before the foremast to twenty feet abaft the mizzen-mast. They are either jogged or dove-tailed down two inches over the beams; the entire depth of the rabbet or dove-tail being cut out of the beam, but on the ledges there is one inch taken out of the thick strakes, and one inch out of the ledges. In most vessels there are three strakes to each deck; the strakes of the spar and gun-deck show no projection above the deck-plank, but on the berth-deck they dove-tail or jog down one and one-half inches into the beam, and usually project four and one-half inches above the berth-deck plank.

These strakes are secured with two bolts in each beam, and two spikes in the ledges; also, with one bolt through every other frame, driven from the outside through frame and water-ways, and riveted on rings on the projecting edges, above or below the deck, as the case may be, so that in repairing the vessel they can be easily backed out.

FRAMING OF HATCHES.

Hatches are framed of four pieces, two placed fore-and-aft, called coamings, and two placed athwartships, called head-ledges. The head-ledges rest on the beams, and the coamings on the fore-and-aft pieces, placed there for that purpose, reaching from beam to beam. The fore-and-aft pieces are worked three inches wider than the coamings, to form a support for the strake of deck-plank that comes on it.

The coamings and head-ledges are chined in above the deck to form a water-course around the hatchway, and are reduced in thickness at the top. The head-ledges and coamings are coaked to the fore-and-aft pieces and beams with round coaks, and when of more than one piece in height above the deck, to each other. In many instances the fore-and-aft pieces for hatches are rabbeted out on the top, leaving a projection of about one-half an inch above the deck-frame (on the inside edge), and the coamings are rabbeted so as to fit over it; this is done to resist the pressure in caulking. The same plan is followed on each piece composing the hatch, and in addition to this the coaks before spoken of are put in. The bolts in the coamings and head-ledges are driven so as to pass through the coaks. The corners of them are dove-tailed together; they are secured with one bolt through each corner, and about eighteen inches asunder, through the head-ledge and coamings, being riveted on rings on the under-side of the beams and fore-and-aft pieces.

The height of the hatch-coamings varies in different ships and on different decks; those on the gun-deck are always the highest, and are from 26 to 30 inches in height.

The hatch coamings either have a rabbet taken out of them to receive the gratings or an ash plank called a capping is placed on top of the coaming, of the same thickness as the depth of the grating, and it is kept back from the inside edge of the coaming, so as to form a rabbet for the gratings; on the spar-deck iron canopy rails are fitted to the forward hatches, and brass to those of the cabin, ward-room and steerage hatches.

When the hatchways are covered, as is the case with the cabin hatch of the yacht *America*, and others, the covering is called a booby-hatch.

SPIRKETING.

(*k*, Figs. 45 and 48.)

The spirketing are composed of thick strakes lying immediately above the water-way on the gun and spar decks, filling up the space from the water-way to the port-sill. On the berth-deck three strakes under the beams are called clamps, and from that to the water-ways is called ceiling.

INSIDE BATTERY PLANK.

(*s*, Figs. 45 and 48.)

The space between the clamps and spirketing on the gun-deck, and the rail and spirketing on the spar-decks, is filled in with oak plank, called inside gun or spar-deck batteries.

Before the hanging-knees are placed under the beams, the water-ways, spirketing, and inside batteries of gun-deck, and ceiling between gun-deck clamps and berth-deck water-ways, must be worked, as the bodies of the knees come over these strakes and fasten through them.

DECK STRINGERS.

Just outside of the coamings of the hatches, on the gun and spar decks, there are generally three or four strakes of plank worked one inch thicker than the deck-plank and jogged that much over the beams, a rabbet being cut on the beam, and the plank carefully fitted over it; the score is taken out of the ledges, and not from the plank; these strakes are called deck stringers.

In some cases a round coak is put in each strake where it crosses the beams. The gun-tackle bolts and deck-stopper bolts are generally placed in these strakes. In some cases they are of white oak, but generally of yellow pine, the same as the rest of the deck plank.

DECK PLANK.

(*b*, Fig. 45.)

The deck plank fills up the space between the deck stringers and deck thick strakes at the sides and between the hatches amidships. The strake running directly through the centre of the deck is generally one-half an inch thicker and wider than the rest, the projection being above the deck, the stanchions which support the deck beams step upon it.

The deck plank is fastened with two spikes in each beam, and one in each ledge that the strake crosses.

All the fastening in the deck plank, deck thick strakes, waterways, spirketing, inside and outside batteries of the gun and spar-decks and channel wales is started in about three-fourths of an inch below the surface, and wooden plugs are dipped in white-lead and then driven in over the heads of the spikes and bolts. These plugs should be made of the same kind of wood as the work they are to be used in, and in putting them in place care should be taken to see that the grain of the wood is in the same direction with that of the strake.

STANCHIONS.

(Figs. 41 and 43.)

The stanchions under the gun and spar-deck beams are of locust or white oak turned and fitted with an iron shoe and cap; those under the beams in the ward-room and cabin are of iron, from 2½ to 3 inches in diameter, and are generally placed one on each side, inside of the line of the bulkheads of state-rooms, leaving a clear space for the table in the centre; these stanchions have metal caps and shoes.

Those in the vicinity of the capstan are also of iron, hinged above, and made to throw up and secure above when the capstan is in use; those to the berth-deck beams are made square, and rest on the centre keelson, the heel being tenoned into the capping, and a wooden cap is placed on the head of it, under the beam, the head of the stanchion being tenoned into it; the cap is spiked to the beam when the stanchions are in place; the metal caps and shoes are secured with large screws to the beams and centre strake of deck.

CHAPTER VI.

Fastenings near the Binnacle—Bitts—Bowsprit Bitts—Mooring or Cable Bitts —Topsail-Sheet Bitts—Towing Bitts—Orlop-Decks—Bulkheads—Poop and Top-Gallant Forecastle Decks—Number and Names of Decks—Bulwarks—Hammock Nettings—Hawse Holes—Manger Board and Manger—Scuppers —Air Ports—Controllers—Compressor—Channels—Cutwater or Head—Gripe—Caulking—Sheathing Vessels with Copper and Yellow Metal.

RULE TO OBTAIN THE SCANTLING OR SIDING SIZES OF THE TIMBER USED IN THE CONSTRUCTION OF WOODEN VESSELS-OF-WAR.

Multiply the moulded breadth of beam by the following decimals for the siding size, in inches and parts of an inch, viz.:—*

Siding size of keel	.42	Hanging knees	.26
Siding size of frame	.28	Deck plank	.1
Moulded square at floor heads	..	Bottom plank	.1
Moulded at throat	.42	Wales and clamps	.15
Moulded at rail	.16	Cable-bitts	.45
Gun-deck beams	.35 to .38	Bowsprit	.4
Spar- " .95 of gun-deck	..	Mast partners	.3
Ledges	.18	Catheads	.4
Carlings	.2	Stanchions in hold	.22
Lodge and lap knees	.18	Stanchions between decks	.2
6 Hanging knees under beams amidships	.7	Coamings	.16
		Timber and Room	.75

FASTENINGS NEAR THE BINNACLES.

All the hatches, decks, and knees in the vicinity of the binnacles are fastened with copper bolts and composition spikes, generally eight feet from the centre of the binnacle each way.

BITTS.

The bowsprit, mooring or cable-bitts, topsail sheet, and towing bitts should all be worked out and secured in their several positions before the decks are laid.

BOWSPRIT BITTS.

The bowsprit bitts are two in number, standing athwartships, and far enough apart to receive the heel of the bowsprit; a chock is dove-tailed into the bitts over the bowsprit to hold it down to

* Rule used by Naval Constructor S. M. Pook, U. S. N.

MANGER.
MANGER BOARD
WATER CLOSET.
WATER CLOSET.
CAPSTAN
PORT-SILL
PORT SILL
CABLE BITT
KNEE
MODERN CAST IRON CABLE BITT
WOODEN BITT WITH IRON CAP
LADDER
MODERN PLAN IN LIEU OF ROUND PIPE
CHAIN SCUTTLE
GALLEY
PIPE
HOLD

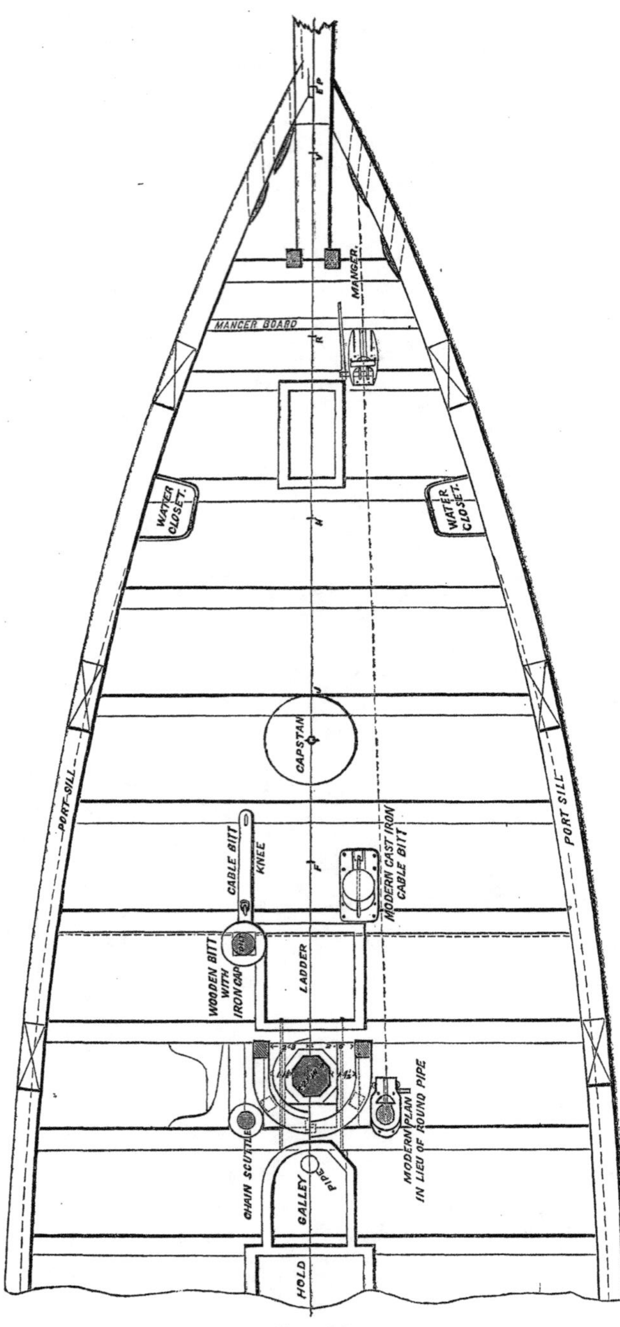

FIG. 52.

its place. They are generally made of live or white oak, and extend from the underside of the top-gallant forecastle or spar-decks to the berth-deck in nearly all vessels-of-war, being scored over and bolted to the gun and berth-deck beams, forward of which they are placed; between the gun and berth-decks they are tapered. In some cases they do not run below the gun-deck. (See Fig. 41.)

MOORING OR CABLE-BITTS.

(Fig. 41, No. 3, and Fig. 52.)

Sloops-of-war and frigates are always fitted with two pair of mooring or cable-bitts on the gun-deck, extending from about three and one-half feet above the gun-deck to the berth-deck beams, being square above and tapered below from the lower side of gun-deck beams to the heel of the bitt; they are scored over and bolted to the beams of both decks. These bitts have a heavy piece of white or live oak timber in front of them, called standards or cable-bitt-knees, being jogged over the beams about two inches, coaked to the fore-and-aft pieces below, and securely fastened to the bitts and beams. There is one ring-bolt placed in the throat of the standards or knees, and one in the next beam, called chain-stopper bolts, and an eye-bolt in the fore end of the knees to hook a tackle in.

These bitts have a cylindrical iron casting over the head of them, with worm flanges cast on them for the cable to rest on, and, as a support to the flanges, pieces of oak are fayed under them and fastened to the bitts; above the flanges, a round iron pin, called a bitt-pin, is placed to prevent the cable from flying off of the bitts when veering rapidly.

In many of our modern vessels, in lieu of the bitts running through the decks, cast iron cable-bitts, with thick broad flanges to secure them by, are used (see Fig. 52). Heavy fore-and-aft pieces of white or live oak are placed between the beams, under the bitts, and the bolts which secure them in place, are driven from the top of the flange and riveted on plates or set up with nuts and washers below; above the flange on the forward side of the bitts, there is a projection to receive the after ends of the supporters, but they are seldom if ever used, as they are deemed sufficiently strong without them; a cavil is placed through the bitt to hold up the parts of the chain, and a bitt-pin above to prevent the chain from flying off when veering rapidly. These cast-iron bitts are used in connection with Brown's Patent Capstan, and are generally used at the present time.

The deck stopper-bolts generally range with the outside of the after pair of bitts, one being placed in each beam from the chain-pipes to the cable-bitts, and riveted on plates under the beam.

TOPSAIL SHEET BITTS.

(Fig. 51.)

The topsail-sheet bitts are generally of locust, and extend to the deck below, tapered between decks; they should stand nearly plumb, placed in the angle of the fore-and-aft partners, and aft side of beam next forward of the masts, secured to the deck beams of both decks.

The bitts should have composition caps and corner pieces, a lignumvitæ cavil through the head, to belay the sheet; eye-bolt for a stopper in the fore side near the deck, and sheaved that the sheets may lead aft.

TOWING BITTS.

Towing bitts are usually of live oak, and are placed directly abaft the mizzen-mast, on the main-deck, against the partner beam; they extend to the deck below, tapered between decks and secured to the beams of both decks; the heads are sometimes fitted with a cylindrical casting, but usually have composition caps, corner pieces, and a heavy bitt-pin.

ORLOP DECKS.

(Figs. 41 and 43.)

The orlop-deck beams require no clamps to rest on; the ends of the beams fay against the timbers and thick strakes, having, in large vessels, one lodging and one hanging knee at the end of each beam, fastened through the bottom with copper and through the beams with iron bolts.

The hatchways of this deck are usually closed with tight hatch covers, provided with iron hatch-bars to secure and lock them up.

In vessels having no regular orlop-deck, light yellow pine beams are fayed against the thick strakes or ceiling with fore-and-aft pieces let in between, instead of a lodging knee, for the purpose of holding the edge of the deck plank up, and on these a light white pine deck is laid. There is also a deck of white pine, about three inches in thickness, laid on top of the keelsons on either side of the main keelson from the engine space forward and aft.

In the space occupied by the boilers this is used to set the boilers on; forward, it answers for the flooring, for the shell-rooms, magazines and chain-lockers; aft, for a flooring for after-hold magazines and shell-rooms.

A bulkhead is usually run up on either side of the shaft-alley, and when there is no regular after orlop-deck a light deck is placed over head; on this deck, forward and aft, store-rooms for various purposes are built.

BULKHEADS.

Bulkheads are sometimes used to give transverse strength to the ship and divide her into water-tight compartments. A water-tight bulkhead is placed in the fore part of all our modern built war steamers; it extends up as high as the berth-deck, made of two thicknesses of yellow pine plank crossing each other at opposite angles, being bolted and riveted on rings on alternate sides and sustained by stanchions on the after side; the seams are caulked and payed on both sides; fitted with a valve and rod on either side of the sister keelson, to let the water run to the pumps.

Bulkheads of lighter construction, and capable of being removed when required, are used to enclose state-rooms, cabins, etc., and to separate apartments in the ship.

Longitudinal or fore-and-aft bulkheads are used to add to the longitudinal strength of the ship. They act like the web of a girder, to resist longitudinal rocking and bending.

POOP AND TOP-GALLANT FORECASTLE-DECKS.

The deck beams of the poop and top-gallant forecastle-deck rest on a shelf-piece instead of clamps, with clamps below. The ends of the beams are bolted through this and secured to the side with a lodge and a lap knee of wood, and an iron hanging knee under the beam. A tenon is cut on the head of each timber in the length of these decks, and an oak plank somewhat thicker than the deck plank, called a plank-sheer, is worked out to the proper shape, mortised to receive the tenons, and bolted to the heads of the timbers.

The forward beam of the poop and after beam of the top-gallant forecastle decks, called a breast-beam, is moulded and sided larger than the others, and rabbeted out to receive the ends of the deck-plank, and projects above the deck the same distance as the plank-sheer; the projection of both is coved out to form a water-course.

The beams of these decks are supported by round iron stanchions fitted with caps and shoes. On top of the plank-sheer a solid piece of oak, called a chock, is sometimes worked, and on top of this a light iron rail is placed, the heels of the rail stanchions being screwed into the chock; over these stanchions and rail, on the outside, a cloth of canvas is sometimes placed.

NUMBER AND NAMES OF DECKS.

Decks in ships, of different sizes and proportions, vary in number from one to six.

The ship is said to be single-decked, two-decked, or three-decked, according to the number of those decks only which are above the load-water-line and complete from stem to stern.

In three-decked ships the lowest deck above water is called the gun-deck, the next above is the middle-deck, the next, the main-deck, the next, the spar-deck.

In two-decked ships, the lowest deck is the gun-deck, the next above, the main-deck, the next, the spar-deck.

In frigates, the lowest deck is the main or gun-deck, the next above it, the spar-deck.

Sloops-of-war usually have but one deck with guns on it, called the spar-deck, unless the deck is covered, as is the case in the *Congress* and *Antietam* class, when it is called the gun-deck, the next above, the spar-deck, and the next below, the berth-deck.

The deck below the berth-deck is called the orlop-deck in frigates and sloops-of-war.

Sloops-of-war having covered gun-decks are called corvettes, among which may be mentioned the *Antietam*, *Congress* and *Savannah*.

In the old line-of-battle ships, the deck below the gun-deck was called the orlop or berth deck; below that the cock-pit.

If a ship has not a top-gallant forecastle or poop, her spar-deck is said to be flush.

Side-wheel steamers have a raised platform extending from side to side, amidships, between the paddle boxes, called a hurricane-deck.

The narrow platform placed athwartships and level with the

Fig. 53.

2
2
3
3
SPARS
4
4
5
10
6
7
8
9
1. Hammock - Rail Stanchions.
2. Hammock-Rails.
3. Tongued and grooved boards.
4. Wood-Screw Bolts.
5. Plankssheer.
6. Head of Top-Timbers.
7. Channel Wales or Strings.
8. Waterways.
9. Deck Thick-Strakes.
10. Rail Moulding.

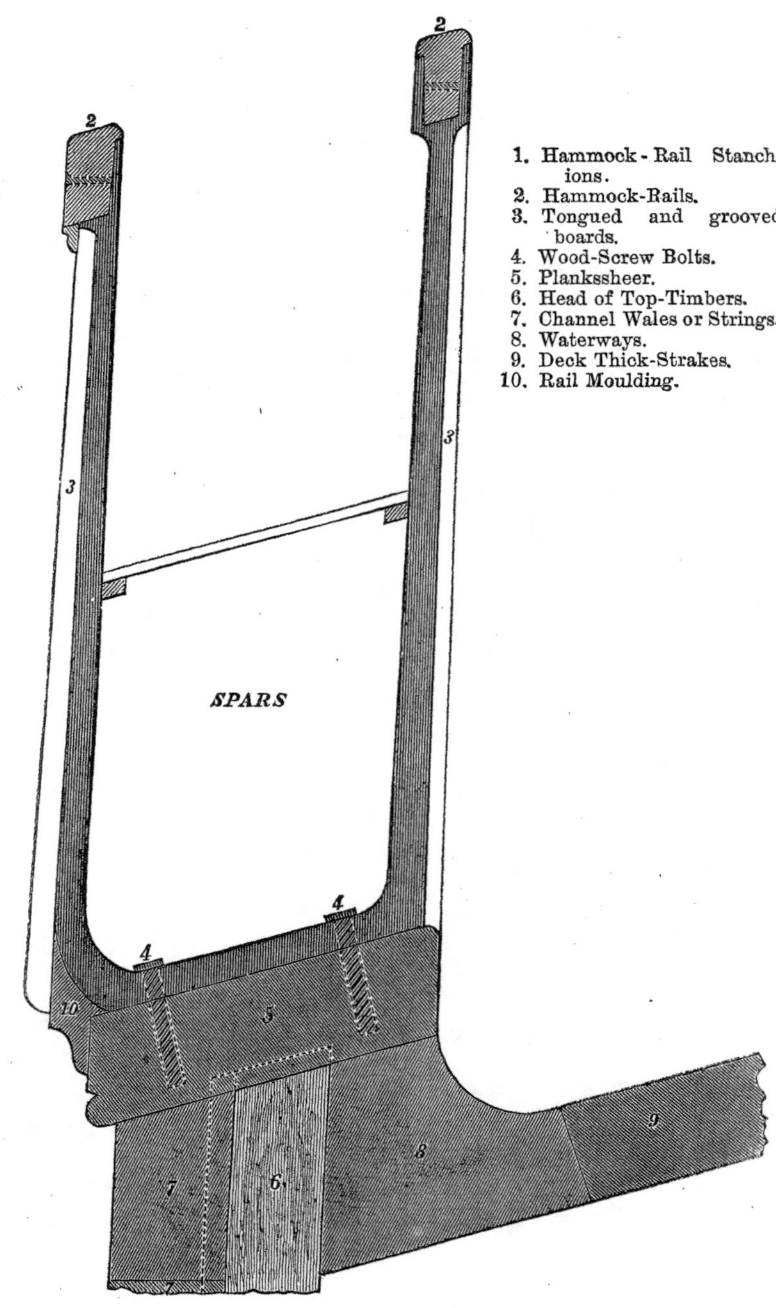

tops of the wheel-houses in side-wheel steamers, and above the hammock netting, forward or abaft the mainmast, in screw-steamers, is called a bridge.

The clear height between decks is measured from the upper surface of the planking of one deck to the under side of the beams of the next deck above; it is seldom less than six feet.

BULWARKS.

Bulwarks are those parts of the ship which rise above the spar-deck. The waist, quarter-deck and forecastle, or the flush-deck of all ships-of-war have close bulwarks; their vertical framing consists of the top-timbers of the frame. The outside and inside of the bulwarks of a man-of-war are usually planked.

Along the top runs a piece of heavy plank, called the main-rail at the waist of a ship, and the plank-sheer at the poop-deck, and topgallant forecastle of a ship with a waist, and throughout the whole length of a flush-decked ship. In the *Antietam* and class there is no main-rail, the piece placed over and secured to the top-timbers between the poop and topgallant forecastle being called the spar-deck plank-sheer (see Fig. 53.) It has a projection outside and inside, with a moulding worked on the outside edge, and a corresponding moulding is put on forward and aft to carry out the sheer-line. In vessels of the *Wabash* class, or any of those without light upper-decks, the piece lying over and covering the edges of the inside and outside planking and top-timber heads, from the topgallant forecastle to the poop-deck, is called the main-rail; it projects beyond the outside and inside planking the same as the plank-sheer spoken of above, having a moulding worked on the outside and inside edges, and corresponding mouldings are put on forward and aft, to carry out the sheer-line and make it look symmetrical.

The plank-sheers and main-rail are secured by cutting a tenon on the head of the top-timber, and a mortise in the rail or plank-sheer, scarphing the pieces together with vertical scarphs and fastening to the heads of the frame-timbers, with bolts driven at opposite angles.

HAMMOCK-NETTINGS.

(Fig. 53.)

On top of the main-rail in vessels without, or on top of the plank-sheer in vessels with, light spar-decks, the hammock-nettings are placed, consisting of a row of upright iron stanchions screw-bolted to the rail or plank-sheer, having a forked end to which the hammock-rails are secured; the opening between the hammock-rails and main-rail, or plank-sheer, being closed up on the outside, with tongued and grooved white-pine boards placed vertically, and panneled on the inside; where the hammock-rails are cut off in the pivot-ports, gangways and break of poop and topgallant forecastle decks, pieces of walnut or mahogany plank are placed, extending up to the height of the chocks on those decks, called head-boards at the fore and after ends, and side-boards in the gangway; against these the hammock-rails finish.

Inside the hammock-nettings shifting-boards are placed to keep the hammocks off the rail and iron work; in vessels with light spar-decks and deep hammock-nettings, the small spare spars and lumber are stowed under them; small scuppers are cut to allow any water to pass off that should get in.

A hammock-cloth is secured on the outside to cover the hammocks when stowed.

The projection of the hammock-nettings should be outside, so as not to interfere with belaying the rigging to the pin-rails.

HAWSE-HOLES.

The hawse-holes for the cables are usually four in number in all vessels-of-war, and are usually placed between the cheek-knees of the head, being cut through the hawse-pieces and lined with heavy sheet-lead, before the heavy cast-iron pipes, called hawse-pipes, are put in; these pipes are cast in two pieces and abut in the centre of their length; a piece called a naval-hood is placed between the cheek-knees, and upon this the outside flange usually rests; the pipes are secured by bolts driven from the outside and inside flanges.

The hawse-holes are stopped when required with bucklers, which work on a hinge, a score being taken out to admit the link of the cable. On account of the extreme sharpness of some of our modern ships, the after hawse-holes cut through the cant-timbers.

A side-pipe is usually placed opposite each mast on the upper-deck, through which a hawser can be led.

A hawse-pipe is also placed on each side aft, for the purpose of riding.

MANGER-BOARD AND MANGER.

(Fig. 52.)

A short distance a baft the hawse-holes on the working-deck, a piece of oak-plank, about ten inches in height and six inches in thickness, called a manger-board, extends across the ship, secured to the water-way and beam over which it is placed, having an iron plate on the top to prevent the chain from cutting it.

The space forward of the manger-board is called the manger; the entire space is lined over the deck and up as high as the lower side of the pipes with heavy lead, and a scupper, called the manger-scupper, is cut in the after-corner through the water-ways and outside planking on either side.

SCUPPERS.

Scuppers are holes lined with lead, cut through the water-way and outside planking, for discharging the water from the deck to the sea. On the outside of each hole a composition-valve is secured, called a scupper-valve, having a lip at the lower part to carry the water clear of the ship's side, and a lid fixed in such a way that when struck by the sea it closes and prevents the water from coming in on deck.

Scuppers should be laid off so that they will come in the opening of a frame, for which a filling must be put in previous to planking; and they should not be placed over a gun or air-port below.

AIR-PORTS.

Air-ports are holes cut through the sides of the vessel in the openings of the frames; there are usually one in each state-room, and in addition, ten or twelve on each side of the berth-deck (in vessels of the *Omaha* and *Antietam* class), and as many as are required for ventilation and light under the poop and topgallant forecastle-decks. The holes are cut first and lined with lead,* and a composition frame, with a heavy glass light in it, made to open inboard, and when closed secured with a thumb-screw, is fitted in outside and fastened with screws. The old-fashioned plan of having an air-port plunger, with the glass secured in it, and a bar on the inside to screw it out on, has been dispensed with in most of our modern vessels.

---

* Hidden's Patent, ordered for all new vessels, by Navy Department.

CONTROLLERS.

(Fig. 52.)

For the purpose of regulating and checking the motion of the cable as it runs towards the hawse-holes, controllers are used, in connection with the bitts and berth-deck compressors.

A controller is a cast-iron block, having a hollow in its upper side of the shape of a link of the chain-cable. There are usually one to each hawse-pipe just aft the manger-board, and in many cases, one directly over the deck-pipe leading to the chain-locker; they are secured by bolts driven through the deck and fore-and-aft pieces, and riveted on plates below.

The cable, while lying on the controller, tends of itself to drop into the hollow slot, and while there it is held by one of its links, which lies flat in the hollow; but at the bottom of the hollow is a jog, or short lever-arm, which can be raised by a longer lever, and so lift the cable out of the slot when it runs out, until the lever is let go and the jog dropped.

COMPRESSOR.

(Fig. 54.)

The compressor is usually a bent lever (iron) which moves horizontally close to the lower end of the chain-pipe, on gun or berth-decks through which the cable passes from the chain locker. It is made with a long arm, having an eye in the end to hook a tackle in, and a short counter balancing arm, pivoting on a heavy bolt running through and riveted on a plate on the top of the deck; an iron plate is let in under the short arm and bolt, to prevent its cutting into the beam.

A strap is placed over the lever arm on one side to assist in supporting the weight of it. By hauling on the tackle at its end, it is made to press the cable firmly against the inside of the pipe, so as to moderate the speed of its running out.

In the beam over the chain locker, an eye-bolt is placed, for the purpose of securing the end of the cable, so that it can be instantly let go when required.

CHANNELS.

(Fig. 55.)

Channels are flat ledges of white oak projecting outboard from the ship's sides for spreading the lower shrouds, and giving

Fig. 54.

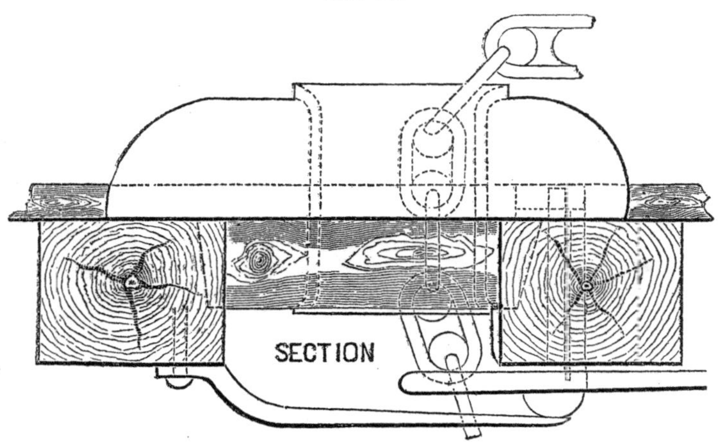

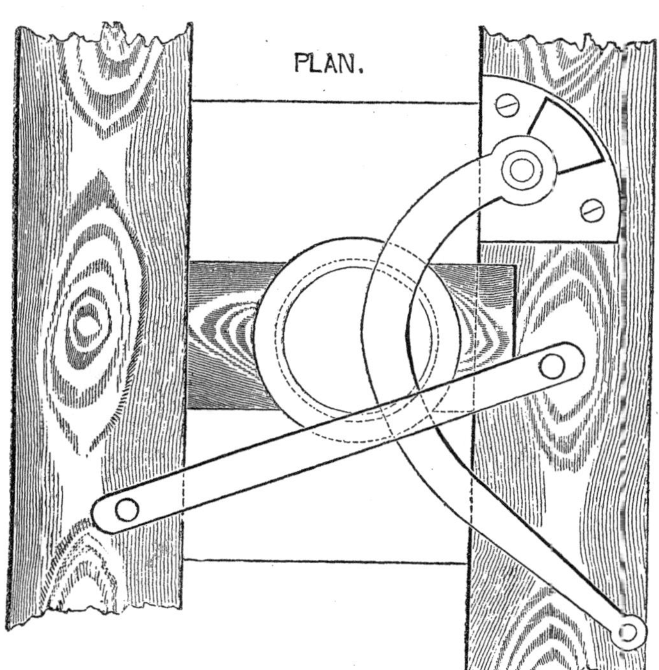

Berth-Deck Compressor.

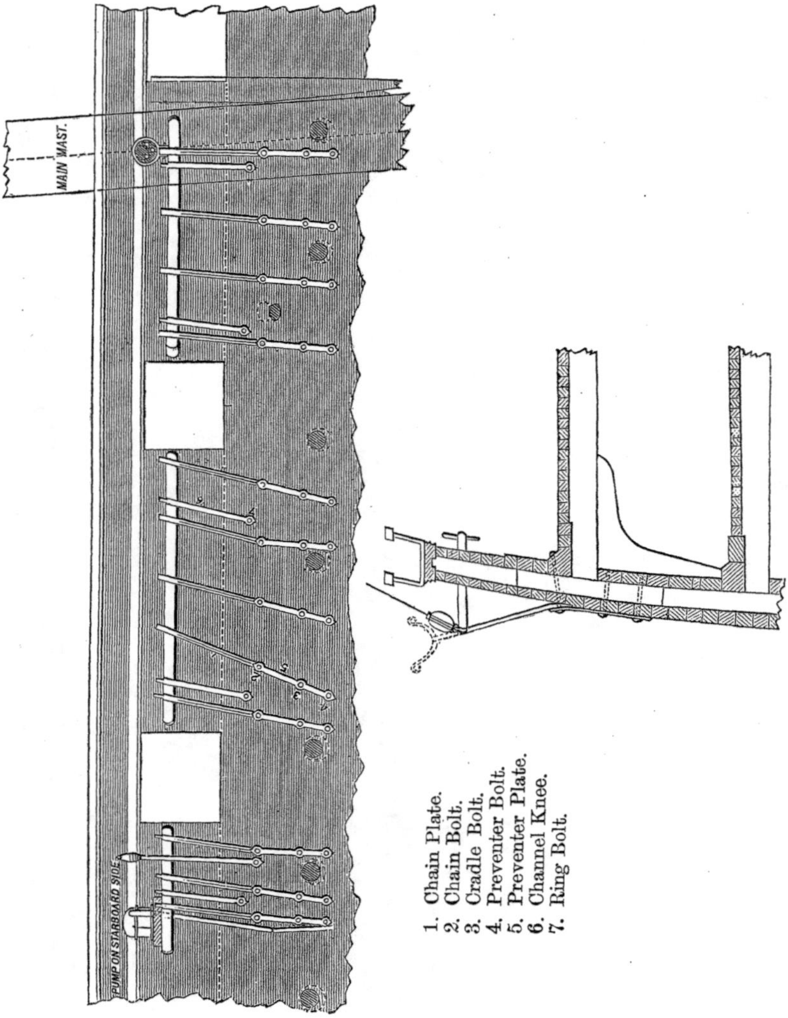

FIG. 55.—Main Channels U. S. Steamer *Brooklyn*.

1. Chain Plate.
2. Chain Bolt.
3. Cradle Bolt.
4. Preventer Bolt.
5. Preventer Plate.
6. Channel Knee.
7. Ring Bolt.

additional support to the masts. The order from the Navy Department now is, that they must be wide enough to allow the shrouds to clear the hammock-rail twelve inches. The extent of the projection usually made was sufficient to carry the shrouds some five inches clear of the hammock-rails, either outboard or inboard. Generally, the shrouds pass outboard of the rail, but in some cases they are made to pass inboard, and are in such cases housed in the hammock-netting.

Ships are often made without channels, the chain-plates being secured to the plank-sheer and channel-wales.*

The side-wheel gun-boats built during the late rebellion, had their chain-plates, in many cases, secured on the inside of the bulwarks.

The foremost end of the channels is usually so placed as to be nearly abreast of the foreside of the lower mast to which they belong.

The length of the channels in a fore-and-aft direction is, on an average, about one-half the length of the lower mast from spar-deck to cap.

One-half the length from hounds to spar-deck is the part usually occupied by the spread of the rigging.

The thickness of the channels is about once-and-a-half that of the skin of the ship's side where they are fastened on, supposing the material to be the same.

Wooden channels are made from one-third to one-fourth thinner than this at the outer edge.

Channels are bolted to the ship's side edgewise, with athwartship bolts, at intervals of about three feet, driven through and riveted on rings on the inside of the vessel, and are supported from below by wrought-iron knees, called channel knees. The plank of which wooden channels are made are tongued together at their edges, and after the chain plates are fastened, a channel batten is placed over the edge of the channel.

The chains made with links are seldom used at the present time; an iron strap, called a chain-plate, passes over the edge of the channel through a score, and is fastened to the side by the preventer-plate; the bolt passing through the preventer-plate and chain-plate is called the chain-bolt; the one at the lower end of the preventer-plate is called the preventer-bolt, and the one

---

* This was the way that the *Antietam* and class were first designed to be finished.

between the two (when used) the cradle-bolt. Under the chain-plate a small iron plate is fitted over the edge of the channel, called a chafing-plate, to prevent the chain-plates cutting further into the channel. The chain, cradle, and preventer-bolts, pass entirely through the ship's side, and rivet on rings or are keyed. An eye is worked on the upper end of the chain-plates to which the dead-eyes are secured. There are usually four channel-knees to the fore and main, and three to the mizzen. The ring-bolts are placed in the lower ends of these instead of every other chain-plate as is frequently seen.

CUTWATER OR HEAD.

(Plate V, Fig. 1.)

The shape of the cutwater or head of a vessel is always laid down in connection with the vessel on the floor of the mould-loft; a mould is made to the shape as laid down, having the position of the several pieces composing it, and the bolts marked upon it.

The pieces composing the cutwater or head are the front-piece, backing-piece, lacing-piece and filling-pieces.

The piece on the front is called the front-piece; the backing-piece, or when made of a knee called the knee piece, comes against the stem; the lacing-piece runs across the top from the backing to the front-piece; the pieces in between these are called filling-pieces; the last-named pieces are of pine, the others of oak. The several pieces have a groove taken out of the edge and a piece inserted between them called a tongue, they are then bolted together edgewise, and when squared and planed off, the cutwater is raised to its position by means of a derrick and secured by driving heavy bolts edgewise through the cutwater, stem and apron, and keying or riveting them on rings or plates on the inside of the apron.

To finish the head there is required cheek-knees, brackets, naval-hoods, trail-boards, sponson-pieces, billet or figure-head, main head-rail, timbers of the head, head-planking, seating and berthing rails, flooring in the head and head-seats. The cheek-knees are pieces worked above and below the hawse-hole in the angle of the bow and cutwater, and are distinguished as the upper and lower cheek-knees.

The brackets are a continuation of the cheek-knees, and are distinguished as the upper and lower brackets; the extreme ends of the brackets where they finish in with the scroll are called hair brackets. The sponson-pieces are of pine and are placed under the lower cheek-knee and bracket.

The naval-hoods are the filling pieces placed between the cheek-knees extending to the rabbet of the stem, on which the outer flanges of the hawse-pipes rest.

The trail-boards abut against the naval-hoods and run up to the billet; they are carved or plain, to correspond with the finish of the billet. They are mitred where they abut the naval-hoods, and are secured with screws, so that they can be removed to caulk the hood ends.

The main head-rail is the lowest; it extends in this *case from the fore-side of the cathead to the billet, and is secured to the side of the vessel and through the end of the cutwater: it is a continuation of the sheer at height of lower port-sill, spar-deck.

The timbers of the head are placed against the side of the cutwater, to which they are secured, their heels resting upon the upper bracket, and their heads coming under and supporting the main head-rail. A light rail, called a middle-rail, is sometimes worked midway between the upper bracket and main head-rail, secured to the outside of the timbers of the head.

The head-planking consists of two thicknesses of oak boards, breaking joints worked fore-and-aft over the timbers of the head, and secured to them.

The seating-rail is next above the main head-rail, running from the bow of the vessel to the billet, and supported on light iron stanchions, with a shoulder worked on them at both ends, and the bolt running through and riveting on rings on the under side of the main and upper part of the seating-rails. The space between the two rails is first boarded vertically with tongued and grooved boards, and then planked fore-and-aft to correspond with the outside bulwarks. * The seating-rail in this case is a continuation of the sheer at main-rail height.

The berthing-rail is next above, running from the bow to the side of the bowsprit, supported and held in place by light iron stanchions, the same as the rails below; the opening between may be boarded up or covered with canvas. * The berthing-rail in this case is a continuation of the sheer at hammock-rail height.

The flooring in the head is put in at the height of the main head-rail, caulked and covered with lead sheathing; on this the

* *Wabash* and class.

head-seats are placed; a scupper is cut through the flooring and head on either side.

GRIPE.

(Plate I., Fig. 1, and No. 29, Fig. 41.)

The gripe is a piece bolted to the fore-side of the stem; it completes the lower part of the cutwater, and runs down according to the shape "laid down for it," falling in fair with the fore-foot or forward end of the keel; the pieces are joined together with plain scarphs.

A composition plate is usually placed on the front of the stem extending from four feet under the keel to the cutwater. At the load-water-line this plate in many cases extends back four feet on the plank, and is securely fastened that it may be used as a ram. The after-edge of the remaining portion extends sufficiently on the stem to be securely fastened to it. The thickness on the front at the load-water-line is about one-and-a-half inches, and the corners are chamfered or rounded.

CAULKING.

The seams of planking, in order to receive the oakum, require to be open to the extent of about one-twentieth of the thickness of the plank. A gauge for the proper width of opening is made by setting the arms of a jointed rule to the angle produced by *one-half inch* of opening between them at a point *ten inches* from the joint, when the opening between the arms of the rule at a distance from the joint equal to the thickness of the plank will show the proper width of opening for the seams at their outer edges.

Seams that are closer than the proper width are opened or reemed by the reeming irons and beetles. This is considered also a test of the sufficiency of the fastenings; and should they prove insufficient, so that the planks are started by the opening, additional fastenings are at once put in. After each seam has been opened or reemed, the proper number of threads of oakum are forced in one after another by means of the caulking iron and mallet. After the oakum has been driven in, it is further compressed by means of a tool called a horsing-iron, held by one caulker and struck with a beetle by another; this is called "horsing up." The wales and bottom plank are caulked solid and home to the timbers, the gun and spar decks with not less than four threads; the berth-deck with three threads; the bulwarks, poop, and topgallant forecastle in proper proportion. The seams of the bulwarks and poop-deck are usually payed with paint and puttied; all other seams are payed with pitch and scraped clean.

The opening and caulking of one seam tends to close the seams near it, so that although some of them may have been previously above the proper width, they may still require to be opened before caulking.

The opening and caulking of seams requires careful superintendence, to see that the seams are really opened to the bottom, and not merely notched into shallow grooves; and that the oakum is actually driven home to the bottom of the seams, and not choked or wedged into a mass near the surface, leaving the bottom empty.

Butts and scarphs of the keel are caulked like seams, and so are any rents or shakes that may occur in the planking.

In caulking decks and light bulwarks the operation of reeming and horsing are usually omitted, particularly where soft wood is used. After the vessel is caulked, she can be planed off fair and smooth, painted, and her bottom covered with copper or yellow metal sheathing.

SHEATHING VESSELS WITH COPPER AND YELLOW METAL.

It was not until the latter end of the last century that copper was introduced for covering the immersed portions of vessels. This coating of copper extends over the whole immersed portion of the vessel. It is formed of sheets 4 feet in length and 14 inches in breadth, the lower edges of the upper sheets lapping over the upper edges of those below them, and the after end of each sheet lapping over the fore end of the one immediately following it. They are fastened with mixed-metal nails, called sheathing nails; yellow metal called Muntz metal, is generally used in the merchant service, and during the rebellion, in the naval service; it is less expensive when compared with copper.

The copper for sheathing is usually made in sheets of the following weight in ounces per square foot:—18, 22, 24, 26, 28, and 32, but oftener is divided into four thicknesses of 24, 26, 28, and 32-ounces, and is applied in the following manner:—[Taking a vessel of the *Brooklyn* class as an example.] The 32-ounce sheathing should cover the bows diagonally from the foremast, at load-line to the fore-foot, and the parts between wind-and-water; 26 and 28-ounce sheathing the rest of the bottom; the keel is covered with a double thickness of 24-ounce sheathing; 28 or 32-ounce sheathing is placed on the rudder.

To ascertain the quantity of copper required to sheathe a vessel, measure the length of the keel, and find how many sheets it will take to extend the whole length, allowing 3 feet 11 inches for the length of a sheet; then ascertain the number of courses required from the keel to the copper-line, allowing 13 inches for the width of a course; multiply the number of courses by the number of sheets required in the length of the keel, and the product will be the number of sheets required on each side.

To the above amount add 25 per cent. for keel, stem, stern-post, rudder and one strake above the load-line.

A full built ship requires one-twentieth more sheathing metal than a sharp one.

Sheets of sheathing metal are usually punched for three and five rows of nails; the sheets punched for three rows require 39 nails, those for five rows, called double nailing, require 49 nails.

The seams under the copper sheathing are filled up flush by laying in a thread of spun-yarn or oakum, and the bottom is sometimes payed with pitch, or tarred paper is put on under the metal.

It is usual to launch a vessel before sheathing her, performing the sheathing process afterwards in the dock.

CHAPTER VII.

Mast Steps—Capstans—Wooden Rudders—Iron Rudders—Equipoise or Balance Rudders—Steering Wheels—Catheads—Boats—Ventilators.

MAST STEPS.

THE steps of the fore and mainmast in all modern built ships are generally cast-iron shoes, fitted over and secured to the main keelson.

The mizzen-mast in all screw steamers steps on the berth or orlop deck.

A piece of white or live oak is jogged down below the top of the beams, and projects above the top of the deck for a length of three feet, and thence is thinned down to the thickness of the deck plank; it is long enough to reach three beams, and is bolted edgewise and to the beams.

A tenon is cut on the heel of the mast, and a corresponding mortise is cut out of the oak piece to receive it.

In the *Wabash* and class the mainmast comes down in the engine room, and could not be stepped on the keelson; consequently an oak beam was placed across the vessel above the line of shafting, kneed off at either end, and on this beam a metal step was secured, and supported from the sides of the main keelson by heavy iron stanchions.

The foremast in the above-named, and nearly all vessels built up to that time, stepped in wooden steps, built up on the main and sister keelsons.

CAPSTANS.

(Fig. 41, No. 2.)

Capstans are machines for winding up ropes or chains; it has its axis vertical, and is especially suited for being driven by hand-power, the men walking or running round it, and pushing before them the capstan bars, which radiate from its head. It is well calculated for making available the strength of a numerous crew.

Capstans are distinguished into single and double, according as they have one or two barrels upon the same spindle, or vertical axis.

The barrel of a single capstan, or the lower barrel of a double capstan, is on the deck on which the cables are worked, and is used for heaving in the cables; the upper barrel of a double capstan is on the deck above. In either case the spindle has the framing of two decks to keep it steady; it turns in a bush or collar in the upper of those decks, and has the pivot at its lower end supported by a step fixed to the lower of them.

The spindle is of tough wrought iron. Its greatest diameter is about the middle, and ranges from 5 to 8 inches. It tapers towards the ends, where its diameter is about two-thirds of the greatest diameter.

The upper barrel is fast on the spindle and turns with it, while the lower barrel is loose on the spindle but can be made fast to it when required, so as to turn along with the upper barrel in the following manner:—On the top of the head of the lower barrel is a circular plate, and just above it, fixed to the spindle a similar circular plate, these are called the connecting plates; they have corresponding holes in them, and by putting bolts called drop-bolts into these holes, the lower barrel is connected with the spindle, and made to turn with it.

The barrel of a capstan ranges from 16 to 28 inches in diameter, and is usually polygonal, with ten or twelve equal sides. From the alternate sides ribs project, called whelps, which are frequently five or six in number, and they are of such a breadth that the mean diameter measured over the whelps, is about double the diameter of the barrel.

They are kept apart at their upper and lower ends by chocks.

They taper towards the upper end, so that the diameter over the whelps is 4 or 5 inches less near the upper end than at the lower end. This is called the surging power, and its object is to make a rope, when wound round the capstan, gradually surge or slip from the larger end where it is led on, towards the smaller end where it is led off, in order that the successive turns of the rope may not override each other at the larger end.

The trundle or drum-head of a capstan ranges from 3 to 5 feet in diameter, being a little greater in diameter than the greatest diameter over the whelps. It has square holes all around its outer rim for inserting the capstan bars, at the rate of about one to every foot of its circumference, or nearly so. These bar holes are from 3 to 5 inches square, tapering inwards, and from 10 to 12 inches deep. The length of the capstan bar is about three times the diameter of the trundle-head, or from 8 to 14 feet long. They are placed in the bar holes and are connected together all round by a rope through their outer ends, called a swifter. The pauls, or catches, for preventing the capstan from running back, are connected to the lower part of the capstan, called the paul-head, and they drop between and take hold of the teeth of the paul-bed, or ratchet—a cast-iron toothed ring which is let down into and bolted to the deck and capstan bed. When required the pauls can be supported clear of the ratchet, by means of small pins in the paul-head.

The lower end of the capstan on the lower deck is formed of cast iron, so as to receive the end of the barrel, which is fixed securely into it. It is called a chain-lifter, and combines the paul-head with it. Its rim is of the form of a deep groove, with projecting ribs on its upper and lower surfaces, so that the alternate links of a chain may fit into the spaces between the ribs.

Forward of the centre of the paul-bed on either side, and abaft opposite the centre of it, are three upright rollers made of cast-iron with wrought-iron spindles; they are for guiding the chain cable so as to make the chain-lifter lay hold of it.

Just forward of the centre of the capstan is a curved wrought-iron bar, called a chain-tripper; the forward end is securely bolted to the deck, the after-end is fork-shaped, and rests close to the inner edge of the chain-lifter; its use is to trip the chain out of the groove should it get jammed and be carried round to that point.

This mode of fitting a capstan, so as to enable it to act directly on a chain cable, is known as Brown's fittings. Capstans of this description have been in use on our naval vessels for a long time; but many of our modern vessels were furnished during the late war with iron capstans, known as Brown's Patent Capstan. These capstans had an arrangement by which the power was increased as 3 to 1, viz.: A cog-wheel, in diameter one-third that of the inside of the paul-head, was keyed to the shaft of the capstan, inside the paul-head; just below this, there was a triangular-shaped piece of plate iron, which was also secured to the shaft; on the upper side of the plate, and secured at either angle, were three corresponding cog-wheels, which were used to transmit the motion from the centre wheel to the inside of the paul-head, which was cast to receive the teeth on the wheels. There were two slides in the paul-bed, which could be shoved in to secure the triangular plate and put the wheels in gear, or pulled out to disconnect them. The capstan head was keyed to the shaft, and was independent of the barrel; when used as an ordinary capstan it was connected to it by two pauls on the inside of the capstan-head, which could be turned by small cranks from the outside.

When heaving with the single purchase, the palls in the capstan head were pointed in the same direction as the men walked, and the slides in the paul-bed were pulled out.

To increase the power they pushed the slides into the paul-bed and walked the contrary way. In consequence of the great difficulty experienced in keeping these capstans in order, they were abandoned, and Brown's capstans of the ordinary kind, having no increase of power, and made of iron, are now generally used.

WOODEN RUDDERS.

(Fig. 41.)

A wooden rudder consists of an assemblage of pieces of timber tongued and bolted together like those of the head.

The forward piece is called the stock; the after piece is called the backing-piece; the centre-pieces are called the filling-pieces and are made of pine; the piece on the bottom covering the ends of the filling-pieces is called the shoe, and, together with the pieces first named, is made of oak.

The rudder is generally bearded to an angle of 38°, and the stern-post is also bearded, so as to allow the rudder to swing to an angle of 42°. The pintles are cast with straps to secure them by, which are let into the sides of the rudder and through bolted.

The wooden rudders used at the present time are round-headed, or patent rudders. The advantage arising from this form of rudder and mode of hanging it is this, that the hole through the counter or stern of the ship, which is called the rudder-port, is wholly closed up by the head or plug of the rudder passing through it, with almost a close joint, as the centre of the rudder-head is in the same axis as the pintles, whereby the round head of the rudder becomes a large pintle working in the counter or rudder-port.

The braces are fixed to the after part of the stern-post to receive the pintles; they are cast with straps, which extend on either side of the post, and are through bolted to it. Great care is taken in letting on the braces to the post and pintles to the rudder, that they may work with each other as one joint. A metal step, called a saucer, is secured to the stern-post below the centre-brace, so that the end of the pintle rests on it, keeping the straps of the braces and pintles from coming close together, thus relieving the braces of the weight of the rudder, and lessening, to a great extent, the friction which there would otherwise be, and allowing it to turn much easier. The pintle which rests on the saucer is called a dumb-pintle. Two saucers are used in large vessels like the *Wabash* or *Franklin*. There is also fitted to the rudder what is called a wood-lock, which is a piece of wood placed in the score, cut out of the rudder under the brace which receives the upper pintle, and which is generally above the water-line. This wood-lock is made to have its upper end bearing against the under side of the brace, and the lower end against the score in the rudder, by which means the rudder is prevented from rising or being unhung.

The wood-lock is made of oak coppered and secured in place by a copper bolt driven through cornerwise, so that it can be readily drifted out when the rudder is required to be unshipped.

The rudder-head has wide iron bands shrunk on to it, let in flush, through which the tiller holes are cut. Quadrants made of composition or wrought iron are generally used (as shown in Fig. 41), but are, or should be, provided with a spare tiller, that can be used in case of any accident.

There is also a short composition tiller, placed in the back of the rudder just above the water, called a preventer-tiller, having composition chains shackled to it for a short distance, the remaining length being made up of rope pendants, called rudder-pendants, which are stopped up to small eye-bolts around the stern, and led to the quarters, where the ends are firmly stopped to eye-bolts driven for that purpose. The use of the rudder-pendants is to provide means for steering the vessel should the rudder-head be sprung or carried away. Above the preventer-tiller a composition yoke, with an eye on either corner, to admit of shackling a chain to, is put on and firmly secured to the rudder. To this yoke two heavy composition chains are shackled, the upper end shackled to heavy eye-bolts driven in the counter of the vessel directly above; the use of these chains is to hold the rudder and prevent its loss, should it be carried away or unshipped from any cause.

The rudder is sheathed with heavy copper; a hole is cut near the heel and lined with lead, large enough to reeve the heel-rope through in shipping it; a large eye-bolt is temporarily placed in the rudder-head, forelocked in the tiller-hole, for the purpose of hooking the top-pendant, to hoist it up through the rudder-port; a bolt is placed through a beam or carling, directly over the rudder-post, and forelocked above, to hook the top-block to in shipping it.

IRON RUDDER.

(Fig. 56.)

The main piece or front of the rudder is almost invariably a solid forging, the pintles being forged in one with it, and in most cases the back of the rudder is also formed by a solid iron frame, which is welded to the main piece. In some cases, however, the body of the rudder has been made of a single plate, and the rudder-head and pintles have been separately forged and riveted to the plate rudder.

The rudder of a large iron ship is now usually made in the following manner:—The main piece is made in one forging, from the head to the heel; lugs in the rough being brought on to receive the other portions of the frame. The forging of the main piece is so formed as to admit of the pintles being worked out of the solid, and they are afterwards shaped out under a slotting machine and completed by hand with chisel and file.

A turning machine has been sometimes used for the purpose of finishing the pintles, and machinery may be advantageously employed also for boring holes in the braces, and taking out the gulleting in the back of the rudder-post. The back of the rudder is formed in a separate forging, and is connected with the main piece by horizontal stays. The stays and back of the rudder are welded to the main piece by means of the stays left on it for that purpose, and thus the rudder frame is made into one solid forging. The back and heel of the rudder are usually tapered considerably from the dimensions of the head, and the sides are made nearly in one plane, and covered with plating worked flush.

The front, back, and stays of the rudder frame are perforated through and through with holes for the riveting of the side plates and the edges of the plates are connected by internal edge strips worked between the stays. After account has been taken of the rivet holes in the rudder frame, and the edge strips have been fitted in place, and the holes for the edge riveting punched, the plating of each side is taken off, the holes for the fastenings in the rudder frame are drilled, and the edge rivets are put in. When this work has been completed, the plating is replaced on the frame, and the through riveting is proceeded with. The edges of the plating are caulked in the ordinary manner, and the whole is supposed to be perfectly water-tight. There is, however, a difficulty in insuring this at first, and when it is remembered that the rudder is very liable to be struck, it will appear that the chances are greatly against the inside of the rudder being free from water. With a view to ensure the exclusion of the water, rudders are frequently filled in between the frames and stays with some light wood, and then covered by the side plates in the usual way.

Between the front and back of the rudder there are four horizontal stays, marked S, and upon the upper and lower stays stop-cleats, marked C, are riveted, and serve to prevent the rudder from being put over past a certain angle, or being driven beyond it by a sudden blow. The number of cross-stays, marked S, varies with the size of the rudder, and in vessels of moderate dimensions they are entirely dispensed with. In very small vessels the back-piece also is omitted, and the plates are secured to the main-piece, their after-ends being brought together and riveted. It will be noticed that the pintles are forged in one with the main-piece, and that their centre is in a line with the centre of the rudder head, as is usually the case in iron rudders. The pintle at the heel fits into a socket in the after-end of the keel piece, and the other pintles fit the braces forged on the rudder-post. The pintle next below the upper one and that next above the lower one are considerably shorter than the other pintles, and they have steel pins screwed into their lower convex surface. These steel-pointed pintles bear on corresponding steel pins fitted in the braces, when the rudder is in place, and the weight of the rudder being taken by these convex surfaces of steel, the friction is reduced to a very small amount, and the rudder is made to turn readily. The importance of this arrangement will appear, when it is considered that the total weight of a frigate's rudder made in this way is about fifteen tons, of which weight the frame makes up twelve tons, and the plating, fillings, &c., the remaining three tons.

EQUIPOISE OR BALANCE RUDDERS.

(Fig. 57.)

Equipoise, or balance rudders, have, within the last few years, been more frequently employed both on ships with single and twin screw propellers. This adoption of balance rudders has been consequent on the recognition of the great advantage they possess as compared with ordinary rudders, in respect both of the increased area of rudder surface thus obtainable, and the ease with which they can be put over to very large angles. Of the total area of the rudder one-third is before the axis and two-thirds abaft it.

As instances of single screw-ships with balanced rudders, we may refer to the *Antietam* and *Congress* (wooden vessels); monitors *Passaic* and *Dictator* (iron vessels). As examples of twin-screw ships with balanced rudders, we may mention the "*light-draught monitors*" (iron vessels). In iron vessels the keel is prolonged for a few feet abaft the stern-post, having a socket worked in it to receive the pintle in the heel of the rudder. The rudder head passes up through a stuffing-box arrangement fitted to prevent the passage of the water inboard. The weight of the rudder is taken inboard, the pintle at the heel only being intended to steady it. A circular casting is secured to the deck around the rudder head, and forms a table, upon the upper bevelled surface of which the friction rollers rest. These rollers are of brass and are conical frustra in shape, being secured in a cone band.

The rudder head is of uniform diameter as far up as the upper side of the cone band; but from that point, and throughout the depth of the forging, the diameter is reduced, forming a shoulder of half-an-inch at the upper and lower edges. By means of this shoulder all the weight of the rudder is transmitted to the friction rollers underneath it, so that the working of the rudder is rendered extremely easy. This arrangement has stood the test of actual employment most satisfactorily, and has been highly approved.

For iron vessels these rudders have a frame of wrought iron plated over and filled in with light wood; for wooden vessels, they are made of composition, with an iron head; no frame is required, as it is cast in a mould around an iron shaft; the shell of the rudder is about seven-eighths of an inch in thickness. Several holes are left open on one side in casting it, in order that the core may be taken out; they are afterwards closed with composition screw plugs.

The heel of the rudder rests in a composition casting or shoe secured to the stern-post. A long ship requires a broad rudder. For every 100 feet in length of the ship, she wants two feet breadth of rudder and one more added, thus 100 feet long will require a three-feet rudder; 200 feet long a five feet rudder; 300 feet long a seven feet rudder.*

STEERING WHEELS.

Steering wheels range from 3 to 6 feet in diameter, the barrel rim and standards of the wheel are made of mahogany, the spokes of locust, the shaft is of copper or composition with patent roller-bushings.

The rudder is so connected with the steering-wheel in every case, that in putting the helm over, the lower rim of the wheel shall be moved in the opposite direction to the rudder, that is, in the same direction with a tiller pointing forward.

Hence, when the tiller points forward, the wheel ropes pass over the barrel first, and when it points aft, under the barrel.

The use of a quadrant becomes necessary in vessels of the *Wabash*, *Juniata* and *Iroquois* classes, which have a lifting-screw, on account of the propeller well occupying the place where the tiller would move; but in the *Juniata* the rudder head projects above the deck, and is made so that a short iron tiller can be shipped readily and worked abaft the well, if required,

CATHEADS.

Catheads are usually made of a pair of white or live oak knees, one projecting on each bow, with stive or upward slope enough to allow the anchor to lay level when stowed, and of a sufficient length to insure that the anchors shall hang from them clear of the ship's side. The projecting part of each cathead is supported by a knee called the cathead supporter, bolted to the cathead and to the ship's side. The inner end of each cathead generally runs down inside the ship's side, through which it is bolted. A wide wrought-iron band is usually let in flush on the

---

* Scott Russell.

top of the inboard portion of the cathead, running a short distance on the outboard portion, to add to its strength, and the bolts which secure it to the vessel's side are driven from the outside and clinched in countersinks on this plate. The outer end of the cathead is hooped to prevent its splitting, and has usually three mortises in it for the sheaves of the catfall. The end is finished off with a carved cat's face or a star. Catheads are sometimes of solid forged iron, and sometimes built of angle-irons and plates. Catheads are fitted with a cast-iron cleat, called a thumb-cleat, secured to the after side, and a tripper on top, on the forward side for the cat-stopper, also an iron belaying cleat on the topgallant forecastle deck. When the anchor is stowed, the inner fluke rests on an iron-covered board, called the bill-board, which projects from the side with a slight outward slope. The bill-boards are fitted with trippers and iron belaying-cleats for the shank-painters. Ring-bolts are also placed where required, to lash the anchors when stowed for sea.

BOATS.

Boats are distinguished as carvel-built and clinker-built, according to the manner of building them. In both of these styles of boat-building, there is a keel, stem and stern-post, rabbeted to receive the planking, as in a ship; the stem is scarphed and the stern-post tenoned to the keel.

Carvel-built boats are built like ships in miniature. They have frames, each generally consisting of a floor and two futtocks; the floors are scored down over the keel and fastened to it with bolts in the larger, and nails in the smaller boats. The frames are sided, moulded and trimmed to their proper bevellings, like those of a ship, and are kept temporarily in their shapes and places by cross-spawls, ribbands, harpins and shores. The planking consists of strakes laid fore-and-aft with flush seams, like those of a ship; they are usually fastened with two nails in each timber of the frame, driven through and clinched on small rings called burs. The strakes first put on are the lowest or garboard strakes, and the uppermost but two, called the binding strake. Above the binding-strake is the landing-strake; the gunwale rests on the timber-heads, and covers the upper edge of the landing-strake, and the uppermost or sheer-strake, has its upper edge flush with the top of the gunwale, and its lower edge overlapping the landing-strake. The stem is usually strengthened by a transom, and the bow by two hooks. Strakes above the gunwale are called wash-strakes.

The thwarts are the transverse planks which keep the sides asunder, like the beams of a ship, and serve as seats for the rowers; some are fixed, and others loose; the fixed thwarts are secured to the sides with knees. The thwarts are spaced about 2 feet 10 inches, from centre to centre, in single-banked boats, and 3 feet in double-banked boats.

Some boats have a fixed inside planking or ceiling, in the bottom; others have moveable bottom-boards; others, gratings.

Clinker-built boats are the lightest class for their strength and size; they are distinguished by the lower edge of each strake of plank overlapping the upper edge of the next strake below. They are not built upon frames, but upon temporary transverse sectional moulds, two, three or four in number, which are fixed at their proper stations on the keel; the strakes are then put on, beginning with the garboard strake, and bent to the figure given by the moulds; each strake is fastened to the next below it by nails driven from the outside through the lands or overlaps, and clinched on burs on the inside.

When two or more lengths of plank occur in a strake, they are scarphed to each other, the outside lip of each scarph pointing aft. The scarphs have a layer of tarred paper between, and are fastened with nails driven from the thin end of each piece.

Towards the hooding-ends, the strakes are chased into each other, that is to say, a gradually deepening rabbet is taken out of each edge at the lands, so that the projection of each strake beyond the next below it gradually diminishes, and they all fit flush with each other into the rabbets of the stem and stern-posts.

Floors, futtocks, and hooks are afterwards put in, and fastened to the planking by nails driven from the outside, and clinched on burrs on the inside of the frame. The keel, stem, stern-post, and frames of boats are usually made of oak; they are planked with cedar, cypress, and juniper boards, excepting the launches which are planked with oak.

Carvel-built boats are "laid down" on a floor—the same as in ship-building—moulds made, and bevellings taken for the timbers.

All boats' bottoms are copper-fastened, and the bands which run down the front of the stem, and on the after-part of the stern-post, are made of copper.

Launches and first cutters for frigates and first-class sloops-of-war, and launches for second, third, and fourth-class sloops, are fitted without knees, the clamps being made sufficiently strong for the bolts in the athwart to pass through them and forelock. The ends of the athwarts are fitted with iron plates, through which the bolt that holds them passes. All launches are sheathed with copper.

All boats have two ring-bolts through their stem and stern-post; the lower bolt is from nine to twelve inches below the upper one, with an oblong link, which is of the same height as the upper one when both are turned up.

All launches are fitted with a stout, copper ring-bolt one-fifth from each end, and another amidships down through the keel and well clinched on the lower side of keel.

Launches are fitted with rollers forward and aft of sufficient length to take the ship's chain.

All boats, except gigs, are fitted with copper pipes or well amidships. Launches are fitted with windlasses for weighing anchors.

The head-sheets of cutters and whale-boats are not laid with the sheer of the boat, but are slightly depressed towards the stem.

All whale-boats are lap-streaked or clinker-built.

Launches and first cutters of vessels which are allowed boat-guns are properly fitted for them, and rigged cutter-fashion. The other boats of large size are rigged lug-fashion, and the smaller boats with sprit-sails. The fixtures required in boats for boat-guns are two eye-bolts on each bow, and two on either side of the stern-post to receive the hooks of the skid; two cross-pieces of yellow pine to bear the carriage, so as to carry the muzzle of the howitzer just above and clear of the gunwale and stem. (Fig. 58.)

One piece of yellow pine scantling, placed lengthwise and amidship, mortised into the rear cross-piece to sustain the carriage in sweeping. The following moveable pieces are required, viz: six pivot-plates and bolts—one at the stem, one at the stern, one at each bow, and one on each quarter; two light wooden tracks to lay along the thwarts for the wheels of the field-carriages and slide of boat-carriage; one midship wheel-track for the trail of field-carriage; two stout skids, each fitted at one end with two hooks, and connected at the shore end by an iron brace.

The chocks, with rollers at the stem and stern-post of launches, are arranged to be removed when the gun is used.

Fig. 58.

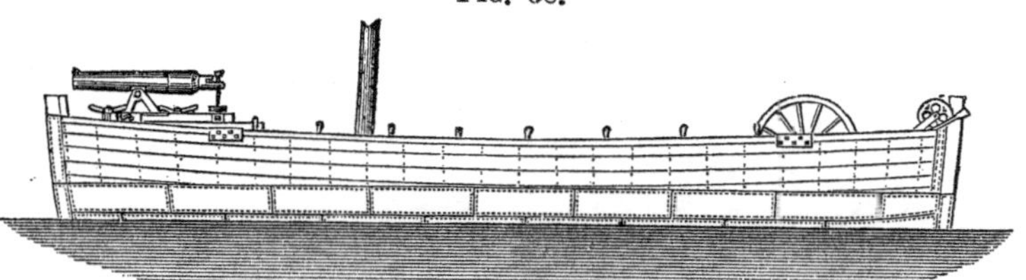

Frigate's Launch.

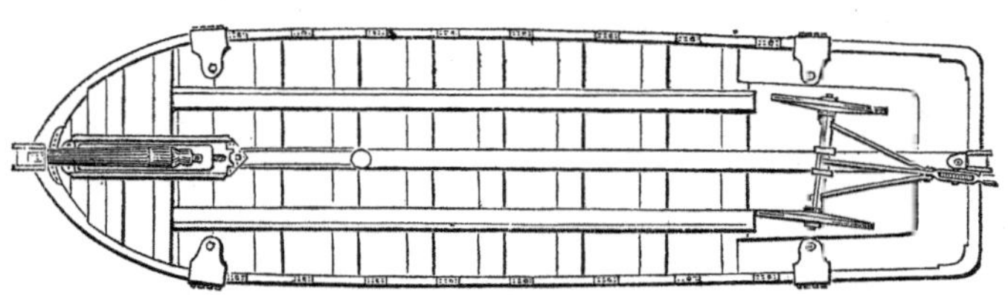

Pivots and Traverses for Bow of Frigate's Launch.

Horizontal Projection Carriage Pivoting on Port Bow.

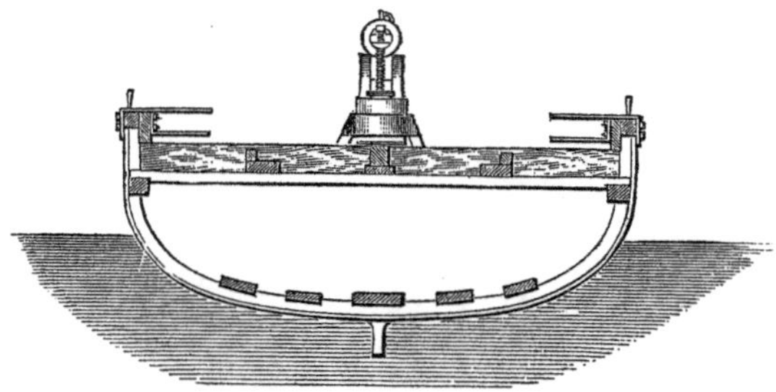

Vertical Section.

VENTILATORS.

Ventilation pipes made of galvanized iron are fitted in all screw-steamers; one aft leading from the shaft-passage to the upper-deck. The portion of the pipe above the berth-deck is divided in the centre, and is made to answer as a ventilator for the after-part of the ward-room. The one forward leads from the berth-deck to the topgallant forecastle. That portion of the ventilators which comes above the poop-deck or topgallant forecastle are made of copper or galvanized iron, and have large bell-mouthed hoods, which are faced to windward at pleasure.

CHAPTER VIII.

Internal Arrangements of the *Antietam*—Berth-Deck of the *Antietam*—Main or Gun-Deck of the *Antietam*—Spar-Deck of the *Antietam*—Magazines—Lighting the Magazine—Shell Rooms—Areas Occupied by one Tier of Shell Boxes—Dimensions, &c., of Powder Tanks—Dimensions of Boxes for Boat Ammunition—Gun-Tackle Bolts—Spaces Required for Working Guns on Truck Carriages—Spaces Required for Working Guns on Pivot Carriages—Sizes of Sockets and Pivot Bolts—Position of Gun-Tackle Bolts for Broadside Guns—Fife Rails—Fore and Main Sheet Chocks—Topsail Sheets—Bolts for Jib and Topmast Staysail Sheets—Bolts for Fore and Main Trysail and Spanker Sheets—Main Brace Bumpkins—Fore-Stay Bolts—Main-Stay Bolts—Bolts for Top-Tackles and Leaders for Top-Tackles—Bolts for Leaders for Yard and Stay-Tackle Fall—Bolts for Leaders for Fore-Stay Tackle-Fall—Bolts for Main-Yard and Main-Stay Tackle-Falls—Chocks for Fore-topmast Studding-sail Tack and Boom Brace—Bolts in Channels for Pendant Tackles—Bolts for Leaders for Fore and Main Topmast and Fore and Main Top-gallant Studding-sail Halliards—Bolts for Leaders for Mast Ropes—Bolts for Leaders for Main-topmast and Main-top-gallant Staysail Sheets—Bolts for Hooking the Cat Backs—Bolts for Sheet Chain Stops—Bolts for Rudder Pendant Stops—Bolts for Securing the Ends of Rudder Chains—Bolts in Lower Brackets for Securing Whisker Jumpers—Bolts for Jib and Flying-jib Guys, Fore-topmast Stays, Backropes and Bowsprit Shrouds, and Links for Bobstays—Method of Setting up the Jib and Flying-jib Stays, Fore-top-gallant and Royal Stays—Bolts for Fore-yard Tackle—Bolts for Fore and Main Lifts—Bolts for Securing Fore-topmast Stays—Bolts for Leaders for Boats Falls—Miscellaneous Fittings.

INTERNAL ARRANGEMENTS OF THE "ANTIETAM."

THE following will give a general idea of the internal arrangements of a screw corvette, such as the *Antietam* and class.

The hold and decks are first subdivided off into compartments by bulkheads.

Commencing forward in the hold there is a water-tight bulkhead about fifteen feet from the bow, running up to the underside of berth-deck beams. Next abaft this is the fore peak, thirty feet in length, appropriated to the storage of boatswain's, carpenter's and other stores.

Next abaft this is the forward magazine for the storage of a portion of the powder. The after bulkhead of the magazine is also the forward bulkhead of the fore-hold.

From this bulkhead to the after one of the fore-hold is a length of about thirty-three feet; against the after bulkhead are stowed six water-tanks holding about 1,200 gallons each, and made to stow in two tiers, side-and-side athwartship. The two after midship tanks are called receiving tanks, and receive the water fresh from the condenser.

All ships are now furnished with an apparatus for aerating the condensed water. A portion of the ship's provisions are stowed in the forward hold. The foremast steps in an iron shoe just abaft the magazine in the fore-hold.

Abaft the fore-hold, a space thirteen feet fore-and-aft, and the entire breadth of the hold at that part, is occupied by the chain lockers for the bower and stream chains in the centre, and a shell-room in either wing. (The construction of the latter are explained further on). Immediately abaft this is the forward or main coal bunker, which communicates directly to the side bunkers, the whole space occupied by the coal enclosing the space occupied by the engines and boilers, and to a certain extent protecting them from shot in action. The coal in the side and main bunkers stows as high as the berth-deck. Inside of the iron bulkheads forming the coal bunkers are, first, the four main and one donkey boilers, and next the engines. The whole space occupied by engines, boilers and coal is one hundred and fifteen feet. The heel of the mainmast steps in a cast-iron shoe secured to the keelsons, between the boiler and engine space. As far aft as the shaft-box is a space enclosing the shaft, formed in this case by a bulkhead running up to the under side of the orlop-deck, and known as the shaft-alley; the bulkhead on the starboard side is close to the shaft-bearing; on the port side there is a passage-way about two feet in width clear of the shaft.

Abaft the after bulkhead of the engine-room is the after-hold, occupying a length of about fifteen feet on either side of the shaft-alley, and used to stow dry provisions. Next, the after magazine on the starboard side, and the after shell-room on the port side of the shaft-alley, occupying a space of about sixteen feet in length.

Abaft the magazine is a store room for boat ammunition. The remaining space is devoted to small store-rooms. The beds or bearings, built up over the main and sister keelsons, to support the line of shafting, are known as the thrust-bearing, bearing-blocks, and pillow-blocks. The thrust-bearing is next to the shaft-box;

there are two pillow-blocks, one just abaft the connection of the main and crank shafts, and one midway between that and the thrust-bearing; the bearing-blocks are placed in the intermediate spaces. In all cases the location of them is determined by the steam engineer.

This vessel has not a regular orlop-deck, framed and kneed, as is the case in vessels like the *Wabash*, but has a light deck below the berth-deck, which answers the same purpose.

The forward orlop-deck is in length about fifty-two and a-half feet, and is divided off, commencing from forward as follows:—The first space bulkhead off is known as the general store-room or yeoman's store-room. Next, the forward bread-rooms (bread-rooms are first lined with tongued and grooved stuff, and then with sheet tin; wooden gratings are placed on the floor over the tin, and shifting boards fitted to the doors, in order that the bread may be stowed properly when carried in bags), extending to the forward bulkhead of the fore-hold. On either side of this deck, aft, a bulkhead is run up enclosing a space, which is entered from the deck above, making a passage to the light-box on the port side and a passage to the magazine on the starboard side. Over the shell-rooms in the fore-hold are situated the sail-rooms, having a passage through them to the shell-rooms.

The after orlop-deck extends about sixty feet abaft the after bulkhead of the engine-room. The forward and after bulkheads of the after-magazine, shell-rooms, and hold, are run up to the under side of the berth-deck beams. The space enclosed on the orlop-deck is divided as follows. Two store-rooms, about six feet square, are located directly in the centre. On either side of them is a passage-way about four feet wide, and in the wings on either side, are two store-rooms. Access is had to the after-hold store-rooms on either side, and to the light-boxes of the magazine and shell-rooms through this passage. Abaft these store-rooms are the after bread-rooms, extending the whole breadth of the deck, with a bulkhead in the centre between them, entered from the deck, above. Next comes the passage to the shell-room, on port side, and to magazine, gunner's store-room and boat-ammunition-room on the starboard side.

The bulkhead forming the shaft-alley abaft the passages last named runs up to the berth-deck; on either side a light deck is put inside of them, about eight feet below the berth-deck, and divided off into four store-rooms for mess and other stores, with a passage-way for the purpose of gaining access to the store-rooms in the hold below.

BERTH-DECK OF THE "ANTIETAM."

Commencing forward on the berth-deck, the first portion bulkheaded off is the sick-bay; the forward berth-deck, appropriated to the crew, fitted with bag-racks, hammock-hooks, swinging-tables, seats, and mess-chests. A bulkhead, with sliding sashes or windows, made to lower into a pocket on the inside, enclose the fire and engine room hatches, with an entrance to each from this deck. It was first intended to put a coal bunker abreast of the fire and engine room hatches, extending further forward on this deck, but that idea has since been abandoned. Next comes the dispensary, engineers' mess store-room, and warrant-officers' mess store-room on the port side; paymaster's issuing-room, marine clothing, and steerage mess store-room on starboard side. Next comes the state-rooms of the warrant-officers, boatswain, gunner, carpenter, and sail-maker; the first two on the starboard side, the others on the port side, abaft which are the starboard and port steerages, occupied by the midshipmen and assistant engineers; finally the ward-room bulkhead, abaft of which are six state-rooms [this is as first designed, but will have to be altered; under the present regulations a larger number of state-rooms will be required] on each side, with pantry abaft, appropriated to the use of the commissioned officers. The cabin store-room is abaft the ward-room pantry, but is entered through a hatch in the cabin on gun-deck.

MAIN OR GUN-DECK OF THE "ANTIETAM."

This deck has no bulkheads, excepting those surrounding the engine-room, and the cabin bulkheads aft. Commencing forward, first is the manger, heel of bowsprit-bitts, water-closets for officers and crew on either side, two pairs of cast-iron mooring-bitts (bow and sheet), with controllers to each, abaft the manger-board, and one directly over the chain locker abreast of the forward main-deck capstan; galley, just abaft the foremast. There is one pair of bilge-pumps located directly forward of the fire-room hatch, and one pair forward of the hatch to the after-hold; finally the main-deck cabin bulkhead, abaft of which are two ordinary sized state-rooms and a bath-room on the starboard side, and a large state-room and water-closet on the port side, with the cabin pantry on the port side, and an armory on the starboard side forward of the cabin bulkhead. A pair of towing-bitts are located abaft the mizzen-mast on this deck. Shot-racks for solid shot and empty shell are put around most of the hatches on this deck. Hammock hooks are put in the spar deck-beams, that a portion of the crew may swing on this deck.

SPAR-DECK OF THE "ANTIETAM."

Commencing forward, first is the bowsprit step, two water closets on either side, capstan directly over the one on main deck, after-capstan forward of steerage-hatch, forward of the fore-hatch are tracks and pivot-bolt sockets for a pivot-gun; finally, directly abaft the main-deck cabin skylight, is the poop cabin bulkhead, abaft of which, there is a state-room, water-closet and pantry, on the port side, and a bath-room, state-room and office on the starboard side.

Topsail-sheet-bitts are placed forward of the fore, main and mizzen masts; fife-rails and leading-blocks around the fore and main, and a brass pin-band on the mizzen, the leading-blocks at the mizzen secured to a brass horse-rail fixed to the mast coaming.

MAGAZINES.

(Figs. 41 and 43, No. 6.)

No detail of internal arrangement should be more carefully considered and executed than those relating to the stowage and delivery of powder, since a defect in these particulars, apparently insignificant, may lead to the instantaneous destruction of the ship, or with the incendiary and explosive projectiles now used, to her becoming, comparatively, an easy prey to an antagonist. In view of the fact that all the powder for great guns is now put up in cubical copper tanks, made water-tight, the form of magazines should be as nearly rectangular as the shape of the vessel will admit, and they should be built strong enough to resist sufficiently the effect of her working in heavy weather, and also the pressure of water they will have to sustain in case of being flooded.

All magazines should have a light-box (Figs. 41 and 43, No. 7), for each alley at one end, and a passage to deliver powder at the other; and the magazine and its passage considered as one, must be made perfectly tight by caulking the (three-inch pine) bulkheads and flooring, and then lining them internally, first with white pine boards, tongued and grooved, battened off one inch from the bulkheads, sides and flooring, and again with sheet lead of six pounds to the square foot on the sides and bulkheads, and eight pounds to the square foot on the floor, soldered together over these boards.

Both of these linings extend entirely over the bottom or floor, and all the way up to the deck above on all the sides.

The athwartship bulkheads are lined externally with sheet-iron as a protection against fire, and to prevent the intrusion of rats. A magazine aft in a ship has its passage for delivering powder adjoining its forward part; and one forward in a ship has this passage adjoining its after part, in order that it may not be necessary to pass the powder over the light-box scuttle. The bulkhead between the passage and magazine room is put in after the magazine is lined; it is generally white pine tongued and grooved plank, two and a-half inches in thickness. As many doors are cut in the bulkhead separating this passage from the magazine room as there are alleys to be left in the latter, between the racks or shelves on which the tanks are stowed, and these doors must correspond with the alleys. They are not only to afford a means of entrance to the magazine room, but also for passing the tanks in and out. Through the upper part of each door a small scuttle is cut, for the purpose of passing the cartridges out of the magazine room with the door itself closed; and has a lid so arranged as to open outward only, and to close of itself when the scuttle is not actually in use.

Sailing frigates should have two alleys for each magazine. In screw vessels of large class, where the shaft will interfere with this arrangement, two alleys for the forward magazine. In smaller vessels one alley will suffice. In all cases the alley is not less than two feet ten inches in breadth, and it ought to be more if practicable, to prevent confusion and delay. Each alley is illuminated by a separate light. If there is room in the magazine, there should be space left, at the end nearest the light, for a man to pass from one alley to the other without going into the passage. Ships with two magazines, one forward and the other aft, should have them as nearly equal, in point of capacity, as the shape of the vessel and other circumstances will admit.

Magazines are constructed as low down as possible. Their floors never come below the tops of the keelsons, but may rest on them. Their height should be equal only to an exact number of times the height of a powder tank when lying on its side, in addition to the thickness of the shelving.

An additional inch for each shelf should be allowed for spring or play.

The whole height in the clear should be limited by the condition that a man standing on the floor may reach the upper tier of tanks with ease. Four tiers of 200 lb. tanks, three of them resting on shelves two inches thick, and the other on inch battens on the magazine floor, will, with an allowance of one and a-half inches for spring and play, require a height, in the clear, of six feet two inches. Three tiers will require a height, in the clear, of about four feet eight inches.

A magazine should be placed, if possible, so as not to include a part of a mast.

All the metallic fixtures about a magazine, delivering passages, and light-rooms, *must* be of copper.

Each delivering passage has, for the distribution of powder, at least as many passing scuttles communicating with the orlop or berth deck as there are chains of scuttles above.

Each magazine, as a whole, that is, including the delivering-passage, being made as stated above, water-tight, is to be provided with an independent cock for filling it rapidly with water; a waste-pipe through the bulkhead at the height of the upper tier of tanks to carry off the superfluous water; and a valve in the floor for letting the water off when the magazine is to be emptied after being flooded. Both cocks are turned from the deck above, each having a lever to its spindle for the purpose, which comes up inside a deck plate, the flange of which is distinctly marked what it is, the wrenches for turning them are kept in lockers built for that purpose, near each cock, locked, and the keys kept with those of the magazine.

LIGHTING THE MAGAZINE.

(Figs. 41 and 43, No. 7.)

The magazine is lighted by means of one regulation lamp, to correspond with each alley of the magazine room, placed in a light-box arranged for that purpose. This box, of which a portion of the magazine bulkhead forms a part, is lined internally, with soldered sheets of copper, and has a few inches of water in it whenever the lamp is lighted. The entrance to it is through a scuttle in the deck large enough to admit the lamp, generally 15½ inches athwartships, 11½ inches fore-and-aft, and 28 inches deep (measured on the inside). In the portion of the magazine bulkhead just alluded to, and so as to throw as much light as possible into the magazine room, an opening 12 inches in diameter and 8 inches above the bottom of the light-box is cut, which is covered by two plain glasses of about two inches in thickness, somewhat separated from each other, one of which, that next to the lamp, must be permanently fixed in the bulkhead, and the other, or that next to the magazine, is let into a wooden frame, so that it may be easily removed, and thus both glasses cleaned at any time with convenience and safety. The glasses are held in place by a rim of copper fastened with brass screws, after being closely fitted and having their edges made perfectly tight. On the back and sides of the light-box inside, there is an inner lining commencing five inches below the top where it is connected to the water-tight lining, and extending to within three inches of the bottom, having an off-set of three-fourths of an inch; holes for the admission of air to form a draught for the lamp, are cut through the back and sides of the box, below the top of the inner lining, covered with copper wire-gauze on the outside of the box. A small dome or reversed funnel of copper, is placed above the lamp and fitted with a pipe of the same metal to convey the smoke off. This pipe is made to screw into the under side of the cover of the light-box, and the hole on top is closed by a metal screw-plug, when not in use. The dome or funnel is fixed to the under side of the light-box cover.

Ledges are placed upon the shelves and cleats between each tank to secure them from getting out of place when the ship rolls.

SHELL ROOMS.

Shell rooms are lined internally the same as magazines, and the provision for lighting and flooding are similar. Each room has one light-box, arranged like those for magazines.

EXTERIOR DIMENSIONS, IN INCHES, FOR SHELL BOXES.

For XV-inch shell,	18. ×	18. ×	20.	high.
For XI-inch shell,	12.75 ×	12.75 ×	14.5	high.
For X-inch shell,	11.65 ×	11.65 ×	13.9	high.
For IX-inch shell,	10.63 ×	10.63 ×	12.9	high
For VIII-inch shell,	10.20 ×	10.10 ×	12.2	high.
For 32-pounder shell,	8.60 ×	8.50 ×	10.2	high.

AREAS OCCUPIED BY ONE TIER OF SHELL BOXES.

XI-Inch.		X-Inch.		IX-Inch.		VIII-Inch.		32-Pounder.	
No.	Ft. In.	No.	Ft. In.	No.	Ft. In.	No.	Ft. In.	No.	Ft. In.
72	15.5½ × 5.8½	75	15.2 × 5.3½	102	15.8¼ × 5.9¼	108	16 × 6	176	16 × 6
52	14.4 × 4.6½	56	14.2 × 4.1½	80	14.9¼ × 4.9½	85	15 × 5	140	15 × 5

POWDER TANKS.

Capacity of Tank for Powder in grain.	Exterior Dimensions.		Weight when empty.	Approximate weight when filled with Cylinders.
	Height in inches including Lid and Handle.	Sides, in inches.		
200 pounds	22¼	16½ × 16½	67½ pounds	218 pounds.
150 pounds	22⅛	15 × 15	59½ pounds	170 to 180 pounds.
100 pounds	20½	13 × 13	....	....
50 pounds	16¾	10¼ × 10¼	....	....

DIMENSIONS OF BOXES FOR BOAT AMMUNITION.

Calibre of Boat Howitzer.	Kind of Projectile.	No. of Projectiles box contains.	Dimensions of Boxes, in inches.	Weight in Powder.	
				Empty.	Filled.
24-pounder,	Shrapnel	9	22 × 20.75 by 13.75 high	35⅓	270⅓
24 "	Canister	9	22 × 20.75 by 15.50 "	36⅓	217⅚
12 " heavy	Shrapnel	9	18.75 × 17.75 by 11.13 "	22⅞	140½
12 " heavy	Canister	9	18.75 × 17.75 by 12.25 "	25½	114¾

GUN-TACKLE BOLTS.

To all the gun-ports on covered gun-decks the following bolts are required: two pairs of breeching-bolts on either side; two eye bolts for train-tackle, one on either side, made with a double eye and flattened on the lower side, that a nib-hooked block may be used; two side-tackles or securing-bolts, one on either side above the breeching-bolts and near the sides of the ports; one eye-bolt or hook over the centre of each port, about five inches below the spar-deck beams, for housing the gun and for shifting it on the carriage; opposite to each port, in the deck, there will be one train-tackle eye-bolt, without there is some other bolt already put in that will answer the purpose. For dismounting guns on covered decks, a composition deck-plate with a metal screw plug, is inserted in the deck above; through this deck-plate a heavy eye-bolt is placed secured above with a nut or key and iron washer, into this eye is hooked the breech-purchase-block.

The hole or plate through which this bolt is put is directly over the cascabel block when the muzzle of the gun is under the housing bolt; it is afterwards stopped with a metal screw-plug.

SPACES REQUIRED FOR WORKING GUNS ON TRUCK CARRIAGES.

(With muzzle 18 inches inside of centre of port.)

	Length of Gun and Carriage. Ft.	In.	Radius. Ft.	In.
IX.-inch shell	11	0	13	0
VIII " of 63 cwt	10	0	11	10
VIII " of 63 " (old)	9	9¼	11	10
VIII " of 55 "	9	6	11	6
100-pounder Parrott Rifle	13	5	15	8
60 " " "	10	4½	12	0
30 " " "	9	4	11	6
20 " " "	8	2½	9	10
50 " Dahlgren "	9	4½	11	6
32 " of 57 cwt	10	5½	12	6
33 " " 51 "	10	1	12	0
32 " " 42 "	9	0½	11	0
32 " " 32 "	7	7	9	6
32 " " 27 "	6	10	9	0

SPACE REQUIRED FOR WORKING DIFFERENT CLASSES OF GUNS ON PIVOT CARRIAGES.

	Distance of Pivot Centre from Water-way. In.	Radius. Ft.	In.
150-pounder Parrott Rifle	45	14	10
100 " " "	45	13	13
60 " " "	38	12	3
30 " " "	38	11	0
20 " " "	27	9	9
XI.-inch shell (iron carriage and slide) pivot at water-way		18	0
XI "	45	14	10
X "	45	13	6
IX "	45	12	0
20-pounder Rifle, or 24 " Smooth-bore	24	7	0

The distance between pivot centres of all XI.-inch, X.-inch, IX.-inch, and 100-pounder carriages shall be either 142 or 117¾ inches, depending on the breadth of beam, position of hatches, and other obstructions, and is not deviated from except by explicit direction from the Bureau of Ordnance. For a 60-pounder Parrott, 130 inches between centres, and for the 30-pounder, 120 inches.

SIZES OF SOCKETS AND PIVOT BOLTS.

	For XI.-inch, X.-inch, IX.-inch, and 100-Pounder. In.	For 60, 30, and 20 Pounder. In.
Length of bolt under the head	18	14
Diameter of bolt	4	3
" hole in socket	4.1	3.5
" boss	10.5	8
Height of boss	1.5	1.1

Slot in the pivot-plate one-sixteenth larger than the boss.

For XI.-inch, X.-inch, IX.-inch, and 100-pounder carriages, the fighting and shifting sockets are bossed, the housing socket plain.

For 60-pounder, 30-pounder, and 20-pounder carriages, the shifting socket alone is bossed.

POSITION OF GUN-TACKLE BOLTS FOR BROADSIDE GUNS.

	20 and 24 inch Port-sills. In.	16 and 18 inch Port-sills. In.
Height of centre of lower breeching-bolt from deck	14.75	10.75
Distance between upper and lower breeching-bolts	3.75	3.75
Distance of centre of first set of breeching-bolts from side of port	14.	14.
Distance of centre of second set of breeching-bolts from side of port	22.	22.
Distance of centre of training-bolt from side of port	36.	36.
Height of training-bolt from deck	21.	14. and 16
Height of securing-bolt (side-tackle bolt) above port-sill	8.	18.

For IX.-inch guns, the port-sill should not be less than 20 inches in height, and no port-sill less than 16 inches, otherwise the carriages will not give sufficient elevation.

FIFE-RAILS.

A fife-rail is placed around the fore and main masts, for the purpose of belaying a portion of the rigging, the remaining portion, that is worked from the deck, belays to the pin-rails, which are secured to the inside of the bulwarks, and should be in length the space occupied by the spread of the rigging. Between the stanchions which support the fife-rail there is an iron rod, called a horse-rail, on which the leading blocks are secured. Several vessels have been fitted with iron-strapped leading-blocks, fitted to turn on a pivot between two horse-rails. This plan was suggested by Rear-Admiral T. O. Selfridge, U.S.N.

The stanchions to the fife-rails are also sheaved for leaders. Under the pin-rails at the side an eye-bolt should be driven in the upper strake of spirketing opposite the space between every two pins, for the purpose of securing leading blocks for the running rigging.

Instead of a fife-rail a composition pin-band, hinged on the fore side and set up with a bolt and nut abaft, is placed on the mizzen-mast; leading blocks around the mizzen-mast are secured on a circular brass horse-rail, which is secured to the top of the mast coaming.

FORE AND MAIN SHEET-CHOCKS.

Fore and main sheet-chocks are fixed blocks, made of lignum vitæ, placed in the bulwarks of the vessel for the purpose of leading the hauling part of the sheets on deck; in some instances they are placed in the gun-deck batteries, but oftener in the spar-deck. The chocks, both inside and out, are fair with the outer surface of the planking; they are put in in two halves, lapping upon the timber to the thickness of the planking, two-thirds of its breadth, two bolts being driven through the laps and timber, and clinched on the inside lap. These chocks should be placed in the opening of the frame. The fore-sheet chock should have three sheaves: the upper one for the sheet, cut with the proper rake; the centre one for the after-guy of the swinging-boom; the third for the lower studding-sail outhauler. The main-sheet chock has only a single sheave. The fore and main sheets are either belayed to large horn-cleats secured to the inside batteries, or, if convenient, to a large cavil placed in the end of the pin-rail. A heavy eye-bolt is placed outside, below the sheet-chocks, for the standing part of the fore and main sheets. An additional bolt is placed below the fore-sheet chock for the standing part of the after-guy of swinging-boom.

Main-tack-bolts are placed in the water-ways—one for the standing part, and one for the leader; they go through, and are clinched on plates on the outside planking.

The fore-tack, if not led to a bumpkin forward, has bolts put in for it on the top-gallant forecastle-deck, properly secured.

The sheet-chocks and bolts for tacks should be properly placed, so that when the tacks are down, and the sheets home, the canvas may present as flat a surface as possible to the wind. *Therefore, that they may be placed in the best position for the tacks and sheets, mark on the deck-plan the point where the foot

* Fincham.

of the fore-course will cut the foremost shroud, and through this point draw a line making an angle with the keel of the ship of 25°; upon this line set off the breadth of the foot of the foresail, which will determine the outer end of the bumpkin, to which the fore-tack is brought.

In fixing the place for the fore-sheet-chock, the same care should be taken, for, when it is brought home to the side, the part of the sail from the after-shroud to the after-leech will become a "back sail." As regards the position of the main-tack-bolts, the same course must be pursued in determining the place for hauling it down, except that the angle of the yard with a fore-and-aft line should not be more than 20°, as the main-sail should always be braced sharper than the fore-sail, because the wind is brought more fore-and-aft when it strikes the main-sail.

The same care should also be observed in regard to placing the main-sheet-chocks as for the fore-sheet.

TOP-SAIL SHEETS.

The hauling part of the top-sail sheets are led through the bitts placed on the forward side of the masts for that purpose, and are belayed to a cavil placed in the head of the bitt. Fore and main topsail-sheet bitts should be sheaved, that the sheets may be led aft. An eye-bolt should be put in below the sheave for a stopper.

BOLTS FOR JIB AND TOPMAST STAY-SAIL SHEETS.

When the vessel has a top-gallant forecastle-deck, there should be an eye-bolt on either side of this deck to hook the standing part of the jib-sheets, and two on each side of the deck for the topmast stay-sail sheets—one for the standing part and one for the leader. The position of these bolts must be such that the sheet, when taut, shall form a line at right angles with the luff of the sail, for, otherwise, either the foot or the leech would become slack, and the sails thus be deprived of a great portion of their efficacy.

BOLTS FOR FORE AND MAIN TRY-SAIL AND SPANKER-SHEETS.

One eye-bolt is placed on either side of the deck, in or near the water-ways, for the fore and main try-sail sheets to hook in, care being taken to place the bolts in such a position that the sail may set as flat as possible. A heavy bolt is placed on each side of the poop or quarter deck in the planksheer or water-way to hook the spanker-sheet. Eye-bolts are required on either side to hook the fore and main try-sail-vangs; the spanker-vangs hook in an eye on the main-brace bumpkin.

BOLTS FOR LEADERS FOR TOP-SAIL HALLIARDS.

One heavy eye-bolt should be placed on either side of the deck opposite their respective backstays, for the purpose of hooking a leading block for the fore, main, and mizzen top-sail halliards. In every case, an eye-bolt is placed in the channels on either side, for the purpose of hooking the lower block of the top-sail halliards. When a vessel carries a battery on her spar-deck, clevis or lewis-bolts should be put in instead of fixed bolts, and placed so as to lead clear of the guns.

MAIN-BRACE BUMPKINS.

Main-brace bumpkins are generally made of wrought iron and placed through the timbers below, or the chock above the poop-deck, and the inner end keyed, fitted with a brace on the forward and after sides and one below. The standing part and leading block of the main-brace are generally secured to it, the hauling part being led in on deck through a fixed block placed above the main-rail or in the bulwarks.

FORE-STAY BOLTS.

In nearly all the modern ships in the United States Navy, the fore-stay bolts are put in on forward end of the top-gallant forecastle deck; the eye is formed to shackle a heart to, the bolt in many instances being driven through the knight-heads and set up on the outside with nuts and washers. In other cases it has been placed through a heavy oak piece let into the deck for that purpose, passing through the deck-hook and breast-hook over the bowsprit, secured on the under side of the breast-hook with nuts and washers; the bolt is made with an arm projecting forward of the eye, which is also secured with bolts clinched on the underside of the hook, adding very much to its strength. The best method for securing the fore-stays, and that which has been adopted on many of our modern vessels, is to have a wrought-iron band placed on the bowsprit just forward of the knight-heads, having a lug welded on either side, to which the hearts for setting up the stays are secured. The latter plan is decidedly the best, as it does not interfere in bracing the fore-yard up sharp.

MAIN-STAY BOLTS.

Bolts for the main-stays, one on either side, are placed through the beam, on the forward side of the mast, secured with washers and nuts below, or in the water-way, the bolt passing through the water-way, timber and outside planking, and riveted on a large plate let in flush with the plank, the bolts being further secured by having an arm forged on the forward side of the eye, which is secured with blunt bolts driven into the water-way. In vessels having a light spar-deck with the main-stays close to the mast, two heavy rods of iron are run between decks and shackled to a heavy bolt, secured to one of the gun-deck beams, the upper end of the rods being made to shackle the dead-eye for securing the stay. This plan is generally used. (See Fig. 41.)

BOLTS FOR TOP-TACKLES AND LEADERS FOR TOP-TACKLES.

Two heavy eye-bolts are required on each side of the several masts for the top-tackles and leaders for the top-tackles and jeer-falls.

BOLTS FOR LEADERS FOR YARD AND STAY TACKLE-FALL.

If the vessel has a top-gallant forecastle, one bolt will be placed on it on each side, and so as to lead well aft, for leaders for the yard and stay tackle-fall.

BOLT FOR A LEADER FOR THE FORE-STAY TACKLE-FALL.

One bolt is required on either side of the deck, forward of main hatch for a leader for the fore-stay tackle-fall.

BOLTS FOR THE MAIN-YARD AND MAIN-STAY TACKLE-FALL.

Two bolts are required forward of, and near the mainmast, for leaders for the main-yard and main-stay tackle-falls.

CHOCK FOR THE FORE-TOPMAST STUDDING-SAIL TACK AND BOOM BRACE.

A chock should be placed in the bulwarks, generally just forward of the gangway, with two sheaves in it, for the fore-topmast studding-sail tacks and boom brace.

BOLTS IN CHANNELS FOR THE PENDANT TACKLES.

Two eye-bolts are required in each channel for the purpose of hooking the pendant tackles to.

BOLTS FOR LEADERS FOR THE FORE AND MAIN TOPMAST AND FORE AND MAIN TOP-GALLANT STUDDING-SAIL HALLIARDS.

Two eye-bolts are required on either side of the spar-deck, in wake of the back-stays near the water-way, both to the fore and main masts, for the purpose of hooking the leader for the fore and main topmast and fore and main top-gallant studding-sail-halliards.

BOLTS FOR LEADERS FOR THE MAST-ROPES.

An eye-bolt is required on deck near the waterway, abaft each mast, for the purpose of hooking the leader for the fore, main and mizzen top-gallant mast-ropes; they should be placed far enough abaft the masts to lead the rope clear of the cross-trees.

BOLTS FOR LEADERS FOR THE MAIN TOPMAST AND MAIN TOP-GALLANT STAY-SAIL SHEETS.

Two eye-bolts are required on either side of the deck near the water-ways, for the purpose of hooking the leaders for the main topmast and main top-gallant staysail sheets.

BOLTS FOR HOOKING THE CAT-BACKS.

Two eye-bolts are required in the cheek-knees over the hawse-holes, for the purpose of hooking the cat-backs.

BOLTS FOR THE SHEET-CHAIN STOPS.

Eye-bolts are required around each bow for sheet-chain stops.

BOLTS FOR THE RUDDER-PENDANT STOPS.

Eye-bolts are required around the stern for the rudder-pendant stops.

BOLTS FOR SECURING THE ENDS OF RUDDER-CHAINS.

Two composition eye-bolts are required in the stern over the rudder yoke, for the purpose of securing the upper end of the rudder-chains.

BOLTS IN LOWER BRACKETS FOR SECURING THE WHISKER-JUMPERS.

An eye-bolt is required in the lower bracket of the head on either side for the purpose of securing the lower end of the whisker-jumper.

BOLTS FOR THE JIB AND FLYING-JIB GUYS, FORE TOPMAST STAYS, BACK-ROPES AND BOWSPRIT SHROUDS, AND LINKS FOR BOBSTAYS.

Eye-bolts are required in either bow for the purpose of securing the jib and flying-jib guys, fore topmast stays, backropes, and bowsprit-shrouds. Links are placed between the projecting eyes on the bobstay plates, for the purpose of securing the lower end of the bobstays.

METHOD OF SETTING UP THE JIB AND FLYING-JIB STAYS, FORE TOP-GALLANT AND ROYAL STAYS.

The jib and flying-jib stays, and fore top-gallant and royal stays are set up to two long shanked bolts in the head, having a double-eye in each bolt; they are driven through the knight-heads and clinched or keyed on the inside. Sometimes the flying-martingale and fore topmast stays are set up in the head, in which case bolts must be put in for them.

BOLT FOR THE FORE-YARD TACKLE.

An eye-bolt should be placed on either side of the top-gallant forecastle, properly placed, for the fore-yard tackle.

BOLTS FOR THE FORE AND MAIN LIFTS.

Eye-bolts are required on either side of the fore and main masts, for the fore and main lifts.

BOLTS FOR SECURING THE MAIN TOP-MAST STAYS.

Two bolts with dead-eyes attached are placed through the mast coaming and deck-frame, properly secured below, on the after-side of the foremast, for the purpose of securing the main topmast stays.

BOLTS FOR LEADERS FOR THE BOATS' FALLS.

Eye-bolts are required properly placed for leaders for the boats' falls.

MISCELLANEOUS FITTINGS.

The bolts before enumerated form only a portion of those required in connection with the rigging of the ship, but they are among the most important, and should be located properly.

In addition to the fittings already considered the following are required:—

Fish-davits and steps to ditto. (iron.)

Stand racks and other fittings for small arms.

Bars, hatch, scuttle, etc.

Benches, armorers', and carpenters'.

Binnacles, and all the fittings connected therewith.

Blocks, beef and chopping.

Boats, stowing of, including chocks, bolts, etc.

Boats' davits, and all fittings therewith.

Buoys, life, including fittings for.

Cleats, belaying and cavils.

Coats to mast and mast wedges.

Companions and hoods, over hatchways and skylights.

Cranks between beams for capstan bars.

Chests, mess, at the rate of one for every 12 men in the crew, marines and firemen included.

Chests, arm and signal.

Galley-bed, work connected with fitting and fixing, including the lead for the bed and tin for covering the beams and deck, and bolts to secure the galley to the deck.

Hand-holds to hatchways.

Hatch-cranes, for striking down and whipping up shot, shell, provisions, etc.

Hawser and hose reels.

Ladders, accommodation, Jacob's hatchways, top-gallant forecastle, and poop, and bridge, including fittings for

Lockers for signals.

Ports, half, and bucklers.

Plugs, scupper, side, hawse, and stern pipe.

Pumps, fitting, and all work connected therewith, including brakes, etc., for working ditto.

Stanchions, awning and manrope.

Steps to ship's side and grab rods for ditto.

Sentry's walk.

Spare spars, stowing of.

Skylights.

Stand for scuttle-butt, and bolts to secure it.

CHAPTER IX.

Iron Ship Building—Preparation of Model and Arrangement of Outside Plating—Mode of ordering Plates and Angle Irons—Laying down of the Ship—Preparations of Frame Angle Irons—Preparation of Keel Work, Stem and Stern Posts—Stems—Forging and Planing of Stems—Stern-Posts—Iron Beams—Preparation of Beams—Process of Framing—Preparations of Floor Plates and Reversed Angle-Irons—Description of Ordinary Mode of Plating a Ship—Mode of Working Deck Stringers—Method of taking the Shape for and Working Plates with a large amount of Curvature and Twist—Ordinary Arrangement of Riveting in Outside Plating—Deck Planking for Iron Vessels—Preparations of Bulkheads—Putting in and Testing Rivet Work—Caulking Laps and Butts of Plating—Bracket Plate System of Framing Iron Ships—Laying off of Ship—Preparation of Model—Disposition of Butts of Keel Work, Bottom Plating, etc.,—Preparation of Moulds for Stem and Stern Post—Preparation of the Keel Work—Preparation of Short Transverse Plate and Bracket Frames—Preparation of Longitudinal Frames—Process of Framing—Working of Bottom Plating—Fitting of Skin-Plating and Girders Behind Armor—Preparation of Beams—Preparation of Bulkheads—Arrangement of Deck Stringers and Plating—Armor Plating.

IRON SHIP BUILDING.

(Fig. 59.)

In this chapter I propose to give a brief outline of the general method of proceeding with the work of building iron ships. The descriptions given are based upon the method practiced by some of the principal firms in this country and England; but as most ship-builders have peculiar methods of performing some portions of the work, it would be impossible to give any general description which would include all these special cases.

PREPARATION OF MODEL AND ARRANGEMENT OF OUTSIDE PLATING.

The order in which the work is usually conducted is as follows: A model of the ship on a scale of ½ inch to a foot is prepared immediately after the drawings have been received, and on the model the general arrangement of the edges and butts of the plating, the directions of the longitudinal work, deck-lines, etc., are drawn. That no confusion may occur in ordering the plates from the manufacturers, and that a correct account may be given to the workmen, it is customary to work the strakes in order, alphabetically, and to number the plates in each strake. The lengths of plates used are regulated by the specification, averaging about 10 feet.

MODE OF ORDERING PLATES AND ANGLE-IRONS.

The lengths of the frames, reversed angle-irons, etc., are taken from the body-plan on the mould-loft floor. The dimensions, actual weights, and particulars of the results obtained by the testing of both plates and angle-irons are recorded in an order-book, and in case where the plates have a peculiar shape, there is a rough sketch given of the form to which they must be brought by the manufacturer. A margin of one inch in length and one-half inch in breadth is allowed in the dimensions recorded in the order-book above the net dimensions of plates on the broadside of an iron ship; but forward and aft, where there is considerable curvature and twist, a greater margin is given. Floor-plates are usually ordered to the required taper, and afterwards bent to the proper curves. When centre-plate keelsons are adopted, each of the floors is in two separate pieces. In ships with bar-keels each floor is usually made up of two pieces welded together, the welds of adjacent frames being placed on opposite sides of the centre-line in order to give a good shift.

LAYING DOWN OF THE SHIP.

The laying down of the ship is proceeded with simultaneously with the preparation of the model, and when it has been completed the lines to which the angle-iron frames are to be bent are transferred to boards prepared for the purpose, and razed in. There are two boards, each being large enough to take the midship section of the ship, the fore-body being transferred to one and the after-body to the other. In order to show the lines more clearly, the upper surface of these boards are covered with a composition of lamp-black, size, and water. The name commonly given to these boards by the workmen is the "schrive," or "schriving" boards, but I shall refer to them as blackboards throughout the following description. In addition to the lines to the outside of the frame, the position of the plate-edges, diagonals, level-lines, heights of floors, beam-ends, etc. (which answer for bevelling spots), are marked upon the blackboards, which are then removed to a place appropriated for the purpose, situated near the furnace, in which the angle-irons are heated. In the transverse system of framing, which this relates to, the frames are formed by a frame angle-iron and a reverse angle-iron riveted to it; the floor-plates riveted to the frame angle-iron at the lower edge, the reverse angle-iron being carried across on the upper edge of the floor-plate, and riveted to it with an angle-iron on the opposite side of the floor-plate, the rivets passing through, and connecting all three together.

The various modes in which floor-plates are fitted are regulated by the arrangement of keel which is adopted.

In vessels which have external solid-bar keels, the floor-plates usually cross the centre-line, while the frame angle-iron ends at the centre-line in many cases. A strap of angle-iron, about four feet long, of the same size as the frame angle-iron, is riveted on the opposite side of the floor-plates in most vessels where this arrangement is adopted, and so keeps up the transverse strength of the frame, and secures the bottom plating. Sometimes, however, the frame angle-iron is continued across the centre-line.

The limber-holes, as a general rule, are cut in the floor-plates, above the frame angle-iron, and to prevent water lodging in the spaces below, they are usually filled up with cement.

When hollow-plate keels* are adopted the arrangements of the floor-plates is exactly similar to that just described for a bar-keel; the frame angle-irons, however, in these cases generally run across the keel, and the hollow keel itself forms the water-course.

PREPARATION OF FRAME ANGLE IRONS.

The leveling-blocks, or bending slabs on which the frames are bent, are made of cast iron, the upper surface being straight and out of winding, and perforated with holes placed at intervals of about six inches. The line to which the frame is to be bent is transferred from the blackboard to the slab by means of a soft iron bar, known as a "set" iron (about $1\frac{1}{4}$ by $\frac{5}{8}$ inch), which is bent to the line on the board, has the bevelling spots, etc., marked on it, and is then removed to the slab, on which the curve is drawn and the spots are marked.

The bevellings are given out on a separate board, as in wood ship building, and are applied to the back of the angle-iron. Care

* The hollow-plate keel was used in the construction of the iron monitors and iron tugs in our service.

has to be taken in bringing the flanges to the correct bevelling to avoid striking too heavily, as the angle-iron, even when of good quality, is liable to open at the root under very heavy blows. The backs of the flanges are also liable to become hollowed while the bevelling is being performed unless special care is taken to keep them straight, which, it will be obvious, is an essential condition for good work, for otherwise the flange would not fit accurately against the plating.

The bending and bevelling having been completed, the angle-iron is allowed to cool, and is then taken to the blackboard and tried to its curve, any unfairness or alteration of form which may exist being corrected. The plate edges, and other stations before enumerated, are notched in on the frames, and the rivet holes for the outside plating are marked, the pitch varying from six to eight diameters, according to the space between the plate edges. The spacing of the rivets for the reversed angle-irons is regulated by the rivets in the outside plating, the rule observed being that no two rivets shall come in the same transverse section of the angle-iron frame, as its strength would otherwise be seriously reduced.

The average pitch of the rivets in the reversed bars also is six to eight diameters. The holes in the frames should be punched from the back, in order that the counter-sink obtained by punching may assist in keeping the rivet in place. The holes in the frames, which receive the rivets in the plate-edges, are generally drilled after the ship is framed and the plate-edges faired and marked in. When the punching has been completed, the frame is again tried to the curve on the board, and any alteration of form caused by punching is corrected.

PREPARATION OF KEEL-WORK, STEM AND STERN-POSTS.

While the frames are being prepared, the keel is proceeded with and temporarily put together on blocks alongside the dock or slip where the ship is to be built. This course is adopted whatever may be the character of the keel, whether bar or flat-keel. When the keel is made ready, the frame stations are painted upon it, and it is taken to pieces and removed to the permanent blocks in the dock or slip, where it is put together again and riveted up.

The fore and after ends of the keel have been previously prepared so as to scarph with stem and stern-posts respectively, and it is usual to make the moulds for the stem and stern-post at as early a stage of the work as possible, in order that they may be forged, and that no time may be lost in waiting for their completion. The work amidship is often well advanced, however, before the stern-post is got in place. It is usual to drill all holes in connection with bar-keels; and in all work where three thicknesses come together, the holes are drilled in the centre thickness, and punched in the outer thicknesses, in order to secure their being well filled by the rivets.

STEMS.

The stem of an iron ship is generally a prolongation of the keel; the iron stem at present in use in ordinary iron vessels is simply a curved solid bar, of uniform section, or nearly so, generally forming the contour of the bow, even where a projecting knee forms an ornamental head. Lloyd's Rule simply provides that the keel and stem shall be scarphed or welded together; if scarphed, the length of the scarph must be eight times the thickness. The Liverpool Rules require that the foot of the stem shall be extended so as to form part of the keel, not less than 4½ feet long.

Stems formed and fitted with special regard to their adaptation for forcing or ramming in the sides of other ships, the consideration of expense, which so largely controls the designs of mercantile vessels, is here subordinate to other considerations; and the forging and planing of the stem into any desired shape is held to be justifiable. The first thing to be accomplished is to give to such a stem the support of all the bow, bottom-plating, and armor-plating, in delivering a horizontal blow. For this purpose all such plating is let into the substance of the stem, abutting squarely and closely against the fore-side of the rabbet; the stem being made deep enough in front of the plate-ends to form a sufficiently stout abutment for them, and deep enough abaft the rabbet-line, or in other words, affording sufficient surface for the skin-plating to receive a double row of bolts through that plating. In the wake of armor, the stem has to be formed sufficiently deep to receive not the armor only but the skin-plating behind it. Sometimes these large stems are formed in two pieces, connected by a carefully fitted hook scarph, eight one-inch rivets passing through the scarph to secure them together.

FORGING AND PLANING OF STEMS.

The stems of all the English iron-clad frigates are formed of the best scrap-iron under the steam hammer. The stem having been forged, is sometimes bent to form and planed afterwards, and at other times planed first and bent. The best method is to plane it first and bend it afterwards; but the planing in that case occupies a long time and is very costly, owing to the planing-tool having to be made to travel round the varying curvature of the stem.

The mode of bending stems varies. The stems of the *Minotaur* and *Northumberland*, English iron-clads, were bent on bevelling slabs used for bending ship-frames, a coke fire being made round a length of about eight feet at a time; and when the heat was sufficient, the fire was removed, and the bending affected by means of wedge-setts, a tackle and crab, and other like appliances. This operation was repeated until the whole length was brought to the required shape.

STERN-POSTS.

The stern-posts of iron ships admit of the same variety as keels and stems. Solid-bar posts are now used, being scarphed or welded to the keel in the same manner as the stem is secured. If the stern-post be scarphed, the length of the scarph must be eight times the thickness of the keel. Stern-posts now in universal use are solid forgings. The forward-post in screw-ships is fashioned to receive the engineer's shaft-tube, in wake of the shaft, and the rudder-post has the lugs and braces for carrying the rudder, either forged upon it, or secured to it by forked arms, embracing it and riveted to it. The two posts are generally forged in one piece.

IRON BEAMS.

Lloyd's Rule with respect to the form and depth of beams is as follows:—Beam-plates to be in depth one-quarter of an inch for every foot in length of the midship beams, and to be in thickness one-sixteenth of an inch for every inch in depth of the said beams, and to be made of H-iron, T bulb-iron, or bulb-plate, with double angle-irons riveted on the upper edge, the two sides of each of these angle-irons to be not less in breadth than three-fourths the depth of the beam-plates, and to be in thickness one-sixteenth of an inch for every inch of the two sides of the angle-iron; or the beams may be composed of any other approved form of beam-iron of equal strength. Where beams below the upper or middle deck (including orlop beams) have no deck laid upon them, the angle-irons on their upper edges are required to be of the same dimensions of the angle-irons of the reverse frames.

The Liverpool Rules require that the beams shall be formed of bulbed iron with strongly bulbed lower edge, with double angle-irons on top edge, or of bulbed T-iron, or of any other approved form, and their regulation as to depth is almost identical with that of Lloyd's Rules. The bulb-iron now generally used for deck beams is rolled in one, and the angle-irons on the upper edge are worked after the bulb-iron has been bent to the round up. The form of beam now commonly employed, especially for upper deck beams, is known as the "Butterley Patent Welded Beam." Up to 12 inches in depth they are rolled in one piece; above that depth, the bulb half is rolled separately from the upper or T half, and the two are welded together along the neutral axis of the beams.

PREPARATION OF BEAMS.

While the frames and keel of the ship are in progress, beam-moulds, with the spring and length marked on them, are given out to the workmen to guide them in making the beams. The processes of bending and straightening the beams are performed by means of screw presses worked by hand or hydraulic presses, the beams being cold. In forming the beam-knees the ends are the only parts put into the fire, and the plan adopted in nearly all instances is to split the beam arm for a short distance, turn the lower part down and weld a piece of plate iron in.

The moulding of the frames determines the number of rows of rivets which may be employed in connecting the beam knee with the frame, double or treble zigzag riveting being preferred for this purpose. In setting off the fastenings in the knees, templates are used. These templates are put in place at the ship, and the holes are arranged so that they may clear the holes in the other flanges of the frame angle-irons, two rivets being usually put in the upper part of the beam arm above the line of the weld made in forming the knee. The templates are then removed to the beams, and the positions of the holes are transferred to the knees. After the holes have been drilled or punched in the knees, the beams are put in place, set fair to the beam line and fixed, and then the holes are drilled through the frames.

PROCESS OF FRAMING.

When the keel has been fixed in position on the permanent blocks, the process of framing is commenced, the frame amidships being first put up, and the work being continued forward and aft simultaneously. Before any frames are raised, staging is erected at the top sides, and the sheer or gunwale harpins are suspended from it, ready to receive the frames when raised in place. When raised, the frames are shored, stiffened by cross-spalls, and temporarily secured at the keel; when a considerable number has been put up, the other harpins and ribbands are fixed in place and the frames regulated. Stages are then made around the ship (without being secured to any part of her), at different heights, for the purpose of proceeding with the plating, the latter operation being commenced as soon as the frames are regulated and secured in place.

PREPARATIONS OF FLOOR-PLATES AND REVERSED ANGLE-IRONS.

In the meantime the floor-plates are prepared from the lines got in on the blackboard, and having been bent to form, are put in place, and have the holes for the fastenings to the frame angle-irons marked. They are then taken out of the ship, the holes in the upper edge for the reversed bars are set off, and all the holes are punched. The floors are then fixed in place and temporarily secured with bolts and nuts. The reversed bars are also prepared while these operations are proceeding, and are bent, bevelled, punched, and faired in a similar manner to the frame angle-irons. In taking account of the holes securing the reversed angle-iron to the frame and floor-plate, it is usual to use a light batten, which is bent around the line of the holes after the frame and floor-plate are fixed in place, and then transferred to the reversed bar. When the preparation of the reversed angle-irons is completed, they are put in place, and the riveting up of both the floors and reversed bars to the frames proceeds simultaneously. Before getting the beams in, it is usual to work a strake of plating at or near the beam ends, and to shore the ship at this part. The whole of the work connected with the construction of the vessel is thus progressing simultaneously. When the ship is properly regulated, the spots notched on the frames at the plate edges, heights of decks, etc., are faired through and corrected by means of battens, and the lines are then marked in on the frames.

DESCRIPTION OF ORDINARY MODE OF PLATING A SHIP.

In plating a ship, the inside strakes are first worked, and the position and shift of butts are made to correspond with the arrangement previously made on the model, the foreman in charge of the work usually having a duplicate of the model to guide him in regulating the plating. According to the plan now in general use, each alternate strake is worked directly on the frames, and the intermediate strake form an outer layer, each strake of which overlaps the edges of the two adjoining strakes of the inner layer. The strakes worked on the frames are termed sunken or inside strakes, and those of the outer layer raised or outside strakes. The lowest strake of the outside plating is generally an inside strake, and is, in most cases, the first strake put on, the work being continued upwards, and the two inside strakes upon which an outside strake laps being fixed in place before it is worked. As soon as the inside strakes are riveted to the frames, the harpins, which were originally placed in wake of the outside strakes, are removed, and the ship is shored under the inside strakes, thus leaving the space free for working the outside strakes.

In taking account of the bottom plating, templates are generally used, the most common form of template consisting of a light batten mould, of which the outside dimensions are a little greater than those of the plates. Cross battens are fixed on the templates at intervals corresponding to the frame space, and when the templates are put in place at the ship, these battens cover the frames. For a plate of an inside strake, it is only necessary to take account of the edges and butts on the battens forming the frame of the template, and of the positions of the rivet-holes in the frame angle-irons on the cross-battens.

The positions of the holes are marked upon the template by means of a wood plug, with a hollow end or a hollow cylinder, which is dipped in white lead and put through the holes from the inside, thus marking the outlines. When the account has been taken, the template is taken down and laid on the plate, and the positions of the lines and rivet-holes are transferred to it. The method of transferring the position of the holes requires some notice, as in many cases bad work is caused by carelessness in this respect. Full particulars of the operation will be given further on. The edges of the plates are next sheared, and the butts planed to the lines obtained from the template, after which the position of the rivets in the edges and butts are set off. In setting off the edge riveting of inside strakes, templates are used which have the positions of the holes marked upon them. As the frame space and the pitch of the rivets in the edges are constant quantities, this mode of setting off the fastenings is a very good one, the only care required being to make the edge fastenings work in well with the butt fastenings with the adjacent strakes. This can be readily done if two templates are employed, the first having the edge fastenings arranged to suit the frame spaces in which a butt comes, and the second being adapted to frame spaces in which there is no butt of the adjacent strakes.

Templates are also used for setting off the butt fastenings. The centres of the holes are generally bored through the templates, and in order to transfer the positions to the plates a sharp-pointed centre-punch is driven through the template. After the holes have been punched the plate is curved by passing it through the rolls, the proper curvature being secured by the use of section moulds made to the frames nearest the butts, the backs of the moulds being out of winding. In some portions of a ship's bottom the amount of curvature is so small as to render this operation unnecessary; but in other portions special care is required, as will be explained more fully hereafter. When the sheet has been sheared, planed, punched, and curved as above described, it is put in place and temporarily secured by bolts and nuts.

In working a plate of an outside strake a similar template is used, and when put in place, in addition to having the positions of the butts and edges of the plate and rivet-holes in the frames marked upon it, account has to be taken of the rivet-holes in the edges of the inside plates which it overlaps. In marking the position of the holes upon the templates the same method is adopted as is described above for the plates of an inside strake. When the holes have been marked the template is removed and laid on the inside of the plate, and the holes are then transferred from the inside of the template to the outside of the plate. This is done by means of a "marker or reverser."

The end of the marker is forked, in order that it may be put over the edge of the template, and have the hole in the upper part brought exactly over the outline of the hole marked on the template. On the lower limb of the marker there is a projecting plug vertically under the hole, and the template is chocked up at such a height above the plate as to allow the lower part of the plug to just clear the surface of the plate when the hole is brought well with the outlines marked on the template.

When the marker has been placed in this position the workman presses down the plug on the plate, and as the plug has been previously dipped in white lead, it marks the position of the hole to be punched. Both the hole and the plug on the marker are of same diameter as the rivets used. The plates of the outside strakes are punched from the inside, on account of the fact that it is the faying surface; but the holes for the edge riveting in the inside strake require, for a similar reason, to be punched from the outside, while the holes for the rivets securing all plates to the frames, and those for the butt fastenings, should always be punched from the inside. The remaining operations involved in the preparation of a plate of an outside strake—punching, shearing, planing, etc.—are identical with those described above for an inside strake, and when they have been completed, the plate is temporarily secured in place with bolts and nuts. The pieces filling up the space between the frames and outside strakes, called liners, are fitted after the plates are prepared and fixed. Wooden templates are used in preparing the liners, being put in place in order to have the position of the rivet-holes marked, and then transferred to the liners. The holes are punched in the liners. When the curvature of the frame is at all considerable the liners are bent to the form required. After their preparation is completed the liners are driven in between the plates and angle-irons by the workmen, and fixed in their proper position. With comparatively light plates the wooden templates are often dispensed with, and the plates themselves are put up and marked; but the ordinary practice is that given above, in order to receive the edge fastenings of the adjacent plates. The liners to the outside strakes are of the breadth of the frame angle-irons, on all except the bulkhead frames, where they extend to the adjacent frames before and aft.

MODE OF WORKING DECK-STRINGERS.

While the plating is being proceeded with, the work in the interior of the ship is also advancing; the riveting of the reversed angle-irons and floor-plates being completed; the beams being got in and fastened; the deck and hold-stringers being fitted, fastened, etc.

The usual mode of fitting deck-stringers consists in laying the plate upon the beams and taking account upon it of the curve of the edge, position of scores, rivet-holes, etc. In the greater number of iron ships the only partial iron deck which is fitted is composed of stringer-plates and of fore-and-aft and diagonal tie-plates. These are of service in adding strength and preventing change in the longitudinal form of the ship. Stringer-plates and angle-irons on the beam-ends act as horizontal knees to the beams, and their efficiency is increased by working upon the stringer-plates continuous angle-irons, which serve both as stiffners to the stringers and as gutter water-ways at the side. The tie-plates usually worked on the various tiers of beams, are arranged so as to have two placed longitudinally, one on each side of the hatchways, and the remainder placed diagonally and running from side to side between the hatchways. These plates serve to prevent the racking forces which are brought into play when the ship is heeled over, or lies across a series of waves. These plates are well riveted to the beams which they cross.

METHOD OF TAKING THE SHAPE FOR AND WORKING PLATES WITH A LARGE AMOUNT OF CURVATURE AND TWIST.

In cases where a plate has a large amount of twist, special means are employed to insure accuracy in taking account of it. The common plan is to take four iron rods about ⅝-inch diameter, to cut them to the lengths of the edges and butts of the plates, and to weld them at the corners. The frame thus formed is put up in place at the ship, and bent to the shape required to give a correct account for the plate. Short pieces of angle-iron are then bent to the curve of the frames, and a bed is formed which has these angle-irons for its transverse framing, their ends being placed well with the twist given by the iron frame. The plate is heated and bent to the form of the bed, after which it is put up in place and fitted, the holes being drilled. All difficult twisted plates with considerable curvature are thus worked, and the iron in the plates requires to be of a superior quality in order to stand the bending. The various processes of marking, bending, punching, etc., are performed by workmen known as "platers," each being assisted by from 4 to 6 helpers, the number of the latter being regulated by the weight of the plates, averaging about one man to every cwt.

ORDINARY ARRANGEMENTS OF RIVETING IN OUTSIDE PLATING.

The edges and butts of bottom-plating are generally double-chain riveted, but in some cases treble-chain riveting is employed for butt fastenings. The pitch of the rivets in the edges is from $3\frac{1}{2}$ to 4 diameters. It is usual to joggle the butt-straps to the outside plates. As the weight of the stringer-plates is not usually very great, and they are easily moved and placed, this is found to be the best mode of procedure, no moulds being required to be made.

DECK-PLANKING FOR IRON VESSELS.

The employment of wood-planking for the decks of iron vessels is almost universal, even when iron decks are laid on the beams. In most cases each plank is secured by a bolt in each beam-flange. The different modes of fastening that have been adopted are as follows, viz.:—

The first, consists of a wood-screw hove up from beneath and passing into the plank for about three-fourths of its thickness; the second is formed by a screw-bolt driven down from above, and secured by a nut hove up underneath the flange or iron deck; the third consists of a screw-bolt hove up from beneath and secured by a nut let down into the plank; and the fourth is formed by combining the first two fastenings, care being taken that the wood-screws on adjacent beams shall fasten opposite edges of a plank. The second plan is that most usually adopted.

PREPARATION OF BULKHEADS.

Watertight bulkheads in iron vessels are always placed transversely, but there are, in many instances, longitudinal watertight divisions also. In many steamships the longitudinal bulkheads enclosing the coal bunkers are made watertight, and thus form subdivisions in the compartments bounded by the transverse bulkheads. In the armour-clad frigates of the English Navy, the wing-passage bulkheads form longitudinal divisions of the hold, while advantage is taken of the subdivisions formed by the bulkheads of magazines, shell-rooms, chain-lockers, shaft-passages, and passages between engines and boilers, all of which are made watertight. The putting up of the transverse bulkheads is delayed as long as is consistent with the progress of the work, in order to allow free access to every part of the hold. The plates, butt-straps, etc., of the various bulkheads are prepared, fitted and punched outside the ship in readiness for being put together, and when the work is sufficiently advanced, they are put in place and riveted.

PUTTING IN AND TESTING RIVET WORK.

After working about three-fourths of the outside plating of the ship, men are set to work at closing up the joints, riming out unfair holes, etc., preparatory to the riveting being commenced. The riveting is generally done by piece-work, a set of riveters being composed of two riveters, a holder up, and two boys to heat and carry the rivets. The rivets used in the outside plating are of a conical form under the head, and the heads of all the rivets in the ship are laid up. Care is taken that the holes are well filled, and the points of the rivets flush with the surface of the plates. In order to try if the surfaces of the plates are brought close, and to test the tightness of the rivets, the following course is adopted: Rivets are marked in different parts of the ship, and the rivet on each side of a marked rivet is cut out. Screw-bolts of the size of the rivet are then placed in the holes and hove up as tightly as possible, in order to try if the rivet between them can be loosened, which will only be the case if the work was not properly drawn together when the rivets were put in.

CAULKING LAPS AND BUTTS OF PLATING.

When the riveting has been advanced to some extent, the edge (when not planed) are chipped fair and cleaned, and then the caulking of the butts and edges is commenced. In caulking a lap-joint the edge of the plate is first fullered with a tool, then it is split with another tool, and lastly, the splitting tool is reversed, and the split part of the edge is driven against the plate which it overlaps.

The caulking of a butt-joint differs from that of a lap-joint in requiring the butts to be first chipped smooth, then split on both sides of the butts, and afterward fullered off.

The closeness of the joints is tested before they are caulked by trying to insert a thin steel blade at various parts.

The caulking being found satisfactory, a painter follows, and thus marks the work complete, while oxidation of the finished portion is prevented.

Three coats of red lead paint is put upon the bottom before launching.

BRACKET-PLATE SYSTEM OF FRAMING IRON SHIPS.

I now propose to describe the bracket-plate arrangement of building an iron ship, which system is universally used in the construction of heavy armor-plated vessels in Europe. *The first vessel built on this plan in the United States, is now in course of construction at the Navy Yard, Brooklyn.

LAYING OFF OF SHIPS.

Directly the drawings are received, the laying-off is proceeded with, and, as soon as the midship-section has been got in upon the mould-loft floor, demands are prepared from it for the framing and plating of that portion of the length amidships of which the transverse form does not differ materially from that of the midship-section. By this means a supply of materials is ensured by the time that the laying-off is completed, and the work of building can be at once commenced.

PREPARATION OF MODEL.

In the meantime a model of the ship is prepared on a scale of ½ inch to the foot, and the position of the edges and butts of bottom plating and armor-plates, the longitudinal frames, deck-heights, and transverse frames are marked upon it. It is found desirable to have the model pivoted at the ends in order to give facilities for drawing these lines upon it.

DISPOSITION OF BUTTS OF KEEL-WORK, BOTTOM-PLATING, ETC.

The disposition of the butts of the flat and vertical keel-plates, keel-angle irons and gutter-plate is first arranged on a separate drawing, and the demands for the plates and angle-irons are made from it. Other expansion drawings are also made from the model, one of which shows the arrangement of the bottom-plating up to the armor-shelf, and another that of the skin-plating behind armor. The lines for the edges of the bottom-plating are first determined on the model, and the longitudinal frames are made to follow the plate-lines, so that the holes for the fastenings of the continuous angle-irons on the outer edges of the longitudinals may be brought, as nearly as possible, to the centre of the strake of plating. In arranging the butts of the bottom-

---

* A vessel designed as a torpedo-boat by Admiral D. D. Porter, U. S. N.

plating and of the longitudinal plates and angle-irons, regard is had to the position of the butts of the keel-work, previously determined on, and care is taken that the butts of the longitudinal framing are well shifted with each other, and with the butts of the outside plating. A drawing is prepared, showing the arrangements of the butts of the longitudinals. The diagonal disposition of butts is now followed for the bottom-plating, there being two passing strakes between consecutive butts. The edges of the plating and stations of the longitudinals are transferred from the model to the body-plan on the floor, and the lines having been faired, the laps of the plating are marked. In demanding the plates for the bottom the breadths are taken from the body-plan. For plates in the midship part of the ship the allowance made over the net length is about one inch, and over the breadth from $\frac{1}{4}$ to $\frac{3}{8}$ of an inch. Care is taken to allow for the curves in the edges and bevellings in the butts of plates with a considerable amount of twist. The longitudinal plates and angle-irons are also demanded from the dimensions taken from the floor, the breadths of the longitudinals being decreased towards the extremities, as previously explained. In tapering the longitudinals, it is usual to reduce the breadths in such a manner as to give sufficient depth at the extremities of the double-bottom, to allow men to enter for the purpose of making repairs or painting.

The moulding of the short transverse plate and bracket frames is, of course, regulated by the breadths of the longitudinals, and when these have been determined, and the inside lines of the frames faired, the dimensions of the plates and angle-irons can be obtained from the floor and the demands prepared.

ARRANGEMENTS OF BUTTS AND EDGES OF SKIN-PLATING AND OUTSIDE PLATING.

It is usual to make an expansion drawing of the continuous transverse frames and the deep frames behind armor, showing the position of the scarphs and butts; and from the lengths taken from the floor in preparing this expansion the angle-irons are demanded. An expansion-drawing is also prepared of the inner bottom, a disposition of the butts and edges is made upon it, the butts being shifted with those of the longitudinals and the bottom plating, and the demands for the plates are made out from the dimensions thus obtained. A similar course is followed with the plating and angle-irons in the wing passage bulkheads.

In arranging the plating behind armor it is first necessary to fix the position of the butts and edges of the armor-plates, and this is usually done on a separate expansion drawing. The edges of the armor-plates being fixed, the position of the longitudinal girders behind armor are known, and these determine the positions of the edges of the inner thickness of skin-plating, as the edge fastenings are made to work in as fastenings in the girders. The edges of the outer thickness of skin-plating are shifted from those of the inner thickness and kept clear of the armor bolts. The butts of both thicknesses are well shifted with each other and with the butts of the armor. An expansion drawing is also prepared showing the disposition of the light plating above the armor belt in the unprotected portions of the ship. The dimensions for this expansion are taken from the floor, and the demand for the plating and light angle-iron frames is prepared in a manner similar to that described above. As the ship advances, dispositions and demands have to be made also for the plating and angle-irons in bulkheads, engine and boiler-bearers, rudder work, etc., as well as demands for beams and the materials required for the various decks. Records of all demands are kept in an order-book, together with the estimates of weights of plates and angle-irons.

PREPARATION OF MOULDS FOR STEM AND STERN POST.

The moulds for the stem and stern posts are prepared at as early a stage of the work as possible, in order to give time for the manufacture, the stern-post especially being in many cases a cause of delay. On this account the engineer's drawing, showing the height of screw-shaft, etc., is required at an early stage of the work.

PREPARATION OF THE KEEL WORK.

As soon as the materials have been received the preparation of the flat and vertical keel-plates, and transverse and longitudinal framing is commenced. Sectional moulds are given out from the loft to guide the workmen in flanging the flat keel-plates, and for the plates forward and aft where there is a considerable amount of twist; the sectional moulds are connected by light battens in order that their correct application may be insured. The flat keel-plates are flanged under a hydraulic press, having been first heated in a furnace placed near the press. In some private yards the flanging is performed by special plate-bending machines. The putting together of the keel-work is conducted in the following manner, viz.: The two midship pieces of the outer flat keel-plate having been flanged by the smiths, are lined to length and breadth, the rivet-holes marked and drilled, and the edges and butts planed; when this has been completed, the plates are placed in position on the blocks. While this is being performed, the corresponding pieces of the inner flat keel-plate are flanged, and when the fixing of the outer keel-plates is completed, they are laid in place and fitted, and the rivet holes marked to correspond with those on the outer plates. They are then drilled and planed and secured with screws to the two outer plates, the three forming a starting length from which to work towards each end of the ship. In doing this the same order is adhered to, namely, first an outer plate, and then the inner plate that butted on it. During this time the vertical keel-plates are planed to width, etc., the rivet-holes punched, and the scores for the continuous transverse angle-irons cut out. When a sufficient number of pieces have been prepared and fixed, a piece of the keel angle-iron is fitted in place, the rivet holes are marked and drilled, after which it is replaced and riveted up. The rivets which pass through the frames are omitted in the keel angle-irons until after the former has been fitted. Before fitting the frames the joints of the keel and keel angle-irons are carefully caulked. In some cases the keel-plates are fitted together on temporary blocks in the workshops or alongside of the dock or slip. In such cases it is also usual to rivet up the flat keel-plates in such lengths as can be conveniently removed to the permanent blocks. In doing this work the foreman is always guided by the expansion drawing prepared at the mould-loft.

PREPARATION OF SHORT TRANSVERSE PLATE AND BRACKET FRAMES.

The short transverse plate and bracket frames are prepared from moulds which give the curves of the inner and outer edges, the bevellings of the ends, and the moulding of the brackets. Amidships one mould will, of course, serve for several frames, but in general a separate mould is made for each frame, and is accompanied by a bevelling board by which the preparation of the short frame angle-irons is regulated. The laps of the bottom plating are marked upon the moulds, and the joggles for the continuous longitudinal angle-irons are cut out. In putting a bracket-frame together, the brackets are moulded and cut to shape, the short frame angle-iron is bent and bevelled, and the holes for the rivets securing it to the brackets are punched, their positions having been set off so as to clear the holes in the other flange; these latter holes, which receive the fastening of the bottom plating, are for the most part drilled, a few being punched before the frame is put together in order to allow the bottom plating to be secured when first put up. The brackets are then put in position on the angle-iron, and the holes are marked and punched. The holes for the rivets in the upper edges and ends of the bracket-plates are set off upon them and punched, and the short connecting angle-irons are marked from the brackets, punched and temporarily secured by cotters and pins. In a water-tight frame, the frame angle-irons are forged staple-fashion to the form given by the mould, the holes are set off and punched in the angle-irons, and, being marked on the plate, are punched in it also. A similar course is followed with the lightened plate-frames. The frame angle-irons and short connecting bars are riveted to the brackets and plates before the frames are put in place, machine riveting being generally adopted.

PREPARATION OF LONGITUDINAL FRAMES.

The longitudinals are prepared from moulds given out from the mould-loft, on which the scores for the continuous transverse angle-irons are marked or cut out, and the positions of the butts of the continuous longitudinal angle-irons, and of the bottom plating, are marked, together with the stations of the transverse frames. The holes for the fastenings in the continuous and short angle-irons on the edges of the longitudinal in the short connecting angle-irons on the transverse bracket and plate-frames, and in the butts of the longitudinal plates themselves, are then set off and punched, and the frames are ready to go in place. A separate mould is made for each length of the longitudinals. The continuous angle-irons on the outer edges are bent cold to the curves required in the midship part of the ship; but forward and aft they require to be heated and bent on slabs to the curves given by the moulds for the longitudinals. The holes in both flanges of these angle-irons are punched before the bars are put in place. The short angle-irons on the inner edges are taken account of, put in place on the longitudinals, and are riveted, after the longitudinals are fixed in the ship.

Separate moulds are also prepared for the continuous transverse angle-irons, and for the deep frames behind armor. The moulds are usually made so that one edge shall give the curve of the frame adjacent to that given by the other edge, one mould thus serving for two frames. The edges of plating, position of butts, scarphs, etc., are marked upon these moulds, and spiling-lines, with check measurements, are given out with them, together with spread battens, showing the proper breadths at the heights of the longitudinals and decks, so that accuracy may be ensured, if the moulds should warp. When all the brackets or plate frames corresponding to any section, have been prepared as far up as the longitudinal next below the armor-shelf, they are fixed in their proper relative position on the floor of the work-shop, and, allowance being made for the longitudinals, the correctness of the form of the section is tested by means of the spread battens and moulds. The continuous transverse frames are bent in the usual manner upon the slabs, and completed as will be described hereafter. The deep reversed frames behind armor are bent and bevelled, and the holes are set off and punched in the outer edge of the transverse flange to receive the fastenings of the double angle-irons. These angle-irons are bent and bevelled, and, being brought to the frames, have the holes marked upon them. They are next taken to the press and punched, and then fixed in place on the frames. The riveting-machine is used in preparing those frames, and care is taken in setting off the holes to avoid bringing them into the same section of the angle-iron with the holes which receive the fastenings of the skin-plating behind armor.

PROCESS OF FRAMING.

The process of framing is commenced as soon as a portion of the keel has been fixed on the blocks, and the riveting and caulking has been sufficiently advanced. The stations of the transverse frames are marked upon the vertical keel-plate from a batten given out from the mould-loft. As soon as these operations are completed, a tier of short transverse frames is put up amidships, and temporarily secured to the vertical keel, the heads being fixed to a ribband, which is afterwards put up and shored.

When this has been done, the fitting of the plates of the lowest longitudinal is proceeded with, they having previously been prepared from the moulds given out from the mould-loft, as described before. When put in place, the longitudinals are temporarily secured, the butt-straps are prepared, and the continuous angle-irons on the outer edges are fixed. A portion of the length of the lowest longitudinal having been completed, another tier of transverse frames is put up, and a ribband is fixed and shored near their heads; then another longitudinal is fitted and fixed, and so on until the longitudinal is reached which forms the upper boundary of the double bottom, and is usually situated at the foot of the wing-passage bulkhead. This longitudinal has to be made water-tight. Previously to completing this water-tight work, the frames behind armor have to be hoisted in, and the continuous transverse angle-irons put in place. The latter are in some cases put in, and have the holes in the brackets and plates marked upon them, the butts fitted, and the holes set off for the fastenings, and are then taken out and have the holes punched. In other cases, the holes have been drilled in place; but the former plan is thought to be cheaper, and is that adopted in recent ships. In getting the frames behind armor into position, it is usual to put up one or two at each end of a sheer-ribband, and to secure the ribband to the inside of the frames, in order to avoid having to hoist the frames in over the ribbands as would require to be done if it were put on the outside. When the ribband has been fixed, the other frames which come upon it are put in, brought to their stations, and secured. The fairing of a portion of the framing is then completed, cross-spalls being fitted to every fourth or fifth frame, and ribbands being but up on the outside of the frames. The lower ends of the vertical frames are scarphed with the continuous transverse angle-irons, and it is usual to punch the holes for the fastenings in either the frame or the angle-iron before it is put in, and to drill them through the unpunched thickness in place.

Between the armor shelf and the longitudinal next below it, the transverse framing is formed by lightened plates with angle-irons on the edges, these frames are prepared from moulds made in the mould-loft, and are completed, with the exception of cutting the heels, in the same manner as the other short transverse frames. In order, however, to secure accuracy in the armor shelf-line, the moulds are put up in place, and a fair line is got around the ship by means of battens, the lower ends of the frames being afterwards cut to the lengths thus obtained.

While the framing amidships has been thus advancing, the keel is being extended both forward and aft, the transverse and longitudinal framing is being put in place in make of it, and the preparation of the remainder of the framing is being proceeded with. Simultaneously with this the riveting up of the various parts of the frame and the connecting angle-irons is being performed, and, as soon as possible, the working of the bottom plating is commenced on the midship part where the framing is most advanced.

WORKING OF BOTTOM PLATING.

The only points requiring notice with respect to the mode of plating adopted, are, that the harpins and ribbands on the bottom are always placed between the edges of an inside strake and a longitudinal, so that they need not be removed until the outside strakes of plating are worked; that the lines for the plate edges are got in upon the frames by a draughtsman from an account furnished from the mould-loft; and that a thin blackboard is used for taking account of the plates instead of a batten template. It has been previously explained that most of the holes in the frame angle-irons for the fastenings of the bottom plating are drilled in place, a few only of the holes between the plate edges being punched previously, in order to allow the plating to be temporarily secured when first put up. The holes for the edge fastenings are always drilled in the frame angle-irons. The position of the holes are transferred to the plates by means of reversers. It is the practice, as far as possible, to complete the riveting of the framing and bottom plating, together with the fitting of the drain-pipes in the double bottom, before the inner skin is worked. The disposition made at the mould-loft is conformed to in working the inside plating, and the mode of taking account of the plates is very similar to that described for outside plating. The plating is flush-jointed both at the edges and butts, and the strips are worked below it. The holes for the fastenings are drilled in the continuous transverse frames, and punched in the plates. The riveting and caulking of the plating in both the inner and outer bottoms are performed in the manner before described.

FITTING OF SKIN PLATING AND GIRDERS BEHIND ARMOR.

The armor shelf having been completed for a portion of the length amidships, the working of the skin-plating behind armor and of the longitudinal girders is commenced. The lines for the plate edges are got in on the frames from an account furnished by the mould-loft draughtsman, and the holes for the fastenings are drilled in the frame angle-irons and longitudinal girders, and punched in the plates. The disposition previously made is carried out by the foreman, who is guided by the expansion drawing, and the butt fastenings are arranged so as to clear the armor bolts. The taking account of the plates, punching, etc., are conducted similarly to the processes before described.

PREPARATION OF BEAMS.

Simultaneously with the work last described, the beams are put in, the deck-lines having previously been got in upon the frames. It is usual for the T-bulb and H-iron beams to be supplied to the builder by the makers, with the knees formed and the proper crown. For this purpose the makers are furnished with sketches of the beam having the figured dimensions marked upon them, with beam moulds giving the crown of the decks, with check-battens marked from the mould-loft floor in order to test the lengths, and with batten moulds showing the bevel of the beam-knees and the inside curves of the beam-arms. The usual allowance made over the true length taken from the mould-loft floor is $\frac{3}{4}$ of an inch on each beam-arm, the additional length being allowed on the outer edges of the arm, and the true lengths taken from the floor being conformed to in making the moulds for the inside curves of the knees. When made beams are adopted, the plate-welds in adjacent beams are carefully shifted, the beam-webs are bent to their proper crown on the slabs, and have the knees formed by splitting the ends and welding in pieces, or by welding the knees on. The holes for the fastenings in the beam angle-irons are set off and punched, the angle-irons are bent to the curves, brought to the beam-plates, have the holes marked, are then taken to the press, and are punched, after which they are temporarily secured to the beam-plates until the riveting is performed. The riveting of made beams is usually done by the machines. In taking account of the beams, the lengths of the beams and bevellings of the knees given from the mould-loft are conformed to, being tested at the ship previously to cutting the beams. The outer edge of the beam-arm is accurately fitted against the transverse flange of one of the double angle-irons on the deep reversed frames. The holes for the fastenings in the beam-arms are usually set off and punched before the beams are put in, templates being used for setting off the fastenings; the holes in the frames are drilled after the beams are in place. The holes for the fastening of deck-planking and plating are always drilled in the beam flanges after the beams have been fixed. The deck-planking is now fastened to the beams only in cases where there is no iron deck.

PREPARATION OF BULKHEADS.

The work in the hold is also being proceeded with during this time. As soon as the inner bottom has been sufficiently advanced the bulkheads are fitted and fastened. A sketch is prepared for each bulkhead from the dimensions taken from the mould-loft floor, and on it the disposition of the plating and stiffeners is made. The plates and angle-irons required for the bulkheads are also demanded from these sketches. The bulkheads are fitted together outside the ship; the holes for the fastenings are marked and punched; the strips and stiffeners fitted, etc.; and the various pieces marked, in order to facilitate the putting together in place. In building the bulkheads in the ship the midship part is first put up, and the ends of the plates coming on the inner bottom are cut to the lengths and curves taken from the ship. The fitting of water-tight doors, sluice-valves, etc., can be proceeded with as soon as the riveting of the bulkheads is completed.

ARRANGEMENT OF DECK-STRINGERS AND PLATING.

The work on the different decks is commenced as soon as the deck-framing is completed for a portion of the length. Plans of the decks are prepared from the mould-loft floor, and the dispositions of the butts and edges of the deck-stringers and plating are made upon them, the demands for plates and angle-irons also being prepared from these drawings. No moulds are used in fitting the stringer-plates, except in places where great care is needed, as for instance where the frames behind armor are run up through the stringer which comes upon the upper edge of the armor-belt. In nearly all instances the stringer-plates themselves are put in place and marked, and this course is thought to be both cheaper and more expeditious. The deck plating is also laid upon the beams, and the holes for the fastenings to the beam-flanges are marked upon it, after which the plates are removed to the press, and the holes are punched. In recent ships the fastenings of the deck planking have been brought out upon the plating clear of the beams, and it is usual to set off the holes upon the plates and to punch them, care being taken to set them off for the strakes of planking and to make good fastenings.

ARMOR PLATING.

The armor plating of the midship portion of the ship is commenced as soon as the skin-plating behind armor has been completed for a sufficient length. The framing and plating of the unprotected parts of the vessel above the armor-belt are commenced as soon as possible. The mode of conducting the work requires no special remark.

The remainder of the work in completing the framing and plating, putting on the armor in the belt, and finishing the bow and stern, is conducted as described in building transverse iron ships. The various fittings in the hold, water-tight flats, engine and boiler bearers, shaft passages, magazines, chain lockers, etc., and the work connected with the decks and topsides, the gunnery arrangements, ports, etc., are completed as the ship advances. The rudder and its fittings are generally prepared and fitted in place before the ship is launched.

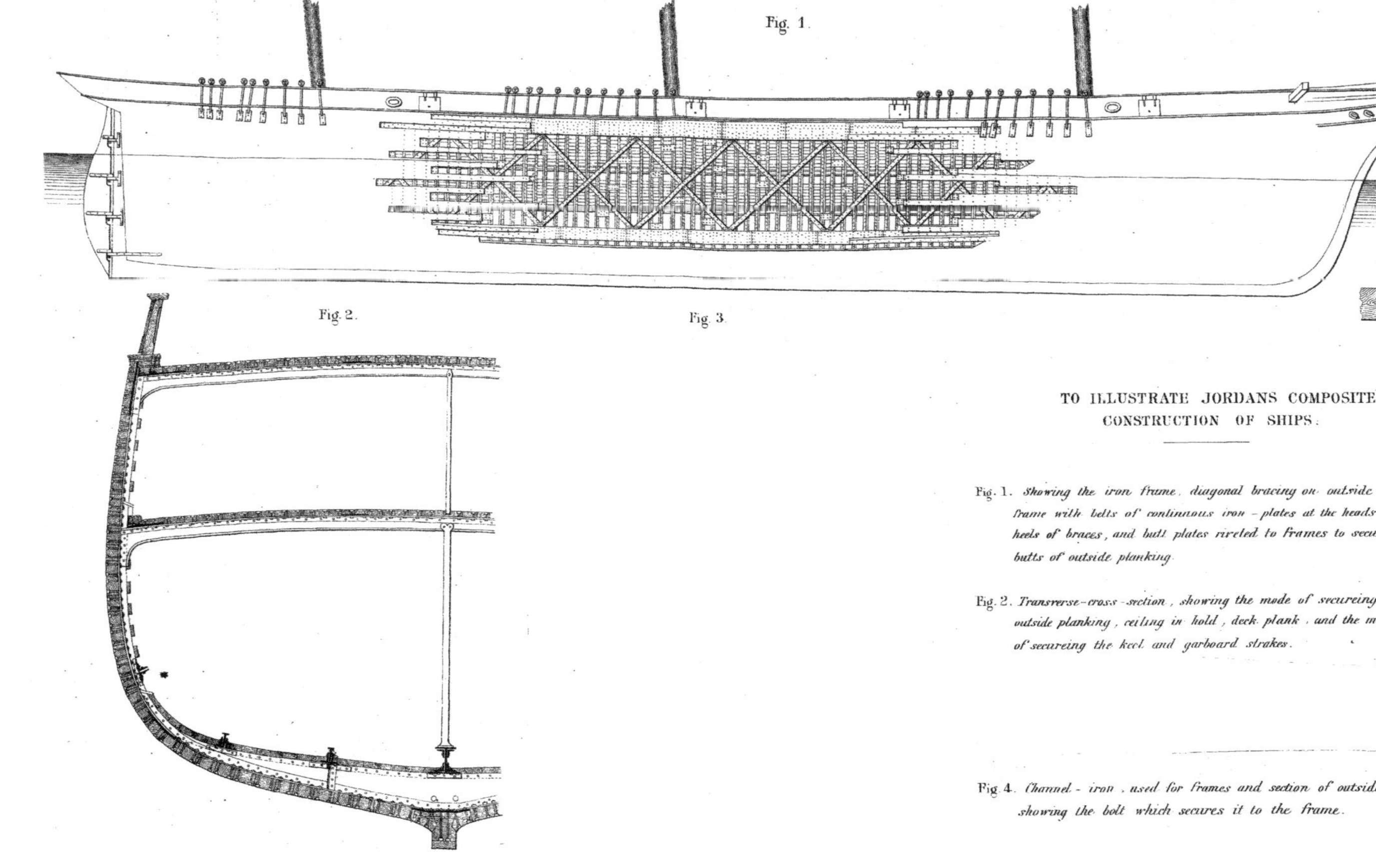

TO ILLUSTRATE JORDANS COMPOSITE CONSTRUCTION OF SHIPS.

Fig. 1. *Showing the iron frame, diagonal bracing on outside of the frame with belts of continuous iron-plates at the heads and heels of braces, and butt plates riveted to frames to secure the butts of outside planking.*

Fig. 2. *Transverse-cross-section, showing the mode of secureing the outside planking, ceiling in hold, deck plank, and the mode of secureing the keel and garboard strakes.*

Fig. 4. *Channel-iron, used for frames and section of outside planking showing the bolt which secures it to the frame.*

J. Bien, lith.

CHAPTER X.

Composite Ships.—Jordan's System of Constructing Composite Ships—McLain's System of Constructing Composite Ships—Scott's System of Constructing Composite Ships—Daft's Method of Sheathing Iron Ships—Grantham's Method of Sheathing Iron Ships—English Admiralty Method of Sheathing Iron Ships.—*Docks.*—Wet Docks—Dry Docks—Method of Docking a Vessel in a Dry Dock—Floating Sectional Dry Docks—Method of Docking a Vessel on a Sectional Dock—Marine Railway—Balance Floating Dock. *Launching.*—The Ways—Breadth of Surface of Ways—Distance of Ways Apart—Launching Ribband—Ribband Shores—Back Shores. *The Cradle.*—Bilge Ways—Packing or Fillings—Poppets—Poppet Ribbands—Poppet Lashings—Preparations for Launching—Launching of Iron-Clad Ships Built on the Longitudinal System—On Completing the Launching of Ships which have Stopped on their Launching Ways—Launching of the *Great Eastern.*

COMPOSITE SHIPS.

THE chief object in all methods of constructing composite ships is to combine the strength of the iron ship with the capability of being coppered afforded by the wooden ship.

In this method of construction special attention is required to see that the iron is completely insulated or cut off from electrical communication with the copper used in the structure. On account of the difference in the expansion of wood and iron by heat, it has been found best to make all pieces which lie fore-and-aft of wood, and all those which lie athwartships vertical or diagonally of iron.

JORDAN'S SYSTEM OF CONSTRUCTING COMPOSITE SHIPS.

The system of composite ship-building most generally practiced is that known as "Jordan's System," in which the whole outer skin, including keel, stem, stern-post and planking, is of wood, arranged as in the skin of an ordinary wooden ship, and the frame-work inside of the skin, including frames, beams, keelsons, stringers, shelf-pieces, water-ways, hooks, transoms, diagonal braces, etc., is of iron, arranged nearly as in an ordinary iron-ship "channel," or trough-shaped iron being used for the frames.

The bolts which fasten the skin to the frames are of iron, generally "galvanized" or coated with zinc, and their outer ends are countersunk in holes of such a depth that the iron bolts can be electrically insulated from the copper sheathing by plugging the holes with pitch, or some other suitable non-conductor of electricity.

McLAIN'S SYSTEM OF CONSTRUCTING COMPOSITE SHIPS.

The difficulties incident to keeping a vessel perfectly tight are very serious, and McLain proposed, in preference, to keep the leakage free from the iron of the structure by building vessels with keel, stem, stern-post, frame and outer planking, nearly the same as those of an ordinary wooden vessel; but, instead of the ceiling or inside planking being composed of wood, it was to be constructed of iron, united all round at the bottom and ends of the vessel, and made thoroughly water-tight, forming a complete inner skin, with beams, stringers, keelsons, bulkheads, platforms, etc., also of iron.

The greater part of the wooden frame is merely of dimensions sufficient for bolting the wooden planking to, and is inserted between iron frames riveted all round the outside of the iron ceiling. The wooden frames are fastened to the iron frames by galvanized iron fore-and-aft bolts, either screwed or plain. The wooden floorings are made deep in the throat and stiffened with plates on each side, riveted to the angle-iron frames, or iron floors are fitted inside the iron ceiling to supply the requisite transverse strength.

The apron, inner-post, and deadwood, are inserted between and bolted to large angle-irons riveted on the iron ceiling. The outer planking within the influences of the copper sheating is fastened to the wooden frame with screw treenails or with yellow metal bolts. The top-timbers of the frame are, by preference, composed of teak, and in the wake of the armor-plating the spaces between the frames are filled in solid with teak, or with any other suitable material; the iron ceiling is also increased in thickness, and additional welt frames are introduced at intervals to resist shot and strengthen the vessel.

DESCRIPTIVE PARTICULARS OF McLAIN'S SYSTEM.

Figs. 1, 2, 3 and 4.—Sections of a composite vessel of about 2,500 tons register.

Fig. 1.—Horizontal section of broadside.

Fig. 2.—Vertical section of ditto at X.

Fig. 3.—Transverse section of keel, keelson, etc.

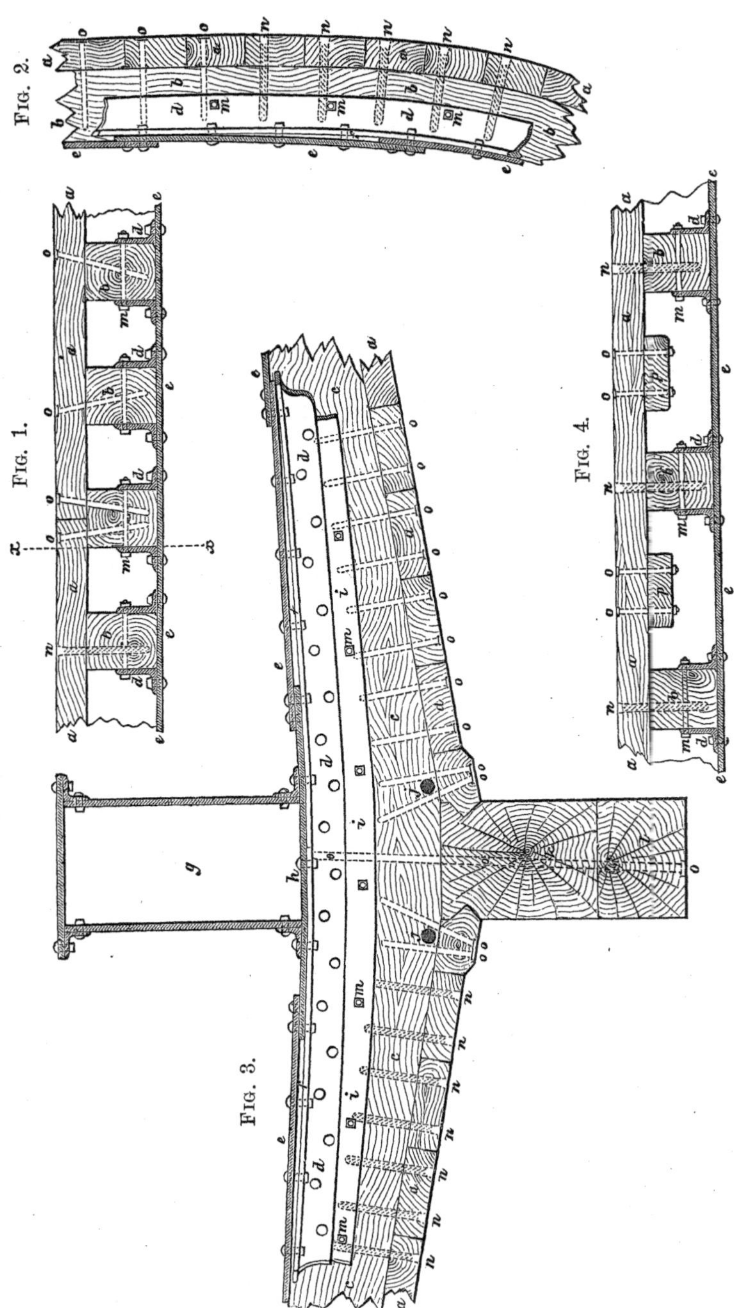

To Illustrate McLain's Method of Constructing Composite Ships.

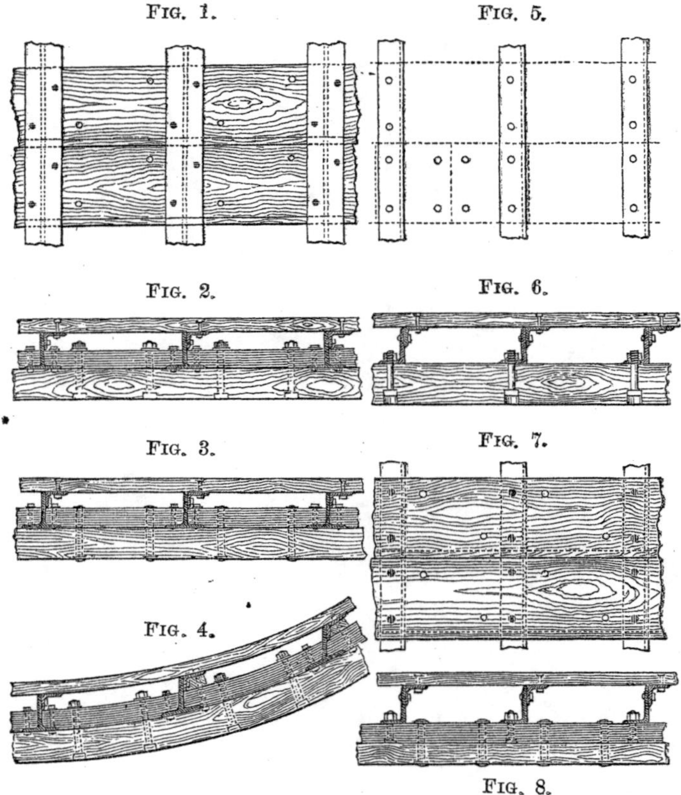

To Illustrate Scott's Improved Method of Constructing Composite Ships.

Fig. 4.—Horizontal section of a broadside, showing mode of increasing frame spacing, when considered desirable.

a a a a, Figs. 1, 2, 3 and 4.—Outer wooden planking, fastened to wooden frame with screw treenails or brass bolts.

b b b, Figs. 1, 2 and 4.—Frame timbers inserted between and bolted to angle-iron frames with galvanized iron screw bolts.

c, Fig. 3.—Wooden flooring inserted between angle-iron frames.

d d d d, Figs. 1, 2, 3 and 4.—Angle-iron frames riveted all round to outside of iron ceiling.

e e e e, Figs. 1, 2, 3 and 4.—Iron ceiling united all round at bottom and ends of vessel, and made thoroughly water-tight, forming a complete inner skin of iron.

f f, Figs. 2 and 3.—Liners, filling clinker spaces of ceiling, in wake of iron frames.

g, Fig. 3.—Box keelson.

h, Fig. 3.—Ventilation aperature through bottom of box keelson into spaces between flooring.

i, Fig. 3.—Stiffening plate, to be fitted on each side of wooden floors, and riveted to angle-iron frames to give transverse strength.

j j, Fig. 3.—Limber holes.

k, Fig. 3.—Main keel.

l, Fig. 3.—False keel.

n n n n, Figs. 1, 2, 3 and 4.—Screw treenails.

o o o o, Figs. 1, 2, 3 and 4.—Brass bolts.

p p, Fig. 4.—Planks bent in one length, from keel upwards, between frames, and fastened to outer planking with brass screw bolts.

SCOTT'S SYSTEM OF CONSTRUCTING COMPOSITE SHIPS.

The frames are of T-iron, instead of angle-iron, all fore-and-aft the ship, and, being stronger, they are spaced further apart.

Betwixt the frames are fitted chocks of teak bolted to the frames with iron bolts, and caulked throughout, forming, in fact, a water-tight ship.

Over these chocks and over the frames is wrought the outside planking, which is fastened, as shown in the drawings, by brass bolts, which pass through the chocks and planking, and which may be either clinched or screwed with nuts.

It will be observed that the planking overlaps the seams of the chocks, so that there are no through seams.

With existing appliances, the frames fore-and-aft will be somewhat more difficult to set to the figure of the ship than frames of angle-iron; but, on the other hand, the number of frames to be set is less than in the ordinary method of building composite ships. Thus, in a vessel 200 feet long, the number of frames would be fewer by at least twenty.

The drawings shown to illustrate the above, represent part of the side of a ship built according to the author's plan.

Fig. 4 shows the construction in an extreme case.

For the purpose of comparison, Figs. 5 to 8 are added, showing some other methods of constructing composite ships.

DAFT'S METHOD OF SHEATHING IRON SHIPS.

Daft's method of sheathing iron ships with copper, mixed metal or zinc, is as follows. The inner layer of the iron skin consists of narrow strips of plate, merely wide enough to make lap joints with the outer layer, and to leave a groove between the edges of each pair of outer plates, about as wide as the plates are thick. Into that groove is inserted a filling of teak or of ebonite (a hard compound of caoutchouc and sulphur). Outside the plating is a layer of tarred felt, about $\frac{1}{4}$-inch thick, upon which the sheathing is laid, and fastened with sheathing nails of the same metal, driven through the felt into the teak or ebonite fillings. Intermediate fastenings are obtained, if required, by inserting ebonite plugs into holes drilled in the iron plates, and driving sheathing nails into them through the felt.

The tarred felt serves to insulate the copper or mixed metal from the iron. It may be used with zinc sheathing also, but is not absolutely necessary; for zinc, being electro-positive to iron, protects the iron against oxidation.

During some experiments made in 1864, in England, it was found that zinc sheathing upon iron lost about .002 inch of its thickness by six months' exposure, to sea-water, and remained free from shell-fish and sea-weed, like copper or yellow metal.

GRANTHAM'S METHOD OF SHEATHING IRON SHIPS.

Grantham's method of sheathing iron ships with copper or yellow metal, is as follows: Outside the iron skin are riveted angle-iron ribs, whose projecting flanges are of a dovetail shape in section. An equal weight of iron is saved in the inside fram-

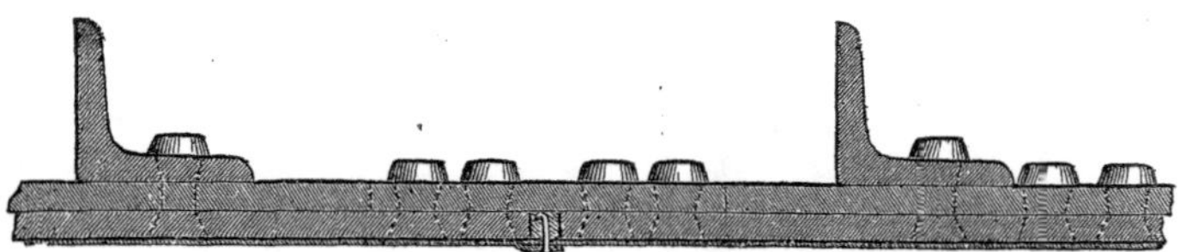

Section (enlarged) through a Sheathing Nail.

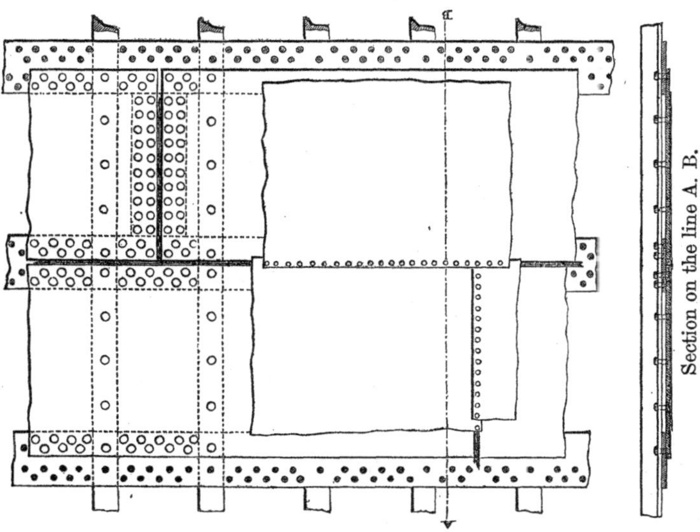

Daft's Construction and Sheathing of Iron Ships.

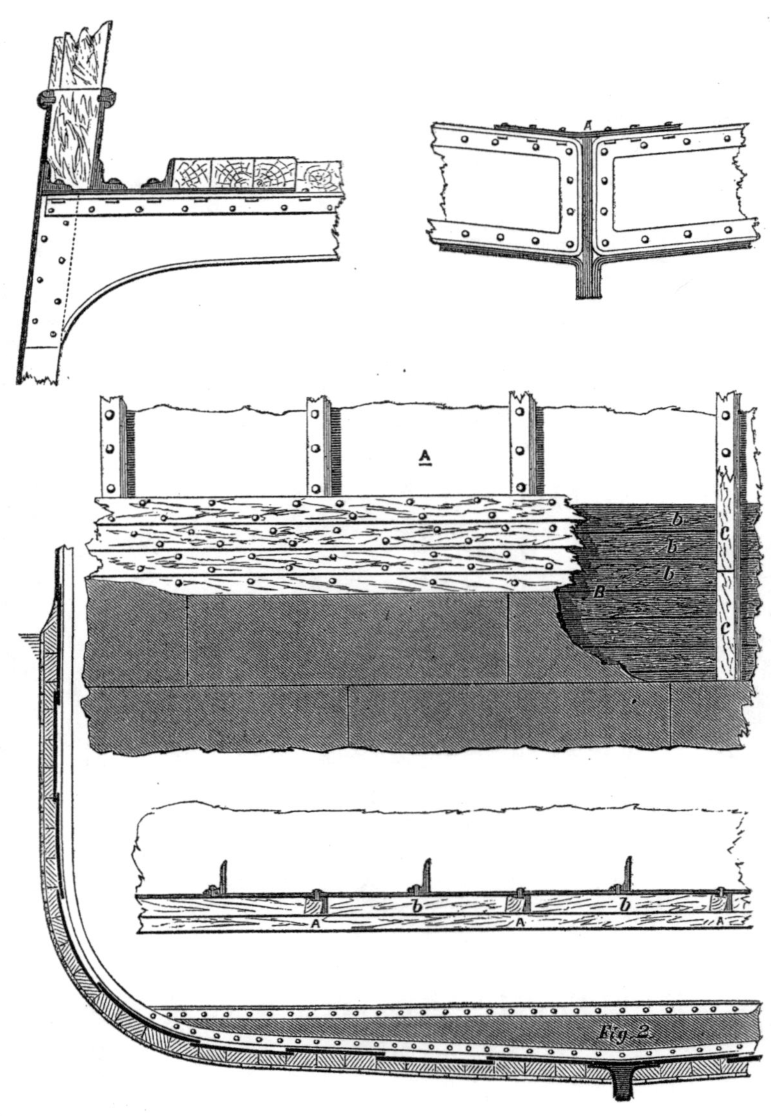

To Illustrate Grantham's Method of sheathing Iron Ships.

ing. The inner skin is then coated with pitch, and the spaces between the dovetail flanges are filled by packing and wedging into them short pieces of plank. The outside ribs, with their wooden filling, rise to a short distance above the water-line, and the upper edge of the filling is guarded by a longitudinal angle-iron. The outer surface of the filling having been payed with pitch, a complete wooden sheathing, about 1½ inches thick, is put on and fastened to the filling pieces with mixed metal nails, which should not pass through those pieces. The wooden sheathing is then pitched, and is sheathed with copper or mixed metal in the usual way—care being taken to keep the metal sheathing two or three inches from any exposed piece of iron.

If the main internal framing be vertical, the external frame may be longitudinal; or, if the main internal framing be longitudinal, the external frame may be vertical; the effect of either plan is, that both frames may be attached direct to the shell, and cross each other's path without either being cut into short lengths, as must be the case when both horizontal and vertical frames are attached on the inner side only.

ENGLISH ADMIRALTY METHOD OF SHEATHING IRON SHIPS.

In 1869, several iron vessels built for the English Navy were sheathed on a plan almost identical to that proposed by Mr. Grantham. They have brass stem and stern-post, a sheathing of teak, 3 inches in thickness, laid fore-and-aft, and tap-bolted to the shell of the ship: over this shifting butts and seams, is an outer course of the same thickness, made of lighter wood, and secured to the inner one by brass wood-screws. The wood sheathing is caulked and payed with pitch, over which the sheathing of copper is to be applied; in all these points the plans correspond. The mode of attaching the inner course is the point on which the respective plans differ.

DOCKS.

There are several kinds of docks: the principal ones are the wet, dry, sectional and balance docks.

WET DOCKS.

Wet docks on the grandest scale are to be seen at London and Liverpool; at these places there is a great rise and fall of the tide, and the wet docks are a kind of artificial harbors, where there is water enough at all times to float the vessels loading and unloading—the vessels being taken in and out of them at high water. These docks are closed by means of iron caissons.

DRY DOCKS.

Dry docks are used for building and repairing vessels in. In England's dock-yards there are at present twenty-seven dry docks completed, and thirteen in course of construction. Most of the English iron-clads are built in docks.

In our navy-yards there are three dry-docks—one at Brooklyn, N. Y.; one at Charlestown, Mass.; and one at Portsmouth, Va. These docks are closed by caissons, or boat gates, which are iron vessels about sixteen feet beam, having a keel and stem made to fit the groves in the masonry at the entrance to the dock. By admitting water in the caisson, it settles down in the grooves and closes the entrance to the dock, or is removed by pumping the water out of it—a small steam pump being used for this purpose. A dry dock is now in course of construction at Mare Island, Cal. Turning gates are placed inside the dock, so that the caisson may be docked, if necessary, to repair it at any time.

METHOD OF DOCKING A VESSEL IN A DRY DOCK.

When a vessel is to be docked, the keel and bilge-blocks are first regulated, that is, the keel-blocks are laid to the shape of the keel, and the bilge-blocks made to fit the bilge of the vessel—moulds of several cross-sections of the vessel being furnished from the mould-loft (if necessary) for this purpose. The blocks having been properly regulated, the filling culverts are opened and the water admitted into the dock until it finds its level. The filling culverts are then closed, as well as the dock chamber to the draining culverts leading to the pump well, and the water is pumped from the latter. The caisson is then floated and hauled out of the way, and the vessel hauled into the dock and secured in the centre of it with hawsers from either bow and quarter and one ahead. The caisson is now placed in its proper position and filled with water, by opening a valve in the bottom, until it rests in the grooves of the dock. The turning gates are also closed. The culvert gates in the dock chamber are now opened and the water allowed to flow into the draining culvert and well. By this means the water is lowered about a foot in a few moments, and an immediate pressure brought upon the gates, to prevent the admission of water and fix them steadily. A complete command of the level at the moment the ship is about to touch the blocks and require the placing of shores is important, as it gives a more perfect control of the operations for the first foot than could be obtained by the best regulated pumps and machinery for driving them. The water remaining in the dock is afterwards pumped out of the well into the reservoir, from which it is discharged through a culvert into the river. The shores are placed first from the side alters to the side of the vessel, called breast-shores; then a set of vertical shores are placed around the vessel at the wale height, called wale-shores, heavy cleats being screw-bolted to the vessel over the heads of them. This is done as soon as the vessel touches the blocks—the pumping being suspended in the meantime; as soon as this is completed, the remainder of the water is pumped out, and the bilge and bottom-shores placed in position. Blocks, called bilge-blocks, are hauled under the bilges as soon as the vessel grounds—ropes lead from them to the top of the dock for this purpose.

FLOATING SECTIONAL DRY DOCKS.

The government owns four floating sectional dry docks, viz., two at Philadelphia, one at Brooklyn, and one at Mare Island, Cal., Navy-yards.

The sectional docks at Philadelphia Navy-yard are composed of seven and nine sections respectively. The sections consist essentially of a main tank, two end-frames, and two floats. A truss and bulkhead extends through the centre of the main tank, directly over which are placed the keel-blocking. At right angles to the line of keel-blocks, bilge-block-ways are fitted to the deck of the tank, upon which bilge-blocks, suited to the proper form of the vessel, are slid (by means of ropes extending to the platform on the inside of the deck above) for the purpose of sustaining the vessel. Horizontal shores, graduated to feet and inches, extend from each end-frame, and are made to slide out and in, to reach the side of the vessel and keep her in the centre of the dock until the keel-blocks are brought against her keel. There is placed in each end-frame, at either side of a section, a float connected with four posts of the framework, by two shafts with small cog-wheels on each end, which work into pinions properly fastened upon one side of each of these posts, by which the machinery raises the end-floats when lowering the sections, and forces them down when raising a vessel; they serve as an equilibrium power, to keep the ends of the main tanks on a level. The sections are joined together by means of a sliding-beam on each side of the main tanks above, so arranged that they can be slid apart from three to six feet, to take up any desired length of vessel, but three feet is the usual distance. At the end of each main tank are one single and one double pump, which, together with the floats, are operated by an engine situated each side and on top of one of the sections. The shafting which conveys the power of the engines from one section to another, runs into a hollow sliding-shaft, and may be slid in or out, corresponding to the distance the sections are spread by the connecting beam. Between the sections there is an universal joint in the shaft, to provide for any deflection there may be in the line of shafting extending along and over the platform.

METHOD OF DOCKING A VESSEL ON A SECTIONAL DOCK.

When a vessel is to be docked, the main tank is filled with enough water to admit of sinking it, the end-floats are run up as the dock sinks down, and their speed regulated so as to keep it level at all times.

When the keel-blocks have been submerged a foot or two more than the draft of the vessel to be docked, the ship is hauled in and placed by the graduated wale-shores in the centre of the dock. The pumps are started and the floats worked down until the keel-blocks have a bearing on the keel of the ship. The engine is now stopped, and the workmen pass rapidly from one section to another on the platforms, and by means of the ropes reaching each platform, haul the bilge-blocks now under water, with great facility, against the bilge of the ship. The pumps and floats are now set to work until the deck of the dock is raised above the water.

If desired, the vessel can now be taken in the basin opposite a marine railway, and the vessel hauled ashore, leaving the dock clear for another vessel.

MARINE RAILWAY.

The marine railway consists of three parallel ways, the top surface of which is level with the deck of the sections. The centre way is intended to sustain the vessel on her keel when under going·repairs; the other two ways, at equal distances from the centre.way, answer the purpose of a launching-way, on which the bilge-way and cradle rest during the operation of hauling the vessel on shore. The cradle is constructed in the same manner as for launching from an inclined slip. Temporary ways are laid upon the deck of the dock, being a continuation of the ways on shore. The bilge-ways are got in place, and the cradle placed in position. The hydraulic cylinder is attached to the head of the sliding frame by large wrought iron hauling beams, and the movement commenced, which draws the vessel along eight feet at a time, until the vessel is off the dock, and on the bed-ways in the navy yard. If the bilge-ways are required for another vessel, they can be taken apart readily. Shoreing ways are arranged on either side of the ways similar to those in the ship houses.

BALANCE FLOATING DOCK.

The government owns one balance floating dock at the navy-yard, Portsmouth, N. H. It may be described in general terms as a combination of a caisson and camel, united in a form of a walled dock, having a middle compartment, in which the vessel rests after the water is pumped out. This combination is made by butting the side compartments or balancing chambers with sloping inner walls into a caisson. It is called a balance dock, from the facility of preserving an exact equilibrium and level by pumping out or letting water into the separate compartments of either of the side-chambers, of which there are eight of the compartments in each side-chamber, all communicating with the pump-well in the centre of the chamber. The portions of the side above the windows is called the ballast-chamber. The dock being entirely constructed of yellow pine, it will not sink of its own specific gravity low enough to admit vessels of great draft, and in order to sink it down to receive vessels of great draft, water is pumped into these ballast-chambers.

There are gates at the end of the dock which can be closed when vessels of great weight are to be raised.

METHOD OF DOCKING A VESSEL ON A BALANCE DOCK.

Preparatory to docking a vessel the discharge-gates are closed, and the pumps set in motion, and the chambers filled to the height of the deck of the dock; it is then allowed to flow into the upper chambers until its weight sinks the dock the required depth. Two hundred and forty tons of water are required to be pumped into the upper chambers to sink it deep enough to take on a ship drawing twenty-five feet of water. When the ship is in the dock and in position to be raised, this ballast is drawn off by opening valves in the lower side-chambers, thereby causing the dock to rise by its own specific gravity until it touches the keel of the vessel. The pumps are now started, the water pumped out of the side-chambers and bottom tank, and as the dock rises with its load, the water in the middle chamber ebbs out. The time ordinarily required to raise a vessel is about two hours.*

LAUNCHING.

(Fig. 61.)

After the carpenters have completed the hull of the vessel, the necessary preparations are commenced for launching. It is the finishing stroke of the ship builder to place her safely in the water.

The transferrence of so great a weight as one, two or three thousand tons out of the building yard into the water appears, at first sight, an arduous and difficult problem, but, with sufficient foresight and forethought, it becomes so easy as to be little more than routine.

It is the object of wise launching arrangements to guard against all casualties. First—the launch ought to take place with certainty at the exact time wanted. Second—it must take place easily and with a moderate speed. Third—provision must be made against straining. These are ordinary conditions to be foreseen; but there are sometimes others—the water is shallow, or there is very little room in the water for the ship to run after leaving the ways, or she may have some distance to run to meet the water, and for such special cases, peculiar provisions are required; and the ship may be launched equally well either head foremost, stern foremost, or broadside on, or at any required angle of obliquity with the keel, provided only the following general precautions are taken.

The ruling condition, however, of every case is this: the ship

---

* For some of the foregoing facts in relation to docks, I have consulted Stewart on Dry Docks.

must remain thoroughly well land-borne, until she becomes thoroughly well water-borne; this is the first difficulty. While the ship is being built she is well supported on the long row of blocks on which her keel rests from end to end; these carry nearly her whole weight. In addition, her hull is kept upright by the long line of shores, which, both under her bilges and all around, prevent her from swaying to either side. In this position the ship is finished, and is perfectly land-borne; but, before she is launched, she must be raised off all these blocks, and all these shores must be knocked away. The first step, then, towards launching, is to provide a new series of supports totally independent of those upon which she has been built, and which shall, nevertheless, support her as perfectly as they have done.

In the mode of launching in our Navy Yards, this is accomplished by laying down on each side of the keel two independent line of supports, resting on blocks built up at the proper declivity. These two lines of supports consist each of an upper layer of logs and an under layer; the upper constitutes the "cradle," and the lower constitutes the "ways" of the launch.

THE WAYS.

The ways consist, essentially, of the blocking, launching-ways, launching-ribband, ribband-shores and back-shores.

The ways or lower line of support, forms nothing more than a kind of railroad, serving to conduct the ship into the water. They are formed by laying, first, blocks from four to six feet apart, until they reach a height of six feet, when recourse is had to cribbing, as in building up the keel blocking, to make up the height, so as to have the depth of the bilge-ways at least in the fullest part of the body, the ways to the proper inclination.

The launching-ways consist of logs of yellow pine or white oak timber laid perfectly smooth, even and continuous, down the slip on the blocking into the water; the butts of the different logs are shifted, and secured together with screw bolts and nuts, and have the butts rounded slightly on top, to prevent any part of the bilgeway from catching as the ship goes off. The inclination of the launching-ways depend altogether upon the weight of the vessel to be launched, ranging from $1\frac{1}{8}$ in the smallest to one-half of an inch to the foot in the largest. Half an inch to a foot is a dangerously slow inclination. Five-eighths of an inch to a foot, is so moderate and gentle that, if we wish to control it, we can easily do so. Ships have been cut in two, one-half launched down this angle to its new place, under the control of cables and capstans, and stopped gently at the precise spot determined for her increased length. The third rate of inclination in use may be called "free launching," namely, six-eighths of an inch to a foot. On this inclination a ship will move steadily and gently down, without ever attaining a very high speed, and this is the inclination one should adopt, if no other circumstances biassed the choice. The next higher rate of inclination is seven-eighths of an inch to the foot; seven-eighths have an advantage over six-eighths for a large and heavy ship, because the lubrication of the ways is somewhat less effectual under a very heavy pressure than under a lighter ship. The fault of this angle is the high speed at which it delivers the ship into the water, and which makes her travel far, so as in narrow water to be both a danger and an inconvenience; it is, however, a good angle for large ships.

As has been stated in the first chapter about the inclination of the launching-way, it will be readily seen that the choice of the place in which the ship is to be built, and the height at which she stands above the water, must all be carefully attended to, when the keel is laid on the blocks. As it is the weight of the ship only which has to take her into the water, we have to see that she is built sufficiently high to allow the proper inclination of ways to run from where she lies to the place where she is to be water-borne; if this be not carefully pre-arranged, it may be impossible to lay the ways at the proper inclination. If the ship, therefore, has to travel 200 feet to get into the water, we must see that she lies 200 inches higher than the place at which she will float, if she go down 1 in 12, and a proportionately smaller height for each smaller inclination.

BREADTH OF SURFACE OF WAYS.

It is the upper surface of the ways which is lubricated with the well known ship-builder's mixture of tallow and soap, along which the ship has to slide. When the tallow has been so well applied as to form a perfectly uniform coating, and that again has been lubricated by oil, the pressure of the ship on the lubricating material may be such as to squeeze it out, and spoil the lubrication. A ship-of-war, when launched, may weigh 1000 tons, and not exceed 200 feet in length. There will, therefore, be 500 tons weight on each way, and we have to see that there is lubricated surface enough to carry this weight. Each square foot will carry up to 3 tons; therefore each way, 200 feet long by 2 feet wide, will contain 400 feet; with only a ton on each square foot, the ways will carry 800 tons; with two tons on the square foot, 1600 tons, and so on: therefore, it is quite plain that ways 2 feet wide have ample surface for an ordinary man-of-war. We have only to increase the breadth of the ways or the number of them, till we get the proper proportion to carry the weight, and so long as we keep between 2 and 3 tons as the maximum pressure on each square foot of surface we have little to fear.

DISTANCE OF WAYS APART.

The usual distance of the launching-ways from each other, from centre to centre, is about one-third of the extreme breadth of the ship at the upper end, and two or three inches wider apart in the length of the ship; this is done to prevent the vessel from becoming ribband-bound, as the cradle sometimes spreads a little when the weight of the ship comes on it.

The launching-ways are also given an in-cant of one-half an inch in a foot of the breadth of the ways, that their surfaces may present less of an acute angle to the cradle, and thus there be less danger of its spreading apart.

LAUNCHING RIBBANDS.

In launching the ship not only tends to slide downwards into the water, but will tend to slide to one side or the other off the ways, on the slightest inclination to either side. To prevent this a piece of oak plank, called a launching ribband, is bolted on the outside of the ways, projecting above it; the butts of the ribband shifting butts with the ways.

RIBBAND-SHORES.

Shores called ribband-shores are placed at frequent intervals on the outside of the launching-ways, with their heads placed against the ribband, and their heels fixed against the sides of the slip or otherwise secured. Their use is to hold the ways in place and prevent the ribband from being torn off. A platform is built the entire length of the vessel, resting on the ribband shores, which answers as a staging to work on, in fitting the packing and poppets, and in launching the vessel.

BACK-SHORES.

Two shores called back-shores are generally placed on the outside and inside of each way, at the lower end of the ship, the head resting against a heavy cleat bolted to the way, the shore placed in line with the way, and the heel properly secured; they are for the purpose of assisting to keep the ways from moving in a fore-and-aft direction, as there is sometimes a tendency of the ways to move that way, when the vessel is launched. The ways are further secured to the blocking by iron dogs.

When a ship is to be launched in a direction at right angles to the water's edge, the lower end of the launching-ways lie in one straight line, perpendicular to the keel of the vessel. But when the vessel is to be launched obliquely to the water's edge it is often convenient to make the lower ends of the launching-ways lie in a line parallel to the edge of the water, care being taken that the upper ends of the bilge-ways lie in a line parallel to the lower end of the launching-ways, so that both bilgeways may quit their bearing on the launching-ways at the same instant.

The lower end of the launching-ways usually run into a depth of water, such that, by the time the bilge-ways quit their bearing on the launching-ways, the ship shall be completely afloat.

THE CRADLE.

Having thus finished the lower line of support, we come to the upper line of support, which forms a cradle for the ship and a carriage on which she may glide along the ways to the water. The cradle is composed of bilge-ways, packing, poppets, poppet-ribbands, sole-pieces, poppet and packing-lashings, and tripping-chain.

The length of the cradle for a wooden ship should be about five-sixths of her length.

BILGE-WAYS.

The bilge-ways are two or more lines of yellow pine, or white oak logs, usually in two or three lengths, having their butts rounded on the lower side to prevent catching on any obstruction there might possibly be on the ways below, and having a hole through the ends where they abut, that a rope lashing may be passed through to secure them together; they lie immediately on the launching-ways, and under the ship, and form the base of the cradle, and directly on these the ship will be supported, that she shall be entirely carried on them as on two sledges. They have been put under such a part of the ship as they could most efficiently support, and also at such a distance asunder that no probable sway of the ship, and no impediment that she might encounter will be likely to upset her.

PACKING OR FILLINGS.

In the full part of the ship the space, from the bilge-ways to the bottom, is filled up with solid pieces of pine, called packing or filling. The quantity of this filling that will be required depends much upon the shape of the ship. Some vessels rise rapidly up from the keel, and vessels with a sharp floor will require a great deal of filling; other vessels with a flat floor, having their bilges low down, lie very near the cradle, and require very little filling. These fillings fit close on the bilge-ways on the inside, but are left about three-fourths of an inch up, on the outside, for wedge-like pieces, called launching-wedges; and before and abaft the solid part of the packing or fillings, the lower piece of filling extends to the extreme ends of the bilge-ways, being left up on the outside the same as the other part and for the same purpose.

POPPETS.

Before and abaft the packing, the ship is supported on the bilge-ways by means of upright or slightly raking square logs of white or yellow pine timber, called poppets. The number of the poppets varies; they are generally from twelve to sixteen inches square, and are placed about that distance asunder. The lower ends of the poppets are kept in their places by being tenoned into the lower piece of packing on which they rest, or by having a piece of oak plank called a sole-piece bolted on top of the lower piece of packing, and the whole size of the heel of the poppet cut out to rest in. The upper ends of the poppets are made to fit against the bottom of the vessel.

Forward, the upper ends of the poppets rake slightly aft, and aft they rake slightly forward, canting in towards the bottom of the vessel the same as the packing. The heels of the poppets are bolted to the lower piece of packing previous to launching.

POPPET-RIBBANDS.

The poppets are held together and braced longitudinally by means of pieces of oak plank called poppet-ribbands; one is generally placed just below the upper, and one above the lower ends of them. Sometimes only one is used forward, when the poppets are short. These ribbands are scored over the poppets, and extend far enough to lap a short distance on the packing. The poppet-ribbands are bolted to the poppets previous to launching.

LASHING FOR PACKING.

In the forward and after ends of the packing, an oblong score is cut through it, and a rope lashing, called a packing-lashing, is first secured to a half-round piece of live oak or lignumvitæ, called a lashing-toggle, which is placed vertically across the score on the outside, having a line secured to its upper end and made fast above on deck; the rope is then rove down under the keel and through the score on the opposite side, passed around the toggle and led back; being continued until it is thought there is sufficient to prevent the packing from being forced out, when the weight is transferred from the middle to the outer line of supports.

POPPET-LASHING.

In the method of launching laid down in many works on this subject, the upper ends of the poppets are prevented from slipping upwards by planks bolted to the bottom of the ship, and these are again secured by cleats, bolted outside of them. This is a dangerous practice, and should not be followed out. The present method is as follows:—

Commencing either at the forward or after-poppet, first, make the end of the chain fast to one of the poppets, at the height of a ribband, passing it under the keel and around the poppet on the opposite side, continuing the operation until each one has had a double turn passed around each poppet, and over the ribband above, and a single turn below, care being taken to see that all the parts are hauled taut as they are passed. The poppets now act as outriggers, the weight of the forward and after ends of the ship resting in the bite of the chains. The size of the chain used would depend altogether upon the weight and dimensions of the vessel.

PREPARATIONS FOR LAUNCHING.

The work on the launching-ways and cradle having been completed the day previous to that appointed for launching the vessel, the whole of the cradle is taken apart, the poppets and packing being placed on the platform opposite to where they belong, and the bilge-ways are shoved in under the bottom, resting on shores placed between the keel and launching-ways for that purpose. The upper part of the launching-ways and lower side of the bilge-ways are next payed over with a composition of tallow and castile soap, and then with fish oil; the tallow to fill up the pores of the wood and give a perfectly smooth surface, and the oil to lubricate that surface.

The bilge-ways are then shoved back again on the launching-ways, and the several pieces which go to make up their length are secured together at their butts by rope lashing, passed through the scores in their ends; they are kept about an inch clear of the inside of the launching-ribband by means of small pieces of wood called toggles, placed between the bilge-way and ribband; this opening is filled up with oakum all fore-and-aft to keep out any dirt; and the portion of the ways below the cradle should be covered over with loose boards for the same reason. The upper end of the bilge-way has an oak plank from four to six inches in thickness, let down flush on top and securely bolted to it, called a sole-piece; it projects some four or five feet on to another piece called a chock, and is securely fastened by screw bolts passing through the chock and launching-ways, and set up below with nuts and washers; it is this plank or sole piece which is finally cut when the time for launching arrives. The cradle is then again replaced, and the launching-wedges are now placed about a foot apart between the bilge-way and packing, all along the cradle; the chain-lashings on the poppets and rope-lashings on the packing are passed and properly secured—the services of the boatswain and a gang of riggers being required for this purpose—the packing-lashings being wet down to shrink them as taut as possible. Meanwhile, other precautions and matters of forethought have been attended to. If the vessel is to be launched in a narrow stream, powerful warps and cables should be carried out from the ship and made fast to anchors or moorings ashore, to bring up the ship and stop her sternway in the water, they should be properly looped up to the ship and laid clear of all possible entanglement, so that, in going down, they may drag no obstacle with them; on board, anchors and cables should be made ready to let go, when the hold of an anchor may be required. Special precautions are required for the immediate removal of the entire cradle, bilge-ways and packing from under the ship the moment she has taken the water. For this purpose a chain-cable of about 1 or $1\frac{1}{8}$ inch link, called a tripping-chain, is provided; it is middled and the bite made fast generally to an anchor buried at the upper ends of the ways, and the ends are secured to bolts in the upper ends of the bilge-ways: the parts of the chain are then led down on the inside of the bilge-ways and stopped up out of the way with rope yarns: the cables are sufficiently long not to come taut until the ship is quite afloat; by this means the bilge-ways are suddenly brought to a stand still, while the ship is still moving powerfully away; thus the ship, of herself, leaves the cradle behind, the weight of the chains on the poppets causes them to turn bottom up, clear of the ship, the toggles in the packing are drawn out and the various portions which compose it are seen floating away from her on both sides. In the space allotted to the engines and boilers, shores or braces are placed to prevent the bilges from springing when the weight of the ship comes on the two outer lines of supports or ways; one set of shores are placed with their heads in the throats of the hanging knees of the deck directly above, and their heels resting on the side or boiler keelson, as near over the line of the ways as they can be got; from the heels of these inclined shores horizontal shores are placed, resting on top of the sister keelsons and against the side of the main keelson. A stanchion or heavy shore is also placed under every beam from the top of main keelson. To prevent the long wooden vessels of the *Wampanoag* or *Florida* class from hogging, the following plan was adopted and successfully used: Three pieces of yellow pine timber 14 inches square called king-posts were placed vertically on top of the main keelson, extending 26 feet above the spar-deck; one piece through the forward-hatch, one through the boiler-hatch, and the other through the after-hatch; all properly braced and secured in the hatches of the respective decks and below in the hold; on the head of each king-post a heavy wrought iron band was placed, having eyes worked on all four sides, at the foot of each king-post wrought iron straps having an eye in the upper end, were securely bolted to the sister keelson; an inch and an-eighth chain-cable was then shackled between each post at their heads and carried down forward-and-aft to a breast or stern-hook to which they were secured; a chain was then led from the head of each post to the strap on the keelson opposite the heel of the post next forward or aft of it, and shackled to the eye in the strap, and, from the eyes in the band on either side of the posts, chains were led to eye-bolts placed through the water-ways of the upper deck. This made as a complete a truss-frame as was required, and no apparent alteration in the sheer of the ship could be detected after launching, as had been the case in vessels of this class that were launched in other navy yards without the truss or hog frame.* A hawser was carried over all parts of the chain and stopped to it at short intervals, to hold it from flying and causing any damage, should it be parted by the great strain brought on it.

The ship still rests as she was built on the slip, and the cradle is merely placed but carries no weight. Two things are now to be done; the whole present supports of the ship are to be removed, and the whole of her weight is to be transferred to the cradle. All the necessary preparations for launching having been made; an hour before the tide will be at its height, a large number of shipwrights are ranged in gangs of from four to six each, at short intervals on each side of the vessel, each gang armed with a battering ram, and at a given signal from the Naval Constructor, they strike the wedges as with one blow from stem to stern, till the whole cradle steadily and strongly rises, pressing the filling pieces up so strongly against the bottom of the ship that they begin to carry a part of her weight and to lighten her load on the building blocks. Every other keel block is now removed commencing from aft, and every other wale and bilge shore taken down. When this is completed, the shipwrights again drive in the wedges until they can do no more; the remaining keel blocks are now removed, and the shores taken down. In heavy ships the desire of the ship to go begins to express itself before the time arrives; a strain visibly comes on everything which tends to keep the ship in its place, and as no materials are perfectly rigid they begin to show that they are under a strain and those that are too much pressed sensibly complain. The only thing that now re-

* This hog or truss-frame was first used by Naval Constructor B. F. Delano, U.S.N., in launching the *Florida* and *Tennessee*, vessels 335 feet in length.

mains to be done is to cut the sole-pieces which connect the bilge-ways to the launching-ways, which is done with a cross-cut saw, by carpenters stationed there for the purpose. The word is passed from aft by the assistant to the constructor—“ All clear, sir ! ” The order is given—“ Cut the ways ! ” and off she goes into the water, (Fig. 62) being baptized by some lady as she commences to move down the ways. In some cases the vessel has refused to move after the sole-piece has been cut, and in event of this happening hydraulic rams are used, one placed against the end of each bilge-way, and if necessary, one under the fore-foot of the vessel; as soon as a strain is put upon them, the vessel will most likely move off.

LAUNCHING OF IRON-CLAD SHIPS BUILT ON THE LONGITUDINAL SYSTEM.

In launching iron vessels built upon the longitudinal system of framing, the launching-ways should be placed in such a position that the weight of the vessel, when transferred from the keel blocks to the launching cradle would come upon a longitudinal, and not between them, on the bracket-plates. In launching the armor-plated ship, *Audacious*, of the English Navy, built by Napier & Sons, of Glasgow, in 1868, considerable damage was sustained by the vessel, caused by placing the launching ways between the longitudinals amidships instead of directly under them. The government inspector objected strongly to this, but the managers objected, preferring that the launching-ways should catch the longitudinals at the ends of the ship. Short pieces of timber were introduced between the inner and outer skins in a vertical position over the cradle, and then a piece of timber was placed in a fore-and-aft direction on the inner bottom, over the vertical pieces, and again passing shores from that fore-and-aft piece to the deck above, so that any strain that might be brought upon the ship, through having the ways in that position, should be distributed throughout the ship. About the time that the ship was ready to be launched a heavy gale of wind was blowing, and as the ship went off it caught her quarter, and tended to twist her, bringing a great strain upon the port-side of the ship while there was a corresponding strain brought upon the starboard bow, which had the effect of buckling two or three frames there ; in the wake of the engine-room several of the bracket plates were buckled and cracked. It took upwards of one week to repair the damages.

FIG. 62.

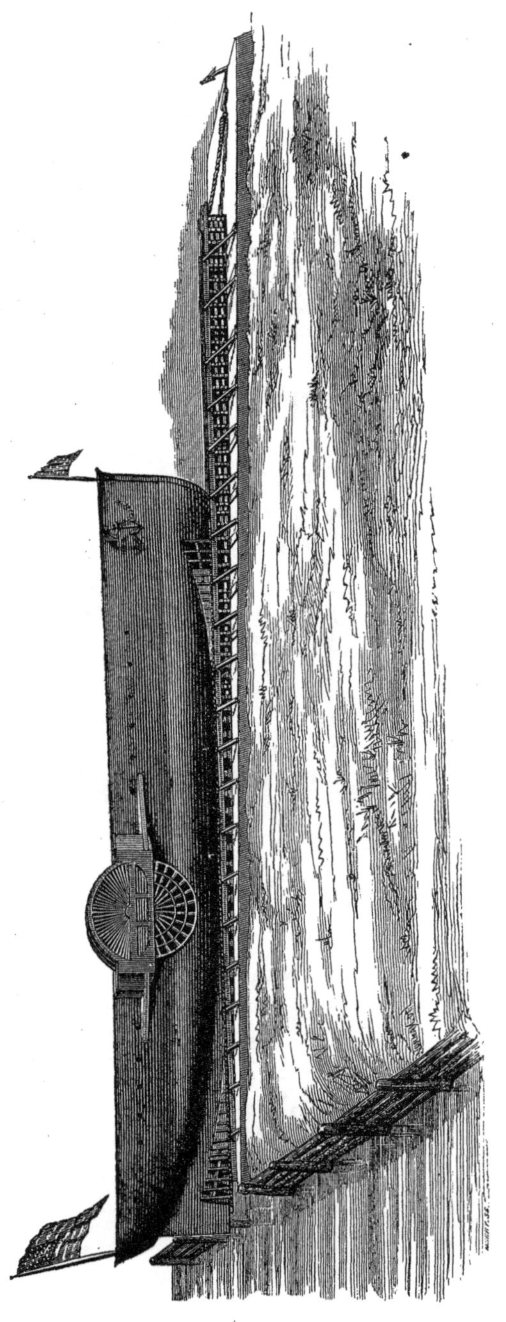

The Naval Constructor, after a careful examination of the damaged parts, reported that the accident was caused by placing the launching-ways improperly between the longitudinal frames.

ON COMPLETING THE LAUNCHING OF SHIPS WHICH HAVE STOPPED ON THEIR LAUNCHING-WAYS.*

The *Cæsar*, a ten-gun two-decker wooden ship, having been prepared for launching, was attempted to be launched on the 21st of July, 1853, at the Royal Dockyard, at Pembroke, South Wales, but after she had slid down the launching ways some eighty feet, and thus immersed her after-part in the water at high tide, she stopped entirely, and all the subsequent effort made that day to move her were of no avail. The declivity given to the launching ways was the usual amount, and the plank and material used in the ways were also of the usual description.

Betweeen the 21st and 26th of July, some small hollow-vessels, built for the purpose, and a few casks, etc., were put under the ship's bottom, below high water-mark, with the view of reducing the weight of the ship on the ways, and at the time of high-tide efforts were then made, by means of purchases, to pull the ship off, but all the measures were unavailing.

The plan was then advocated of the necessity of building camels, for breaking the too close contact that appeared to be established between the bilge-ways and launching-ways, by lifting the stern of the ship, so as to take its weight off of the launching ways. Three large camels were therefore ordered to be laid off in the mould loft, in a few hours, to fit each buttock, seventy-two feet long, to be planked with four-inch plank, and one for the stern, twenty feet square in section and forty-eight feet long, to be built of five-inch plank; the collective lifting power, when properly in place, being estimated equal to 1,100 tons. In nine days these camels were finished and launched; they were got in place at low-water, and secured by bearers put out at the quarter-ports on the lower-deck, and shored to the main-deck upper sills, to keep in place the quarter camels; a similar plan having also been adopted to keep down the stern camel; without any pulling power being applied, the ship about one-and three quarter hours before high water, abandoned her unworthy connection with the land and glided gracefully into the water.

---

* From Transactions of the Institute of Naval Architects.

*On the 17th of March, 1866, the *Northumberland*, an iron frigate, 400 feet in length, and weighing over 3000 tons, stopped on her launching slip; a second set of ways were laid with the same inclination as the first, and mooring lighters were placed under her quarters and alongside aft, but they failed to launch the ship.

Immediately after this failure, four camels, two for each quarter, were built in a very few days, and they were secured in place by the 17th of April (just one month from the first attempt to launch the ship being made), and on the rising of the tide they lifted the ship abaft off the launching ways, when she glided into the river without the help of the large pulling power which had been provided.

The advantages obtained by the use of camels, are due to the fact that they take all the weight of the ship off the bilge ways, except the extreme fore-end, so that the after-part is lifted clear of any obstruction that may exist, or where the grease used is bad or insufficient in quantity, the adhesion of the surfaces in contact is overcome, and they are left free to slide upon each other.

To the foregoing it may be added that due consideration should at all times be given in preparing the "launch" of a ship to the relative weight of the ship and area of launching ways, declivity of the launching slip, and to the time it is intended the ship shall rest in her cradle before the launch takes place; then, finally, on the kind and quantity of grease to be used between the sliding surfaces. All these points affect the *friction* to be overcome in launching the ship.

LAUNCHING OF THE GREAT EASTERN.

The launching arrangements of this vessel, in most of their features, differed little from those of any other vessel, with the exception only that she was launched broadside on. It is only necessary to supply a sufficiently large surface, well lubricated, and the weight of the ship can be just as easily carried down an incline broadside on, as end on. The blunder made in launching the *Great Eastern* was the determination to try the experiment of launching her on iron ways. The folly of such an arrangement is shown by a very simple experiment. There was in the yard where the *Great Eastern* was built, a railway incline of 1 in 24.

* From Transactions of the Institute of Naval Architects.

On that inclination, a single wheel of a railway track, locked fast, was enough to stop the descent of the truck, and just enough. That proves that friction of an iron wheel, on an iron rail, to be nearly equivalent to an inclination of 1 in 6, and this with so large a bearing as that of a smooth wheel on a used rail. In the launch of the *Great Eastern*, one set of rails with a round top crossed another set of rails with a round top, and, of course, they bit each other under pressure, and bit each other with a force certainly not less than one-sixth part of the whole load. In short, they bit as the wheel of a locomotive bites the rail, only somewhat more severely. This biting of rail on rail was the whole cause of the failure of the launch of the *Great Eastern*. The launching arrangements were duly carried out by the owners of the ship, as originally designed, but with the addition of a set of iron bars on the upper surface of the ways, and another set of iron bars on the lower surface of the cradle. When abandoned to the sliding force of these bars, the ship slid a few feet until the lubricating stuff was rubbed off, and then the rails simply bit one another, as the wheels of a locomotive engine bite the rails, and they held the ship firmly in its place; so firmly, that not only was the inclination of 1 in 12 with the whole weight of 12,000 tons of ship on it unable to move it down the inclined plane, but some thousands of tons of additional pressure by hydraulic rams were unable to force it down into the water in a less period than some three months from starting. Had the surface on which she was carried been simply the ordinary plank surface, well lubricated with tallow and grease, the phenomenon of launching the *Great Eastern* would have been no other phenomenon than the ordinary launch of a large ship. The area of the ways covered by the two cradles was nearly 20,000 square feet, and that surface was far more than sufficient to conduct the weight smoothly and gently down into the water in the manner of an ordinary launch.

[From Scott Russell's Naval Architecture.]

DIVISION FOURTH.

MAST AND SPAR-MAKING;

WITH A NUMBER OF USEFUL TABLES, AND PROPORTIONS OF DIFFERENT PARTS OF SPARS; ALSO PROPORTIONS FOR ALL KINDS OF IRON-WORK FOR SPARS.

MAST AND SPAR-MAKING.

REMARKS ON THE BENEFIT OF HAVING MASTS ELASTIC.

1. If masts or other spars in a vessel are stiff or stubborn "they will cramp her in sailing," for this reason, iron masts will never come in use as a general thing, unless they can be made more elastic.

In making masts due regard ought to be had to their strength to support their weight and pressure of setting up their rigging.

The masts that are in use in the U. S. Navy, at the present time (1872), and that were invented by me in 1839, contain all the above qualities; they are lighter, more elastic, and stronger than the old plan, to say nothing of their beauty and economy in building them.

Without any further remarks in this part of the work, I will commence my system of sparring vessels for war, and other purposes.

MAIN-MAST.

2. Multiply the moulded breath of beam by two, and add two-thirds the depth of the hold* for the length of the main-mast.

The main-mast to be in the partners one inch to every three feet of its length.

The heels of all lower masts to be sixth-sevenths of their greatest diameter.

At the stop of hounds nine-tenths of their greatest diameter.

At the trestle-trees three-quarters of their greatest diameter.

At the upper part of the mast-head six-sevenths of the diameter of the mast in the trestle-trees.

The mast to be lined with a fair curve, from the stop of hounds to the heel, so as to make the mast at the first setting off, above the partners, a little larger than the partners; this will give the mast

* The depth of the hold is here calculated from the top of keelson to top of the main-deck, and all three masts are calculated to bury the same; but if the "fore and mizzen-mast" buries less, then the difference is to be deducted from them.

strength where it is required; the more barrelling you make the mast the greater strength it will have.

The length of all lower-mast heads are five-fourteenths of the length of their respective topmasts without the head.

FORE-MAST.

3. The fore-mast to be in length nine-tenths of the length of main-mast; the diameter the same as main-mast, and in all other respects the same.

MIZZEN-MAST.

4. The mizzen-mast, at cap, to be on a level one-third of the length of main-mast head, above the bottom of main trestle-trees.

Head of mizzen to be in length five-sevenths of main-mast head; diameter five-sevenths of the diameter of main-mast.

BOWSPRIT.

5. The bowsprit to be in length ten-sixteenths of the length of main-mast.

The diameter the same as the main-mast; diameter at heel to be six-sevenths of its greatest diameter.

Outer-end to be two-thirds of its greatest diameter, two-thirds of its length out-board (top-side) from the rabbet.

MAIN-TOPMAST.

6. The main-topmast is three-fifths of the length of the-main-mast.

The head of the topmast is one-third of the length of its respective top-gallant-mast; diameter one inch to every three feet of its length; heel-blocks for the sheave are added, in length one and a quarter of its diameter.

To be lined straight, and the same size from heel to stop of hounds; to be in the trestle-trees five-sevenths of its greatest diameter; to be at the top of the head six-sevenths of the trestle-trees.

FORE-TOPMAST.

7. The fore-topmast to be in length nine-tenths of the main top-mast, and in all other respects the same proportions as the main-topmast, and the same diameter as the main-topmast.

MIZZEN-TOPMAST.

8. The mizzen-topmast to be in length five-sevenths of the main-topmast, and in all other respects the same proportions as the main-topmast; diameter five-sevenths of the diameter of the main-topmast.

JIB-BOOM.

9. The length of the jib-boom outboard is one-half of the length of the main-topmast.

The length of the inboard part of the jib-boom is two-thirds of the outboard part.

Pole included one-twentieth part of the whole length; the diameter is twelve-thirteenths of the diameter of main-topmast.

FLYING-JIB-BOOM.

10. The length of the flying-jib-boom (outboard part without the pole) is two-thirds the length of the outboard part of the jib-boom, pole added one-ninth of its whole length; the diameter is twelve-thirteenths of the diameter of the main top-gallant-mast; at the heel five-eighths of the greatest diameter; at the stop of hound four-fifths of its greatest diameter; at the grommet two-thirds of its greatest diameter; outer end of pole one-half the size of the grommet.

JIB-BOOM (*again*).

11. The heel of the jib-boom is three-quarters of its greatest diameter, at the stop of the hounds four-fifths of the greatest diameter, at the end of the pole seven-eighths of its grommet.

MAIN TOP-GALLANT-MAST.

12. The length of the main top-gallant-mast is one-half of the length of the main-topmast, diameter nine-eighths to every three feet, and lined straight from the heel to the stop of the hounds.

FORE TOP-GALLANT-MAST.

13. The fore top-gallant-mast in length is nine-tenths of the length of the main top-gallant-mast and the same size and proportions in other respects.

MIZZEN TOP-GALLANT-MAST.

14. The length of mizzen top-gallant-mast is five-sevenths of the length of the main top-gallant-mast, and in all other respects the same proportions.

MAIN ROYAL-MAST.

15. The length of the main royal-mast is two-thirds of the length of its top gallant-mast. The diameter is four-fifths of the diameter of the main top-gallant-mast.

At the upper part or stop of hound is ten-elevenths of the diameter of its respective royalmast. Poles are in length the length of their respective topmast heads, diameter of pole is three-quarters of the diameter of royal-mast; end of pole half the diameter of heel of pole.

FORE ROYAL-MAST.

16. The length of the fore royal-mast is nine-tenths of the main royal-mast, and the same size and the same proportion of the main royal-mast.

MIZZEN ROYAL-MAST.

17. The mizzen royal-mast in length five-sevenths of the length of the main and the diameter five-sevenths of the main; all other proportions the same as the main.

MAIN-YARD.

18. To get the length of the main-yard multiply the moulded breadth of beam by two and add the length of arm, one-twentieth of this length. The diameter one inch to every four feet the ends of the yard-arm is three-sevenths of its greatest diameter.

FORE-YARD.

19. The fore-yard is nine-tenths of the main-yard, and in all other respects the same proportions as the main-yard.

CROSS-JACK-YARD.

20. The cross-jack-yard is five-sevenths of the main-yard, the length of arms are one-tenth of its length; the diameter is one inch to every four and a half of its length.

MAIN-TOPSAIL YARD.

21. The main-topsail yard is three-fourths of the length of the main yard. The diameter is one inch to every four feet in length; the arms are one-eleventh of its length; the ends are three-sevenths of its greatest diameter.

FORE-TOPSAIL YARD.

22. The fore-topsail yard is nine-tenths of the main-topsail yard, in all other respects the same proportions.

MIZZEN-TOPSAIL YARD.

23. The mizzen-topsail yard is five-sevenths of the main-topsail yard, in all other respects the same proportion.

MAIN TOP-GALLANT YARD.

24. The main top-gallant yard is nine-fourteenths of the length of the main top-sail yard. The diameter is seven-eighths of an inch to every four feet of its length. The arms are one-twentieth of its length. The ends of the yard are three-sevenths of its greatest diameter.

FORE TOP-GALLANT YARD.

25. The fore top-gallant yard is nine-tenths of the main top-gallant yard and in all other respects the same proportion.

MIZZEN TOP-GALLANT YARD.

26. The mizzen top-gallant yard is five-sevenths of the length of the main top-gallant yard, and in all other respects the same proportions.

MAIN ROYAL-YARD.

27. The main royal-yard is nine-twentieths of the length of the main top-sail yard. The diameter is seven-eighths to every four feet of its length; the arms are one-twentieth of its length; the ends of the yard are three-sevenths of its greatest diameter.

FORE ROYAL-YARD.

28. The fore royal-yard is nine-tenths of the length of the main royal-yard, and in all other respects the same proportions.

MIZZEN ROYAL-YARD.

29. The mizzen royal-yard is five-sevenths of the main royal-yard, and in all other respects the same proportion.

SPANKER-BOOM.

30. The spanker-boom is one-half the length of the main-mast, the pole one-fourteenth of its length included; the diameter is one inch to every four feet of its length; the inner end is four-fifths of its greatest diameter; at the shoulders or stops it is two-thirds of its greatest diameter; at the grommet it is two-thirds of its inner end; and at the outer end of pole it is six-sevenths of the grommet.

SPANKER-GAFF.

31. The spanker-gaff is four-fifths of the length of the spanker-boom, the pole included one-sixth of its length; the diameter is one inch to every four feet of its length; the inner end is six-sevenths of the greatest diameter; the outer end at stops is three-quarters of its greatest diameter; in the grommet it is two-thirds of its greatest diameter; and at the end of the pole it is one-half the size of the grommet.

MAIN AND FORE-GAFFS.

32. The main and fore-gaffs are four-fifths of the length of the spanker-boom; pole is one-thirtieth of its length included; diameter one inch to every four feet of its length; inner end six-sevenths of its greatest diameter; outer end or stops three-quarters of the greatest diameter; end of pole three-quarters of the grommet.

DOLPHIN-STRIKER.

33. The dolphin-striker to be in length one-half of the length of the out-board part of the jib-boom; pole included one-sixth of its length; the diameter is one inch and one-eighth to every two feet; the inner end is three-quarters of its greatest diameter; the outer end at stop is eight-ninths of its greatest diameter; in the grommet it is five-sevenths of its greatest diameter; and at the end of the pole it is three-quarters of the grommet.

WHISKER-BOOMS.

34. The whisker-booms are the same length as the dolphin-striker, and the same diameter; the inner ends are four-fifths of their greatest diameter; the outer ends at stop is the same size as the greatest diameter; in the grommet it is five-eighths of the greatest diameter; they should be lined with a neck.

NOTES ON YARDS.

35. When yards are made with poles for arms, they should be made of the following dimensions, viz.:

Lower-yards, top-gallant yards, and royal-yards are in the grommet one-half of their greatest diameter. The shoulders to be from three-quarters to one-quarter of an inch in thickness, according to the size of the yard; and the end of the poles three-sevenths of the greater diameter of the yard.

TOP-SAIL YARDS.

36. Top-sail yards are in the grommet five-eighths of their greatest diameter, the shoulder to be from one-half an inch to three-quarters of an inch in thickness, according to the size of the yard; the end of the poles should be three-sevenths of the greatest diameter of the yard.

ENSIGN-STAFF.

37. The ensign-staff is one-third of the length of the main-mast, above the main-rail; the diameter is one-inch to every six feet of its length, and at the top it is two-thirds of its greatest diameter.

JACK-STAFF.

38. The jack-staff is one-half of the length of the ensign-staff above the top of the jib-boom; the diameter is one inch to every five feet of its length; the top end is two-thirds of its greatest diameter.

CAP-SHORES.

39. The length of the cap-shore is the length of the mast-head; the diameter is one inch to every four feet of its length.

SWINGING-BOOMS.

40. The swinging-booms are in length five-eighths of the length of the fore-yard. The diameter is one inch to every five feet of

their length; the inner ends are four-fifths of their greatest diameter; and the outer ends are two-thirds of their greatest diameter.

TOPMAST STUDDING-SAIL BOOMS.

41. The topmast studding-sail booms in length are one-half the length of their respective yards, and twice the diameter added to them.

The diameter of the booms is one inch to every five feet of their length.

The inner ends are four-fifths of their greatest diameter.

The outer ends are two-thirds of their greatest diameter.

TOP-GALLANT STUDDING-SAIL BOOMS.

42. The top-gallant studding sail-booms are of the same proportions as the top-mast studding-sail booms, according to their respective yards.

TOPMAST STUDDING-SAIL YARDS.

42½. The topmast studding-sail and top-gallant studding-sail yards are in length two-fifths of their respective yards, and the lower studding-sail yard the same length as the topmast studding-sail yard.

The diameter is one inch to every four feet of their length.

MAIN-TOP.

43. The main-top in breadth is one-half of the moulded breadth of beam.

The length of the top is five-eighths of its breadth.

The breadth of the lubber-hole is two-fifths of the breadth of the top.

The forward part of the top is two-ninths of its length.

The after part of tops is three-ninths of its length.

The length of the lubber-hole is two-sevenths of the breadth of tops.

The forward topmast shroud to be opposite the middle of the lower-mast head.

The forward cross-trees to be even with the lubber-hole; the after cross-trees to be the width of the lubber-board aft of the lubber-hole.

FORE-TOP.

44. The fore-top to be nine-tenths of the main-top, and in all other respects it is the same proportion.

MIZZEN-TOP.

45. The mizzen-top is five-sevenths of the main-top, and in all other respects it is the same proportion.

LOWER TRESTLE-TREES.

46. The lower trestle-trees in depth are the diameters of their respective topmasts, and one-half of the depth of their thicknesses.

The ends of trestle-trees are tapered to four-fifths of their depth.

The nuts are in thickness three-sevenths of the diameter of their respective topmasts.

TOPMAST TRESTLE-TREES.

47. The topmast trestle-trees in depth are the diameters of their respective top-gallant masts, and one-half the depth of their thickness; the ends are tapered to four-fifths of the depth.

The nuts are in thickness two-fifths of the diameter of their respective top-gallant masts.

LOWER CROSS-TREES.

48. The lower cross-trees in width are one-half of the depth of their respective trestle-trees.

The thickness of the cross-trees is two-thirds of their widths.

The thickness of the ends of cross-trees is one-half of the middle-part of the cross-trees.

TOPMAST CROSS-TREES.

49. The after topmast cross-trees should be in length three-fifths of the breadth of the tops.

The forward topmast cross-trees should be five-sevenths of the after cross-trees in length; they should curve about four inches in sixteen feet.

The forward cross-trees should be placed between the heel of the top-gallant mast and the topmast head.

The topmast cross-trees should be in width one-half the depth of the trestle-trees.

The width of the ends should be three-quarters of the width at the centre.

The depth of the centre of cross-trees should be three-quarters their width.

The depth of the ends of the cross-trees is three-fifths of the depth at the centre.

CAPS.

50. The caps are in width one and five-elevenths of the diameter of their respective topmasts and top-gallant masts.

The depth of the caps should be one-half of their width.

The wood on the ends of the caps should be five-twelfths of the diameter of their respective topmasts and top-gallant, etc.

BIBBS.

51. Bibbs for lower-masts should be in length four-elevenths of the length of the mast-head.

The length of the arms of bibbs is the width of the trestle-trees the width of the nut and two-thirds the diameter of the topmast added together.

The thickness of the bibbs is nine-eighths to every foot in length.

The lower end of the bibbs is one-half of the width of the mast in the trestle-trees.

The thickness of the lower end of the bibbs is one-quarter of its greatest thickness.

LONG BEES ON BOWSPRIT.

52. The length of the bees to be long enough to reach three feet inside of the head-rail.

The size of the bees to be one-quarter of the greatest diameter of the bowsprit, "*square*."

NOTES ON MASTS AND BOWSPRITS.

53. All made masts and bowsprits should be put together with lignumvitæ dowels or coaks, one coak under each hoop on the first two strakes put together, and the next two strakes to have coaks half way between the hoops. The coaks in the scarphs to be about two feet apart, and placed so as not to come in contact

with the bolts through the coaks in each strake. The coaks or dowels for all masts of twenty-eight inches in their greatest diameter or under, to be three inches in diameter.

All over twenty-eight inches to be three and a half inches in diameter.

NOTES ON BIBBS.

54. The bibbs to be put on with two reverse diagonal shoulders and from three to four coaks, the upper shoulder in thickness one-eighth to every three inches of the greatest diameter of the mast.

The lower shoulder to be one-eighth to every four inches of the greatest diameter of the mast.

NOTES ON SCARPHS AND HOOPS.

55. The scarphs to be equally divided throughout the length of the mast, and kept out of the neck of the mast as much as possible. The hoops on the fore and main-mast of a sloop-of-war and a frigate's mizzen-mast, to be in width four and a quarter inches, and in thickness one-half inch.

The hoops on the fore and main-mast of a frigate and line-of-battle ship's mizzen-mast to be in width four and three-quarters, and in thickness nine-sixteenths of an inch.

The hoops on a fore and main-mast of a line-of-battle ship to be in width five inches, and in thickness five-eighths of an inch.

NIBS OF SCARPHS OF MASTS.

56. The outside nibs of scarphs to be one-tenth of the greatest diameter of the mast; the inside nib to be one-seventeenth of the greatest diameter of the mast.

CHAFING BATTENS.

57. Chafing battens on the front side of masts to cover the keys of bands, are in width three-twelfths of the greatest diameter of the mast; the thickness is one-half of the width.

SQUARE HOLE IN LOWER MASTS.

58. The square hole in the centre of the lower masts should be one-tenth of the greatest diameter of the mast.

PREPARING TO BUILD A MAST.

59. In making masts out of plank stock or other timber on the plan at the present time in use in the U. S. Navy,—in the first place take a long rod, the proper length of the mast, set off the length of the head, and the depth of hold or partners of the mast, divide the part between the partners and stop of hounds into eight equal parts, and between the partners and heel into four equal parts, make a mark for a hoop thirty inches above the partners, and another one two inches below the stop of hounds, then divide the spaces for hoops into equal parts, so that they will be, for a sloop-of-war, about three feet from centre to centre; for a frigate, about three feet three inches; and for a line-of-battle ship, about three feet six inches; then mark the hoops below the deck so as to clear the wedges.

The length of scarphs to be regulated by the hoops so that for a sloop-of-war's mast, and frigate's mizzen-mast, there shall be four hoops on each scarph; on a frigate's fore and main-mast, and a line-of-battle's ship mizzen-mast five hoops on each scarph, and all larger masts the same.

FASTENINGS FOR MASTS.

60. Masts of all sizes should be bolted with three-quarter iron bolts, spaced about nine feet apart on each strake.

FUTTOCK-BAND.

61. The futtock-band should be placed seven-fifteenths of the breadth of the tops from the top of the hound to the centre of the band.

TRUSS-BAND.

62. The truss-band should be one-half the length of the mast-head from the top of the hound to the centre of the band.

NOTES ON YARDS.

63. The scarphs of all yards should be in length about one-third of the length of the yard.

If your timber should not be long enough, then less than one-third will do.

They should be put together with lignumvitæ dowels or coaks spaced about two feet apart.

Three inch coaks should be used for small yards, and three and a half for large yards.

The nibs of scarphs of yards should be in thickness one-fourteenth of the greatest diameter of the yard.

The hoops to be spaced from centre to centre one and one-quarter the diameter of the yard. The hoops that cover the nibs should be wider and thinner than the others.

The chafing battens on lower and top-sail yards should be in length one-half the length of the yard; the width to be a little less than the eight square in the centre, and the ends to be three-quarters of the centre. Chafing battens on top-gallant and royal yards, are in length twice the length of the arms, and in width the eight square.

IRON WORK FOR YARDS.

64. Pacific irons for lower yards to be in length three and a half times the diameter of the end of the yards.

The width of straps to be one-half the diameter of the end of the yards.

The inner end of the straps should be five-sixths of the width of the outer end.

The length of the neck should be one-half of the diameter of the end of the yard, which is added to the length of the pacific irons.

The size of the neck is one-half the length of the neck; size of the square part is two-fifths of the length of the neck added.

TOP-SAIL YARDS.

65. Pacific irons for top-sail yards should be in length four times the diameter of the ends of yards.

The width of the strap is one-half the end of the yard.

The inner end of the strap is five-sixths of the outer end of the strap.

The length of the neck is three-fifths of the end of the yard.

The size of the neck is seven-fifteenths of the length of the neck.

The size of the square part is two-sixths of the length of the neck added.

QUARTER-IRONS.

66. The quarter-iron in the neck between the yard and boom should be one-half the diameter of the boom, and should be placed one-sixth of the length of the yard from the end of it.

BOOM-IRONS.

67. The boom-irons for all yards, from the centre of the yard to the lower side of the booms, is six-thirteenths of the diameter of the yard at the slings.

The size of iron should be the same size as the neck of their respective pacific irons.

The rollers to be in length one-half of the diameter of the booms. (No roller in top-sail yard iron.)

The width of the irons should be one-third the end of the yard.

BURTON-BANDS, LOWER YARDS.

68. The burton-bands on the lower yards should be placed one-seventh of the length of the yard from the end of it, with an eye and shackle on the top side of the yard.

BURTON-BANDS, TOP-SAIL YARDS.

69. The burton-bands on the top-sail yards should be one-sixth of the length of the yard from the end of it.

DISTANCE BETWEEN MASTS AND YARDS.

70. The distance between the lower yards and masts is one-fourth of the length of their respective mast-heads.

IRON JACKS.

71. The jack on the head of the top-gallant mast should be, in length, one-third of the length of the royal-mast.

The diameter in the centre should be seven-eighths to every four feet of their length; the ends should be six-tenths of the centre.

IRON FIDS.

72. Iron fids are in depth five-sixteenths of the diameter of their respective topmasts and top-gallant masts; and in width, two-thirds of their depth.

Wooden fids are one-half of their masts in depth, and two-thirds of their depth for their width.

NOTES ON TOPS.

73. The tops should be made in two equal parts so that each part may be removed separately; the futtock-plate for the forward topmast shroud should be placed opposite the centre of the lower-mast head.

The tops should be light, with upper cross-trees on the tops and over the lower ones, and fayed down over the battens, and well-keyed or screw-bolted together.

The forward part of the top should be sufficiently rounded to prevent the chafing of the sail. The forward cross-tree should be made with a sweep.

74. TOP TABLES.

	Ships-of-the Line.		Frigates.		Sloops.		Brigs.
	Main and Fore.	Mizzen.	Main and Fore.	Mizzen.	Main and Fore.	Mizzen.	Main and Fore.
	In.	In.	In.	In.	In.	In.	In.
Plank to be of two thicknesses yellow-pine.	1¼	1	1⅛	⅞	⅞	¾	¾
" " " " white-pine..	1½	1¼	1¼	1	1	⅞	⅞
Breadth of rim, white-oak..............	13	10	11	9	9	7	7
Thickness " " "	2½	1¾	2	1½	1¼	1¼	1¼
Breadth of lubber-board, white-oak.......	9	8	8	7	7	5½	5½
Thickness " " " "	3	2½	2½	1¾	1¾	1½	1½
Breadth of battens.......................	3½	3	3	2½	2½	2	2
Thickness "	3½	3	3	2½	2½	2	2
Tapered to.............................	2½	2	2	1½	1½	1¼	1¼
Iron plates, breadth.....................	5	4½	4½	4	4	3½	3½
" " thickness..................	½	7/16	7/16	⅜	⅜	5/16	5/16
Upper cross-trees of oak, breadth the same as lower ones............................	....	....	....	....	....	....	....
Thickness...............................	6½	5	5½	4¼	4¼	3½	3½
Tapered to..............................	4	3½	3½	3	3	2	2

75. TOP-STANCHIONS AND RAILS.

There should be four or five holes in each stanchion, and an iron cleat should be riveted on between the first and second hole from the top, on the forward side of it.

The iron rail should have a nut on each end, on the inside and outside of the outboard stanchion, to keep the rail steady.

Top Stanchions.	Ships-of-the-Line.				Frigates.				Sloops.				Brigs.	
	Main and Fore.		Mizzen.		Main and Fore.		Mizzen.		Main and Fore.		Mizzen.		Main and Fore.	
	Ft.	In.	Ft.	In.	Ft.	In.	Ft.	In.	Ft.	In.	Ft.	In.	Ft.	In.
In length	3	6	3	3	3	3	3	....	3	....	2	9	2	9
Diameter at bottom	....	1¾	....	1⅜	....	1½	....	1¼	....	1¼	....	1⅛	....	1⅛
" " top	....	1¼	....	1	....	1⅛	....	⅞	....	⅞	....	¾	....	¾
" of rail	....	1½	....	1⅛	....	1¼	....	1	....	1	....	$\frac{13}{16}$	....	$\frac{13}{16}$

76. CONVERTING AND LINING TIMBER FOR MASTS AND OTHER SPARS.

The conversion of timber to the best advantage is of great importance, otherwise much unnecessary expense and waste must occur, and the greater number of pieces any mast is made of, the more judgment is required to suit each with a stick the nearest to its size.

The most approved method is to delineate the various pieces the mast is composed of by a convenient scale of any part of an inch to a foot upon a smooth board, that the different lengths and thicknesses may be taken, and the most suitable stick of timber be provided.

Sticks of timber not quite straight, if sufficiently large, may be used, the workmen having always an opportunity of setting them straight when required.

Every stick of timber appointed to make a mast, yard, or bowsprit, or any part thereof, should be examined to ascertain whether it is sound and fit to be used.

For which purpose a short piece is cut off the butt, to see whether the heart of the stick is sound; if it has white pithy veins, is rotten or shaky at the heart, it is bad; if so, continue taking off more pieces while there remains sufficient length. When the butt is approved of search along the sides, dubbing spots at a little distance asunder; and carefully examine every knot, rindgall, &c. If sound and clear of sap, then line and commence working it.

77. NOTES AND EXPLANATIONS ON THE FOLLOWING TABLES OF DIMENSIONS.

These tables are numbered from one to thirty-three (1–33).

Take any number that will suit you for a main-mast, and then take the same number in the other tables for all the spars belonging to the main-mast, and the following: Bowsprit, jib-boom, and flying-jib-boom, dolphin-striker, whisker-booms, spanker-boom, and spanker-gaff.

Then take any number to suit you for a fore-mast, and take the same in other tables for all the spars belonging to the fore-mast.

Then take any number to suit you for a mizzen-mast, and take the same number in other tables for all the spars (except spanker boom and gaff) for all the spars belonging to the mizzen-mast.

78. Tables of Dimensions. Nos. 1 and 2.

LOWER MASTS.						LOWER YARDS.					
No.	Length.		Diam.	Heads.		No.	Length.		Diam.	Arms.	
	Feet.	In.	In.	Feet.	In.		Feet.	In.	In.	Feet.	In.
1	50	..	$16\frac{5}{8}$	8	11	1	45	5	$11\frac{2}{8}$	2	3
2	52	6	$17\frac{4}{8}$	9	3	2	49	8	$11\frac{6}{8}$	2	4
3	55	..	$18\frac{2}{8}$	9	9	3	50	..	$12\frac{3}{8}$	2	6
4	57	6	19	10	3	4	52	3	13	2	7
5	60	..	20	10	8	5	54	6	$13\frac{4}{8}$	2	8
6	62	6	$20\frac{7}{8}$	11	2	6	56	9	14	2	10
7	65	..	$21\frac{5}{8}$	11	6	7	59	1	$14\frac{6}{8}$	2	11
8	67	6	$22\frac{4}{8}$	12	..	8	61	4	$15\frac{1}{8}$	3	..
9	70	..	$23\frac{2}{8}$	12	6	9	63	7	$15\frac{6}{8}$	3	2
10	72	6	24	12	11	10	65	10	$16\frac{1}{8}$	3	3
11	75	..	25	13	4	11	68	2	17	3	5
12	77	6	$25\frac{7}{8}$	13	10	12	70	5	$17\frac{4}{8}$	3	6
13	80	..	$26\frac{5}{8}$	14	3	13	72	8	18	3	7
14	82	6	$27\frac{4}{8}$	14	8	14	75	..	$18\frac{6}{8}$	3	8
15	85	..	$28\frac{2}{8}$	15	2	15	77	3	$19\frac{1}{8}$	3	10
16	87	6	29	15	7	16	79	6	$19\frac{6}{8}$	4	..
17	90	..	30	16	..	17	81	9	$20\frac{2}{8}$	4	1
18	92	6	$30\frac{7}{8}$	16	6	18	84	..	21	4	2
19	95	..	$31\frac{5}{8}$	16	10	19	86	4	$21\frac{4}{8}$	4	3
20	97	6	$32\frac{4}{8}$	17	4	20	88	7	22	4	5
21	100	..	$33\frac{2}{8}$	17	10	21	90	10	$22\frac{3}{8}$	4	6
22	102	6	34	18	3	22	93	2	$23\frac{1}{8}$	4	7
23	105	..	35	18	9	23	95	5	$23\frac{6}{8}$	4	9
24	107	6	$35\frac{1}{4}$	19	2	24	97	8	$24\frac{1}{8}$	4	10
25	110	..	$36\frac{5}{8}$	19	7	25	100	..	25	5	..
26	112	6	$37\frac{4}{8}$	20	..	26	102	3	$25\frac{4}{8}$	5	1
27	115	..	$38\frac{2}{8}$	20	6	27	104	6	26	5	2
28	117	6	39	20	11	28	106	9	$26\frac{4}{8}$	5	4
29	120	..	40	21	5	29	109	..	$27\frac{1}{8}$	5	5
30	122	6	$40\frac{7}{8}$	21	11	30	111	4	$27\frac{6}{8}$	5	6
31	125	..	$41\frac{5}{8}$	22	3	31	113	7	$28\frac{2}{8}$	5	8
32	127	6	$42\frac{4}{8}$	22	9	32	115	10	$28\frac{6}{8}$	5	9
33	130	..	$43\frac{2}{8}$	23	2	33	118	2	$29\frac{4}{8}$	5	11

79. Tables of Dimensions. Nos. 3 and 4.

TOPMASTS.

No.	Length.		Diam.	Heads.	
	Feet.	In.	In.	Feet.	In.
1	30	..	10	5	..
2	31	6	$10\frac{4}{8}$	5	3
3	33	..	11	5	6
4	34	6	$11\frac{4}{8}$	5	9
5	36	..	12	6	..
6	37	6	$12\frac{4}{8}$	6	3
7	39	..	13	6	6
8	40	6	$13\frac{4}{8}$	6	9
9	42	..	14	7	..
10	43	6	$14\frac{4}{8}$	7	3
11	45	..	15	7	6
12	46	6	$15\frac{4}{8}$	7	9
13	48	..	16	8	..
14	49	6	$16\frac{4}{8}$	8	3
15	51	..	17	8	6
16	52	6	$17\frac{4}{8}$	8	9
17	54	..	18	9	..
18	55	6	$18\frac{4}{8}$	9	3
19	57	..	19	9	6
20	58	6	$19\frac{4}{8}$	9	9
21	60	..	20	10	..
22	61	6	$20\frac{4}{8}$	10	3
23	63	..	21	10	6
24	64	6	$21\frac{4}{8}$	10	9
25	66	..	22	11	..
26	67	6	$22\frac{4}{8}$	11	3
27	69	..	23	11	6
28	70	6	$23\frac{4}{8}$	11	9
29	72	..	24	12	..
30	73	6	$24\frac{4}{8}$	12	3
31	75	..	25	12	6
32	76	6	$25\frac{4}{8}$	12	9
33	78	..	26	13	..

TOP-SAIL YARDS.

No.	Length.		Diam.	Arms.	
	Feet.	In.	In.	Feet.	In.
1	34	..	$8\frac{2}{8}$	3	1
2	35	9	9	3	3
3	37	6	$9\frac{4}{8}$	3	4
4	39	2	$9\frac{6}{8}$	3	6
5	40	10	10	3	8
6	42	6	$10\frac{4}{8}$	3	10
7	44	3	11	4	..
8	46	..	$11\frac{4}{8}$	4	2
9	47	9	$11\frac{6}{8}$	4	4
10	49	4	$12\frac{2}{8}$	4	5
11	51	1	$12\frac{6}{8}$	4	7
12	52	9	13	4	9
13	54	6	$13\frac{4}{8}$	4	11
14	56	3	14	5	1
15	57	11	$14\frac{4}{8}$	5	3
16	59	7	$14\frac{6}{8}$	5	5
17	61	3	$15\frac{2}{8}$	5	6
18	63	..	$15\frac{6}{8}$	5	8
19	64	9	16	5	10
20	66	5	$16\frac{4}{8}$	6	..
21	68	1	17	6	2
22	69	10	$17\frac{4}{8}$	6	4
23	71	6	$17\frac{6}{8}$	6	6
24	73	3	$18\frac{2}{8}$	6	7
25	75	..	$18\frac{6}{8}$	6	9
26	76	8	19	6	11
27	78	4	$19\frac{4}{8}$	7	1
28	80	..	20	7	3
29	81	9	$20\frac{2}{8}$	7	5
30	83	6	$20\frac{6}{8}$	7	7
31	85	2	$21\frac{2}{8}$	7	8
32	86	10	$21\frac{4}{8}$	7	10
33	88	6	$21\frac{6}{8}$	8	..

80. Tables of Dimensions. Nos. 5 and 6.

TOP-GALLANT MASTS.						TOP-GALLANT YARDS.					
No.	Length.		Diam.			No,	Length.		Diam.	Arms.	
	Feet.	In.	In.				Feet.	In.	In.	Feet.	In.
1	15	..	$5\frac{5}{8}$	..	..	1	21	10	$4\frac{6}{8}$	1	2
2	15	9	$5\frac{7}{8}$	..	..	2	22	11	$5\frac{1}{8}$	1	3
3	16	6	$6\frac{1}{8}$	..	..	3	24	1	$5\frac{2}{8}$	1	4
4	17	3	$6\frac{3}{8}$	..	..	4	25	2	$5\frac{4}{8}$	1	4
5	18	..	$6\frac{6}{8}$	..	..	5	26	3	$5\frac{6}{8}$	1	5
6	18	9	$7\frac{1}{8}$	..	..	6	27	3	6	1	6
7	19	6	$7\frac{2}{8}$	..	..	7	28	5	$6\frac{1}{8}$	1	7
8	20	3	$7\frac{4}{8}$	..	..	8	29	6	$6\frac{4}{8}$	1	7
9	21	..	$7\frac{7}{8}$	..	..	9	30	7	$6\frac{6}{8}$	1	8
10	21	9	$8\frac{1}{8}$	..	..	10	31	8	7	1	9
11	22	6	$8\frac{3}{8}$	..	..	11	32	10	$7\frac{1}{8}$	1	9
12	23	3	$8\frac{5}{8}$	..	..	12	33	10	$7\frac{3}{8}$	1	10
13	24	..	9	..	..	13	35	..	$7\frac{6}{8}$	1	10
14	24	9	$9\frac{2}{8}$	..	..	14	36	1	$7\frac{7}{8}$	2	..
15	25	6	$9\frac{4}{8}$	..	..	15	37	2	$8\frac{2}{8}$	2	..
16	26	3	$9\frac{6}{8}$	..	..	16	38	3	$8\frac{5}{8}$	2	1
17	27	..	$10\frac{1}{8}$	..	..	17	39	4	$8\frac{6}{8}$	2	2
18	27	9	$10\frac{3}{8}$	..	..	18	40	6	$8\frac{7}{8}$	2	3
19	28	6	$10\frac{5}{8}$	..	..	19	41	7	$9\frac{1}{8}$	2	3
20	29	3	$10\frac{7}{8}$	..	..	20	42	8	$9\frac{2}{8}$	2	4
21	30	..	$11\frac{2}{8}$	..	..	21	43	9	$9\frac{4}{8}$	2	5
22	30	9	$11\frac{4}{8}$	..	..	22	44	10	$9\frac{6}{8}$	2	5
23	31	6	$11\frac{6}{8}$	..	..	23	45	11	$10\frac{1}{8}$	2	6
24	32	3	12	..	..	24	47	1	$10\frac{3}{8}$	2	7
25	33	..	$12\frac{3}{8}$	..	..	25	48	2	$10\frac{4}{8}$	2	8
26	33	9	$12\frac{5}{8}$	..	..	26	49	3	$10\frac{6}{8}$	2	8
27	34	6	$12\frac{7}{8}$	..	..	27	50	4	11	2	9
28	35	3	$13\frac{1}{8}$	..	..	28	51	6	$11\frac{3}{8}$	2	10
29	36	.	$13\frac{4}{8}$	..	..	29	52	6	$11\frac{4}{8}$	2	11
30	36	9	$13\frac{6}{8}$	..	..	30	53	8	$11\frac{6}{8}$	2	11
31	37	6	14	..	..	31	54	9	12	3	..
32	38	3	$14\frac{2}{8}$	..	..	32	55	9	$12\frac{2}{8}$	3	..
33	39	..	$14\frac{5}{8}$	..	..	33	56	10	$12\frac{3}{8}$	3	1

81. Tables of Dimensions. Nos. 7 and 8.

ROYAL-MASTS.					
No.	Length.		Diam.	Poles.	
	Feet.	In.	In.	Feet.	In.
1	10	..	$4\frac{4}{8}$	5	..
2	10	6	$4\frac{5}{8}$	5	3
3	11	..	$4\frac{6}{8}$	5	6
4	11	6	5	5	9
5	12	..	$5\frac{3}{8}$	6	..
6	12	6	$5\frac{5}{8}$	6	3
7	13	..	$5\frac{6}{8}$	6	6
8	13	6	6	6	9
9	14	..	$6\frac{2}{8}$	7	..
10	14	6	$6\frac{4}{8}$	7	3
11	15	..	$6\frac{5}{8}$	7	6
12	15	6	$6\frac{7}{8}$	7	9
13	16	..	7	8	..
14	16	6	$7\frac{2}{8}$	8	3
15	17	..	$7\frac{4}{8}$	8	6
16	17	6	$7\frac{6}{8}$	8	9
17	18	..	8	9	..
18	18	6	$8\frac{1}{8}$	9	3
19	19	..	$8\frac{4}{8}$	9	6
20	19	6	$8\frac{5}{8}$	9	9
21	20	..	9	10	..
22	20	6	$9\frac{1}{8}$	10	3
23	21	..	$9\frac{3}{8}$	10	6
24	21	6	$9\frac{4}{8}$	10	9
25	22	..	$9\frac{7}{8}$	11	..
26	22	6	10	11	3
27	23	..	$10\frac{2}{8}$	11	6
28	23	6	$10\frac{4}{8}$	11	9
29	24	..	$10\frac{6}{8}$	12	..
30	24	6	11	12	3
31	25	..	$11\frac{1}{8}$	12	6
32	25	6	$11\frac{3}{8}$	12	9
33	26	..	$11\frac{5}{8}$	13	..

ROYAL-YARDS.					
No.	Length.		Diam.	Arms.	
	Feet.	In.	In.	Feet.	In.
1	15	3	$3\frac{3}{8}$	..	10
2	16	3	$3\frac{4}{8}$	..	10
3	17	3	$3\frac{6}{8}$	..	11
4	17	7	$3\frac{7}{8}$	..	11
5	18	4	4	1	..
6	18	10	$4\frac{1}{8}$	1	..
7	19	10	$4\frac{3}{8}$	1	1
8	20	8	$4\frac{4}{8}$	1	1
9	21	5	$4\frac{6}{8}$	1	2
10	22	2	$4\frac{7}{8}$	1	2
11	22	7	5	1	3
12	23	9	$5\frac{2}{8}$	1	3
13	24	6	$5\frac{3}{8}$	1	4
14	25	3	$5\frac{4}{8}$	1	4
15	26	4	$5\frac{6}{8}$	1	5
16	26	9	$5\frac{7}{8}$	1	5
17	27	6	6	1	6
18	28	4	$6\frac{2}{8}$	1	6
19	29	1	$6\frac{3}{8}$	1	7
20	29	10	$6\frac{4}{8}$	1	7
21	30	1	$6\frac{5}{8}$	1	8
22	31	5	$6\frac{7}{8}$	1	8
23	32	2	7	1	9
24	32	11	$7\frac{1}{8}$	1	9
25	33	3	$7\frac{3}{8}$	1	10
26	34	6	$7\frac{5}{8}$	1	10
27	35	3	$7\frac{6}{8}$	1	11
28	36	..	$7\frac{7}{8}$	1	11
29	36	9	8	2	..
30	37	9	$8\frac{1}{8}$	2	..
31	38	3	$8\frac{3}{8}$	2	1
32	38	8	$8\frac{4}{8}$	2	1
33	39	1	$8\frac{7}{8}$	2	2

82. Tables of Dimensions. Nos. 9 and 10.

No.	Bowsprit. Length.		Diam.	Bees Square.		No.	Dolphin-Striker and Whisker-Boom. Length.		Diam.	Poles.	
	Feet.	In.	In.	Feet.	In.		Feet.	In.	In.	Feet.	In.
1	31	3	16 5/8	..	4 1/8	1	8	11	4 3/8	1	3
2	32	9	17 4/8	..	4 3/8	2	9	6	4 5/8	1	4
3	34	4	18 2/8	..	4 4/8	3	9	11	4 6/8	1	5
4	35	11	19	..	4 6/8	4	10	4	5	1	5
5	37	6	20	..	5	5	10	10	5 2/8	1	6
6	39	..	20 7/8	..	5 1/8	6	11	2	5 5/8	1	7
7	40	7	21 5/8	..	5 3/8	7	11	9	5 6/8	1	8
8	42	2	22 1/8	..	5 5/8	8	12	3	6	1	9
9	43	9	23 2/8	..	5 6/8	9	12	8	6 2/8	1	9
10	45	3	24	..	6	10	13	1	6 4/8	1	10
11	46	10	25	..	6 2/8	11	13	6	6 6/8	1	11
12	48	5	25 7/8	..	6 3/8	12	14	1	7	2	..
13	50	..	26 5/8	..	6 5/8	13	14	5	7 2/8	2	..
14	51	6	27 4/8	..	6 7/8	14	14	11	7 3/8	2	1
15	53	1	28 2/8	..	7	15	15	5	7 5/8	2	2
16	54	8	29	..	7 2/8	16	15	10	7 6/8	2	3
17	56	3	30	..	7 4/8	17	16	4	8	2	4
18	57	9	30 7/8	..	7 6/8	18	16	9	8 3/8	2	4
19	59	4	31 5/8	..	7 7/8	19	17	2	8 4/8	2	5
20	60	11	32 4/8	..	8	20	17	8	8 6/8	2	6
21	62	6	33 2/8	..	8 2/8	21	18	1	9	2	7
22	64	..	34	..	8 4/8	22	18	6	9 2/8	2	7
23	65	7	35	..	8 6/8	23	19	..	9 4/8	2	8
24	67	2	35 7/8	..	8 7/8	24	19	6	9 6/8	2	9
25	68	9	36 5/8	..	9	25	20	..	10	2	10
26	70	3	37 4/8	..	9 3/8	26	20	5	10 2/8	2	11
27	71	10	38 2/8	..	9 4/8	27	20	10	10 3/8	2	11
28	73	5	39	..	9 6/8	28	21	4	10 5/8	3	..
29	75	..	40	..	10	29	21	9	10 6/8	3	1
30	76	6	40 7/8	..	10 2/8	30	22	3	11	3	2
31	78	1	41 5/8	..	10 4/8	31	22	9	11 2/8	3	3
32	79	8	42 4/8	..	10 5/8	32	23	1	11 4/8	3	3
33	81	3	43 2/8	..	10 6/8	33	23	7	11 5/8	3	4

83. Tables on Dimensions. Nos. 11 and 12.

JIB-BOOM.						FLYING JIB-BOOM.					
No.	Length.		Diam.	Poles.		No.	Length.		Diam.	Poles.	
	Feet.	In.	In.	Feet.	In.		Feet.	In.	In.	Feet.	In.
1	26	9	$8\frac{7}{8}$	1	3	1	28	4	$5\frac{1}{8}$	3	1
2	28	1	$9\frac{3}{8}$	1	4	2	29	8	$5\frac{5}{8}$	3	3
3	29	5	$9\frac{6}{8}$	1	5	3	31	2	$5\frac{6}{8}$	3	5
4	30	9	$10\frac{2}{8}$	1	5	4	32	8	6	3	7
5	32	1	$10\frac{5}{8}$	1	6	5	34	1	$6\frac{3}{8}$	3	9
6	33	5	$11\frac{1}{8}$	1	7	6	35	5	$6\frac{4}{8}$	3	11
7	34	9	$11\frac{4}{8}$	1	7	7	36	10	$6\frac{6}{8}$	4	1
8	36	1	12	1	8	8	38	4	7	4	3
9	37	6	$12\frac{4}{8}$	1	9	9	39	9	$7\frac{4}{8}$	4	5
10	38	9	$12\frac{7}{8}$	1	10	10	41	1	$7\frac{5}{8}$	4	7
11	40	1	13	1	10	11	42	6	$7\frac{6}{8}$	4	9
12	41	6	$13\frac{6}{8}$	1	11	12	44	..	8	4	11
13	42	10	$14\frac{2}{8}$	2	..	13	45	5	$8\frac{3}{8}$	5	1
14	44	1	$14\frac{5}{8}$	2	1	14	46	9	$8\frac{6}{8}$	5	2
15	45	6	$15\frac{1}{8}$	2	2	15	48	3	9	5	3
16	46	10	$15\frac{5}{8}$	2	2	16	49	8	$9\frac{2}{8}$	5	5
17	48	2	16	2	3	17	51	1	$9\frac{4}{8}$	5	7
18	49	6	$16\frac{4}{8}$	2	4	18	52	6	$9\frac{6}{8}$	5	9
19	50	10	$16\frac{7}{8}$	2	5	19	53	11	10	5	11
20	52	2	$17\frac{3}{8}$	2	5	20	55	4	$10\frac{2}{8}$	6	1
21	53	6	$17\frac{6}{8}$	2	6	21	56	9	$10\frac{4}{8}$	6	3
22	54	10	$18\frac{2}{8}$	2	7	22	58	2	$10\frac{6}{8}$	6	5
23	56	2	$18\frac{5}{8}$	2	8	23	59	7	11	6	7
24	57	6	$19\frac{1}{8}$	2	8	24	61	..	$11\frac{3}{8}$	6	9
25	58	11	$19\frac{5}{8}$	2	9	25	62	5	$11\frac{6}{8}$	6	11
26	60	2	20	2	10	26	63	10	12	7	1
27	61	7	$20\frac{4}{8}$	2	11	27	65	3	$12\frac{2}{8}$	7	3
28	62	11	$20\frac{7}{8}$	2	11	28	66	8	$12\frac{4}{8}$	7	5
29	64	3	$21\frac{3}{8}$	3	..	29	68	2	$12\frac{6}{8}$	7	7
30	65	7	$21\frac{6}{8}$	3	1	30	69	7	13	7	9
31	66	11	$22\frac{2}{8}$	3	2	31	70	11	$13\frac{2}{8}$	7	11
32	68	3	$22\frac{6}{8}$	3	3	32	72	5	$13\frac{4}{8}$	8	1
33	69	7	$23\frac{1}{8}$	3	3	33	72	10	$13\frac{6}{8}$	8	3

84. Tables of Dimensions. Nos. 13 and 14.

No.	SPANKER-BOOM. Length. Feet.	In.	Diam. In.	Poles. Feet.	In.	No.	SPANKER-GAFF. Length. Feet.	In.	Diam. In.	Poles. Feet.	In.
1	25	..	$6\frac{2}{8}$	1	9	1	20	..	5	3	4
2	26	3	$6\frac{4}{8}$	1	10	2	21	..	$5\frac{2}{8}$	3	6
3	27	6	$6\frac{7}{8}$	1	11	3	22	..	$5\frac{4}{8}$	3	8
4	28	9	$7\frac{1}{8}$	2	..	4	23	..	$5\frac{6}{8}$	3	10
5	30	..	$7\frac{4}{8}$	2	1	5	24	..	6	4	..
6	31	3	$7\frac{6}{8}$	2	2	6	25	..	$6\frac{2}{8}$	4	2
7	32	6	$8\frac{1}{8}$	2	3	7	26	..	$6\frac{4}{8}$	4	4
8	33	9	$8\frac{3}{8}$	2	4	8	27	..	$6\frac{6}{8}$	4	6
9	35	..	$8\frac{6}{8}$	2	6	9	28	..	7	4	8
10	36	3	9	2	7	10	29	..	$7\frac{2}{8}$	4	10
11	37	6	$9\frac{3}{8}$	2	8	11	30	..	$7\frac{4}{8}$	5	..
12	38	9	$9\frac{5}{8}$	2	9	12	31	..	$7\frac{6}{8}$	5	2
13	40	..	10	2	10	13	32	..	8	5	4
14	41	3	$10\frac{2}{8}$	2	11	14	33	..	$8\frac{2}{8}$	5	6
15	42	6	$10\frac{5}{8}$	3	..	15	34	..	$8\frac{4}{8}$	5	8
16	43	9	$10\frac{7}{8}$	3	1	16	35	..	$8\frac{6}{8}$	5	10
17	45	..	$11\frac{2}{8}$	3	2	17	36	..	9	6	..
18	46	3	$11\frac{4}{8}$	3	3	18	37	..	$9\frac{2}{8}$	6	2
19	47	6	$11\frac{7}{8}$	3	4	19	38	..	$9\frac{4}{8}$	6	4
20	48	9	$12\frac{1}{8}$	3	5	20	39	..	$9\frac{6}{8}$	6	6
21	50	..	$12\frac{4}{8}$	3	6	21	40	..	10	6	8
22	51	3	$12\frac{6}{8}$	3	7	22	41	..	$10\frac{2}{8}$	6	10
23	52	6	$13\frac{1}{8}$	3	9	23	42	..	$10\frac{4}{8}$	7	..
24	53	9	$13\frac{3}{8}$	3	10	24	43	..	$10\frac{6}{8}$	7	2
25	55	.	$13\frac{6}{8}$	3	11	25	44	..	11	7	4
26	56	3	14	4	..	26	45	..	$11\frac{2}{8}$	7	6
27	57	6	$14\frac{3}{8}$	4	1	27	46	..	$11\frac{4}{8}$	7	8
28	58	9	$14\frac{5}{8}$	4	2	28	47	..	$11\frac{6}{8}$	7	10
29	60	..	15	4	3	29	48	..	12	8	..
30	61	3	$15\frac{2}{8}$	4	4	30	49	..	$12\frac{2}{8}$	8	2
31	62	6	$15\frac{5}{8}$	4	5	31	50	..	$12\frac{4}{8}$	8	4
32	63	9	$15\frac{7}{8}$	4	6	32	51	..	$12\frac{6}{8}$	8	6
33	65	..	$16\frac{2}{8}$	4	7	33	52	..	13	8	8

85. Tables of Dimensions. Nos. 15 and 16.

Swinging-Boom.						Lower Studding-Sail Yard.					
No.	Length.		Diam.			No.	Length.		Diam.		
	Feet.	In.	In.				Feet.	In.	In.		
1	25	2	5	..	..	1	14	4	$2\frac{7}{8}$	..	..
2	26	5	$5\frac{3}{8}$	..	..	2	15	1	3	..	..
3	27	9	$5\frac{5}{8}$	..	..	3	15	10	$3\frac{1}{8}$	..	..
4	29	..	$5\frac{7}{8}$	..	..	4	16	6	$3\frac{2}{8}$	..	..
5	30	3	6	..	..	5	17	3	$3\frac{3}{8}$	..	..
6	31	6	$6\frac{1}{8}$	..	..	6	18	..	$3\frac{4}{8}$	..	..
7	32	9	$6\frac{4}{8}$	..	..	7	18	8	$3\frac{5}{8}$	..	..
8	34	..	$6\frac{7}{8}$	..	..	8	19	5	$3\frac{6}{8}$	..	..
9	35	3	7	..	..	9	20	1	4	..	..
10	36	6	$7\frac{2}{8}$	..	..	10	20	10	$4\frac{1}{8}$	..	..
11	37	10	$7\frac{4}{8}$	..	..	11	21	7	$4\frac{2}{8}$	..	..
12	39	1	$7\frac{7}{8}$	..	..	12	22	4	$4\frac{3}{8}$	..	..
13	40	4	8	..	..	13	23	..	$4\frac{4}{8}$	..	..
14	41	7	$8\frac{2}{8}$	..	..	14	23	9	$4\frac{6}{8}$	..	..
15	42	11	$8\frac{5}{8}$	..	..	15	24	6	$4\frac{7}{8}$	..	..
16	44	2	$8\frac{7}{8}$	..	..	16	25	2	5	..	..
17	45	5	9	..	..	17	25	11	$5\frac{1}{8}$	..	..
18	46	8	$9\frac{2}{8}$	..	..	18	26	8	$5\frac{2}{8}$	..	..
19	47	11	$9\frac{5}{8}$	..	..	19	27	4	$5\frac{3}{8}$	..	..
20	49	2	$9\frac{7}{8}$	..	..	20	28	1	$5\frac{4}{8}$	..	..
21	50	5	10	..	..	21	28	9	$5\frac{6}{8}$	..	..
22	51	9	$10\frac{2}{8}$	..	..	22	29	6	$5\frac{7}{8}$	..	..
23	53	..	$10\frac{5}{8}$	..	..	23	30	3	6	..	..
24	54	3	$10\frac{7}{8}$	..	..	24	31	..	$6\frac{1}{8}$	..	..
25	55	6	11	..	..	25	31	8	$6\frac{2}{8}$	..	..
26	56	9	$11\frac{2}{8}$	..	..	26	32	5	$6\frac{3}{8}$	..	..
27	58	..	$11\frac{5}{8}$	..	..	27	33	1	$6\frac{4}{8}$	..	..
28	59	3	$11\frac{7}{8}$	..	..	28	33	10	$6\frac{6}{8}$	..	..
29	60	6	12	..	..	29	34	6	$6\frac{7}{8}$	..	..
30	61	9	$12\frac{2}{8}$	..	..	30	35	3	7	..	..
31	63	1	$12\frac{5}{8}$	..	..	31	36	..	$7\frac{1}{8}$	..	..
32	64	4	$12\frac{7}{8}$	..	..	32	36	9	$7\frac{2}{8}$	..	..
33	65	7	13	..	..	33	37	5	$7\frac{3}{8}$	..	..

86. Tables of Dimensions. Nos. 17 and 18.

Top-mast Studding-sail Boom.						Top-mast Studding-sail Yard.					
No.	Length.		Diam.			No.	Length.		Diam.		
	Feet.	In.	In.				Feet.	In.	In.		
1	23	7	4 5/8	..	..	1	13	5	2 5/8	..	..
2	24	9	4 7/8	..	..	2	14	1	2 6/8	..	..
3	26	..	5	..	..	3	14	10	2 7/8	..	..
4	27	3	5 3/8	..	..	4	15	6	3	..	..
5	28	4	5 5/8	..	..	5	16	2	3 2/8	..	..
6	29	6	5 7/8	..	..	6	16	10	3 3/8	..	..
7	30	9	6	..	..	7	17	6	3 4/8	..	..
8	31	11	6 3/8	..	..	8	18	2	3 5/8	..	..
9	33	1	6 5/8	..	..	9	18	10	3 6/8	..	..
10	34	3	6 7/8	..	..	10	19	6	3 7/8	..	..
11	35	6	7	..	..	11	20	3	4	..	..
12	36	8	7 3/8	..	..	12	20	11	4 1/8	..	..
13	37	10	7 5/8	..	..	13	21	7	4 2/8	..	..
14	38	11	7 7/8	..	..	14	22	2	4 3/8	..	..
15	40	2	8	..	..	15	22	11	4 4/8	..	..
16	41	4	8 2/8	..	..	16	23	7	4 5/8	..	..
17	42	8	8 4/8	..	..	17	24	4	4 6/8	..	..
18	43	9	8 6/8	..	..	18	25	..	5	..	..
19	44	11	8 7/8	..	..	19	25	8	5 1/8	..	..
20	46	1	9	..	..	20	26	5	5 2/8	..	..
21	47	3	9 3/8	..	..	21	27	..	5 3/8	..	..
22	48	4	9 5/8	..	..	22	27	7	5 4/8	..	..
23	49	6	9 7/8	..	..	23	28	3	5 5/8	..	..
24	50	10	10	..	..	24	29	..	5 6/8	..	..
25	52	1	10 3/8	..	..	25	29	9	5 7/8	..	..
26	53	3	10 5/8	..	..	26	30	5	6	..	..
27	54	5	10 7/8	..	..	27	31	1	6 1/8	..	..
28	55	7	11	..	..	28	31	9	6 2/8	..	..
29	56	9	11 3/8	..	..	29	32	5	6 3/8	..	..
30	57	11	11 5/8	..	..	30	33	1	6 4/8	..	..
31	59	1	11 7/8	..	..	31	33	9	6 5/8	..	..
32	60	3	12	..	..	32	34	5	6 6/8	..	..
33	61	6	12 3/8	..	..	33	35	1	6 7/8	..	..

87. Tables of Dimensions. Nos. 19 and 20.

TOP-GALLANT STUDDING-SAIL BOOMS.						TOP-GALLANT STUDDING-SAIL YARD.					
No.	Length.		Diam.			No.	Length.		Diam.		
	Feet.	In.	In.				Feet.	In.	In.		
1	17	8	$3\frac{4}{8}$	..	..	1	10	..	2	..	..
2	18	7	$3\frac{5}{8}$	..	..	2	10	7	2	..	..
3	19	6	$3\frac{7}{8}$	..	..	3	11	..	$2\frac{1}{8}$	..	..
4	20	4	4	..	..	4	11	7	$2\frac{2}{8}$	..	..
5	21	3	$4\frac{2}{8}$	..	..	5	12	1	$2\frac{3}{8}$	..	..
6	22	1	$4\frac{3}{8}$	..	..	6	12	7	$2\frac{3}{8}$	..	..
7	23	..	$4\frac{4}{8}$	..	..	7	13	1	$2\frac{4}{8}$	..	..
8	23	11	$4\frac{6}{8}$	..	..	8	13	8	$2\frac{5}{8}$	..	..
9	24	10	$4\frac{7}{8}$	..	..	9	14	2	$2\frac{6}{8}$	..	..
10	25	8	5	..	..	10	14	8	$2\frac{7}{8}$		..
11	26	7	$5\frac{2}{8}$	..	..	11	15	2	3	..	..
12	27	5	$5\frac{3}{8}$	..	..	12	15	8	$3\frac{1}{8}$	..	..
13	28	4	$5\frac{5}{8}$	..	..	13	16	2	$3\frac{1}{8}$	..	..
14	29	3	$5\frac{6}{8}$	..	..	14	16	8	$3\frac{2}{8}$	..	..
15	30	2	6	..	..	15	17	2	$3\frac{3}{8}$	..	..
16	31	..	$6\frac{1}{8}$	..	..	16	17	8	$3\frac{4}{8}$	..	..
17	31	10	$6\frac{3}{8}$	..	..	17	18	2	$3\frac{5}{8}$	.	..
18	32	9	$6\frac{4}{8}$	..	..	18	18	8	$3\frac{5}{8}$	..	..
19	33	8	$6\frac{5}{8}$	..	..	19	19	2	$3\frac{6}{8}$	..	..
20	34	7	$6\frac{7}{8}$	..	..	20	19	9	$3\frac{7}{8}$	..	..
21	35	5	7	..	..	21	20	3	4	..	..
22	36	2	$7\frac{2}{8}$	..	..	22	20	9	$4\frac{1}{8}$	..	..
23	37	2	$7\frac{3}{8}$	..	..	23	21	3	$4\frac{2}{8}$	..	..
24	38	1	$7\frac{4}{8}$	..	..	24	21	9	$4\frac{2}{8}$	..	..
25	39	..	$7\frac{6}{8}$	..	..	25	22	3	$4\frac{3}{8}$	..	..
26	39	10	$7\frac{7}{8}$	..	..	26	22	9	$4\frac{4}{8}$	..	..
27	40	9	8	..	..	27	23	3	$4\frac{5}{8}$	..	..
28	41	8	$8\frac{2}{8}$	..	..	28	23	9	$4\frac{6}{8}$	..	..
29	42	6	$8\frac{3}{8}$	..	..	29	24	3	$4\frac{6}{8}$	..	..
30	43	5	$8\frac{4}{8}$	..	..	30	24	9	$4\frac{7}{8}$	..	..
31	44	3	$8\frac{6}{8}$	..	..	31	25	3	5	..	..
32	45	2	9	..	..	32	25	9	$5\frac{1}{8}$	..	..
33	46	..	$9\frac{1}{8}$	..	..	33	26	3	$5\frac{2}{8}$	..	..

88. NOTES ON THE FOLLOWING TABLES OF LOWER MASTS.

Divide the mast from the heel to the partners, into four parts, and from the partners to the stop of hounds, into eight parts; then number the settings off, beginning at the heel, No. 1, and so continue up to the head of the mast.

The partners is No. 5.

The stop of hounds No. 13.

The trestletrees No. 14.

The top of head No. 15.

The size of the mast is given in inches and eighths.

These dimensions will give the mast its greatest diameter at No. 7, but in making masts from these tables, keep the masts in the partners the size given you in the preceding tables, and let them be as much larger above the partners as these tables give you.

NOTES ON TOPMASTS.

All topmasts should be the same size from the heel to the stop of the hounds, and if they have heel-blocks for sheaves, it should be added; the heel should be square; and if it is not large enough to fill the trestle-trees, then box the trestle-trees to fit.

NOTES ON TOP-GALLANT MASTS.

All top-gallant masts should have a link in their heel to slide up and down.

All royal-masts with sheet poles should be in their grommet two-thirds of the greatest diameter of the royal-masts.

LOWER MASTS.

Heel of Mast.								Partners of Mast.																Stop of Hounds.		Trestle-trees.		Top of Head.	
1		2		3		4		5		6		7		8		9		10		11		12		13		14		15	
in.	8ths	in.	8ths	in.	8ths	in.	8ths	in.	8ths	in.	8ths	in.	8ths	in.	8ths	in.	8ths	in.	8ths	in.	8ths	in.	8ths	in.	8ths	in.	8ths	in.	8ths
15	3	16	6	17	4	17	6	18	-	18	1	18	2	18	1	18	-	17	6	17	3	16	6	16	1	13	4	11	4
15	7	17	2	18	-	18	2	18	4	18	6	18	6	18	5	18	4	18	2	18	7	17	2	16	4	13	6	11	6
16	2	17	6	18	4	18	6	19	-	19	1	19	2	19	1	19	-	18	6	18	3	17	6	17	-	14	-	12	-
16	5	18	2	19	-	19	2	19	4	19	5	19	6	19	5	19	4	19	2	18	7	18	2	17	3	14	4	12	2
17	1	18	5	19	3	19	6	20	-	20	1	20	2	20	1	20	-	19	6	19	3	18	6	18	-	15	-	12	6
17	4	19	1	19	7	20	2	20	4	20	5	20	6	20	5	20	4	20	2	19	7	19	2	18	4	15	2	13	-
18	-	19	5	20	3	20	6	21	-	21	1	21	2	21	1	21	-	20	6	20	2	19	6	18	7	15	6	13	3
18	3	20	1	20	7	21	3	21	4	21	5	21	6	21	5	21	4	21	2	20	6	20	2	19	2	16	-	13	5
18	6	20	4	21	4	21	7	22	-	22	1	22	2	22	1	22	-	21	6	21	2	20	6	19	6	16	4	14	2
19	4	20	7	21	7	22	3	22	4	22	5	22	6	22	5	22	3	22	2	21	6	21	1	20	3	16	7	14	4
19	5	21	4	22	4	22	7	23	-	23	1	23	2	23	1	22	7	22	5	22	1	21	4	20	6	17	2	14	6
20	-	21	7	22	7	23	3	23	4	23	5	23	6	23	5	23	4	23	2	22	5	22	-	21	2	17	5	15	1
20	4	22	3	23	3	23	7	24	-	24	2	24	3	24	2	24	-	23	6	23	2	22	4	21	6	18	-	15	4
21	-	22	7	24	-	24	3	24	4	24	6	24	7	24	6	24	4	24	2	23	6	23	-	22	2	18	3	15	-
21	3	23	3	24	3	24	7	25	-	25	2	25	3	25	2	25	-	24	6	24	1	23	4	22	5	18	6	16	1
21	7	23	7	24	7	25	3	25	4	25	5	25	7	25	6	25	4	25	2	24	5	23	7	23	-	19	1	16	3
22	2	24	2	25	3	25	7	26	-	26	2	26	3	26	2	26	-	25	6	25	1	24	3	23	4	19	4	16	6
22	5	24	6	25	6	26	3	26	4	26	5	26	7	26	6	26	4	26	2	25	5	24	7	24	-	19	7	17	-
23	-	25	2	26	2	26	7	27	-	27	2	27	3	27	2	26	7	26	5	26	1	25	2	24	3	20	3	17	3
23	4	25	5	26	6	27	2	27	4	27	5	27	7	27	6	27	4	27	2	26	5	25	6	24	7	20	5	17	5
24	-	26	1	27	2	27	7	28	-	28	1	28	3	28	2	28	-	27	5	27	-	26	2	25	2	21	-	18	-
24	3	26	5	27	6	28	2	28	4	28	5	29	-	28	7	28	4	28	1	27	4	26	5	25	5	21	3	18	3
24	6	27	-	28	2	28	6	29	-	29	2	29	3	29	2	29	-	28	5	28	-	27	1	26	1	21	7	18	5
25	2	27	4	28	6	29	2	29	4	29	6	29	7	29	6	29	4	29	1	28	4	27	5	26	5	22	1	19	-
25	5	28	-	29	6	29	6	30	-	30	2	30	4	30	3	30	2	29	5	29	-	28	1	27	-	22	4	19	3
26	1	28	4	29	6	30	2	30	4	30	6	31	-	30	7	30	5	30	2	29	4	28	5	27	4	22	7	19	5
26	5	28	7	30	1	30	6	31	-	31	2	31	4	31	3	31	1	30	5	30	-	29	-	28	-	23	2	20	-
27	-	29	3	30	6	31	2	31	4	31	6	32	-	31	7	31	4	31	1	30	4	29	4	28	3	23	5	20	2
27	3	29	7	31	1	31	5	32	-	32	2	32	4	32	3	32	-	31	5	30	7	30	-	28	7	24	-	20	5
27	6	30	2	31	5	32	2	32	4	32	6	33	-	32	7	32	5	32	1	31	3	30	2	29	2	24	3	21	-
28	2	30	6	32	1	32	6	33	-	33	2	33	4	33	3	33	1	32	5	31	7	30	7	29	5	24	6	21	2
28	6	31	2	32	5	33	1	33	4	33	6	34	-	33	7	33	5	33	1	32	3	31	3	30	1	25	1	21	4
29	1	31	5	33	-	33	5	34	-	34	2	34	3	34	2	34	1	33	5	32	7	31	7	30	5	25	4	21	7
29	4	32	1	33	4	34	1	34	4	34	6	35	-	34	7	34	5	34	1	33	3	32	3	31	1	25	7	22	2
30	-	32	5	34	-	34	5	35	-	35	2	35	4	35	3	35	1	34	5	33	7	32	6	31	7	26	2	22	4
30	3	33	1	34	4	35	1	35	4	35	6	36	-	35	7	35	5	35	1	34	3	33	2	32	-	26	5	22	6
30	6	33	4	35	-	35	5	36	-	36	2	36	4	36	2	36	-	35	5	34	6	33	5	32	3	27	-	23	1
31	2	34	-	35	4	36	1	36	4	36	6	37	-	36	7	36	4	36	-	35	2	34	1	32	6	27	3	23	3
31	5	34	4	36	-	36	5	37	-	37	2	37	4	37	3	37	1	36	5	35	6	34	5	33	-	27	6	23	6
32	1	35	-	36	4	37	1	37	4	37	6	38	-	37	7	37	4	37	1	36	2	35	1	33	6	28	1	24	-
32	5	35	4	37	-	37	5	38	-	38	2	38	4	38	3	38	1	37	5	36	6	35	5	34	2	28	4	24	3
33	-	36	-	37	4	38	1	38	4	38	5	39	-	38	7	38	5	38	1	37	2	36	1	34	5	28	7	24	6
33	3	36	3	37	7	38	5	39	-	39	2	39	4	39	3	39	-	38	4	37	6	36	4	35	-	29	2	25	-
33	7	36	7	38	3	39	-	39	4	39	6	40	-	39	7	39	5	39	1	38	2	37	-	35	4	29	5	25	3
34	2	37	3	38	7	39	5	40	-	40	2	40	4	40	3	40	1	39	4	38	7	37	4	35	7	30	-	25	6
34	6	37	7	39	3	40	-	40	4	40	7	41	1	40	7	40	5	40	1	39	1	38	-	36	5	30	3	26	-
35	1	38	2	39	7	40	4	41	-	41	2	41	4	41	3	41	-	40	4	39	5	38	3	36	7	30	6	26	3
35	4	38	6	40	3	41	-	41	4	41	6	42	-	41	7	41	5	41	-	40	1	38	7	37	2	31	1	26	5
36	-	39	2	40	7	41	5	42	-	42	3	42	4	42	3	42	1	41	4	40	5	39	3	37	5	31	4	27	-
36	4	39	5	41	3	42	-	42	4	42	7	43	1	43	-	42	5	42	-	41	-	39	6	38	1	31	7	27	2
36	6	40	1	41	7	42	4	43	-	43	2	43	5	43	4	43	1	42	4	41	5	40	2	38	5	32	3	27	5
37	1	40	5	42	2	43	-	43	4	43	6	44	1	44	-	43	5	43	-	42	-	40	5	39	-	32	6	27	7
37	6	41	1	42	6	43	4	44	-	44	2	44	5	44	4	44	-	43	4	42	4	41	1	39	4	33	-	28	2
38	1	41	5	43	2	44	-	44	4	44	6	45	1	45	-	44	4	44	-	43	-	41	5	40	-	33	3	28	5

TOPMASTS.

Heel and Cap.		Stop of Hounds.		Trestle-trees.		Top of Head.		Heel and Cap.		Stop of Hounds.		Trestle-trees.		Top of Head.	
In.	8ths.	In.	8ths.	In.	8ths.	In.	8ths	In.	8ths.	In.	8ths.	In.	8ths.	In.	8ths
13	—	12	7	9	2	7	7	19	4	19	2	13	7	11	7
13	2	13	1	9	3	8	—	19	6	19	4	14	—	12	—
13	4	13	3	9	5	8	2	20	—	19	6	14	2	12	1
13	6	13	5	9	6	8	3	20	2	20	—	14	3	12	2
14	—	13	7	10	—	8	4	20	4	20	2	14	4	12	4
14	2	14	1	10	1	8	5	20	6	20	4	14	6	12	5
14	4	14	3	10	2	8	6	21	—	20	6	15	—	12	6
14	6	14	5	10	4	9	—	21	2	21	—	15	1	12	7
15	—	14	7	10	5	9	1	21	4	21	2	15	2	13	—
15	2	15	1	10	7	9	2	21	6	21	4	15	4	13	2
15	4	15	3	11	—	9	3	22	—	21	6	15	5	13	3
15	6	15	5	11	2	9	5	22	2	22	—	15	7	13	4
16	—	15	6	11	3	9	6	22	4	22	2	16	—	13	5
16	2	16	—	11	4	9	7	22	6	22	4	16	2	13	7
16	4	16	2	11	6	10	—	23	—	22	6	16	3	14	—
16	6	16	4	11	7	10	1	23	2	23	—	16	4	14	1
17	—	16	6	12	1	10	3	23	4	23	2	16	5	14	2
17	2	17	—	12	2	10	4	23	6	23	4	16	7	14	3
17	4	17	2	12	4	10	5	24	—	23	6	17	1	14	5
17	6	17	4	12	5	10	6	24	2	24	—	17	2	14	6
18	—	17	6	12	6	10	7	24	4	24	2	17	4	15	—
18	2	18	—	13	—	11	1	24	6	24	4	17	5	15	1
18	4	18	2	13	1	11	2	25	—	24	6	17	6	15	2
18	6	18	4	13	3	11	3	25	2	25	—	18	—	15	3
19	—	18	6	13	4	11	4	25	4	25	2	18	1	15	4
19	2	19	—	13	6	11	6	25	6	25	4	18	3	15	5

TOP-GALLANT MASTS.

Top-gallant Masts.				Royal-Masts.				Poles.				Top-gallant Masts.				Royal-Masts.				Poles.			
Heel and Cap.		Stop of H'nds.		Heel.		Stop of H'nds.		Heel.		Top of Pole.		Heel and Cap.		Stop of H'nds.		Heel.		Stop of H'nds.		Heel.		Top of Pole.	
In.	8	In.	8	In.	8	In.	8	In.	8	In.	8	In.	8	In.	8	In.	8	In.	8	In.	8	In.	8
7	–	6	7	5	4	5	–	4	1	2	–	10	7	10	6	8	5'	7	6	6	4	4	–
7	1	7	–	5	5	5	1	4	1'	2	–	11	–	10	7	8	6	7	7	6	4'	4	2
7	2	7	1	5	6	5	1'	4	2	2	–	11	1	11	–	8	7	8	–	6	6	4	2
7	3	7	2	5	7	5	2	4	3	2	–	11	2	11	1	9	–	8	1	6	5	4	2
7	4	7	3	6	–	5	3	4	4	2	–	11	3	11	2	9	–'	8	1'	6	6	4	2
7	5	7	4	6	1	5	4	4	4'	2	–	11	4	11	3	9	1	8	2	6	6'	4	2
7	6	7	5	6	1'	5	4'	4	5	2	–	11	5	11	4	9	2	8	3	6	7	4	2
7	7	7	6	6	2	5	5	4	5'	2	–	11	6	11	5	9	3	8	4	7	–	4	2
8	–	7	7	6	3	5	6	4	6	2	4	11	7	11	6	9	4	8	5	7	–'	4	2
8	1	8	–	6	4	5	7	4	6'	2	4	12	–	11	7	9	4'	8	5'	7	1	4	5
8	2	8	1	6	4'	5	7'	4	7	2	4	12	1	12	–	9	5	8	6	7	1	4	5
8	3	8	2	6	5	6	–	4	7'	2	4	12	2	12	1	9	6	8	7	7	2	4	5
8	4	8	3	6	6	6	1	5	–	2	4	12	3	12	2	9	7	8	7'	7	2'	4	5
8	5	8	4	6	7	6	1'	5	–'	2	4	12	4	12	3	10	–	9	–	7	3	4	5
8	6	8	5	7	–	6	2	5	1	2	4	12	5	12	4	10	–'	9	1	7	4	4	5
8	7	8	6	7	–'	6	3	5	2	2	4	12	6	12	5	10	1	9	2	7	4'	4	5
9	–	8	7	7	1	6	3'	5	2'	3	–	12	7	12	6	10	2	9	2	7	5	4	5
9	1	9	–	7	2	6	4	5	3	3	–	13	–	12	7	10	3	9	3	7	6	4	6
9	2	9	1	7	3	6	5	5	4	3	–	13	1	13	–	10	4	9	4	7	6'	4	6
9	3	9	2	7	4	6	6	5	4'	3	–	13	2	13	1	10	4'	9	4'	7	7	4	6
9	4	9	3	7	5	6	7	5	5	3	–	13	3	13	2	10	5	9	5	7	7'	4	6
9	5	9	4	7	5'	6	7'	5	6	3	–	13	4	13	3	10	6	9	6	8	–	4	6
9	6	9	5	7	6	7	–	5	6'	3	–	13	5	13	4	10	7	9	7	8	1	4	6
9	7	9	6	7	7	7	1	5	7	3	–	13	6	13	5	11	–	10	–	8	1'	4	6
10	–	9	7	8	–	7	2	6	–	4	–	13	7	13	6	11	–'	10	–'	8	2	4	6
10	1	10	–	8	–'	7	2'	6	–'	4	–	14	–	13	7	11	1	10	1	8	2'	4	6
10	2	10	1	8	1	7	3	6	1	4	–	14	1	14	--	11	2	10	1'	8	3	5	–
10	3	10	2	8	2	7	4	6	2	4	–	14	2	14	1	11	3	10	2	8	4	5	–
10	4	10	3	8	3	7	4'	6	2'	4	–	14	3	14	2	11	4	10	3	8	5	5	–
10	5	10	4	8	4	7	5	6	3	4	–	14	4	14	3	11	4'	10	3'	8	5'	5	–
10	6	10	5	8	5	7	6	6	3'	4	–	14	5	14	4	11	5	10	4	8	6	5	–

N.B.—Royal-Masts with short Poles are to be in the grommet ⅔ of the greatest diameter of Royal-Masts.

(') *indicates* ($\frac{1}{16}$) *of an inch.*

YARDS WITH CLEATS.

Lower Top-Sail, Top-Gallant, and Royal.

Slings. No. 1.		No. 2.		Quarters No. 3.		No. 4.		Ends No. 5.		Slings No. 1.		No. 2.		Quarters No. 3.		No. 4.		Ends No. 5.	
In.	8ths	In.	8ths	In.	8ths	In.	8ths	In.	8ths	In.	8ths	In.	8ths	In.	8ths	In.	8t's	In.	8t's
4	—	3	6	3	4	2	6	1	5	16	4	16	1	14	5	11	7	7	—
4	4	4	2	4	—	3	1	1	7	17	—	16	4	15	—	12	2	7	2
5	—	4	6	4	3	3	4	2	1	17	4	17	—	15	4	12	4	7	4
5	4	5	2	4	5	3	7	2	2	18	—	17	4	16	—	12	7	7	5
6	—	5	6	5	2	4	2	2	4	18	4	18	—	16	3	13	2	7	7
6	4	6	2	5	7	4	5	2	6	19	—	18	4	16	7	13	5	8	—
7	—	6	6	6	2	5	—	3	—	19	4	19	—	17	2	14	—	8	2
7	4	7	2	6	5	5	3	3	1	20	—	19	4	17	6	14	3	8	4
8	—	7	6	7	—	5	5	3	3	20	4	20	—	18	1	14	6	8	6
8	4	8	2	7	4	6	—	3	5	21	—	20	4	18	5	15	1	9	—
9	—	8	6	7	7	6	3	3	6	21	4	21	—	19	1	15	4	9	1
9	4	9	2	8	3	6	6	4	—	22	—	21	4	19	4	15	7	9	3
10	—	9	6	8	7	7	1	4	2	22	4	22	—	20	—	16	1	9	5
10	4	10	2	9	2	7	4	4	4	23	—	22	3	20	3	16	5	9	6
11	—	10	6	9	5	7	7	4	5	23	4	22	7	20	7	16	7	10	—
11	4	11	1	10	1	8	2	4	7	24	—	23	3	21	3	17	2	10	2
12	—	11	5	10	4	8	4	5	1	24	4	23	7	21	6	17	5	10	4
12	4	12	1	11	—	8	7	5	2	25	—	24	3	22	1	18	—	10	5
13	—	12	5	11	4	9	2	5	4	25	4	24	7	22	5	18	3	10	7
13	4	13	1	12	—	9	5	5	6	26	—	25	3	23	1	18	6	11	1
14	—	13	5	12	3	10	—	6	—	26	4	25	7	23	6	19	1	11	3
14	4	14	1	12	7	10	3	6	1	27	—	26	3	24	—	19	4	11	5
15	—	14	5	13	2	10	6	6	3	27	4	26	7	24	4	19	7	11	7
15	4	15	1	13	6	11	1	6	5	28	—	27	3	24	7	20	1	12	—
16	—	15	5	14	1	11	4	6	6	28	4	27	7	25	2	20	5	12	2

YARDS WITH SHOULDERS.

Lower Top-Gallant and Royal.

Slings.		Shoulders on Stop of Hounds.		Grommet.		End of Yard.		Slings.		Shoulders on Stop of Hounds.		Grommet.		End of Yards.	
In.	8ths	In.	8ths	In.	8ths	In.	8ths	In.	8ths	In.	8ths	In.	8ths	In.	8ths
4	—	2	4	2	—	1	5	17	—	1	6	8	4	7	2
4	4	2	6	2	2	1	7	17	4	10	—	8	6	7	4
5	—	3	—	2	4	2	1	18	—	10	2	9	—	7	5
5	4	3	2	2	6	2	2	18	4	10	4	9	2	7	7
6	—	3	4	3	—	2	4	19	—	10	6	9	4	8	—
6	4	3	6	3	2	2	6	19	4	11	—	9	6	8	2
7	—	4	2	3	4	3	—	20	—	11	4	10	—	8	4
7	4	4	4	3	6	3	1	20	4	11	6	10	2	8	6
8	—	4	6	4	—	3	3	21	—	12	—	10	4	9	—
8	4	5	—	4	2	3	5	21	4	12	—	10	6	9	1
9	—	5	2	4	4	3	6	22	—	12	4	11	—	9	3
9	4	5	4	4	6	4	—	22	4	12	6	11	2	9	5
10	—	6	—	5	—	4	2	23	—	13	—	11	4	9	6
10	4	6	2	5	2	4	4	23	4	13	2	11	6	10	—
11	—	6	4	5	4	4	5	24	—	13	4	12	—	10	2
11	4	6	6	5	6	4	7	24	4	13	6	12	2	10	4
12	—	7	—	6	—	5	1	25	—	14	—	12	4	10	5
12	4	7	2	6	2	5	2	25	4	14	2	12	6	10	7
13	—	7	6	6	4	5	4	26	—	15	—	13	—	11	1
13	4	8	—	6	6	5	6	26	4	15	2	13	2	11	3
14	—	8	2	7	—	6	—	27	—	15	4	13	4	11	5
14	4	8	4	7	2	6	1	27	4	15	6	13	6	11	7
15	—	8	6	7	4	6	3	28	—	16	—	14	—	12	—
15	4	9	—	7	6	6	5	28	4	16	2	14	2	12	2
16	—	9	2	8	—	6	6	29	—	16	4	14	4	12	4
16	4	9	4	8	2	7	—	29	4	16	6	14	6	12	6

YARDS WITH SHOULDERS.

Top-sail Yards.

Slings.		Shoulder on Stop of Hounds.		Grommet.		End of Yards.		Slings.		Shoulder on Stop of Hounds.		Grommet.		End of Yards.	
In.	8ths.	In.	8ths.	In.	8ths.	In.	8ths	In.	8ths.	In.	8ths.	In.	8ths.	In.	8ths
4	....	3	....	2	4	1	5	17	....	12	1	10	5	7	2
4	4	3	2	2	6	1	7	17	4	12	3	10	7	7	4
5	....	3	5	3	1	2	1	18	....	12	6	11	2	7	5
5	4	3	7	3	3	2	2	18	4	13	....	11	4	7	7
6	....	4	2	3	6	2	4	19	....	13	3	11	7	8	...
6	4	4	4	4	...	2	6	19	4	13	5	12	1	8	2
7	....	4	7	4	3	3	..	20	....	14	....	12	4	8	4
7	4	5	1	4	5	3	1	20	4	14	2	12	6	8	6
8	....	5	6	5	....	3	3	21	....	14	5	13	1	9	...
8	4	6	....	5	2	3	5	21	4	14	7	13	3	9	1
9	....	6	2	5	4	3	6	22	....	15	2	13	6	9	3
9	4	6	5	5	7	4	...	22	4	15	4	14	....	9	4
10	....	7	2	6	2	4	2	23	....	15	7	14	3	9	6
10	4	7	4	6	4	4	4	23	4	16	1	14	5	10	..
11	....	7	7	6	7	4	5	24	....	16	4	15	....	10	2
11	4	8	1	7	1	4	7	24	4	16	6	15	2	10	4
12	....	8	4	7	4	5	1	25	....	17	3	15	5	10	5
12	4	8	6	7	6	5	2	25	4	17	5	15	7	10	7
13	....	9	1	8	1	5	4	26	....	18	....	16	2	11	1
13	4	9	3	8	3	5	6	26	4	18	2	16	4	11	3
14	....	10	....	8	6	6	...	27	....	18	5	16	7	11	5
14	4	10	2	9	....	6	1	27	4	18	7	17	1	11	7
15	....	10	5	9	3	6	3	28	....	19	2	17	4	12	...
15	4	10	7	9	5	6	5	28	4	19	4	17	6	12	2
16	....	11	2	10	....	6	6	29	....	19	7	18	6	12	4
16	4	11	4	10	2	7	..	29	....	20	2	18	4	12	6

JIB-BOOMS.

Heel No. 1.		No. 2.		Cap. No. 3.		No. 4.		No. 5.		No. 6.		Sh'lder. No. 7.		Grom'et No. 8.		End of Pole. No. 9	
In.	8th	In.	8th	In.	8th	In.	8th	In.	8th	In.	8th	In.	8th	In.	8th	In.	8th
7	4	9	3	10	...	9	7	9	4	9	..	8	...	6	5	6	...
7	5	9	5	10	2	10	1	9	5	9	1	8	1	6	6	6	1
7	7	9	7	10	4	10	3	9	7	9	3	8	3	7	...	6	2
8	...	10	...	10	6	10	5	10	1	9	5	8	4	7	1	6	3
8	2	10	2	11	...	10	7	10	3	9	7	8	6	7	2	6	4
8	3	10	4	11	2	11	1	10	5	10	1	9	...	7	4	6	6
8	5	10	6	11	4	11	3	10	7	10	3	9	1	7	5	6	7
8	6	11	...	11	6	11	5	11	2	10	5	9	3	7	6	7	...
9	...	11	2	12	...	11	7	11	3	10	6	9	4	8	...	7	1
9	1	11	4	12	2	12	1	11	5	11	...	9	6	8	1	7	2
9	3	11	5	12	4	12	2	11	7	11	2	10	...	8	2	7	4
9	4	11	7	12	6	12	4	12	1	11	3	10	1	8	4	7	5
9	6	12	1	13	...	12	6	12	3	11	5	10	3	8	5	7	6
9	7	12	3	13	2	13	...	12	5	11	7	10	4	8	6	7	7
10	1	12	5	13	4	13	2	12	6	12	1	10	6	9	...	8	...
10	2	12	7	13	6	13	4	13	...	12	3	11	...	9	1	8	2
10	4	13	1	14	...	13	6	13	2	12	5	11	1	9	2	8	3
10	5	13	2	14	2	14	...	13	5	12	7	11	3	9	4	8	4
10	7	13	4	14	4	14	2	13	6	13	...	11	4	9	5	8	5
11	...	13	6	14	6	14	4	14	...	13	2	11	6	9	6	8	6
11	2	14	...	15	...	14	6	14	2	13	4	12	...	10	...	9	...
11	3	14	2	15	2	15	...	14	3	13	5	12	1	10	1	9	1
11	5	14	4	15	4	15	2	14	5	13	7	12	3	10	2	9	2
11	6	14	6	15	6	15	4	14	7	14	1	12	4	10	4	9	3
12	...	15	...	16	...	15	6	15	1	14	3	12	6	10	5	9	4

Heel. No. 1.		No. 2.		Cap. No. 3.		No. 4.		No. 5.		No. 6.		Sh'lder. No. 7.		Gro'net. No. 8.		Cap. No. 9.	
In.	8th	In.	8th	In.	8th	In.	8th	In.	8th	In.	8th	In.	8th	In.	8th	In.	8th
12	1	15	2	16	2	16	–	15	3	14	5	13	–	10	6	9	6
12	3	15	3	16	4	16	2	15	5	14	6	13	1	11	–	9	7
12	4	15	5	16	6	16	4	15	7	15	–	13	3	11	1	10	–
12	6	15	7	17	–	16	6	16	1	15	2	13	4	11	2	10	1
12	7	16	1	17	2	17	–	16	3	15	4	13	6	11	4	10	2
13	1	16	3	17	4	17	2	16	4	15	6	14	–	11	5	10	4
13	2	16	5	17	6	17	4	16	6	15	7	14	1	11	6	10	5
13	4	16	7	18	–	17	6	17	–	16	1	14	3	12	–	10	6
13	5	17	–	18	2	18	–	17	2	16	3	14	5	12	1	10	7
13	7	17	2	18	4	18	2	17	4	16	5	14	6	12	2	11	–
14	–	17	4	18	6	18	4	17	6	16	7	15	–	12	4	11	2
14	2	17	6	19	–	18	6	18	–	17	–	15	1	12	5	11	3
14	3	18	–	19	2	19	–	18	2	17	2	15	3	12	6	11	4
14	5	18	2	19	4	19	2	18	4	17	4	15	5	13	–	11	5
14	6	18	4	19	6	19	4	18	6	17	6	15	6	13	1	11	6
15	–	18	6	20	–	19	6	19	–	18	–	16	–	13	2	12	–
15	1	19	–	20	2	20	–	19	2	18	1	16	1	13	4	12	1
15	3	19	2	20	4	20	2	19	3	18	2	16	3	13	5	12	2
15	4	19	3	20	6	20	4	19	5	18	5	16	4	13	6	12	3
15	6	19	5	21	–	20	6	19	7	18	7	16	7	14	–	12	4
15	7	19	7	21	2	21	–	20	1	19	1	17	–	14	1	12	6
16	1	20	1	21	4	21	2	20	3	19	2	17	1	14	2	12	7
16	2	20	3	21	6	21	4	20	5	19	4	17	3	14	4	13	–
16	4	20	5	22	–	21	6	20	7	19	6	17	4	14	5	13	1
16	5	20	6	22	2	22	–	21	1	20	–	17	6	14	6	13	2

FLYING JIB-BOOM.																BOWSPRIT.														
Heel.				Boom Irons.								Sho'l-ders.		Grom-met.		End of Poles.		Heel.		Bed.								Outer End.	
No. 1		No. 2		No. 3		No. 4		No. 5		No. 6		No. 7		No. 8		No. 9		No. 1		No. 2		No. 3		No. 4		No. 5		No. 6	
in.	8ths	in.	8ths	in.	8ths	in.	8ths	in.	8ths	in.	8ths	in.	8ths	in.	8ths	in.	8ths	in.	8ths	in.	8ths	in.	8ths	in.	8ths	in.	8ths	in.	8ths
2	5	4	3	5	—	4	7	4	6	4	4	4	—	3	2	1	5	11	1	13	–	12	6	11	7	10	6	8	5
2	6	4	5	5	2	5	1	5	—	4	5	4	1	3	3	1	6	12	–	14	–	13	6	12	7	11	5	9	2
2	7	4	7	5	4	5	3	5	2	4	7	4	3	3	5	1	7	12	6	15	–	14	6	13	6	12	4	10	–
3	—	5	1	5	6	5	5	5	4	5	1	4	4	3	6	2	—	13	5	16	–	15	6	14	6	13	3	10	5
3	1	5	2	6	—	5	7	5	6	5	3	4	6	4	—	2	1	14	4	17	–	16	5	15	5	14	1	11	2
3	2	5	4	6	2	6	1	6	—	5	5	5	—	4	1	2	2	15	3	18	–	17	5	16	4	15	–	12	–
3	3	5	6	6	4	6	3	6	1	5	7	5	1	4	2	2	3	16	2	19	–	18	5	17	4	15	7	12	5
3	4	5	7	6	6	6	5	6	3	6	—	5	3	4	4	2	4	17	1	20	–	19	5	18	3	16	5	13	2
3	5	6	1	7	—	6	7	6	5	6	2	5	4	4	5	2	5	18	–	21	–	20	5	19	2	17	4	14	–
3	6	6	3	7	2	7	1	6	7	6	4	5	6	4	6	2	6	18	6	22	–	21	4	20	2	18	3	14	5
3	7	6	4	7	4	7	3	7	1	6	6	6	—	5	—	2	7	19	5	23	–	22	4	21	1	19	2	15	2
4	—	6	6	7	6	7	5	7	3	7	—	6	1	5	1	3	—	20	4	24	–	23	4	22	–	20	–	16	–
4	1	7	—	8	—	7	7	7	5	7	1	6	3	5	2	3	1	21	3	25	–	24	4	23	–	20	7	16	5
4	2	7	2	8	2	8	1	7	7	7	3	6	4	5	4	3	2	22	2	26	–	25	4	23	7	21	6	17	2
4	3	7	4	8	4	8	3	8	1	7	5	6	6	5	5	3	3	23	1	27	–	26	3	24	6	22	4	18	–
4	4	7	6	8	6	8	5	8	3	7	7	7	—	5	6	3	4	24	–	28	–	27	3	25	6	23	3	18	5
4	5	7	7	9	—	8	7	8	4	8	1	7	1	6	—	3	5	24	6	29	–	28	3	26	5	24	2	19	2
4	6	8	1	9	2	9	1	8	6	8	3	7	3	6	1	3	6	25	5	30	–	29	3	27	4	25	–	20	–
4	7	8	3	9	4	9	3	9	—	8	4	7	4	6	2	3	7	26	4	31	–	30	3	28	3	25	7	20	5
5	—	8	5	9	6	9	5	9	1	8	6	7	6	6	4	4	—	27	3	32	–	31	3	29	3	26	6	21	2
5	1	8	7	10	—	9	7	9	4	9	—	8	—	6	5	4	1	28	2	33	–	32	3	30	2	27	4	22	–
5	2	9	—	10	2	10	—	9	6	9	2	8	1	6	6	4	2	29	1	34	–	33	3	31	3	28	3	22	5
5	3	9	2	10	4	10	3	10	—	9	3	8	3	7	—	4	3	30	–	35	–	34	2	32	1	29	1	23	2
5	4	9	4	10	6	10	5	10	1	9	5	8	4	7	1	4	5	30	6	36	–	35	2	33	–	30	–	24	–
5	5	9	5	11	—	10	7	10	2	9	7	8	6	7	2	4	6	31	5	37	–	36	2	33	7	30	7	24	5
5	6	9	7	11	2	11	1	10	6	10	1	9	—	7	4	4	7	32	4	38	–	37	2	34	4	31	6	25	2
5	7	10	1	11	4	11	3	10	7	10	2	9	1	7	5	5	—	33	3	39	–	38	2	35	6	32	5	26	–
6	—	10	2	11	6	11	5	11	2	10	4	9	3	7	6	5	1	34	2	40	–	39	1	36	6	33	3	26	5
6	1	10	4	12	—	11	7	11	4	10	6	9	4	8	—	5	2	35	1	41	–	40	1	37	5	34	2	27	2

SPANKER-BOOMS.

Fore End.								Greatest D.am.				Shoulder.		Grommet.		End of Pole.	
No. 1		No. 2		No. 3		No. 4		No. 5		No. 6		No. 7		No. 8		No. 9	
In.	8ths	In.	8ths	In.	8ths	In.	8ths	In.	8ths	In.	8ths	In.	8ths	In.	8ths	In.	8ths
4	—	4	4	4	5	4	7	5	—	4	5	3	3	2	5	2	1
4	1	4	5	4	7	5	1	5	2	4	6	3	4	2	6	2	2
4	3	4	7	5	1	5	3	5	4	5	1	3	5	2	7	2	3
4	4	5	1	5	3	5	5	5	6	5	2	3	6	3	–	2	4
4	6	5	3	5	5	5	2	6	—	5	4	4	—	3	1	2	5
5	—	5	5	5	7	6	1	6	2	5	6	4	1	3	2	2	6
5	1	5	6	6	1	6	3	6	4	6	–	4	2	3	3	2	7
5	3	6	–	6	3	6	5	6	6	6	2	4	4	3	4	3	—
5	4	6	2	6	5	6	7	7	—	6	4	4	5	3	5	3	1
5	6	6	4	6	7	7	1	7	2	6	5	4	6	3	6	3	2
6	—	6	6	7	1	7	3	7	4	6	7	5	—	4	–	3	3
6	1	6	7	7	3	7	5	7	6	7	1	5	1	4	1	3	4
6	3	7	1	7	5	7	7	8	—	7	3	5	2	4	2	3	5
6	4	7	3	7	6	8	1	8	2	7	4	5	4	4	3	3	6
6	6	7	5	8	–	8	3	8	4	7	6	5	5	4	4	3	6
7	—	7	6	8	2	8	5	8	6	7	7	5	6	4	5	3	7
7	1	8	–	8	4	8	7	9	—	8	2	6	—	4	6	4	—
7	3	8	2	8	6	9	1	9	2	8	4	6	1	4	7	4	1
7	4	8	4	9	–	9	3	9	4	8	6	6	2	5	–	4	2
7	6	8	6	9	2	9	5	9	6	9	–	6	4	5	1	4	3
8	—	9	–	9	4	9	7	10	—	9	3	6	5	5	2	4	4

Fore End.								Greatest Diam.				Shoulder.		Grommet.		End of Pole.	
No. 1		No. 2		No. 3		No. 4		No. 5		No. 6		No. 7		No. 8		No. 9	
In.	8ths	In.	8ths	In.	8ths	In.	8ths	In.	8ths	In.	8ths	In.	8ths	In.	8ths	In.	8ths
8	1	9	2	9	6	10	1	10	2	8	5	6	6	5	3	4	5
8	3	9	4	10	–	10	3	10	4	8	7	7	–	5	4	4	6
8	4	9	6	10	2	10	5	10	6	9	1	7	1	5	5	4	7
8	6	10	–	10	3	10	7	11	—	9	4	7	2	5	6	5	–
9	–	10	1	10	5	11	1	11	2	9	6	7	4	6	–	5	1
9	1	10	3	10	7	11	2	11	4	10	–	7	5	6	1	5	2
9	3	10	5	11	1	11	4	11	6	10	2	7	6	6	2	5	3
9	4	10	7	11	3	11	6	12	—	10	4	8	–	6	3	5	4
9	6	11	1	11	5	12	–	12	2	10	6	8	1	6	4	5	6
10	–	11	3	11	7	12	2	12	4	11	1	8	2	6	5	5	7
10	1	11	4	12	1	12	4	12	6	11	3	8	4	6	6	6	–
10	3	11	6	12	3	12	6	13	—	11	5	8	5	6	7	6	1
10	4	12	–	12	4	13	–	13	2	11	7	8	6	7	–	6	2
10	6	12	2	12	6	13	2	13	4	12	1	9	–	7	1	6	3
11	–	12	3	13	–	13	4	13	6	12	3	9	1	7	2	6	4
11	1	12	5	13	2	13	6	14	—	12	5	9	2	7	3	6	5
11	3	12	7	13	4	14	–	14	2	12	7	9	4	7	4	6	7
11	4	13	–	13	6	14	2	14	4	13	2	9	5	7	5	7	–
11	6	13	2	14	–	14	4	14	6	13	4	9	6	7	6	7	1
12	–	13	4	14	2	14	6	15	—	13	6	10	–	8	–	7	2
12	1	13	6	14	4	15	–	15	2	14	–	10	1	8	1	7	3

SPANKER GAFF.

Heel.		Greatest Diameter.								Shoulder.		Grommet.		End of Pole.	
No. 1		No. 2		No. 3		No. 4		No. 5		No. 6		No. 7		No. 8	
In.	8ths	In.	8ths	In.	8ths	In.	8ths	In.	8ths	In.	8ths	In.	8ths	In.	8ths
3	3	4	-	4	2	3	6	3	4	3	-	2	5	1	2
3	6	4	4	4	3	4	2	4	-	3	3	2	7	1	4
4	2	5	-	4	7	4	6	4	3	3	6	3	2	1	5
4	5	5	4	5	3	5	2	4	6	4	1	3	5	1	6
5	1	6	-	5	7	5	5	5	2	4	4	4	-	2	-
5	4	6	4	6	3	6	1	5	5	4	7	4	2	2	1
6	-	7	-	6	7	6	4	6	1	5	2	4	5	2	2
6	3	7	4	7	3	7	-	6	4	5	7	4	7	2	4
6	6	8	-	7	7	7	4	7	-	6	-	5	2	2	5
7	1	8	4	8	3	8	-	7	3	6	3	5	5	2	6
7	5	9	-	8	7	8	3	7	7	6	6	6	-	3	-
8	1	9	4	9	2	8	7	8	2	7	1	6	2	3	1
8	5	10	-	9	6	9	3	8	6	7	4	6	5	3	2
9	-	10	4	10	2	9	6	9	1	7	7	6	7	3	3
9	3	11	-	10	6	10	2	9	4	8	2	7	2	3	5
9	6	11	4	11	2	10	6	10	-	8	5	7	5	3	6
10	2	12	-	11	7	11	2	10	4	9	-	8	-	4	-

DOLPHIN-STRIKER.

Heel.		Greatest Diameter.								Shoulder.		Grommet.		End of Pole.	
No. 1		No. 2		No. 3		No. 4		No. 5		No. 6		No. 7		No. 8	
In.	8ths	In.	8ths	In.	8ths	In.	8ths	In.	8ths	In.	8ths	In.	8ths	In.	8ths
3	-	4	-	4	-	3	7	3	6	3	4	2	6	2	-
3	3	4	4	4	3	4	3	4	2	3	7	3	1	2	2
3	6	5	-	4	7	4	7	4	5	4	3	3	4	2	4
4	1	5	4	5	3	5	2	5	1	4	6	3	6	2	6
4	4	6	-	5	7	5	6	5	5	5	2	4	1	3	-
4	7	6	4	6	3	6	2	6	-	5	5	4	4	3	3
5	2	7	-	6	7	6	6	6	4	6	1	4	7	3	5
5	5	7	4	7	3	7	2	7	-	6	4	5	2	3	7
6	-	8	-	7	7	7	6	7	4	7	-	5	5	4	1
6	3	8	4	8	3	8	2	8	-	7	3	6	-	4	3
6	6	9	-	8	7	8	6	8	3	7	7	6	2	4	6
7	1	9	4	9	3	9	2	8	7	8	3	6	5	5	-
7	5	10	-	9	7	9	5	9	3	8	6	7	-	5	2
7	7	10	4	10	3	10	1	9	7	9	2	7	3	5	4
8	2	11	-	10	7	10	5	10	2	9	5	7	6	5	6
8	5	11	4	11	3	11	1	10	6	10	1	8	1	6	-
9	-	12	-	11	7	11	5	11	2	10	5	8	4	6	3

WHISKER-BOOMS.

Heel.				Greatest Diameter.				Shoulder.		Grommet.		End of Pole.	
No. 1		No. 2		No. 3		No. 4		No. 5		No. 6		No. 7	
In.	8ths	In.	8ths	In.	8ths	In.	8ths	In.	8ths	In.	8ths	In.	8ths
3	1	3	6	4	-	3	5	4	-	2	4	2	1
3	4	4	2	4	4	4	1	4	4	2	6	2	3
3	7	4	6	5	-	4	4	5	-	3	1	2	5
4	2	5	1	5	4	5	-	5	4	3	3	2	7
4	6	5	5	6	-	5	4	6	-	3	6	3	1
5	1	6	1	6	4	5	7	6	4	4	-	3	3
5	4	6	5	7	-	6	3	7	-	4	3	3	5
5	7	7	1	7	4	6	6	7	4	4	5	3	7
6	3	7	5	8	-	7	2	8	-	5	-	4	2
6	6	8	-	8	4	7	6	8	4	5	2	4	4
7	1	8	4	9	-	8	1	9	-	5	5	4	6
7	4	9	-	9	4	8	5	9	4	5	7	5	-
8	-	9	4	10	-	9	-	10	-	6	2	5	2
8	3	10	-	10	4	9	4	10	4	6	5	5	4
8	6	10	3	11	-	10	-	11	-	6	7	5	7
9	1	10	7	11	4	10	3	11	4	7	1	6	-
9	4	11	3	12	-	10	7	12	-	7	4	6	3

MAIN AND FORE-GAFF.

		Greatest Diameter.								Shoulder.		Grommet.		End of Pole.	
No. 1		No. 2		No. 3		No. 4		No. 5		No 6		No. 7		No. 8	
In.	8ths	In.	8ths	In.	8ths	In.	8ths	In.	8ths	In.	8ths	In.	8ths	In.	8ths
3	3	4	-	4	-	3	6	3	4	3	-	2	5	2	2
3	6	4	4	4	3	4	2	4	-	3	3	3	-	2	4
4	2	5	-	4	7	4	6	4	3	3	6	3	2	2	6
4	5	5	4	5	3	5	2	4	6	4	1	3	5	3	-
5	1	6	-	5	7	5	5	5	2	4	4	4	-	3	3
5	4	6	4	6	3	6	1	5	5	4	7	4	2	3	5
6	-	7	-	6	7	6	4	6	1	5	2	4	5	4	-
6	3	7	4	7	2	7	-	6	4	5	7	5	-	4	2
6	6	8	-	7	6	7	4	7	-	6	-	5	2	4	4
7	1	8	4	8	2	8	-	7	3	6	3	5	5	4	7
7	5	9	-	8	6	8	3	7	7	6	6	6	-	5	1
8	1	9	4	9	2	8	7	8	2	7	1	6	2	5	3
8	5	10	-	9	6	9	3	8	6	7	4	6	5	5	6
9	-	10	4	10	2	9	6	9	1	7	7	7	-	6	-
9	3	11	-	10	6	10	2	9	4	8	2	7	3	6	2
9	6	11	4	11	-	10	6	10	-	8	5	7	5	6	4
10	2	12	-	11	2	11	2	10	4	9	-	8	-	6	6

NOTE.—Whisker booms should be lined like a Yard, then make a neck to them by lining off the shoulders to the size of the greatest diameter of the boom.

SWINGING-BOOMS.							
Out-Board End.		Greatest Diam.				In-Board End.	
No. 1.		No. 2.		No. 3.		No. 4.	
In.	8ths.	In.	8ths.	In.	8ths.	In.	8ths
2	5	4	..	3	5	3	1
3	..	4	4	4	1	3	4
3	2	5	..	4	4	3	7
3	5	5	4	5	..	4	2
4	..	6	..	5	4	4	6
4	2	6	4	5	7	5	1
4	5	7	..	6	3	5	4
5	..	7	4	6	7	5	7
5	2	8	..	7	3	6	3
5	5	8	4	7	6	6	6
6	..	9	..	8	2	7	1
6	2	9	4	8	6	7	4
6	5	10	..	9	1	8	..
7	..	10	4	9	5	8	3
7	3	11	..	10	1	8	6
7	5	11	4	10	4	9	1
8	..	12	..	11	..	9	4

FORE AND MAIN TOP-MAST STUDDING-SAIL BOOMS.							
Heel.		Greatest Diam.				Outer End.	
No. 1.		No. 2.		No. 3.		No. 4.	
In.	8ths.	In.	8ths.	In.	8ths.	In.	8ths
3	1	4	..	3	5	2	5
3	4	4	4	4	1	3	..
3	7	5	..	4	4	3	2
4	2	5	4	5	..	3	5
4	6	6	..	5	4	4	..
5	1	6	4	5	7	4	2
5	4	7	..	6	3	4	5
5	7	7	4	6	7	5	..
6	3	8	..	7	3	5	2
6	6	8	4	7	6	5	5
7	1	9	..	8	2	6	..
7	4	9	4	8	6	6	2
8	..	10	..	9	1	6	5
8	3	10	4	9	5	7	..
8	6	11	..	10	1	7	3
9	1	11	4	10	4	7	5
9	4	12	..	11	..	8	..

FORE AND MAIN TOP-GALLANT STUDDING-SAIL BOOMS.									
Heel.				Middle Greatest Diam.				Outer End.	
No. 1.		No. 2.		No. 3.		No. 4.		No. 5.	
In.	8ths	In.	8ths	In.	8ths	In.	8ths	In.	8.
3	1	3	6	4	..	3	5	2	5
3	4	4	2	4	4	4	1	3	..
3	7	4	6	5	..	4	4	3	2
4	2	5	2	5	4	5	..	3	5
4	6	5	6	6	..	1	4	4	..
5	1	6	1	6	4	5	7	4	2
5	4	6	5	7	..	6	3	4	5
5	7	7	1	7	4	6	7	5	..
6	3	7	5	8	..	7	3	5	2
6	6	8	..	8	4	7	6	5	5
7	1	8	4	9	..	8	2	6	..
7	4	9	..	9	4	8	6	6	2
8	..	9	4	10	1	9	1	6	5
8	3	10	..	10	4	9	5	7	..
8	6	10	3	11	..	10	1	7	3
9	1	10	7	11	4	10	4	7	5
9	4	11	3	12	..	11	..	8	..
..	..	..	..	..	..	..	..	..	..
..	..	..	..	..	..	..	..	..	..
..	..	..	..	..	..	..	..	..	..
..	..	..	..	..	..	..	..	..	..
..	..	..	..	..	..	..	..	..	..
..	..	..	..	..	..	..	..	..	..
..	..	..	..	..	..	..	..	..	..
..	..	..	..	..	..	..	..	..	..

LOWER, TOPMAST, AND TOP-GALLANT STUDDING-SAIL YARDS.									
End.				Slings Greatest Diam.				End.	
No. 1.		No. 2.		No. 3.		No. 4.		No. 5.	
In.	8ths	In.	8ths	In.	8ths	In.	8ths	In.	8.
1	4	1	6	2	..	1	6	1	4
1	5	2	1	2	2	2	1	1	5
1	6	2	2	2	4	2	2	1	6
1	7	2	4	2	6	2	4	1	7
2	..	2	6	3	..	2	6	2	..
2	1	3	..	3	2	3	..	2	1
2	2	3	2	3	4	3	2	2	2
2	3	3	3	3	6	3	3	2	3
2	4	3	5	4	..	3	5	2	4
2	5	3	7	4	2	3	7	2	5
2	6	4	..	4	4	4	..	2	6
2	7	4	2	4	6	4	2	2	7
3	..	4	4	5	..	4	4	3	..
3	1	4	6	5	2	4	6	3	1
3	2	5	..	5	4	5	..	3	2
3	3	5	2	5	6	5	2	3	3
3	4	5	3	6	..	5	3	3	4
3	5	5	5	6	2	5	5	3	5
3	6	5	7	6	4	5	7	3	6
3	7	6	..	6	6	6	..	3	7
4	..	6	2	7	..	6	2	4	..
4	1	6	4	7	2	6	4	4	1
4	2	6	6	7	4	6	6	4	2
4	3	7	..	7	6	7	..	4	3
4	4	7	1	8	..	7	1	4	4

103. *A plan*, for iron screw-fids for topmasts, and wood wedge-fids, for top-gallant masts, was ordered by the Navy Department, August 9th, 1870, to be used hereafter as directed by Commodore T. O. Selfridge, U.S.N., the designer of them.

Iron-screw fids for top-masts are in length one inch less than the widths of their respective trestle-trees.

In depth, three-tenths of the greatest diameter of their respective topmasts. In thickness, the same as their depth. Whole length of the screw is the greatest diameter of its respective topmast.

The screw in diameter is three-seventeenths of the greatest diameter of its respective topmast.

Head of screw to be about one inch larger than the screw.

Length of the head of screw the depth of the fid.

The diameter of the heaving bar is one-tenth of the diameter of the topmast. The length of the bar is the diameter of the topmast.

104. *Wood-wedge Fids for Top-gallant Mast.*—Fids of locust for top-gallant masts are in length the breadth of their respective trestle-trees.

In depth, three-fifths of the greatest diameter of their respective top-gallant mast, and in thickness five-ninths of their depth.

REVENUE CUTTERS AND OTHER SCHOONERS.

105. *Main-Mast.*—The main-mast, in length, should be three times the breadth of beam, and two-thirds the depth of hold.

The head should be one-tenth the length of the mast. The diameter in the partners should be one inch to every four feet of its length. Diameter of the heel twelve-thirteenths of the partners. Diameter of the stop of hounds, seven-eighths of the partners. Diameter in the trestle-trees, two-thirds of the partners. Diameter of the top of head, six-sevenths of the trestle-trees.

106. *Fore-mast.*—The fore-mast should be in length seventy-four seventy-sixths of the length of the main-mast, and in all other respects, the same as the main-mast.

107. *Bowsprit.*—The bowsprit out-board from the rabbet should be one-quarter of the length of the main-mast.

The diameter in the bed is the same as the diameter of the main-mast.

The diameter of the outer end is two-thirds of the bed.

The diameter of the heel is twelve-thirteenths of the bed.

The in-board part of the bowsprit is one-half the length of the out-board part.

108. **Main Topmast.*—The main-topmast in length should be two-sevenths of the length of the main-mast.

The diameter, one and one-quarter of an inch to every three feet of its length;

And at the stop of the hounds, one-quarter less than the given diameter.

109. *Top-gallant Masts.*—The top-gallant masts should be ten twenty-firsts of the lengths of topmasts.

The diameter of the top-gallant masts should be four-fifths of the diameter of the topmasts.

The diameter at the stop of hounds is ten-elevenths of the diameter of the top-gallant masts.

The pole is in length one-fifth of the length of the top-gallant mast.

The diameter of the pole is three-quarters of the diameter of the top-gallant mast.

110. *Fore Topmast.*—The fore topmast is the same length and diameter as the main topmast, and in all other respects the same.

111. *Jib-Boom.*—The jib-boom (out-board) to be four-fifths of the out-board part of bowsprit, the in-board part to run into the knight-head.

The diameter to be one-half of the diameter of the bowsprit. At the stop of hounds or shoulder, it is four-fifths of its greatest diameter.

In the grommet it is two-thirds of its greatest diameter.

The inner end of jib-boom should be one-half of its greatest diameter.

Pole included in the length should be one-twelfth of the out-board part of the jib-boom.

The end of the pole is the same size as the flying jib-boom.

112. *Flying-Jib-Boom.*—The flying-jib-boom (out-board) should be four-fifths of the out-board part of the jib-boom.

The pole included one-fifth of the out-board part of the flying jib-boom.

The diameter, two-thirds of the greatest diameter of the jib-boom.

NOTE.—*The following dimensions of masts, etc., are intended for yellow pine; but if white pine is used, then they should be about two inches larger in diameter.

At the shoulders it is four-fifths of its greatest diameter.

In the grommet it is two-thirds of its greatest diameter.

The end of the pole is one-half of the grommet.

113. MAIN-BOOM.

The main-boom in length should be three-quarters of the length of the main-mast.

The diameter, one inch to every five feet of its length; inner end four-fifths of its greatest diameter; outer end two-thirds of its greatest diameter.

114. MAIN-GAFF.

The main-gaff is one-half of the length of the main-boom; pole included one-tenth of its length.

The diameter should be one inch to every four feet of its length; the inner end should be six-sevenths of its greatest diameter, and the outer end at shoulder three-quarters of its greatest diameter.

In the grommet it should be two-thirds of its greatest diameter.

115. FORE-GAFF.

The fore-gaff is one-half the length of the main-boom.

The diameter, the same as main-gaff.

The inner end is six-sevenths of the greatest diameter.

The outer end is three-quarters of its greatest diameter.

116. FORE-YARD.

The fore-yard in length should be twice the breadth of beam.

The diameter is one inch to every five feet of its length.

The end of yard half the greatest diameter.

The arms in length are one-twentieth of the whole length of the yard.

117. FORE TOP-SAIL YARD.

The fore top-sail yard in length is three-quarters of the lower yard.

Arms included one-eleventh of its length.

The diameter should be one inch to every five feet of its length.

The ends of yard is one-half the diameter.

118. FORE TOP-GALLANT YARD.

The fore top-gallant yard is in length nine-fourteenths of the length of the top-sail yard.

The arms one five-hundredth of its length.

The diameter one inch to every five feet.

The end of the yard is one-half the greatest diameter.

119. SQUARE-SAIL YARD.

The square-sail yard is once and a-half the breadth of beam.

Arms included one-fortieth of the length.

The diameter one inch to every five feet of its length.

The shoulder is two-thirds of the diameter.

The grommet is four-sevenths of the diameter.

The end of arm is one-half of the diameter.

PROPORTIONS AND DIMENSIONS FOR MASTS, YARDS, &c.

ON MASTING BOATS.

*In determining the lengths of masts, &c., for boats, the proportion that exists between the areas of their different sails is of little use, as boats are soon affected by an alteration of the stowage, &c.; nor are we guided by experiment in fixing the best proportions, for there is a great difference in the moments of sails of boats of the same size, and this frequently when they are similarly rigged, and employed for the same purposes, arising from the ideas and various modes of managing them by different officers. All that can be useful, therefore, is to state the limits taken from the greatest and smallest sails of those boats that are best rigged, and fully approved of by the most experienced managers, and from them to form tables which shall give the same moment of sail (nearly) for every kind of rigging.

The sails of boats are subject to the same rules for placing of the centre of effort, as those of vessels of the largest magnitude; but as the effect of the wind on a boat's sails is very considerable,

---

* Fincham.

in comparison to its stability, as they can be more easily taken in, the centre of effort must be so situated, that the boat may have a strong tendency to fly up in the wind, and so diminish its effect on the sails. It is, however, of little importance, that the form of the boat should be such as would ensure their being ardent, since the quality of being ardent may be so easily procured by varying the position of the stowage.

The proportions given in the following tables, for the sizes of the sails in relation to the masts, yards, &c., are all taken as they were actually found in boats that were considered as properly rigged, and with well-proportioned sails; but the proportions in general given are for *sprit-sails*, for the fore leech 12 inches less than the depth from the sheave at the mast-head to the gunwale, with one or two gore cloths; or for the foot to have a proper spread for the sheet and head, to be for the fore, .88 and for the main .8 of the foot, with each cloth gored from 12 to 14 inches. The head of the mizzen has seldom more than a gore of 11 inches to each cloth, and the depth of the fore leech from the sheave, so as just to clear the gunwale. To *lug-sails*, the head spreads the yard to about 4 inches of the cleats, and has about a 6-inch gore to each cloth; the fore leech has two or three gored cloths, and is generally two-thirds the length of the after leech; the foot is gored to have a small sweep. The hoist of most sails for the main and fore are, at the mast, 12 inches less than the depth from the sheave to the gunwale. Jibs have in general the leech 12 inches less than the depth from the sheave to the gunwale, and the foot to spread the distance from the sheave in the bowsprit or stem, to the mast.

DIVISION FIFTH.

VOCABULARY OF TERMS USED.

VOCABULARY OF TERMS USED.

ABUT.—When two timbers or planks are united end-ways, they are said to *butt* or *abut* against each other.

ADZE.—A cutting tool of the axe kind, for dubbing flat and circular work, much used by shipwrights.

AFTER-HOODS.—The after plank of all in any strake, outside or inside.

AFTER-BODY.—That portion of the ship's body abaft dead-flat.

AIR-PORTS.—Circular apertures cut in the side of a vessel to admit light and air to the berth-deck, state-rooms, etc. Closed by the old-fashioned air-port plunger, or fitted to close with a light of glass, set in a composition-frame and turning on a hinge, secured when closed by a heavy thumb-screw.

AMIDSHIPS.—Signifies the middle of the ship, as it regards both the length and the breadth.

ANCHOR-HOOPS.—Strong iron hoops binding the stock to the end of the shank and over the nuts of the anchor.

ANGLE-IRON.—A pair of plates, or bars, at right angles to one another, but manufactured solid in one piece. These two bars form a letter **L**, and are really a couple of small plates at right angles to one another.

AN-END.—The position of any mast, etc., when erected perpendicularly on the deck. The topmasts are *an-end* when hoisted up to their stations. This is also a common phrase made use of among ship-carpenters for expressing the forcing of anything in the direction of its length, as to force one plank in working a strake to meet the butt of the one last worked.

ANVIL.—The massive block of iron on which shipsmiths hammer forge-work.

APOISE.—Said of a vessel properly trimmed.

APRON.—A timber conforming to the shape of the stem, and fixed in the concave part of it, extending from the head to some distance below the scarph joining the upper and lower stem-pieces.

ARM-CHEST.—A portable locker on the upper deck or tops, for holding arms, and affording a ready supply of cutlasses, pistols, etc.

ASH.—This timber is used for making ladders for hatchways, gratings for hatches, mess-chests, swinging-tables for the crew, oars, etc.

AUGER.—An instrument for boring holes for bolts, treenails, and other purposes.

BACK-BOARD.—A board across the stern-sheets of boats to support the backs of passengers, and also to form the box in which the coxswain sits.

BACKING.—The timber behind the armour-plates of a ship.

BALLAST-PORTS.—Square holes cut in the sides of merchantmen for taking in ballast.

Barge.—A boat of a long, slight and spacious construction, generally carvel-built, double-banked, for the use of admirals and captains of vessels-of-war.

Ballast.—Heavy substances placed in a vessel's hold to regulate her trim, and to bring the centre of gravity of the system to its proper place.

Barque.—A ship having three masts, square-rigged on the fore and main masts.

Batten.—Hatch-battens are strips of oak, half-inch by three inches, used for securing the tarpaulins over the hatchways in a heavy storm, to prevent the sea from getting between decks. Mould loft-battens are of yellow and white pine of different sizes, square and flat, used in laying down the lines of a vessel on the mould-loft floor.

Bearding.—The diminishing of the edge or surface of a piece of timber, etc., from a given line, as on the stem, deadwood, etc.

Bevel.—An instrument composed of a stock and movable tongue, used by shipwrights in getting out frame-timber, plank, etc., to the proper angle.

Bevelling-Boards.—Pieces of white pine-boards on which the bevellings of the frame-timbers are described.

Beams.—The largest pieces of timber in the deck-frame extending across the vessel resting on the clamps, for the purpose of holding and securing the sides of the vessel in proper shape.

Bed of the Bowsprit.—A bearing formed out of the head of the stem and apron, to support the bowsprit; it is lined with lead to prevent the water from getting below on account of any shrinkage or shakes in the timber.

Bends.—The main wales are frequently called by seamen the bends of the ship.

Bevelling.—The angles formed between one surface and another, as between the sides of the timber and the outer surface, on the side and end, etc. When it is without a square or an obtuse angle, it is called a standing bevelling; when within, or an acute angle, an under bevelling.

Bed-Bolt.—A horizontal bolt passing through both brackets of a gun-carriage near their centres, and on which the forward end of the stool-bed rests.

Bee-Blocks.—Pieces of oak bolted to the outer end of the bowsprit at the sides, to reeve the fore-topmast stays through, commonly called bees.

Bill-Boards.—Projections of oak plank secured to the bow of the ship abaft the cat-heads for the bill of the anchor to rest on.

Bitts.—Large pieces of timber, oak or locust, placed vertically projecting above the deck, to which the vessel rides at anchor, also smaller ones for leading and belaying ropes to, such as topsail-sheets, &c.

Bilge.—The flat part of a ship's body on each side of the keel at the floors, or that part which is in contact with the supporting surface when the ship is aground.

Bilgeways.—A series of logs placed on either side of the vessel placed on the launching ways to form the cradle upon, for supporting the body as it descends the inclined plane in launching.

BINDING STRAKES,—Thick planks on the decks, running just outside the line of hatches, jogged down over the beams and ledges.

BITT-PINS.—Similar to belaying pins but larger. Used to prevent the cable from slipping over the heads of the bitts in veering rapidly.

BIBBS.—Pieces of timber bolted to the hounds of the mast to support the trestle-trees.

BINNACLE.—A case to contain the compass, light, &c., by which the ship is steered.

BOLTS.—Pieces of round iron, copper, or *mixed metal*, used in uniting into one mass the different parts of the structure. The longest bolts are generally those driven through the deadwood forward and aft, and those used in securing the cutwater to the stem.

EYE-BOLTS.—Are bolts that have an eye formed upon one end, to project out for hooking tackles, &c.

RING-BOLTS.—Have a ring welded into the eye, they are used for deck stoppers, anchor lashings, &c. When intended for lashings they are triangular in form, that the lashing may lie easy.

FIXED-BOLTS.—Are the ring and eye-bolts that are fixed for different purposes, as the eye-bolts for the standing parts of sheets and tacks, &c.

DRIFT-BOLTS.—Are bolts used for driving or starting out other bolts in repairing vessels.

BODY-POST.—The main stern-post in a screw steamer is often called a body post.

BOOBY HATCH.—A small companion, readily removed; it is in use for merchantmen's half-decks, and lifts off in one piece.

BOOM-IRONS.—Are metal rings fitted on the yard-arms, through which the studding-sail booms traverse; there is one on each top-sail yard-arm, but on the lower yards a second, which opens to allow the boom to be triced up.

BOAT-CHOCKS.—Clamps of wood upon which a boat rests when stowed upon a vessel's deck.

BOATS.—Small open vessels impelled by oars or sails.

BOARD.—Distinguished from plank by being less than 1¼ inches in thickness.

WRAIN-BOLTS.—They are used in planking a vessel, being secured to the frame with two screws bolts, and have a cylindrical piece of wood, called a wrain-stave, placed through the ring for the purpose of setting to (called bringing to), by means of wedges, the different planks to the frame of the ship, &c.

BOOM-KIN.—A boom made of iron or wood projecting from the bow of the ship, for hauling down the fore-tack; also from either quarter, for securing the standing part and leading block for the main-brace.

BOOMS.—The *main boom* is for extending the fore-and-aft main sail; the *spanker boom* for the spanker; the jib boom for the jib and the *flying jib boom* for the flying jib. The *studding-sail booms* are for the fore and main lower, top and top-gallant studding-sails and swinging booms for bearing out the lower studding-sails.

Bows.—The curved part of the ship forward.

FULL OR BLUFF Bow, in proportion as the horizontal tangent to the curve of the bow approaches a perpendicular to the longitudinal axis, the bow is said to be full or very full.

LEAN OR SHARP Bow.—In proportion as the horizontal tangent to the curve of the bow approaches a fore-and-aft line, or forms more acute angles with the longitudinal axis, the bow is said to be sharp, or very sharp, or lean.

FLAREING Bow.—The bow flares more or less as it falls out or increases in breadth in the upper part, and it rakes in degrees, as it is without a perpendicular vertically to the longitudinal axis; when it is perpendicular the bow or stem is said to be upright.

BODY-PLAN.—One of the plans used in delineating the lines of a ship, showing the sections made by a series of vertical planes perpendicular to the length of the ship.

BOWSPRIT.—The use of the bowsprit is to secure the foremast and extend the head sails.

BOWSPRIT CHOCK.—A piece placed between the knight-heads, fitting close upon the upper part of the bowsprit.

BOXING.—The boxing is any projecting wood, forming a rabbet, as the boxing of the knight-heads, center counter timber, etc.

BOLSTERS.—Pieces of wood placed on the lower trestle-trees to keep the rigging from chafing.

BOBSTAY PLATES.—Plates let in on either side of the stem and extending up on the side of the cutwater having an eye worked in them to secure the bobstays.

BREECHING-BOLTS.—Bolts placed on either side of the gun-ports, to which the gun-breechings are secured.

BREAST-BEAMS.—Those beams at the fore-part of the quarter-deck, and the after-part of the forecastle, in vessels which have a poop and top-gallant forecastle.

BRIDLE-PORT.—A square port in the bows of a ship for taking in mooring-bridles. They are also used to fire a gun as near a line ahead as possible.

BROAD AXE.—A light, broad-bladed axe used by shipwrights and sparmakers.

BRACKETS.—Pieces resembling knees, with their outer parts formed generally with an inflective curve; they are either for support or ornament.

HAIR BRACKETS.—A piece, which is a continuation of the upper bracket, and terminates with a scroll at the back of the billet-head.

BREADTH, EXTREME.—It is the breadth at the greatest transverse-section to outside of wale-strakes; whereas moulded breadth is only to the outside of the frame-timbers.

BREAK.—When the quarter-deck or forecastle has a rise to give height between the decks, the part where the rise terminates towards the waist is called the break of the quarter-deck or forecastle.

BREECH.—Where the outside of two arms of any two pieces formed of knee timber meet.

BRIG.—A two-masted, square-rigged vessel.

BRIGANTINE.—The same as a brig, but without a square main-sail.

BRIG (Hermaphrodite).—A vessel with two masts, square-rigged on the fore mast only.

BREAST-HOOKS.—Large pieces of compass timber or knees fitted in the bows of ships against the apron and stemson, and the arms running back across the timbers of the bow. Those in the line of the decks are called *deck hooks*.

BRACES.—Composition castings secured to the stern-post, used in connection with the pintles to hang the rudder.

BULKHEADS.—Partitions that separate one part of the ship from the other.

BUTT.—The root or largest end of any timber or plank; the joint where two planks meet endwise.

BUTTOCKS.—The after-part of the ship on each side below the knuckle.

BUTTOCK-LINES.—Represented on the sheer-draught as curve lines, cutting the ship into vertical longitudinal sections, parallel to the centre line.

BUCKLERS.—Lids or shutters used for closing the hawse-holes, holes in the port-shutters and side-pipes.

BUSH.—Metal in the sheaves of blocks which have iron pins.

BUTT-END.—The end of a plank in a ship's side. The root or largest end.

CAISSON.—A boat-gate, having generally both ends similar in form to the bows of a vessel, used to close the entrance to a dock or basin.

CAMBERING.—An arching upwards, contrary to sheer or hanging.

CANT.—A term used by shipwrights, signifying the inclination that anything has from a square.

CANT-TIMBERS.—Timbers at the forward and after ends of a vessel, whose planes are not at right angles to the centre line of the vessel.

CAP BLOCKS.—The upper piece of each pile of building-blocks on which the keel is laid.

CAPS.—Pieces fixed upon the heads of the lower and top masts and bowsprit for the top masts, topgallant masts, and jib-boom to pass through.

CAPSTAN.—A machine used for weighing anchor, etc.

CARLING.—Pieces of the deck-frame running fore-and-aft between the beams.

CARVEL-BUILT.—A method of building boats in which the planks are put on edge to edge, and the seams caulked as the planking of ships.

CATHEAD.—A timber projecting from the bow of the ship used for hoisting the anchor after the capstan has brought it clear of the water.

CAULKING.—The operation of forcing oakum or cotton into the seams, butts, and rents by means of mallets and irons.

CABOOSE.—The cook-room or kitchen of merchantmen on deck.

CAP-SHORE.—A supporting spar between the cap and the trestle-trees.

CAULKING-IRONS.—The peculiar chisels used for the purpose of caulking; they are the caulking-iron, the making-iron, the reeming-iron, and the rasing-iron.

Caulking-Mallet.—The wooden instrument with which the caulking-irons are driven.

Cavil.—A large cleat for belaying the fore and main tacks, sheets, and braces to.

Centre of Displacement.—The centre of gravity of the immersed body of the vessel, and also the centre of the vertical force that the water exerts to support the vessel.

Centre of Effort of Sails.—That point in the plane of the sails at which the whole force of the wind is supposed to be exerted.

Centre of Gravity.—The point about which, if suspended, all the parts would be in equilibrium.

Ceiling.—Strakes of plank worked between the clamps and water-ways on berth-decks, and between the thick strakes and clamps, and thick strakes and bilge strakes in the hold.

Centre of Cavity, of Displacement, of Immersion, and of Buoyancy, are synonymous terms in naval architecture for the mean centre of that part of a vessel which is immersed in water.

Chined.—Timber or plank slightly hollowed out.

Channel-Bolts.—The bolts driven through the channels edgewise, and through the frame and planking to secure them to the ship's side.

Chains.—Iron links which secure to the side the dead-eyes connected with the channels.

Chain-Bolts.—The bolt which passes through the toe-links, and secures the chains to the side.

Chain-Plates.—Iron plates to which the dead-eyes are secured; they are often substituted for chains, being considered preferable.

Channels.—Flat ledges of white oak plank projecting outboard from the ship's side, for spreading the lower shrouds and giving additional support to the masts.

Cheek-Blocks.—Blocks placed upon the side of bitts for fair leaders.

Cheek-Knees.—Knees worked above and below the hawse pipes in the angle of the bow and cutwater, the brackets being a continuation of them to the billet or figurehead.

Chine.—That part of the waterway which is left above the deck, and hollowed out or bevelled off to the spirketting.

Chinse.—A slight mode of caulking any seams or butts.

Clapms.—The strakes of plank on which the deck beams rest.

Cleats.—Pieces of wood having projecting arms, used for belaying ropes to.

Clinch or Clench.—To spread the point, or rivet it upon a ring or plate; to prevent the bolt from drawing out, same as riveting.

Clincher Built, or Clinker Built.—A term applied to boats built with the lower edge of one strake overlapping the upper edge of the one next below. It is opposed to the term *carvel built.*

Coaking.—The placing of pieces of hard wood, either circular or square, in the edges or surfaces of any pieces that are to be united together, to prevent their working or sliding over each other.

COAMINGS.—The pieces that lie fore-and-aft in the framing of the hatchways and scuttles. The pieces that lie athwart ship, to form the ends, are called head-ledges.

COMPANION.—A wooden hood or covering placed over a ladderway to a cabin, etc.

COMPRESSOR.—An iron (bent) lever, having one end secured to the beam nearest to the chain pipe by a bolt, round which it is made to turn; its use is to prevent the cable from running out too fast when letting the anchor go. A tackle is secured to the end of it, the standing part being brought to the beam.

COPING.—To turn the ends of iron knees to form a hook in the beams, etc.

CORVETTE.—A flush-decked vessel, ship-rigged, or a ship with one entire battery, without a quarter-deck and forecastle, except that it commonly has a top-gallant forecastle for the shelter of the crew.

COUNTER.—In round-sterned ships that portion of the stern from the water-line to the knuckle of the stern.

COUNTER TIMBERS.—Timbers worked on each side of the stern-post in all round and elliptical sterned ships to form the rake and contour of the stern.

COLD-CHISEL.—A stout chisel, made of steel, used for cutting iron.

COMPASS-SAW.—A narrow saw, inserted in a hole bored by a centre-bit, it follows out required curves.

CRANK.—A vessel by her construction or her stowage, inclined to lean over a great deal, or from insufficient ballast or cargo incapable of carrying sail, without danger of overturning. The opposite term is *stiff*, or the quality of standing up well under her canvas.

CRAB.—A small capstan fixed in a frame, and made portable that it may be used for different purposes; likewise a wooden spindle, with its lower end working in a socket, having two holes at right angles to each other at the upper end, passing through the spindle to receive the bars; it has great power on account of the length of the bars and smallness of the spindle.

CRADLE.—The frame-work which supports the vessel during the operation of launching.

CRANKS.—Iron rods bent at each end, and placed between the beams of a ship for stowing capstan bars, etc.

CROSS-SPALLS.—Pieces of plank that keep the frame to the proper breadth until the beams are in.

CUPPY.—A defect sometimes found in timber, where a portion of the heart has separated from the outside; probably caused by lightning or severe frosts.

CUP.—A socket let into the deck, in which the heel of the capstan spindle rests.

CUTWATER.—The head of a vessel, or that part forward of the stem.

CUTTING DOWN OR THROATING LINE.—A curve bounding the inside of the timbers of the ship at the centre line.

DAGGER.—A term given to all timbers lying diagonally, as dagger-knees.

DEAD-EYES.—Pieces of lignumvitæ, of an oblate form, for receiving the lanyards for setting up the shrouds; those attached to the ship are shackled to the chain plates.

Dagger-Knees.—A name given to any hanging knee that has its body inclined forward or aft.

Davits.—Pieces of wood or iron projecting from the sides or stern of the ship, for the purpose of raising or lowering the boats. The *fish davits* are used for fishing the anchor, they are sometimes made of heavy iron, shaped like a boat davit, and secured in a socket near the bill-boards, or when a wooden boom is used, goose-necked to the foremast.

Dead-flat.—A term used to denote the greatest transversed section of the ship. and always distinguished by the symbol ⊗.

Deadwood.—A body of timber built up on top of the keel forward and aft, for the purpose of getting solid wood to land the heels of the cant frames against.

Decks.—The several platforms in ships, distinguished by different names according to their situations and purposes.

Deck Planks.—The flooring or covering of the beams.

Deck Transom—A timber extending across the ship at the after extremity of the deck, on which the ends of the deck plank rests.

Depth of Hold.—One of the principal dimensions of a ship; it is the depth in midships, from the upper side of the upper deck beams, in flush-decked vessels, and from the upper side of the lower deck beams in all others, to the throats of the floor timbers.

Displacement.—The volume of water displaced by the immersed body of the ship, and which is always equal to the weight of the whole body.

Diagonal Lines.—Lines used principally to fair the bodies, shown as straight lines in the *body-plan* where they are made to indicate the position of the heads and heels of the timbers of the frame.

Dowel.—To fasten two boards or pieces together by pins inserted in their edges. This is similar to coaking but used in a diminutive sense.

Doubling.—The covering of a ship's bottom or side, without taking off the old plank, a method sometimes resorted to in the merchant service when the plank get thin or worn down.

Dog.—A tool (iron) used by shipwrights; it is made of round iron having both ends sharpened and one turned over making a right angle. In planking the decks or outside it is first driven a short distance into the beams or frame timbers and wedges introduced between that and the strake's edge to force the plank up to the one last worked.

Dove-Tailing.—Joining two pieces together with a mortise and tenon resembling in the shape of them a dove's tail.

Dove-Tail Plates.—Metal plates resembling dove-tails in form, let into the heel of the stern-post and the keel, to bind them together.

Drag.—A term used to denote an excess of draft of water aft.

Dry Rot.—A disease destructive of timber, occasioned by a fungus, the *Merulius lachrymans*, which softens wood and finally destroys it; it resembles a dry pithy cottony substance, whence the name dry-rot, though when in a perfect state, its sinuses contains drops of clear water, which has given rise to its specific Latin name. Free ventilation and cleanliness appear to be the best preservatives against this costly evil.

DRAUGHT.—A design given on paper for the several parts of a ship.

DRAUGHT OF WATER.—The line at which the surface of the water cuts the body, when the hull is entirely clear it is called the light-water-line; and the draught of water to this line the light draught of water; and when fully loaded, the line at the surface of the water is called the load-water-line; and the draught of water, the load draught of water. The depth that the vessel swims is shown by marks placed on the stem and stern-posts, the lower part of the mark shows the feet and the upper part six inches.

DRUMHEAD.—The upper part of the capstan, in which the bars are inserted.

DRUXEY.—A decay in timber which has a dark appearance with white spongy veins.

DUMB PINTLE.—When the pintle is short and works in a socket-brace.

DUMB BATTENS.—Battens of oak nailed across the cable tier to keep the cables up and allow the air to circulate under them; gratings are used in sail-rooms for this purpose.

DUBB, TO.—To smooth and cut off with an adze the superfluous wood.

ENTRANCE.—The forward part of a vessel below the water-line.

EVEN-KEEL.—When the vessel has the same draught of water forward and aft, she is said to be on an even-keel.

FALLING HOME OR TUMBLING HOME.—A term applied to the upper part of the topside of a ship, when it falls very much within a vertical line from the main breadth.

FALSE KEEL.—A thin keel, coppered in lengths of from 12 to 16 feet, and put on below the main keel after it has been coppered, fastened with composition spikes or short copper bolts, that it may be torn off without injury to the main keel, should the vessel touch the ground.

FASHION PIECES.—Timbers that give the form or fashion of the after extremity, below the wing transom, when they terminate at the tuck in square-sterned ships.

FAY.—To fit with a close joint.

FELLOES.—The arch pieces which form the rim of the steering wheel.

FID.—A bar of wood or iron used to support the top-masts and top-gallant masts when they are on end.

FID-HOLE.—Mortises in the heels of top-masts and topgallant-masts.

FIFE RAIL.—Rails placed around the mast in which the pins are placed to belay the running rigging to.

FIGURE OR BILLET.—The principal ornament of carved work at the head of the ship.

FILLINGS.—Pieces placed in the openings between the frames wherever solidity is required.

FILLING TRANSOMS.—Transoms placed between the wing and deck transom, or between two deck transoms.

FILLET.—A small square moulding, which accompanies or crowns a larger.

Fire-Ship.—A ship having combustible materials on board, that they may be readily set on fire, to produce a conflagration in an enemy's fleet, &c.

Fore-Jack Bolts.—Bolts used to confine the fore-mast lower corners of the fore-course in a fixed position.

Foretop, Trestle, and Cross-Trees.—Foretop, a platform surrounding the foremast-head: it is composed of the trestle-trees, which are strong bars of oak timber fixed horizontally on the opposite sides of the foremast; and the cross-trees, which are of oak, and supported by the cheeks and trestle-trees.

Fit-Rod.—A small iron rod with a hook at the end, which is put into the holes made in a vessel's side, etc., to ascertain the lengths of the bolts required to be driven in.

Fishes.—Pieces used in made masts; also cheek pieces, carried to sea on board vessels to secure a crippled mast or yard.

Fixed Blocks.—Sheet chocks, or any other chock placed in the side of a vessel to lead a rope through.

Flaring.—Falling out from the main breadth; the reverse of tumbling home.

Flight.—A sudden rise; as the height at which the cheeks and brackets curve above the sheer before the stem is called the flight of the cheeks.

Floor.—All that part of a ship, on either side of the keel, which approaches nearer to a horizontal than a perpendicular direction, and that would be in contact with the supporting surface if inclined.

Floor Timbers.—Timbers of the frame which lay directly across the keel; in a white-oak frame there are generally two to each frame, having a long and a short-arm on alternate sides; in a live-oak frame there is a single-floor timber extending an equal distance on either side of the centre-line, the first futtocks abutting over the keel on the opposite side.

Floor-Heads.—The outer ends of the floor-timbers.

Floor-Ribband.—The ribband next below the floor-heads.

Flush.—Fair, or any parts being on the same surface.

Fore-and-Aft.—In the direction of the ship's length, ranging from end to end.

Fore-Foot.—The forward end of the keel.

Forelock.—A thin circular or straight wedge of iron, made to pass through a mortise at the point of a bolt, to prevent its being drawn when a direct strain is brought upon it.

Fore-Body.—That portion of the vessel forward of dead-flat.

Fore-Peak.—The contracted part of a vessel's hold close to the bow; close forward under the lower deck.

Fore-Sheet Traveller.—An iron ring which travels along on the fore-sheet horse of a fore-and-aft rigged vessel.

Futtock-Plates.—Iron plates to which the dead-eyes of the top-mast rigging and futtock-shrouds are connected, crossing the sides of the top-rim.

Futtocks.—Timbers of the frame between the floors and top-timbers.

GANG-BOARDS.—The boards on either side at the entrance from the accommodation-ladder to the deck.

GARBOARD STRAKES.—The first two or three strakes on either side of the keel, through which they fasten edgewise.

GAMMONING.—A strap of iron placed around the bowsprit, just outside of the knight-heads, and secured through the cutwater, to enable it to support the stays of the fore-mast.

GOOSE-NECK.—An iron bolt, made with a strap and hinge, used on the spanker, lower and fish booms. The bolt is made with a shoulder, to rest on a brace and forelock underneath.

GRATINGS.—Lattice-work made of ash, to cover the hatchways, &c.

GRIPE.—A piece bolted to the foreside of the stem, to complete it below the cutwater.

GRAVING.—The paying over of tar, &c., on a vessel's bottom while in dock.

GUNWALE.—The same as main rail.

HALF-BREADTH PLAN.—That on which is shown the form of the vessel by horizontal and diagonal longitudinal sections.

HAMMOCK-STANCHIONS.—Iron stanchions fixed on the main-rail or plank-sheer, having a forked end to which the hammock rails are secured.

HANCE.—The sudden breaking-in from one form to another as when a piece is eight square on one part, and the other part cylindrical; the part between the termination of these different forms is called the hance, or the parts of any timber where it becomes suddenly narrower or smaller.

HANGING.—The same as sheer, or a bending down.

HANGING-KNEES.—Knees placed vertically under the deck-beams.

HARPINS.—A continuation of the ribbands at the fore and after extremities of the ship, fixed to keep the cant-frames, etc., in position, until the outside planking is worked.

HAWSE-HOLES.—The holes at the fore part of the ship through which the cables pass.

HAWSE-PIPES.—Iron pipes fitted in the hawse-holes to take the chafe of the cables, a lead lining being placed under the iron pipes.

HAWSE-PLUGS.—Plugs made to stop up the hawse-pipes when the cables are unbent, and prevent the passage of the sea through them.

HAWSE-PIECES.—Pieces in the frame to the number of from three to six next aft of the knight-heads, through which the hawse-holes are cut.

HACK-SAW.—Used for cutting-off bolts by shipwrights.

HANGING-STAGE.—Any stage hung over the sides of a vessel for caulking, painting, or temporary repairs.

HATCH-RINGS.—Rings to lift or replace hatches by.

HEAD-BOARDS.—Boards placed at the forward and after ends of the hammock-nettings.

HEAD-TIMBERS.—Small timbers used in building up the head, situated on each side to receive the planking of the head.

HEEL.—The lower end of any timber. To incline.

Helm.—The rudder, tiller and wheel, taken as a whole.

Hollows and Rounds.—Plane-tools used for making mouldings.

Horse.—The iron rod placed between the fife-rail stanchions on which the leading blocks are rove or secured. Also in fore-and-aft rigged vessels, it is a stout bar of iron, with a large ring or thimble on it, which spans the vessel from side to side just before the foremast, for the fore-staysail sheet; and when required one is also used for the fore and main-boom sheets to haul down to and traverse on.

Hounds.—Those projections at the mast-heads serving as supports for the trestletrees of large, and rigging of smaller, vessels to rest upon. With lower masts they are termed cheeks.

Hogging.—The arching up of the body, occasioned frequently by the unequal distribution of the weights. Most ships hog in launching, caused by the after part of the vessel not being properly water-borne till she is clear of the ways.

Hood.—The foremost and aftermost plank in each strake.

Hooding Ends.—The ends of the hoods where they abut in the rabbet of the stem and stern-post.

Horsing-Irons.—A caulking-iron, with a long handle attached, which is struck with a beetle by a caulker in hardening up the oakum in the seams and butts, called *horsing-up.*

Horse Shoes.—Straps of composition in the form of a horse shoe, used for securing the stem to the keel, placed on opposite sides, let in flush and bolted through; rings are now generally used instead.

Hounding.—The length of the mast from the heel to the lower part of the head.

Hutch-Hooks.—Small pieces of oak used for the temporary fastening of any work, generally placed over the heads of shores in building or in docking a vessel, secured to the vessel with ribband-screws.

Hull.—The body of a ship.

In-and-Out.—The bolts that are driven through the ship's side are said to be in-and-out bolts.

Inner Post.—Worked on the inside of the main post running down to the throat of the stern-post knee.

Joint of Frame.—The line at which the two inner surfaces of the frame-timber meet.

Iron-Sick.—The condition of vessels when the iron-work becomes loose in the timbers from corrosion by gallic acid.

Keel.—The first timber laid upon the blocks, it is one of the principals in the fabric, and forms a basis for raising the superstructure.

Keelson.—A timber in the interior of the ship, placed immediately over the keel, lying upon the upper part of the floors (*Main Keelson.*)

Key Model.—In shipbuilding, a model formed by pieces of board laid on each other horizontally, and held in place by wooden keys and screws.

KEVEL.—Large wooden cleats to belay ropes and hawsers to, commonly called *Cavils.*

KNIGHT-HEADS.—Timbers worked on each side of the stem and apron.

KNUCKLE OF THE STERN.—The sudden angle made by the counter-timbers and after cants.

LACING-PIECE.—The piece running across the top of the head from the backing-piece to the front-piece.

LANDING STRAKE.—The upper strake but one in a boat.

LAUNCH.—The slip upon which the ship is built, with the cradle and all connected with launching.

LAYING DOWN.—The delineation of the different parts of a ship to their full size upon the mould-loft floor.

LAUNCHING RIBBAND.—An oak plank bolted to the outside of the launching ways, to guide the cradle in its descent in launching.

LAP SIDED.—A term expressive of the condition of a vessel when it will not float or sit upright in the water.

LATERAL RESISTANCE.—The resistance of the water against the side of a vessel in a direction perpendicular to her length.

LEE BOARDS.—Similar to centre-boards, affixed to the sides of flat bottomed vessels, such as Dutch schuyts, &c.; these on being let down, when the vessel is close-hauled, decrease her drifting to leeward.

LEDGES.—The pieces of the deck frame lying between the beams jogged into the carlines and knees.

LIMBER HOLES.—Holes cut out of the fillings and through bulkheads for a water passage.

LIPS OF A SCARPH.—The thin parts or laps of the scarph.

LIFE BUOY.—An apparatus fitted to the sterns of war vessels, formed of two copper oblong tanks fitted in a frame of wood, fitted with a port-fire and lock, and so arranged as to be readily detached should a man fall overboard. It is held in an upright position by means of an anchor attached to the staff of the buoy.

LIGHTER.—A large open flat bottom sloop-rigged vessel.

LOCKERS.—Compartments built in the cabin, ward-room, etc., for various purpose.

LUFF OF THE BOW.—The roundest part of the bow.

MANGER BOARD.—A piece of oak plank fitted over the deck and running from side to side a short distance abaft the hawse pipes.

MANGER.—The space forward of the manger board.

MARGIN.—A line in ships having a square stern, at a parallel distance down from the upper edge of the wing transom forming the lower part of a surface for seating the tuck rail; it terminates at the ends of the exterior planking, or what is called the tuck.

MAST-COAT.—A canvas covering fitted over the upper ends of the mast wedges and nailed to the mast and mast combing to prevent any leakage around the mast.

MAIN WALES.—An assemblage of planks placed upon the widest part of the body.

MAULS.—Large single-faced hammers used by shipwrights for driving spikes, bolts, and treenails. Heavy hammers having two faces are called double-headers.

META CENTRE.—The meta centre of a floating body is the point where the vertical passing through the centre of buoyancy, in the position of equilibrium, meets the vertical drawn through the new centre of buoyancy, when the body has been slightly displaced from this position. It is a point in a ship above which the centre of gravity of weight must never be placed, because if it were the vessel would at once roll bottom up.

MITRE.—The joining of two pieces together, that when connected, the joint shall make an angle with the side of each piece that shall be common to both.

MORTISE.—A hole cut in any piece to receive the end or tenon cut in another piece.

MOULD.—A piece of pine board used by shipwrights as a pattern to mould the timbers of the frame, etc., by.

MOULDED.—The way in which it is formed by the mould as the in-and-out dimensions of the frame. The breadth is called the *siding*.

MOULDED BREADTH.—The greatest breadth of a ship to the outside of the frame timbers.

MUNIONS.—Pieces placed up-and-down to divide the panels in framed bulkheads.

NAVAL HOODS.—Filling pieces placed between the cheek knees extending to the rabbet of the stem, on which the outer flanges of the hawse pipes rest.

NOG.—A short treenail that projects to keep a piece of timber in place.

OARS.—Instruments made of ash for propelling a boat.

OAKUM.—Old rope picked apart and loosened like hemp, to be used in caulking the seams and butts of a vessel.

OGEE.—A moulding with a concave and a convex outline, like to an S.

OUTBOARD.—On the outside of a vessel.

PROOF-TIMBER.—An imaginary timber used to prove the fairness of the body at the ends of the vessel.

PORT SILLS.—Pieces of oak dove-tailed into the frame timbers to form the upper and lower part of the ports.

PORT-STOPS.—The rabbet cut on the outside of the ports to receive the port shutters.

PORT-STOPPER.—Heavy iron bars made to swing round and close the ports in a turreted vessel.

PREVENTER-BOLTS.—Bolts passing through the lower end of the preventer plate.

PREVENTER-PLATES.—Short plates of iron bolted to the lower part of the chain plates, to help take the strain.

PROFILE PLAN.—A vertical longitudinal view of the vessel, showing the inboard works; it has upon it the height and sheer of decks and ports.

PUMP-CISTERNS.—A cistern fixed over the pump heads, lined with lead to receive the water until it is discharged through the scuppers.

PARTNERS OF THE MAST.—Pieces placed in the deck-frame to form the mast-hole and give the necessary strength to the deck-frame at those points.

PINTLES AND BRACES OF THE RUDDER.—A composition bolt having straps attached to secure it to the back of the rudder, with the bolt resting and entered into the braces fixed upon the stern-post.

PADDLE-WHEEL.—Wheels used in steam vessels propelled by side-wheels. On many of the western rivers a single paddle-wheel is used at the stern of the boat.

PADDLE-BEAMS.—Two large beams, extending out sufficiently from the sides of paddle-wheel steamers, to receive the spring-beam; a frame is thus formed on which to erect the paddle-box.

PADDLE-BOX.—The covering of the paddle wheels.

PAUL.—Short arms of iron placed on a capstan or windlass to hold it from recoiling.

PANEL.—A square or oval framed in a bulkhead or door.

PAY.—To pay a seam is to pour hot pitch and tar into it after caulking, to prevent the oakum from getting wet.

PADDLE-BOX BOATS.—Boats made to fit the paddle-boxes in paddle-wheel steamers; they are stowed bottom up. They are carried on the *Susquehanna* and *Powhatan.*

PILE.—Spars pointed at one end, and driven into soil to support a superstructure; sometimes found necessary in building a foundation to build a vessel on.

PINK STERNED.—Having a very narrow stern.

PLANK.—All timber from one-and-half to six and eight inches in thickness has this name given to it.

PLANKSHEER.—(See Main Rail.)

POPPETS.—Large logs placed on top of the bilgeways and lower piece of packing at the ends of the cradle, standing in an inclined position, the upper ends resting against the vessel.

POPPET-RIBBANDS.—Pieces of oak plank running across the poppets, fore-and-aft to which they are secured.

POPPET-LASHING.—Chain cables passed around the poppets and over the poppet-ribbands, from side to side, to support the extremities of the vessel in launching.

PORT-FLANGE.—A wooden batten coved out and fitted on the ship's side over the ports to prevent the water from running into the port.

QUARTER GALLERYS.—Projections from the quarters of a vessel, and intended as an ornament as well as for the convenience of the cabin.

RAM-LINE.—A small line used in regulating the frame, etc., of a vessel.

RAZING.—The operation of marking timber from a mould with a *razing-knife.*

RAVE-HOOK.—A hooked-iron tool used in cutting butts of planking to afford sufficient opening to caulk them.

RABBET.—A groove cut in the stern-post, keel, etc., to receive the ends or edges of plank.

RAG-BOLT.—A bolt having its surface cut so as to prevent its being easily drawn out.

RAKE.—To incline, as the inclination of the stern or stern-post, and masts from a vertical line.

REEMING.—The opening of the seams of plank for caulking by driving in irons called reeming irons.

RENDS.—Large shakes or splits in timber or plank, most common to plank.

RING-BOLTS.—Eye-bolts having a ring passed through the eye of the bolt.

ROOM AND SPACE.—The distance from the joint of one frame to that of the adjoining one.

ROWLOCKS.—Places either raised above or sunk in the gunwale of the boat to place the loom of the oar in rowing.

RUDDER.—The machine by which the ship is steered.

RUN.—The narrowing of the after-part of the ship; thus a ship is said to have a full, fine, or clean run.

RUDDER-STOCK.—The main piece of a rudder.

SAGGING.—The contrary of hogging.

SCARPHING.—The uniting of two pieces together by lapping one piece on the other, so as to make them appear as one solid, and with even surfaces.

SCARPHS.—Scarphs are called vertical when their surfaces are parallel to the sides, and flat or horizontal when their surfaces are opposite, as the scarphs of the keelson and keel. They are hook-scarphs when formed with a hook or projection, as the scarphs of the stem; and key-scarphs, when their lips are set close by wedge-like keys at the hook, as the scarphs of the beams.

SCANTLINGS.—The dimensions that are given for the different timbers.

SCUPPERS.—Holes cut through the water-ways and side, and lined with lead, to convey the water to the sea.

SEAMS.—The spaces between the planks when worked.

SEATING.—That part of the floor which rests on the keel.

SAUCERS.—Metal steps bolted to the aft-side of the rudder-post below a brace, so that the plug of the pintle will rest on it, and keep the straps of the pintles and braces from coming in contact, thereby lessening the friction to be overcome in turning the rudder. The pintles which rest on these saucers are made with longer plugs, and are called saucer-pintles.

SHEERS.—Elevated spars, connected at the upper ends, used in masting and dismasting vessels, etc.

SHORE.—An oblique brace or support, the upper end resting against the body to be supported.

SHIFT.—A term made use of to denote the disposition of the position of butts and scarphs of planks and timber, so as to gain the proper strength.

SHAKY.—A defect in plank or timber when it is full of shakes or splits.

SHEATHING.—A thin covering of planks or boards. A covering of copper or yellow metal placed on the submerged part of a vessel to prevent the worms from cutting it, and to maintain a clean smooth surface.

SHEER.—The longitudinal curve of the rails, decks, etc., of a ship.

SHEER-PLAN.—That on which all lines are projected as to height and length; it gives the vertical longitudinal form.

SHEER-STRAKES.—The first strakes worked, being the upper strake of main-wales and upper and lower strakes of channel-wales or strings.

SHOE, ANCHOR.—A flat block of hard wood, convex on the back, and scored out on the flat side to take the bill of the anchor; it is used in fishing the anchor to prevent tearing the plank on the vessel's bow, and is placed under the bill of it, and is hauled up with it.

SHELF-PIECES.—A strake worked for the deck beams to rest on where iron hanging knees are to be used.

SIRMARKS.—Stations marked upon the moulds for the frame timber, etc., indicating where the bevellings are to be applied.

SKEG.—The after-end of the keel. The composition piece supporting the heel of an equipoise rudder.

SNAPING.—Cutting the end of a stick off bevelling so as to fay upon an inclined plane.

SNY or HANG.—When the edges of the strakes of plank curve up or down, they are said to *sny* or *hang;* if down, to hang; if up, to sny.

SPINDLE.—The iron shaft upon which a capstan revolves.

SPECIFIC GRAVITY.—The relative weight of any body when compared with an equal bulk of any other body. Bodies are said to be specifically heavier than other bodies when they contain a greater weight under the same bulk; and when of less weight, they are said to be specifically lighter.

SPILES.—Wooden pins used for driving into nail-holes. Those for putting over bolt-heads and deck-spikes are cylindrical, and are called plugs.

SPIRKETTING.—The strakes of plank worked between the lower sills of ports and the waterways.

SPRUNG.—A yard or mast is said to be sprung when it is cracked or split.

SQUARE-BODY.—The square body comprises all those frames that are square to the centre line of the ship.

SQUARING OFF.—The trimming off of the projecting edges of the strakes after the vessel is planked.

STANDARDS.—Knees placed against the fore-side of the cable or riding-bitts, and projecting above the deck.

STANCHIONS.—Upright pieces of wood or iron placed under deck beams to support them in the centre.

STAPLES.—A bent fastening of metal formed as a loop, and driven in at both ends.

STEALER.—A name given to plank that fall short of the stem or stern-post, on account of the amount of sny given sometimes in planking full-bowed ships.

START-HAMMER.—A steel bolt, with a handle attached, which is held on the heads of bolts, and struck with a double-header to start them in below the surface of the wood.

STIVEING.—The elevation of a vessel's bowsprit, cathead, etc.

STRAKE.—A breadth of plank.

STEM.—The foremost boundary of the ship, being a continuation of the keel to the height of the vessel at the fore extreme of her.

STERN-POST.—The after boundary of the frame of the ship, being the after continuation of the keel to the height of the deck.

STEMSON.—A piece of live or white oak timber placed in the angle of the apron and top of deadwood or keelson.

STEPPING-LINE.—Same as bearding line.

STEPS OF THE MAST.—Steps of the mast are for stepping the heels of the masts in. At the present time, the fore and main masts, are stepped in cast iron mast steps, made to fit down over the main keelson, with a broad flange on the sister keelsons, to which they are secured. The mizzen mast steps in a piece of live oak timber scored down over the berth or orlop-deck beams to which it is secured.

STEPS OF THE SIDE.—Pieces of oak worked with mouldings, and fastened on the ship's side, at the gangway, for the convenience of ascending and descending when the accommodation ladder is unshipped.

STILES.—The up and down pieces in a section of a bulkhead or those that form the two sides of it. The rails lie across and are tenoned into the stiles; these are the upper, lower and middle rails. When the panels would be too large, or out of proportion to fill in wholly between the stiles, pieces are placed between them in the same direction, and tenoned into the rails, called munions.

STOPPER-BOLTS (*deck*).—Large ring bolts driven through the deck and beam for stoppering the cable to.

STABLE.—A body which is free to move is said to be *stable*, if, when disturbed from its balance of steadiness, it tends to *right itself* or return to that position. If, on the other hand, it tends to deviate further from that position, or upset, it is said to be *unstable.*

STABILITY.—The power of standing up against the action of any inclining force, and the power of returning to the upright or normal position when the inclining force is removed.

STRAIGHT-EDGE.—A long flat ruler used by draughtsmen.

SUPPORTERS.—Knees placed under the cat-heads.

SHOT-LOCKER.—Apartments in the hold for containing shot.

SWAGE.—A tool use by shipwrights in driving in eye-bolts, gun-starts, etc., it is made to fit the head of the bolt so that in driving or striking on the swage the bolt is forced in without bruising the head of it. It is also used by ship-smiths in making the various kind of bolts, starts, etc.

TENON.—The end of one piece diminished and cut with shoulders, to fit in a hole of another piece, called a mortise.

THOLE-PINS.—Small flat wooden pins put perpendicularly in the gunwale of a boat, and forming the fulcrum for the oar, which acts as a lever in rowing.

THWARTS.—Seats in a boat.

THROAT.—The hollow of any piece or curved part, that connects the two parts of knees or compass timber.

TILLER.—An arm of wood or iron fitted into the rudder-head to steer a ship or boat by.

TIMBER-HEADS.—Projecting timbers for belaying towing lines, etc.

TONNAGE OF CAPACITY.—The capacity which the body has for carrying cargo, estimated at 100 cubic feet to the ton.

TONNAGE OF DISPLACEMENT.—The weight of the ship in tons with all on board; found by computing number of cubic feet of the immersed body to the deep load line and dividing by 35.

TOPSIDE.—That part of the ship above the main wales.

TOP-RAIL.—An iron rail at the after part of ship's tops.

TOP-RIM.—The circular sweep or the fore-part of a vessel's top and covering in the ends of the cross-trees and trestle-trees, to prevent their chafing the topsail.

TOP AND HALF TOP-TIMBERS.—The upper timbers of the frame.

TRAIL-BOARDS.—The filling pieces, sometimes carved, placed between the brackets on the head.

TRANSOMS.—Transverse timbers in square-sterned ships, connected and placed square with the stern-posts.

TREENAILS.—Pins of oak or locust, of a cylindrical form, used as a fastening for plank below the water-line, being used in place of through-bolts. This kind of fastening is much used in building merchant vessels; but seldom in the naval service.

TUCK-RAIL.—A rail placed at the upper part of the wing transom forming an abutment and finish to the ends of the plank in square-sterned vessels.

TUCK.—That part in which the after extremities of the outside planking end, either on the wing transom or against the tuck timber.

WALES.—*Main-wales* are the strakes from the lower port-sill of the gun-deck to the bottom plank. *Channel-wales* sometimes called strings, are those strakes between the spar and main-deck ports in ships of three decks, and spar-deck ports in those of two decks. *Middle-wales*, are placed between the main and gun-deck ports in ships of three decks.

WATERWAYS.—Pieces of oak or yellow pine timber lying in the angle made by the top of the deck beams and inside of the frame timbers.

WASHBOARDS.—Thin plank placed above the gunwale of a boat forward and aft to increase the height.

WATER-LOGGED.—The condition of a leaky ship when she is so full of water as to be heavy and unmanageable.

WATER-LINES.—Sections of the vessel parallel to the plane of flotation.

WHELPS.—The projecting parts on every other square of a capstan barrel.

WINCH.—A machine similar to a windlass, but much smaller, often placed on the fore side of the lower masts of merchant vessels, just above the deck, to assist in hoisting the topsails, etc.

WINDLASS.—A machine used in small vessels for hoisting the anchor instead of a capstan.

WING-PASSAGES.—Places next the side of the ship upon the orlop, parted off in foreign ships of war, to afford facilities for the carpenter's gang to gain access to, and plug up shot-holes in time of action.

WOODLOCK.—A piece put in the throating or score of the pintle, above the load-water-line, or as near to it as possible; to prevent the rudder from unshipping, one end abuts under the lower side of the brace, and the other against the score. It is coppered before being put in, and when in place is secured by driving a copper bolt through it into the stock of the rudder.

New York, March, 1873.

JOHN WILEY & SON'S

LIST OF PUBLICATIONS,

15 ASTOR PLACE,

Under the Mercantile Library and Trade Salerooms.

AGRICULTURE.

DOWNING. **FRUITS AND FRUIT-TREES OF AMERICA;** or the Culture, Propagation, and Management in the Garden and Orchard, of Fruit-trees generally, with descriptions of all the finest varieties of Fruit, Native and Foreign, cultivated in this country. By A. J. Downing. Second revision and correction, with large additions. By Chas. Downing. 1 vol. 8vo, over 1100 pages, with several hundred outline engravings. Price, with Supplement for 1872.......................... $5 00

"As a work of reference it has no equal in this country, and deserves a place in the Library of every Pomologist in America."—*Marshall P. Wilder.*

" **ENCYCLOPEDIA OF FRUITS;** or, **Fruits and Fruit-Trees of America.** Part 1.—APPLES. With an Appendix containing many new varieties, and brought down to 1872. By Chas. Downing. With numerous outline engravings. 8vo, full cloth.. $2 50

" **ENCYCLOPEDIA OF FRUITS;** or, **Fruits and Fruit-Trees of America.** Part 2.—CHERRIES, GRAPES, PEACHES, PEARS, &c. With an Appendix containing many new varieties, and brought down to 1872. By Chas. Downing. With numerous outline engravings. 8vo, full cloth......... $2 50

" **FRUITS AND FRUIT-TREES OF AMERICA.** By A. J. Downing. First revised edition. By Chas. Downing. 12mo, cloth.. $2 00

" **SELECTED FRUITS.** From Downing's Fruits and Fruit-Trees of America. With some new varieties, including their Culture, Propagation, and Management in the Garden and Orchard, with a Guide to the selection of Fruits, with reference to the Time of Ripening. By Chas. Downing. Illustrated with upwards of four hundred outlines of Apples, Cherries, Grapes, Plums, Pears, &c. 1 vol., 12mo.... $2 50

" **LOUDON'S GARDENING FOR LADIES, AND COMPANION TO THE FLOWER-GARDEN.** Second American from third London edition. Edited by A. J. Downing. 1 vol., 12mo $2 00

DOWNING & LINDLEY. **THE THEORY OF HORTICULTURE.** By J. Lindley. With additions by A. J. Downing. 12mo, cloth....... $2 00

DOWNING. **COTTAGE RESIDENCES.** A Series of Designs for Rural Cottages and Cottage Villas, with Garden Grounds. By A. J. Downing. Containing a revised List of Trees, Shrubs, and Plants, and the most recent and best selected Fruit, with some account of the newer style of Gardens. By Henry Winthrop Sargent and Charles Downing. With many new designs in Rural Architecture. By George E Harney, Architect. 1 vol. 4to................................ $6 00

DOWNING & WIGHTWICK. **HINTS TO PERSONS ABOUT BUILDING IN THE COUNTRY.** By A. J. Downing. And **HINTS TO YOUNG ARCHITECTS,** calculated to facilitate their practical operations. By George Wightwick, Architect. Wood engravings. 8vo, cloth........................$2 00

KEMP. **LANDSCAPE GARDENING; or, How to Lay Out a Garden.** Intended as a general guide in choosing, forming, or improving an estate (from a quarter of an acre to a hundred acres in extent), with reference to both design and execution. With numerous fine wood engravings. By Edward Kemp. 1 vol. 12mo, cloth..........................$2 50

LIEBIG. **CHEMISTRY IN ITS APPLICATION TO AGRICULTURE, &c.** By Justus Von Liebig. 12mo, cloth....$1 00

" **LETTERS ON MODERN AGRICULTURE.** By Baron Von Liebig. Edited by John Blyth, M.D. With addenda by a practical Agriculturist, embracing valuable suggestions, adapted to the wants of American Farmers. 1 vol. 12mo, cloth..$1 00

" **PRINCIPLES OF AGRICULTURAL CHEMISTRY,** with special reference to the late researches made in England. By Justus Von Liebig. 1 vol. 12mo.................75 cents.

PARSONS. **HISTORY AND CULTURE OF THE ROSE.** By S. B. Parsons. 1 vol. 12mo.............................$1 25

ARCHITECTURE.

DOWNING. **COTTAGE RESIDENCES; or, a Series of Designs for Rural Cottages and Cottage Villas and their Gardens and Grounds,** adapted to North America. By A. J. Downing. Containing a revised List of Trees, Shrubs, Plants, and the most recent and best selected Fruits. With some account of the newer style of Gardens, by Henry Wentworth Sargent and Charles Downing. With many new designs in Rural Architecture by George E. Harney, Architect.........................$6 00

DOWNING & WIGHTWICK. **HINTS TO PERSONS ABOUT BUILDING IN THE COUNTRY.** By A. J. Downing. And **HINTS TO YOUNG ARCHITECTS,** calculated to facilitate their practical operations. By George Wightwick, Architect. With many wood-cuts. 8vo, cloth..................$2 00

HATFIELD. **THE AMERICAN HOUSE CARPENTER.** A Treatise upon Architecture, Cornices, and Mouldings, Framing, Doors, Windows, and Stairs; together with the most important principles of Practical Geometry. New, thoroughly revised, and improved edition, with about 150 additional pages, and numerous additional plates. By R. G. Hatfield. 1 vol. 8vo..$3 50

NOTICES OF THE WORK.

"The clearest and most thoroughly practical work on the subject."

"This work is a most excellent one, very comprehensive, and lucidly arranged."

"This work commends itself by its practical excellence."

"It is a valuable addition to the library of the architect, and almost indispensable to every scientific master-mechanic."—*R. R. Journal.*

HOLLY **CARPENTERS' AND JOINERS' HAND-BOOK,** containing a Treatise on Framing, Roofs, etc., and useful Rules and Tables. By H. W. Holly. 1 vol. 18mo, cloth........$0 75

" **THE ART OF SAW-FILING SCIENTIFICALLY TREATED AND EXPLAINED.** With Directions for putting in order all kinds of Saws. By H. W. Holly. 18mo, cloth...$0 75

RUSKIN **SEVEN LAMPS OF ARCHITECTURE.** 1 vol. 12mo, cloth, plates...$1 75

RUSKIN. **LECTURES ON ARCHITECTURE AND PAINTING.** 1 vol. 12mo, cloth, plates....$1 50

" **LECTURE BEFORE SOCIETY OF ARCHITECTS.** 0 15

WOOD. **A TREATISE ON THE RESISTANCE OF MATERIALS,** and an Appendix on the Preservation of Timber. By De Volson Wood, Prof. of Engineering, University of Michigan. 1 vol. 8vo, cloth....$2 50

This work is used as a Text-Book in Iowa University, Iowa Agricultural College, Illinois Industrial University, Sheffield Scientific School, New Haven, Cooper Institute, New York, Polytechnic College, Brooklyn, University of Michigan, and other institutions.

" **A TREATISE ON BRIDGES.** Designed as a Text-book and for Practical Use. By De Volson Wood. 1 vol. 8vo, numerous illustrations, cloth (shortly)....$3 00

ASSAYING—ASTRONOMY.

BODEMANN. **A TREATISE ON THE ASSAYING OF LEAD, SILVER, COPPER, GOLD, AND MERCURY.** By Bodemann and Kerl. Translated by W. A. Goodyear. 1 vol. 12mo, cloth....$2 50

MITCHELL. **A MANUAL OF PRACTICAL ASSAYING.** By John Mitchell. Third edition, edited by William Crookes. 1 vol. thick 8vo, cloth....$10 00

NORTON. **A TREATISE ON ASTRONOMY, SPHERICAL AND PHYSICAL,** with Astronomical Problems and Solar, Lunar, and other Astronomical Tables for the use of Colleges and Scientific Schools. By William A. Norton. Fourth edition, revised, remodelled, and enlarged. Numerous plates. 8vo, cloth....$3 50

BIBLES, &c.

BAGSTER. **THE COMMENTARY WHOLLY BIBLICAL.** Contents:—The Commentary: an Exposition of the Old and New Testaments in the very words of Scripture. 2264 pp. II. An outline of the Geography and History of the Nations mentioned in Scripture. III. Tables of Measures, Weights, and Coins. IV. An Itinerary of the Children of Israel from Egypt to the Promised Land. V. A Chronological comparative Table of the Kings and Prophets of Israel and Judah. VI. A Chart of the World's History from Adam to the Third Century, A. D. VII. A complete Series of Illustrative Maps. IX. A Chronological Arrangement of the Old and New Testaments. X. An Index to Doctrines and Subjects, with numerous Selected Passages, quoted in full. XI. An Index to the Names of Persons mentioned in Scripture. XII. An Index to the Names of Places found in Scripture. XIII. The Names, Titles, and Characters of Jesus Christ our Lord, as revealed in the Scriptures, methodically arranged.

2 volumes 4to, cloth....$19 50
2 volumes 4to, half morocco, gilt edges.... 26 00
2 volumes 4to, morocco, gilt edges.... 35 00
3 volumes 4to, cloth.... 20 00
3 volumes 4to, half morocco, gilt edges.... 33 00
3 volumes 4to, morocco, gilt edges.... 40 00

BLANK-PAGED BIBLE. **THE HOLY SCRIPTURES OF THE OLD AND NEW TESTAMENTS;** with copious references to parallel and illustrative passages, and the alternate pages ruled for MS. notes.

This edition of the Scriptures contains the Authorized Version, illustrated by the references of "Bagster's Polyglot Bible," and enriched with accurate maps, useful tables, and an Index of Subjects.

1 vol. 8vo, half morocco....$10 00
1 vol. 8vo, morocco.... 15 00

THE TREASURY BIBLE. Containing the authorized English version of the Holy Scriptures, interleaved with a Treasury of more than 500,000 Parallel Passages from Canne, Brown, Blayney, Scott, and others. With numerous illustrative notes.

1 vol., half bound....................................$7 50
1 vol., morocco.......................................10 00

COMMON PRAYER, 48mo Size.

(Done in London expressly for us.)

COMMON PRAYER.

No. 1. Gilt and red edges, imitation morocco...........$0 62½
No. 2. Gilt and red edges, rims.......................... 87½
No. 3. Gilt and red edges, best morocco and calf....... 1 25
No. 4. Gilt and red edges, best morocco and calf, rims.. 1 50

BOOK-KEEPING.

JONES. **BOOKKEEPING AND ACCOUNTANTSHIP.** Elementary and Practical. In two parts, with a Key for Teachers. By Thomas Jones, Accountant and Teacher. 1 volume 8vo, cloth..$2 50

" **BOOKKEEPING AND ACCOUNTANTSHIP.** School Edition. By Thomas Jones. 1 vol. 8vo, half roan.......$1 50

" **BOOKKEEPING AND ACCOUNTANTSHIP.** Set of Blanks. In 6 parts. By Thomas Jones..............$1 50

" **BOOKKEEPING AND ACCOUNTANTSHIP.** Double Entry; Results obtained from Single Entry; Equation of Payments, etc. By Thomas Jones. 1 vol. thin 8vo...$0 75

CHEMISTRY.

CRAFTS. **A SHORT COURSE IN QUALITATIVE ANALYSIS;** with the new notation. By Prof. J. M. Crafts. Second edition. 1 vol. 12mo, cloth..............................$1 50

JOHNSON'S FRESENIUS. **A MANUAL OF QUALITATIVE CHEMICAL ANALYSIS.** By C. R. Fresenius. Edited by S. W. Johnson, Professor in Sheffield Scientific School, Yale College. With Chemical Notation and Nomenclature, old and new. 1 vol. 8vo, cloth...$4 50

" **A SYSTEM OF INSTRUCTION IN QUANTITATIVE CHEMICAL ANALYSIS.** By C. R. Fresenius. From latest editions, edited, with additions, by Prof. S. W. Johnson. With Chemical Notation and Nomenclature, old and new...$6 00

KIRKWOOD **COLLECTION OF REPORTS (CONDENSED) AND OPINIONS OF CHEMISTS IN REGARD TO THE USE OF LEAD PIPE FOR SERVICE PIPE,** in the Distribution of Water for the Supply of Cities. By Jas. P. Kirkwood. 8vo, cloth.................................$1 50

MILLER. **ELEMENTS OF CHEMISTRY, THEORETICAL AND PRACTICAL.** By Wm. Allen Miller. 3 vols. 8vo..$18 00

" Part I.—**CHEMICAL PHYSICS.** 1 vol. 8vo.......... $4 00

" Part II.—**INORGANIC CHEMISTRY.** 1 vol. 8vo..... 6 00

" Part III.—**ORGANIC CHEMISTRY.** 1 vol. 8vo.......10 00

"Dr. Miller's Chemistry is a work of which the author has every reason to feel proud. It is now by far the largest and most accurately written Treatise on Chemistry in the English language," etc.—*Dublin Med. Journal.*

" **MAGNETISM AND ELECTRICITY.** By Wm. Allen Miller. 1 vol. 8vo..$2 50

MUSPRATT. **CHEMISTRY—THEORETICAL, PRACTICAL, AND ANALYTICAL**—as applied and relating to the Arts and Manufactures. By Dr. Sheridan Muspratt. 2 vols. 8vo, cloth, $18.00; half russia..........................$24 00

NOAD. **A MANUAL OF QUALITATIVE AND QUANTITATIVE CHEMICAL ANALYSIS.** For the use of Students. By H. M. Noad, author of "Manual of Electricity." 1 vol. 12mo. (London.) Complete..........................$6 00

" **QUANTITATIVE ANALYSIS.** 1 vol. cloth.......... 4 00

PERKINS. **AN ELEMENTARY MANUAL OF QUALITATIVE CHEMICAL ANALYSIS.** By Maurice Perkins. 12mo, cloth..$1 00

DRAWING AND PAINTING.

BOUVIER AND OTHERS. **HANDBOOK ON OIL PAINTING.** Handbook of Young Artists and Amateurs in Oil Painting; being chiefly a condensed compilation from the celebrated Manual of Bouvier, with additional matter selected from the labors of Merriwell, De Montalbert, and other distinguished Continental writers on the art. In 7 parts. Adapted for a Text-Book in Academies of both sexes, as well as for self-instruction. Appended, a new Explanatory and Critical Vocabulary. By an American Artist. 12mo, cloth....................$2 00

COE. **NEW SERIES OF DRAWING CARDS,** by Benj. H. Coe, viz.:

" **DRAWING FOR LITTLE FOLKS;** or, **First Lessons for the Nursery.** 30 cards. Neat case.................$0 30

" **FIRST STUDIES IN DRAWING.** Containing Elementary Exercises, Drawings from Objects, Animals, and Rustic Figures. Complete in *three numbers* of 18 cards each, in neat case. Each.......................................$0 30

" **COTTAGES.** An Introduction to Landscape Drawing. *Containing 72 Studies.* Complete in four numbers of 18 cards each, in neat case. Each..........................$0 30

" **EASY LESSONS IN LANDSCAPE.** Complete in four numbers of 40 Studies each. In neat 8vo case. Each, $0 30

" **HEADS, ANIMALS, AND FIGURES.** Adapted to Pencil Drawing. Complete in three numbers of 10 Studies each. In neat 8vo case. Each..........................$0 30

" **COPY BOOK, WITH INSTRUCTIONS**.............$0 37½

RUSKIN. **THE ELEMENTS OF DRAWING.** In Three Letters to Beginners. By John Ruskin. 1 vol. 12mo...........$1 00

" **THE ELEMENTS OF PERSPECTIVE.** Arranged for the use of Schools. By John Ruskin.......................$1 00

SMITH. **A MANUAL OF TOPOGRAPHICAL DRAWING.** By Prof. R. S. Smith. Second edition. 1 vol. 8vo, cloth, plates..$2 00

" **MANUAL OF LINEAR PERSPECTIVE.** Form, Shade, Shadow, and Reflection. By Prof. R. S. Smith. 1 vol. 8vo, plates, cloth......................................$2 00

WARREN. **CONSTRUCTIVE GEOMETRY AND INDUSTRIAL DRAWING.** By S. Edward Warren, Professor in the Massachusetts Institute of Technology, Boston:—

I. ELEMENTARY WORKS.

1. ELEMENTARY FREE-HAND GEOMETRICAL DRAWING. A series of progressive exercises on regular lines and forms, including systematic instruction in lettering; a training of the eye and hand for all who are learning to draw. 12mo, cloth, many cuts.................................. 75 cts.
Vols. 1 and 3, bound in 1 vol...................... .$1 75

ELEMENTARY WORKS.—Continued.

WARREN

2. PLANE PROBLEMS IN ELEMENTARY GEOMETRY. With numerous wood-cuts. 12mo, cloth..................$1 25
3. DRAFTING INSTRUMENTS AND OPERATIONS. Containing full information about all the instruments and materials used by the draftsmen, with full directions for their use. With plates and wood-cuts. One vol. 12mo, cloth, $1 25
4. ELEMENTARY PROJECTION DRAWING. Revised and enlarged edition. In five divisions. This and the last volume are favorite text-books, especially valuable to all Mechanical Artisans, and are particularly recommended for the use of all higher public and private schools. New revised and enlarged edition, with numerous wood-cuts and plates. (1872.) 12mo, cloth..$1 50
5. ELEMENTARY LINEAR PERSPECTIVE OF FORMS AND SHADOWS. Part I.—Primitive Methods, with an Introduction. Part II.—Derivative Methods, with Notes on Aerial Perspective, and many Practical Examples. Numerous wood-cuts. 1 vol. 12mo, cloth..........................$1 00

II. HIGHER WORKS.

These are designed principally for Schools of Engineering and Architecture, and for the members generally of those professions; and the first three are also designed for use in those colleges which provide courses of study adapted to the preliminary general training of candidates for the scientific professions, as well as for those technical schools which undertake that training themselves.

1. GENERAL PROBLEMS OF ORTHOGRAPHIC PROJECTIONS. The foundation course for the subsequent theoretical and practical works. A new edition of this work will soon appear.
2. GENERAL PROBLEMS OF SHADES AND SHADOWS. A wider range of problems than can elsewhere be found in English, and the principles of shading. 1 vol. 8vo, with numerous plates. Cloth.......................... $3 50
3. HIGHER LINEAR PERSPECTIVE. Distinguished by its concise summary of various methods of perspective construction; a full set of standard problems, and a careful discussion of special higher ones. With numerous large plates. 8vo, cloth..$4 00
4. ELEMENTS OF MACHINE CONSTRUCTION AND DRAWING; or, Machine Drawings. With some elements of descriptive and rational cinematics. A Text-Book for Schools of Civil and Mechanical Engineering, and for the use of Mechanical Establishments, Artisans, and Inventors. Containing the principles of gearings, screw propellers, valve motions, and governors, and many standard and novel examples, mostly from present American practice. By S. Edward Warren. 2 vols. 8vo. 1 vol. text and cuts, and 1 vol. large plates....... $7 50

A FEW FROM MANY TESTIMONIALS.

"It seems to me that your Works only need a thorough examination to be introduced and permanently used in all the Scientific and Engineering Schools." —Prof. J. G. FOX, *Collegiate and Engineering Institute, New York City.*

"I have used several of your Elementary Works, and believe them to be better adapted to the purposes of instruction than any others with which I am acquainted."—H. F. WALLING, *Prof. of Civil and Topographical Engineering, Lafayette College, Easton, Pa.*

"Your Works appear to me to fill a very important gap in the literature of the subjects treated. Any effort to draw Artisans, etc., away from the 'rule of thumb,' and give them an insight into principles, is in the right direction, and meets my heartiest approval. This is the distinguishing feature of your Elementary Works."—Prof. H. L. EUSTIS, *Lawrence Scientific School, Cambridge, Mass.*

"The author has happily divided the subjects into two great portions: the former embracing those processes and problems proper to be taught to all students in Institutions of Elementary Instruction; the latter, those suited to advanced students preparing for technical purposes. The Elementary Books ought to be used in all High Schools and Academies; the Higher ones in Schools of Technology."—WM. W. FOLWELL, *President of University of Minnesota.*

DYEING, &c.

MACFARLANE. **A PRACTICAL TREATISE ON DYEING AND CALICO-PRINTING.** Including the latest Inventions and Improvements. With an Appendix, comprising definitions of chemical terms, with tables of Weights, Measures, &c. By an experienced Dyer. With a supplement, containing the most recent discoveries in color chemistry. By Robert Macfarlane. 1 vol. 8vo....................................$5 00

REIMANN. **A TREATISE ON THE MANUFACTURE OF ANILINE AND ANILINE COLORS.** By M. Reimann. To which is added the Report on the Coloring Matters derived from Coal Tar, as shown at the French Exhibition, 1867. By Dr. Hofmann. Edited by Wm. Crookes. 1 vol. 8vo, cloth, $2 50

"Dr. Reimann's portion of the Treatise, written in concise language, is profoundly practical, giving the minutest details of the processes for obtaining all the more important colors, with woodcuts of apparatus. Taken in conjunction with Hofmann's Report, we have now a complete history of Coal Tar Dyes, both theoretical and practical."—*Chemist and Druggist.*

ENGINEERING.

AUSTIN. **A PRACTICAL TREATISE ON THE PREPARATION, COMBINATION, AND APPLICATION OF CALCAREOUS AND HYDRAULIC LIMES AND CEMENTS.** To which is added many useful recipes for various scientific, mercantile, and domestic purposes. By James G. Austin. 1 vol. 12mo....................................$2 00

COLBURN. **LOCOMOTIVE ENGINEERING AND THE MECHANISM OF RAILWAYS.** A Treatise on the Principles and Construction of the Locomotive Engine, Railway Carriages, and Railway Plant, with examples. Illustrated by Sixty-four large engravings and two hundred and forty woodcuts. By Zerah Colburn. Complete, 20 parts, or 2 vols. cloth..$20 00
Or, half morocco, gilt top.............................. 25 00

KNIGHT. **THE MECHANICIAN AND CONSTRUCTOR FOR ENGINEERS.** Comprising Forging, Planing, Lining, Slotting, Shaping, Turning, Screw-cutting, &c. Illustrated with ninety-six plates. By Cameron Knight. 1 vol. 4to, half morocco..$15 00

MAHAN. **AN ELEMENTARY COURSE OF CIVIL ENGINEERING,** for the use of the Cadets of the U. S. Military Academy. By H. P. Mahan. 1 vol. 8vo, with numerous woodcuts. New edition, with large Addenda, &c. Full cloth.....$4 00

" **DESCRIPTIVE GEOMETRY,** as applied to the Drawing of Fortifications and Stone-Cutting. For the use of the Cadets of the U. S. Military Academy. By Prof. D. H. Mahan. 1 vol. 8vo. Plates....................................$1 50

" **INDUSTRIAL DRAWING.** Comprising the Description and Uses of Drawing Instruments, the Construction of Plane Figures, the Projections and Sections of Geometrical Solids, Architectural Elements, Mechanism, and Topographical Drawing. With remarks on the method of Teaching the subject. For the use of Academies and Common Schools. By Prof. D. H. Mahan. 1 vol. 8vo. Twenty steel plates. Full cloth..$3 00

" **A TREATISE ON FIELD FORTIFICATIONS.** Containing instructions on the Methods of Laying Out, Constructing, Defending, and Attacking Entrenchments. With the General Outlines, also, of the Arrangement, the Attack, and Defence of Permanent Fortifications. By Prof. D. H. Mahan. New edition, revised and enlarged. 1 vol. 8vo, full cloth, with plates...$3 50

" **ELEMENTS OF PERMANENT FORTIFICATIONS.** By Prof. D. H. Mahan. 1 vol. 8vo, with numerous large plates. Cloth...$6 50

MAHAN. **ADVANCED GUARD, OUT-POST**, and Detachment Service of Troops, with the Essential Principles of Strategy and Grand Tactics. For the use of Officers of the Militia and Volunteers. By Prof. D. H. Mahan. New edition, with large additions and 12 plates. 1 vol. 18mo, cloth......$1 50

MAHAN & MOSELY. **MECHANICAL PRINCIPLES OF ENGINEERING AND ARCHITECTURE.** By Henry Mosely, M.A., F.R.S. From last London edition, with considerable additions, by Prof. D. H. Mahan, LL.D., of the U. S. Military Academy. 1 vol. 8vo, 700 pages. With numerous cuts. Cloth...$5 00

MAHAN & BRESSE. **HYDRAULIC MOTORS.** Translated from the French Cours de Mecanique, appliquée par M. Bresse. By Lieut. F. A. Mahan, and revised by Prof. D. H. Mahan. 1 vol. 8vo, plates..$2 50

WOOD. **A TREATISE ON THE RESISTANCE OF MATERIALS**, and an Appendix on the Preservation of Timber. By De Volson Wood, Professor of Engineering, University of Michigan. 1 vol. 8vo, cloth..........................$2 50

A TREATISE ON BRIDGES. Designed as a Text-book and for Practical Use. By De Volson Wood. 1 vol. 8vo, numerous illustrations, cloth (shortly)...................$3 00

GREEK.

BAGSTER. **GREEK TESTAMENT, ETC.** The Critical Greek and English New Testament in Parallel Columns, consisting of the Greek Text of Scholz, readings of Griesbach, etc., etc. 1 vol. 18mo, half morocco..........................$3 00

" ——— do. Full morocco, gilt edges................ 4 50

" ——— With Lexicon, by T S. Green. Half-bound........ 4 50

" ——— do. Full morocco, gilt edges................. 6 00

" ——— do. With Concordance and Lexicon. Half mor., 6 00

" ——— do. Limp morocco......................... 7 50

" **THE ANALYTICAL GREEK LEXICON TO THE NEW TESTAMENT.** In which, by an alphabetical arrangement, is found every word in the Greek text *in every form in which it appears*—that is to say, every occurrent person, number, tense or mood of verbs, every case and number of nouns, pronouns, &c., is placed in its alphabetical order, fully explained by a careful grammatical analysis and referred to its root, so that no uncertainty as to the grammatical structure of any word can perplex the beginner, but, assured of the precise grammatical force of any word he may desire to interpret, he is able immediately to apply his knowledge of the English meaning of the root with accuracy and satisfaction. 1 vol. small 4to, half bound..............................$6 50

" **GREEK-ENGLISH LEXICON TO TESTAMENT.** By T. S. Green. Half morocco $1 50

HEBREW.

GREEN. **A GRAMMAR OF THE HEBREW LANGUAGE.** With copious Appendixes. By W. H. Green, D.D., Professor in Princeton Theological Seminary. 1 vol. 8vo, cloth....$3 50

" **AN ELEMENTARY HEBREW GRAMMAR.** With Tables, Reading Exercises, and Vocabulary. By Prof. W. H. Green, D.D. 1 vol. 12mo, cloth.....................$1 50

" **HEBREW CHRESTOMATHY**; or, Lessons in Reading and Writing Hebrew. By Prof. W. H. Green, D.D. 1 vol. 8vo, cloth...$2 00

LETTERIS. **A NEW AND BEAUTIFUL EDITION OF THE HEBREW BIBLE.** Revised and carefully examined by Myer Levi Letteris. 1 vol. 8vo, with key, marble edges.....$2 50

"This edition has a large and much more legible type than the known one volume editions, and the print is excellent, while the name of LETTERIS is a sufficient guarantee for correctness." —*Rev. Dr.* J. M. WISE, *Editor of the* ISRAELITE.

BAGSTER'S GESENIUS. **BAGSTER'S COMPLETE EDITION OF GESENIUS' HEBREW AND CHALDEE LEXICON.** In large, clear, and perfect type. Translated and edited with additions and corrections, by S. P. Tregelles, LL.D.

In this edition great care has been taken to guard the student from Neologian tendencies by suitable remarks whenever needed.

"The careful revisal to which the Lexicon has been subjected by a faithful and Orthodox translator exceedingly enhances the practical value of this edition." —*Edinburgh Ecclesiastical Journal.*

Small 4to, half bound..............................$7 50

BAGSTER'S **NEW POCKET HEBREW AND ENGLISH LEXICON.** The arrangement of this Manual Lexicon combines two things—the etymological order of roots and the alphabetical order of words. This arrangement tends to lead the learner onward; for, as he becomes more at home with roots and derivatives, he learns to turn at once to the root, without first searching for the particular word in its alphabetic order. 1 vol. 18mo, cloth..............................$2 00

"This is the most beautiful, and at the same time the most correct and perfect Manual Hebrew Lexicon we have ever used."—*Eclectic Review.*

IRON, METALLURGY, &c.

BODEMANN. **A TREATISE ON THE ASSAYING OF LEAD, SILVER, COPPER, GOLD, AND MERCURY.** By Bodemann & Kerl. Translated by W. A. Goodyear. 1 vol. 12mo, $2 50

CROOKES. **A PRACTICAL TREATISE ON METALLURGY.** Adapted from the last German edition of Prof. Kerl's Metallurgy. By William Crookes and Ernst Rohrig. In three vols. thick 8vo. Price..............................$30 00

Separately. Vol. 1. Lead, Silver, Zinc, Cadmium, Tin, Mercury, Bismuth, Antimony, Nickel, Arsenic, Gold, Platinum, and Sulphur..............................$10 00
Vol. 2. Copper and Iron.............................. 10 00
Vol. 3. Steel, Fuel, and Supplement.............................. 10 00

FAIRBAIRN. **CAST AND WROUGHT IRON FOR BUILDING.** By Wm. Fairbairn. 8vo, cloth..............................$2 00

FRENCH. **HISTORY OF IRON TRADE, FROM 1621 TO 1857.** By B. F. French. 8vo, cloth..............................$2 00

KIRKWOOD **COLLECTION OF REPORTS (CONDENSED) AND OPINIONS OF CHEMISTS IN REGARD TO THE USE OF LEAD PIPE FOR SERVICE PIPE,** in the Distribution of Water for the Supply of Cities. By I. P. Kirkwood, C.E. 8vo, cloth..............................$1 50

LESLEY. **THE IRON MANUFACTURER'S GUIDE TO THE FURNACES, FORGES, AND ROLLING-MILLS OF THE UNITED STATES.** By J. P. Lesley. With maps and plates. 1 vol. 8vo, cloth..............................$8 00

MACHINISTS—MECHANICS.

FITZGERALD. **THE BOSTON MACHINIST.** A complete School for the Apprentice and Advanced Machinist. By W. Fitzgerald. 1 vol. 18mo, cloth..............................$0 75

HOLLY. **SAW FILING.** The Art of Saw Filing Scientifically Treated and Explained. With Directions for putting in order all kinds of Saws, from a Jeweller's Saw to a Steam Saw-mill. Illustrated by forty-four engravings. Third edition. By H. W. Holly. 1 vol. 18mo, cloth..............................$0 75

KNIGHT. **THE MECHANISM AND ENGINEER INSTRUCTOR.** Comprising Forging, Planing, Lining, Slotting, Shaping, Turning, Screw-Cutting, etc., etc. By Cameron Knight. 1 vol. 4to, half morocco..............................$15 00

TURNING, &c. **LATHE, THE, AND ITS USES, ETC.; or, Instruction in the Art of Turning Wood and Metal.** Including a description of the most modern appliances for the ornamentation of plane and curved surfaces, with a description also of an entirely novel form of *Lathe* for Eccentric and Rose Engine Turning, a Lathe and Turning Machine combined, and other valuable matter relating to the Art. 1 vol. 8vo, copiously illustrated. Including Supplement. 8vo, cloth......$7 00

"The most complete work on the subject ever published."—*American Artisan.*

"Here is an invaluable book to the practical workman and amateur."—*London Weekly Times.*

TURNING, &c. **SUPPLEMENT AND INDEX TO LATHE AND ITS USES.** Large type. Paper, 8vo....................$0 90

WILLIS. **PRINCIPLES OF MECHANISM.** Designed for the use of Students in the Universities and for Engineering Students generally. By Robert Willis, M.D, F.R.S., President of the British Association for the Advancement of Science, &c., &c. Second edition, enlarged. 1 vol. 8vo, cloth...........$7 50

*** It ought to be in every large Machine Workshop Office, in every School of Mechanical Engineering at least, and in the hands of every Professor of Mechanics, &c.—Prof. S. EDWARD WARREN.

MANUFACTURES.

BOOTH. **NEW AND COMPLETE CLOCK AND WATCH MAKERS' MANUAL.** Comprising descriptions of the various gearings, escapements, and Compensations now in use in French, Swiss, and English clocks and watches, Patents, Tools, etc., with directions for cleaning and repairing. With numerous engravings. Compiled from the French, with an Appendix containing a History of Clock and Watch Making in America. By Mary L. Booth. With numerous plates. 1 vol. 12mo, cloth.................................$2 00

GELDARD. **HANDBOOK ON COTTON MANUFACTURE; or, A Guide to Machine-Building, Spinning, and Weaving.** With practical examples, all needful calculations, and many useful and important tables. The whole intended to be a complete yet compact authority for the manufacture of cotton. By James Geldard. With steel engravings. 1 vol. 12mo, cloth...................................$2 50

MEDICAL, &c.

BULL. **HINTS TO MOTHERS FOR THE MANAGEMENT OF HEALTH DURING THE PERIOD OF PREGNANCY, AND IN THE LYING-IN ROOM.** With an exposure of popular errors in connection with those subjects. By Thomas Bull, M.D. 1 vol. 12mo, cloth...........$1 00

FRANCKE. **OUTLINES OF A NEW THEORY OF DISEASE,** applied to Hydropathy, showing that water is the only true remedy. With observations on the errors committed in the practice of Hydropathy, notes on the cure of cholera by cold water, and a critique on Priessnitz's mode of treatment. Intended for popular use. By the late H. Francke. Translated from the German by Robert Blakie, M.D. 1 vol. 12mo, cloth...$1 50

GREEN. **A TREATISE ON DISEASES OF THE AIR PASSAGES.** Comprising an inquiry into the History, Pathology, Causes, and Treatment of those Affections of the Throat called Bronchitis, Chronic Laryngitis, Clergyman's Sore Throat, etc., etc. By Horace Green, M.D. Fourth edition, revised and enlarged. 1 vol. 8vo, cloth..................................$3 00

" **A PRACTICAL TREATISE ON PULMONARY TUBERCULOSIS,** embracing its History, Pathology, and Treatment. By Horace Green, M.D. Colored plates. 1 vol. 8vo, cloth.......................................$5 00

GREEN. **OBSERVATIONS ON THE PATHOLOGY OF CROUP** With Remarks on its Treatment by Topical Medications. By Horace Green, M.D. 1 vol. 8vo, cloth...............$1 25

" **ON THE SURGICAL TREATMENT OF POLYPI OF THE LARYNX, AND ŒDEMA OF THE GLOTTIS.** By Horace Green, M.D. 1 vol. 8vo..................$1 25

" **FAVORITE PRESCRIPTIONS OF LIVING PRACTITIONERS.** With a Toxicological Table, exhibiting the Symptoms of Poisoning, the Antidotes for each Poison, and the Test proper for their detection. By Horace Green. 1 vol. 8vo, cloth..................................$2 50

TILT. **ON THE PRESERVATION OF THE HEALTH OF WOMEN AT THE CRITICAL PERIODS OF LIFE.** By E. G. Tilt, M.D. 1 vol. 18mo, cloth..............$0 50

VON DUBEN. **GUSTAF VON DUBEN'S TREATISE ON MICROSCOPICAL DIAGNOSIS.** With 71 engravings. Translated, with additions, by Prof. Louis Bauer, M.D. 1 vol. 8vo, cloth..$1 00

MINERALOGY.

BRUSH. **ON BLOW-PIPE ANALYSIS.** By Prof. Geo. J. Brush. (In preparation.)

DANA. **DESCRIPTIVE MINERALOGY.** Comprising the most recent Discoveries. Fifth edition. Almost entirely re-written and greatly enlarged. Containing nearly 900 pages 8vo, and upwards of 600 wood engravings. By Prof. J. Dana. Cloth...$10 00

"We have used a good many works on Mineralogy, but have met with none that begin to compare with this in fulness of plan, detail, and execution."—*American Journal of Mining.*

DANA & BRUSH. **APPENDIX TO DANA'S MINERALOGY,** bringing the work down to 1872. By Prof. G. J. Brush. 8vo.....$0 50

DANA. **DETERMINATIVE MINERALOGY.** 1 vol. (In preparation.)

" **A TEXT-BOOK OF MINERALOGY.** 1 vol. (In preparation.)

MISCELLANEOUS.

BAILEY. **THE NEW TALE OF A TUB.** An adventure in verse. By F. W. N. Bailey. With illustrations. 1 vol. 8vo......$0 75

CARLYLE. **ON HEROES, HERO-WORSHIP, AND THE HEROIC IN HISTORY.** Six Lectures. Reported, with emendations and additions. By Thomas Carlyle. 1 vol. 12mo, cloth...$0 75

CATLIN. **THE BREATH OF LIFE; or, Mal-Respiration and its Effects upon the Enjoyments and Life of Man.** By Geo. Catlin. With numerous wood engravings. 1 vol. 8vo, $0 75

CHEEVER. **CAPITAL PUNISHMENT.** A Defence of. By Rev. George B. Cheever, D.D. Cloth...........................$0 50

" **HILL DIFFICULTY,** and other Miscellanies. By Rev. George B. Cheever, D.D. 1 vol. 12mo, cloth.........$1 00

" **JOURNAL OF THE PILGRIMS AT PLYMOUTH ROCK.** By Geo. B. Cheever, D.D. 1 vol. 12mo, cloth........$1 00

" **WANDERINGS OF A PILGRIM IN THE ALPS.** By George B. Cheever, D.D. 1 vol. 12mo, cloth.........$1 00

" **WANDERINGS OF THE RIVER OF THE WATER OF LIFE.** By Rev. Dr. George B. Cheever. 1 vol. 12mo, cloth...$1 00

CONYBEARE. **ON INFIDELITY.** 12mo, cloth.................. 1 00

CHILD'S BOOK **OF FAVORITE STORIES.** Large colored plates. 4to, cloth..$1 50

EDWARDS. **FREE TOWN LIBRARIES.** The Formation, Management, and History in Britain, France, Germany, and America. Together with brief notices of book-collectors, and of the respective places of deposit of their surviving collections. By Edward Edwards. 1 vol. thick 8vo..............$8 00

GREEN. **THE PENTATEUCH VINDICATED FROM THE ASPERSIONS OF BISHOP COLENSO.** By Wm. Henry Green, Prof. Theological Seminary, Princeton, N. J. 1 vol. 12mo, cloth..................................$1 25

GOURAUD. **PHRENO-MNEMOTECHNY; or, The Art of Memory.** The series of Lectures explanatory of the principles of the system. By Francis Fauvel-Gouraud. 1 vol. 8vo, cloth, $2 00

" **PHRENO-MNEMOTECHNIC DICTIONARY.** Being a Philosophical Classification of all the Homophonic Words of the English Language. To be used in the application of the Phreno-Mnemotechnic Principles. By Francis Fauvel-Gouraud. 1 vol. 8vo, cloth..........................$2 00

HEIGHWAY. **LEILA ADA.** 12mo, cloth.......................... 1 00

" **LEILA ADA'S RELATIVES.** 12mo, cloth........... 1 00

KELLY. **CATALOGUE OF AMERICAN BOOKS.** The American Catalogue of Books, from January, 1861, to January, 1866. Compiled by James Kelly. 1 vol. 8vo, net cash.......$5 00

" **CATALOGUE OF AMERICAN BOOKS.** The American Catalogue of Books from January, 1866, to January, 1871. Compiled by James Kelly. 1 vol. 8vo, net...........$7 50

MAVER'S **COLLECTION OF GENUINE SCOTTISH MELODIES.** For the Piano-Forte or Harmonium, in keys suitable for the voice. Harmonized by C. H. Morine. Edited by Geo. Alexander. 1 vol. 4to, half calf.........................$10 00

NOTLEY. **A COMPARATIVE GRAMMAR OF THE FRENCH, ITALIAN, SPANISH, AND PORTUGUESE LANGUAGES.** By Edwin A. Notley. 1 vol., cloth......$5 00

PARKER. **POLAR MAGNETISM.** First and Second Lectures. By John A. Parker. Each..................................$0 25

" **NON-EXISTENCE OF PROJECTILE FORCES IN NATURE.** By John A. Parker.........................$0 25

STORY OF **A POCKET BIBLE.** Illustrated. 12mo, cloth........$1 00

TUPPER. **PROVERBIAL PHILOSOPHY.** 12mo............... 1 00

WALTON & COTTON. **THE COMPLETE ANGLER; or, The Contemplative Man's Recreation, by Isaac Walton, and Instructions how to Angle for a Trout or Grayling in a Clear Stream, by Charles Cotton,** with copious notes, for the most part original. A bibliographical preface, giving an account of fishing and Fishing Books, from the earliest antiquity to the time of Walton, and a notice of Cotton and his writings, by Rev. Dr. Bethune. To which is added an appendix, including the most complete catalogue of books in angling ever printed, &c. Also a general index to the whole work. 1 vol. 12mo, cloth......................................$3 00

WARREN. **NOTES ON POLYTECHNIC OR SCIENTIFIC SCHOOLS IN THE UNITED STATES.** Their Nature, Position, Aims, and Wants. By S. Edward Warren. Paper....$0 40

WILLIAMS. **THE MIDDLE KINGDOM.** A Survey of the Geography, Government. Education, Social Life, Arts. Religion, &c., of the Chinese Empire and its Inhabitants. With a new map of the Empire. By S. Wells Williams. Fourth edition, in 2 vols.......................................$4 00

RUSKIN'S WORKS.

Uniform in size and style.

RUSKIN. **MODERN PAINTERS.** 5 vols. tinted paper, bevelled boards, plates, in box.......................................$18 00

" **MODERN PAINTERS.** 5 vols. half calf............ 27 00

" " " " without plates 12 00

" " " " " half calf, 20 00

Vol. 1.—Part 1. General Principles. Part 2. Truth.
Vol. 2.—Part 3. Of Ideas of Beauty.
Vol. 3.—Part 4. Of Many Things.
Vol. 4.—Part 5. Of Mountain Beauty.
Vol. 5.—Part 6. Leaf Beauty. Part 7. Of Cloud Beauty. Part 8. Ideas of Relation of Invention, Formal. Part 9. Ideas of Relation of Invention, Spiritual.

" **STONES OF VENICE.** 3 vols., on tinted paper, bevelled boards, in box.......................................$7 00

" **STONES OF VENICE.** 3 vols., on tinted paper, half calf...$12 00

" **STONES OF VENICE.** 3 vols., cloth............... 6 00

Vol. 1.—The Foundations.
Vol. 2.—The Sea Stories.
Vol. 3.—The Fall.

" **SEVEN LAMPS OF ARCHITECTURE.** With illustrations, drawn and etched by the authors. 1 vol. 12mo, cloth, $1 75

" **LECTURES ON ARCHITECTURE AND PAINTING.** With illustrations drawn by the author. 1 vol. 12mo, cloth...$1 50

" **THE TWO PATHS.** Being Lectures on Art, and its Application to Decoration and Manufacture. With plates and cuts. 1 vol. 12mo, cloth..........................$1 25

" **THE ELEMENTS OF DRAWING.** In Three Letters to Beginners. With illustrations drawn by the author. 1 vol. 12mo, cloth.......................................$1 00

" **THE ELEMENTS OF PERSPECTIVE.** Arranged for the use of Schools. 1 vol. 12mo, cloth..................$1 00

" **THE POLITICAL ECONOMY OF ART.** 1 vol. 12mo, cloth...$1 00

" **PRE-RAPHAELITISM.**
NOTES ON THE CONSTRUCTION OF SHEEPFOLDS.
KING OF THE GOLDEN RIVER; or, The Black Brothers. A Legend of Stiria.
} 1 vol. 12mo, cloth, $1 00

RUSKIN. **SESAME AND LILIES.** Three Lectures on Books, Women, &c. 1. Of Kings' Treasuries. 2. Of Queens' Gardens. 3. Of the Mystery of Life. 1 vol. 12mo, cloth..........$1 50

" **AN INQUIRY INTO SOME OF THE CONDITIONS AT PRESENT AFFECTING "THE STUDY OF ARCHITECTURE" IN OUR SCHOOLS.** 1 vol. 12mo, paper...$0 15

" **THE ETHICS OF THE DUST.** Ten Lectures to Little Housewives, on the Elements of Crystallization. 1 vol. 12mo, cloth.......................................$1 25

" **"UNTO THIS LAST."** Four Essays on the First Principles of Political Economy. 1 vol. 12mo, cloth.. ... .$1 00

RUSKIN. **THE CROWN OF WILD OLIVE.** Three Lectures on Work, Traffic, and War. 1 vol. 12mo. cloth................$1 00

" **TIME AND TIDE BY WEARE AND TYNE.** Twenty-five Letters to a Workingman on the Laws of Work. 1 vol. 12mo, cloth....................................$1 00

" **THE QUEEN OF THE AIR.** Being a Study of the Greek Myths of Cloud and Storm. 1 vol. 12mo, cloth $1 00

" **LECTURES ON ART.** 1 vol. 12mo, cloth........... 1 00

" **FORS CLAVIGERA.** Letters to the Workmen and Labourers of Great Britain. Part 1. 1 vol. 12mo, cloth, plates, $1 00

" **FORS CLAVIGERA.** Letters to the Workmen and Labourers of Great Britain. Part 2. 1 vol. 12mo, cloth, plates, $1 00

" **MUNERA PULVERIS.** Six Essays on the Elements of Political Economy. 1 vol. 12mo, cloth...............$1 00

" **ARATRA PENTELICI.** Six Lectures on the Elements of Sculpture, given before the University of Oxford. By John Ruskin. 12mo, cloth, $1 50, or with plates. $3 00

" **THE EAGLE'S NEST.** Ten Lectures on the relation of Natural Science to Art. 1 vol. 12mo...............$1 50

" **THE POETRY OF ARCHITECTURE:** Villa and Cottage. With numerous plates. 1 vol. 12mo, cloth (shortly)....$2 00

" **FORS CLAVIGERA.** Letters to the Workmen and Laborers of Great Britain. Part 3. 1 vol. 12mo, cloth (shortly).$1 50

BEAUTIFUL PRESENTATION VOLUMES.

Printed on tinted paper, and elegantly bound in crape cloth extra, bevelled boards, gilt head.

RUSKIN. **THE TRUE AND THE BEAUTIFUL IN NATURE, ART, MORALS, AND RELIGION.** Selected from the Works of John Ruskin, A.M. With a notice of the author by Mrs. L. C. Tuthill. Portrait. 1 vol. 12mo, cloth extra, gilt head...$2 50

" **THE TRUE AND THE BEAUTIFUL IN NATURE, ART, MORALS, AND RELIGION.** Selected from the Works of John Ruskin, A.M. With a notice of the author by Mrs. L. C. Tuthill. Portrait. 1 vol. 12mo, plain cloth, $2 00

" **PRECIOUS THOUGHTS:** Moral and Religious. Gathered from the Works of John Ruskin, A.M. By Mrs. C. L. Tuthill. 1 vol. 12mo, cloth extra, gilt head..................$2 00

" **PRECIOUS THOUGHTS:** Moral and Religious. Gathered from the Works of John Ruskin, A.M. By Mrs. L. C. Tuthill. 1 vol. 12mo, plain cloth.................................$1 50

" **SELECTIONS FROM THE WRITINGS OF JOHN RUSKIN.** 1 vol. 12mo, cloth extra, gilt head........$2 50

" **SELECTIONS FROM THE WRITINGS OF JOHN RUSKIN.** 1 vol. 12mo, plain cloth.................$2 00

" **SESAME AND LILIES.** 1 vol. 12mo................$1 75

" **ETHICS OF THE DUST.** 12mo..................... 1 75

" **CROWN OF WILD OLIVE.** 12mo.................. 1 50

RUSKIN'S BEAUTIES.

" **THE TRUE AND BEAUTIFUL**
PRECIOUS THOUGHTS.
CHOICE SELECTIONS.
} 3 vols., in box, cloth extra, gilt head..........$6 00; do., half calf...10 00

RUSKIN'S POPULAR VOLUMES.

CROWN OF WILD OLIVE. SESAME AND LILIES. QUEEN OF THE AIR. ETHICS OF THE DUST. 4 vols. in box, cloth extra, gilt head.......... .....$6 00

RUSKIN'S WORKS.

Revised edition.

RUSKIN. Vol. 1.—**SESAME AND LILIES.** Three Lectures. By John Ruskin, LL.D. 1. Of Kings' Treasuries. 2. Of Queens' Gardens. 3. Of the Mystery of Life. 1 vol. 8vo, cloth, $2 00. Large paper....$2 50

" Vol. 2.—**MUNERA PULVERIS.** Six Essays on the Elements of Political Economy. By John Ruskin. 1 volume 8vo, cloth....$2 00
Large paper.... 2 50

" Vol. 3.—**ARATRA PENTELICI.** Six Lectures on the Elements of Sculpture, given before the University of Oxford. By John Ruskin. 1 vol. 8vo....$4 00
Large paper.... 4 50

RUSKIN—COMPLETE WORKS.

THE COMPLETE WORKS OF JOHN RUSKIN. 27 vols., extra cloth, in a box..$40 00
Ditto 27 vols., extra cloth. *Plates*... 48 00
Ditto Bound in 47 vols., half calf. do.... 70 00

SEAMANSHIP.

ALSTON. **SEAMANSHIP.** New edition, revised and enlarged, by Commander R. H. Harris, R. N. With a Treatise on Nautical Surveying by Staff-Commander May. Also, Instructions for Officers of the Merchant Service by W. H. Rosser. With two hundred illustrations. 1 vol. 12mo, cloth, price.......$5 00

SHIP-BUILDING, &c.

BOURNE. **A TREATISE ON THE SCREW PROPELLER, SCREW VESSELS, AND SCREW ENGINES,** as adapted for Purposes of Peace and War. Illustrated by numerous woodcuts and engravings. By John Bourne. New edition. 1867. 1 vol. 4to, cloth, $18.00; half russia....$24 00

WATTS. **RANKINE (W. J. M.) AND OTHERS.** Ship-Building, Theoretical and Practical, consisting of the Hydraulics of Ship-Building, or Buoyancy, Stability, Speed and Design—The Geometry of Ship-Building, or Modelling, Drawing, and Laying Off—Strength of Materials as applied to Ship-Building —Practical Ship-Building—Masts, Sails, and Rigging—Marine Steam Engineering—Ship-Building for Purposes of War. By Isaac Watts, C.B., W. J. M. Rankine, C.B., Frederick K. Barnes, James Robert Napier, etc. Illustrated with numerous fine engravings and woodcuts. Complete in 30 numbers, boards, $35.00; 1 vol. folio, cloth, $37.50; half russia, $40 00

WILSON (T. D.) **SHIP-BUILDING, THEORETICAL AND PRACTICAL.** In Five Divisions.—Division I. Naval Architecture. II. Laying Down and Taking off Ships. III. Ship-Building. IV. Masts and Spar Making. V. Vocabulary of Terms used—intended as a Text-Book and for Practical Use in Public and Private Ship-Yards. By Theo. D. Wilson, Assistant Naval Constructor, U. S. Navy; Instructor of Naval Construction, U. S. Naval Academy; Member of the Institution of Naval Architects, England. With numerous plates, lithographic and wood. 1 vol. 8vo. Shortly........

SOAP.

MORFIT. **A PRACTICAL TREATISE ON THE MANUFACTURE OF SOAPS.** With numerous wood-cuts and elaborate working drawings. By Campbell Morfit, M.D., F.C.S. 1 vol. 8vo....$20 00

STEAM ENGINE.

TROWBRIDGE. **TABLES, WITH EXPLANATIONS, OF THE NON-CONDENSING STATIONERY STEAM ENGINE,** and of High-Pressure Steam Boilers. By Prof. W. P. Trowbridge, of Yale College Scientific School. 1 vol. 4to, plates....$3 50

TURNING, &c.

THE LATHE, **AND ITS USES, ETC.** On Instructions in the Art of Turning Wood and Metal. Including a description of the most modern appliances for the ornamentation of plane and curved surfaces. With a description, also, of an entirely novel form of Lathe for Eccentric and Rose Engine Turning, a Lathe and Turning Machine combined, and other valuable matter relating to the Art. 1 vol. 8vo, copiously illustrated, cloth..........$7 00

" **SUPPLEMENT AND INDEX TO SAME.** Paper...$0 90

VENTILATION.

LEEDS (L. W.). **A TREATISE ON VENTILATION.** Comprising Seven Lectures delivered before the Franklin Institute, showing the great want of improved methods of Ventilation in our buildings, giving the chemical and physiological process of respiration, comparing the effects of the various methods of heating and lighting upon the ventilation, &c. Illustrated by many plans of all classes of public and private buildings, showing their present defects, and the best means of improving them. By Lewis W. Leeds. 1 vol. 8vo, with numerous wood-cuts and colored plates. Cloth.........$2 50

"It ought to be in the hands of every family in the country."—*Technologist.*

"Nothing could be clearer than the author's exposition of the principles of the principles and practice of both good and bad ventilation."—*Van Nostrand's Engineering Magazine.*

"The work is every way worthy of the widest circulation."—*Scientific American.*

REID. **VENTILATION IN AMERICAN DWELLINGS.** With a series of diagrams presenting examples in different classes of habitations. By David Boswell Reid, M.D. To which is added an introductory outline of the progress of improvement in ventilation. By Elisha Harris, M.D. 1 vol. 12mo, $1 50

WEIGHTS, MEASURES, AND COINS.

TABLES OF WEIGHTS, MEASURES, COINS, &c., OF THE UNITED STATES AND ENGLAND, with their Equivalents in the French Decimal System. Arranged by T. T. Egleston, Professor of Mineralogy, School of Mines, Columbia College. 1 vol. 18mo.....................$0 75

"It is a most useful work for all chemists and others who have occasion to make the conversions from one system to another."—*American Chemist.*

"Every mechanic should have these tables at hand."—*American Horological Journal.*

www.ingramcontent.com/pod-product-compliance
Lightning Source LLC
LaVergne TN
LVHW020932110826
845150LV00004B/835

* 9 7 8 1 4 2 5 5 5 2 7 9 4 *